P9-DDX-336

The Kingdom, the City
& the People of God

# Urban
## ministry

HARVIE M. CONN
& MANUEL ORTIZ

InterVarsity Press
Downers Grove, Illinois

*InterVarsity Press*
*P.O. Box 1400, Downers Grove, IL 60515-1426*
*World Wide Web: www.ivpress.com*
*E-mail: mail@ivpress.com*

*InterVarsity Press® is the book-publishing division of InterVarsity Christian Fellowship/USA®, a student movement active on campus at hundreds of universities, colleges and schools of nursing in the United States of America, and a member movement of the International Fellowship of Evangelical Students. For information about local and regional activities, write Public Relations Dept., InterVarsity Christian Fellowship/USA, 6400 Schroeder Rd., P.O. Box 7895, Madison, WI 53707-7895.*

*Cover photograph: Tomek Sikora/Image Bank*

*ISBN 0-8308-1573-2*

*Printed in the United States of America* ∞

**Library of Congress Cataloging-in-Publication Data**

*Conn, Harvie M.*
   *Urban ministry: the kingdom, the city, and the people of God/Harvie M. Conn &*
*Manuel Ortiz.*
     *p. cm.*
   *Includes bibliographical references.*
   *ISBN 0-8308-1573-2 (hardcover: alk. paper)*
     *1. City churches. 2. City missions. I. Ortiz, Manuel, 1938- II. Title.*
*BV637.C586 2000*
*253'.09173'2—dc21*

                                                                              *00-063359*

| 22 | 21 | 20 | 19 | 18 | 17 | 16 | 15 | 14 | 13 | 12 | 11 | 10 | 9 | 8 | 7 | 6 | 5 | 4 | 3 | 2 | 1 |
|----|----|----|----|----|----|----|----|----|----|----|----|----|----|----|----|----|----|----|----|----|----|
| 20 | 19 | 18 | 17 | 16 | 15 | 14 | 13 | 12 | 11 | 10 | 09 | 08 | 07 | 06 | 05 | 04 | 03 | 02 | 01 |

*Dedicated to students and servants*
*in God's vineyard*
*throughout the cities of this world*

# Contents

# Preface

As I think through the process leading up to this book, I recall how Harvie Conn spoke of his desire to provide a textbook for students moving into urban ministry, for those wrestling with the complexities of the city as pastors, for evangelists, for missionaries who are planting urban churches in the United States and throughout the world, and for faculty who have taken the lonely road of teaching urban mission studies in Christian institutions. When he asked me to labor with him in this project, I was both delighted and fearful that I would not meet his expectations. But we worked hard at embracing the mission of this book. I gladly submitted to his demands on time and writing style as I recognized the excellent opportunity for me to work with a master writer.

Harvie was ill and struggled with his last chapters until it was impossible for him to continue. He was extremely apologetic when I spoke with him a few days before his death. How badly he wanted not to let the readers down. Nothing would comfort him—there was still more he wanted to include in the book. We hugged and kissed as we knew his departure was imminent. He went home to be with his Lord on August 28, 1999.

Harvie always excelled in writing and research. He left enough behind to allow the completion of this volume, and you now have in your hands the final work of Dr. Harvie Conn.

On behalf of Harvie I want to thank those friends at Westminster and his family who greatly supported him as he undertook this project while gravely ill. I myself am greatly indebted to his mentoring during this process. I also want to thank my family, who helped me carry out much of what is written in these pages. I thank the faculty of Westminster for their ongoing support and encouragement. Finally, I thank my colleague in ministry and in teaching at Westminster, Sue Baker, who gave valuable input and evaluation throughout the writing of this book and assisted in its completion upon Harvie's passing.

*Manuel Ortiz*

# Introduction

During the wilderness wandering, the spies returned to Moses with their mixed report. The land truly was flowing with milk and honey. "But the people who live there are powerful, and the cities are fortified and very large" (Num 13:28). The providence and promises of God took a back seat in a majority report that measured urban challenge only in terms of size, density and population.

Have things changed, or are God's people still afraid of what cities hold? This book aims to address today's urban reality in all its complex and interrelated facets.

## How to Use This Text

The content of this book was carefully structured for students to work through sequentially in order to get a full-orbed understanding of urban ministry. Yet the work can also be used as a reference book; any section can be read by itself.

The first three sections provide a foundation for what follows. Part one is a historical section, attempting to lay out a global view of urban history and demographics. We wanted our treatment to be as comprehensive as possible. This historical analysis provides perspective and renewed vision for what the sovereign Lord is doing in his world. It identifies some missiological concerns that have not yet been addressed fully by present-day mission strategies.

The second section takes a biblical-historical look at God's concern for cities. Drawing on both Old and New Testaments, this material helps the reader put together the present contemporary world with the world of biblical times. Actually very little has changed regarding either issues or solutions. Biblical strategies must be operative in contemporary society if there is to be kingdom reign.

The third section—"Understanding the City"—presents ways to interpret and define the city. It is strong on sociological information. How do we do theology in the midst of the historical reality of where and how people live? The city's complexity can be overwhelming; this section assists the student and practitioner in wrestling with the various aspects of the city as a Christian.

Now that the foundation has been laid, section four looks at practical skills and highlights the importance of the social sciences. In the early 1970s Donald McGavran and C. Peter Wagner from the School of Church Growth at Fuller Theological Seminary introduced social-scientific perspectives and methods into church planting and church growth. Their work was helpful but was often dismissed as too secular and not Christian enough. Again and again, both in classes and other forums, we have insisted on the utilization of the social sciences as an applied science for mission. This section leads the reader to grasp the need for doing serious field work before embarking on any mission endeavor. Bible translation work since the beginning of the twentieth century exemplifies how insights from anthropology and sociology help us understand cultures and societies for the purpose of bringing the gospel to unreached peoples.

Section five addresses Christian community development among the poor. The church has to reckon with its inescapable responsibility to the poor. The Lord Jesus has summoned his body to be what he is in the world. Mercy ministry is not optional but is demanded of all Christians, reflecting God's concern for the value of life and his image bearers (Rom 5:21-26).

Much will depend on the development of leaders, which is the subject of our final section. This section may be one of the most important, because all the ministry described in preceding sections is vitally dependent on biblical leadership. The city will not see effective kingdom ministry if leaders are not preaching and living the whole counsel of God. Reductionism will not do. Sociology without biblical theology misses the mark. Justification without justice will not be divine salt that penetrates and preserves our God's world.

All across the world urbanization is proceeding apace, not waiting for us to decide whether the city is a legitimate place for mission. The Lord of history is calling us to be servants of his gospel in the cities of his world.

Lima, Peru, one of the major cities of South America, can serve as a specific example of contemporary urban challenges. This will lead us to formulate a contemporary agenda for reflection which lays out the many questions this book seeks to address.

## Lima, Peru: Looking for Clues

Indigenous peoples have inhabited the area we now call metropolitan Lima for nearly seven thousand years. But 1535 was a crucial turning point. Conqueror Francisco Pizarro saw Lima's safe harbor advantages and began its transformation into his "City of Kings." City-minded Spanish colonialists shaped Lima into one of the two most important urban centers of what became Latin America (the other is Mexico City). "As both the political-administrative capital for the viceroyalty and its principal economic center, Lima also took on the role of the social capital of Spanish South America" (Kent 1994:459).

***Population patterns.*** For a little over four hundred years, Lima grew slowly. By 1796 its population accounted for a little over 6 percent of Peru's total. By 1940 the city had grown to 645,000 people, about 8.6 percent of the nation's population.

Then came the last half of the twentieth century. And Lima, like the world's major urban centers, underwent a demographic explosion. By the early 1990s well over six million people, nearly one-third of Peru's population, were calling themselves Limeños.

The city is now a center of political and economic power. By 1988 Lima was thirteen times larger than the country's second city. Its metropolitan boundaries enclose more than 50 percent of Peru's entire urban population (León 1992:201). And paralleling this demographic growth have come significant urban challenges.

***Religious directions.*** Over 90 percent of Lima's residents are formally attached to the Roman Catholic Church. Some of the church's 136 parishes are home to tens of thousands of constituents. But, reflecting a long history, there is a divorce between church and religion. Few fulfill Catholicism's minimal requirements of participation in Sunday Mass. Faith expresses itself in a more individualistic way, often disconnected from the official church. It is to the confraternities and brotherhoods, in what is termed "popular religion" that one looks for manifestations of serious commitment (Klaiber 1992:16).

"Popular religiosity" is a genuine expression of Catholic piety fitted to native traditions and the painful marginalization of the poor. It is "a people's way of crying and remembering and aspiring" (Cox 1973:117) the faith of those who have been least integrated into the mainstream of urban society.

Processions and feast days, the multiplicity of saints, the prominence and popularity of religious relics bespeak rural backgrounds of devotion and veneration. Those less linked to the agricultural cycle turn to more secularized forms of faith, to horoscopes and astrology (Candelaria 1990:9-14).

"Without doubt the most important popular religious manifestation in Peru is the great procession of Our Lord of Miracles, which takes place three times during the month of October in Lima" (Klaiber 1992:91). Clothed in purple penitential robes, the faithful accompany the image of the crucified Christ, the "Purple Lord," carried on a heavy platform through the streets of Lima. The Brotherhood of the Bearers of the Lord of Miracles had three hundred members in the 1920s; by the 1980s the membership had reached some four thousand.

But such expressions of "popular religiosity" are often less (or more) than the church expects or wants. The distance between private faith and ecclesiastical practice is a concern.

Some in the 1990s looked to the papal push of the Lumen 2000 movement, the "new evangelization" of Latin America, to narrow the gap. Others, like Gustavo Gutiérrez, Lima's "father" of liberation theology, struggle with the connection between popular religion and the poor. In his earlier writing Gutiérrez expressed fear of its opiate impact on the poor. Conversion, he noted, demands society's transformation, not just a personal change of heart. Can these expressions of popular religion deaden the poor, those very agents of change, to their identity as the church of the poor, for the poor? In more recent years Gutiérrez appears to be looking for more positive connections.

**Poverty's expansion.** The recent expansion of migration has underlined the challenge of poverty in Lima. Since 1950 the people of the Peruvian countryside have been slipping through the city's back door. Pushed by poverty and fear of the violent activities of the *Sendero Luminoso* (Shining Path), they are pulled by an optimistic urban hope. Most settle in the *pueblos jóvenes* ("young towns"), an aristocratic euphemism for the 598 squatter areas that ring the metropolitan area.

Between 9 and 10 percent of the city's population lived in these "slums of hope" in 1955; by 1985 that figure had reached 50 percent. There are also hundreds of thousands in old, overcrowded inner-city tenements called *tugurios* (Grigg 1992a:24, 103). Marginalized by poverty and a government simply unable to keep up with the flow, these urban migrants form cities within the city.

Relatively untouched by large-scale industrialization, the new Limeños join the 49 percent of Latin America's work force who find their livelihood in the informal sector. By 1984 nearly 70 percent of Lima's working population was linked to this nonformal sector, which the government does not regulate. "Many join the 200,000 to 300,000 army of street vendors, who sell everything from brooms to artichokes" (Maust 1984:10). Cars are repaired in backyards, and furniture gets repaired and clothing is manufactured in people's homes. "This trade does not get registered in the country's economic statistics. It pays no taxes to governments strapped for cash. And millions of citizens in the informal sector are outside government health programs and have no provision for their old age" (Berg and Pretiz 1992:91).

*Poverty's youth.* Old age is not always a problem in Lima; youth is. Typical of Latin America's cities is the youthful age of Lima's population. One-third of the country's population aged fifteen to twenty-four—1.2 million—are Lima residents.

Typical also is the marginalization of the young. By the mid-1980s officials estimated there were ten thousand abandoned children in the city. They shine shoes, change tires, wash cars or go begging during the day. At night they sleep in parks or on sidewalks. A major in the Salvation Army comments, "I know of children who live on a cup of tea and a couple of bread rolls a day."

## Contemporary Urban Challenges

The story of Lima is reproduced with variations in many cities. By looking at these cities we become aware of the challenges facing the church today. But just what are these challenges, and how is the church responding?

*Population explosion.* Whatever else we see, we see the city as *more of everything*—more people, more buildings and expanding neighborhoods.

Isolated voices speak of a "decline in the growth rates of cities nearly everywhere. The era of rapid urban growth is about to finish" (Prud'Homme 1989:45). But usually these predictions are limited to so-called developed countries, suggesting more slowdown than decline.

Many continue to affirm the 1985 predictions of Rashmi Mayur, then president of the Global Futures Network. "Ninety percent of the earth's population," he suggested, "will likely be urbanized by the end of the next century. Much of this urbanization will take place in 'supercities' in Third World countries" (Mayur 1985:28).

Urban populations will continue to grow at almost twice the rate of national growth, and large cities at a rate three to four times as high. Does the church show any indication of interest in these expanding urban centers? Vital signs are beginning to appear in the Southern Hemisphere. In Latin America, Protestants "have now reached a critical mass of about 15% (with wide variations from country to country). Although the vast majority of Latin Americans when polled still identify themselves as Catholics, relatively few attend mass regularly. The upshot is that the number of active Protestant churchgoers is comparable to that of practicing Catholics" (Berryman 1994:7).

How much of that Protestant presence is urban? Full figures are not yet available. And hints are sometimes not consistent. Between 1990 and 1992, 710 new churches—five a week—were established in greater Rio de Janeiro. Typical of elsewhere, 90 percent of these were Pentecostal. During the same period one new Catholic parish was established. El Salvador claims 390,000 evangelicals in its capital, 26.4 percent of the city's population. On the other hand, in Venezuela 4 percent of the total population is Protestant, but in Caracas the figure is just 1.16 percent. Lima now boasts an evangelical community of 212,000, 3.2 percent of its total (Pretiz 1995:8-9).

A full recognition by the church of the potential of the world's cities seems yet to appear. Commenting on Africa, a Catholic observer remarks that "about 80% of missionary personnel in Africa are engaged in rural parish work, while there are very few actually involved in ministering to the slum dwellers of the towns and cities" (Zanotelli 1988:283). An evangelical addressing the same context adds, "Churches . . . have failed to recognize fully the tremendous needs of the multitudes who left their homes and went to the cities" (Falk 1979:426).

***Socioeconomic gap.*** Everywhere the global city is becoming identified with the poor. In the United States past practices of housing discrimination have locked blacks and Hispanics into isolated urban neighborhoods. In the meantime, the work base of the American city has shifted from industry to service orientation. Factories spring up in industrial parks in the suburbs far from these urban communities, while new office buildings transform the urban skyline. Entry-level and low-education-requirement jobs become scarcer in the city. Blue-collar employment opportunities shrink as white-collar openings expand.

Economically marginal communities are finding more doors of occupational opportunity closed to them. Federal aid resources for the city are greatly reduced, and a crumbling urban infrastructure must look to a diminishing tax base among the growing poor. Help is not there to give. The white middle class, now joined by a rapidly emerging black middle class, continues its movement to the suburbs with its tax dollars, while central-city expenses skyrocket.

In England's urban priority areas (UPAs) the patterns are similar. The gap between rich and poor becomes a gulf. The poor, both unemployed and working, bear both the brunt of recession and the blame as "social security scroungers." By 1981, just over 2.6 million unemployed people and members of their families were living in poverty or at its margin—

three out of every ten people under pension age.

And what lies at the heart of the problem? "The national decline in the number of manual jobs, and the concentration of manual workers in the UPAs" (*Faith in the City* 1985:202). As in the United States, the major source of new British jobs (with some shifting between the 1970s and 1980s) is the service sector.

But outside the historically industrialized world, poverty speaks even louder. "Nowhere else is the economic, political, and social distance between the few rich and the masses of the poor greater than in towns of the Third World" (Gutkind 1974:35). And nowhere is poverty more visible than in the slums and shantytowns that spread out from the edges of Lima or Bangkok. In San Francisco and Philadelphia, Houston and Boston, the word *suburb* denotes home for the middle and upper classes. But in the Matheri valley of Nairobi and high on the hills above Caracas, the suburbs are where we find the poor and marginalized. It is estimated that half the urban populations of Africa, Asia and Latin America live in slums. Africa's cities have become what one author has called "centers of despair." An estimated 79 percent of Addis Ababa residents live in squatter settlements, as do 70 percent of Casablanca's residents and 65 percent of Kinshasa's. "More than one-third of the populations of Nairobi and Dakar are slum dwellers. In Nairobi, the population of the lowest squatter settlements has been growing more than twice as fast as that of the city as a whole" (Rondinelli 1988:304).

The overall pattern is staggering:

> By the year 2000, 2,116 million, or 33.6 percent of the world population, will be in Third World cities, and 40 percent of these (a low figure) will be squatters (846 million people). This would indicate a world that is about 13.6 percent squatters by the year 2000—a bloc nearly the size of the Muslim or Hindu populations, doubling each decade. Squatters thus constitute an immense people group—a distinct entity deserving specific strategies for evangelization. (Grigg 1992a:25)

The picture becomes even more compelling if we include the decaying inner-city areas as well as the street people living in cities. That brings our estimate of the urban poor up to one billion by the year 2000, a figure totaling 30 percent of these cities, or 16.9 percent of the world's population.

Where is the church in all this? The picture is not uniform. In Latin America the majority of the churches are among the poor. In ranges varying from 60 to 90 percent, Mexico City's 1,200 churches, Sao Paulo's 5,294 congregations, Lima's 610 fellowships reach out to the marginalized (Grigg 1992a:102-7).

Leading the way in church planting in this social class have been Pentecostal churches. While mainliners and evangelicals have moved up the social ladder, Pentecostal churches have concentrated their evangelistic efforts on the lower classes in mushrooming cities:

> Millions of rural-to-urban immigrants, their village life left behind forever, were ripe for new ideas, including religious teaching. The Pentecostals provided them the opportunity to hear the gospel free of intimidation from relatives or neighbors, to experience warm Christian fellowship in the impersonal city, and be treated with dignity as children of God. (Greenway 1994:190)

By contrast, "nowhere in Asia, with the exception of Korea, does the church in the slums make up more than four percent of the existing church in the city" (Grigg 1992a:95). In 1986 over 19 percent of Bangkok's population lived in its 1,024 slum areas. Only three churches and two house groups were located there at the time. In Calcutta, between 48,000 (officially) and 200,000 (the generally accepted figure) live on the streets. No figures exist for residents of squatter areas, but some estimate that a million may be living there in tents and mud or thatched huts. Of the 132 churches in Calcutta, only one has targeted this population.

Also missing from the Asian church is the blue-collar factory worker. In patterns similar to the past in England and the United States, Christianity in Hong Kong and Taipei is perceived as a middle-class institution.

In Taiwan that perception is not far off. By 1984 almost 23 percent of Taiwanese church members had a college-level education (compared with 5.1 percent of the general population). It is easy to understand why the working class see most church programs as geared toward the needs of the intellectual or the middle class.

Three million strong by 1984 and increasing at the rate of ten thousand a month, working-class Asians tend to hang on to their folk religions. Living in company-built dormitories, their weekly work hours are long—fifty-two in Korea, forty-eight in Singapore (1979), fifty in Taiwan (1983). And their expectations are low. A high percentage are women, who enter the factories "as a means of liberation or as a new and exciting experience" (Tsai 1985:125). That optimism quickly turns to cynicism and passivity; women workers soon see themselves as mere assemblers who count for very little.

There are signs that the church* may be awakening to the needs of this

---

*Throughout this book when the word *church* is used with no referrant to Roman Catholic, Protestant or universal church, it should be construed to mean both the Protestant Church and the Roman Catholic Church.

forgotten group. But the signs are still geographically isolated. In Hong Kong, visionaries like Agnes Liu of the China Graduate School of Theology saw the need years ago. And that awareness has spawned over one hundred lay-led factory fellowships. A dozen churches have started. In Taiwan the Fellowship of Covenant Churches initiated a church-planting project in the central part of the island among the more settled factory workers—those married or planning to stay in the area after marriage. Making initial contact through the factories, particularly those with Christian management, the Fellowship planned to create home meetings to meet the need (Fredericksen 1993:16-18).

***The public arena.*** There is still another dimension to the urban world that the gospel cannot ignore: public life and the policies shaped by it.

Politics and economics, real estate matters and city planning, history and socioeconomic policies shape the directions of population demographics and cultural systems. Here global movements mold local responses to issues of poverty and development; powerlessness listens as power speaks. Political and military colonialism fades into the urban past, to be replaced by what many call economic neocolonialism. The global reach of the world-class city marginalizes rural and small-town interests—and now it is shifting even national concerns to the periphery.

Across the globe, urban realities require that Christianity develop an agenda that addresses more than church planting or evangelism. South Africa's explosive urbanization led to population shifts that helped topple the oppressive pass laws and the structures of apartheid. Human rights abuses, government corruption, sexism and racism have become urban questions in Kampala and Recife, Seoul and Chicago. Pressures mount on society and the family. New urban financial struggles strain human relationships. Roles shift as Korean immigrant wives in the United States find themselves transformed from rural homemakers to second-income earners. Families in Zaire and Thailand wrestle with splitting their time between the city and their country roots. New questions arise: kin obligations on narrowed incomes; conflicts between parents and children as rural value systems are challenged by urban values adopted by the children; newly emerging patterns of sociability, based now not only on family but on vocation. Children and youth encapsulate these challenges of rapid urbanization on more than simply a private level. As the poor become visible, they become younger. A Roman Catholic study notes that in Africa "youth are the most affected by the rural exodus and the consequent urbanisation" (Meeting on African Collaboration 1983:3).

City dwellers in the United States have a median age of about thirty. In

Mexico City the average age is 14.2. Sixty-eight percent of the urban populations of Argentina, Chile, Uruguay and Costa Rica are made up of young people between the ages of fifteen and twenty-four. In Brazil, Mexico and Venezuela it is 75 percent. By the year 2010 more than 10 percent of the world's population will be children living in the urban slums and squatter settlements of Asia, Africa and Latin America.

> How exploited are the children? Forty million abandoned children live on the streets of the poorest cities. In São Paulo, Brazil, for example, 700,000 live by their wits in that city's streets. Abandoned by their parents, they survive by begging, stealing or selling their bodies.
>   City children who work in order to stay alive number, worldwide, between 100 million and 200 million. Sixty percent of all children in Asian cities are full-time wage earners. Child prostitution is one of the principal means of making money. Forty thousand of the estimated 100,000 prostitutes in Bangkok are 14 or younger. In Manila, 15,000 children are in prostitution, most purchased from their parents to be sex slaves. (Linthicum 1994:21)

The West is not exempt from this victimization of children. In the United States "every day 15 children are killed by firearms; 2,660 babies are born into poverty; 8,493 children are reported abused or neglected and 3 die from it; 2,756 teens become pregnant; 2,833 students drop out of school; and 100,000 children are homeless" (*Rachel's Tears* 1996:4).

The Christian community faces a new urban generation. They are less idealistic and considerably more pessimistic. Jaded and old before their time, without hope and marginalized by broken promises, they become easy prey to the temptations of cynicism and meaningless violence. How do we respond to their needs?

In the recent past the church often found itself sharply divided in seeking solutions. The Anglo-Saxon church world expressed that division more quickly and sharply than the minority churches within its cities or the more holistically oriented congregations of the developing world. Mainline and Catholic voices have turned more easily to face the public side of these issues. Their agenda concerns incorporate with relative ease topics of homelessness, political power brokering, rapid social change. They call readily for a partnership of theology, politics and urban policy.

Evangelical bodies find themselves more comfortable with responses that reflect the private dimensions to these questions. Evangelism, church planting and traditional expressions of charity toward the poor, they argue, will ultimately effect "redemption and lift." Beyond this limit they are extremely reticent to speak.

Reinforcing these proposals is their legitimate concern for past capitulation to theological liberalism. Will a both/and mixture of the public and the private lead once more to the theological reductionism that previously minimized the gospel and maximized the social? And further, is entrance into the urban public sector a legitimate role for the church in its institutional form? What, after all, is the calling of the church? Where does the limited competence of the church end?

These concerns and warnings have affected the daughter churches of the mission fields in a similar way. And reinforcing an inherited theological reluctance have been other contextual factors. How will the church speak to public issues in countries where it is often socially and politically restricted to a closet existence? In Muslim-majority countries where the church can exist only as a ghetto, forbidden growth by Qur'anic legislation? In the People's Republic of China and North Korea, where even its private life is subject to constant scrutiny and intrusive suspicion? How will a marginalized church of the poor in Latin America shift the weight of global power forces that shape local economies and larger development programs? How can African church leaders trained and experienced in rural settings carry rural-shaped worldviews of social connection into urban settings and styles of ministry (P. Fritz 1995:33-34)?

There are encouraging signs of change. Asia's evangelicals "recognize that our ministry demands a clear and intelligent understanding of the complexities of our economic, environmental, social and cultural context. . . . Our gospel must reach the poor, down-trodden and marginalized as well as the rich, powerful, and comfortable sections of urban population" (Ro 1989:1).

In Latin America many evangelicals support a holistic approach to the city. A 1988 consultation of the Latin American Theological Fraternity calls for the churches to be agents of transformation in the city. Five areas are targeted for that process: (1) better understanding by the church of the city's social and economic structures, (2) the incarnation of the church in those social and cultural realities, (3) sensitivity to all social levels in the city, and particularly affirmative action on behalf of the poor, (4) a clearer definition of the prophetic role of the church in the city and (5) a reemphasis on the church as a community of compassion by way of a Christ-centered message of hope and incarnation ("Seeking the Peace" 1989:22-24).

## Agenda for Reflection

The challenges we have summarized are large and complicated. What kinds of questions flow out of all this for our mission reflection? What are some of the issues we must engage?

1. *What is the basis of urban mission?* What place does the city occupy within the total framework of Scripture's commands and promises?

The history of urbanization points to many motivations in the church's interaction with the city. Frequently that motivation was a Western desire to connect "Christianizing" with "civilizing." The city has been seen as the venue for spreading what was seen as a superior white culture. In more recent times the urban interests of the church often became tied to the colonial interests of the sending church's home base. Concerned over those very connections, some mission agencies have turned to rural areas for church planting, fearful of the watchful eye of government on urban activities.

Also affecting the mission of the church to the city has been a growing antiurbanism in the mentality of Europe and North America. Overwhelmed by the impact of the industrial revolution, these traditional centers of evangelistic activity have turned with approval to a nostalgic rural ideology of mission. Remembering the recent rural successes of the gospel, an increasingly middle-class church is paying less attention to the sudden growth of the developing world's cities. The growing visibility of the poor in those cities reinforces middle-class suspicions of poverty and makes antiurbanism an obstacle to mission. God's providential opening of the cities becomes a secularized history of mixed motives and ideas.

a. *How does Scripture view the city?* Is the Bible a rural book, promoting a rural understanding of mission? Where do we find the proper patterns to read that revelation? In sample models and case studies drawing principles from cities like Ur and Sodom, Jerusalem and Antioch, Athens and Rome? Or from the larger hermeneutical structures of the history of special revelation?

b. *How do we fashion a full-orbed urban mission from the Bible?* Is the work of urban mission to be restricted exclusively to the work of evangelism and church growth? What is the connection between urban mission and the kingdom of God? Is that kingdom emphasis fully exhausted by the preaching of Christ? Or is it more comprehensive? Does it also include urban social transformation? If so, does that transformation spread out to the life of the non-Christian? In what way?

2. *How do we understand the city as a process and urbanism as a way of life?* The city, we are learning, is a holistic system of networks. Those networks are geographical, social, institutional, political, cultural and religious. Through them social community takes on new forms.

a. *How are ties of ethnicity and kinship affected by the city?* What new challenges face them in secondary relationships such as friendships and work partnerships? How are human norms and values reexamined? How is the concept of neighborhood changed by the city? How do these new perceptions affect the congruity, the link, between neighborhood and local church? How far does the impact of the city extend? How do new urban influences reinforce or question traditional patterns of religion and faith?

b. *Wrestling with these questions draws us deeply into definition of the term* urban—*and that definition will have a crucial effect on our perception of urban mission.* We can make it an adjectival addendum. But this will add little to a radical, basic understanding of a theology of mission. A second possibility makes the term *urban* into a "definitive category, part of a new core that will create a new sub-discipline, urban missiology" (Conn 1994b:viii). The first choice can leave Christian discipleship as a calling to witness, church attendance, Bible study and prayer. The second choice can add to that list the practice of justice and love in every sphere of urban life.

Will our vision for urban ministry be holistic enough to meet these new perceptions of the city? Will the theology of mission we develop be merely a theology of mission *in* the city or a theology of mission *for* the city? Will the first choice treat the city only as a place in which mission operates? Will the second choice go further and treat the city as a fundamental variable in the design of urban mission?

3. *What tools does God provide to help us see the city and urban church growth more clearly?* How do we develop urban church growth eyes?

Urban mission studies in recent decades have followed earlier academic interests in focusing on demographics. The reasons may be different, but the bottom line has been the same. Built into the nature of the church, after all, is its deep yearning that men and women everywhere come to Christ in repentance and faith. It is a missiological concern that does not stop at any geographical or political boundary of the world.

Those boundaries expanded particularly in the world's urban centers during the last half of the twentieth century. Massive urbanization has brought explosion of the cities of the so-called Third World.

a. *Demographics has taken a prominent place in mission research, given these population shifts.* Discussions of unreached peoples and their size, number and location in this world has accelerated. Through its institutions, the church continues to expand its efforts to collect more reliable statistical information on these groups.

More recently still, that search began to zero in on the least evangelized cities. Preliminary strategy plans are emerging, built around the transformation not merely of people groups but of cities (Grigg 1995). The term "gateway cities" is applied to the most significant entry points for evangelizing unreached people groups.

b. *But demographics alone is not enough. Other tools must be used also.*

What use can be made of the social sciences as we analyze class systems in city and church? How can urban ethnographies aid us in looking past statistical surveys to the cultural settings in which a church might grow?

c. *How do we link all this research with God's plan for the evangelization of the cities?* All truth, no matter where we find it, comes from God. But how do we prevent this search for truth from losing its Christian edge and becoming research exuberance instead of spiritual discernment? Recent Christian literature, wrestling with this temptation, calls for "spiritual mapping" as a key to the process of research and planning and praying. How should we evaluate this new appeal?

4. *Where should our research and planning be directed?* Where do we look to see signs of the kingdom of God in the city?

a. *We must begin with a drive for new churches and their growth.* Writing in 1970, Donald McGavran noted that "after a hundred and fifty years of modern missions, the plain fact is that churches have not done well in most cities" of Africa, Asia, and Latin America (McGavran 1970:280). Reinforcing that judgment is the decline of Christianity in the cities of North America and Europe.

In the twenty-first century the need for urban church planting is growing. "We will live in a world of seventy-nine supercities (fifty-nine of them in developing countries), each with over four million inhabitants. Our globe will have 433 mega-cities with over one million people in each. Our urban population will increase by 1.6 million people per week. Poverty in our urban areas will continue to expand, producing a 'planet of slums' " (D. Barrett 1987:84).

b. *Where should we look to accomplish this task?* How will the concept of reachable people groups aid us? What potential for church planting will we find among the world's poor, among the global movement of border-crossing migrants and immigrants? What of neglected industrial factory workers, or government employees who make up a large percentage of the world's primary cities, or new ethnic and tribal groups settling in urban areas?

c. *What unmined treasures can we still find in the Scriptures to help us shape new contextual forms of worship and message for these peoples?* How can Spirit-directed promptings stirred by these new cultural encounters with the gospel help us look at the Bible in a fresh way? What new theological light still waits to break forth with evangelistic force from the cities of Brazil and Japan, from the slums of Philadelphia and Cairo?

d. *The theological paradigms that have shaped the church's self-under-*

*standing in its dialogue with the city can create a measure of distortion.* Hidden behind stone and mortar are the philosophies of ministry that have shaped the urban church. And basic to these are unseen assumptions that dictate those church statements of purpose. Our image of the city and of urban ministry is affected by the paradigms, the presuppositions, out of which we create our models for mission.

Can we construct a historical typology of paradigms fashioned by the church's perception of the city? What are the paradigms available to us in the dialogue of church and city? How do the paradigms shape the models that shape self-understanding? How many of these paradigms are shaped by an antiurban bias? Where are the boundaries we cannot cross and remain the people of God in urban mission? What are the boundaries we must break down to be the people of God?

5. *Most of the boundaries of our paradigms are structured to define church Sunday morning. Where are those boundaries Monday morning?* Can we look for signs of the kingdom in the public sector of the city?

Across the globe, cities have become concentration points for problems not exclusively urban. Massive poverty, human exploitation, government corruption and the abuse of human rights cry out for answers. Racism and ethnic cleansing devastate East Los Angeles and Lusaka. Sydney wrestles with a massive influx of non-European immigration. Prostitution becomes a major tourist industry for Bangkok. Trade imbalances create joblessness in Houston, put people to work in Shanghai, and accelerate shouting matches between Tokyo and Washington, D.C. Industrialization in Seoul marginalizes rural and small-town interests.

a. *What is the responsibility of the people of God in this public sector?* Will the pursuit of some sort of social calling leave evangelism in the dust? Does biblical shalom incorporate social justice activities in the task of urban mission? Is mercy, not justice, our part in social transformation? Should the church be only a servant of righteousness? Can it also be an advocate for righteousness? Prison Fellowship, set up by Charles Colson, carries on Bible studies for inmates and helps the families of prisoners. Should it also press, as it does, for changes in social legislation to bring prison reform?

b. *Where do the agenda boundaries end for the church as an institution?* Should Christians alone or in community take action in the public square? How does our holistic understanding of the kingdom of God affect the boundary lines of the church's work? Can we shape a legitimate public theology?

c. *How do we determine where we can establish incarnational ministries?* Many churches are incarnating their social conscience in Christian community development. Free medical clinics for the poor, reconstruction of deteriorating housing in the inner cities, legal services for the "underclass" and food distribution programs are appearing in the world's cities. Base Ecclesial Communities are reshaping perceptions of the nature of the church and its relation to the poor and to the community.

How do we determine what we can and cannot do? How are Christian community development projects related to the shalom of the kingdom of God?

6. *How do we prepare Christian leaders for these tasks?* What shape should discipleship training for the city take?

Experts warn us that "when training Christian leaders for ministry in the city, the church is going to have to abandon assembly-line, denomination-oriented, systems-associated ministries" (Elliston and Kauffman 1993:135). People and task orientation, rather than institution orientation, they tell us, will have to carry the day.

Spiritual formation and technical skills must be shaped to meet new demands and confront new needs—worldview adjustments, increasing ethnic diversity, more easily discernible differences between the classes, moral demands that cannot always be addressed by traditional patterns of behavior, the growing visibility of the poor, urban openness to change and the accumulated effect of new ideas.

Past models of decision making will face adjustments. Hierarchical patterns of African group thinking will cope in the city with the pressure of a more individualistic style of choosing. First- and second-generation Koreans in the United States will struggle to cross a gulf of alternate leadership models as wide as that between Japanese and Anglos.

a. *In the cultural and social diversity of the world's cities, how will we discern leadership gifts?* Where do we look to find gifts that are appropriate to the cultural context and faithful to biblical demands? How will those gifts be tested in ministry?

b. *How will the training of leaders be carried on?* The formal schooling model of learning has severe drawbacks in cultural settings where education moves on nonformal lines. Can mentoring avoid the one-way concept of learning, where instruction is deposited in student receptacles as money is deposited in a bank? How can we develop mentoring models in which content is not detached from the real world of the learner, where every mentor/teacher is also a learner?

c. *How do we develop a model for mentoring laity that equips unpaid as well as paid leaders of the church?* That instructs every Christian in equipping skills? That leaves out no generation in the church—youth or adult? How do we create a holistic program of discipleship that encourages the people of God to take their ministry outside the church into the urban public world?

The agenda just outlined is the focus of this book. It is what might be termed a calling to spiritual warfare and ultimately to the urban mission of God himself. We cannot improvise; we may only ask at each step what it is that God demands (Bavinck 1960:5). How does God see the mission of his people in this world of cities?

# Part 1

## The City
## Past & Present

# 1

## From the Present
## to the Past

GRAFFITI MESSAGES ON THE TERMINAL WALL of Tegucigalpa's airport in the mid-1980s introduce the intention of this chapter. "Poor Honduras—oppressed and occupied," reads one plaintive, angry line. Below it, a second line in dialogue with the first, scrawled by another hand: "You s.o.b. communist: go back to Cuba." And under that, a third and last word by yet another writer: "Christ is the answer!" (Berg and Pretiz 1992:13-14).

That third line needs some filling out. How can Christ be the answer to the glory and misery, the order and chaos, the sanctity and sin of our vast cities? If Christ is the urban answer, what are the questions?

If we pluck phrases and adjectives at random from the literature, the verbal impressions become strong: religious "syncretism," "people who know only despair," "a population deprived of security and stability," "an outcast subculture," a working class caught in a cycle of "insecurity, instability, and low wages," "a ruling class of some lineage and power," children as "the victims of economic depression." How did our cities get this way? Can we find clues from the cities' past? parallels? connections?

Moving to the urban present requires at least four stopovers along the way. This chapter will review the first two great urban waves—urban empires and feudal and commercial cities—but let's begin before the territorial state borders of nation and empire, past the boundaries of Rome and Athens, in the hazy world of the city-state.

## Shrine City-States

In this world people take their name not from their identity as a people (e.g., Israel) but from their connection with an isolated urban nucleus of political power (e.g., Sumer, Ur). In this world there are no national capitals. There is only one city with its hinterland surroundings. And that city and its monarchy are the state (Buccellati 1967:12-15).

In keeping with the Genesis narrative, the beginnings of these city-states are found in the Tigris-Euphrates river valleys of Mesopotamia (Gen 4:17, 22; 11:1-9). Here, before 4000 B.C., on sites like Al Ubaid in modern Iraq, people built temples on city terraces surrounded by dwellings. Here other cities emerged about the same time—Ur, Eridu and Uruk (probably the Erech of Gen 10:10). Here around 3500 B.C. the Sumerians migrated, drawn by the twin magnets of sea trade and metal, to usher in the bronze age (Moholy-Nagy 1968:37-38).

From these beginnings came years of urban development and struggle. The city-states of Sumer and Akkad battled for dominance. Lagash, Umma, Eshnumma, Kish and Ur, each in its turn, sought to gain hegemony over others. The new city-states of Knossos and Mallia developed on Crete. In the Nile Valley grew centers like Heliopolis, Thebes and Akhetaten (Tell el Amarna). By 1400 B.C., over two millennia later, urbanization was languishing. The cities in the very regions where urban life first appeared went into eclipse. They would not flourish again until the fourth century B.C.—and then with a new shape.

What social, technological and physical conditions created these early city-states? That is a question still widely argued by archaeologists and social scientists. Much of the debate appears to us to be too heavily dependent on evolutionary assumptions of social and cultural development (Adams 1966; Childe 1950:3-17; Kempinski 1983:235-41; Redman 1982:375-82). The biblical record, by comparison, associates the appearance of the city with the first family on earth (Gen 4:17).

***Power and the city-state.*** What links today's Lima or Jakarta to the early city-states? Certainly not size. Defining these city-states by size is relatively problematic. There was, to be sure, a concentration of people in one place. But the concentrations were small by modern standards. "The walls of ancient Babylon, for example, embraced an area of very roughly 3.2 square miles, and 'Ur with its canals, harbors, and temples, occupied some 220 acres; the walls of Erech encompassed an area of just two square miles.' This suggests that the famous Ur could hardly have boasted more than 5,000 inhabitants and Erech hardly more than 25,000" (Davis 1960:430-31).

Where then do we go to find the link between Lima and Akkad? And what enables the archaeologist, as he or she searches among the oldest remains of settlements, to differentiate between small sites considered to have been cities and others labeled villages? The answer may be power.

Signs of it are in evidence everywhere. Craft production and the distribution of trade goods, the presence of monumental buildings like temples and palaces, marks of creativity and innovation, and the fortresslike walls of Jericho all point to a place of radiating power and expanding influence.

Whether small or large the city-state was the anvil of civilization, the center of power, a physical metaphor of human society itself. In the city converged piety and trade, security and politics. Its walls marked it as protector, its shrines and temples its place as the center of the world.

***Religion and power.*** At the heart of power's expression in the city-state was its religious role, a prologue to the later religiosity of the world's Limas. Ancient Eridu and Ur, Sumer and Uruk were marked by elaborate temple structures raised on platforms or mounds, the forerunners of the later ziggurats. The temple was central to the life of these cities.

In these urban centers "every feature . . . revealed the belief that man was created for no other purpose than to magnify and serve his gods. That was the city's ultimate reason for existence" (Mumford 1961:74-75). Citizenship was defined in terms of service to the gods. Family, agriculture and economy were bound together by their religious commitment to the local gods in a seamless experience of everyday life.

Idolatry was not simply an isolated worship of deity. It was the foundation of community, "the shared conviction that the land and all humankind, indeed nature itself, were the property of the gods" (Lapidus 1986:265). Each city was ruled by a king seen as the representative of the city's tutelary deity. His voice was the voice of the gods, his whim the whim of the gods (Frankfort 1978). Temple priests were judges and politicians; society was sharply divided between the temple elite and the masses who executed the will of the gods. A stratified class system appeared to divide the social hierarchy. Standing at the pinnacle "were small numbers of princely families who seem to have been vigorously extending their control of land by purchase" (Adams 1966:109). At the bottom of the hierarchy? A concentration of slaves. As in Lima, society was polarized.

### The First Great Urban Wave: Urban Empires
Mesopotamia's urban model would have its wider influence. From its cultural cradle ancient cities like Mohenjo-Daro and Harappa would appear

in the Indus Valley of present-day Pakistan, Anyang and Zhengzhou in the Huang-Ho valley of China. Egypt bore its Memphis and its Thebes. But the urban achievement of the Indus Valley proved abortive. And in Egypt cities sprang out of the idea of a unified territory, not vice versa (Hammond 1972:57-76). In fact, the first great city-building wave would come not from Mesopotamia at all but from Greece.

The history of Mesopotamia's city-states would still make contributions to the new urban drive. Emerging from these early city-states was a new twist to urban power that would shape a new direction—the expansion of the city past local borders through conquest. The urban empire was born, and the shrine city became also the imperial city.

Sargon of Akkad (born about 2400 B.C.) was one of the earliest to add this geographical dimension to armed conflict between the cities. And others followed. Asshur, the city named after its god (Gen 10:22), became Assyria the empire, Babel Babylon.

Invested with the divine authority of the city gods, the city kings grew in pride and greed (Dan 4:30) that could not be contained by one city's borders. The city's trade routes, its monopolizing control of resources, its manpower demands became structural routes along which spread sin's quest for power (Jas 4:1-2). The dark side of colonialism that would one day engulf Latin America, Africa and Asia had been born.

***Hellenism and the Greco-Roman Empire.*** Alexander the Great saw the imperial city as a tool for the colonization of his conquered world. By 323 B.C. that world included the Persian empire and stretched from Macedonia on the Balkan peninsula across Asia Minor, Mesopotamia and Persia into India. At strategic points Alexander built Greek cities to serve as administrative centers. Through these cities a new cultural vision began to penetrate the world of the East: "urbanization became the means of hellenization" (Meeks 1983:11). For six and a half centuries from Alexander to Constantine, through Greek and Roman empires, the cities were founded and refounded. Political, sociocultural and religious changes were to reshape them and be shaped by them in return.

In the ancient Near East the formation of far-flung empires was already reducing the integrating religious power of king and temple. With their growing institutionalization, "the temples, cities, and city-states ceased to be territorial governments, municipalities, communalities of worshippers, or communities of economic exchange" (Lapidus 1986:281). Cities began to lose their totalitarian roles as representatives of the gods.

In the Hellenistic and Roman empires that process continued. The gods, though ever present (Acts 17:16), slowly lost their place as integrating centers of the city. And the city itself replaced them as a civil sanctuary, a *polis,* from whose center flowed political, economic, military and cultural power.

Under the influence of Hellenism, urban government shifted from the top-down of Mesopotamian theocracy to the bottom-up of local authority. In place came a formally enrolled citizen body *(demos)* and a governing body *(boule).* The Roman empire in its early years continued that practice. The empire became a commonwealth of self-governing cities, functioning, by Hellenistic heritage, in a general spirit of tolerance and openness.

This was to change in the later years of the empire. As Rome expanded, so did the need for administration and defense. More centralizing control imposed limits on local urban autonomy. Popular sovereignty was fading by the end of the second century A.D. as Rome vested political power in the hands of the well-to-do.

But in the early days of transition and growing imperial power, the cities remained the centers of power. The city was where the empire was. A growing antagonism between city and country appeared to accent this urban emphasis. Ownership of land became concentrated more and more in the hands of fewer and fewer. Tenancy and slavery reduced the number of small independent landowners, a social characteristic reflected in the New Testament.

The city shaped a common Greco-Roman culture. "When Rome conquered Greece, Greece conquered Rome" (Stockwell 1993:30). The pluralistic nature of the globe-spanning empire was united by a common culture and a common Greek language. "It is no accident that all the documents of the New Testament and virtually all other extant writings from the first two centuries of Christianity were written in Greek" (Meeks 1983:15). And that language was not the language of the classical world but the language of the urban marketplace.

Rome's military conquests carried the urban model far and wide. Full-fledged cities began to form around Rome's colonial settlements and military forts. Ancient Italy was said to contain 1,197 cities, Spain 360. "North Africa had hundreds of cities, and north of the Alps major cities rose from Vienna to Bordeaux. Even in far-off Britain there were major cities at York, Bath, and London. . . . Rome's domination resulted in an urban imperialism" (Palen 1992:38). At its height, close to half the world's population would be included in its grasp.

**Rome.** Linking all this together was Rome, "goddess of the earth and of its people," the most powerful city of the world at that time. Gargantuan by all previous urban standards, its population may have been 650,000 by A.D. 100 (Chandler and Fox 1974:303), perhaps as high as a

million. Some fifty-two thousand miles of roads crisscrossed its conquered world to link them to the mother city.

Its lifestyle matched its size. "If the Greek conception of the 'good life'
was to build the city around the principles of moderation, balance, and
human participation, the Roman conception was centered on a celebration of sheer excess and unremitting domination" (Spates and Macionis
1982:179). Its best efforts to establish a universal commonwealth, comments Lewis Mumford, "succeeded only in achieving a balance of privileges and corruptions" (Mumford 1961:210). Rome's authors, from the
elegance of their rural villas, made few attempts to conceal their con-
tempt for the city (Lowenstein 1965:110-23).

Megalopolis became Necropolis, the city of death. Rome's unique contributions to urban life were the arena and the bath, "one contaminating
it, the other purifying it" (Mumford 1961:234). Its order, its justice, its *pax
Romana* were all built on savage exploitation and suppression. By the
second century after Christ a third of Rome's population was slaves, and
between a third and a half of its people were on government and private
benefactor doles. The entertainments of the circus, carnivals of sadism
and death, satiated a depressed populace.

**The church and the city of God.** In the midst of all this came Jesus
and the church, and a new kind of citizenship was formed. Its roots were
not shaped by birth in Roman city or colony but by new birth in the death
and resurrection of Jesus Christ. To a culture of injustice and social division
it offered a new society in which slave and owner became brothers (Philem
16), service the sign of power, and righteousness the partner of justice.

Along the Roman roads it moved in triumph, planting this new kind of
city, the *civitas Dei*. By the beginning of the third century Edessa in northern Mesopotamia had become the first city-state to make Christianity its
official religion. By the middle of that century seven missionary bishops
had been sent to cities in Gaul (including Paris). In southern Italy there
were over one hundred bishoprics, all centered on cities. Rome's Christian community was 5 percent of a decreasing population (D. Barrett
1986:40).

In A.D. 313 Christianity emerged from persecution and oppression to
become a licensed religion of the empire. And a hundred years after that,
in A.D. 410, it numbered twelve hundred bishops in the urban centers of
North Africa when the Visigoth army of Alaric sacked Rome and this
urban empire moved toward its final collapse.

The poet Rutilius Namatianus could say in his epitaph to Rome, "You
made a city of the far-flung earth." The poet's words were a good description of the past but useless as a prediction of the immediate future. For at

least the next six hundred years the cities of the West entered into a period of either minimal survival or nonexistence.

## The Second Great Urban Wave: Feudal and Commercial Cities

The reasons for the urban decline in the West are many and much debated. The decay of the Roman Empire, the impact of barbarian invasions, the throttling of trade by an expanding Islam through the Mediterranean basin in the seventh century all played their part.

Outside the Western world, however, great cities were making their appearance. By A.D. 800 in China, Chang'an with a population of 800,000 and Loyang with 245,000 were two of the five largest cities in the world. Around the same time in Mexico, Teotihuacan's future was abruptly ended for unknown reasons. At one point in its previous thousand-year history it had sheltered a population of nearly 100,000 inhabitants (Lezama 1994:352).

But in the ruins of what once was the Roman Empire the picture was different. Once great cities became isolated hamlets, marked by the architectural return of the wall. From the fifth through the eleventh century the Western world became a rural mosaic of feudal manors, autonomous villages and small towns. All roads no longer led to Rome; they led to the feudal lord. Service on his lands was bartered for security.

At least two factors began to prompt a return to the city during the closing years of this period—gold and God. The city was reborn, and commerce and the church were its midwives.

*The church and urban revival.* As the barbarian populations of northern and central Europe swung over to Christianity, the urban role of the church began to grow. After the fall of the Roman Empire, the church became the one powerful and universal community in western Europe. The fundamental political divisions of society, the parish and the diocese, took their forms from the church that had once taken them from the empire.

"From the smallest village with its parish church to the greatest city with its Cathedral, its many churches, its monasteries and shrines, the Church was visibly present in every community; its spires were the first object the traveler saw on the horizon and its cross was the last symbol held before the eyes of the dying" (Mumford 1961:265-66; see Brooke 1970:59-83). Other aspects of church architecture kept alive these intended connections between church and city. For a thousand years the cathedral form was cast in the shape of a stylized and miniaturized fortress city. "The orb atop St. Peter's dome proclaims the church's power over *urbs* and *orbis;* the towers of Notre Dame de Paris, with rows of kings below, assert the absolute kingship of God and the endurance of His city against all assaults" (Dougherty 1980:46).

**Commerce and urban revival.** But the church was not the only instrument for urban reawakening. Commerce also had its partnership role to play. Around the physical shell of the ancient Roman city was growing up the walled fortress, the *bourg* now occupied by bishop or church official. Surrounding it was the *faubourg,* the merchants' settlement, growing up on the hills or slopes just outside the *bourg.* Primarily a trading center, it was sometimes adjacent to the city gates leading into the *bourg.*

Its residents formed an emerging merchant class of entrepreneurs and traders. These residents were referred to as "burghers" or "bourgeoisie" (from the root *burg* or *bourg*). Later to become a Marxist epithet in the industrial age, it was initially a label to denote a new direction for the city as it moved from the Mediterranean basin into western Europe. The city had started as a shrine and been transformed into a military and colonial center. Now it was finding a new identity as a permanent marketplace under the protection of fortress and church.

In the thirteenth and fourteenth centuries that shift to the city as economic marketplace would be symbolized even more dramatically. A new model for city building, the *bastide,* appeared in southern France, England and Spain.

No longer built on previously settled land, the *bastide* was virtually the first "planned" city in history. Its purpose? To increase wealth through the trade of agricultural products. It was normally laid out with a regular street plan, often a rectangular grid. Settlers were treated equally, with no feudal hierarchies or imposition of stringent guild rules from the past. And at its symbolic center was neither church nor fortress but the market (J. Vance 1990:178-205).

English settlers in North America in the seventeenth century would bring this new city form with them. Cities like Cambridge, Massachusetts, and New Haven, Connecticut, would exemplify them. Like their European counterparts, they were designed to be working places. They lacked massive housing or imposing churches. At their center was the public square, the "green" that was the marketplace. Here on the commons the practice of economics and trade was thought to be the great equalizer.

The Crusades (1096-1291) played their part in this shift. That unique military mixture of God and gold gave new life to the cities as commercial centers. They expanded local and regional trade to routes linking Europe and the Middle East. Cities formed steppingstones in the march of goods (Mumford 1961:255-56). In return, the reopening of such trade brought new ideas and products to Europe's reawakening cities (Pirenne 1952).

As commerce and trade expanded, so did the cities. In the year 1000 Europe boasted some thirty-five to forty-five cities with populations of more than twenty thousand. By 1340 that figure had probably risen to more than one hundred (Bairoch 1988:136).

By the start of the fourteenth century there were five European cities with populations likely exceeding 100,000. Paris had jumped from 20,000 in the year 1000 to around 160,000 in 1300. Venice may have been a city of 110,000, Milan and Genoa around 100,000.

At the same time, the level of urbanization remained stationary in comparison to the rapid growth in overall population. From a population of about thirty-four to forty-two million in the year 1000, Europe probably reached seventy to eighty million in 1300. By the middle of the fourteenth century, however, the opened trade routes also became the path along which the Black Death of bubonic plague spread through the Middle East and Europe. In its first three years, from 1348 through 1350, one-fourth of Europe's population died. Percentages were especially high in the cities. Over half the population of most cities was wiped out. Not until the end of the fifteenth century did the continent's urban population return to its 1340 level.

***The questioning of Christianity and the church.*** In spite of these losses, however, Western sociocultural history was again to be the history of cities. Urban populations began their unsteady but gradual climb again. From 1500 to 1800, "in every single fifty-year interval the urban percentage rose, reaching 10 percent by 1800" (de Vries 1984:38). In 1500 Europe included 154 cities with at least ten thousand inhabitants. By 1800 that number had more than doubled to 364.

But they were to be cities with new direction. A final blow to the rural-based feudal system had been struck. A new urban culture was evolving—and at its heart a new worldview was forming.

Undoubtedly the Renaissance, which was to reach its apex in the fifteenth and sixteenth centuries, played a part in this change. Urban man was heralded as the competent architect of an urban future. For many, this did not mean a rejection of the institutional church. But it did mean marginalization of a more radical sort.

The medieval ideal of the Christian knight and the Christian prince was being replaced. Disappearing with it was urban respect for the church and the gospel. Cities were beginning to look for a new way to define themselves without God at the core. More and more they saw Christianity, represented by the clergy, tied to another world, outsiders to the city and its citizens.

Late medieval Flanders, for example, was a city of only external, formalized religiosity among laypeople. A significant number of its citizens never darkened the doors of the confessional for years on end (Ozment 1975:18). Germany's cities were in a similar state.

Ecclesiastical bureaucracy had preserved the cities in earlier years. Now it was seen as having the opposite effect. Town councils struggled with the bishops' right to intervene, with the muscle of patronage and the well-entrenched benefice system of the church (Moeller 1979:263-64). With feudalism gone, cities were tasting a new freedom for the first time. And their residents were beginning to wonder whether the church was not a leftover of feudalism and a deterrent to freedom. Bishops, after all, were traditionally appointed from the nobility. And how many of those holding church office had any knowledge of and sympathy with local urban problems?

A new vision for the city was appearing. With the last fetters of feudal restraint being broken, disenchantment with the church's medieval theopolis grew. But the new urban freedom was feeling pressure from another direction. The structure of social organization was shifting to the economic power of the nation-state, not the chartered city.

The Greco-Roman world had integrated religion and the city by asking, Am I a good person? The medieval world had asked, Am I a church person? The modern question, prompted by the Renaissance mentality, was becoming, Am I a secular person?

**The Reformation interlude.** Interrupting this time of urban transition came the sixteenth-century Reformation, a uniquely urban event. Neither medieval nor Renaissance in character, it posed a different question to the urban dweller: Am I a Christian? The Reformation called for a return to a new cosmopolis. It rediscovered a sovereign God unleashed by an open Bible in the life of the city.

The Reformation, as we have said elsewhere (Conn 1992a:256-59), cannot be understood as reinforcing the iconoclasm of the late medieval period. Nor can it be understood as simply a call for the church's purification. Its attractiveness to the cities and towns did not lie simply there.

> Protestant preachers pointed out what many laymen had evidently also come to suspect—that the church and her clergy would first have to undergo a major redefinition before they could be integrated as good citizens into society. The root of the problem . . . was not the privileges of a special clerical class or even its administrative or moral failings but the most basic beliefs and practices of the church it represented. (Ozment 1975:44)

To be sure, this was a call to a religious transformation, and it was sounded loudly by voices like those of Martin Luther, John Calvin and

Menno Simons. The ultimate purpose of the city, whatever its form, was to be God's righteousness fulfilled in the death and resurrection of Jesus Christ. Grace, not the works of the law, was to mark our path through the cities of this world.

But this call to the obedience of faith also involved a new social ethic for the city. The Protestant concept of the clerical ministry as an activity, not a passive sacramental state, appealed to burghers who had fought to curtail clerical privileges and immunities. The Reformation slogan of the priesthood of all believers opened the path of service to all the urban citizenry. The importance of secular life and vocations was confirmed. Conversely, the Reformation also worked to secularize the clergy.

The urban citizen saw the Reformation as inner freedom from religious superstition and nominalist uncertainty. It was perceived as a new ethic of urban service (Ozment 1975:83), an unprecedented religious flattering of life outside the institutional church but without the medieval separation of the sacred from the secular.

Before the century ended, the Reformation's urban impact was widespread. Fifty of the sixty-five imperial cities subject to the emperor officially recognized the Reformation either permanently or periodically, as either a majority or a minority movement. Of Germany's almost two hundred cities and towns with populations exceeding one thousand, most witnessed Protestant movements. Some of the largest—Nürnberg, Strasbourg, Lübeck, Augsburg and Elm, all with populations in excess of twenty-five thousand—became overwhelmingly Protestant. Geneva under Calvin became the Jerusalem of Europe, its impact stretching far and wide.

But ultimately the Reformation remained a parenthetical interruption. It provided no brake on the growing pressure for the secularization of the city. A new urban order was taking over. Christopher Wren's plan for the reconstruction of London after the Great Fire of 1666 symbolized it. The dominating site did not go to St. Paul's Cathedral. Wren planned the new avenues so as to give this honor to the Royal Stock Exchange.

# 2

## Into the
## Industrial Age

THE THIRD URBAN WAVE IN HISTORY, the topic of this chapter, flowed around the machine. The industrial revolution was to shape city, church and civilization for years to come. Someone has said that it "marks the most fundamental transformation of human life in the history of the world recorded in written documents" (Hobsbawm 1968:1).

It changed family lifestyles, our understanding of social strata, our politics. It gave some nations special prominence and helped push others toward independence. And it made new demands on the church. It did more than merely coincide with colonialism and the global expansion of the church. Those histories are, in many ways, inseparable.

### Preindustrial Colonialism and Commerce
Rome's had been the last successful, far-flung urban dream of an empire. In the fifteenth and sixteenth centuries western Europe began to dream also. Supported by a revolution in ship building and seamanship, and the developing science of cartography, the Atlantic age of colonial capitalism was about to begin.

Portugal was first in the field. The ships of Spain, in commemoration of its constitution as a nation in 1492, soon followed. By 1532 "Portugal was firmly established in West and East Africa, in India and Malacca, and at the mouth of the Persian Gulf. Spain had opened up the route to America, and was supreme for thousands of miles on both sides of the Equator" (Neill 1966:37). Conquest, catechization, trade, fame and wealth motivated the drive.

Others later joined in the pursuit. By the seventeenth century, France had surpassed the faltering activities of Spain and Portugal and had undertaken colonial and commercial empire building in the West Indies, North America and India. England was expanding its power in Africa, Asia and North America.

**Colonization and the city.** Before colonization, many areas already had a long but limited urban tradition. By 1519 the island city of Tenochtitlán, the center of the Aztec empire in the valley of Mexico, covered more than twelve square kilometers. It may have contained as many as 200,000 people then. Its conqueror, Hernando Cortés, said it was as large as Seville or Cordoba. To the south, the Inca empire of the Andes flourished between 900 and 1463. Cuzco, its administrative center, may have contained a population between 100,000 and 300,000 at the height of its power (Butterworth and Chance 1981:4-5).

Africa's history was similar. Until it was destroyed, Carthage in North Africa was the greatest rival of Rome. From the eleventh to the late seventeenth century, the cities of the Ghana, Mali and Songay empires in West Africa were of considerable importance, primarily as market and trade centers. The Nigerian Yoruba had lived in towns long before colonization. "Each of the Yoruba towns was ruled by a king and was in fact the capital of a kingdom which was itself a network of smaller towns whose chiefs were subject to the king at the capital" (Shorter 1991:21-22).

Colonization was also an urban venture but in a new direction. In the majority of cases it bypassed indigenous cities and created new ones to serve the colonizing power's own commercial, military and administrative interests. The colonial city became a vehicle of conquest and exploitation. All wealth and power flowed into the cities.

> The Spanish were the first to inaugurate such a colonial urban network. Of Latin America's twenty largest metropolitan cities in 1970, sixteen were founded before 1620. In fact, most of the cities created by the Spanish were founded in the sixteenth century, in particular between 1530 and 1560. "The Portuguese cities, on the other hand, were founded two centuries later." (Bairoch 1988:385)

Exploitative patterns were similar elsewhere. Africa's early stages of colonization, between 1500 and 1850, were marked by the inhumanity of the slave trade.

The Spanish and Portuguese imported slaves to Latin America to replace the decimated Indian population; the English and Americans shipped them in vast numbers to the New World to do the backbreaking work of building a new country. Other European countries participated as well. All enlisted the aid of a professional cadre of slave traders—Europeans, Muslims, Africans—whose job it was to bring the "black gold" to market at Dakar in Senegal, Elmina on the coast of Ghana, Zanzibar in Tanzania and other slave-trade towns established up and down the continent's coasts. (Spates and Macionis 1982:271-72)

In Asia the cities created, transformed or enlarged by European impact were very few. The west coast Indian city of Goa, taken by the Portuguese in 1510, got little attention from its captors despite its early fame as "the Rome of India." By 1619 Batavia (now Jakarta) had been made over into a veritable Dutch city. British trade interests either created new port cities (Calcutta, 1690; Singapore, 1819) or occupied them by concession (Bombay, Hong Kong).

These cities would not feel a very strong impact from European colonization until the nineteenth century. "At no time before the second half of the eighteenth century did these cities, including their non-European population, have more than 1% of the total urban population of Asia, the exact figure in all likelihood being some 0.3-0.6%" (Bairoch 1988:396).

**Early colonization and the church.** Where was the church in these new urban directions? Economics was the driving force behind colonial expansion. And the church rode on its coattails as it opened evangelistic doors into Africa, Asia, China and the Americas.

The Spanish conquest of the Southern Hemisphere Americas in the sixteenth century and beyond was far more than a remarkable military and political exploit. It was, at the same time, one of the greatest and most fractured attempts the world has seen to make Christianity prevail outside the boundaries of the *corpus Christianum.*

One cannot talk about Spanish colonial imposition without talking about the evangelization and catechization of America. "The official intentions of the conquest were twofold: to annex the newly conquered lands to the Spanish domains, and to incorporate the baptized indigenous peoples into the Catholic Church" (Floristan 1992:137).

The colonial cities were keys to both these goals. Borrowing the mother country model of Spain, the city became the spearhead for settling and appropriating land, for "civilizing" and "Christianizing" people. It was "a microcosm of the imperial and ecclesiastical order" (Morse 1992:5).

In the seventeenth century the Netherlands, England and Denmark became important sea powers. Protestant mission, slowed by Reformation interests in the renewal of the European church, also took to the colonial seaways. " 'The religion of truth' accompanied 'the religion of trade' " (Jongeneel 1995:225). Dutch missionaries came with the East Indies Company to the Gold Coast in Africa, to southern Africa, to Ceylon, Malacca, the Dutch East Indies and Taiwan. North America became the object of early missionary concern for England. Before the century was over, the largest transoceanic passage in all history had been launched toward North American shores. The movement was migrant rather than missionary. But the colonization was interpreted by its Puritan minority as a chapter in the gospel epic of transforming the wilderness into the garden paradise of God. The formation of the Society for the Propagation of the Gospel in New England in 1649 supported these concerns.

In these early years, and stretching through the eighteenth century, the paternalistic identity between mission and colonialism was very strong. Too often mission societies and orders, whether Catholic or Protestant, identified the best interests of the nation in which they served with the "civilizing" cultural values of their homeland in Europe, the British Isles or the United States.

Those "civilizing" values came with the price tag of racism and cultural arrogance. In Latin America Iberian conqueror and priest lived in social isolation in the cities they created. In large metropolitan centers like Mexico City, Lima and Bogotá, the majority of the population was Spanish. Indians were forcibly resettled into towns or "reductions," ostensibly to achieve the goals of "civilizing" and "Christianizing" them (Estragó 1992:351-62).

Similar patterns of elitist superiority could be seen among Protestants. In the early New England colonies they encouraged a policy of "civility with religion" for Native Americans who professed Christianity. The praying Indians (as they were called) were formed into Christian communities (praying towns) isolated from both the colonist and their indigenous cultures. And paralleling Catholic social isolation, evangelists kept their distance. "Of the 309 Atlantic-coast agents of the (Anglican) Society for the Propagation of the Gospel in the eighteenth century, not one lived among the Indians" (Hutchison 1987:29).

But the most inhuman sample of colonialist arrogance was the colossal evil of the African slave trade. Kenneth Latourette calls it "the most extensive selfish exploitation of one set of races by another which history has seen" (Latourette 1943:320). For approximately three hundred years its trade enriched West Africa's colonial ports of embarkation. Liverpool, England, and Nantes, France, grew rich as slave-trading centers. From 1783 through 1793 Liverpool traders were responsible for the passage of over 300,000 slaves through their city.

In these early years of African colonialism, Christianity and the church were linked to this trade.

> Some priests traded in slaves. The Church in Angola derived much of its income by baptizing and instructing the enslaved, and the end of the slave trade caused a financial crisis. Exported slaves were branded as proofs of ownership *and* of baptism. It was a peculiar irony that only Christians could be sold, and that they could be sold only to Christians. Catholic debates about the slave trade tended to focus not on its intrinsic evils, but on matters such as whether or not slaves should be sold to heretics. Protestants shared this same myopia. John Newton made three slaving voyages after his conversion: "I never knew sweeter or more frequent hours of divine communion than in my last two voyages to Guinea." (Isichei 1995:71)

But there were other voices also speaking for Christianity in those early days of the colonial city. Some, like the Dominican bishop of Chiapas, Bartolomé de Las Casas (1474-1566), pled at great risk for compassion and justice on behalf of the indigenous populations. Between 1504 and 1620 one-third of the Latin American bishops are said to have aligned themselves with Las Casas's concerns. His denunciation of the Spanish conquerors' "insatiable greed and ambition" would not be forgotten (Floristan 1992:144-46).

In colonial centers outside the Americas there were still others whose missionary strategy questioned the validity of "civilizing." Francis Xavier (1506-1552), one of the first six members of the Society of Jesus, went to the colonial port of Goa in south India in 1542. Initially he "had shared the usual European assumption that non-Christian cultures offer nothing on which the missionary can build" (Hutchison 1987:21). That view changed with his three-year experience in the highly developed civilization of Japan at the end of his life. The missionary, he decided, refines and re-creates; he need not destroy.

Other Jesuit examples supported Xavier's final conclusions. Matteo Ricci (1552-1610) in Beijing, Roberto de Nobili (1577-1656) in Madura, India, and Jean de Brebeuf (1593-1649) among the Hurons in Canada were learning the same lessons. Eventually their calls for accommodation (as it came to be termed) would win the day. "Civilizing" as a task of Catholic mission would begin to fade. But not before papal debate over the views of Ricci and de Nobili and heated disagreement among the missionary orders. And not before the pope, under pressure, dissolved the Jesuit Order in 1773.

## The Third Great Urban Wave: The Industrial City
The colonial city had begun as a global front door for Western expansion-

ism. Toward the end of the eighteenth century that mentality was showing severe signs of fatigue. The wars of the Napoleonic era had turned
European interests away from overseas ventures. Capital needed for
colonial mercantile trade had been consumed.

Industrialization, linked to the strength of the nation-state, gave
expansionism a new lease on life. As the need for cheap raw materials
grew, Europe looked once more to Africa, Asia and Latin America; only
now it would seek a new kind of political, economic and social leverage
for control. Colonialism would begin to take on a territorial form that
extended beyond its earlier interest in trading-port toeholds (Drakakis-
Smith 1990:13-17). England's early industrial dominance would give it an
equally dominant role in this new shape of colonialism.

This new shift would underline what earlier centuries have continued
to teach: cities are not isolated blips of society, independent nodes of
administration and commerce. They connect things rural and urban,
powerful and powerless, religious and cultural in connecting networks of
dependency, holism and mutual interaction.

***Western technology and the population boom.*** Up until now, one
might say that three buildings symbolized the main functions of the city
in history: the market, the castle and the temple. The third urban wave
has added still another: the factory.

For about two hundred years, from the mid-eighteenth to the mid-
twentieth century, that symbol was largely located in the Western city.
Infatuated with capitalism, the cities of Europe and North America
embraced the machine. The medieval city represented protection and
security. The industrial city represented the priority of the individual and
the calculated risks that promoted the individual. England in particular
was its point of inauguration. By 1790-1810, it had become what others
later would call the "workshop of the world."

Those beginnings were in the textile mills of the late 1700s. In two
generations a cottage industry of textile workers laboring on hand looms
was replaced by an urban-industrial proletariat toiling in giant spinning
factories. By 1825, the output of an average worker in a spinning mill was
equal to that of two to three hundred workers at the end of the previous
century.

Other business realms also witnessed the power of change. The production of cast iron using coal instead of charcoal began to accelerate
around 1750. By 1806, 97 percent of iron was being produced in coke
blast furnaces. Production had increased tenfold. By 1825, with only
2 percent of the world's population, England was producing a volume of
ironworks equal to that of the rest of the world.

Water and steam power replaced hand labor. Machinery grew in complexity. The small-scale family workplace was replaced by massive industrial establishments. Transportation technology expanded to meet the demands. The first railroad line was opened in 1825, and by 1835 nearly four thousand kilometers of canals had been constructed for shipping.

London especially grew to dominance in these years. Already a growing city before the industrial revolution, it had a population of nearly 900,000 by 1800, twice the size of Paris. By 1861 its population had reached nearly three million, making it the largest city in the world; within a few years, it was the first to exceed the three-million mark. By 1901, that figure had passed almost four and a half million.

Other English cities shared in industrial and population growth. Liverpool and Manchester had populations of only five to eight thousand in 1700. By 1831 Manchester's population had increased nearly six times in sixty years and by nearly 45 percent in the decade just ending. "No one doubted that the cotton industry explained the increasing size and wealth of the town. . . . Manchester became 'one of the commercial capitals of Europe' long before it became an incorporated town in 1838" (Briggs 1993:89). By 1910 Manchester and Liverpool each exceeded 700,000.

Continental Europe's cities were slower to enter the industrial age and slower to feel the population boom. Between 1800 and 1850 England accounted for 35 percent of all growth in urban population in the developed world. As late as 1910, its ratio of urban to rural population was twice as great as that of continental Europe (Bairoch 1988:290).

In the meantime, another industrial power was beginning to emerge— and urbanization was growing with it. The United States, no longer a colonial outpost of the British empire, had moved quickly toward industrialization. By 1830, manufacturing had turned from home-produced products to factories. And the process was accelerated following the country's civil war in the mid-nineteenth century.

The massive growth of rail transportation was a key factor. Chicago illustrates it well. A fort established in 1804 for trade, it had only a few hundred residents right up to the start of the 1830s. By 1852 the railroad reached the city, and ten years later its population had more than tripled in size to 109,000. By 1890 it was the second largest city in the United States.

Urbanization had became a controlling factor in the country's national life by the 1880s (Conn 1994a:49-58). In the one hundred years between 1790 and 1890, the total U.S. population grew sixteen-fold, but urban population increased 139 times. By 1920 the urban population had passed 50 percent.

Unlike developments in England and Europe, the earliest history of the

United States displayed no vested colonial interests of a political sort. But its dreams of world impact and global markets were expanding. Developing since the 1840s was a compelling sense of manifest destiny, "of a national mission assigned by Providence for extending the blessings of America to other peoples" (Anderson 1995:374). In the 1890s manifest destiny would refocus beyond the limits of continental expansion to a global calling. Encouraged by nativistic fears over its crowded cities and growing Roman Catholic and Jewish populations, U.S. leaders began to see the country as "the primary agent of God's meaningful activity in history" (Anderson 1995:375).

*The pains of urban industrial childbirth.* None of this urban growth was achieved without grief or cost to human life. The factory had become the symbolic instrument of the modern worldview initiated by the Renaissance. And the essence of that religious worldview is the polarizing struggle between autonomous freedom and the world of nature. Given such a mindset, with grace marginalized in both freedom and nature, Mammon, always a hard taskmaster, was harder still. Now it came clothed in the iron armor of the machine, and one could see its evil marks in many areas.

The urban interconnection of Western industry and colonialism was one such display case. As in the shrine cities of old, power remained the chief indicator of the presence of the gods. And power belonged to the machine. The colonial city was only the launching pad, never the winner; only the market, never the marketer.

> By the nineteenth century, the goods manufactured from Europe's and North America's own resources, above all coal and iron, had knocked out much of the old luxury handicraft exports from Asia. India and China, too, became exporters of raw materials—tea, jute, cotton—Malaysia of rubber and tin, Latin America of cocoa, coffee, tin, and copper in exchange for Manchester textiles and Pittsburgh ironware. Africa was brought into the system on the same basis. Having long supplied slaves and gold, it began to be developed for new materials. Palm oil for soap became an indispensable commodity amid unspeakable filth in the new industrial order. Cocoa and coffee were added, diamonds and gold simply appropriated. In the twentieth century, the most fateful of all raw materials came into play—petroleum from Arabia and the Caribbean and the West Indies. This underlying pattern of trade—raw materials from the then colonial or near-colonial world in exchange for manufactured products from Europe and North America—provided the larger framework within which Western industrialization took place. (B. Ward 1976:25)

The stimulation of manufacturing in the growing colonies was not a part of colonial policy.

Within the industrial city itself the pursuit of power and wealth brought its own Midas curse. History's traditional urban social patterns that divided the powerful from the powerless were reinforced. Industrial wealth accumulated in the hands of the few at the expense of the many. In the United States, robber barons like John D. Rockefeller could say, "I believe the power to make money is a gift of God" (Wauzzinksi 1993:90). Meanwhile "the main elements in the new urban complex" would become "the factory, the railroad, and the slum" (Mumford 1961:458).

> England asked for her profits and received profits. Everything turned to profit. The towns had their profitable dirt, their profitable smoke, their profitable slums, their profitable disorder, their profitable ignorance, their profitable despair. The curse of Midas was on this society. . . . For the new town was not a home where man could find beauty, happiness, leisure, learning, religion . . . [but] a bare desolate place without color, air, or laughter, where man, woman, and child worked, ate, and slept. (Hammond and Hammond 1975:232)

Social critics and writers were quick to see the pain. Charles Dickens's novels chronicled the grim decay of London's slums and workhouses. Nineteenth-century reformer William Cobbett spoke of the same city as "the Great Wen" (literally, a tumorous cyst). "Civilization works its miracles," wrote the great French liberal Alexis de Tocqueville of Manchester, "and civilized man is turned back almost into a savage" (quoted in Briggs 1993:115). "Wretched, defrauded, oppressed, crushed human nature, lying in bleeding fragments all over the face of society," lamented American visitor Henry Colman in 1845. "Every day I live I thank Heaven that I am not a poor man with a family in England" (Briggs 1993:116).

The United States, however, fared no better. Its industrial cities were swollen by vast numbers of new immigrants from southern and eastern Europe near the end of the nineteenth century. The term *slum* was coined to refer to their already aged housing on the edge of the central business districts. Urban reformer Jacob Riis spoke for many when he described the urban poor in his 1890 work *How the Other Half Lives.* "The half that was on top cared little for the struggles, and less for the fate of those who are underneath so long as it was able to hold them there and keep its own seat. . . . How shall the love of God be understood by those who have been nurtured in sight only of the greed of man?" (quoted in Riis 1971:1-2).

### The Industrial City and the Church
How did the church respond to these needs? And how did the industrial city affect the church?

**Urban church growth.** In England and the United States, the most industrialized countries, early indications pointed to significant improvement in church attendance compared to the previous century. In 1851 the only official census of religion ever taken in England was conducted. It indicated that somewhere between 47 and 54 percent of the total population over the age of ten were in church on census Sunday. By comparison, over a hundred years later (1979) adult church attendance was 11 percent.

At the same time, the census signaled a growing gap between rural and urban churchgoing. By 1850 the urban population of the United Kingdom was 10.2 million. The official 1851 census indicated that "the index of attendance (total attendance as a percentage of the population) was 71.4 for rural areas and small towns; but for large towns with a population of more than 10,000 it was 49.7. All eight London boroughs and Birmingham, Manchester, Liverpool, Leeds, Sheffield, and Bradford recorded an index of attendance below 49.7" (Bebbington 1989:107).

The urban population swing in the United States was later in coming, making exact comparisons more difficult. In 1850 it stood at only 3.4 million. Not until 1900 did it reach 28.6 million and surpass the United Kingdom (then 27.8 million) in its rate of urbanization.

At this point of growth, the United States conducted the only two religious censuses in its history, those of 1890 and 1906. The results were equally impressive. Total church membership grew 60 percent nationally between 1890 and 1906. In cities the rate of growth was more than 87 percent. "By 1906, 39 percent of Americans belonged to some church, while over 46 percent of city residents were affiliated with a local congregation" (Christiano 1987:20).

How much of America's urban church growth came from the massive infusion of immigration in the latter part of the nineteenth century, especially from the largely Catholic areas of southern and eastern Europe? To be sure, large numbers of immigrants came from these areas, and a heavy percentage of them settled in the major cities of the north. The Italian population in the United States, for example, numbered fewer than 4,000 in the middle of the nineteenth century, but fifty years later it had reached 500,000.

Recent scholarship has questioned the ease with which a large and vital Catholic population has been numbered in this period. "In truth, most of the millions of immigrants from 'Catholic' nations . . . were at best *potential* American Catholic parishioners" (Finke and Stark 1992:109). But even factoring in overcounting and the nominalism of the European immigrant, there were still slightly more than a million American Catholics in 1850 (5 percent of the total population). By 1860 that total had doubled, to nearly 2.5 million adherents. The largest increase came between 1890 and 1906, when Catholic membership went from more than seven million to more than fourteen million (Finke and Stark 1992:113). In 1908 Pope Pius X terminated the mission status of the American church.

This early demographic concentration has remained to this day. The U.S. Roman Catholic community has continued to retain a significant place in largely urban areas. So much so, in fact, that urban mission as a category loses any defining sense for that church's ministry. Sixty percent of all U.S. Catholics are concentrated in 30 metropolitan dioceses out of a total of over 180.

**The working classes and church growth.** At the same time there were ominous social trends in the demographic patterns of British and American urban churches. These patterns would accelerate as the churches moved into the twentieth century.

In England the urban working class viewed the church as aligned with the powerful and the privileged. Its clergy were suspect because of their middle-class character and comfortable lifestyle. Class divisions in society were carried over into the church. The gulf between the church and the poorer classes grew.

> The 1902-03 census of church attendance in London gave a clear indication of the close association between the social status of a district and the level of Anglican church-going. Adult attendance at Anglican services averaged 4 percent in the poorest working-class districts, 5 percent in average working-class districts, 7 percent in upper working-class districts, 9 percent in lower middle class, 11 percent in middle class districts, 18 percent in wealthy suburban districts, and 22 percent in wealthy West End districts. . . . Although most cities had a few conspicuously flourishing working-class parishes, the hundreds who attended these churches were few if set beside the thousands who stayed away. (*Faith in the City* 1985:31)

Outside the Anglican fold the picture was less stark but still apparent. The growth of class-specific suburbs in the later nineteenth century accentuated the tendency. "By 1902 in London there was a close correspondence between levels of churchgoing and the position of a suburb in the social hierarchy" (Bebbington 1989:110). Unskilled workers, usually the majority of the working classes, attended in smaller numbers. Even evangelicalism, though it enjoyed substantial working-class support, could not count on the allegiance of the laboring masses.

In the United States the picture was similar. Its great industrial transformation took place in the middle third of the nineteenth century, and it "saw Protestant church leaders reacting to urban and early industrial change by huddling up to the self-made men of the middle and, when possible, the upper classes. Most of the clergymen came from these classes, had most successes with them, shared their values, and tried to help people make their way upward in them. . . . The Church born among the poor and developed for their passion and their solace was coming to despise the outcasts" (Marty 1970:107).

The American revivalism prominent during this same period did little to change the picture. The urban campaigns of Dwight L. Moody (1837-1899) reached their peak in 1885. But they did not reach the poor of the city.

> His audiences were essentially middle-class, rural-born native Americans who had come to the city to make their fortunes; they believed that he spoke God's truth in extolling hard work and free enterprise. But he was not a spokesman for those who were becoming discouraged or disillusioned with the success myth; nor did he reach the foreign-born or Catholic poor who made up so large a proportion of the labor class. His revivals represented an effort to reassure the middle-class (or those rising into it) that urban industrial problems were minimal and temporary. (McLoughlin 1978:144-45)

The urban revivals of Charles Finney (1792-1875), reaching their high-water mark before midcentury, showed similar characteristics. Finney was far more deeply involved in social reform than Moody, and he sought through his revivals to "gather in all classes." But the revivals apparently found their greatest success not in the laboring classes but among those higher on the social scale. "Such success as urban Protestantism did enjoy in these years was primarily among the more settled and comfortable ranks; the families of professional men, merchants, clerks, and skilled artisans; the more successful of the native-born newcomers" (Conn 1994a:46).

***The urban church and industrialization.*** In the face of the industrial city's mounting pain and squalor, there were those outside the church who saw little hope in change through the individual. "The unfeeling isolation of each in his private interest becomes the more repellent and offensive, the more these individuals are crowded together. . . . This isolation of the individual, this narrow self-seeking is the fundamental principle of our society everywhere [but] it is nowhere so shamelessly barefaced, so self-conscious as just there in the crowding of the great city" (Engels 1950[1845]:24). When Friedrich Engels (1820-1895) looked at industrialized Manchester, England, he saw "the marvels of civilization" for the few linked to "nameless misery" for the many. With Karl Marx (1818-1883), an observer of London's growing gap between the rich and the poor, he saw hope for the future in the inevitability of class struggle.

Within the Christian community, these needs were not unrecognized. In England, legislation initiated by Christian leaders in Parliament sought to address many of the open sores of British industrial life. Child labor in factories, female labor in mines and collieries, overlong hours, the lack of safeguards and medical protection, unhealthy working conditions, prison abuses, housing needs among the working class—all were affected by Christian political commitment. Moral crusades were mounted in both England and the United States against the slave trade, against alcoholism.

But these signals of Christian concern were not always unmixed or completely supported by the church. Social evils were assaulted, but not always from a clear sense of public justice or righteousness as a social calling. Often the campaigns were essentially protest movements against individual evils played out on a large scale. In England (compared to the United States), the establishment connection between church and state made legislative recourse easier in the "anti-" policies of reform.

England's (and America's) evangelical community, for example, "was aware of the cruelties perpetuated by slaveholders long before the sudden upsurge of demands for the termination of slavery. Inhumanity in itself did not prod their consciences" (Bebbington 1989:133). Slavery became the target of Christian assault in England in the early 1830s only when it began to be seen for the first time as a barrier to missionary progress in the Caribbean. Similarly, the struggle to reduce working hours may have been motivated in part by the desire to allow workers more time to attend church meetings. Some saw the individual's sabbath observance at risk.

Concern over individual misbehavior may have partly propelled outrage against mining conditions and overcrowded housing. Families living in single rooms, Christians were told, were prone to incest. A Royal Commission report indicated that mining conditions required that male and female children be lowered to work together half naked. Christians were shocked into action (Bebbington 1989:134).

Individualism led churches to turn most naturally to charities and voluntarism to respond to urban needs. And on both sides of the Atlantic they appeared. The motivating compassion of Christ, coupled with the acculturated individualism of a middle-class church, produced large-scale religious philanthropy and organized charity programs for the city— the rescue mission, the Salvation Army "slummers," cheap hotels for the impoverished, shelter homes for women and children, the settlement house, the "institutional church" movement (Conn 1994a:62-65).

**Industrial modernity and the church.** What lay behind this Christian mindset that found itself more comfortable with charity than with jus-tice—that could reduce questions of social structures to individualist dimensions? Part of the answer may lie in the failure of the church to understand well enough the challenge of modernity.

Modernity was a worldview in internal conflict. Basic to that conflict was an inherent struggle between individual autonomy and a view of nature now isolated from God and dominated more and more by the machine. How would the Christian community respond to it? Repeatedly the church resorted to dualisms in this face-off, sometimes moving toward the individualist end of the modernity pole, sometimes the social end. The dualisms can be seen in several areas.

The attitude toward the labor movement was one example. Protes-tants reached out in charity toward the poor but saw "something almost indecent about the lowly members of the nation's labor force banding together in an effort to improve their lot in life and to claim a greater share of the national product" (Wirt 1968:59). Organizing labor found itself contending against more than management and ownership. Middle-class churchgoers saw the fledgling labor movement as marked by ingrat-itude, disrespect, sedition and worldliness.

The voting record of English bishops in the House of Lords on labor and factory reform issues was hardly anything like "good news to the poor." In America the picture was similar. The gulf that placed " 'huge capital alongside huge misery, . . . over-production on the one side and starvation on the other' found most Protestants embarrassingly silent" (Greenway 1973:33).

The Catholic Church in America had a more positive response. With Roman Catholic immigrants making up a great part of the urban working force, it eventually positioned itself as a supporter of organized labor— but not without controversy of its own as it struggled with the issue of its participation in "Americanism" (Marty 1984:277-80).

In all this a pattern was being set. Protestant church growth in England and the United States was isolating itself from the industrial worker. This pattern would be repeated in the future in the expanding mission field.

Also placing its stamp on the future would be the growing Christian dualism that looked for individual converts in the city but turned against the city as a perversion of nature. A growing transatlantic antiurbanism divided the poor of the cities into worthy and unworthy (D. Ward 1989) and would eventually isolate evangelism from social transformation. Class sensitivities in England and Anglo-Saxon racist attitudes in Amer-ica toward blacks and new immigrants molded negative opinions about the city. Urban slums began to be seen as blighted ghettos, centers of hereditary depravity.

A corollary of this antiurbanism was a resurgence of the Arcadian myth of back to nature. Virtue was to be sought in the wilderness, nature unsullied by urban traces. A variety of movements arose to institutionalize this mentality. Campfire Girls and Boy Scouts (begun in 1908), landscape gardening and conservation crusades, the establishment of national parks and other means of retreat to the solitude of the wilderness became middle-class responses to urban pressures (Schmitt 1990).

Theological formulations began to reflect the antiurban dualism of individual and society. They revolved around attitudes to what was eventually called the Social Gospel. On both sides of the Atlantic (Bebbington 1993:195) the debates were to become more prominent in the twentieth century. In its early stages the center of the theological struggle was the poverty and despair of the city. How were those urban needs to be met? Initially the Christian response had been to make common cause (White and Hopkins 1976:5-13). But gradually differences began to appear. Evangelical confidence in the piety of the energized individual insisted, "Change the person and you change the setting." Supporters of a wider program and those fearful of quietism demanded, "Change the setting and you change the person."

Strategies employed to deal with the urban crisis reflected these same commitments. The Social Gospel movement focused strongly on the need for change in social setting. Evangelicals began to fear this focus.

Collaboration dwindled as theological differences became clearer. Moving into the twentieth century, the Social Gospel movement swung toward the public, the political, the social, while the evangelical movement, in reaction, emphasized a private, individualized outlook. Evangelical hope for urban change turned from the public square to the private world of regenerated individuals who might change society. The long partnership of evangelism and social transformation was moving toward divorce in what came to be called the evangelicals' Great Reversal.

### Later Colonialism, Industrialization and Mission
The industrial revolution was to open other doors for Christianity. It "became a kind of irresistible bulldozer, forcing a way for Western civilization into the non-Western areas of the world" (Van Leeuwen 1964:317). And with it came a new shape to the old question of modernity.

Earlier colonialism had searched for wealth and markets. From the latter half of the nineteenth century it began to search for more. Colonialism turned to political expansion. In India a half century of quasi-sovereign domination by the British East India Company came to an end after the Indian mutiny of 1857. British governmental rule took its place.

In China the picture was similar:

> Cannon balls smashed open the gates of China in the Anglo-Chinese War of 1839-1842 and the War of 1856-1860, in both of which China was beaten. Treaties signed in 1858 between China on the one hand and Britain, France, Russia and the United States on the other hand gave western businessmen, diplomatic officials, and missionaries the right of entrance and residence in China. (Mathews 1951:159)

Africa's turn was not far behind. The electrifying words of missionary explorer David Livingstone (1813-1873) before the University of Cambridge in 1857 spurred on more than mere missionary interest. "I go back to Africa," he proclaimed, "to make an open path for commerce and Christianity. Do you carry on the work which I have begun." Between the death of Livingstone in 1873 and the end of the century, Britain and the powers of Europe "carved up Africa like a gigantic Thanksgiving turkey" (Mathews 1951:138). They arrived at an agreement in Berlin in 1885 to regulate the "scramble for Africa." By 1900 some eleven million square miles had come under white domination—British, French, German, Belgian, Portuguese and Italian (Groves 1955:3-43). Tribal and ethnic rights of domain were disregarded. And from Africa flowed rubber for Western tires, tin for Western canning, cocoa for Western chocolate, gold and diamonds for the Western economy.

***Colonialism, the city and Christian missions.*** Everywhere that the colonial powers were at work, pushed by industrialization's search for new frontiers, Christian missions were also to be found. The nineteenth century became "the great century" of the global expansion of Christianity.

At the beginning of that epoch the total Protestant missionary force hardly exceeded several hundred persons. The majority of those came from the British Empire. By 1910 there were over twenty-one thousand missionaries, single women making up about one-fourth of that number. A new Christian force was emerging.

Thirty-four percent of the 1910 missionaries came from the United States and Canada (Hogg 1977:369). After all, "the main missionary achievement of the nineteenth century was the Christianizing of the United States" (Walls 1990:8). Energized by this shift, North America's churches were turning their attention from home to foreign mission. Reinforcing their concern was America's sense of manifest destiny, underlined to some extent by fears over its own urban changes. It began now to define this sense of self in missiological terms (Marty 1984:338-43). The twentieth century of mission would become "the American century."

What impact did all this have on the world's cities? In 1800, notes David Barrett, thirty-six million people lived in cities (4 percent of the world's total). Thirty-one percent (11.2 million) of that urban total were Christians. By 1900 the world urban community had jumped to 14.4 percent of the total—and the Christian population in those cities (159.6 million) stood at 68.8 percent (Barrett 1986:16).

These statistics showing the emerging urban strength of Christianity need balancing. A large part of the world's urban community was still Western (or Northern Hemisphere) in its base. By the year 1900, the world's five largest cities—in order of size, London, New York, Paris, Berlin, Chicago—had become strongholds of Christian life and evangelism. To be sure, this represented a major achievement in urban mission. But the gospel's urban impact was not yet fully global.

The demographic world of the nineteenth century was rural, and most missionary leaders appropriately focused their efforts on rural areas. Antiurbanism also reinforced this rural strategy. Nineteenth-century British Protestant missionaries came from churches that had ignored the massive urban problems brought by the industrial era in their own country. The Catholic Church all over Europe continued to be identified with conservative rural communities (Shorter 1991:62). Similarly, the emerging American missions contingent was motivated to some degree by a desire to flee the decaying American cities.

Political circumstances also played their part in the rural mission focus. In areas like China, trading treaties restricted foreign activity, political or missionary, to port cities. Not until the Tientsin and Peking treaties of 1858 and 1860 could mission personnel travel beyond the approximately sixteen urban centers where they had been restricted by law. "In 1865, no Protestant missionary was to be seen in eleven of the eighteen provinces of China; and in the seven 'occupied' provinces the area of missionary penetration had not reached far from the coast, except for a number of stations in the Yangtze valley" (Neill 1964:332). In Africa also, early mission activities were limited to coastal ports.

Breaking out of these limitations was not always wise. In Asian civilizations like China, cities were centers of a highly controlled bureaucratic system. Depending on the desires of the ruler, gospel progress might be obstructed rather than encouraged.

Colonial rulers too could prove resistant to the missionary impulse. In

Africa in some cases they "were hostile to Christianity, or at best uncomfortably impartial, favouring Islam, for example, as a counterweight to the Church" (Shorter 1991:58-59). In such situations, missionaries found themselves between a rock and a hard place: they could not do without government approval, yet remaining in the cities and working under the close scrutiny of a hostile government was not wise.

Thus missionary direction turned from the coastal ports of China and Africa to the interior. Following the lead of the China Inland Mission (founded in 1865) and its intentional march to the hinterlands, stirred by the African explorations of David Livingstone, they began to dream new dreams. But the dreams remained largely rural. Peter Scott, the founder of Africa Inland Mission (1895), envisioned a chain of mission stations across Africa to bar the southward progress of Islam and open the door to Africa's heartland. Other bodies like Sudan Interior Mission (founded in 1896) and the Heart of Africa Mission (founded in 1912) shared this dream.

The mission-station model that emerged from this rural drive was not unique to Africa. It was repeated around the world (McGavran 1955:42-67), and it bore some striking resemblances to the praying towns of earlier American colonial days. The mission stations embodied the continuing colonial association of Christianization with civilization. Converts drawn to them formed colonies in isolation from their traditional societies and found themselves stigmatized as foreigners to their own cultural roots and people.

In the end, suggest some, the mission-station strategy may well have been the instrument that "turned away great numbers of workers from the cities" (Hildebrandt 1993:44). The mission station was developed originally as an outpost ministry when cities were small and rural areas neglected. But increasingly it became a substitute instead of a supplement.

***Colonialism, mission and modernity.*** The age we have described was, par excellence, the age of the "white man's burden." The two streams of colonialism and Christianity were seen by the West as the confluence of civilization and Christianity. "Colonial officials and missionaries alike gladly but consciously took it upon themselves to be the guardians of the less-developed races. The peoples of Africa and Asia were wards dependent upon the wise guidance of their white patrons who would gradually educate them to maturity" (Bosch 1991:308).

Later years would reveal the tragic results of these flawed judgments. In areas where the ties were strong, the collapse of colonialism would signal a national judgment against Christianity. Theological divisions would erode the holistic certainty of the gospel as sides chose one or the other of the two alternatives. Liberalism, as it had done in Europe and North America, would move toward the Christianizing pole in a comprehensive approach that gave equal space to preaching, education, medical assistance, and technical and socioeconomic aid (Bavinck 1960:107-12). In knee-jerk reaction to civilizing as the wrong path to follow, some evangelicals would reduce their calling to personal evangelism. Christianity's mandate for social transformation became charitable service. The spiritual formation of national churches would omit social and public ministries as a significant part of Christian discipleship.

Recent scholarship, however, is painting a more nuanced picture of the complicity of the missionary enterprise in the colonial expansion. "It is simply inadequate to contend that mission was nothing other than the spiritual side of imperialism and always the faithful servant of the latter" (Bosch 1991:310). To the colonial powers, the church was often a nuisance. In China the missionaries opposed the British introduction of opium in their quest for imperial power. In 1923 the British declared that Kenya was African territory and that in the event of any clash of interests those of the African must be paramount. That ruling was obtained almost entirely as a result of missionary and Christian pressure. After American rule had been established in the Philippines in 1898, "missionaries spent more time challenging the government to adhere to the high purpose that they had assigned to it than they did in praising its accomplishments" (Foreman 1982:55).

The list goes on—the missionary production of the first ethnologies of human cultures and religions, the Christian crusade against the slave trade, the promotion of vernacular languages and revitalization of indigenous literary movements, the defense of national rights. Medicine as a social service, educational movements open to women as well as men, and literacy campaigns would promote a growing taste for independence and self-reliance that would eventually become colonialism's downfall.

An anthropologist paints this summary of the complex and often contradictory picture: "Christian missions have thus been sometimes the forerunners, sometimes the followers of colonial government and frequently an enlightened and liberal controlling influence, but never permitted by events to have much lasting influence beyond the colonial frontiers" (Southall 1961:3). Where does one go to find the sources for these contradictions—a Christian mission that could both embrace colonialism and oppose it?

Was a compromise with the worldview of modernity once more in evidence? Was there a naiveté regarding colonialism as there was regarding industrialization—a naiveté that stumbled into the dualistic polarizations that lay implicit in modernity's own contradictions? Should Christianity choose again to isolate the world of faith from the colonial world of public policy and law, thus splitting the expression of individual faith in Jesus from its expression in the open secular marketplace (Boer 1984:132-37)? Such a split could also engender a fear of the emerging spirit of nationalism in colonized protectorates and a blindness to the nationalism implicit in the mother country's own colonial quest for God and gold.

What legacy would these choices leave the global church of the city in the twentieth century?

# 3

# The Fourth
# Great Urban Wave

"FUTURE HISTORIANS WILL RECORD THE twentieth century as that century in which the whole world became one immense city" (Cox 1966:273).

If we stick strictly to statistics, Cox's assertion is not hard to support. In the year 1800, the world's population was 97 percent rural. Only 1.7 percent of the world's peoples lived in communities of 100,000 or more. Almost 2.5 percent could be found in communities of 20,000 or more, and 3 percent in towns of 5,000 or larger. By 1992, however, some 45 percent of the world's population is recorded as urban; by 2000, it was expected that those figures would top 50 percent. "Today we are on the threshold of living in a world that for the first time will be numerically more urban than rural" (Palen 1992:3).

This fourth great urban wave began in the 1950s. Before the children born in 1985 become adults, half of the world's population will be urban. And half of that half will be living in cities with over a million inhabitants.

## The Urban Present: Global Explosion
The new wave is distinctive in its location and its accelerated velocity. The wave is breaking on the shores of Africa, Asia and Latin America. And urban metropolises like Mexico City, Seoul and Kinshasa are compressing into a few decades growth that took North American cities over a century to achieve.

***Africa and Latin America.*** Africa's urban population jumped from
10.5 percent in 1950 to 26 percent in 1985, and by 2000 it rose to 42.5
percent—almost a 50 percent increase rate in only fifteen years. "For
every urban African in 1985 there will be two in the year 2000" (Monsma
1989:20). It was expected that by the end of the 1990s, more than 345 million Africans would be living in cities (Rondinelli 1988:292). At the end of
the nineteenth century in black Africa south of the Sahara, Ibadan was
the only city with a population of more than 100,000 people. By 1970
there were some thirty-seven cities with populations of 100,000 or more,
seven surpassing half a million. By 1980 such cities were likely in excess
of fifty (Bairoch 1988:431).

As a whole, Latin America is far more urbanized than Africa or Asia.
During the same 1950-1985 period its urban community moved from
40 percent to 67.4 percent, and the percentage of those living in cities of
a million people or more escalated from 23 to 31 percent. Before the
industrial revolution the general level of urbanization in Europe never
exceeded 13 percent. By 1950 it had reached 40 percent in Latin America (Bairoch 1988:457). "The greatest growth has been in the very largest cities. Latin America is a continent of primate cities, with half (49
percent) of its population in cities of over 100,000 inhabitants" (Palen
1992:439).

***Asia.*** Asia's urban history is a long one. Until two hundred years ago it
contained more city dwellers than the rest of the world combined. In 1800
six of the ten largest cities in the world were located there (four in China
alone)—Beijing, Canton, Hangchow, Yedo (Tokyo), Soochow and Osaka.
By 2000 Asia was expected to have more city dwellers than any other
continent, with 40-50 percent of its population living in cities. That represents a 665 percent growth rate since 1920. By comparison, its rural
growth over the same period was only 95.6 percent (Costa et al. 1989:5-
6).

As of 1990, in fact, Asia still boasted six of the ten largest cities in the
world—Tokyo/Yokohama (depending on the scope of one's measurement, the largest city in the world), Shanghai, Beijing, Bombay, Calcutta
and Seoul. From 1950 to 1985, Asia's overall urban growth rate (except-
ing China) had moved from 14.5 to 27.6 percent, placing it slightly higher
than Africa's figure for the same time period.

Nevertheless, the large populations of China, India and Indonesia have
only recently entered their time of rapid urban growth. In the industrializing nations like Taiwan and Korea the pace has been much more rapid.
China deserves special attention here (and special care also). Its massive
population of over one billion people, for one thing, makes urban macro-

regional generalizations difficult. It is roughly equal to the combined population of all the twenty-one nations of western Europe, all the thirty-six nations of Latin America and the Caribbean, plus the populations of the United States and Canada.

In addition, a succession of government urban policies since the 1950s have helped keep China's urban population trends a demographic mystery. Mao's early policies, described by some as "resolutely antiurban," promoted urban control and rural relocation. But these ran up against economic realities.

What does urbanization look like in today's less restrictive post-Mao China? Scholarship has treaded lightly in looking for answers. Not until the mid-1970s, in fact, did China's cities become a major focus of historical research (Stapleton 1996:1-2). "The most likely figure for 1982 is an urban population of some 207 million and a [1985] rate of urbanization of 21%" (Bairoch 1988:435). That percentage rate is a significant increase from the 1950 estimate of 12 percent (and an urban population of 121 million people).

**North Africa and the Middle East.** North Africa and the Middle East have been a Muslim world for centuries, and that world has always been predominantly urban. Scholarship, in fact, has long debated the uniqueness of the shape of the "Muslim city" (Haneda 1994:1-10). But recently these discussions have taken a new turn. Researchers are recognizing the Western assumptions about Orientalism that controlled the earlier debate, along with generalizations that were based largely on acquaintance with only North African cities (Abu-Lughod 1987:155-76).

However that debate goes, scholars are still generally agreed that "for Muslims, cities often possess a special sanctity and are regarded as the sole places in which a full and truly Muslim life may be lived" (Lapidus 1969:v). Relatively unencumbered by Western conflicts between city and country, rural and urban, the spread of Islam in the centuries after its birth has followed an urban path. While European urbanism was declining in the so-called Dark Ages, the Arabs were busy founding new towns and regenerating the old Roman towns of Egypt and the Levant and the Sassanian towns of Persia. Cities took on military and administrative significance as radiating centers for Islamization. Urban artisans, merchants and tradesmen used the city's commercial webs to spread Islam along the caravan and sea routes.

In the late fifteenth and early sixteenth centuries, urban decline began in the Middle East. By the end of the nineteenth century, the preindustrial world of urban Islam had lost much of its vitality in the face of European expansionism. Since the 1920s, however, and especially since the last three decades of the twentieth century Islam's urban expansion has accelerated. So-called city-states like Kuwait and Qatar are becoming urbanized at phenomenal rates of 10 and 15 percent annually. Damascus, with a population of 850,000 in 1970, was projected to reach 3 million by 2000. Baghdad was expected to grow from 2.2 million in 1970 to 12 million by 2000.

In 1922 Tehran's first official census reported a population of 210,000. By 1956 it had reached 2,980,000. Current estimates range from 8 to 10 million. More people now live in Iran's capital than the populations of Israel, Lebanon or Jordan.

The picture in North Africa is similar:

> In the period between 1950 and 1970, urban growth in Northern Africa surpassed that of North America and all of Europe. The percentage increase of urban population growth in North Africa reached 51.6% (19.1% rural). In North America it was only 17.6%; in western Europe 18.7%; northern Europe was 9.8%. By 1970, 42.9% of Algeria's population was living in urban areas with over 5,000 inhabitants. In Tunisia, the figure was 43.5%, Morocco 32.5%. (Conn 1989:64)

And the future? Algiers was projected to hit 4.8 million in 2000 (from 1.2 million in 1970), Tunis 2.3 million (from 755,000 in 1970). Casablanca was expected to grow from its 1970 population of 1.4 million to 5 million by 2000.

***Looking for reasons.*** How do we explain this rapid urban growth? What has transformed the global village into the global city?

Industrialization may be too easy a generalization. To be sure, it has changed the recent fortunes of large Asian cities like Seoul, Hong Kong and Tokyo, where it tends to be concentrated. Taipei, for example, is the location for one-third of industrial establishments in Taiwan that employ more than five hundred people. And 79 percent of those employed in manufacturing in the Philippines work in Manila.

But "it is uncommon to find the majority of urban residents incorporated into this type of employment. . . . Large-scale industrialization has . . . occurred only in about ten countries and several of these are European" (Drakakis-Smith 1987:53, 56). Unlike England and North America in the nineteenth century, the fourth urban wave does not feature urbanization and industrialization as equal partners. Currently urbanization is sometimes developing without industrialization (Bairoch 1988:462).

Where then should we look for causes? Population growth overall is a major factor (Phillips and LeGates 1981:105). Since World War II a stable birth rate and a declining death rate have marked the developing worlds of Asia, Africa and Latin America. Between 1950 and 1970, while world population grew from 2.5 billion to 3.6 billion, populations in the developing countries grew four times as much. And in their cities the picture is the same: between 54 and 60 percent of current growth in these areas comes from natural increase (Palen 1992:364).

Migration into cities is the other major reason. In a push-pull dynamic the rural population turns in hope to the city. Too often the push factors reflect tragedy or frustration. Wars and civil strife send thousands of refugees from Ethiopia to Khartoum, from Sierra Leone and Liberia to Abidjan. Vietnamese and Cambodians find their way to Sydney and Los Angeles. Exiles make Miami the second largest Cuban city. Successive years of drought in the Calcutta region drive the desperate off their small subsistence farms. Many East Africans find their way to townships and cities in Kenya and Tanzania. They come "from thinly populated rural areas where the soil is of poor quality, and from the so-called 'marginal' or semi-arid areas where scratching a living from the soil is the only prospect for the peasant farmer" (Shorter 1991:16-17).

But the pull factors are stronger and more optimistic: the promise of jobs in Nairobi, better education in Seoul, medical treatment and healthcare in Mexico City. In Fiji the lure of wealth turns people to Suva and Nausori, now accounting for some 60 percent of Fiji's urban community. Over the last few decades there urban income has been growing six times as rapidly as rural income. In Africa many young men and women are drawn to cities by a desire for freedom from the social constraints of a close-knit rural community. The antiurban bias of the West is not yet a match for the developing world's sense of urban optimism.

## Shift from the Old Center of Gravity

Another factor magnifies the impact of this new geographically global location of the city: the slowing down and reshaping of urbanization in countries where it first achieved prominence. The world's urban center of gravity is not just getting larger; it is moving. The majority of the world's urban peoples no longer speak English, French or German at home; the languages of the global city are becoming mother tongues like Chinese, Spanish and Swahili.

Urban growth in the old centers of Europe and North America accelerated from 1920 to 1980. Europe moved from an urban population of 46.2 percent to 75.9 percent, North America from 51.9 percent to 73.3 percent. But the years since then have seen a leveling off in urban growth patterns. From 1980 to 1987, the average annual urban growth rate in the United States was 1.0 percent, in Sweden 0.2, in France 0.6. The Federal

Republic of Germany recorded 0.1 percent. By comparison, in the same period the urban growth rate was averaging 3.2 percent in Ghana and 4.1 percent in India (Abu-Lughod 1991:57).

By the year 2000, according to United Nations predictions, the slow-up rate would continue in Europe and North America (Palen 1992:4). Other long-urbanized areas are following this trend. For example, with 70 percent of Australia's people living in its ten largest cities, that nation's enthusiasm for the city may be changing.

What is happening? How do we explain the new direction? No single reason will fit everywhere. But two are prominent.

**Suburbanization.** A major trend in this devolution of the Western industrial city is the growth of the suburb. Tributaries flowing away from the urban core, to some they have offered a kind of class refuge. In England and the United States, the lure is that of a single-family home. The suburbs are a shelter primarily for the middle and upper classes.

In Europe, as popular as they are, the suburbs often represent just a move from one rental high-rise to another, in this case the condominium (Adler 1995:711). The European norm is not a detached house but an apartment or a terraced or row house. It is the cities, not the suburbs, that are the chosen home of the middle and upper classes of continental Europe.

In the English-speaking world the inner-city core is increasingly reserved for the poor and for non-Anglo-Saxon immigrants. In non-English-speaking Europe, by comparison, people of different income groups live intermingled in the city while preserving class distinctions within and among buildings (Hohenberg and Lees 1995:351).

If current scholarship is correct, the suburban ideal of the English-speaking world was the creation of London's evangelicals in the late eighteenth and early nineteenth centuries. Christian statesmen like William Wilberforce and John Thornton saw the suburban villa as a temple dedicated to the ideals of domestic purity—a notion predicated on a sharp divide between the public and private worlds. In the suburb would be built separate spheres for work and family, men as breadwinners and women as homemakers. In a time when industrialization was devaluating women's work, the single-family home became the ideal for the professional homemaker (Adler 1995:698). Linking home and work would be commuter transportation. In the village of Clapham, five miles from London Bridge, evangelicals modeled their suburban retreat. Here moral purity could be safeguarded in class isolation "from the dangers, cruelties, bad language, suffering, and immorality that filled the crowded London streets" (Fishman 1987:58).

In the years that followed, the model became a pattern. The growth of London's inner city began to stall as migration from city to suburb expanded. After the interwar period, and especially in the 1950s and 1960s, Britons, aided by a vast increase in private transportation, became commuters. In 1931 inner London had boasted a population of 4,397,000 people, with 1,899,000 living in "outer metropolitan London." By 1971 there were only 2,723,000 living in inner London, but the outer edge of the city had a population of 5,290,000 (Gulick 1989:94). Between 1961 and 1974 the metropolitan counties and greater London lost 5.4 percent of their people, while the rest of Great Britain had a population increase of 12.8 percent (*Faith in the City* 1985:7).

U.S. patterns of suburbanization have been similar. They flowed out of a quintessential passion for privacy, an ideology of "we keep ourselves to ourselves" (Mumford 1961:493). Repelled by urban growth and decay associated with industrialization, the wealthy upper classes were the first to follow that ideology out to the commuting suburbs. By the beginning of the twentieth century, with the expansion of public transportation, those with white-collar positions could begin to follow the trolley tracks through urban fragmentation to the suburban dream. With the help of Henry Ford and the private automobile, the working classes would eventually follow also (Conn 1994a:56-58, 76-78, 83-85). With the mass building of prefabricated homes on large suburban tracts of land in the years immediately following World War II, the single-family home became a reality as well for the blue-collar, white working class.

In 1920 city dwellers were a majority of the U.S. population. In 1970, however, more Americans were living in suburbs than in cities. "Of two hundred million people, seventy-six million lived in areas around but not inside cities, sixty-four million in cities themselves" (Chudacoff 1981:264).

**Inner-city transformations.** What factors reinforced white flight from early industrial cities to the idealized suburbs? In England it was a dominating perception of the urban priority areas (UPAs) as "districts of specially disadvantaged character" (*Faith in the City* 1985:9). Opportunities for jobs, housing, social services, schools and leisure have shifted out of the industrial city. Greater London has lost at least 50 percent of its manufacturing jobs since 1960. New white-collar jobs attract people from the outer rings of the city; left behind are residents of the central areas who are disproportionately unskilled or in many cases employed at a lower level of skill.

The city becomes the land of those left behind—the poor, the underemployed, the ethnic outsider. The conditions they inherit are economic decline, physical decay and social disintegration. In once-prosperous

Manchester unemployment reached 20 percent in 1981, in Birmingham almost 25 percent (40 percent among ethnic minorities). "To describe the UPAs is to write of squalor and dilapidation. Gray walls, littered streets, boarded-up windows, graffiti, demolition and debris are the drearily standard features of the districts and parishes" (*Faith in the City* 1985:18).

Though untouched by war and the disintegration of an empire, the industrial city of the United States also looks less and less like a launching pad for hope and more and more like a repository of despair. The shift in American cities from an industrial to a service-oriented economy creates a "rust belt" in older urban centers of the Northeast. The middle-class identification of the city with crime and social disintegration has left the metropolis with a collapsing tax base, a failed attempt at urban reform in the 1950s, and a marginalized life of social and political powerlessness.

Reinforcing such trends are white assumptions about the ethnic changes that are also reshaping these inner cities. In Europe

> a fortress mentality is being adopted in the East and West with foreigners, especially from the Third World, more and more regarded as second-class people. Millions of immigrants from Northern Africa, Turkey, the Commonwealth countries were once welcomed by sheer political and economic opportunism. For the same reason they are now being offered one-way tickets back to their countries of origin. (Companjen 1993:8)

Everywhere in the industrialized Western city there is ethnic change. In the 1950s and 1960s Western Europe—especially the "golden triangle" of Birmingham/Milan/Düsseldorf—was undergoing economic expansion. It needed more labor than it could recruit from its own rural areas. "So Turks and West Indians, North Africans and Asians came to the cities of Europe in response to the invitations of government and commerce to provide a new work force, and to do some of the dirty jobs which the indigenous Europeans preferred not to do" (Milligan 1984:84). But when the economic tide turned and jobs became scarce, the new work force became surplus labor. Now "they" have become a part of "us." And white Europe has become reluctantly multicultural. "Resentment of the outsiders has been widespread, notably in working-class districts where contacts at work and in school are close and there is competition for housing and jobs" (Hohenberg and Lees 1995:350).

England's urban priority areas have moved in the same multicultural direction. One of the largest mosques outside the traditional Muslim world now stands in central London near Regents Park. By 1985 Britain's Muslim community numbered over 1.5 million people; they came from Pakistan and Bangladesh, from the Near and Middle East, from

Africa, Malaysia and the Caribbean. The second largest ethnic community is the Chinese and the Vietnamese boat people. In 1989 the black community, coming largely from the Caribbean and the West Indies, made up only about 4 percent of English society. They are newcomers to the racial mix.

That mix is largely an urban mix.

> While it is possible to sit on the top deck of a London bus and hear for mile after mile never a word of English, it is equally possible to visit some rural community whether in Lincolnshire or Cornwall where there has never yet set foot anybody of Asian or African descent. Even in a city like Leeds or Bradford it is perfectly possible to go over the brow of a hill and there to find that the outer suburb reflects nothing of the mixing of races and cultures and religious grouping that its neighbouring inner city area so obviously indicates. (Marchant 1985:108)

The deep-rootedness of England's class system is in conflict with this multiethnic presence (Bradbury 1989:13). Urban graffiti sprays its welcome on the walls of the city: "Slums for Filthy Wogs," "Burn Black Babies," "Pakis Stink."

Urban ethnic patterns in North America's industrial centers are similar. The United States, long an immigrant nation, found a new kind of immigrant shaping its move to industrialization in the late nineteenth century. From 1870 to 1920 over twenty-six million entered the country, a figure a little less than four times the number from the previous fifty years (Glaab 1963:236-37). But this time they came not from northern Europe and the Anglo-Saxon community but from the less developed countries of eastern and southern Europe. America's cities found themselves speaking Italian, Polish and Yiddish. New York City now had more foreign-born residents than any city in the world. By far the majority of these immigrants settled in the industrial cities of the Northeast and Midwest. By 1920 the American city was home to three-fourths of the foreign-born.

The twentieth century brought still more ethnic changes to American cities. Between the two world wars great numbers of blacks moved from the South to the North, from the farm to the city. It was the beginning of the largest single migration movement within the country. By the end of World War I well over half a million blacks had moved north to the cities; by midcentury that figure would total almost three million (Conn 1994a:78).

The closing decades of the twentieth century witnessed an acceleration of these patterns. Over three million legal immigrants entered the country during the 1960s; by the 1980s that figure had doubled, to six million. In the twenty-first century other racial and ethnic groups will outnumber Anglos for the first time. An article from *American Demographics* sums up the future: "You'll know it's the twenty-first century when everyone belongs to a minority group" (Waldrop 1990:23-27). By 2056 the "average" U.S. resident will trace his or her descent to Africa, Asia, the Hispanic world, the Pacific Islands, Arabia—almost anywhere but white Europe.

As elsewhere, ethnic pluralism has enlarged the gap between city and suburb, and racism has encouraged it. The half-century after 1880 witnessed a tidal wave of intolerance and racist violence. The blame for urban decay was laid at the feet of the immigrant "unworthy poor" (D. Ward 1989). Immigration quota systems effectively barred Chinese entrance from 1882 to 1943. Race riots in 1943 welcomed African Americans to Detroit and Harlem, Oakland and San Francisco. And in cities—northern and southern—the civil rights movement of the 1950s and 1960s marked its progress despite police resistance, burned-out churches and indifference.

Urban Australia is a relative newcomer to such multiethnic changes, but they are significant nonetheless. It has become one of the most ethnically diverse populations in the world. "Since World War II, no other country, with the exception of Israel, has accepted so many immigrants relative to the size of its existing population. Multiculturalism, the maintenance of the distinctive languages and cultures of various ethnic groups within a general Australian identity, has become government policy" (Cooper 1994:3). Over three and a half million people have come to Australia within the last thirty years, an unprecedented boom in assisted migration. Including the children born there, at least one in three Australians now has an immediate link with migration. Eighty-five percent of these have settled in the continent's major cities (Soulos 1994:32). Today its cities are an amalgam of 140 ethnic groups speaking one hundred languages and practicing over forty religions.

The source of this migrant intake has also shifted significantly since World War II. Initially immigrants came in largest numbers from the British Isles. But by 1986 only 35 percent of the overseas-born could trace their ancestry to the British empire's roots. Now 34 percent come from elsewhere in Europe while 13 percent are from Asia, 8 percent from Oceania and 4 percent from the Middle East. Still another 4 percent claim North and South America as their origin. Three percent come from Africa.

Lebanese and Vietnamese settle in Sydney's outer western suburbs. Italians take advantage of cheap housing in the Sydney suburbs of Annandale and Leichhardt (known popularly now as Little Italy).

But no matter where newcomers settle, their presence, as elsewhere in the world's white cultures, is met with resistance and sometimes protest. "Violent prejudice and tolerant, easy-going prejudice both find a place in Australian society" (Lawton 1988:42). An Australian commissioner for human rights maintains that "the immigration debate has become our national pastime." And behind that debate are signs that "many Australians still harbour a desire for a homogeneous British-based society" (Lawton 1988:42).

## Growth of Non-Christian Urban Population

As the cities grow, the percentage of urban Christians decreases. In 1900, notes David Barrett, Christians numbered 68.8 percent of urban dwellers, a total of 159,600,000 people. By 1996 the number of urban Christians had risen to 1,269,954,000—but the percentage had fallen to 45.7 percent (D. Barrett 1996:25). The number of new non-Christian urban dwellers per day now totals 123,000. In 1900 that figure was 5,200.

Is the church losing the cities? That language can be misleading to some degree. Remember the massive urban population increases we have been chronicling in parts of the world traditionally hostile to Christianity. In countries where non-Christian world religions have been strongly entrenched, urban population figures have swelled, supported by massive migration and natural birth increases.

Reinforcing this population boom among non-Christians has been the identification of the church with its rural heritage. The evangelical church in Latin America, for instance, has experienced tremendous growth in recent years. But most of it has been in rural areas, towns and smaller cities. "With the exception of Central America's cities and Santiago, Chile, there has been proportionately little church growth in the larger cities until recently" (Berg and Pretiz 1992:93). In megacities like Buenos Aires, Rio de Janeiro, Lima, Caracas and Mexico City, the total evangelical population has not exceeded 3 percent. A 1986 survey of Mexico City discovered a total Protestant community of only 240,000 out of a population of over twenty million.

*An African sample.* Africa is a clear example of this history. As mentioned in the previous chapter, late-nineteenth-century missionaries to Africa, like their counterparts elsewhere, tended to concentrate their activities around mission stations in rural areas. The church, whether Catholic or Protestant, appeared to perceive "towns as a godless environment, where evil flourished and little good could be found" (Peil 1982:6). This meant settlement at a distance from towns and cities. "After 1914, the ideal of the Christian village was gradually abandoned, as it was realized that it was essentially a ghetto, and unlikely to transform society as a whole" (Isichei 1995:196). But a pattern had been set that rapid urbanization could only reinforce with its poverty, prostitution and powerlessness.

Attitudinal changes within the Catholic Church have slowly begun to change the old urban images. A growing body of literature on the church's social role has created new understandings of the complexities of the city, and specifically the urban and African dimensions of secular issues (J. Kelley 1977:29-36). But this sophistication has been missing from Protestant and particularly evangelical circles. Too often Christians have moved with more enthusiasm to the cities that have the churches.

Given the past missionary strategy that used rural mission stations as centers for evangelism and church growth, most African Protestant denominations today have been left with a very rural outlook. They are poorly equipped to minister to the African cities of the twenty-first century (Hildebrandt 1993:44).

Nairobi is an example. At the time of the 1979 census, close to four out of ten Kenyans lived in the capital. The city grows at the rate of more than five hundred people a day. Roughly half that figure are new immigrants. The city doubles in size every ten years (Niemeyer 1989:13). What about the church? In 1963 the total attendance in all the churches of Nairobi was 30,000. By 1986 that number had increased fivefold, to over 150,000. However, other statistics offer warning signals. The percentage of those attending church remained fairly constant at 9-12 percent over this period. In view of population increase, this means that "the number of unchurched people has risen significantly from 270,000 (1963) to over a million (1986). . . . By growing at the same rate as the population grows, the church is actually falling behind because more and more people are living outside its influence" (Niemeyer 1989:19).

When church size in the areas outside Nairobi is taken into account, the urban challenge becomes even more problematic. "Nairobi has one church for every 2000 people, but it has been estimated that in the entire nation there is one church for every 1000 people" (Niemeyer 1989:25). This disparity shows also in the average size and location of the eight hundred churches of Nairobi. Most are relatively small. Over half have one hundred or fewer people in attendance on a given Sunday. Most of these are growing by adding Christians from other places and other churches, not by converting Christians. To reach out and minister to all of the city's 1,600,000 residents (1988), each church should be targeting two thousand people.

Complicating this further is the unevenness in the churches' geographical spread through the city. The congregations are not uniformly distributed through the city's forty wards. In some wards like Kaloleni and

Kangemi there is one church for every 600-800 people. In Parklands it is one church for every 8,000 and in Uhuru one church for every 15,400. "The economically depressed areas of the city continue to be among the areas most in need of additional churches" (Niemeyer 1989:30).

Full participation in the life of Nairobi's church is also problematic. In a city where perhaps as many as 80 percent claim to be Christians, under one-third are members of a Nairobi church. More surprising still, fewer than one-half of that number are in church on a given Sunday.

These urban churches are undergoing a crisis in qualified leadership as well. "Less than one percent of Nairobi pastors are trained for urban ministry" (Mutunga 1993:26). Integrating urban mission into the whole life of the theological training schools of Nairobi—its faculty and administration, its curriculum and its students—is a priority only beginning to be adopted (Austin 1992b:28-38).

***Megacities outside the orbit of Christendom.*** At the beginning of the twentieth century, there were only twenty cities with a population exceeding one million. By 1980 that figure had reached 235, with some 118 located in less developed areas (Palen 1992:4). Since 1950 there has been a tenfold increase in the population living in such cities.

In 1900 all of the world's five largest cities—London, New York, Paris, Berlin and Chicago—were centers of Christianity and bases for global evangelism. By comparison, "what we may call the opposition to Christian world missions has mushroomed phenomenally from five non-Christian mega-cities in the year 1900 to 121 today, and to 510 by A.D. 2050. Non-Christian or anti-Christian supercities are also exploding from nil in 1900 to 20 today, and to 180 by A.D. 2050" (Barrett 1986:10).

This is powerfully demonstrated in the recently emerging urban giants with over ten million inhabitants each. In 1958 Tokyo became the first to reach ten million. Then came Shanghai in 1967, Beijing in 1976, Calcutta and Osaka in 1984, and Bombay in 1985. By 2000, it was expected that as many as seven Muslim cities were expected to join that select group— Jakarta, Cairo, Baghdad, Istanbul, Teheran, Karachi and Dacca.

***Christian decline in the West.*** When we look at the state of Christianity in its former Western base, we can speak more easily of losing the cities. Here nominalism and decline are prevailing. Here the church faces not a pre-Christian urban world but a post-Christian one. Christian missions ask, Can the West be converted?

The picture in Europe is not always easy to read. A 1989 survey asserts that "the overall number of practising church people in the last twenty years in Western Europe is declining" (Brierley 1989:2). In countries like Finland, Sweden, France, Switzerland and Italy, the rate of decline may be over 10 percent. On the other hand, in a few areas a minority of new churches appear as larger numbers record closure. In the Netherlands between 1975 and 1985 twenty Catholic churches and thirty associated with the Reformed churches closed—but during the same time twenty other Reformed churches opened their doors (Brierley 1989:48).

Equally frustrating for evangelical evaluation is the uneven placement of Protestant churches. Seventy-three percent of the Spanish population live in 1,110 cities with a population of at least five thousand people. But 62 percent of these cities have no evangelical witness. Protestant strength in France is found in the southern and eastern parts of the country. In Portugal the farther north one goes, the fewer churches will be found. Mismatch of this sort hardly indicates decline. But it most certainly indicates absence.

Overall, observers tend to be gloomy. By 1989, comments one source, while the church in Africa was adding four thousand new members per day, in Europe the church was said to be losing seven thousand per day (Gili 1989:17). A more conservative source speaks of a net decline each year of 1.8 million (Cotterell 1989:37). An average of 5-6 percent of western Europeans attend church regularly, compared with 40-45 percent of Americans. Marc Spindler describes the European scene in terms of "a resurgence of paganism" (Spindler 1987:8). Should we then speak of the reevangelization of Europe? Anton Wessels looks in depth at its early contact with Christianity and wonders, "Was it ever really Christian?" (Wessels 1994).

A 1985 British report, *Faith in the City,* found an average of ninety adults attending church out of an Anglican urban parish population of 10,560 (0.85 percent). For every one person who went to an Anglican church in an urban parish there were ninety-nine who did not. In contrast "are the increasing number of growing and developing Black-led churches—at present over 160 denominations involving perhaps 100,000 people in about 2,500 congregations" (*Faith in the City* 1985:43).

Australia's recent church history moves generally in the same direction. Unlike England and Europe, however, the Australian church never experienced a demographically significant golden age of faith from which to fall. Furthermore, some argue that even in its first two hundred years on the Australian continent the church's major role was moral policeman. It kept the people within boundaries of acceptable behavior and was seen as the killjoy promoter of a puritanical fanaticism that Australians have dubbed "wowserism." Even today that thesis continues; the churches are seen primarily as sources of morality and civilization rather than as repositories of supernatural truth (Mol 1985:137).

Similar to trends in Canada, current Australian "church attendance rates are the same for both rural and metropolitan areas. This challenges the common belief that country areas are more religious than the cities. Country towns in particular demonstrate similar patterns to the cities. It is only in small country villages that attendance rates tend to be higher than the national average" (Brookes 1990:9). But significant drops in church participation signal deep cause for concern. In 1960 around 41 percent of the population claimed to attend church at least monthly. By the mid-1980s that figure had dropped to around 24 percent (Kaldor 1987:22).

Christian writers look at this decline and at the impact of the gospel in the last half of the twentieth century and ask questions. "Advance Australia where?" (J. Smith 1988), "Can God survive in Australia?" (B. Wilson 1983), "Faith without the church?" (Bentley, Blombery and Hughes 1992). "Socially speaking," judges one concerned author, "God has retreated to places like churches, which now appear as a speciality leisure industry catering for the religiously musical" (B. Wilson 1983:55).

Preliminary reports from the 1991 National Church Life Survey appear to suggest that over the previous five years "such declines have not been evident across Anglican/Protestant churches" (Kaldor 1992:19). It would seem that, based on statistics collected from participating congregations in the survey, these Australian churches are keeping up with population growth. But further analysis is still needed.

Urbanization in Canada is a more recent trend. In 1940 only half of its population lived in urban areas. Now cities account for 75 percent of its people, and some expected that percentage to reach 90 by the year 2000 (Tunnicliffe 1990:18). As in much of the Western world, urban Canadian church attendance and participation continues its decline. In 1945 "some 60% of the population maintained that they were attending services on close to a weekly basis. . . . The 60% figure fell to around 50% by 1960, to about 30% by 1980, and now stands at just over 20%" (Bibby 1995:15-16).

The future provides little hope. Churchgoers are disproportionately old. Today's fifty-five-and-overs—the group most supportive of Canada's churches—will disappear from the scene, and today's adults under thirty-five (only 14 percent of whom attend church) will replace them in the demographic picture. What, then, can we expect? Within twenty years, the proportion of people attending church weekly will drop from today's 23 percent level to around 15 percent (Bibby 1995:117).

But as in Australia, the gulf between Canadian urban-based churchgoers and rural-based participants is not significant. Whether metropolitan area, smaller city, village or farm, "fewer than five in ten people in each community-size category claim to be committed to Christianity, or to any other religion, for that matter" (Bibby 1987:92-93). The stereotype of a religiously committed rural area and an urban secular one does not exist in Canada. Fewer than three in ten Canadians, no matter where they live, attend services weekly.

## Conclusion

The global village in which we began our survey has become a global city, whose demographic center of gravity has shifted through history from industrialization in Europe and the English-speaking world to explosive changes in Africa, Asia and Latin America. It is a long journey from the cities of the Roman Empire to the cities of Sydney and São Paulo, Dakka and Djibouti.

The journey is particularly confusing for the church. Where has this review of urban history taken us? What new urban realities face us? What preliminary clues can these realities offer us for creating a mission agenda for the people of God in the global city? Which directions should we take to bring together the city, the kingdom of God and the church?

For its first three hundred years beyond the coming of Christ, the church saw cities as gifts of God, royal routes to the evangelization of the world. Now the picture is not so bright. In the Western world the church moves to the outer edges of the city, fearful of what it perceives as emerging urban patterns. In the worlds of Africa, Asia and Latin America the cities expand as the population flows toward them, but with notable exceptions, the church feels overwhelmed and moves only slowly to face urban challenges.

What are some of the major challenges we face? And what agenda issues do they create for our reflection? Where do we turn to discern appropriate urban assignments for the global people of God?

# Part 2

Biblical Perspectives

# 4

# God & the
# Old Testament City
## *Love or Hate?*

IN THE CUNEIFORM WRITING OF SUMER it was called *uru*. In Akkadian it was *alu, happiras* in Hittite (Hallo 1971:58). The ancient Hebrews generally called it *ir,* and the Greeks of the Hellenistic world spoke of *polis.* For the English-speaking world, it is *city.* But jumping too quickly from the cities of the twentieth century to the urban vocabulary of the Old Testament can be hazardous to one's hermeneutical health, for several reasons.

For one thing, most of the cities of the ancient Near East were relatively small, possibly only five to ten acres in area. If one estimated 240 inhabitants per urban acre, the population of such cities would range from one to three thousand (Frick 1977:79). Contrary to English translations like the New International Version, the Hebrews had no separate word like *town* to indicate an area of smaller population than *city.* To indicate larger size than normal, one could simply speak of a city as great (Num 13:28; Deut 1:28; Jon 3:2-3). Even then there was an implication of strength and power, not simply size.

Why so? In the world of the ancient Near East what made a city (as opposed to a village) was its role as a fortified guardian. Located on an elevated place or surrounded by a wall, the city meant security and defense from one's enemies, not necessarily density and size (Thompson 1983:5-38; Zimmermann 1967:582-92).

Even more significant was the intimate link between the city—its power and place—and religion in the very ancient world. The city was a shrine. On its streets the gods and humankind lived in community. The citizen who passed through its gates approached "the center of the world." Its walls surrounded a miniature cosmos, the four points of the compass joining at its center, "a shrine or tower where the union of earth and heaven, man and god, is ritually consummated" (Dougherty 1980:2).

The ancient world echoed with these religious themes. Long before walls served a military purpose, they were a "magic defense." They divided the chaotic world of demons and phantoms outside from the holy and ordered center within (Eliade 1963:371).

The great city of Ur in southern Mesopotamia was likely such a shrine city. It occupied some 220 acres with its canals, harbors and temples. Its ziggurat tower, called "the mountain of God" or "the hill of heaven," rose high above the alluvial plain. Built and rebuilt, it was a symbol of the reunion of the gods and society, of heaven and earth (DeWitt 1979:21). Its three staircases each led up to a gate-tower and access to the two upper stories and the shrine at the summit. Here in the shrine reigning over the city as king was the moon god Nannar. Here the exalted Lord, the crown of heaven and earth, the beautiful Lord who shines in heaven united politics and agriculture, worship and warfare in an urban theocracy.

Out of this urban worldview, linked by the Genesis author with the Babel tower history (Gen 11:1-9, 31), God called his servant Abram. " 'Leave your country and your people,' God said, 'and go to the land I will show you' " (Gen 12:1; Acts 7:3). "Despite Ur's glory, it was for the Israelites a city to be left behind for the sake of God's even better promises" (Selman 1985:284). From Ur of the Chaldeans the patriarch went, "looking forward to the city with foundations, whose builder and maker is God" (Heb. 11:10).

Ancient extrabiblical texts appear to indicate that in the work of temple building there was self-glorification and name making for the builders (DeWitt 1979:22). By contrast, Abram's departure from Ur is rewarded by the assurance that God would make his name great (Gen 12:2). In confidence in that promise Abram builds neither tower nor city. He erects instead an altar to the God who made the moon and its heavenly retinue (Gen 12:7). And the patriarchs who followed him pitched their tents and built their altars as he did (Gen 12:8; 13:18), on the outskirts of the shrine centers (Gen 33:18-20; 35:27). The "habitations of Jacob" (Ps 79:7; Lam 2:2) become "edge cities," encampments that affirm urban reality without embracing urban shrine theology.

## The City: Enemy or Ally?

Since those days almost three millennia ago, other pilgrims have continued to wrestle with choices similar to Abram's. The shrine cities of the ancient world with their integrated network of totalitarian theological demands have disappeared. Today our choices to obey God may involve less radical breaks than Abram had to make. But the difficult choices are still difficult. Do we love the city or leave it? Did God make the country and the devil make the city? Are we closer to God in the country than in the city? What is our urban mission? How is it related to God's urban mission? Isn't that urban mission an antiurban pattern?

**The antiurban debate.** In the search for editorial sources to the Old Testament, liberal scholarship has often made use of this alleged antiurban ideal (Halligan 1975). Nineteenth-century Romanticism painted the ideal human society as nomadic and settled urban life as decadent. In keeping with this, and affected by growing sociological approaches to the Scriptures, much biblical research began to paint Israel's religious ideals as antiurban (Hahn 1966:157-84). Israel's nomadic-wilderness past became the perceived source of its faithfulness to God (Flight 1923:158-224).

After all, goes the argument, didn't the downfall of Lot, Abraham's nephew, begin when "he pitched his tents near Sodom" (Gen 13:12)? And didn't Lot's eastward path to the city (Gen 13:11) trace the eastward path of Adam and Eve, Cain and the Babel tower builders—always away from the presence of God (Gen 3:24; 4:16; 11:2)? Wasn't God's mission in the city always to involve destruction of Babel towers (Gen 11:8-9) or angelic visitations of fire and brimstone (Gen 19:24)?

The prophets have been appealed to for reinforcement. After all, doesn't Jeremiah seem to look nostalgically at Israel's wanderings in the wilderness as a time when the nation was completely faithful to God (Jer 2:2)? Doesn't Hosea condemn the corruption of the cities and look forward to the day when God will take Israel back to the wilderness, where the pure worship of the Lord will be restored (Hos 2:14-20)? On this understanding, the prophets are seen as preservers of Israel's nomadic traditions, critics of life in the Canaanite cities.

More recently theological antiurbanism has taken a new scholarly turn. The model of Israel as a nomadic people has been questioned. Israel, argues Norman Gottwald, was essentially an agricultural, egalitarian society based in towns, not a nomadic and pastoral society (Gottwald 1977). Contrary to the book of Joshua, Israel did not possess the land through mass invasion. Rather, the great urban feudal states were overthrown in a peasant revolt by a small band of slave-labor captives (Israel) who had escaped Egypt in the thirteenth century B.C.

In this revolt model the antiurbanism still remains, only now the polarization is between urban life and rural town life. The conflict is between two disparate social organizations—the urban statism created by a military aristocracy and the rural tribalism and egalitarianism of the Israelite serfs and oppressed allies who joined in revolt. Israel's faith in Yahweh was adopted as a religious expression of their egalitarian hopes for freedom.

A lengthy examination of these antiurban judgments is not possible or necessary here. We only want to show this view's influence on biblical studies. Yet critical scholarship has not totally yielded to any of these forms of antiurbanism. A 1983 study of ten key texts focusing on the city in Deuteronomy concludes that the passages show a clear "urban tradition . . . which goes all the way back to Jahwists who lived together in cities during the 13th century BCE." Its conclusion? "Biblical histories and theologies can no longer consider early Israel to be completely nonurban" (Benjamin 1983:305).

Others have questioned at length the alleged antiurbanism of the prophets, arguing that we cannot find in the prophets a fundamental difference between a religion of the city and a religion of the country. They perceived the city only as "one instrument that could be used in the plan of God. As such, the city had no final value" (Frick 1977:230). The city is condemned by the prophets only "as a symbol of man's attempt to provide for his own material security" (Frick 1977:231).

Even the recent twists to the antiurban model proposed by Gottwald and others have not undergone modifications (Brandfon 1981:101-10) or even criticism (Finkelstein 1988:306-14; Malamat 1982:24-35). Gottwald's reconstruction of Israel's history is highly speculative and lacks biblical and extrabiblical support.

Was there then a latent antiurban bias in ancient Israel? The conclusion of Robert Wilson is ours: "it cannot be found in the Old Testament texts" (R. Wilson 1986:5). How then do we perceive the Hebrew Scriptures' view of the city?

**The city as divine intention.** In the world of the ancient Near East, city building was the pinnacle of a society's success. Associated with it were order, creation, civilization, life and beauty. A city's magnificent buildings spoke of prosperity and power; its walls symbolized security and peace. Its rebuilding meant a return to life, the restoration of order and rebirth from chaos.

These positive urban perspectives carried over into Israelite culture. Even in the midst of the garden setting of Genesis 1—2 such perceptions emerge. A perfect creation completed by God and unmarred by sin stood poised to begin its historical development. And in that setting God calls Adam and Eve and their future descendents to rule the earth and subdue it (Gen 1:28). This calling has been aptly termed the cultural mandate. It is a calling to "image God's work for the world by taking up our work in the world" (Spykman 1992:256). But it could just as easily be called an urban mandate. It will be accomplished through more than farming or husbandry; the founding of the first city will be one of the first achievements of this enduring mandate to expand the borders of the garden (Gen 4:17). The future of humankind outside the garden was destined to play out in cities.

> The couple in the garden was to multiply, so providing the citizens of the city. Their cultivation of earth's resources as they extended their control over their territorial environment through the fabrication of sheltering structures would produce the physical architecture of the city. And the authority structure of the human family engaged in the cultural process would constitute the centralized government by which the life and functioning of the city would be organized, under God. (Kline 1983:23)

In keeping with this urban intention of God, Genesis images of the garden elsewhere in Scripture become urban images. The river that waters the garden (Gen 2:10) is pictured in Psalm 46:5 as watering "the city of God." Zechariah combines the Edenic features of the river and life into "living waters" that go out from Jerusalem (Zech 14:9). And preeminently the Eden allusions reappear in the New Jerusalem of Revelation, "the holy city coming down out of heaven from God" (Rev 21:2). In this shrine city there is no temple as of old; the Lord God Almighty and the Lamb are its temple (Rev 21:22). Eden's river is there, its banks now lined with multiple trees of life "for the healing of the nations" (Rev 22:1-2).

Did the fall of Adam and Eve change this positive perception of the city or God's concern for the city? Did the city become, as some have argued, "an institution in which the tribes during their desert wanderings were simply not interested, [because of] so many hateful obstacles" (MacKenzie 1963:61)? Despite sin's radical distortion of God's urban purposes, the city remains a mark of grace as well as rebellion, a mark of preserving, conserving grace shared with all under the shadow of the common curse. Urban life, though fallen, is still more than merely livable.

Even Cain, skeptical of a divine response to retaliation, acknowledges the shelter that the city offers for his posterity (Gen 4:14, 17). And the creators of Babel's tower, in their proud effort to defy heaven, turn to city building after they have been scattered (Gen 11:4, 8-9). In the eyes of the builders, the city will be their protection.

Even the Lord's intervention at Babel recognizes the city's common-grace potential for unification: "If as one people speaking the same language they have begun to do this, then nothing they plan to do will be impossible for them" (Gen 11:6). His judgment is in fulfillment of his saving promise to Noah (Gen 9:15-16). "If the whole of humanity had remained concentrated, the power of sin would likewise have remained united, and doubtless soon again would have reached stupendous proportions" (Vos 1948:71). God saves the urban world of the future by destroying this city's power of unity.

Justice and order throughout the history of Israel's sojourn in the land should be expected at the gates of the city (Deut 21:19; 22:15; Ruth 4:1-12; Job 29:7-11; Amos 4:10, 12, 15 [AV]; Zech. 8:16 [AV]). But when these common-grace blessings of justice and order are transformed instead into displays of violence and oppression, God hears the outcry of those offended (Gen 18:20).

In response to such oppression Abraham, in alliance with five urban rulers, rescues his nephew Lot and restores the wealth of Sodom and Gomorrah (Gen 14). When these same cities, intended for refuge and safety, later threaten to transform Lot's hospitality into perversion (Gen 19:1-3, 6-8). Abraham intercedes once more—but this time with God, not on behalf of Lot but on behalf of Sodom (Gen 18:22-33).

The Lord's willingness to hear Abraham's remarkable prayer plea is linked in Genesis 18:18 with the divine promise that "all peoples on earth will be blessed through you" (Gen 12:2). This is striking for two reasons. First, God's covenant blessing on the patriarch is to be demonstrated in Abraham's intercession *for* the city, not against it. Second, to speak of "all nations on earth" *(eretz)* is to speak of the cities of the earth like Sodom and Gomorrah. The parallelism of *earth* and *city* will occur frequently in Scripture. In some instances the two terms become almost synonyms (Gen 11:28; 1 Kings 8:37; 22:36).

So God's later promise of the Israelites' possession of the Promised Land *(eretz)* will be fulfilled in the possession of the cities of the land. Divine blessing will be defined in gifts that are more than merely agrarian. God's benefactions will include "a land *[eretz]* with large, flourishing cities you did not build" (Deut 6:10). Symbolizing preeminently the positive link between these gift cities and the redemption of God that secured them will be the divinely consecrated six cities of refuge (Num 35:9-34; Josh 20:1-9).

Cain had built his city for self-protection from vengeance. In the cities of refuge to be set apart by God, that purpose was retained, but in accord with the justice of the divine builder-kinsman. Here those guilty of involuntary manslaughter could find asylum from the retribution of the kinsman.

The cities of refuge were to be symbols of life, not death, of divine protection rather than self-protection. Thus the cities were appointed chronologically after the exodus history. They were to be the urban firstfruits of the redemption of the divine kinsman (Job 19:25; Is 41:14; 44:21-22) and a preview of "the glory of the heavenly Jerusalem, when the murderer's place of exile will become the place of refuge for all the pardoned" (Ellul 1970:92). There the shelter of God will no longer wait to be finalized until a high priest's death (Num 35:25). It will already have been guaranteed by the death of the redeeming kinsman, the work of Christ, who has become both high priest and sacrificial lamb (Heb 7:26-27; Rev 21:22-23).

Signifying an even larger role for the cities of refuge was their inclusion among the forty-eight cities set apart for use by the tribe of Levi (Josh 21:1-42; 1 Chron 6—7). Spread throughout the Promised Land, the forty-eight cities were selected by lot, underlining their divine appointment (Num 26:55; Josh 14:2; 1 Sam 14:41-42).

Were these forty-eight cities to be models for God's new urban society? Some hints suggest this possibility. Certainly their allotment in the wilderness pointed to a new source of Israel's confidence, unknown in the ancient Near East. These urban gifts would come not from the power of the Baal gods but from the faithfulness of Yahweh the divine warrior (Num 35:1-8). He had promised, "I myself will drive [the Canaanite nations] out before the Israelites" (Josh 13:6). Would that promise be kept?

At the conclusion of the conquest period under Joshua, not all of the designated cities were yet in the hands of Israel. Only later would centers like Gezer (1 Kings 9:16), Taanach (Judg 1:27) and Rebob (Judg 1:30-32) be secured. God's "already" was still "not yet." Faith was still needed as God's people awaited the link between promise and fulfillment.

Unlike the lifestyle of the captured cities, compassion, justice and righteousness were to mark the teaching to come from these forty-eight cities. They were to be Torah centers of instruction by the Levites. The Levites' calling was to guard the covenant and teach the precepts of the law to God's people (Lev 10:11; Deut 33:8-10). And obedience to that teaching would "be our righteousness" (Deut 6:25). They were to exemplify the larger Israel's vocation to be a holy nation, a kingdom of priests (Ex 19:5-6). Distributed among the tribes, the cities where they dwelt would bring the whole people under the dissemination of God's directing word.

**The missionary intention of God's cities.** What of the mission impact of this new urban lifestyle beyond the circle of the people of God? What of the mixed population in cities like Shechem (Judg 9)? Were there other cities among the designated forty-eight, their full conquest not yet completed, that were spectators of a new divine intruder and a new way of life? Some scholars, in fact, have wondered if the texts in question really restrict the residents of Levitical cities to the Levites (Ashley 1993:645).

In these urban kingdoms Israel, through its Levite priests, could uniquely fulfill its role as a people in the midst of the peoples. In keeping with its calling Israel would "represent God in the world of nations. What priests are for a people, Israel as a people is for the world" (Blauw 1962:24). The glory of a God not limited to territorial boundaries could attract its Rahabs once more (Josh 2:11).

This territorial transcendence of Israel's Yahweh would stand out in missionary contrast to the geocentric orientation of the gods whose cities the Israelites would occupy. Those urban deities "were primarily attached to specific geographic territories and only secondarily concerned with the inhabitants of these areas. . . . The gods are concerned primarily with the land ascribed to them; the identity of the inhabitants of these lands is relatively immaterial" (Block 1988:23). In contrast, Yahweh had chosen Israel to be the special objects of his love (Deut 4:37; 7:7-8). But this God of the Hebrews was also the "God of all the earth" (Is 54:5). "He was not merely a divinity who had acquired a plot of real estate and then accepted as his own whatever population happened to inhabit his land" (Block 1988:23). And whatever geographical territory those outside Israel enjoyed, they enjoyed as the inheritance of the Most High (Deut 32:8).

A radical shift in understanding the link between deity and urban people had been introduced. It would spill over into the New Testament, where the church would replace Israel as the people of God.

But before it did, Jerusalem, the mother of all peoples (Ps. 87), would exemplify the glory of this geocentric universalism. In Jerusalem the sovereign Lord chose to erect his temple house (2 Sam 7). Here on the mountain citadel of Zion, God would dwell (Ps 74:2). And here the dynastic house of David would fulfill its task as the royal covenant caretaker (2 Sam 7:11-16). The perfections of beauty (Ps 48:2; 50:2; Ezek 16:14), the security of peace (Is 2:2-4) and unity (Ps 122:6-9; 133) were typified in Jerusalem. "Walk about Zion," rejoiced the psalmist, "go around her, count her towers, consider well her ramparts, view her citadels" (Ps 48:12-13).

Here Israel's missiological task would be engaged in a unique way. In the grip of the centripetal force of God's glory manifest in Jerusalem, the peoples of the earth would flow to the holy city (Is 2:2-4). Life in the cities of the ancient Near East provided joy for their own citizens. Jerusalem, however, was to be "the joy of the whole earth" (Ps 48:2; cf. Ps 68:31; 86:9; 137:1-2, 5-6).

Eventually the Gentile cities would come in pilgrimage (Is 60:3) to participate in Jerusalem's messianic feast (Ps 25:6). Hiram of Tyre who helped build the city (2 Sam 5:1) and Cyrus of Persia who rebuilt it (Ezra 1:2-3) were only forerunners of a new registry role of citizens. The census of a future Jerusalem would include Rahab and Babylon, Philistia, Tyre and Ethiopia (Ps 87:4-5; Is 56:3-8). Egypt and Assyria would worship the Lord with Israel (Is 18:9-24); Philistia would be like a clan in Judah (Zech 9:7).

**God's urban alternative.** In this prourban world of Israel, what were the alternatives? Neither rural village nor urban tribalism. The alternatives were chaos, disorder, desolation, emptiness. The urban inversion would substitute stench for perfume, rope for party sash, sackcloth for rich robes, burning for beauty. The gates of the city emptied of population would become gathering places for echoing a liturgy of despair, not joy (Is 23:24-25).

A number of metaphors underline this urban alternative. The upheaval of chaos reminiscent of the beginning of creation (Gen 1:2) is one. Urban Nineveh's downfall is pictured in terms of the Near Eastern metaphor of the conflict between God and the sea (Longman and Reid 1995:75). "He rebukes the sea and dries it up; he makes all the rivers run dry" (Nahum 1:4). Outside the refuge stronghold of God, described as a city in Psalm 46:1-3, trembling mountains fall into the roaring and foamy waters.

Even the fall of Jerusalem, its security taken for granted by the psalmist, is dramatized in the imagery of watery chaos. How shall we explain the destruction of urban Zion's temple, asks Psalm 74:2-8. How can the Creator, the divine conqueror of the Red Sea, possibly return the place of his dwelling to the chaos of old? The psalmist's assumption is expressed in the poetic metaphor of the Canaanite chaos myth of Baal's triumph over Leviathan (Curtis 1978:244-56). After all, he recalls, "it was you who split open the sea by your power; you broke the heads of the monster of the waters. It was you who crushed the heads of Leviathan" (Ps 74:13-14). From watery chaos God had brought victory and the glory of urban order. How can he now return us to chaos?

The desert-wilderness metaphor becomes another foil in picturing God's urban alternative. The series of fortresses that dot Edom's borders will become "nettles and brambles," Edom's palaces "a haunt for jackals, a home for owls" (Is 34:13; cf. 14:21-22; 17:2; 23:13). The cup of God's wrath, poured out on the cities of the ancient Near East, will leave behind it a desolate land (Jer 25:17-26, 38). In the coming day of the Lord, his appointed locust warriors will transform "land like the garden of Eden" into "a desert waste" (Joel 2:3).

Linking all these metaphors is the common theme of shame and disgrace that accompanies the loss of the city. There is no pride in the glory of the ruined city, whether Jerusalem or Tyre (Is 22:6-9), Babylon (Is 13:19-22) or Damascus (Is 17:1-3; Jer 49:24-27). The same motifs of shame and disgrace are applied to all. The ruined city is a despised remnant (Is 24:13), its "high fortified walls" brought down and humbled "to the very dust" (Is 25:12; 26:5).

In the ancient world cities were symbols of success, of order, of life. But vanquished, their walls fallen, they are like a widow, isolated and in mourning (Lam 1:1-2). Without a comforter, she is transformed by defeat from a princess into a forced laborer (Lam 1:3). The city descends from a position of honor to a place of shame (Olyan 1996:215-17). Thus with pride its enemies, seeing gates "sunk into the ground," can mock in parody, "Is this the city that was called the perfection of beauty, the joy of the whole earth?" (Lam 2:15-16). Nehemiah, feeling this shame, pleads, "Come, let us rebuild the wall of Jerusalem, and we will no longer be in disgrace" (Neh 2:17).

Antiurbanism does not mark the prayer of Joab, David's general, as he battles the Aramean city-states. His war cry is an exhibition of his faith in the true divine owner of even these enemy cities: "Be strong and let us fight bravely for our people and the cities of our God" (2 Sam 10:12). With confidence that the Lord will do what is good, he claims the cities as the possession of God. We can do no less.

### The City as a Reflector of Religious Commitment
The link between the city and religion in the ancient Near East was more explicit than it is in our world today. Western scholarship is used to treating religion as one isolated component of urban life—and a private, individualistic component at that. But in the ancient world and in the Bible it was, and still is, the hub connecting all the urban spokes. It is as integral to understanding the city then and now as it is to understanding life, selfhood and culture.

As the human response to the revelation of God, religion is more than a functionalist, isolated response to a basic human need (Conn 1984:118-20). It is the holistic response of the whole human self, the image of God. It is the voice of the heart (Prov 4:23; Mt 12:34). And that voice shapes its creaturely worldview either for or against the Creator.

So the heart builds a city either in defiance of God (Gen 11:4) or out of covenant obedience. It commits the city as a monarchy, its people and its sociocultural systems either to the tyranny of sin and self-rule or to service to the divine King of the city. The lifestyle of the city is religion made visible, faith reflected either toward God or against him. "The essential Old Testament assumption about the city is that it is the battleground between Yahweh and Baal" (Linthicum 1991a:27).

**The city as rebel.** The Baal gods were local territorial gods. Each city carried the name of its particular Baal ("lord" or "master") as more than a symbolic hope. It was the mortgage designation of the property owner; the city was the estate of the city-god whose name it bore. The Canaanite naming of cities like Baal-Zephon (Ex 14:2), Baal-Peor (Num 25:3), Baal-Meon (Num 32:38) and Baal-Gad (Josh 11:17) illustrates this.

In the same way, west Semitic cities carried the names of the wives of various gods. The city of Baalah (Josh 15:9) reflects the feminine form of the god-husband's name. Ashteroth-Karnaim (Gen 14:5) and Ashtaroth (Josh 9:10; 12:4) were named after Ashtoreth, the local Canaanite fertility goddess (1 Sam 31:10; 1 Kings 11:5). The Canaanite goddess Anath gave her name to Anathoth (Josh 21:18) and Anath (Judg 3:31). It was apparently a long-standing tradition for capital cities in this region to be regarded as goddesses who were married to the patron god of the city (Galambush 1992:20-23).

More than personification, the names were a matter of theopolitical identification (Fitzgerald 1972:403-16). Could piety then have motivated the Israelites to change the name of Baalah ("wife of Baal"), where the ark of the covenant rested for a time (1 Chron 13:5-6), to Kiriath Jearim ("city of forests")?

The feminine metaphors of the ancient Near East did find their way into Israelite vocabulary, but in a limited way. The Israelites found ways to distance themselves from the original idolatrous connotations of urban female imagery without radical name changes. In the religions of the ancient Near East the urban marital language referred to the relation between the city's goddess and god. Israel took up imagery of a marriage between Yahweh and the city (J. Schmitt 1985:568-69). The city became only the city-as-a-woman, demoted from divine to mortal status. In keeping with this shift, prominent cities became "mothers," and towns within their sphere of influence were "daughters" (Num 21:25; 32:42; Josh 15:45).

But even then the idolatrous background could be recalled when the urban society turned from its covenant purposes before the Lord. In a polytheistic urban society the worship of other gods in addition to the patron god or consort goddess of a city was perfectly acceptable. The image of the city-goddesses in the ancient Near East remained positive. But for the people of God the only possible way to view this, within the metaphor of a city as the wife of the patron deity, was negative. The marriage metaphor was extended to condemnations of the infidelity of a city as adultery and prostitution (Nah 3:4-5).

The prophets made use of the pagan associations to condemn the idolatry and injustice of Israel's cities as adultery with foreign gods (Deut 31:16; Jer 2:32-36; 3:12-13; Hos 2:2-13; Ezek 23:7). Even an unrighteous Jerusalem could not escape the charge: "See how the faithful city has become a harlot!" (Is 1:21). Though Yahweh could be described as father in his relation to Israel, there was no room for his having a consort.

**The city as tyrant.** In these ancient city-states with their autocratic territorial gods, the ruler or king interpreted the will of the gods. And the people served as slaves of the gods and of their earthly, royal regents. The religious mythologies that shaped the sociopolitical world made resistance to the ruler a form of treason against the gods. In fact, in keeping with this mythic connection, the ruler often bore the designation "son of the god" (Engnell 1967:80-81, 137, 153-54, 170).

The will and whim of the ruler were the will and whim of the gods. "Unquestioning obedience is the highest virtue, and order the highest religious value. 'The king's word is right, his utterance, like that of a god, cannot be changed!'" (Wink 1992:15).

In this social system, people "were tyrannized by the political and economic structures the gods legitimated" (Walsh 1987:56). Domination, oppression and violence were the handmaidens of idolatry. Burning incense to Baal was not a solitary cultic act of religion; joined to it were theft and murder, adultery and perjury (Jer 7:9). *Justice* (*mispat* in Hebrew) in this context meant "having the say," "calling the shots" (Walsh 1987:2-4). It was the arbitrary power exercised by the king in the name of the gods; it could say what is and make it stick.

As "sons of the gods" (Gen 6:2-3), the tyrannical monarchs could compel women to join their polygamous harems (Kline 1963a:187-204). They promulgated law codes to ratify their own mythic authority. In contrast to Yahweh's instructions (Deut 17:16; Judg 7), they relied on a large army and superior weapons (Josh 17:16; Judg 1:17) to guarantee support for their rule. They held title to all lands in the name of the patron gods. Their subjects farmed as dependent tenants, driven into poverty by heavy taxation and the luxurious living of the monarch (1 Sam 8:11-17).

Ahab's royal confiscation of Naboth's vineyard (1 Kings 21) may have been a violation of the obligation of Israel's king to protect human rights (Deut 17:19-20), and it was certainly a violation of the inalienable right of ancestral inheritance (1 Kings 21:3-4). But for Jezebel, Ahab's wife and the daughter of a Canaanite king, it was simply his right. "Are you king over Israel or not?" she railed (1 Kings 21:7). There were no limitations on royal power.

The historical expansion of the city-state to a territorial state and again to a national state (Buccellati 1967:19-23) only enlarged the borders within which dictatorial religious power could be exercised. The steady expansion of Babel to Babylon and Babylonia serves as an example.

Babel's origins are traced to Nimrod, the prototype of rebellion (Gen 10:8-12). The possible etymology of his name ("let us revolt") is lived out in the history of violence and conquest that marked Babel's national successor, the Babylonian empire. Babylon was the sword "made ready for the hand of the slayer" (Ezek 21:11; 32:11), the hammer even God would use against its Israelite imitators (Jer 51:20-23).

The same divine rewards would judge Babylon's pride and violence. Babel's rebellious pride in tower building brought its overthrow by God. Those tower symbols of human strength reappear repeatedly in the Old Testament, symbols also of God's power to bring them down (Is 2:12-17; 25:2-3; 30:25; Jer 51:53). So too Babylon would be overthrown again (Is 3—11). Nebuchadnezzar's urban boasting (Dan 4:30) would meet its divine reward.

In the final conflict of the ages, that judgment is secured forever. Babylon reappears again, this time as the worldly alternative to the new Jerusalem. Babylon is Rome, sitting on the seven hills (Rev 17:3; cf. 1 Pet 5:13); even more, she is "the great whore" (Rev 17—18), the urban counterpart of the bride of the Lamb. For the last time we see embodied in Babylon all the magnetic pull of the urban symbols of the Old Testament—regal power (Rev 17:3-4), wealth (Rev 18:13-17), the allure of beauty (Rev 17:2; 18:3). And behind it all we see the demonic origins of this power, wealth and allure (Rev 17:3-14). This city's blasphemous names, its sins piled up to heaven, herald its final ruin.

**The city's covenant king.** In dramatic contrast to all this, Yahweh called his people to a new model for urban life. Israel was to be the exhibition place for God's redemptive grace in the city and the empires that formed around God's people in history. At the heart of the model was a new theological vision, a covenant relationship between the suzerain God and his servant community. At the core of that vision was a concept of divine kingship new to the ancient world, and to demonstrate it, a new sociopolitical organization.

Unlike the urban religions of the ancient Near East, the divine overlord in this covenant relationship was not incarnate in his people. He could "discipline his people, deliver them to their enemies, afflict them in wrath with sickness and cause them to sigh in bondage for many years, but he himself suffers no defeat. It is rather precisely in the need and confusion of his people that God proved himself to be the Holy One of Israel, the one who bears his people with unsearchable faithfulness throughout the ages" (Bavinck 1960:14).

In further contrast to the surrounding urban religions, this divine king could tolerate no rivals in this covenant (Ex 20:3-6). His was a universal realm, not limited by one city's geographical boundaries; heaven was his throne and the earth his footstool (Is 66:1).

The opening chapter of Genesis, to which Isaiah 66 alludes, reflects this covenant universalism. Yahweh appears "not as a king among kings for whom the Canaanite term *melek* was proper, but as 'Suzerain,' a technical term in political science for a monarch who acknowledged no other power the equal of his own. In his sphere all power was derivative from him" (Wright 1969:207). The royalty of the sovereign Lord of creation was antithetical to that of the local city-kings. He simply speaks, and the world comes into being.

At the heart of God's covenant reign was the exhibition of unfailing, initiating grace. Again unlike contemporary urban mythology, God was no divine sheriff whose sole duty was to enforce the ordinances of the city, keeping watch on its walls and patrolling it for evildoers, club in hand (Jacobsen 1946:188, 192). Nor was he some capricious minor deity whose favoritism and influence with the higher gods might or might not win favors for his human protegé (Jacobsen 1946:203, 207). His theocratic rule was a benevolent dictatorship, consistently exercised. It could be traced from the goodness endowed in his creation work (Gen 1:10, 12, 18, 21, 25, 31) through his divinely initiated covenant with the patriarchs (Gen 12:2-3; 26:3-6; 28:4, 12-15).

Those promises of grace to Israel's founders echo again in the deliverance from Egypt (Ex 6:2-8). With compassion he had heard the earth's outcry against the murder of Abel (Gen 4:10) and promised to protect (Gen 4:15). Again he hears the outcry of the misery of his children in Egyptian bondage (Ex 3:7-10), and once more in compassion he redeems.

In that exodus history of the redemption and formation of the people of God the conscious apologetic with the urban ideology of the ancient Near East continues. The biblical record draws on literary motifs from this collective background to describe the deliverance history—house, throne, mountain, warfare with the gods. Yahweh's triumph over Egypt is a triumph over the gods of Egypt (Ex 12:12; 15:13; Num 33:4) and Pharaoh, the god-king (Ex 15:3-5). Later passages will describe this triumph of the divine warrior with the urban metaphor of the slaying of the dragon (Ps 74:12-13; Is 51:9-10). Complementing this imagery is the jubilant song of Moses, who sees in this deliverance God's guiding his people to his holy dwelling (Ex 15:13). Yahweh, through this act of redemption, builds a house for himself, a royal sanctuary on the mountain of his inheritance (Ex 15:17-18).

Such poetic allusions linking sanctuary city and divine house were common coin in the literature of the ancient Near East (Fleming 1986:690-92). Other biblical passages continue their parallel pairing (Ps 127:1; Jer 26:6, 9, 12), particularly picturing Jerusalem and its temple as the city-house of Yahweh (1 Kings 8:43-44). The "temple of the LORD" (1 Kings 6:1: 8:30) is "the city of God" (Ps 7:3; 46:4).

**The city and covenant mission.** Where was this covenant house-building to be prominently displayed in the urban centers of the ancient Near East? In the kingdom-house of Israel as the divine Artisan's earthly dwelling place. Israel's social and political identity as a people of righteousness was to mirror the righteousness of God. The mission of God to the cities of the world was to be lived out in Israel's theocratic self-understanding.

Covenantal commitment to Yahweh carried with it a rejection of loyalty to the gods of city-state and empire and a rejection, therefore, of how those urban societies were ordered. Out of the covenant notion that Yahweh is king and Israel is Yahweh's kingdom (Is 43:15) was to come a new social and political order of rule.

*Retribalization* does not adequately describe this new direction. A new state was formed at Sinai out of the exodus history, not an amphictyony or tribal league (Ex 19:4-6; 1 Pet 2:9-10). Further, there are suggestions in the history that this newly formed people will fulfill a role unlike other similar localized and particularistic monarchies.

The Lord who reigned over Israel had global and universalistic intentions. In forming Israel, he could claim that "the whole earth is mine" (Ex 19:5). In demonstration of that universal reign, his gift to his people was the cities of the land (Deut 6:10; 13:12; 19:2; 20:13, 16). Jericho's walls would fall not with battering rams but with exultant shout: "the LORD has given you the city" (Josh 6:16).

Ancient covenant treaty forms designated the gods as witnesses to the fulfillment of covenant promises. In Yahweh's covenant, the cities and the nations would, with God himself and his creation, bear witness to the faithfulness of God's word (Josh 2:8-11). His sovereign redemption and judgment, authenticated "in the presence of Pharaoh" (Ex 7:20; 9:8), would not escape "the sight of the nations" (Lev 26:45; Ezek 5:8,14; 16:41).

These urban centers were to see at the heart of this covenant social order the new demands of a holy God. Yahweh was that God. And he showed himself "holy by his righteousness" and "exalted by his justice" (Is 5:16). When this God looked at cities, He looked for justice *(mispat)* and not bloodshed *(mispach)*, righteousness *(tsedaqah)* and not cries of distress *(tse'aqah)* (Is 5:7).

This pairing of justice and righteousness is common in the Old Testament, often used, in fact, to define the rule of a righteous king (2 Sam 8:15; 1 Kings 10:9; 2 Chron 9:8; Ps 72:1). The terms had strong associative force and sometimes could be used interchangeably (Stek 1978:157). Thus "to deal honestly and seek the truth" in Jeremiah 5:1 becomes the same as to "do what is just and right" in Jeremiah 22:3. They provided a startling contrast between Israel's self-understanding and the royal ideology of its urban neighbors.

In the Canaanite world into which Israel would soon travel, justice *(mispat)* meant only the promise of survival—a survival ensured by centralized, absolute power. Righteousness was the guarantee of no more than security and abundance (Walsh 1987:24-32). In Israel justice and righteousness flowed from the holiness and unfailing love of Yahweh (Ex 15:11, 13). "Righteousness and justice are the foundation of your throne," exulted the psalmist, "love and faithfulness go before you" (Ps 89:14). And these characteristics were to be reflected in Israel's life as a community (Amos 5:24). Should they fail to follow that path, the same judgments that God promised for the Canaanite cities would fall on the cities he gave them (Lev 26:25; Deut 28:15-16, 52-55).

Also unique to this pairing of justice and righteousness were its connections with *hesed,* translated variously as "compassion" or "mercy" (AV), "steadfast love" (RSV), "kindness" or "love" (NIV). The person who sowed justice would reap compassion (Hos 10:12).

*Hesed* is the covenant alternative to ritual without heart, sin without grace and forgiveness (Hos 6:6; Mt 9:13; 12:7); it is part of the marriage dowry of righteousness and justice, love and *hesed* compassion to be paid for betrothal to Yahweh (Hos 2:19-20). The one who shows *hesed* to another acts to promote that person's well-being (Gen 21:23; 39:21; Josh 2:12; 2 Sam 9:1-7; 1 Kings 20:31).

Over against an urban world where justice and righteousness could mean oppression and disregard for the weak and poor, *hesed* love forbade taking advantage of others in the name of law (Mt 23:23). In God's new social order it was not simply justice that must be maintained; it was love and justice (Hos 12:6). Yahweh's delight was "kindness, justice and righteousness on earth" (Jer 9:24; Is 16:5). "He has showed you, O man, what is good. And what does the LORD require of you? To act justly and to love mercy *[hesed]* and to walk humbly with your God" (Mic 6:8).

In the Torah law of Israel's new covenant society these connections are exhibited clearly. That law, in the deepest sense, was not secular law or civil law, nor was Israel's identity as a people established simply by the nation's attitude toward law and order. Israel's identity was established by the doing of justice, righteousness and love to the cosmic God and to the Israelites' neighbors.

The Torah pointed to the social reflection of that calling. Israel was to be a benevolent and just society embodying the exclusive kingship of Yahweh, its benevolent and just Lord. As a people, Israel was to be the image of God, exhibiting the glory of God in love toward God and human beings. By the time of the first century A.D., Judaism would be distinguishing between lighter and weightier, smaller and greater commandments. Jesus recalls Judaism to the core of the covenant demand: the inseparability of a wholehearted love for God from selfless concern for neighbor (Mt 22:36-40; Mk 12:28-32; Lk 10:27-28). To know Yahweh is to hear the cry of one in need. And to hear the cry of one in need is to recognize a neighbor and to know Yahweh (Lk 10:36-37).

That love of neighbor was to make no economic or class distinctions. The urban world of promised inheritance that the Israelites entered would be a world of haves and have-nots, a class society of powerful and powerless, ethnic divisions of insider and outsider/stranger. By contrast, Israel's formation in covenant was to create no such unbreachable barriers for the expression of justice and compassion. Any gulf between insider and alien outsider was theological, not biological. After all, Israel too had once been "not my people" (Hos 1:9-10; 1 Pet 2:10), a worshiper of foreign gods (Josh 24:14-15, 23). Covenant, not ancestry, had left room for a mixed multitude to accompany the Israelites from Egypt (Ex 12:38).

It was also covenant that opened Israel's doors of worship and community to the alien or stranger within its gates (Ex 12:48-49; 20:10; Lev 22:18-19; 23:22; 25:35). Justice (Lev 24:22) and compassion for the resident alien (Lev 19:9-10) were to flow from Israel's collective theological memory of who it had once been in Egypt. "Do not mistreat an alien or oppress him, for you were aliens in Egypt" (Ex 22:21; cf. Lev 19:33-34; 25:23; Deut 10:18-19; 23:7).

Poverty and oppression were also enemies to overcome in the mission of this new community. The stated reality that there would always be poor people in the land only underlined Israel's calling to be "openhanded toward your brothers and toward the poor and needy" (Deut 15:11). Faithfulness to the jubilee sabbath system instituted by God to obviate debt and guarantee land security (Lev 23:10-11; 25:1-55; Deut 15:2-18) would offer a different alternative: "there should be no poor among you" (Deut 15:4).

In contrast to an urban world of self-promoting economy built on greed and land grabbing, the land and its cities are Yahweh's (Lev 25:23). The suzerain Lord of glory grants his tenant people not ownership of private property but ownership in the use of the land.

> Only the use of the land is to be bought and sold. Thus only the productivity of the land is to have economic value in the life of the nation. Economic factors may not disinherit Yahweh's servant from Yahweh's land. In the Year of Jubilee, each Israelite is to return to the inheritance granted him and his family by Yahweh. Meanwhile, the right of redemption of land sold under economic distress is to remain open (Lev. 25:24ff). Nor will a family lose its place in Yahweh's land if there be no son, only daughters. In that case, the daughters inherit, as with the daughters of Zelophehad (Numb. 27:5ff; 36:1-9). (Stek 1978:153)

In contrast to an urban world of royal power politics, no one, not even a king, is beyond covenant keeping of the Torah (Deut 17:18-20). And no one, not even the disabled (Lev 19:14) or disadvantaged (Ex 22:23-24; Lev 19:9-10), is beyond the law's protection. Even legal punishment has its limits; degradation and the humiliation of the guilty are not part of it (Deut 25:2-3). In contrast to an urban world of exploitation, the wealthy are to freely lend money (or other commodities) to the poor without interest (Ex 22:25; Lev 25:35-38). The poor man's garment taken as pledge for a loan must be returned "by sunset so that he may sleep in it" (Deut 24:12-13; Ex 22:25-27). Wages for the poor must be paid "each day before sunset, because he is poor and counting on it" (Deut 24:14-15). And sharing together, slave as well as family, alien as well as animal are to enjoy the shelter of sabbath rest (Ex 20:8-11).

Surveying even a minimal number of stipulations for this new social order, as we have, underlines its novelty (Stek 1978:150-54). It is not hard to see why many now argue that God is biased toward the poor. That phrasing probably says too much. But to say that God is on the side of the poor in a ruthless world where the poor are oppressed nonpersons surely does not.

The Torah thus becomes a scenario of how the urban world should be under the structure of covenant, of "how the world could be alternatively organized under the metaphor of kingdom" (Brueggemann 1984:92-93).

# 5

## Temptation & Testing,
## Promise & Fulfillment

HUNDREDS OF YEARS AFTER ITS EARLY HISTORY, Babel the city had become Babylon the urban empire. The independent city had become a conquering political network of urban centers. Its long succession of rulers had carried out a policy of deliberate urbanization. Throughout their territories, cities had become for the Babylonians the instruments of administration and defense, and for their subjugated peoples the symbols of oppression and lost hopes.

To the Israelites now living in this urban diaspora God, through the prophet Jeremiah, outlined a different and surprising mission. "Seek the peace and the prosperity of the city to which I have called you into exile. Pray to the LORD for it, because if it prospers, you too will prosper" (Jer 29:7).

False prophets had encouraged the exiles to see their captivity as temporary and to expect a quick deliverance (Jer 29:8). Now the prophet gives them a new perspective on their exile and their mission among the Gentiles. Their seventy-year wait was to be more than a delay frustrated by false confidence (Jer 29:10). They were to seek the blessing, not the destruction of their enemies. God was calling them to be salt and light in the world of their oppressors.

Such seeking was to be more than a state of mind. It meant practicing what was promoted. To *seek* justice meant to *do* justice, to *practice* justice

(Is 16:5). To seek the peace and good of the city meant to spend one's energies and activity in praying for its peace and blessing it by the doing of good works. Urban refugees were to be urban public benefactors.

God's promised blessing to the pilgrim from Ur was to be fulfilled again through the pilgrims in Babylon's cities: "all peoples on earth will be blessed through you" (Gen 12:3). And the focus of that blessing was to be the cities that barred their way home.

In this mission the exiles would be reminded again that their identity as the people of God was not dependent on those things they had seen as crucial in their past. The inviolability of Jerusalem (Jer 26:6), the temple and its rituals (Jer 7:4; 27:16-17) were trappings that could disappear. But God's presence would accompany people faithful to his covenant, whoever they might be and wherever they might gather to celebrate his grace.

Israel would one day return to the city of God, but not alone. With it would also come the Gentile nations "from the ends of the earth" (Jer 16:19). Partners in repentance, they too would be blessed by God as they gloried in him (Jer 4:2). In the urban renewal work of the new covenant the foreigner also would serve the Lord as God and David as the restored king (Jer 30:9). What had been the center of Jewish hopes would become a multinational gathering place for the tribute of the earth.

How did Israel move from exile in Egypt to exile in Babylon? How do we explain what seems to be a shift from God's particular love of Israel in the Torah to his universal concern for the world reflected in the prophets? How are these emphases in God's urban mission reflected in the urban mission of the people of God?

### God's Urban Commission Unfulfilled

The connections between the exodus and the exile are rooted in Israel's response to the temptations of urban life in the Promised Land and to their understanding of Yahweh as their exclusive monarch and divine warrior. "If the Exodus shows God's power on behalf of Israel, the Exile displays God's power against Israel. The Exodus is an expression of God's grace; the Exile displays his judgment. In the Exodus event we witness God as Israel's warrior; in the Exile, he is Israel's enemy" (Longman and Reid 1995:52).

The exodus was a call to shape a new people marked by the holiness of God in their cities. The exile was God's response to their failure to display that urban holiness. The exodus history placed the redeeming God in Israel's midst to be its city security (Ps 46:4-7). The exile marked God's departure from an apostate people who presumed on that presence (Jer 7:4-7). The exodus redemption was the foundation for the planning and raising of the tabernacle (Ex 25—40), the tent dwelling place of the Lord (Ex 40:34-38). In the exile judgment God's glory abandoned his city/temple (Ezek 9:3; 10:18; 11:23).

How do we explain these changes?

*Israel's quest for a king.* Before entry to the Promised Land, the establishment of a monarchy in Israel had received divine sanction as permissible (Deut 17:14). Depending on the kind of monarchy and socioreligious system that emerged, it would not be a threat to the theocratic rule of Yahweh. "If the king conformed to the spirit of the present provision, ruling under Jahweh and by the covenant law, he would actually enrich the Old Testament's symbolic prefiguration of the messianic reign" (Kline 1963b:97).

To do so, the king was to be "one from among your own brothers" (Deut 17:15). The issue was not pure blood or tribal connection; the king had to be one who would lead in servant loyalty to covenant. He was to be steeped in the Torah, a vassal not above the law of Yahweh but subject to it like others (Deut 17:18-20). In his rule he was to exemplify it.

Unlike the city-state monarchies that Israel would encounter soon, the normal guarantees of royal power and self-reliance were to be avoided— the multiplication of horses, wives and wealth (Deut 17:16-17). Lust for Pharaoh's famed horses and chariots (1 Kings 10:28-29; Is 30:2) meant lustful reliance on military and political strength; Israel's reliance must remain on the Lord.

Proscription of the multiplication of wives was more than a judgment on sexual self-indulgence. Royal multiple marriages were political ploys, aimed at gaining security in a reliable social network of alliances. Solomon's fall would exemplify this (1 Kings 11:1-6). The prohibition of wealth and gold alluded to the same temptation to self-security, the normal way of being king among Israel's urban neighbors.

The path to monarchy was not a smooth one nor always faithfully followed by Israel. The jubilant keynote of the book of Joshua is its focus on the fulfillment of God's promise to give his people the land. As noted already, "the land" is defined in terms of the cities and their kings given to Israel in the "holy wars" of the conquering Yahweh. Jericho, Ai, the battle with the five kings of the Amorite cities (Josh 10:1-28) are exemplars of gifts won by the divine warrior. Later, the book of Acts in the New Testament shows a similar pattern of conquest as the word of God continues its growing spread through the cities of the world (Acts 6:7; 9:31; 12:24; 16:5; 19:20; 28:31).

But the Promised Land's conquest was not complete, contrary to the command of God (Deut 7:1-5; 20:16-18; 25:17-19). There were lands and cities yet to be possessed and occupied (Josh 13:1-7, 13; 15:53; 16:10; 17:12). The same pattern continued following the death of Joshua, particularly among the tribes whose assigned territory was the north (Judg 1:22-36). Strategic urban centers like the Esdraelon valley and its cities (Judg 1:27-28), Gezer (Judg 1:29), the cities of the northern plain (Judg 1:31) and Jerusalem (Judg 1:21) were unoccupied. The tribe of Dan was completely dispossessed (Judg 1:34).

In the religious and social order of those unoccupied cities, predicted the Lord, was Israel's temptation: "they will teach you to follow all the detestable things they do in worshiping their gods, and you will sin against the LORD your God" (Deut 20:18). Idolatry with Canaan's fertility gods, intermarriage and violent injustice would accelerate the Canaanization of Israel's worship and life (Ps 106:34-40).

That temptation appeared early in Israel's conquest history. The lure of wealth and the taking of booty for victories won was a pattern of long standing in the city-states of the ancient Near East. Achan at Jericho (Josh 7:1) yielded to it in violation of the covenant ban on the city (Josh 6:21). He had forgotten that the victory was won by God, not Israel. Later Saul, the first king of Israel, would forget it as well. Taking the flocks of the Amalekites as plunder and sparing their king, Agag (1 Sam 15:7-26), would seal Saul's doom as king.

In the book of Judges, however, Israel's departure from covenant becomes even more apparent in the disunity of the tribes. "At no point were more than six tribes (Judg 5:14-18) united to stave off an aggressor; usually one or two tribes were left to defend themselves as best they could" (Cundall 1969-1970:179).

Archaeological studies are apparently now going through a radical reexamination of earlier models. This, coupled with meager information from this period, makes research conclusions much more tentative than in the past (J. Flanagan 1988:46, 112-16). But even the more skeptical studies of Canaanite society point to extrabiblical similarities that strongly parallel Israel's disunity within its covenant structure.

The Amarna Letters portray Canaan between 1550 and 1200 B.C. "as a time of chaos, dissension, and selfish competition among heads of city-states vying for their own survival and the economic resources of their closest neighbors. . . . Town is pitted against town, neighbor against neighbor. Tributes of agricultural products, trade taxes, women, and slave labor increase" (J. Flanagan 1988:193). Regional independence and autonomy become instability, disruption and expansionist aggression. Political and social systems are legitimized by belief in the divine right of local power. The resemblances with Israel during the time of the judges are too striking to be simply coincidence. Was syncretism affecting the people of God?

Surely it shows its face at the Baal shrine of Gideon's father (Judg 6:12) and in Gideon's action in making an ephod that led the people astray (Judg 8:27). Jephthah's rash vow that led to the sacrifice of his own daughter (Judg 11:30-31) and the frailty of Nazirite Samson's commitment to his vows point in the same direction.

The closing five chapters of Judges underline this near anarchy of the premonarchy period. Before the narrative of its two stories concludes, we have observed a breakdown of religious and social life and witness. The breakdown begins with idolatry (Judg 17:3-5) and moves on to include priestly irregularities (Judg 17:10-13), syncretism (Judg 18:17-26,30-31) and lawlessness (Judg 18:27-28), a collapse of the social code reminiscent of the history of Sodom and Gomorrah (Judg 19), brutality (Judg 19:29-30), and intertribal warfare (Judg 21). All of this within Israel itself! Linking these narratives is the plaintive repeated commentary "In those days Israel had no king; everyone did as he saw fit" (Judg 17:6; 18:1; 19:1; 21:25).

Evangelical scholarship still wrestles with the specific purpose behind these judgments and with the exact time they were written. Is the author constructing an apologetic for the Davidic monarchy (Cundall 1969-1970:178-81)? Is he reminding his people at some later date that the covenant ideal of Israel had been preserved through this period in spite of Israel (Dumbrell 1983:30-32)?

Perhaps these two answers are not too divergent. Yahweh, the architect and achiever of Israel's victories, still displays his grace as he hears the cries of his oppressed people. He delivers them again and again through the judges. In spite of Israel's repeated covenant disobedience, the nation survives because of the mercy of God. And against that record of her disunity and apostasy, the Davidic monarchy comes as a model of God's continuing grace to his people.

***Royal quest fulfilled in city and temple.*** Particularly in the rule of David the earlier metaphors of kingdom and covenant—mountain, city and house—come together. With David's enthronement the urban "house of the LORD" (Ps 122:1, 9) becomes the dynastic "house of David" (Ps 122:5; 2 Sam 7:5-12). The path along which God's covenant of grace has led Israel through the years takes us to the establishment of the throne of David (Ps 78:67-72). Unlike his judgment on Saul (1 Sam 13:13; 15:22-23), Yahweh will deal in unfailing mercy with David's house and kingdom (2 Sam 7:16).

Parallel to that theme of God's choice of David as his anointed is his choice of Zion as his sanctuary (Ps 132:11-18; Is 14:32). The Lord, through his servant David, had completed the conquest of the urban enemies. And to the city David had brought the ark of the covenant, the symbol of God's deliverance from Egypt and his presence among his people. The divine warrior had come to "his dwelling place in Zion. There he broke the flashing arrows, the shields and the swords, the weapons of war" (Ps 76:1-2). Now that victorious warrior would make great the name of its human builder (2 Sam. 7:9).

Jerusalem as a royal centerpiece thus becomes a unique sign, a witness to Yahweh's work of gracious adoption. The city's pagan origins were never forgotten. Like an unwanted child aborted and abandoned, she lay dying in her own blood until the Lord came and called, "Live!" (Ezek 16:3-6). Naked, she was covered by God her lover (Ezek 16:7-9).

Jerusalem stood as a covenant testimony to the cities of the world of the unity and peace of God (Ps 122:6-9). Its past was marked by that unity. The writer of the royal history saw this. Immediately following his description of the coming together of all the tribes with Judah under David's rule (2 Sam 5:1-5), he narrates the history of David's seizure of Jerusalem from the Jebusites (2 Sam 5:6-10).

At the core of that unity and peace was to be a centralization of worship. The portable tabernacle shrine of the wilderness wandering was to disappear when God chose one place in which to dwell (Deut 12:5). No longer would "everyone [do] as they saw fit" in any place they happened to be (Deut 12:8-14). The extended description of the construction of the temple (1 Kings 6-7) thus becomes a central focus in the building program of Solomon. It is not a blueprint for construction nor, as in the shrine cities of the ancient Near East, some localization of God's presence (1 Kings 8:22). The text is careful to point out that Yahweh's true dwelling place is heaven (1 Kings 8:30, 43, 49). The temple is to be a witness to God in stone, bronze and gold of his covenant faithfulness (1 Kings 8:22-26), of his promise of forgiveness and mercy for the repentant and oppressed (1 Kings 8:29-40). And it is to be a witness to the nations of that same divine salvation. Solomon prays that the awe of its glory and grandeur will bring more than Israelites to worship. It is to be a missionary incentive that will draw one day "all the peoples of the earth" (1 Kings 8:41-43).

In addition to this covenant primacy given to the temple as the city-house of God, the writer of Chronicles in particular finds still another way to add to the urban glory of the Davidic line of succession. Writing in the postexilic period (2 Chron 36:22-23), he relies on the community's familiarity with the earlier written history and offers additional theological commentary. The commentary emphasizes the postschism city-building history as an indication of God's blessing on the Davidic succession.

In doing so the Chronicler is providing eschatological hope to an exiled people. "The path to freedom and to the amelioration of Judah's difficulties lay in seeking God and humbling oneself before him, while turning from that path could only lead to disaster" (Dillard 1987:101-2).

"At a time when Israel was subject to the Persians, the Chronicler still cherished hopes of a restoration of Davidic rule, and he describes the glorious rule of David and Solomon [and their royal line of succession] in the past in terms of his hope for the future" (Dillard and Longman 1994:175). He underlines that hope for the blessing of God in a past of urban expansion and restoration, in the strengthening of the security provided by city fortresses (1 Chron 11:5; 14:6-7; 16:6; 17:1-2, 12; 26:2, 6, 9-10; 27:3-4; 32:3-5, 29-30; 33:14; 34:10-13). In Chronicles urban building projects become signs of divine blessing, and wicked kings neither strengthen nor build or rebuild cities.

Israel's growing urban base was intended to be more than a system of administering land and people for the sake of a socioeconomic monopoly. Nor was its goal, as Gottwald has argued, a social experiment in egalitarianism over against hierarchical bureaucratic statism. "Israelitization" was a call to live under Torah in covenant with the only true God.

### Theocratic Failure and the City
The history of the Davidic succession in Chronicles was a positive apologetic for temple and city. The larger scope of the books of Samuel and Kings points to the darker side of the introduction of monarchy and urban development.

Samuel heard this dark side with regret in the official appeal of the people of God: "Now appoint a king to lead us, such as all the other nations have" (1 Sam 8:5, 19-20). It was a rejection of the nation's divine election (Ex 19:5-6; Lev 20:26; Deut 7:6; 14:2; 1 Sam 12:22), of its unique covenant relationship with God (Deut 4:6-8) and, founded on it, the social institution of the theocracy (1 Sam 8:7-8; 10:17-19).

More was at stake in the request than a simple rejection of the existent judgeship, and more also than an isolated battle over gods. What was threatened was Israel's covenant identity and with it, its theocratic expression (Eslinger 1985:256-58). It was rebellion against covenant and the social values and social organization that flowed out of the covenant theocracy. It meant a reversion to pagan models of statecraft and rule, to be extended now by centralization past city-state to larger territorial borders (Mendenhall 1975:157-60).

The Lord's response to Israel's request was judgment as much as assent. Israel would taste the power of the city monarch it sought to emulate in the conscription of its sons and daughters (1 Sam 8:11, 13). Its lands, its agricultural products, its servants and flocks would be taken (1 Sam 8:14-17).

Israel's kings would be like the urban monarchs of the ancient Near East who claimed divine prerogatives and exercised power and control within the deity's domain. Taxation, conscription, royal luxury, slavery and the monopolizing power of armed force were the expressions of that regal authority. So it would be in the monarchy for which Israel now pled. Once more Israel would be reduced to a bondage like the one they had known in Egypt. They would cry out again as they had before Pharaoh (Deut 17:16; 1 Sam 8:18). "The royal apparatus designed to keep and enhance the land will cause Israel to lose it" (Brueggemann 1977:79).

The glorious height of the monarchy, as we have underlined, was with David and Solomon. But here too it begins its plunge—especially with Solomon. Other kings fell lower than he, but none from such a height.

At the dedication of the temple Solomon asks only for wisdom, and wisdom understood as discernment in administering justice (1 Kings 3:9, 11). In response to that request for the justice that lies at the heart of the covenant, God adds the blessings of riches and honor (1 Kings 3:13). "Those who honor me I will honor" (1 Sam 2:30; cf. Ps 91:15; Is 43:4).

Gifts like honor in the ancient Near East were rewards commonly associated with covenant connection (Olyan 1996:202-4). In the reciprocity of suzerain and vassal, such a gift called for the exercise of vassal responsibility. That responsibility Solomon quickly forsakes. Solomon's urban accessions and city-building projects are part of the background against which his failure is played out.

The writer of Kings appears generally to commend the extension of the borders of Solomon's realm and their fortification through the rebuilding of garrison cities and cities for his chariots and his horses (1 Kings 9:15-23; cf. 2 Chron 8:1-6). But even as he does he also points to signs of decay.

Solomon's rebuilding activity uses conscripted slave labor (1 Kings 9:15), as he had done in the building of the temple (1 Kings 5:13-14). Later the northern tribes use this "harsh labor" and "heavy yoke" put upon them by Solomon as a reason for dividing the nation into two (1 Kings 12:4).

Bypassing the divine ownership of the cities of the Promised Land, Solomon cedes twenty of them to Hiram of Tyre. The writer of Kings describes it as done "either to satisfy an outstanding debt (I Kings 9:11) or as payment for additional gold needed to complete the work (I Kings

9:14)" (Dillard 1987:62). By comparison, the negative response of Hiram (1 Kings 9:12-13) is deleted by the Chronicler, who also says that Hiram gave the cities to Solomon (2 Chron 8:1-2). As we have indicated before, the Chronicler's account "is best understood as both preserving the image of Solomon and providing a less onerous sequel to Kings" (Dillard 1987:63). The Chronicler's theological airbrushing, however we ultimately harmonize it, only accentuates Solomon's weakness.

From Pharaoh comes devastated Gezer as a wedding gift to Solomon for his daughter (1 Kings 9:16). The connection of the gift of the city with Solomon's marriage outside the covenant would appear to be a preview act later condemned by the author (1 Kings 11:1-6).

Behind all this is Solomon's desire to consolidate control of the kingdom through expansive urbanization. Earlier biblical references speak more frequently of a city's "daughters," "villages" or "surrounding areas" (*benot, hatzer,* cf. Num 21:25, 32; 32:42; Josh 13:23, 28; 15:32, 36, 41, 44-47; 17:11; Judg 11:26; 1 Chron 2:23). These, some argue, would appear to suggest that a premonarchy majority of the population lived "in villages surrounding the cities or spread out between them" (Ahlstrom 1982:136). But from the time of the monarchy, there would be a new face to Israel's social structure. It was a "wave of new city foundations," largely replacing the previous village type of settlement (V. Fritz 1995:76).

**Fruits of failure.** From a purely sociopolitical point of view, urbanization fit in well with the erection of the Israelite monarchy. City building was a royal enterprise in the ancient Near East generally and a useful political tool as well. It enabled the royal authority to bind together diverse populations and regions in a more unified community.

For Israel's monarchy that unification through urbanization could have served a more profound purpose. It could have provided another instrument for teaching the various peoples the way of the covenant. After all, unlike the territorial states now emerging in these days, Israel was a covenant state.

But monarchy and urbanization moved in other directions, as Samuel had prophesied. The failure of Israel to drive out all the Canaanites from the land reinforced its attraction to the urban idolatry of its neighbors. The centralization of worship before Yahweh (Deut 12) faded into royal obeisance both north and south before the rival shrines of the high places. Jeremiah eventually cried, "You have as many gods as you have towns, O Judah" (Jer 11:13).

This idolatry touched deeply the social life of God's people. Vast sums of money were needed to maintain the consumptive luxury of the monarchy and its extensive building program from Jerusalem to the borders of the state. From faith in God as the theocratic divine warrior the people of God turned instead to royal power exhibited in a standing army of men, chariots and horses (1 Kings 4:26; 9:22). Such a military retinue was characteristically associated with oppression and intimidation (cf. Ex 14:9, 23; Deut 20:1; 2 Sam 15:1; 2 Kings 18:23; 23:11).

Rebuilt fortifications and garrisons placed at crucial places marked turning points away from the security that could be found only in Yahweh. And the division of the monarchy into northern and southern kingdoms only multiplied on both sides that drive to fortification (Na'aman 1981; Pienaar 1981).

With the kings as exemplars not of justice and righteousness but of faithlessness, the cities built by the kings became political demonstrations of disobedience to God. In Jerusalem (1 Kings 11:7-8; 12:31-32) and Samaria (1 Kings 16:24-26, 32), Bethel (1 Kings 12:28-33) and Beersheba (Amos 5:5; 8:14)—everywhere one could see worship on the high places, covenants with unbelieving Gentiles, marriage rituals of state mirroring the betrothal of God's people to Baal rather than Yahweh.

Against this background, apostasy also becomes urban injustice. The gulf between rich and poor grows. Land is accumulated by the wealthy (Is 5:8), and farmers become landless tenants in debt to pitiless creditors (Amos 2:6-8; 8:4-6). The covenant scandal of the city becomes the exploitation of the poor and helpless (Ps 9:12; 103:6), the sign of covenant obedience their rescue (Ps 72:12-14; Mic 6:8). Yahweh "defends the cause of the fatherless and the widow, and loves the alien, giving him food and clothing. And you are to love those who are aliens, for you yourselves were aliens in Egypt" (Deut 10:18; cf. Ps 12:5).

Repeatedly the prophets speak out against the rich who speculate and defraud (Hos 12:7): "They covet fields and seize them, and houses, and take them. They defraud a man of his home, a fellowman of his inheritance" (Mic 2:2). Bribery is condemned (Mic 3:11; 7:3), not simply because it is dishonest but because it closes the eyes of the rulers and judges to the needs of the poor (Ex 23:8; Is 1:23).

Righteousness expressed in justice thus becomes "the indispensable qualification for worship—no justice, no acceptable public worship" (Mays 1983:7). The functional criterion of a just society is found in the treatment of the poor and weak (Is 3:14-15).

Underlining the covenant connections in all this, the vocabulary of the Old Testament transforms key sociological terms into theological categories as well. Words like *poor, humble, needy, godly, righteous* and *those who trust in God* become virtual synonyms (Ps 86:1; 109:22-25; 140:12-13). The poor are Yahweh's "afflicted people" (Ps 74:19; 149:4).

Similarly, the contrast between the poor and the rich becomes a contrast between the poor and the unrighteous (Ps 10:2; 68:5-6; 146:9; 147:6; Is 32:7-8). To maintain the rights of the poor and oppressed, to rescue the weak and needy, is to "deliver them from the hand of the wicked" (Ps 82:4).

The rejection of God means the rejection of the poor (Coggins 1987:11-14; Gowan 1987:341-53). "Not wealth and luxury in themselves the prophets attack. Of social burdens, such as heavy taxation and cruel exactions they do not even speak, but to the reflex indignity offered through social maltreatment to Jehovah in the persons of his people" (Vos 1948:296).

***Judgment and promise.*** God gave the cities to his people as a covenant gift. They were signs of God's grace in the present, their walls signs of God's security for the future.

But as their passion for Yahweh fades in their passion for wealth, as the place of the divine warrior is usurped by horses and chariots, these same cities taste the jealousy of God (Is 2:6-11). The cities will no longer share in the glory of the king of kings; "the LORD alone will be exalted in that day."

The cities will be burned with fire (Is 1:7), their highways deserted (Is 33:8), desolate in their ruin (Is 24:10). Even outside the people of God, none will escape the day of the Lord. Damascus will become a heap of stones (Is 17:1). The fortified city will disappear from Ephraim (Is 17:3). God will stir up the cities of Egypt in an orgy of mutual self-destruction (Is 17:2). Nineveh, the Assyrian capital, will be plundered and carried away into exile (Nahum 2:6-10). And preeminently Babylon, "the jewel of kingdoms, the glory of the Babylonians' pride, will be overthrown by God like Sodom and Gomorrah" (Is 13:19; cf. Jer 50:35-38; 51:44-58).

The strongest language of the prophets, however, is reserved for Samaria, the capital of the northern kingdom, and particularly for Jerusalem. "As my hand seized the kingdoms of the idols, kingdoms whose images excelled those of Jerusalem and Samaria—shall I not deal with Jerusalem and her images as I dealt with Samaria and her idols?" (Is 10:10-11).

For the prophet Micah:

> Samaria is described as "Rebellion" par excellence, the concrete symbol of Jacob's sinful stance, and Jerusalem is merely the "high place" (1:5 in Hebrew text) of Judah. With allusion to the fertility cults of the north Micah sees the wealth of Samaria as "the price given to a prostitute" (1:7), and the cities filled with illegal seizure of property (2:1), "skinning" the poor (3:2ff), and the cultivation of prophets who proclaim peace when their mouths are full (2:6;

3:5). The cities are pervaded with evil since in them dwell the responsible leaders "who build Zion with blood and Jerusalem with wrong" (3:10). There is no alternative but that both Samaria and Jerusalem become twisted heaps of ruin (1:6; 3:12). (Sklba 1976:41)

Why does God judge the city that he has designated as his dwelling place? Nowhere is Jerusalem judged because it is a city, nor is its condemnation exclusively because of idolatry. Isaiah points to the bloody hands that offer up the ritual sacrifices (Is 1:15-17), a city once "full of justice" and now a "companion of thieves" (Is 1:23). Jeremiah sees streets without a single person "who deals honestly and seeks the truth" (Jer 5:1-2), burnt offerings without obedience (Jer 7:21-23), city walls that protect oppression, violence and destruction (Jer 6:6-7). Chosen as instruments of divine judgment are the nations that were to witness Israel's covenant life of obedience. In keeping with the role of the witness (Deut 17:7), they serve also as the executors of judgment for covenant violation.

Assyria's hand sweeps away the ten northern tribes. In memorial to the forgotten poor of the southern kingdom and the neglected cycle of sabbath years that could have been their salvation, the Babylonian empire sends Jerusalem and the remaining tribes into exile. The land finally enjoys its sabbath rest. "All the time of its desolation it rested, until the seventy years were completed in fulfillment of the word of the LORD" (2 Chron 36:21).

But judgment is not irreversible. The prophets also speak of a coming day of the Lord when "the poor will eat and be satisfied; they who seek the LORD will praise him" (Ps 22:26). Solomon, the bringer of much oppression, sees a future when God "will deliver the needy who cry out, the afflicted who have no one to help. He will take pity on the weak and needy and save the needy from death" (Ps 72:12-13).

This kingdom reversal of the place of the poor already suggests an urban renewal of a new kind. And other prophetic emphases underline the difference. The restoration will not be nationwide. It will focus on a righteous remnant (Amos 5:15; Rom 11:1-5), a "smaller group who were in practice what the whole community was in theory, who took seriously the obligations of the covenant and endeavoured to carry them into effect" (Bruce 1968:57).

Without these "consecrated ones" (Ps 50:5), these few survivors, the cities would have been like Sodom and Gomorrah (Is 1:9). With them God preserves his promise of an unbroken Davidic succession and the continued existence of a true Israel. The saved remnant becomes the saving remnant; "not all who are descended from Israel are Israel" (Rom 9:6).

The term *poor* and its related images in fact become synonyms for that remnant of Israel who will in that day "return to the Mighty God" (Is 10:20-21). In the sociopolitical context of Israel terms like *the meek* and *the humble* suggest the oppressed, those who suffer under the power of injustice. And more besides. The meek are at the same time those who remain faithful to God and expect their salvation from his kingdom alone (Ridderbos 1962:188-89). Their distress, and their faith in the midst of distress, is a title to God's love (Ps 19:28; 34:5-11).

In this restoration Jerusalem will be reborn. "The LORD builds up Jerusalem; he gathers the exiles of Israel" (Ps 147:2). "The delight of donkeys, a pasture for flocks" (Is 32:14) will be called "Sought After, the City No Longer Deserted" (Is 62:12). God will return to Jerusalem with mercy. And that divine urban renewal blessing will overflow into Yahweh's other cities also (Zech 1:17). "God will save Zion and rebuild the cities of Judah" (Ps 69:35).

Even in these promises there are hints of radical changes in the coming Jerusalem as a restored center of worship. Foreigners and eunuchs will no longer be barred from entrance into temple worship. God's house "will be called a house of prayer for all nations" (Is 56:3-7; Mk 11:15-17).

The restoration of Zion will encompass the peoples of the earth. In the darkness that covers the earth, Zion will become a beacon that attracts the world to the glory of God displayed in it. Nations will be drawn to Zion's light, kings to the brightness of its dawn (Is 60:3). "Many nations will be joined to the LORD in that day and will become my people" (Zech 2:11). This universalism "is not an ideological abstraction. It is an invitation, addressed to the whole world, to sit at the banquet of the Covenant, to become heirs of the promises made to the Fathers, to Abraham, and to his seed forever" (LeGrand 1990:27). It is the universalism of salvation to be offered now to all the cities and peoples of the earth.

The invitation often is described in political or geographical categories. Isaiah pictures it in terms of the customary tribute offered to Zion by conquered nations (Is 60:5-6). Ezekiel sees the restored boundaries of the Messiah's land incorporating Syrian Damascus (Ezek 47:6-18; 48:1). And along with native-born Israelites, these aliens will share in the inheritance of the tribes (Ezek 47:22-23).

At the same time, the political language is interwoven with that of worship. The tribute becomes offerings for worship at the altar (Is 60:7-8), brought "to the honor of the LORD." The coming of the nations to Jerusalem is for instruction in the way of the Lord (Is 2:3; Mic 4:2).

To call this universalism "missionary" would be to use language that is anachronistic and overly strong. Zion's mission is not a campaign to convert the pagans. It consists rather in testimony rendered "in the sight of all the nations" (Isa. 52:10) by the mighty arm of God stretched forth in behalf of his people and assuring their salvation. . . . The "light of the nations" is not a teaching transmitted by human missionaries. It is the power of God manifested to the entire world through Israel. (LeGrand 1990:20)

Above all else, one feature transforms this description of urban renewal. At its heart will be the coming of David's greater son, the Messiah. The Spirit of the sovereign Lord will rest upon him, and the ancient ruins will be rebuilt, the places long devastated repaired; "they will renew the ruined cities that have been devastated for generations" (Is 61:1, 4). With his coming the tent of childless Zion will be filled with her descendants, who "will dispossess nations and settle in their desolate cities" (Is 54:1-3; cf. Amos 9:12; Acts 15:17).

Through the Messiah's anointed rule there will be justice for the poor (Is 11:4), saving judgment with righteousness for God's afflicted ones (Ps 72:2). The Lord himself will come to plead the case of the poor and take the life of those who rob them (Prov 22:22-23; 23:10-11). He will participate in their oppression by bearing it for them. He will be oppressed and afflicted, yet he will not open his mouth (Is 53:7). As the poor are despised, so will the Messiah-servant be despised—forsaken by all, a man of sorrows and acquainted with grief (Is 53:3).

## God's Urban Commission Fulfilled

Six hundred years after God's call through Jeremiah to seek the peace of the city (Jer 29:7), the fuller significance of the words of Jeremiah would begin to unfold in history. His prophecies to the exiles were filled with many themes—the raising up of David and the Davidic line, future blessing for Israel in God's shalom peace, Gentiles sharing in those blessings, cities tasting the fruits of Israel's good works.

In the city of David a royal child would be born, and the threads of promise would begin to form a divine tapestry of fulfillment. In the temple a widowed prophet named Anna would see in that child's coming the restoration of the ruined city, "the redemption of Jerusalem" (Lk 2:38; Is 52:9). In the same temple courts righteous Simeon would hold the child in his arms, staring at God's glory-giving salvation, "a light for revelation to the Gentiles" (Lk 2:32; Is 60:3). Simeon, Israel and the nations would wait in exile no longer; the messianic day of consolation had come at last in Jesus (Lk 2:25).

Jesus' healing miracles would remind multitudes of the coming of the Son of David (Mt 12:22-23; 20:30). Even the Gentiles would see in his divine power that of David's greater son (Mt 15:22). The crowds would hail his coronation path to Jerusalem with hallelujah exclamations of praise to him as the Son of David (Mt 21:8-9). And the high priest would convict him of blasphemy for his taking that title for himself (Mt 26:63-65).

Jeremiah's disparaging of a temple-centered faith would be expanded to a message of temple displacement. Jesus' redemptive ministry would signal the coming of One greater than the temple (Mt 12:6). His act of temple cleansing at the beginning of his ministry would be done with the authoritative zeal of the Messiah (Jn 2:14-17). And in that enacted parable his disciples would eventually see in the resurrected Christ God's temple alternative (Jn 2:19-22).

In all this the prophetic urban dimension is not lost. The promised Savior does not stand apart from the city. Jesus' widening proclamation of God's redemptive kingdom come in himself cannot be restricted to one place; he must preach the good news "to the other cities also" (Lk 4:43 NKJV). "To every city and place where he himself was about to go" he sends in advance his envoys (Lk 10:1 NKJV). They are to function as benefactors, healing the sick and proclaiming the presence of God's kingdom reign of grace in Jesus (Lk 10:8-9). This urban embassy resembles "a rhetorical dress rehearsal for [Luke's] description in Acts of the church's worldwide mission" (Danker 1976:16).

Eight hundred years before, God had invited his herald to bring good news to Jerusalem and to the cities of Judah. The long night of sin and warfare was to end. And the messenger's voice on the mountain summed it up: "Here is your God!" (Is 40:9).

In Jesus that announcement to the cities becomes reality. In Jesus the covenant is renewed, the law and the prophets are fulfilled, justice and righteousness are incarnated, salvation becomes more than promise, the perfect sacrifice for sin is offered. The kingdom of God comes in the person of the King, the jubilee year of God begins, the poor are lifted up, the cities hear the good news, and God inaugurates his time of urban restoration.

# 6

# Jesus, the Spirit
# & the Church

To MOVE FROM THE CITIES OF THE ANCIENT Near East to those of Jesus' day is to take a large leap. Cities, after all, change and adapt in function as the social systems of which they are a part change. Scholarship is learning that we cannot judge the Bible's preindustrial cities by industrial city models (Rohrbaugh 1991a:68-74; Sjoberg 1960). It is also important to remember that Ur is not Elam and Philistine cities are not Roman ones. More than years separate these histories; social twists and turns also divide them.

## Urban Shifts and Stabilities
Mesopotamia's simplest city systems, for example, were fundamentally economic communities based on agriculture and the interdependence of the city and its surrounding villages. The city (usually walled) was the center of a two-tiered system. And its (usually unwalled) village "daughters" were the peripheral second tier (Josh 13:28; 15:32, 36, 41, 44, 46-47). These networks controlled very little territory (Frick 1997:15). As late as the postexilic period this model sheltered the dispossessed Levites and temple attendants living in the shadow of a devastated Jerusalem (Neh 11:25, 30; 12:28-29). It survived under different political conditions at least into the Hellenistic period; Mark 8:27 speaks of "the villages around Caesarea Philippi."

**Urban transitions.** As these city-village systems expanded, they began to encroach on neighboring systems. Overlapping friction led to power alliances or competition and strife. Abraham's collaboration with the five kings of the plains against the four kings (Gen 14) was typical of this kind of Mesopotamian power politics within the period c. 2000-1750 B.C. (Kitchen 1966:43-47).

With this expansion the simpler two-level organization was often transformed into a larger regional, three-tiered league of cities, with a central city administering several connected city-village systems. Israel's march to the Promised Land appears to have touched these spreading territorial systems. The Israelite defeat of Sihon of the Amorites swept away not only the capital "Heshbon and all its surrounding settlements" but all the cities to whose realm it belonged (Num 21:25-26). Victory over the Midianites, possibly a league of tribes (Dumbrell 1975), whose five kings were vassals to Sihon (Josh 13:21), meant God's victory over all the cities where the Midianites had settled, as well as all their encampments.

In this growing process of territorial expansion, the role of the city shifted to administration over a widening political and military base. The symbiotic interaction of the city with its neighboring villages was transformed into an expanded state based not solely on cities but on territorial control by a hereditary monarchy. God's answer to Israel's appeal to Samuel for "a king to lead us, such as all the nations have" (1 Sam 8:5) suggests some of the characteristics of this new urban model and the darker side associated with them: a highly structured state built around centralized control of the monarchy; a growing bureaucracy fed by a socially fixed labor force; a standing, not voluntary, army; the involuntary conscription of the people as servants; capital concentration of the economy and agriculture in the will of the monarchy; the rise of one city as magnet capital for economic and military power (1 Sam 8:10-18).

The final stage in this transition from control by a city and its ruler was the empire, "control on a territorial basis, perhaps exercised through cities but not connected with any specific one" (Frick 1997:17). In the hand of God it would be the judging power against the northern kingdom of Israel under the Assyrians (2 Kings 17:3-18; 18:9-12) and later, against the southern kingdom of Israel under the Babylonians (2 Kings 24:1-5; 25:1-21). No longer a relatively independent center, the city had become a territorial tool of empire builders. With the succession of the Persian, Greek and Roman empires, that role was solidified. "Cities no longer represented society, civilization, or the gods" (Lapidus 1986:282). Now they became physical settings in the functioning of a larger and different form of society.

That pattern is stamped on the urban background of the New Testament. To solidify conquests and advance Greek influence, Alexander and his successors had built new urban settlements and rebuilt existing ones. He himself was reputed to have established seventy such cities. In the centuries that followed, Hellenization became closely linked to urbanization. Cities became local administrative communities within the colonial system. Following Greek practice, they were permitted to retain their changing cultural identity and keep, within limits, a strong measure of political autonomy.

In the Roman provincial network that was to overlay the Greek system, the basic pattern repeated itself. Greek culture found a partnership in Roman institutions. Kings devolved from a monarchy into a titular ruling status by Roman appointment (Acts 25:13). Behind and beside them stood a Roman shadow government of governors (Acts 23:24) and tetrarchs (Lk 3:1). "When 'Jesus was born in Bethlehem of Judea in the days of Herod the king' (Matt. 2:1), he was born into a Jewish kingdom ruled by an Idumean king with a Greek name, installed and sponsored by the Romans" (Stambaugh and Balch 1986:13).

**Urban continuities.** But with all these shifts in what we call the city, some features, with modifications, remained constant. Whether in Ur or empire, religion was intertwined with the life of the city. The worldviews of cities were faith commitments foreign to any separation between the sacred and the secular. Religion and ethnicity, whether Canaanite or Roman, "were bound together in an unbreakable bond. To have an ethnic identity was to have a religious identity; to define a particular people was to define that people's gods" (Berlin 1996:1).

So too with public life. The religious dimensions of politics and the political dimensions of religion were not separate tracks in the public domain. They were embodied in temple and shrine, in the Greco-Roman perception of the city's charter as a gift from the patron deity and in the obligation of citizen and special officials to carry out religious functions on behalf of the city.

Nor was private life isolated from matters of faith. The dedication of meat to the gods in the marketplace made eating a struggle of conscience for the Christian (1 Cor 8). Temple prostitution at Corinth transformed sexual activity into a religious act of devotion (1 Cor 6:15-20). For the citizens of Athens, reason or wisdom was more than an intellectual attainment; it was the gift of its patroness Athena, the daughter of Zeus (Grant 1986:64).

Another constant remained amidst these centuries of urban shifting: the integration/interaction of city and village within the societal system.

Past research has slighted connections like these in promotion of an urban-rural polarization of closed systems (Conn 1987:18-20, 39-40). Anachronisms drawn from perceptions of the industrial city have been imposed on the preindustrial cities we are looking at now. Recent research suggests cities and villages should be seen as "nodal points within societal systems" (Leeds 1994:71). Like the cities in the ancient Near East, the Greco-Roman city of the New Testament was not a closed system or a tightly bound entity in isolation from other nucleations like villages or towns.

Even after the state component in city-state had lost its strict meaning, the closely interlocked town-country unit remained basic in an empire "more urbanized than any other society before the modern era" (Edwards 1988:178). Larger urban and commercial centers incorporated smaller urban areas and village networks within their trading spheres. Import and export networks bound city and village in ties of economic reciprocity. Hellenism's cultural and linguistic influence reinforced the continuum of city and village (Edwards 1988:172-82).

In keeping with this interaction, *cities* and *villages* are easily linked terms in the New Testament (Mt 9:35; 10:11; Mk 6:56; Lk 10:1; 13:22—though recall that the NIV often substitutes *towns* for *cities*). Sometimes what other Gospels call a village *(kome)* Luke will call a city *(polis)*. Bethlehem, a village in John 7:42, becomes "the city of David" in Luke 2:3-4, 11, perhaps due to its physical proximity to Jerusalem. Bethsaida is a village in Mark 8:23, but in a switch similar to that in Matthew 11:20-21, it becomes a city in Luke 9:10.

What was the difference between the two? The very pairing of the coordinate terms in couplets argues for some kind of distinction, though some scholars are not convinced of this (Feyne 1980:146). A. N. Sherwin-White offers a possible solution of a politico-administrative sort. Judea and the tetrarchies, he notes, were administered under the house of Herod and the procurators alike by the Ptolemaic system of villages *(komae)* grouped into districts known as toparchies. A large village acted as the administrative center of the toparchy. Josephus, Sherwin-White continues, may have often used the term *city* to denote merely the capital of toparchies (Sherwin-White 1963:126, 130). Gadara was such a toparchic capital, called a *polis* in Luke 8:26-30. So was Bethsaida, also designated as *polis* in Luke 9:10.

Research still struggles with the ambiguity of this issue (Rohrbaugh 1991b:125-29; Edwards 1988:169n3). Does Luke use the term *city* in a nontechnical sense? Is this in keeping with Luke's "relative indifference to geographical and temporal setting" (Stonehouse 1953:98)? Is a city, after all, just a grander village—one with administrative functions, walls (as in the past), cultural institutions, public buildings? Whatever solution is reached, city and village remain integrated wholes, and that tightly knit relationship would ensure the flow of the gospel from city to village and village to city.

## Jesus' Urban Context

Was Jesus a man of the country in contrast to the urban Paul? Some scholarship argues that way. Jesus' early ministry, it is argued, was located in the Galilean countryside's small and often anonymous places. "Where Hellenistic cities are in fact mentioned, Jesus enters only the surrounding territory, and not the cities themselves. He touches on the 'villages of Caesarea Philippi' (Mark 8:27), the 'region of Tyre' (Mark 7:24, 31), the 'country of the Gerasenes' (Mark 5:1). He goes through the Decapolis without entering the actual ten cities (Mark 7:31)" (Theissen 1978:47). "The Jesus movement," agree other scholars, "was socially located in the rural village culture alienated from Graeco-Roman cities" (Stambaugh and Balch 1986:106). And not until the Jesus movement decided to "leave the village culture of Palestine behind," continues the thesis, did it turn toward the Greco-Roman urban world (Meeks 1983:11).

*Jesus and the villages.* How do we respond to this argument? Without a doubt, Jesus' transition from his public ministry to his postresurrection church generally involved a transition from smaller population centers to larger ones. Nazareth, where Jesus was raised (Mt 2:23; Lk 2:51), was what today might be called a small village. Even Capernaum, where he went to live following his rejection in the Nazareth synagogue (Lk 4:31; Mt 4:13), may have had a population no larger than twelve to fifteen thousand (Overman 1988:162).

At the same time, such judgments based on population size may also involve anachronistic assumptions imposed on preindustrial nodules by industrial city standards. Both Nazareth (Mt 2:23; Lk 1:26; 2:4) and Capernaum (Lk 4:31) are designated cities in the Gospels.

But even if we assume the propriety of these population judgments, the province of Galilee where these cities were located needs a second look. An area of about 750 square miles, it supported a population of about 200,000 during the reign of Herod Antipas (Batey 1991:136). In lower Galilee, a geographical zone roughly fifteen by twenty-five miles, we enter "one of the most densely populated regions of the entire Roman Empire" (Overman 1988:165). Through this area Roman road systems ran, placing lower Galilee at the center of trade and travel in the entire region (Avi-Yonah 1950-1951). Linked to the roads were the regional centers of Roman power, culture, and influence—Capernaum; the walled city of Magdala; Scythopolis or Beth Shean, the largest city of the Decapolis (Mt 4:25; Mk 5:20); Tiberias; and Sepphoris, the seat of the Sanhedrin and the capital and "ornament" of Galilee.

Sean Feyne's massive study of Galilee of the Gentiles (Mt 4:15) also paints a picture of the growing Hellenization of the area through urbanization. And Josephus gives the impression of a fairly densely populated and urbanized province: "The cities [poleis] lie very thick and the very many villages that are here are everywhere so full of people by the richness of their soil that the very least of them contained about 15,000 inhabitants" (*Wars of the Jews* 3.43). Feyne still sees Galilean life as mainly organized on village lines, but he concludes, "Even allowing for notorious exaggeration of population figures, it seems likely that quite a few Galilean settlements were anything but villages by the modern use of that term, and clearly some criterion other than that of population is operative" (Feyne 1980:104).

Crowded into a fifteen- to twenty-five-mile area, how could these urbanized centers not dramatically influence the social world around them? Recall the already-described symbiotic relationship between agricultural and urban environments of the time. "One could not live in any village in lower Galilee and escape the effects and ramifications of urbanization" (Overman 1988:165). Life here was as urbanized and urbane as anywhere else in the Empire.

Did these urban influences escape the attention of Jesus and his disciples whose principal ministry was in this region? Not if we judge by a vocabulary studded with references to urban institutions like courts (Mt 5:25) and city market squares (Mt 23:7; Mk 5:56), and with financial analogies built on interest-bearing accounts (Mt 25:27; Lk 19:23) and metaphors of God as an absentee landlord (Mk 12:1-12). Centurion leaders of one thousand soldiers (Mt 8:5) and bureaucratic tax collectors controlling even fishing rights (Mt 9:10; Lk 5:27) dot the Galilean narratives.

***Jesus and the Gentiles.*** What of the claim mentioned earlier that Jesus touched only the borders and boundaries surrounding Hellenistic cities and not the cities themselves? That too needs modification. Did Jesus, for example, touch only the edge of Tyre (Mk 7:24, 31)? The Greek word *horion* in the singular means boundary, but in the plural (as used here) it signifies territory or district (Arndt and Gingrich 1957:584-85). Further, the same preposition *(eis)* used for Jesus' entering *into* the house (Mk 7:24) is used in speaking of his passage *into* the district of Tyre.

In the same vein, what of his going into "the villages around Caesarea Philippi" (Mk 8:27)? We need to remember that Caesarea Philippi was not a district but a toparchic capital, controlling an extensive number of subordinate villages, as all such capitals did. It even possessed the privilege of minting its own money. Isolating too radically a toparchic capital from its villages, as the argument under consideration does, damages the city-village connection built into such a relationship.

Why, though, do the Gospels not record visits to Sepphoris, only an hour's walk from Nazareth, or the thoroughly Gentile city of Tiberias (mentioned only in Jn 6:23)? Whatever reluctance Jesus may have felt about entering these Hellenistic cities, their absence does not indicate an oversight or a village-oriented rabbi's avoidance of cities per se. The Gospels note the ministry of Jesus and his disciples in cities frequently enough to put that possibility to rest (Mt 9:35; 10:23; 11:1, 20; Mk 6:33, 56; Lk 13:22).

The answer lies not in oversight but in a strategy shaped by the history of redemption. Any reluctance is toward the Gentiles who formed a part of their populace. The focus of Jesus' ministry in the cities is the synagogue (Mt 9:35). His disciples are sent to the lost sheep of the house of Israel who live in the "cities of Israel" (Mt 10:23; cf. 2:20; 19:28). The time has not yet come for a full proclamation to the Gentiles. That time will begin to come with the death and resurrection of our Lord (Mt 21:33-43). Until then, salvation must be offered to Israel before the Gentiles can be received into the people of God. "Many will come from the east and the west, and will take their places at the feast with Abraham, Isaac and Jacob in the kingdom of heaven" (Mt 8:11). But not yet.

### Jesus' Urban Mission

Into this urban world came Jesus of Nazareth. And with his coming came the inauguration of God's urban renewal plan. Babel's human quest for unity in rebellion is finally fulfilled in God's gift of unity in "one Lord, one faith, one baptism" (Eph 4:5). God comes down again (Gen 11:5) not to judge but to save in Christ.

On a stairway-tower God stood promising blessing to a fleeing Jacob and all the families of the earth (Gen 28:13-14). Out of that site emerged a city, Bethel, "the house of God." Reflecting on that history, Jesus promises to Nathanael that a new reality has surpassed Jacob's dream: "You shall see heaven open, and the angels of God ascending and descending on the Son of Man" (Jn 1:51). Jesus is the stairway, that One in whom heaven comes down to the cities of the world and through whom we ascend to the heavenly city. "Heaven stands open through Him whom the angels serve" (Clowney 1988:69).

After three days in the belly of the great fish, a reluctant Jonah went forth, virtually resurrected from the dead, to promise God's redemption to a repenting Nineveh. Now Jesus' preaching, "something greater than Jonah," calls the cities to repentance. And the sign of his power will be his Jonah-like resurrection from the dead after three days (Mt 12:39-40).

Ezekiel spoke of the day when God himself would return to Zion and take up residence as its rightful King, when the shekina glory that had departed (Ezek 11:22-23) would once more fill the house of God (Ezek 43:4-5). The name of the city from that time on would be "THE LORD IS THERE" (Ezek 48:35). Near the Bethlehem birthplace of Jesus, shepherds quaked as "the glory of the Lord shone around them" (Lk 2:9). Angels herald the fulfillment of the promise as they sing of "glory to God in the highest" (Lk 2:14). "One greater than the temple is here" (Mt 12:6).

After the cleansing of the exile, the prophets had cried, there would be an eschatological restoration for Zion and the people of God. God the shepherd-king himself would come to gather his lost sheep (Ezek 34:16, 23-24). The ruined cities would be rebuilt (Amos 9:14; Acts 15:14-18), and even the desolate cities of the Gentiles would be repopulated (Is 54:3).

At the center of this urban restoration work would be God. All the urban domains of royalty would be fulfilled in him. His would be the sacred city kingship "in the order of Melchizedek" (Gen 14; Ps 110:4). In the echoed but transformed language of national kingship Isaiah sees the glory of sun and moon fade in shame before the coming glorious reign of the Lord "on Mount Zion and in Jerusalem, and before its elders" (Is 24:23). "On that day they will say to Jerusalem, 'Do not fear, O Zion; do not let your hands hang limp. The LORD your God is with you' " (Zeph 3:16-17). His kingship would extend past the boundaries of empire: "the LORD will be king over the whole earth" (Zech 14:10). Before the redeemer "servant of rulers," kings and princes will bow down (Is 49:7).

The message of Jesus is that these promises of God's royal saving reign have begun to be fulfilled. The coming of the divine King to reclaim, redirect and redeem is the coming of Jesus. The new age of righteousness and grace, God's jubilee year for the cities (Is 61:1-2), has dawned: "Today," announces Christ of his preaching, "this scripture is fulfilled in your hearing" (Lk 4:21). To the cities he sends his Twelve with a message: "The kingdom of heaven is near" (Mt 10:7; cf. Lk 10:1, 11). Because Jesus is in their midst, the kingdom of God is in their midst (Lk 17:21). He is the incarnate form of the saving rule of God, the kingdom present in the King, the agent of urban restoration through his life, death and resurrection.

**Luke's urban emphasis.** Such a view of Jesus and the city is uniquely underlined in Luke's Gospel and his "second chapter" book of Acts. The word *polis* occurs about 160 times in the New Testament, and half of these occurrences are in Luke's writings. The closest competitors are Matthew (26 times) and the book of Revelation (27), then only four times each in Paul's writings and Hebrews. Of particular interest is the wide usage of *polis* in Luke's Gospel. Approximately half of its occurrences (thirty-nine verses) are found here, rather disquieting in view of the marked rural-urban contrasts alleged between Jesus and Paul. To underline this again, the New Testament names ninety different places that may have been cities. Of these, twenty-eight specific names are used in Luke and Acts "in direct or implied association with the word 'city' *(polis)*" (Rohrbaugh 1991b:126).

Luke's interest becomes all the more remarkable when we observe the stylistic ways he appears to spotlight the *polis*. In Luke and Acts, for example, the term in question is often added to the proper names of localities, an addition not characteristic of the other Gospels. The angel Gabriel is not sent simply to Nazareth but to "Nazareth, a city in Galilee" (Lk 1:26, rendered "town" in NIV). The home of Zechariah is located specifically in "a *polis* in the hill country of Judah" (Lk 1:39). In Mark's Gospel, Jesus in the synagogue heals a man possessed of an evil spirit. This takes place at Capernaum (Mk 1:21), which in Luke's Gospel becomes "a *polis* in Galilee" (Lk 4:31). It is not simply at Nain where the widow's only son is raised from the dead, but "a *polis* called Nain" (Lk 7:11). Joseph, pictured in Luke 23:51 as "waiting for the kingdom of God," is described as not simply from Arimathea but "from the Judean *polis* of Arimathea."

We have already mentioned Luke's designation as *polis* what other Gospels call "village." Bethlehem, a village in John 7:42, is called a city in Luke 2:3-4, 11. Bethsaida is a village in Mark 8:23 but a city in Luke 9:10.

Yet this is no doctrinaire usage overriding the historical in favor of a controlling theological interest. Luke

> does not automatically apply the term *polis*, however, as seen when he uses *kome* "village" for the hostile Samaritans (9:52), the home of Mary and Martha (10:38), the sources of the colt for his entrance into Jerusalem (19:30), and Emmaus (24:13,28). Not all editorial summaries make a reference to city (9:6). These examples, usually in close proximity to Jerusalem, may only illustrate his desire to contrast the role of the great city with lesser neighboring settlements. (Sklba 1976:54-55).

H. J. Cadbury remarks that "Luke seems to think it is worth while to note the city as the scene or scope of what he has to tell, even when he has made no mention of the city by name" (Cadbury 1961:247). Thus in the house of the Pharisee, Jesus' feet are anointed with perfume and kissed by a woman who was a sinner; Luke also notes that she was a woman "in that *polis*" (Lk 7:37). In chapter 8 we are introduced to Luke's variation of the parable of the sower. While both Matthew (Mt 13:2) and Mark (Mk 4:1) draw attention to the crowds, the multitude who heard Jesus, only Luke notes that they came from various cities (Lk 8:4). A similar urban detail characterizes a parable unique to Luke's Gospel. The judge figure at the center of the parable of importunate prayer is from "a certain *polis*"; the widow heroine is also "in that *polis*" (Lk 18:2-3).

In parables parallel or similar to other Synoptic materials, Luke's details underline the urban. Matthew relates the story of the great banquet. When the invited guests do not appear, he continues, the servants are sent "to the street corners" to invite in passersby (Mt 22:9). Luke's description is more particular still: "Go out quickly into the streets and alleys of the *polis*" (Lk 14:21). In Matthew the parable of the ten talents speaks of the reward given to good and faithful servants. "Come and share your master's happiness!" says the master (Mt 25:21). In Luke's variation, obedient servants are made masters of cities (Lk 19:17, 19).

Even what appear to be the most rural scenes in Luke are given an urban coloring. Large crowds that come to hear our Lord's parables are drawn "from *polis* after *polis*" (Lk 8:4; cf. 8:1). In commissioning the seventy to announce the arrival of the eschatological harvest of God (Is 27:12; Joel 3:13; Amos 9:13-15), Luke tells us that Jesus sent them "to every *polis* and place where he was about to go" (Lk 10:1). It is the city that Jesus has in view as the audience that is unreceptive to the message of the seventy (Lk 10:8, 10-12). He heals a demoniac living in the tombs across the Sea of Galilee, whom only Luke tells us came "from the *polis*" (Lk 8:27). Sent home by Jesus to describe what great things God had done for him, he returns to the Decapolis, according to Mark 5:20. Luke omits the proper name of this federation of Hellenistic cities and says only that the man carried the word of the Messiah's healing throughout the whole *polis* (Lk 8:39). Again, in the account of the miracle of the multiplication of loaves and fishes, the other Gospels' only topographical allusions are to the isolation and solitary character of the area (Mt 14:13; Mk 6:32). Luke speaks of the isolated location but ties it to a city called Bethsaida (Lk 9:10).

**Jesus and Jerusalem.** The centerpiece of Gospel attention, however, remains the mission of Christ. Luke orients that mission uniquely toward Jerusalem, the city of the great king (Lk 9:41; 22:10; 23:19; 24:49), and to Jesus' urban pilgrimage toward his atoning death and resurrection (DeRidder 1975:128-200). Jesus is called to that city for the fullness of his mission, and Luke's Gospel takes on the appearance of an extended processional toward the city and the temple as its messianic goal.

Jerusalem, without doubt, plays an important role in Luke's writings. "In his Gospel alone, Luke refers to the city twice as often as does any of the other Evangelists" (DeYoung 1960:15). Even more striking are the instances in Luke's materials where the phrase "the *polis*" occurs by itself, virtually without antecedent, and yet clearly referring to Jerusalem (cf. Lk 19:41; 22:10; 23:19; 24:49). Unaccompanied by definitive genitive or demonstrative pronoun, *polis* par excellence is Jerusalem.

Jesus' march to his cross and resurrection is a march to Jerusalem, the city. So the Gospel begins with the angelic announcement of the birth of John in the city of the King (Lk 1:5-25), and it ends with the disciples joyfully returning to that city and temple after the risen Lord's command to remain "in the city until you have been clothed with power" (Lk 24:46-52). In contrast to the other Gospels (Mt 28:7, 10, 16: Mk 16:8), Luke describes no resurrection appearances in Galilee but only in the environs of Jerusalem.

And between these events everywhere the shadow of Jerusalem's city walls and its temple center as the Father's house falls on Jesus' path. A tax census takes the pregnant Mary and Joseph on the first of Luke's pilgrimages to the city (Lk 2:3). And there in Bethlehem, which Luke designates "the city of David," the child is born (Lk 2:4). To Jerusalem's temple Jesus returns as a young boy, conscious that he must be in his Father's house (Lk 2:50). In the temptation that inaugurates his public ministry (Mt 4:1-11; Lk 4:1-12), Luke reverses the sequence "to allow the final encounter to take place, not on a remote mountain, but on the Temple's pinnacle" (Sklba 1976:52).

The same journey-pilgrim motif shapes the so-called travel section of the Gospel (Lk 9:51—19:44); it occupies nearly 40 percent of Luke's history, in contrast to only two chapters in Matthew (Mt 19—20) and one in Mark (Mk 10). Throughout the long narrative we are reminded of the pilgrimage's final goal: "Jesus resolutely set out for Jerusalem" (Lk 9:51, 53; 13:22; 17:11; 19:11). The exodus of the eschatological Moses, the Savior of his people, has begun (Lk 9:31). "Surely no prophet can die outside Jerusalem!" (Lk 13:33). The fulfillment of the redemptive plan for the city—the accomplishment of the Messiah pilgrim's saving purposes—is oriented to Jerusalem.

The final phase of the journey closes with Jesus' messianic entrance into the city that belongs to him. The crowds echo the words of Psalm 117:26, "Blessed is he who comes in the name of the LORD." Luke's rendering elaborates by reading, "Blessed is the king" (Lk 19:38).

But coupled with the jubilation, Luke—and only Luke—takes note of Jesus' weeping over the city (Lk 19:41). The temple and the city have become the focus of opposition to the Messiah. The Lord has come to his temple (Mal 3:1). But his "house" has abandoned him in the abandonment of his Son. So ownership of God's dwelling house is transferred to Jerusalem; the temple, "his house," becomes "your house" (Lk 13:35).

Jesus' final temple cleansing, coming immediately after his judgment of the city of Jerusalem (Lk 19:41-44), links these again in the suggestion of that same judgment theme. "The city's blindness (v. 42) is manifested most acutely in the Temple which is blind to its true purpose and which, just like the city, fails to 'recognize the time of God's coming' (v. 44)" (Walker 1996:63). Jesus' use of the language of exodus to describe his death/departure had effectively cast Jerusalem in the role of Egypt (Lk 9:31). The same linguistic allusion to the exodus appears in Luke 24:50, when the resurrected Christ "had led [his disciples] out" to the vicinity of Bethany. Once more Jerusalem is recast as Egypt.

### Jesus' Urban Ministry Continued

The Gospel interest in the wide geographical distribution of Jesus' ministry is widened still further in the book of Acts. It is stretched by the missionary history of the ethnic expansion of Christianity from Galilee to the ends of the earth. As in the Gospels, that expansion continues to move in an urban direction. In the Gospels the urban geographical outlook takes us "from Galilee to Jerusalem"; in Acts we move from "Jerusalem to Rome" (Filson 1970:75). And the movement from place to place in these journeys is dotted by urban stopping points and allusions.

***The urban emphasis of Acts.*** Scholarship has long been ready to assume literary connections between Luke's Gospel and the book of Acts. The renewed dedication in Acts 1:1 to Theophilus, its backward glance to the "first book," and the retrospective summary of the earlier history all argue for such connections. And when the author describes the former volume as an account of "all that Jesus began to do and to teach," we are encouraged to see more than mere common authorship. "The implication of Luke's words is that his second volume will be an account of the things which Jesus *continued* to do and teach after his ascension—by His Spirit in His followers" (Bruce 1954:32).

Redaction criticism has attempted to demonstrate this continuing feature by underlining the theological contribution of the author, some designating him as Luke out of convenience more than historical necessity. Growing interest has focused on the author as "a consummate literary artist" and searched for formal literary parallels and patterns (Talbert 1974; Flender 1967). Charles Talbert, for example, remarks that

> the Evangelist definitely wanted to portray the deeds and teachings of Jesus as the pattern for the acts and instruction of the apostolic church. It is, therefore, near impossible to avoid the conclusion that these correspondences

> between Jesus and the church serve the same *imitatio magistri* theme. . . .
> The tradition of Jesus is passed on to posterity through the life and teaching
> of the apostolic church. (Talbert 1974:98-99)

There is no need to diminish in any way the historical reliability of the
book of Acts if we acknowledge these correspondences. The architectural
patterns do exist, and among other things, they take urban shape.

As in the Gospel, Luke is not content simply to speak of Joppa, Lystra
or Derbe, Thyatira or Lasea. It is "the city of Joppa" (Acts 11:5), "the cities
of Lystra and Derbe" (Acts 14:6), "the city of Thyatira" (Acts 16:14) and
"the city of Lasea" (Acts 27:8, rendered "town" in NIV). And again Luke
displays a preference for speaking of cities when others might speak of
villages or districts and areas. So the fame of the Christian miracles
spreads outside Jerusalem, and from the cities round about (Acts 5:16) the
crowds gather.

Ernst Haenchen remarks that "there are of course no real *poleis* in the
vicinity" and "Luke had no exact ideas of the geography of Palestine"
(Haenchen 1971:243). But this does injustice to Luke's preference in his
Gospel for speaking of "various cities" instead of provinces or districts (Lk
8:1, 4; 10:1). It also misses a significant difference in the ways Luke and
Paul separately speak of their work. "While Paul's letters show that for his
missionary work he treats the Roman provinces as units (Galatia, Asia,
Macedonia, Achaia, and even Illyricum and Spain . . . ), we can best
understand his biographer as one who thought in terms of cities, or of city
states, or city stations or itineraries" (Cadbury 1961:246). So the apostles
in Jerusalem rejoice that "Samaria had accepted the word of God" (Acts
8:14). But it is to "a city in Samaria" (Acts 8:5, 8) that Philip goes.

The province of Galatia to Paul becomes, by at least one exegetical
choice of harmonization open to us, the cities of Iconium, Derbe and
Lystra to Luke. Macedonia to Paul (2 Cor 8:1) becomes Thessalonica,
Berea and Philippi to Luke (Acts 16:9-17:14). Luke is not unaware of the
provincial titles in Acts (Acts 16:9; 18:5). His political sensitivity can
designate Gallio as proconsul of Achaia (Acts 18:12). But his urban
interest defines the gospel work there in terms of Corinth and Athens
(Acts 17:15—18:18). It is no exaggeration to say that the book of Acts
deals almost entirely with cities; missionary work is almost limited to
them.

Adolf von Harnack, hardly noted for his apologetic defense of the his-
toricity of the New Testament record, included in his 1909 study of Acts a
careful search of the book's geographical terms. He notes how rarely
there is reference to the country in the rural sense. And he includes these
interesting remarks about the use of the word *city* in Acts:

The mission was for the most part carried on in cities, as also the Jews of the Diaspora were chiefly settled in the cities. Hence we read in 8:40 of Philip: "he preached the gospel to all the cities"; again James says (15:21) that Moses has "in every city in the synagogues them that preach him"; and Paul admits (26:11) that he persecuted the Christians not only in Jerusalem, but also followed them up "even unto the cities outside"; Paul and Silas pass through (16:4) "the cities" and revisit (15:36) city by city the communities that were founded on the first journey; Paul declares that the Spirit "city by city" prophesied sufferings that were about to come on him (20:23) and "the multitudes of the cities round about Jerusalem" crowded into the city to be healed by the apostles (5:16). It is characteristic of the exactness of the author that he often marks the fact that something took place outside the city. Stephen was stoned "outside the city" (7:58); the temple of Zeus in Lystra was situated "before the city" (14:13); Paul was dragged "outside the city" (14:19); the place of prayer in Philippi lies "outside the gate" (16:13); and the disciples in Tyre accompany Paul "even to outside the city" (21:5). (Harnack 1909:61-62)

***Jerusalem and the temple fulfilled.*** Another important bridge between the two volumes and their urban interest is the function of Jerusalem as "a sort of geographical sign-post" (Maddox 1982:10). As in the Gospel, the book of Acts invests theological significance in the city. Jerusalem, the place of resurrection, ascension and Pentecost, becomes the starting point and the measuring stick for all apostolic mission ventures. Talbert sums up its significance:

(a) It is from Jerusalem the universal preaching of the gospel is to begin (Lk. 24:37; Acts 1:4, 8). (b) Every new expansion of the church in apostolic times had to receive the approval of Jerusalem (e.g., Acts 8:12, 14-15; 11:1-2, 18, 19-22; 15:2, 12ff). (c) Paul's entire ministry is given a Jerusalem frame of reference (9:27ff); his work at Antioch is undertaken at Barnabas' initiative (11:25ff); his missionary commission is given by a church which was Jerusalem approved (13:1-3); each of his missionary journeys ends at Jerusalem (15:2; 18:22; 21:17); he recognizes the validity of and appeals to the witness of the Twelve (13:31); he refers difficult questions to Jerusalem (15:2), accepts Jerusalem decisions (21:23-26), and appeals to Jerusalem authority (16:5). In sum, Jerusalem controls the mission enterprise in Acts. (Talbert 1982:100)

In keeping with this significance of Jerusalem and parallel to Luke's practice in the Gospel, *polis* appears again in the book of Acts as a solitary designation for Jerusalem (Acts 7:58; 12:10). The city, without specified context, is Jerusalem.

Eric Franklin suggests that this centrality of Jerusalem serves a twofold purpose in Acts. "In the first place, though she does not inaugurate the succeeding stages of the mission, it is her approval which regularizes them, and, secondarily, their relationship with her alone secures their incorporation into the renewed people of God" (Franklin 1975:128). Thus Luke, through the significance he gives to Jerusalem, can show the early Christian mission to be the fulfillment of eschatological expectations. In keeping with the judgment of James at the Jerusalem Council (Acts 15:15-18), the pilgrimage of the nations to Jerusalem is linked to the renewal of Israel and to the restoration of the city of God (Is 2:2-24; 55:5; Zech 2:10-11; 8:20-23; Joel 2:32). The constant return to Jerusalem throughout the history recorded in Acts becomes a reflection of the magnetic power of Mount Zion drawing the peoples to its light.

At the same time, a third and more negative purpose may also help to explain another feature of Luke's treatment of Jerusalem in Acts: the new geographical focus that concludes Luke's second volume. The church's mission must begin from Jerusalem (Lk 24:47-49; Acts 1:8). But it concludes at Rome, "the ends of the earth." "For Luke the coming of Paul to Rome signals and symbolizes the entrance of Rome into the role of focal center of the church and missionary home base of its gospel outreach. The center of the church is no longer Jerusalem; it now moves to Rome" (Filson 1970:75).

Stylistically Luke paints this shift throughout his history as away from Jerusalem as the center of the new people of God. The seven and their followers are driven out from Jerusalem, and this opens the door to the rapid extension of the mission in other places (Acts 6:9—8:4). Paul is denied justice in Jerusalem, and this leads to his preaching in Rome. Paul's repeated confrontation with the Jews of the urban dispersion is a counterpart to that of Jesus with Jerusalem. The shift away from Jerusalem is emphasized uniquely in the significance Luke gives to the journey Paul makes to Rome (Acts 19:21—28:31). That journey, undistinguished even by current scholarship as a missionary journey, occupies the final, climactic third of the second volume. Why?

Floyd Filson sees it as a direct literary parallel to Jesus' Jerusalem journey in Luke's Gospel. And Talbert suggests as least thirty-six structural comparisons between the two passages, an architectonic pattern too deliberate to ignore (Talbert 1974:16-23). Both journeys climax in a turning away from those who themselves have turned away. Jesus weeps over the city and announces its downfall (Lk 19:41-44). Paul calls the leaders of the Jews and, in a tone of finality, announces that "God's salvation has been sent to the Gentiles, and they will listen" (Acts 28:28). Jesus comes to the great city and its leaders spurn the divine Messiah. Now Paul is spurned by the same city and, in his march to Rome, symbolizes the turning from the city by the divine Messiah (Walker 1996:89-94).

In the language of Filson:

It is the repeated emphasis of the closing chapters (and indeed of the earlier chapters) of the Acts that the gospel is the fulfillment of God's promises to Israel as found in the Old Testament; the church is the divinely given continuation of the life of Israel and so the church is the true Israel. Jerusalem could have continued to be the focal geographical and spiritual center of that new and true Israel. But it failed to avail itself of its privilege. With the mob attack on Paul in the temple and the active attempt of the Jewish leaders to put Paul out of the way, Luke sees the failure of Jerusalem to accept and fulfill its role; and so Luke in this final third of the Acts is presenting the lost opportunity which Jerusalem had and the essential transfer of the center of the church from Jerusalem to Rome. (Filson 1970:75)

The pattern of urban invitation moved inward in the Gospel, from Galilee through Samaria to Judea and Jerusalem. In the book of Acts it moves outward from Jerusalem through Judea and Samaria to the uttermost parts of the earth. "As Israel's rejection in Jerusalem led to opportunity for the outcasts in Luke, so also in Acts, the Jews' rejection resulted in the preaching to the Gentiles" (Miesner 1978:201). In the chronicling of the urban dispersion, the association of Israel and church has also become the alternative of Israel or church.

## Mission by the Church Through the Spirit

This transition to Israel or the church was a gradual one. While they could, the disciples continued to participate in temple fellowship (Acts 2:46), to teach in the temple (Acts 3:1; 5:20-21, 42), to fulfill their vows in it (Acts 21:26; 24:17-18). But a new consciousness gripped them. The day when they would worship the Father neither at Gerizim nor in Jerusalem had come (Jn 4:21). Jesus the Messiah by his death and resurrection (Jn 2:19-22) had built a new temple. "The symbolic temple yields to the person of the present Lord. He is the topstone. His body is the temple. He bears the glory" (Clowney 1971:79). Zion was where God was pleased to dwell (Deut 12:5; Ps 68:16), out of which his glory would fill the whole earth (Is 6:3). Now Jesus has become the One in whom all God's fullness was pleased to dwell (Col 1:19).

Isaiah looked forward to the day when "the Redeemer will come to Zion" (Is 59:20). Paul sees that prophecy as fulfilled in Christ's coming (Rom 11:26). But in a striking switch, he replaces Isaiah's phrase "to Zion" with his own "from Zion." His attention has turned to Zion as the channel of divine blessing to the Gentiles. The centripetal ("to Zion") had become the centrifugal ("from Zion"). "Paul's own focus was not so much on what Zion might continue to be in the future but rather on what God had done there in the recent past in order to move his purposes forward onto a world-wide canvas" (Walker 1996:142).

***The gathered and gathering house of God.*** The instrument for that ingathering of the Gentiles was to be the church, the new temple in whom the Spirit of Christ dwells (1 Cor 3:16; 6:19; 2 Cor 6:16), the temple/house of God (Eph 2:19-22). As both Acts and Paul's letters suggest, that ingathering, and the instrument for that ingathering, was urban. Patterning the new community after the synagogue model dispersed through the Empire and turning from one centralized temple worship center opened new urban doors. In the cities power was located, and changes could occur; the mobility of a traveling population could carry the gospel (Meeks 1983:14-23).

Thus Paul could speak of his proclamation of the gospel as a breakthrough to all the peoples, an extensive missionary building of the house of God that has been completed. He could boast to the Romans, "From Jerusalem all the way around to Illyricum, I have fully preached the gospel of Christ" (Rom 15:19, 23; cf. 1 Tim 3:16). Practically, how had this been accomplished? He had "planted small cells of Christians in scattered households in some of the strategically located cities of the northeast Mediterranean basin" (Meeks 1983:9-10).

The Roman Empire before and after Paul's day decried the urban life and romanticized the rural way of life (Lowenstein 1965). But that seems remote from the pages of the New Testament and its picture of the church. Even the term *ekklesia*—a word we translate as "church"—had an urban ring in the days of the empire. In common usage it referred to the town meeting of free male citizens of a city of Greek constitution. It continued to be so used through the Hellenistic period and (with modifications) in the Roman world (Meeks 1983:108). Even acknowledgment of the term's source and deeper roots in the Septuagint translation of the Old Testament does not eradicate that wider sense in the world outside the Christian community.

Other social organizations in Greek and Roman cities also provided interesting parallels to the church. Clubs or voluntary associations resembled Christian communities in several ways. These clubs (called *thiasoi* in Greek and *collegia* in Latin) each worshiped some patron god. They held regular (usually monthly) meetings, shared a common meal and required special rituals for admission into membership. The groups were small, usually homogeneous associations of socially or trade-oriented people. Supporting them was the generosity of a patron.

It would not have been hard for society to identify the church as one of these urban clubs. They too had a patron god in Jesus. They held regular meetings for fellowship (Acts 2:46-47). Love feasts and the Lord's Supper were their common meals, baptism their admission ritual. In the house churches of Corinth and Rome, people like Stephanas (1 Cor 16:15-18) and Phoebe (Rom 16:1-2) are described in terms used of the host patron. In fact, in the second century Roman officials and literary opponents of Christianity often identified the church with such groups. And Christian apologists as late as the third century could plead for the legitimacy of the church on the basis of these parallels (Stambaugh and Balch 1986:140-41).

But beyond the similarities there were differences not always recognized immediately by society. Jesus, the "patron god," allowed no room for alternate choices. The names of municipal offices adopted by such clubs are virtually absent from the letters of Paul. No clubs spoke of their members as the holy ones, the elect, the beloved of God. Membership in the *ekklesia* broke the bounds of ethnicity and rank, wealth and professions. In this "club" there was "neither Jew nor Greek, slave nor free, male nor female" (Gal 3:28). Boundary lines vanished in oneness "in Christ Jesus." Even the local character of the "club" was minimized in the face of the church's self-understanding as a worldwide community.

If we do not look to voluntary clubs and associations to find the nature and mission of the urban church, where can we turn? We turn to Old Testament images of divine house and temple, kingdom and Zion, and to their fulfillment in the gathering church gathered by Jesus. Not in Jerusalem's rubble but "scattered throughout Pontus, Galatia, Cappadocia, Asia and Bithynia" (1 Pet 1:1) and its cities we find a new temple of "living stones, . . . being built into a spiritual house" (1 Pet 2:5). Paul's first missionary journey sweeps in gospel triumph through cities like Pisidian Antioch, Lystra and Derbe, and the church sees in that the rebuilding of David's fallen tent/tabernacle in Jerusalem (Acts 15:16). The believers at Ephesus rise from a new foundation "to become a holy temple in the Lord" (Eph 2:21), with Jesus himself as its chief cornerstone. Jesus, "the ruler of the kings of the earth," takes the seven urban churches of Asia (Rev 1—3) and "makes . . . a kingdom" (Rev 1:5; 5:10). To a church of Jew and Gentile, people and no people, God gives the privileged title holy nation and calls them to the witness of praise (1 Pet 2:9-10). God's praises are to rise from the new Zion (Is 25:6-8).

**The divine witness who gathers.** How could this thin little collection of Christian groups in no more than a dozen or so cities of the Roman Empire see themselves as a restored Zion? Where do we go to find the reason for their self-understanding as a new urban world rebuilt by God? How did they break out of their Hebrew particularism to make the transition to a universal ministry? The answer lies in the overshadowing gift and presence of the Holy Spirit.

Through ingratitude and rebellion, the people of God had grieved his Holy Spirit (Is 63:10; 1 Thess 4:8). But in the last days, say the prophets, the Spirit will return in renewing power. The suffering servant will be anointed by the same Spirit "to preach good news to the poor," the good news of the coming of the jubilee year of the Lord's favor (Is 61:1-2; cf. 11:1-5). Included in that jubilee ministry of the Spirit will be the rebuilding of the ancient ruins, the renewing of ruined cities (Is 61:4). God will perform a heart transplant in his people; hearts of stone will be replaced by hearts of flesh (Ezek 36:26). And how will he do this? "I will put my Spirit in you . . . I will resettle your cities, and the ruins will be rebuilt" (Ezek 36:27, 33).

When will God keep that promise? The focus of Luke and Acts is on the reply to that question.

In the once-for-all event of Pentecost the ecclesiastical wait for that "gift my Father promised" (Acts 1:4) is ended. The covenant promise is the Spirit himself (Lk 24:49; Acts 2:33), come in his fullness to dwell in the new house of God not built with hands (Rom 8:9-11; 1 Cor 3:16; Eph 2:22). He is both a fulfillment of the promise and the promise of fulfillment, himself the down-payment guarantee of the new age to come (2 Cor 5:4-5; Eph 1:14) and the firstfruits of God's universal harvest to come (Rom 8:23). His presence is the new covenant fulfillment of the covenant word to Abraham (Gen 12:2; 17:5-10) and, beyond Abraham, for all who are far off (Acts 2:38-39; language used of the Gentiles in Acts 22:21). "The epochal significance of Pentecost raises the whole course of salvation-history to a new plane" (Dunn 1970:53). At Pentecost a reconstitution of the people of God takes place.

> Up to Pentecost the central place of worship had been the temple; the central office-bearer, the priest; the central cultic object, the altar; the central cultic act, the sacrifice. With the coming of the Spirit this entire cultic complex was abrogated. For a while the members of the *ekklesia* continued to have a place in the *qahal* [assembly], but this dual loyalty was a transitional phenomenon. Pentecost was the death-knell of temple, priest, altar, sacrifice, law and ceremony. All disappeared, and in their place came the preaching of the gospel and the sacraments, together bearing witness to the completed work of Christ. (H. Boer 1961:113)

This perspective controls the meaning of Acts 1:6-8. The disciples are pressing on Jesus their eschatological question: "Are you at this time going to restore the kingdom to Israel?" The language of restoration is the language of expectation (Mal 4:5-6), perhaps asked with some Jewish nationalist hopes. Jesus' response turns their power expectations in a new direction, to be shaped by a new source: "You will receive power when the Holy Spirit comes on you; and you will be my witnesses in Jerusalem, and in all Judea and Samaria, and to the ends of the earth" (Acts 1:8). Power in the life of the new Israel will be a gift of the Spirit. And that power will be exhibited in the publishing of the jubilee good news about Christ to all peoples.

Old Testament prophecies underlined the centripetal coming of the nations to the Lord: the spontaneous streaming of the peoples drawn to God's magnet house (Is 2:2-3) for his end-time banquet (Is 25:6), mountains flattened into roads and highways elevated to provide travel safety and security for those who "will come from afar" on their pilgrimage to Zion (Is 49:11-12), Gentile cities coming to Jerusalem to seek the Lord Almighty (Zech 8:21), "ten men from all languages and nations" eagerly snatching the robe of a Jew and pleading to go with him "because we have heard that God is with you" (Zech 8:23).

Acts points repeatedly to the fulfillment of that theme of spontaneity as the Spirit draws people from cities to Jesus. The emphasis on numerical response pushes in that direction. At Peter's Pentecost preaching about three thousand souls were converted (Acts 2:41). In a short time this grew to five thousand men alone (Acts 4:4). Through the witness of the apostles, "more and more men and women believed in the Lord and were added to their number" (Acts 5:14). "The word of God spread. The number of disciples in Jerusalem increased rapidly, and a large number of priests became obedient to the faith" (Acts 6:7). In the cities of Samaria "the crowds . . . paid close attention" to Philip's preaching (Acts 8:6). In fact, the response was so great that Luke comments, "Samaria had accepted the word of God" (Acts 8:14).

Luke's catalog of spontaneous urban response continues. Peter heals a paralytic in Lydda, and news of this spreads through the semi-Gentile coastal plain of Sharon: "all those who lived in Lydda and Sharon . . . turned to the Lord" (Acts 9:35). In Joppa he raises Dorcas from the dead and "many people believed in the Lord" (Acts 9:42). Missiological innovators fleeing from Jerusalem's persecution begin evangelizing Greeks in Antioch, and "a great number of people believed and turned to the Lord" (Acts 11:21). What may have been an incredulous church at Jerusalem sends Barnabas to authenticate the ministry. And it continues unabated: "a great number of people were brought to the Lord" (Acts 11:24). In Antioch of Pisidia, in striking contrast to the antagonism of the Jews, "almost the whole city" gathers to hear Paul and Barnabas (Acts 13:44-45). As a result of this witness, "the word of the Lord spread through the whole region" (Acts 13:49). In Derbe "they preached the good news in that city and won a large number of disciples" (Acts 14:21). In Thessalonica "some of the Jews were persuaded . . . [as were] a large number of God-fearing Greeks and not a few prominent women" (Acts 17:4).

Underlining the divine source of that spontaneity is Luke's focus on the Spirit as the true presence of God (in Christ) in the world. The centrifugal march of the church out "among the nations" in the new diaspora (Lk 24:47 KJV) is also a centripetal movement to God. "Nothing is left to men, not even to apostles; *that,* however, is why everything *can* be delegated to the Church" (Blauw 1962:90). The church's witness is ultimately the witness of the Holy Spirit.

The Pentecost coming of the Spirit in Acts 2 begins the pattern. All the disciples "were filled with the Holy Spirit and began to speak in other tongues" (Acts 2:4). Why was the gift of tongues given now? It was a sign of assurance that the Holy Spirit would enable them to communicate the truths of the gospel to the whole world. What, after all, is a tongue but the instrument of human communication? And in keeping with this exhibition of the Spirit's power, the text immediately records the growth of the church (Acts 2:41). There is a symbiosis between Spirit and witness that is rooted in the authentication of God-centered centripetal prophecy.

The same connections between the Pentecost event and the gift of tongues occur possibly three other times in the narrative. All come at points where the spontaneous expansion of the church moves past the boundaries of perceived redemptive history. Samaria hears the word of God, and the Samaritans' inclusion into the household of God is certified to a skeptical delegation from Jerusalem with the receiving of the Holy Spirit (Acts 8:14-17). The reception of a Roman centurion is sealed by the "gift of the Holy Spirit" and of tongues (Acts 10:44-46). At Ephesus the disciples of John the Baptist are moved from the margins of the covenant community to its center when the presence and reality of the Holy Spirit was certified again with tongues (Acts 19:1-6).

The Spirit's role in widening the horizon of the mission and thus affirming God's wider intentions is carried through the rest of the book. Philip's encounter with the Ethiopian eunuch is through the agency of the Spirit (Acts 8:29, 39); doors that once were closed to this man for temple worship (Deut 23:1) have now been opened (Is 56:4-5). The coming of the Holy Spirit on all the believers, circumcised and uncircumcised, at Cornelius's baptism is seen as linking Gentile also to the earlier Pentecost history of the same Pentecost Spirit. "They have received the Holy Spirit just as we have" (Acts 10:47; 11:12-18).

In his report to the Jerusalem community Peter underlines this connection again (Acts 11:15). Gentiles and Jews now enter the new age of the Spirit together, both incorporated into the Pentecostal history of redemption, both sharers in the "the same gift" (Acts 11:17). An astonished church affirms it as well: "God has granted even the Gentiles repentance unto life" (Acts 11:18).

The same God-centered emphasis on the work of the church as the work of the Spirit continues in Luke's description of Paul's ministry. It is a ministry initiated at his conversion with the fullness of the Spirit (Acts 9:17). The same Spirit instructs the church to set Paul and Barnabas apart for mission (Acts 13:2). They are described in Acts 13:4 as sent not by the Father or by Christ but "by the Holy Spirit." The same Spirit of God even guides the geographical direction of Paul's ministry. The Spirit is that specific agent who prevents him from going into Asia in order that he might take the momentous step of entering Macedonia and Europe (Acts 16:6-10). The fateful trip to Rome (which concludes the narrative) is also Spirit-inspired; Paul is "compelled by the Spirit" to go to Jerusalem (Acts 20:22), and his arrest and trial process there take him to the imperial capital.

Centripetal and centrifugal, particular and universal, the end time has broken into urban history. "Pentecost publicly marks the transition from the old to the new covenant, and signifies the commencement of the 'now' of the day of salvation (2 Cor. 6:2)" (Ferguson 1996:57). There is more to come—the second coming of Christ in full glory, the time of consummation, the throne judgment of the cities (Lk 10:14). But between the present "already" and the coming "not yet" there is the church's mission of grace in the Spirit to the ends of the earth, until the end of time.

How should it be carried on?

# 7

# A New Lord, a New
# People, a New World

ACCORDING TO PHILO, THE ESSENES described the Hellenistic cities as an "infectious germ," an unclean world they sought to avoid. Jerusalem, despoiled by illegitimate priests, offered only defiled sacrifices. Zealots and *sicarii,* ethnocentric resistance fighters of the day, had an equally negative view of the city. Their resistance to idolatry barred their entrance to any city; "no one had to go through a gateway with a statue on it" (Theissen 1978:50-51).

But for Paul, divine commentator on the history of salvation, Hellenistic cities posed no such barrier. They were strategic centers, not cloisters, from which the gospel would be spread. "All the cities, or towns, in which he planted churches were centres of Roman administration, of Greek civilization, of Jewish influence, or of some commercial importance" (Allen 1962:13).

> He concentrates on the district or provincial capitals, each of which stands for a whole region: Philippi for Macedonia (Phil. 4:15), Thessalonica for Macedonia and Achaia (I Thess. 1:7f), Corinth for Achaia (I Cor. 16:15; II Cor. 1:1), and Ephesus for Asia (Rom. 16:5; I Cor. 16:19; II Cor. 1:8). . . . In each of these he lays the foundation for a Christian community, clearly in the hope that, from these strategic centers, the gospel will be carried into the surrounding countryside and towns. (Bosch 1991:130)

## The City, World Mission and Redemptive History

But in all this there was more than simply strategic planning by someone who was himself born and rooted in urban culture, "a citizen of no ordinary city" (Acts 21:39). At the heart of Paul's missionary method was his perspective on the history of redemption.

God's new world order had been initiated through the coming of Christ and his death and resurrection (Gaffin 1978). Through the coming of the Holy Spirit a new age was being constructed while the old age still existed (Eph 1:20-21). The jubilee day of salvation, the time of favor when God would restore the land (Is 49:8), was no longer a promissory note; "now," affirmed Paul, "is the time of God's favor, now is the day of salvation" (2 Cor 6:2). Upon the scattered house churches of the empire "the fulfillment of the ages has come" (1 Cor 10:11).

More is still to come. Now people reap the harvest of grace in the cities; the day is coming when angels will reap in judgment "outside the city" (Rev 14:17-20). Salvation still awaits the consummation (Rom 13:11) and the return of the triumphant Christ (1 Pet 1:4-5). The "already" points to the "not yet."

Linking the "already" and the "not yet," and at the center of that redemptive history, is Jesus the Lord. The title *kyrios* (Lord) was a favorite designation of Paul (Warfield n.d.:223). Within the urban world it was used widely of revered beings, local deities or high rulers (Kittel 1965:1049-58). But when Paul used it of Jesus, he spoke of more than one revered being among many (1 Cor 8:5). Paul went back for his source to the Greek translation of the Old Testament, the Septuagint. There it was— the term marking the name of the only true God, Yahweh. In startling fashion, Paul used it also to point to Jesus as that Yahweh/*kyrios*/Lord.

The day was coming, said the prophet, when "every knee will bow . . . every tongue shall swear, 'In the LORD alone are righteousness and strength' " (Is 45:23-24). Now, says Paul, "at the name of Jesus every knee should bow"; the confession of every tongue is that "Jesus Christ is Lord" (Phil 2:10-11). In the coming day of the Lord "everyone who calls on the name of [Yahweh/*kyrios*] will be saved" (Joel 2:32). Now, comments Paul on that Joel prophecy, Jesus as Lord is the saving name confessed by Jew and Gentile (Rom 10:12-13).

***The Day of the Lord and Paul's mission.*** Paul sees his own ministry as deeply linked to that eschatological day. It is embedded in his striking phrase of self-evaluation: "I have fulfilled the gospel of Christ" (Rom 15:19, our translation). Favored English translations (KJV, NKJV, NIV) render this "I have fully preached," which may give the mistaken impression that he is reflecting on the fullness with which he set forth the gospel (cf. Acts

20:20, 27). The Jerusalem Bible translates it "I have preached Christ's Good News to the utmost of my capacity," underlining the strenuous self-efforts of the apostle. All these translations miss the link between the apostle's commission that he expounds here and the sense of complete-ness that he now expresses. The language is similar to Colossians 1:23, where Paul speaks of the gospel "that has been proclaimed to every crea-ture under heaven" (cf. Col 1:25).

What does Paul mean? It surely cannot mean that he had preached the gospel in every locality and to every person. Is this cosmic hyperbole? In what sense has the preaching of the gospel of hope been completed, or proclaimed to all humanity?

Behind the language is, again, Paul's sense of the place of world mis-sion in the history of redemption. In his ministry to Jews and Gentiles he saw the triumph of the Lord as peoples "from Jerusalem all the way around to Illyricum" found their way to God in Christ. The eschatological expectations of the ingathering of the Gentiles had become eschatologi-cal experience in the mission of Paul. "The universality of the gospel is matched by the universality of the apostle's task, that is, to herald God's saving victory over His creation" (Beker 1980:7).

This vocational self-consciousness flowed out of no mistaken notion on Paul's part that the second coming of Christ was to immediately fol-low. It flowed rather from his understanding that with the death and res-urrection of Christ the last days had begun. Paul's global mission was both exhibition and anticipation, both overture and guarantee, of that coming triumph of God. "While there is indeed a future aspect to his eschatological understanding of mission, the dominant orientation is upon the 'already' rather than the 'not yet' " (Bowers 1976:149).

**The city and Paul's mission.** The scope of Paul's geographical refer-ence—"from Jerusalem all the way around to Illyricum"—also suggests more than sporadic forays and random skirmishes in Gentile lands. In the Hellenistic world to speak of the inhabited world, the *oikoumene,* was to speak of the city (Friedrich 1967:157n1). And into that urban world the gospel is to be heralded as widely as creation itself speaks of God (Ps 19:4; Rom 10:18; cf. Mt 24:14).

Cities for Paul, then, become representatives of the entire world (Theissen 1982:38). In the planting and maturation of churches in those cities Paul sees the formation of new urban communities created and loved by God. Even urban legal vocabulary is assimilated freely into the Pauline dictionary to describe those communities (Lyall 1984:60-66).

*Citizenship,* the term we use today for membership in a state or nation, had a narrower political connection in the days of Paul. It was legal terminology ordinarily used to denote the rights obtained by birth or purchase in a city (Acts 22:26-28). Paul uses it of the readers of his circular letter to the Ephesians; Gentile foreigners now share joint "city-zenship" with the saints of Israel (Eph 2:12-13). With the Philippian believers he pleads, "Continue to exercise your 'city-zenship' *[politeuesthe]* in a manner worthy of the gospel of Christ" (Phil 1:27, our translation).

Because Philippi was a Roman colony, its residents' names were inscribed on the citizenship rolls at Rome; they could live in Philippi "in the enjoyment of the same privileges which would be theirs if they moved to Rome itself" (Motyers 1966:158). But the Philippian believers had an even better urban connection: "our city-zenship is in heaven" (Phil 3:20). Their names were on the census roll in glory, placed there by their being in Christ (Phil 3:21). So they lived at Philippi in the enjoyment of the privileges that would be theirs when they moved to heaven.

## Urban Mission's Action Agenda

How was that urban, heavenly citizenship to be exercised? What were the key features in Paul's understanding of the churches' urban mission? Where should the cities look to see this new work of divine restoration?

***Mission and the praise of God's glory in worship.*** For Paul the taproot of that mission was the glory of God and its display and acknowledgment in global worship. Mission was not the ultimate goal of the churches Paul planted. Nor was the goal church growth. "Worship is. Missions exist because worship doesn't" (Piper 1993:11). God's glory fuels our mission and draws our worship. "Worship is not a mere function of the church; it is her *ultimate* purpose" (Costas 1974:38).

Repeatedly Paul echoes the sentiment of the psalmist in his addresses to the city churches: "May the peoples praise you, O God; may all the peoples praise you. May the nations be glad and sing for joy" (Ps 67:3-4). The opening lines of his second letter to Corinth focus on God's work of compassion and comfort as an incentive to praise (2 Cor 1:3-7). Interjected into his opening reflections on the lavished riches of God's grace in Ephesians is the repeated refrain "to the praise of his glorious grace" (Eph 1:6, 12, 14). Song, whether in Old Testament worship or New (Ps 18:49; Rom 15:9), is not only a vehicle for "teaching and admonishing one another" (see Deut 31:19; Col 3:16); it is also the voice of "thanks to God the Father for everything" (Eph 5:19-20). "Christ," Paul proclaims, "has become a servant of the Jews . . . so that the Gentiles may glorify God for his mercy" (Rom 15:8-9). In confirmation he quotes Scriptures that call for praise and rejoicing by the Gentiles (Deut 32:43; Ps 18:49; 117:1).

To describe his ministry to the Gentiles Paul borrows the language of worship and liturgy. His proclamation of the gospel to the Gentiles is an act of worship (Rom 1:9 JB), the service of a "liturgical priest" (Rom 15:16, "minister" NIV), the Gentiles his offering. The anticipation of his possible death becomes the pouring out of a libation, a drink offering to God (Phil 2:17; cf. 2 Tim 4:6). The collection he gathers for the saints at Jerusalem becomes a liturgical act of worship offered up by the Gentiles (Rom 15:27; 2 Cor 9:12).

Enriching and reshaping this doxology of worship and praise are the realities of the new covenant. The Old Testament phrase for formal Israelite worship was "to call on the name of the LORD" (Gen 4:26; 12:8; 26:25; 1 Kings 18:24; 2 Kings 5:11; Ps 105:1). In the coming day of the Lord, God would purify even the lips of "the peoples, that all of them may call on the name of the LORD" (Zeph 3:9). Now, says Paul, it is "the name of our Lord Jesus" that is to be glorified in us (2 Thess 1:12). Our thanks in song to God the Father is to be offered "in the name of our Lord Jesus Christ" (Eph 5:20). In fact, everything we do, whether in word or deed, is to be done "in the name of the Lord Jesus" (Col 3:17). Israel's tabernacling God has come to be with us, and Immanuel/Jesus is his name (Mt 1:21-23).

With his coming worship is transformed. The Jerusalem temple-shrine had centered worship "upon the concept of sacrificial death as a means of gaining access into God's presence. There was a new center, Christ himself. It was he who had secured this 'access' for believers (Rom. 5:1-2) which could be appropriated directly through exercising 'faith' in his 'blood' (Rom. 3:25; cf. Eph. 2:13; 3:12). The temple's role in the past had been vital, not so in the future" (Walker 1996:123-24). With Jesus' death and resurrection, the temple is to be found wherever two or three are gathered in his name. And the service of worship becomes the "living sacrifice" to God of the day-by-day practice of transforming holiness (Rom 12:1-2).

This living sacrifice can now be offered by both Jew and Gentile. The temple boundary marker is gone; through the cross Christ has broken down the dividing wall (Eph 2:14). The burnt offerings of foreigners can now be accepted on God's altar (Is 56:6-7); Zion's gates stand open to receive their wealth (Is 60:10-11). Those "who serve[d] wood and stone" (Ezek 20:32) can now enter to serve the living God in Christ.

***Mission and the planting and nurturing of the church.*** If the glory of God was the ultimate center of Paul's mission methodology, its penultimate base was the church: "to him be glory in the church and in Christ Jesus throughout all generations, for ever and ever" (Eph 3:21). If Christ was the last Adam who had subdued all things to himself and "fills everything in every way" (Eph 1:22-23; cf. Gen 1:28), the church was his body, "the fullness of him who fills." The church was the assembly arena whose meaning was to be filled with his life and power and whose mandate was to seek its fullness in the fullness of its risen Head (Ridderbos 1975:390-92).

Can we speak of the church as a goal of urban mission, as an end as well as a means of mission? Some theorists have been fearful of defining the church as anything more than the church in terms of its function or task in and for the world (Hoekendijk 1967). But this is to isolate the church from its nature as the holy temple/house in which God now dwells between the times (Eph 2:19-22). Repeatedly Paul's imagery returns to that larger eschatological picture to describe the church (Roels 1962:83-152).

The church is the body of Christ, that community in whom Christ dwells, turned outward in action toward the world (1 Cor 12:12-27). It is that end-time "community which the Christ, in action as Spirit, forms and equips to continue His work of reconciling men in every city, village, and town of our time, reconciling them to God and one another" (Smedes 1970:231). The church is the bride of Christ (Eph 5:23-32), the Israel once called deserted but now, in this last day, called back in compassion by the heavenly bridegroom (Is 54:6-7; 62:4-5). From every city the faithful husband had promised to bring his faithless bride back to Zion (Jer 3:14), to renew his marriage covenant (Jer 31:32). Now, in a wedding garment "without stain or wrinkle or any other blemish" (Eph 5:27), the radiant church is presented to Christ.

The church, in other words:

> is both a means and an end, because it is a foretaste. It is the community of the Holy Spirit who is the earnest of our inheritance. The Church can only witness to that inheritance because her life is a *real* foretaste of it, a real participation in the life of God Himself. . . . Precisely because the Church is here and now a real foretaste of heaven, she can be the witness and instrument of the kingdom of heaven. It is precisely because she is not *merely* instrumental that she can be instrumental. (Newbigin 1953:147-48)

Conscious of this identity, Paul crosses the urban world, planting these instrumental samples of his already redeemed creation. The term *ekklesia* dignifies a scattering of believing communities in a dozen or so cities of the empire, "so many 'pockets' of an alternative lifestyle that penetrates the mores of a society around them" (Bosch 1991:150). Meeting in houses, they live out the new age of the Spirit in cities like Corinth (Rom 16:5), Ephesus (1 Cor 16:19) and Colossae (Col 4:15; Philem 2). And with a regularity uncommon in the Old Testament Paul uses the plural to speak of those same communities within larger areas—"the Galatian churches" (1 Cor 16:1; Gal 1:2), "the churches in the province of Asia" (1 Cor 16:19), "the Macedonian churches" (2 Cor 8:1).

But never forgotten is the deeper identity of these base cells of the Christian movement. They are the "churches of God" (1 Cor 11:16; 2 Thess 1:4). They are proclaimers of the kingdom of the Father, sharing the life of the Son, bearing the witness of the Spirit (Newbigin 1978). Their calling is to nurture the body's membership in the richer growth and display of already exhibited marks of divine ownership.

Because the planting of churches is both means and end, both goal and instrument, growth is to be measured in numbers and more. It is to be measured also "by their participation in the bringing about of a new order, in establishing a community of love, in struggling for justice and peace as an *anticipation of the ultimate revelation of God's kingdom*" (Costas 1979:57).

So Paul correlates his mixed images of the church as the restored house, temple and building of God with metaphors centering on the cultivation of growth and the continuing work of God with his people (Rom 14:19-20). The temple is also a cultivated field where "only God . . . makes things grow" (1 Cor 3:7, 9); Christ is the foundation upon which we build (1 Cor 3:11-15). The goal of the church as the fullness of Christ is to be "fully mature with the fullness of Christ himself" (Eph 4:13 JB). The once-for-all grounding in Christ as foundation and cornerstone (1 Cor 3:11; Eph 2:20) demands an ever-continuing nurturing, upbuilding and growth. And the goal of that nurturing and upbuilding? "To *know* the Lord, to *do* the Lord's will, and to *be* like the Lord" (Clowney 1995:143).

"For the sake of this upbuilding God equips the church with all sorts of gifts and powers that he places at its disposal, as also with various kinds of ministries that must further its upbuilding" (Ridderbos 1975:432). Given and directed by the Spirit, these nurturing ministries (Eph 4:11-13; 1 Cor 12:7-11) become "spiritual gifts" (1 Cor 12:1) for "mutual edification" (Rom 14:19).

***Mission and the conversion of the Gentiles.*** The grafting in of the Gentiles becomes another of the goals of the new eschatological day for Paul. Like a victorious general leading his captives in the public spectacle of a triumphal march, Christ leads Paul through the city streets of the world. The gospel he preaches, like the traditional burning of spices in such processions, becomes "the fragrance of the knowledge of Christ" (2 Cor 2:14). In this last-days harvest inaugurated by Jesus, "the firstfruits" of the resurrection (1 Cor 15:20), the Spirit as firstfruits gathers Epaenetus and the household of Stephanus as "the firstfruits of Achaia unto Christ"

(Rom 16:5; 1 Cor 16:15 KJV). God lays claim again to the world as his creation by reconciling it to himself "in Christ," thus making the church "a new creation" (2 Cor 5:17). The eschatological macrocosm of "new heavens and a new earth" (Is 65:17) is unveiled in the microcosm of the people of God.

Paul sees his own ministry as a key part of that renovation and ingathering. From the regions along the African coast of the Red Sea to the distant isles of the Mediterranean, Israel's Gentile brothers would one day come to God's "holy mountain in Jerusalem as an offering to the LORD" (Is 66:20). Now, in his "priestly duty of proclaiming the gospel of God," Paul brings that offering of the Gentiles to God (Rom 15:16). No longer are the Gentile outsiders prevented from approaching the great altar of the temple; they become themselves "the offering acceptable to God, sanctified by the Holy Spirit."

Tyre, "the gateway to the sea," after a thirteen-year siege lost its vaunted security to Nebuchadnezzar and the judgment of God (Jer 27:3-11; Ezek 26—28). Hundreds of years later its Christian community of disciples offers rest and security to Paul (Acts 21:3-4). Antioch of Syria, a commercial center in the Roman Empire and a citadel of Greco-Roman culture, becomes the urban entry point for Christianity into the Gentile world (Acts 11:19-21; 13:1-3; 14:26; 15:22-31; 18:22-23).

In concrete expression of the breaking down of the barrier between Jew and Gentile, Paul carries to the Jerusalem saints a collection gathered from Gentile believers (Rom 15:26-27). The thank offering to Zion becomes an eschatological sign of the Gentiles as self-thank offering, a sign that the wealth of the nations was being brought to the "Jerusalem that is above" (Is 60:5; Gal 4:26; O'Brien 995:30-32; 50-51).

How was this ingathering of the Gentiles to take place? Once again, the centripetal and centrifugal are merged in Paul. And the church becomes the point where the two directions cross.

The lifestyle of the church becomes the centripetal drawing point, pulling the Gentile peoples to itself and, beyond it, to God. Thus the planting and nurturing of the church ministers also to the world in witness. The God-centered life of the church is part of its missionary calling to the world. The church's exemplary existence is to be a missionary magnet, drawing inside those whom Paul calls outsiders (Col 4:5; 1 Thess 4:12; 1 Tim 3:7).

Like stars in the universe, the churches are to shine in blamelessness and purity (Phil 2:15). Even legitimate ecstatic demonstrations of the gifts of the Spirit are to be curbed in public worship lest visiting unbelievers think the Christians possessed or insane (1 Cor 14:23). By their love of all people (1 Thess 3:12), by giving no occasion for valid criticism (1 Cor 10:32), by their service of others, they are to be "the only hermeneutic of the gospel." The gospel's power and credibility are to be interpreted and authenticated in the community of men and women where it is believed and lived (Newbigin 1989:227).

Merging with this centripetal role of the church as the God-centered magnetic drawing point for the Gentiles is the God-centered centrifugal role of the church. It is to move out past Israel among all the world's peoples in witness. That witness inevitably has a verbal dimension; invitations to repent and believe, after all, are not written with invisible ink (Rom 10:14-15).

But the focus of Paul's concern for witness is not primarily how it is done; the focus is Christ and his work as the incarnate good news of the gospel. Taking the good news to the Gentiles is bringing to them "the unsearchable riches of Christ" (Eph 3:8). The call to conversion is a declaration of what God in Christ has done, is doing and will do. And first and foremost the proclamation focuses on what God has already done in the Savior (1 Cor 15:3-4).

The kingdom has come; God has manifested his justice through Jesus Christ (cf. Rom 3:21-27); he has conquered the powers of darkness (cf. Col 1:13) and triumphed over the power of death (cf. 2 Tim 1:10); he has, in Christ, broken down the wall of partition between Jews and Gentiles (Eph 2:14-17), which means he has shattered all the barriers that divide the human family and has made possible a new community (Bosch 1981:68).

Did Paul expect that the churches, like him, should also proclaim this message? He was deeply conscious that his apostolic calling was a heralding of the good news; he was "set apart for the gospel of God" (Rom 1:1), "compelled to preach" (1 Cor 9:16). Was it also the calling of the churches?

It is most certainly true that a review of Paul's letters finds few exhortations to verbal witnessing. Some scholars, like David Bosch, argue that "the primary responsibility of 'ordinary' Christians is not to go out and preach, but to support the mission project through their appealing conduct and by making 'outsiders' feel welcome in their midst" (Bosch 1991:138).

But such arguments ignore the spontaneous character of the churches' witness, referred to in our previous chapter. The church testified also through the "unexhorted and unorganized activities of individual members of the Church explaining to others the Gospel which they have found for themselves" (Allen 1960:7). This activity "is simply taken for granted"

(Gilliland 1983:188). Writing probably from Rome, Paul notes that because of his imprisonment "most of the brothers in the Lord have been encouraged to speak the word of God more courageously and fearlessly" (Phil 1:14). And whatever their motives may be, "Christ is preached" (Phil 1:15-18).

From Thessalonica the word of the Lord has rung out, and the believers' "faith in God has become known everywhere" (1 Thess 1:8). Is Paul's reference to the inspiration provided to the wider church by the believers in Thessalonica simply a commendation of their Christian lifestyle? It appears to be more. He links it to the sounding forth of the "word of the Lord," language used also in 1 Thessalonians 2:13 and 2 Thessalonians 3:1 and easily understood in those passages as referring to preaching (cf. Acts 4:31; 6:7; 13:5; 16:5; 18:11; 19:20).

Paul saw the church in the city as a railway station, not an exhibition hall. By both word and deed the gospel was to spread to Jew and Gentile from those communication centers.

***Mission and the transformation of urban society.*** Though peripheral to urban society as far as its size was concerned, the church for Paul existed as an alternative to that urban lifestyle. It was to be society's new direction, modeling before the city God's divine intentions for his creation.

Repeatedly the church found itself at points of tension in cities divided socially, economically and ethnically (Stambaugh and Balch 1986:110-16). At these points, the church's calling was to demonstrate a new kind of community, one where rich and poor were to share the same table (1 Cor 11:18-22) and where runaway slaves became brothers (Philem 15-16). In a society where the brutal disparities of power and powerlessness were political realities, the Christian community echoed with Paul and Jesus, "My grace is all you need, for my power is strongest when you are weak" (2 Cor 12:9 TEV).

In a top-down society where ranking was measured by such standards as occupational prestige, income, education and family position (Meeks 1983:53-55), the church found room for all, with a particular concern for those at the social ladder's bottom rung (1 Cor 1:26-28). In the death and resurrection of Christ to which we are united by faith, there is a new route to social transformation in the city, "an intrusion of the power, principles, and reality of the consummation into the period of delay" (Kline 1972:156).

In this involvement with urban society, the church is under no illusion that its participation will bring final political or social change; that it can bring about full cosmic transformation, the final resurrection and the liberation of the creation from its bondage to decay (Rom 8:21). Unlike the state, the church can carry no sword to enforce justice (Mt 26:52; Rom 13:4). When justice is delayed, the church's recourse is ceaseless prayer (Lk 18:1-8). In the face of righteousness denied, God's people can only "groan inwardly" in expectant hope for what is not yet (Rom. 8:22-25). The church cannot bring the salvation that Christ lived, died and rose again to win (Sider and Parker 1986:85-107). The only sign of the kingdom come and coming remains Jesus himself (Mt 12:39-40; 16:4).

Are prayer and patience and suffering, then, the churches' only calling in this sinful and rebellious world between the times? Not all divine activity, we must remember, is saving activity. God's exiles in Babylon, after all, had been called before to "seek the peace and prosperity of the city" in which they lived (Jer 29:7); they "were not to plot the destruction of their conquerors, but to seek their blessing" (Winter 1994:16).

Now, once more as exiles and templeless strangers, they were to "silence the ignorant talk of foolish men" by doing good (1 Pet 2:15). Through participation in public life, Christians would counter accusations that they were evildoers who warranted prosecution (1 Pet 2:11-15). They were to repay evil with blessing, insult with gentleness (Ps 34:12-16; 1 Pet 3:9-17).

Through its lifestyle the church was to oppose the evils that God hates—harsh treatment of wives and children (Col 3:19, 21), unjust oppression of slaves (Col 4:1), the discord that, in society then, promoted litigation (1 Cor 6:1-11). The church's good works were to be neighbor-loving demonstrations of God's love for the troubled and poor (Acts 9:36; 2 Cor 9:8-9; 1 Tim 5:10; 6:18).

As carbon copies of the kindness of God shed on the just and unjust alike (Mt 5:45), God's people were to be city lights shining before the Gentiles, "that they may see your good works and praise your Father in heaven" (Mt 5:14-16; Phil 4:8). The Lord rains down his providential goodness no matter how the world responds. Should not his pilgrim children do the same?

Recent scholarship is uncovering that world-affirming ministry of the church in the political arena. It comes through a deeper look at terms like "good works" and "doing good."

> The welfare of the city in the Graeco-Roman world depended on the ongoing contributions of civic-minded benefactors. They paid for public works from their private resources in order to enhance the environs of their cities and, in times of famine, to ensure the supply of grain at a cost affordable to every citizen. (Winter 1994:26)

In extrabiblical literature the language used to describe these acts of civic benefaction by the members of the ruling classes was "the good," "to do good." The municipal benefactor was sometimes called "a good man" (Winter 1994:34-35; Clarke 1990:128-42).

The clients of these benefactors, in turn, reciprocated with acts of gratitude, doing the bidding of the benefactor. Their chain of obligations could also include boisterous social activity and political rabble-rousing on behalf of their patrons. A frequent side effect was a sort of welfare dependency, participation in a continual cycle of giving and receiving.

Paul's letters indicate that the churches had their share of well-to-do Christians who may have been benefactors (1 Cor 1:26). Aristarchus from Thessalonica (Acts 19:29; 20:4) "is possibly one such person—if he is the same person as Aristarchus, son of Aristarchus who heads a list of politarchs in that city" (Winter 1989:306). Stephanas's patronage supported the Christian groups in Corinth; Paul commends him as deserving respect from the church because of it (1 Cor 16:15-18). Gaius, Paul's host at Corinth, had home and wealth large enough to accommodate, and provide hospitality for, "the whole church" (Rom 16:23). Erastus, "the city's director of public works" (Rom 16:23), may well have fit the role (Winter 1994:180-97).

Were these Christian benefactors to forsake their past commitments to the city, to exempt themselves from public duty, fearful of the reaction of officialdom to their new standing in Christ? "Do what's good," exhorts Paul, using the language of public benefaction, "and you will have praise from the same [civil authority]" (Rom 13:3 NKJV; cf. 1 Pet 2:14). After all, it was a binding obligation in this Greco-Roman world that one would honor one's benefactor (Rom 5:7).

Yet even in this, the role of the Christian as benefactor—and as client—was transformed. And the center of the transformation, again, is Jesus. Notice Clarke's unique reading of Romans 5:7-8:

> While it is almost inconceivable that someone would give up their life merely for an upright citizen, it is not unthinkable in the first century that someone—because of the ties of patronage—would give up their life for their benefactor, *ho agathos* [a good man]. Yet Christ gave up *his life for us*—when we were yet sinners without any claim on him. (Clarke 1990:141-42)

In Christ every believer becomes a benefactor, called to "do good to all people, especially to those who belong to the family of believers" (Gal 6:10). Even a Christian widow, to qualify for support by the church, had to exhibit a life given to benefactions; she had to be "well known for her good deeds, . . . devoting herself to all kinds of good deeds" (1 Tim 5:10).

Wealth no longer defines the role of patron. Out of "extreme poverty" can well up "rich generosity." It flows from "overflowing joy" in the grace of Christ our divine Benefactor, who, "though he was rich, yet for your sakes . . . became poor" (2 Cor 8:2, 9).

"Sharing" becomes "the privilege" of Christian ministry (2 Cor 8:4; Phil 4:14-20). In the world of benefactions, gifts could be called loans, to be repaid with gratitude to the giver. In the church the gratitude was offered to God and repaid with service.

Nor is the Christian benefactor to restrict his or her gifts to the influential. By settled custom, "patrons did not establish client relationships with 'the urban poor.' . . . They did so with those who possessed the same status as they did, but not their wealth, or with those who were their former slaves but were now their freedmen" (Winter 1994:45). By contrast, Christian beneficence reached out to the poor and unjustly treated (Acts 6:1-4), to older widows without the support of family (1 Tim 5:16). The office of deacon as a ministry of mercy emerged to reflect that calling to serve the weak in matters of physical need (Rom 16:1-2).

All this meant, as well, a transformation of the client relationship. The social conventions of dependency and fawning support for the patron's cause in public could not be characteristic of those who now, by God's grace, were also benefactors.

Paul's demand that a believer "lead a quiet life, . . . mind your own business and . . . work with your hands" (1 Thess 4:11) may be much more than a simple exhortation to keep out of trouble and work hard. He may have been warning believers neither to continue dependency on the patron's expected dole nor to create strife in the city in support of a patron's cause. His reasons given in 1 Thessalonians 4:12 fit that picture: "Christians were not only to command the respect of outsiders by being self-sufficient, but they were to seek the welfare of their city by having the wherewithal to do good to others" (Winter 1989:314). Paul's second letter to the Thessalonians repeats the injunction (2 Thess 3:6-13) and closes with language appropriate for the new benefactors in Christ: "but, as for you brethren, do not grow weary of doing good" (2 Thess 3:13 NASB).

## Then and Now

Paul believed, as we have suggested, that through his own apostolic commission "the gospel has been proclaimed to every creature under heaven" (literally, "fulfilled the word of God," Col 1:23). What does that leave for us to do? How do we explain the centuries-long efforts of the church to reach the world and its cities that followed Paul? If the job was done, why did the church press on, often stumbling into gospel betrayal and political compromise, evangelistic forgetfulness and tattered holiness, but stretching past the borders of the Roman Empire to make the gospel trail a superhighway through the world?

*Our place on God's timeline.* The clue lies in the enlarged eschatology that dominates the thinking of Paul and the New Testament. Eschatology has become Christology. "The fullness of times" has begun because God has sent his Son to redeem (Gal 4:4; Eph 1:10); God's "mystery," the Messiah promised "for long ages," has been revealed (Rom 16:25-26; 1 Cor 2:7; Col 1:26). The great framework of redemptive history has arrived at its turning point in Jesus' coming. And it will reach its final turning point in his coming again (Ridderbos 1975:44-49).

Between these two turning points runs the course of urban mission. The language describing it may shift, but its center in Jesus remains the same. Jesus proclaims the kingdom of God, and that kingdom language virtually disappears in Paul's letters. But the message of the kingdom is not lost. The kingdom is present in Jesus; the Proclaimer is the Proclaimed. He who preaches the good news is the very content of that good news. Jesus spoke about the kingdom; Paul and the church spoke about Jesus. But these were not two separate messages. Declaring "the kingdom of God" is linked to teaching "about the Lord Jesus Christ" (Acts 28:23, 31).

What is the place of the church now in this redemptive framework? Jesus' preaching stands at that stage in the history of the gospel before the resurrection. Paul looks back to the resurrection as the highest point of the fulfillment of that history. And the church in the millennia since Paul? It stands past Paul on the eschatological timeline, looking back through his interpretive eyes but closer to the final consummation of all things.

Thus the kingdom of God is no longer a distant hope; it is a promised reality that has been set in motion by the life, death and resurrection of Jesus Christ. And "as long as Christian faith is oriented by the history of promise and the eschatological significance of Christ, there will be a Christian mission in world history" (Braaten 1977:54).

*Our continuing task on God's timeline.* Marking today's path of that mission through the cities of the world are Paul's footprints. They can be spotted in verbal clues left from the old urban world's reshaped vocabulary. And they form an integrity and wholeness for carrying on Paul's action agenda in urban mission.

*Leitourgia* in extrabiblical Greek was a term originally used to denote specific services performed by the public benefactor for the urban public welfare (Kittel 1967:216-19). In the Bible it becomes worship, mission as the celebration of God before the nations (Ps 107:21-22), the people of God assembled for worship on Mount Zion (Is 56:6-8). The distance between then and now does not substantially change that focus. It directs it, as the New Testament did, to Christ. The Mount of God is indeed exalted. It is exalted to where Christ is, seated at the right hand of the Father (1 Pet 2:9-11). And toward that same mountain stronghold the contemporary church moves in worship.

*Kerygma* provides another connection between urban mission then and now. In the Greco-Roman city the announcement call to worship was the responsibility of the herald *(keryx)*. Similar to the town crier of later centuries, the herald was a messenger vested with public authority. His news *(kerygma)* carried the weight of the one who commissioned him, his demands those of urban king or god whom he represented before the city (Kittel 1965:683-94).

Twice Paul uses that term, *herald,* to refer to his appointment by God to preach (1 Tim 2:7; 2 Tim 1:11). And repeatedly the verb form invades his language to describe his message and its declaration. The object of the heralding was the "good news" *(euangelion,* 2 Cor 11:4; Gal 2:2; 1 Thess 2:9). That heralded good news for the cities was Jesus (1 Cor 1:23; 2 Cor 1:19; Phil 1:15; Col 1:23).

This *kerygma* links then to now, Paul's urban mission to ours. The past lives in the present through the proclamation of apostolic *kerygma* received by the church (2 Cor 11:4). It is a divine trust committed to Paul and from Paul to the church (1 Cor 15:1, 3; 2 Cor 5:19). From generation to generation (2 Tim 1:4; Tit 2:3) we are to pass it on (2 Thess 2:15) by confessing it as our faith (1 Cor 12:3; Col 2:6). Then and now the church is to guard the deposit of sound doctrine by giving it away in evangelism (1 Tim 6:20).

If it is from *kerygma* that the Christian faith is taught, it is within the setting of *koinonia* (fellowship) that it is caught. Again, this word was not uncommon in the urban context of the Greeks. Plato had long before structured his ideal urban republic on a community of goods and wives. Stoicism pled for a common sense of brotherhood.

But in the Hellenistic world *koinonia* was much less than a dream. Class and status divided the honorable and the humble, those with wealth and property from those without it, master from slave. "The upper classes enjoyed great privileges, and they guarded them vigilantly" (Stambaugh and Balch 1986:113). Gender roles entrenched in law and custom reinforced hierarchical patterns "in which the male was always superior to the female, as surely as parents to children and masters to slaves" (Meeks 1983:23). Any erosion of these sociocultural standards was assaulted by rhetoricians and satirists.

Against this the church offered, and still offers, a community the urban world cannot match. It was, and still is, to be a family, Jew and Gentile "foreigner" both now part of "God's household" (Eph 2:19). In contrast to the urban clubs of Paul's day, wealth, occupation and ethnicity did not form its base. Baptism, not circumcision, as a sign of membership now opened the community more widely to women. Mutual submission, not female subjugation, transformed spousal relations (Eph 5:21-33). Caring, sacrificial love for others, then and now, summed up the law of God (Rom 13:8-10; Gal 5:14).

*Diakonia* (service) exemplified, and still does, that communal ministry of love. In the city life of the empire the term was often used of the work of slaves. And Rome had more to use than had any previous society. As an integral but distant part of the extended household, slaves waited at table (Lk 17:7-8) while the worthy reclined (Jn 12:2).

In the kingdom of God *diakonia* is transformed by Jesus' service on the cross (Mk 10:45), the compulsion of the messianic servant's "I must" (Mt 16:21; Lk 24:26). Human ideas of greatness and rank are reversed again as Jesus the Lord who was the servant becomes the object of our joyful and patient service in suffering (Rom 12:11; 14:17-18). Apostles become servants (1 Cor 3:5; 2 Cor 11:23), and the freedom of sonship demands that we "serve one another in love" (Gal 5:13). Through gifts of service and the ministry of mercy the church grows in maturity (Eph 4:7-16). Giving, not receiving, becomes the blessed reward for those who help the weak (Acts 20:35).

Running alongside this idea of service is the church's calling to *dikaioma* (justice). Justice had an urban environment. In the social world of Old Testament Israel, the village threshing floor could become a meeting place for the execution of justice. But particularly in cities, the gates served as courthouses where the elders met in deliberative assembly (Deut 21:18-21; 22:13-21; 22:23-27). In the Greco-Roman world justice was the responsibility of civic communities grouped into administrative units called provinces; "in each of the Pauline Epistles the [urban] church addressed was situated where Roman law was likely to be known" (Lyall 1984:237).

But whether in Israel or in the empire, justice for the weak and needy was not always to be found in the city. The Old Testament repeatedly laments how bribery upends justice for the poor (Ex 23:8; Deut 16:19) and oppresses the righteous (Is 1:23; Amos 5:10-12; 6:12; 8:5).

Roman law was not admirable in its treatment of the underling. "Generally lawsuits were conducted between social equals who were from the powerful of the city, or by a plaintiff of superior social status and power against an inferior" (Winter 1994:108). In 1 Corinthians 6:1, Paul adds that the Roman judges were ungodly (literally, "the unjust"). Extrabiblical materials appear to affirm that Paul's word was a judgment of corruption (Winter 1994:109-10).

God's promise was that this would change. He was "the LORD, who exercises kindness, justice and righteousness on the earth, for in these I delight" (Jer 9:24). When he came, it would be on behalf of justice for all, fairness for the afflicted of the earth (Is 11:1-5). The Old Testament promise of the Messiah's jubilee year would mean justice and freedom for the oppressed and broken (Is 61:1-2).

The good news of the Gospels is that in Christ the jubilee year of restoration for society has begun (Lk 4:17-21). Those who hunger and thirst for righteousness, God's kingly justice, are filled (Mt 5:6). God's perfect righteousness has been fulfilled through the redemption of Christ (Rom 4:21-26); justice and peace have kissed one another at the cross.

To his people who came through the city's gates, he had cried of old, "Do what is just and right" (Jer 22:3). Now, in the fulfillment time of the new Jerusalem, God's new benefactor people move through other city gates with the same mandate and a victorious Messiah to make it happen.

"We live *now* in that new space created by the powerful invasion of Christ; therefore we can no longer tolerate Old Age distinctions in the social and political order" (Bosch 1991:175). So Christian masters, themselves under their Master in heaven, are exhorted, "Grant to your slaves justice and fairness" (Col 4:1 NASB). Elder-bishops are to be sought who exhibit justice mixed with their self-control and love of what is good (Tit 1:8). And Christians are to fill their minds with everything that is noble and pure, lovely and honorable—and just (Phil 4:8).

Now as then, this call to justice interlocks with all other urban mission pieces into a whole. The nurtured Christian community draws the world to its fellowship of mercy, service and justice and becomes itself the path to joint worship. Evangelism by word and deed points to the source of the new world order it preaches—Jesus the kingdom come. That kingdom manifesto sends the people of God, then and now, embarking on a great campaign, advance previews of coming attractions.

# Part 3

## Understanding the City

# 8

## Place, Process
## & Misperception

WHAT IS THIS THING CALLED "CITY" around which God's mission and ours revolves? That is harder to answer than one might suppose. Scholarship devoted to the city has yet to find a commonly accepted definition of either *a* city or *the* city (Gulick 1989:1-21).

The diversity of cities makes such a question extremely difficult. In some ways it is easier to focus on cities in the plural than on the city as a monolith. Are we speaking of precolonial West African settlements built of grass houses? Or Aztec holy cities like Tenochtitlán, with its boulevards carefully laid out in geometric patterns to mirror its view of the four-quartered universe? Or the clay houses of Mesopotamia's ancient cities, built on the remains of earlier centers?

Where is the point of comparison between Beijing in the fifteenth century and Los Angeles in the twentieth? Beijing was reconstructed then to reflect the order and harmony of the universe. At its walled center was the Hall of Divine Harmony, the sacred core of the world, and the Temple of Heaven. Here earth and sky met, the four seasons merged, and yin and yang were in harmony. Its architectural design symbolized the role of China as the Middle Kingdom. It united the will of heaven to the will of earth, power and cosmic harmony merged.

By contrast, modern Los Angeles exists virtually without a downtown center. It is fragmented by freeways and distance into a complex of clustered suburbs in search of a city. Some say that in the twenty-first century it will spread 150 miles from San Diego to Santa Barbara, from ocean to desert Palm Springs. If Los Angeles has a walled center, it is probably Disneyland, an amusement park of fantasy and order, the Magic Kingdom of la-la land. Its unity is not readily apparent. It is the second largest Mexican city in the world, the second largest Guatemalan city, the second largest Cambodian city.

Of crucial importance: If we cannot find common connections between cities past and present, how shall we link the biblical perceptions of the city and urban mission discussed in previous chapters with the city today? Is the link we think we see between the remote, preindustrial cities of the Bible and cities like Copenhagen and Colorado Springs an artificial, imposed one? Is religion a part of it? Is the gulf so large that it isolates radically the walled city of Jericho from the double-beltway-circled Washington, D.C., or the island-mainland harbors of Tyre from those of Kowloon-Hong Kong?

In the face of such great differences, can we reach any conclusions about this thing called city? Where do we look for commonality?

## The City as Place

Pioneering European studies of the city in the nineteenth and early twentieth centuries largely set the direction in the search for commonality. Following the lead of Ferdinand Tonnies (1855-1936), a sharp contrast was drawn between two types of human social life. The one was *Gemeinschaft* or community, the quality said to be characteristic of the small country village. Here people worked for the common good, linked by ties of family and neighborhood, common interests, common purposes. The lifestyle of this "living organism" was "intimate, private, and exclusive living together," its members bound by a sense of "ourness," of "us" (Tonnies 1957).

In sharp contrast was *Gesellschaft*, the urban society. A "mechanical aggregate and artifact," the urban lifestyle of association was said to be characterized by disunity and hostility, rampant individualism and selfishness. There was no belief in common good. Ties of family and neighborhood tended to be of little significance.

Other interests and developments also emerged in this early stage of reflection. Georg Simmel (1858-1918), for example, moved in Tonnies's direction but focused on the social psychology of the city. In the midst of overwhelming stimulation and the call for rational response, the urbanite, he argued, finds relief in the development of social reserve and a blasé mindset. Out of that more calculating and rational mindset, he feared, might come indifference and even aversion.

Out of these early emphases was emerging a strong antiurban pattern, oriented to the city as a place in contrast to the rural setting (Karp, Stone and Yoels 1991:12-44). What became known as the Chicago school of sociology amplified and modified these directions. In the period between about 1913 and 1940 it formulated the problems and provided the research that would virtually define the whole field of study (Bulmer 1984). How do we understand the ecology of the city as a place? How do we see the human community shaped by and shaping the city as place?

Sociologist Louis Wirth, a prominent member of the Chicago School, produced a classic definition in 1938 that scholars still debate, deny, correct or modify. "A city," he argued, is "a relatively large, dense, and permanent settlement of socially heterogeneous individuals" (Wirth 1980:35).

Wirth's focus was fixed on definite physical boundaries, on population size and density. Contrasted sharply with the homogeneity of the rural setting, the city was perceived as heterogeneous, a place of specialization and diversity. And, asked Wirth and his supporters, what was the effect of this on our way of life in the city, on what he called urbanism?

Kinship ties are eroded by social contacts. Individualism grows, competition dominates. Community is replaced by noncommunity, simplicity by sophistication. In the city the sacred becomes secular, the integrated life moves toward anomie, toward life without norm. The warmth of personal relationships is exchanged for rational, impersonal anonymity.

Scholarship has continued to modify or challenge Wirth's thesis with a variety of emphases over the years. Studies have pointed out, for example, Wirth's heavy dependence on the industrial city for his urban model. Chicago, after all, cannot be a paradigm for the whole urban world. Researchers have asked in response, what about the preindustrial city (Sjoberg 1960)? Was Wirth's model really universal enough?

What of modern cities like Cairo where over one-third of the inhabitants were born outside the city? How many of these newcomers are urban in residence but, by Wirth's definition, are still rural in outlook and behavior? In extensive research, Janet Abu-Lughod found thirteen communities or subcities of Cairo in that city's last hundred years. Scattered through the thirteen subcities, past and present, was a spectrum of four lifestyles from rural to urban, traditional to modern (Abu-Lughod 1971).

Other contrasts suggested by Wirth and refined by his supporters have been attacked or modified severely. Is it true, to cite one significant debate example, that migration from a peasant village to a large urban center leaves the newcomer disorganized and marginalized? Can one really find in the village, as Robert Redfield contended from his neo-Romantic bias, all the moral virtues and communal solidarity and homogeneity missing from the city (Redfield 1941)? Isn't it actually true, responded Oscar Lewis, that life in a Mexican village like Tepotzlan shows much of the fragmentation and dislocation imagined in the city? Isn't Redfield's evolutionary model of cultural development from the simple to the complex, from tribal to rural to urban, an oversimplification? And conversely, in the urban environment of Mexico City cannot one find the continued maintenance of kinship lines and the healthy support of religious systems thought to have been eroded (Lewis 1963:31-41)?

**Liabilities and modifications.** We will return throughout this book to the heavy baggage that comes with this paradigm of the city as a place. But at least two major flaws must be uncovered before we move on now. They both can play a strong role in an understanding of urban mission—and in damaging it.

One of those flaws is the strong antiurban direction taken by the paradigm. The eulogy it pronounced over the city has been bane, not blessing (Conn 1987:20-22). The city was observed through a bipolar moralistic model of rural versus urban. Everything rural was good, everything urban was bad. Urbanism as a way of life was ultimately an acid that would eat away traditional rural values and undermine meaningful relationships and institutions.

Linked to this was a second major flaw: static determinism. In this ethical stereotyping of rural versus urban, all the destructive patterns of life were peculiarly, essentially or exclusively urban. As urbanism increases, the thesis argues, neighbors become less important, social norms are enfeebled. We are left with "peculiarly urban phenomena—stress, estrangement, individualism, and, especially, social disorganization" (Fischer 1984:31-32).

Abstracted from these flaws, there is still some wisdom in using population size, density and social heterogeneity in the beginnings of a sketch of urbanism and the city (Gulick 1989:18). After all, the demographic criterion is common to virtually all definitions of urban or city. Other dimensions—institutional, social, cultural or behavioral—must also be added. Yet these demographic qualities are relative: "they are not all-or-nothing characteristics" (Fischer 1984:25). Ultimately, regardless of where we put our emphasis, "definitions largely consist of threshold criteria that describe minimal levels of demographic, institutional, or structural complexity beneath which city or urban levels cannot be applied" (Press and Smith 1980:12).

In keeping with this reminder, even size of area and density of population provide no uniform measure for definition. A feudal city like Damascus could be crossed in a morning's leisurely walk. To cross modern Tokyo or Mexico City would take an automobile. "The populations of all but a few of the greatest medieval cities could be dropped into our modern urban centers and make scarcely a ripple. The Los Angeles metropolis was in 1980 over 150 times greater in area and about 14 times greater in population than Cairo at its most glorious around 1500" (Fischer 1984:8).

Scholarship still stumbles over relative questions of size, population and their measurement. How, for example, do we deal with history's early urban settlements? Archaeological evidence is fragmentary. And research struggles with finding uniform standards for measuring those early settlements (Shiloh 1980:25-35).

Even in our contemporary world, government census takers continue to find little agreement when it comes to statistical definitions. In Denmark and Sweden it takes only two hundred inhabitants for a place to be defined a city. In the United States there needs to be at least twenty-five hundred, in Greece and Senegal ten thousand. Sensitive to the diversities particularly between developed and less developed countries, the United Nations has set up its own classification system. Urban characteristics on an international scale, UN thinkers argue, are most readily found in population areas exceeding twenty thousand people.

All this underlines that the value of demographics in defining city is only relative. There are other more significant pieces to add to the urban mix.

**The church's early response.** During the first stage of emerging great cities Christians joined in the antiurban bias toward the city as a place. As early as the 1830s and 1840s church sentiment in Europe was turning against the cities as strongholds of irreligion, as religious deserts. That view quickly took on traditional status: urbanization leads to the decline of faith.

By 1880 Horatius Bonar (1808-1889), an evangelical pastor in Edinburgh, was writing a series of missionary tracts to Parisian working men and speaking of cities as "great centers of human evil." Pleading that his readers not forget "the warnings of Noah's days and the doom of Sodom and Gomorrah," he asked, "Does God care for our Great Cities or has he given them up?" (Bonar 1880:83-84, 90-92). Others were asking the same question but with less compassion.

For Pietists Berlin was a "Babel . . . where all ties were broken and nothing was sacred." A London clergyman in an 1844 sermon spoke of the life of cities as "essentially a worldly life," in contrast to "the country with its pure serenity" (McLeod 1995:8). Catholic clergy supported the negative judgments of Francois Courtade, who, writing in 1871, saw cities like Paris as "without faith and without God" (Kselman 1995:165). Cities had become a threat to faith.

In the rapidly urbanizing United States a similar pessimism was growing. Protestant churches were feeling overwhelmed by urban growth and change. Dwight L. Moody's early enthusiasm over the church's role in the city was dying. Urged to resume his urban revival campaigns, he was becoming reluctant. By 1896 he was writing, "The city is no place for me" (quoted in Conn 1994a:60). "The city as a menace to be resisted and redirected into familiar Protestant patterns—this was the predominant understanding among Protestants at the turn of the century" (Handy 1969:94).

To a greater degree in America than anywhere else, Protestant clergy took the lead during the latter half of the nineteenth century in publicizing what they perceived as "the urban peril"—pauperism and chronic poverty, crime and political disorder, alcoholism, the new immigrants from southern Europe and the concomitant growth of Roman Catholicism. Fear replaced hope as the city became "a serious menace," "the fever sores of the land," the ultimate challenge to religious commitment and faith (Lees 1985:165-68). Frequently accented was the demographic disproportion between the growth of the city and the availability of clergy and churches to respond to the needs.

American Catholics voiced similar pessimism regarding the city. By the 1920s the church's membership was largely urban. But there were those like Father John Ryan who concluded somberly, "The future will be with the Church that ministers to the rural population" (quoted in Cross 1962:41). Critics saw the weakening of the territorial parish and the rapid multiplication of national ethnic parishes as telltale signs of the present disunity of the city and warnings of further demoralization. "Imbued with respect for the past, nostalgic for a life close to nature, and bemused . . . by an urban sociology that clothed similar sentiments in a majestic scientific terminology, they yielded too readily to impulses of dismay" (Cross 1962:51).

Industrializing Europe and long industrialized Britain underlined similar concerns. Many of England's Protestant clergy "saw the city as at worst a den of iniquity and at best a serious challenge that could be effectively countered only through constant vigilance" (Lees 1985:153). In the 1870s an Anglican bishop remarked to Prime Minister Benjamin Disraeli that "the Church would probably lose the city." Replied Disraeli, "Don't be mistaken, my Lord, the church has nothing to lose, for she has never had the city."

Around 1850, life in Germany was still predominantly agrarian. Two generations later it had become the leading industrial power on the European continent. Already its Protestant clergy were joining England's voices of despair, denouncing the urban way of life for its destructive "impact on the religious and ethical standards of the previously faithful. Traditionally allied with the conservative forces in state and society to an even greater extent than their British counterparts, they perceived the big city as a milieu in which all their efforts to retain and guide their parishioners continually faced attack by the forces of secular individualism" (Lees 1985:158). The cities were "shapeless giants . . . comparable to powerful vacuum cleaners," "a wildly fluctuating chaos of human beings" in which the forces of Christianity would be placed inevitably on the defensive.

**History revisited.** Revisionist looks at these early prophecies of urban downfall question the full historical accuracy of these judgments. Did the rural-urban polarization and the migration to the city produce a real decay in faith? The clergy's verbal "for example" is apparently no proof. The polarization is too simplistic, too ideological, to explain the full picture. The late anthropologist Margaret Mead, noted for her wit as well as her scholarship, provides another evaluation of such migration: " 'At least 50 percent of the human race doesn't want their mother-in-law within walking distance.' Mead's remark may tell us as much about life in the countryside as the typologies do" (Phillips and LeGates 1981:129).

> **An Indictment of the Urban Context**
>
> "All dangers of the town may be summed up in this: that here, withdrawn from the blessed influence of Nature, and set face to face against humanity, man loses his own nature and becomes a new and artificial creature—an inhuman cog in a social machinery that works like a fate, and cheats him of his true culture as a soul. The most unnatural fashions and habits, the strangest eccentricities of intellect, the wildest and most pernicious theories in social morals, and the most appalling and incurable barbarism, are the legitimate growths of city life."
> REV. AMORY D. MAYO, SYMBOLS OF THE CAPITAL: OR, CIVILIZATION IN NEW YORK, 1859.

Further, where should the final judgment be placed—on the city as an unresponsive place? Even when we restrict gospel impact to the demographics of church attendance, there are enough historical examples from this early history of industrialization to indicate that urban unresponsiveness is too easy an answer.

In 1851 the city of Glasgow had a church attendance rate higher than a quarter of Scotland's rural counties. And in nearly all cases major Scottish towns had higher rates than their immediate hinterlands (Brown 1995:251). After a complex evaluation of England's industrializing cities,

Callum Brown concludes that "taking mainland Britain as a whole, the degree to which industry contributed to a city's economy is probably a poor predictor of church participation" (Brown 1995:253).

Also ignored in early judgments against the city were the immigrants who brought their own faith to the cities from their rural heritage. The ghettos built by Catholic and Protestant newcomers to European and North American cities were more than forced retreats in the face of Anglo-Saxon racism. They were that, to be sure. But they were also efforts by the newcomers to deal with the city's pluralism. In these enclaves their people would be safe from over-close contact with commitments alien to their faith.

Subsequent history underlined this impact of the new migrants. In England the initial period of rapid immigration was a time of religious growth. But as immigration declined from 1870 to 1914, religious stagnation and decline accelerated. Another explanation for the decline of faith was also being offered during this time. It laid the blame not on the unresponsive city but on the church's neglect of urban need. The city was a God-given opportunity as much as a diabolical threat.

For evangelicals like General William Booth (1829-1912), founder of the Salvation Army, the decaying state of the city was a call to Christian action. Beyond the city as a place, he was alert to the processes that made up the city. "As there is a darkest Africa," he asked, "is there not also a darkest England? Civilisation, which can breed its own barbarians, does it not also breed its own pygmies? May we not find a parallel at our own doors, and discover within a stone's throw of our cathedrals and palaces similar horrors to those which Stanley has found existing in the great Equatorial forest?" (Booth 1890:11-12).

Booth's pleas, along with those of others in the United States (Conn 1994a:62-70), drew attention to the church's isolation from the working classes. To be sure, class patterns of church involvement showed considerable variations from country to country (McLeod 1995:27). Even so, were class distinctions that had long divided churched from unchurched more to blame than the city as a place? Was revulsion at the irreligiosity of the urban lower classes in the cities of England, Germany and the United States as much revulsion at lower classes as at irreligiosity?

***Responses from contemporary Christian scholarship.*** One hundred years later, Christian reflection has still not caught up completely with these revisionist discoveries—or, for that matter, with modifications of the early flaws. The defect of static determinism in the rural-urban polarization can be quickly acknowledged. After all, such determinism strikes at the very heart of the Christian notion of conversion, of radical change. With it hope for change will quickly vanish.

There still appear to be traces of a defeatism regarding city life. This shows in a tendency to resist the city's impact on the church instead of developing the church's impact on the city.

The stereotypical negativism spawned by antiurbanism still surfaces, from various directions. For some the reality of God's common-grace blessings in the city is still minimized as the city is primarily perceived as a place of Satanic power. Its inhabitants are still described as powerless, alone, vulnerable, lost, rejected, bewildered, insecure, used, void of meaning. Others, in a proper assault on the Enlightenment background of modernity and modernization, speak of urbanization as one of the main realities that drives the process.

Happily, the earlier version of the rural-urban contrast has undergone revision or readjustment among some Christian theorists. Some speak of a rural-urban continuum rather than of polarization; they underline the damage caused by the negative and simplistic stereotype of the past. "The city does not exist in opposition to the countryside" (Hiebert and Meneses 1995:262). Others speak of it as an "idealized contrast" (DuBose 1978:34-35) or a heuristic typology to provoke analysis and discussion of society and social change (Filbeck 1985). The proposed continuum is seen as a meaningful channel, not a barrier, for spreading the gospel (DuBose 1983:515-16). Whether these revisions are adequate to offer a new path for healthy urban mission is a question awaiting more in-depth Christian research.

## The City as Process

The interests of cultural anthropology and sociology in urbanism as a way of life have moved in many directions in the last few decades. Some of those interests are still tied to past discussions. What social relations have been generated by these areas of relatively heavy population, density and heterogeneity we call cities? Will we find these relationships exclusively in the city? Can we find them also in places other than cities? Cities are mosaics of institutions, family and kinship groups, ethnic enclaves, and associations. How do we understand the complex interactions that go on between them, and the interactions with areas beyond the city?

*Burgeoning study agenda.* In the 1960s and 1970s, a heyday of urban anthropology and sociology, interest in urban processes created a wide but limited agenda. How do we understand urban poverty? What happens in the process we call rural-urban migration? How do we describe life in a residential neighborhood? What goes on in the struc-tures and functions of associations not built on kinship? How can we best explain the persistence of extended kinship relationships? How do role relationships work in an urban setting? What is this thing called "ethnic-ity" (Sanjek 1990:152)?

In the 1980s the scope of these studies expanded. The liabilities of ear-lier studies were recognized and modified as new directions were pur-sued. In the process, less formal attention has been devoted to issues of definition (Sanjek 1990:153). But a consensus has been growing on the significance of the socializing process for understanding urbanism.

In the development of this consensus Marxist-oriented scholars have pressed the hardest in the most radical terms. Some, like Anthony Leeds and Leonard Plotnicov, have decided that the city under capitalism can-not be distinguished from complex society as such. Words like *city* and *town, village* and *rural,* become relative in any society, ancient or modern, integrated as they are by class differences in the area of production (Plot-nicov 1985:50-51). In such a world, "No Towne is an Islande of Itselfe" (Leeds 1994:71-79). Cities and towns, villages and metropolises, goes the argument, are simply nodal points within societal systems. They are only distinct specialties of an urban society linked (under any technology known) to specific geographical spaces.

The impact of this radical emphasis, we argue, has played some part in further confusing significant areas of study. Urban anthropology now struggles more than ever with defining its area of research. What really is urban? Has the virtual equation of urban with civilization and human cul-ture not left us with something too diffuse and too large to be studied with anthropology's traditional method of participant observation and intense fieldwork? If everything is urban, then nothing is urban.

The Chicago School saw the development of cities as a natural pro-cess. However, others take a different stance. Neo-Marxist political econ-omists take into consideration the manipulative capacities of those in power. Primarily viewing the development of cities through the economic maneuvering of government and big business, they focus on such phe-nomena as exploitation and discrimination. The question we must ask is, does the neo-Marxist orientation to economics restrict our understanding of urbanism to the point of imbalance and one-sidedness? When eco-nomics are absolutized at the center of urban studies, what happens to the significance of history and the arts, politics and religion, for under-standing the city and urbanism? Are they really useful—or only when they are redefined within a Marxist framework?

At the same time, out of this ferment of discussion, Marxist and otherwise, have come new issues for study that add to an interdisciplinary picture of urbanism. Political and class questions begin to explore work relations, enrich urban migration studies, and expand interests beyond the urban poor to gender and public culture issues. Even the study of urban religion, long neglected in contemporary sociology and anthropology, seems to be making an appearance (Kemper 1991:383-84; Sanjek 1990:154-55).

Above all else, scholarship, even outside the Marxist orbit, now finds itself wrestling with the social connections between the city and the world outside the city. Urban history does touch, and is touched by, widening circles beyond its own. "Paris sneezes and France blows its nose." Urban and rural are not simply bipolar, isolated opposites but distinct entities integrated by mutual action and reaction. How will we understand that interaction? In the process how does the city act? And how is it acted upon? How is power exercised, and who benefits from it?

The restrictive demographic definitions of the past are breaking down. Scholarship appears to be recognizing more and more that cities are places but also participators in, and respondents to, social process (Palen 1992:339-56).

***Christian research reflections.*** Urban mission studies in recent decades have not moved as quickly as larger scholarship concerns into considering the city as process. Among evangelicals the worldwide growth of cities, coupled with pragmatic interests in personal evangelism and church planting, has led to a narrow study agenda dominated by demographics. The gathering of reliable statistical information on urban growth—particularly on world-class cities—and on unreached people groups has been a central focus of concern (Conn 1997:26-28). Urbanization, in this light, has been understood more as a demographic process than as a process of sociocultural shifting.

Also restricting progress has been a lack of interfacing between Christian mission and the social sciences most useful in analyzing the city. Linguistics, cultural anthropology and communication theory are becoming more comfortable, though still debated, instruments in research. But little serious attention is being paid to sociology, economics or political science.

Studies also remain disproportionate geographically, ecclesiastically and topically. A growing body of studies from America's mainline churches focuses on North American urban history and mission (Hartley 1996:308-63). Deeply sensitive to social and institutional context, these studies add a much-needed dimension missing from more explicitly evangelical research. But their ties to biblical and evangelistic concerns can sometimes be weak, and their connections with the American geographical scene and to theological pluralism can hamper wider usefulness.

Outside the Anglo-Saxon world both macro-level and micro-level research on urban mission is much more limited. The churches of Asia and Latin America, for example, "recognise that our ministry demands a clear and intelligent understanding of the complexities of our economic, environmental, social and cultural context" (Ro 1989:1; cf. "Seeking the Peace" 1989:18-24). But Christian research has still not caught up fully with the shift of ecclesiastical gravity from the Northern to the Southern Hemisphere.

Some agenda topics related to broader studies of the urban process have received considerable attention. The interest of the church growth school in the homogeneous unit principle has fostered wide research into questions of family and kinship groups. But little, comparatively speaking, has yet been done to relate these issues to the urban setting. General inactivity in sociological research and reluctance among some toward a holistic approach to ministry has minimized such mission studies. Issues of neighborhood, role relationships, societal structures and networks receive some attention, but it is often hit and miss.

If there was one issue that gained mission ascendancy in the 1980s, it was poverty and social transformation. The global city is reminding the church of our calling to serve the poor. Why poverty exists and how the church should fulfill that calling are still debated. Mainline discussions within the Anglo-Saxon world join with many minority communities in underlining a systemic approach to the problem. A substantial number of evangelicals from the Two-Thirds World, joined by many from the Anglo-Saxon world, plead for a holistic balance that will unite the systemic and the personal in a vital connection with evangelism and church planting (Nicholls 1986). Others are concerned that such a balance is too fragile and evangelism will be minimized in such a wedding.

## Urban Misperception

Left behind from this history of academic study and popular perception are accumulating images of the city. Scholarship through the years has rejected some and corrected or modified others. We will be dealing in more detail with some of these images in future chapters.

One particular image continues to capture and summarize many others into one popular ideology—the city as an urban wasteland. Christian joins with non-Christian in a stereotype of concentrated chaos and disorder, the city as a maze of disruption and dislocation, bewildering sprawl and confused worldviews. Everything about the city then becomes "too much": too much crowding, too much noise, too much stress.

Just how realistic is this chaotic image, particularly as a negative barrier? Why do migrants with enthusiastic optimism still seem to ignore it and move into the cities across the developing world? They continue to pour into what the expert perceives as the disorder of Jos and Lima, Tokyo and Cairo, pulled by the attractions of cities struggling with the chaotic growth that their presence helps create. The pull factors are usually stronger than the push factors. Why? For the migrants growth, however disordered, means change and progress. It means educational and medical benefits, improvement of family income. For many young men and women it means freedom from social constraints and traditions. How do they cope? They create positive mental maps of the city that allow for mobility, communication and enough organization for emotional security (Krupat 1985:70-71).

> ### Cities and Chaos
>
> Whatever has been my taste for solitude and natural scenery, yet the thick, foggy, stifled elements of cities, the entangled life of so many men together, sordid as it was, and empty of the beautiful, took quite a strenuous hold upon my mind. I felt as if there never could be enough of it.
> NATHANIEL HAWTHORNE, THE BLITHEDALE ROMANCE
>
> New York City, the incomparable, the brilliant star city of cities, the Cyclopean paradox, the inferno with no out-of-bounds, the supreme expression of both the miseries and splendors of contemporary civilization . . . at once the climactic synthesis of America and yet the negation of America.
> JOHN GUNTHER, AUTHOR
>
> New York is great. I've got so much noise. Subways. Horns. I can't stand something quiet, I go nuts.
> MILES DAVIS, JAZZ MUSICIAN
>
> President Anwar el-Sadat and I, separately considering the Egyptian capital city of Cairo, recently arrived at the same conclusion; it was about to explode. . . . I do not mean seismically. Cairo is not a city of meteorological extremes. . . . No, I am speaking of the metaphysical condition of the place, its political, social, historical state, which is never languid or lethargic, but which seems to me now almost to be almost lethally excitable. . . . Hush and tumult: the ancient and majestic streaked indefinably, somewhere among the city lights, with the ominous.
> JAN MORRIS, DESTINATIONS

***Creating the chaos image.*** Where then do the ideological images of chaos and disorder come from? They come in large part from the spectacled presuppositions through which we filter what we want to see. The images are shaped by more than objective reality; they are shaped also by our social, cultural and human ideologies. Chaos is in the eye of the beholder.

The rural-urban polarization outlined in this chapter surely affects us. It assumes our response will be, "The city is too much." On the other hand, some research has looked at the rural model and affirmed, "The noncity is too little." There is a human need for complexity, novelty, excitement and exploration. And those are needs uniquely met by the city (Geller 1980).

Change, linked to the rural-urban polarization, can also be seen as a part of negative chaos and disorientation—moral and cultural. "Human beings need the framework of ideas, images, and behavioural norms that culture provides in order to develop, to communicate and to interact with one another. Culture gives significance to experience and is the basis for the human articulation and creation of meaning" (Shorter 1991:141). So when Koreans move from their homeland to North American cities and members of ethnic tribal groups make their way to African cities, they find themselves a cognitive minority bombarded by new cultural signals. Traditional norms and comfortable social institutions are not quickly at hand. The result can be a profound cultural alienation and moral upheaval. In Africa "family life, sexual mores and the socialization of children all suffer, and crime, alcohol, drug-taking and sexual promiscuity appear as viable survival strategies" (Shorter 1991:141). In Korean-American homes there are role changes for husbands and wives and frequent conflicts between first and second generations as the new culture is either assimilated or ignored.

Change, as part of the human process of adjustment, can also mean growth and transformation. The Mataco Indians of the northern Argentine Chaco plain, twenty-five thousand strong, are traditionally a hunting, fishing, gathering society. Their traditional society now faces rapid urbanization, many being drawn by the "glitter of the city" syndrome. Crowded in barrios at the very edges of the urban centers, they often lose the dignity and security of their cultural identity and forest existence. Their concepts of ownership and property are threatened, their traditional extended family system undergoes change; white Argentinean racism continues its harassment of them (S. Barrett 1997:29-30).

Yet the Matacos, with the encouragement of the Anglican Church, are seeing change in a new light. "We can't resist or reject change," some acknowledge, "but we must know how to distinguish between good and bad change." Apprehension for the future of the culture, a sense of insecurity, remains. But it is not a fear of chaos. In the language of one church leader, "In the past, the Indians did not have salt, herbs, and spices to flavor their food. When these condiments became available to them, their food took on a new and more appealing taste. Positive changes can have a similar effect on the life of our communities" (Barrett 1997:37-38).

The negative judgments of social class, especially outsider (etic) judgments, surely play a part in the discovery of chaos. Middle- and upper-class observers assume the good life is defined by order and the choices that wealth makes possible. They look at the inner-city slums of Chicago and the vast peripheral squatter settlements of Calcutta and see congestion, a cluttered sea of huts constructed from sacking, packing cases and rusting sheets of corrugated iron. Four miles from the beauty of downtown Nairobi, along the sides of the Mathare River, there is a squatter settlement of some 200,000 people. "The area . . . is ugly," writes one sympathetic commentator, "the houses crammed together in an apparently haphazard fashion. . . . The roads are makeshift, garbage is piled high in open areas, and the children play in the dust." Its inhabitants, the report continues, are "highly marginal in every sense of the term" (quoted in Lloyd 1979:17). Note the consistent language of rootlessness, disorder, and chaos used to describe this area—*ugly, crammed, haphazard, makeshift, marginal.* Do these descriptive words not point to an ideological judgment that the outside observer has added, and in the adding missed other features clearer to the (emic) insider?

In the maze of Mathare Valley, what of the kinship and ethnic ties that still bind Akamba to Akamba, Luhya to Luhya in community? An outsider also could easily miss the highly organized and politically integrated organization that a 1973 observer perceived in the life of Village Two in the valley: a "clearly identifiable group of community leaders who direct the village committee," a village-run cooperative society that maintains nursery schools and has a social hall for dances to finance the schools and pay beer fines (Lloyd 1979:17-18).

Is there nothing but chaos and disorder in the inner-city slums of the United States? Gerald Suttles, in his classic 1968 study of the Taylor Street area of Chicago, found otherwise. He noted a social order structured around ecologically settled ethnic areas, boundaries invisible to the outsider but well known and respected by insiders. Ordered segregation marked the Italian, Mexican, Puerto Rican and African American communities. And within that negotiated order of stability among competing groups one found a stable moral order based on shared values. Within those ethnic borders were safety and comfort, in-group membership designating churches, parks and business establishments as in-group territory. Frequently even distinctive ways of dressing and local speech patterns marked off social order (Suttles 1968), and graffiti at strategic corners was a means for youth gangs to mark off their territoriality and zones of safety.

***Seeing a new way.*** Changing the chaos mindset from fear to favor has not been easy for the Christian community. In 1900 a statement of the bishops of the Methodist Episcopal Church looked at the American city and saw "the menace of the American State and Church. To penetrate this alien mass by an evangelical religion is as difficult as it is imperative. The question of the city has become the question of the race. How to reach the heart of the city and to change its life is, indeed, the question of questions" (quoted in Handy 1969:94).

As late as 1962 the question remained, unanswered perhaps in part because of the high proportion of Protestant ministerial students coming from rural backgrounds. Out of a sampling of 1,079 students, only 36 percent came from cities of more than 250,000 people. Concluded Truman B. Douglass, "Because of their rural and small-town origins many ministers bring to their work in a city church a distaste for city ways—a distaste which is the more disabling because it is largely unconscious" (Douglass 1962:90).

In 1994 evangelical urbanologist Fletcher Tink suggested a new path for investigation in the future. In a survey of 265 urban laity, pastors and missionaries, both international and U.S.-based, he focused on perceptions of the city in terms of order and chaos. He found among them a strong view of the city as a place of heightened disorder. In a comparison of metaphors of ministry, he found a high majority turning repeatedly to less-ordered descriptors like "three ring circus," "a community clinic," "a sandlot 'pickup' game," "a flea market," "a fiesta," "a lifeboat" (Tink 1994:210-12). But along with these metaphors, there was also "common consensus that disorder is not necessarily hostile" (Tink 1994:300). Like a jazz combo, urban ministry aims not for order but resolution into harmony. Tink's own conclusions, drawn out of a rich biblical investigation of the role of chaos, suggest that a healthy skepticism toward order is an appropriate stance for the urban practitioner of ministry.

"Malignant chaos" will need exorcising as surely as an order chosen primarily because it is secure and comfortable. Is the manifestation of chaos truly disordered or only apparently so? Is the urban practitioner equipped emotionally and theologically to see chaos as an ingredient of harmony? Or will a phobia or reticence toward chaos as a path to harmony step around it or trample it? What discernment gifts are needed to mete out order for those governed by chaos and offer some measure of appropriate disorder for those bound by exaggerated order (Tink 1994:301-2)? Safety, after all, is not always salvific, nor is security always sound. Boundaries, Tink reminds us, are not always beneficial, and surprises are not always subversive.

Randy White, a former realtor who became national director of urban projects for InterVarsity Christian Fellowship, describes his family's awakening to these new images of urban reality at Oxford, England. There they met Michael and Robyn Duncan and their "three very young, bouncy children," a family from New Zealand who had been working and living in a squatter settlement in urban Manila. The photograph albums they showed one another painted two worlds.

> Our pictures were filled with smiling, well-dressed children amidst their toys. Michael and Robyn's were of smiling children too, but amidst the rubble surrounding the cardboard and tin shacks they lived in. Ours were filled with extended family, healthy and affluent, treasuring the grandchildren. Theirs were filled with Filipino friends, barely surviving, treasuring their "adopted" grandchildren. Ours were filled with the well-ordered, edged and trimmed world of suburbia; theirs with chaos, pollution and the ceaseless efforts of the urban poor trying to clear a space to raise and feed their families. (White 1996:21)

Puzzled, Randy commented, "You must be an amazing person, and your family must be an amazing family, to be able to do this."

Michael's reply was an eye-opener to the upside-down urban kingdom of God: "No, we're not. Jesus lives in our neighborhood, in the slums, and we've moved there to be with him."

# 9

# Religion in the City

WHAT IS THE CONNECTION BETWEEN THE CITY and religion? In some cases the link seems obvious. The regal-ritual cities of Swaziland, for example, are almost entirely governed by religious ideology. Often very small places, hardly larger than villages in their society, they are embodiments of the sacred. They are symbolic locations, drawing sacred significance from the residence of the ruler-chief (Fox 1977:39-50).

What of "the Muslim city," a label created by past Western scholarship? In recent years this category has become more problematic. It is now questioned in academic reinvestigations (Haneda 1994:1-10). Does its architectural shape really speak largely of religious ideology? Or is such a city a complex of shaping forces?

The shape is neither unique nor geographically universal. But it is widespread enough to recognize in western Asia and North Africa. Its pattern divides the public space of mosque and great market from the private space of courtyard-type houses and blind alleys. Gender segregation regulates the placement of windows, the height of adjacent buildings, the guarding of visual privacy. Since the 1970s scholars have been asking more probingly, how has Islam as a religion influenced these urban structures and shapes in the Muslim world? The academic concept of the Muslim city slowly fades, but the role of Islam as a religion remains a part of the current discussion. Underrated or overrated, how does Islam as a religion shape the city?

Can one expect to find religion in the cities of a strongly antireligious state? For a number of decades the People's Republic of China has promoted religious disaffection, even antagonism. In the early years of the Marxist takeover urban Protestant churches, to cite one example, saw one door closed after another. Their organizational structures had been concentrated in the major cities, where they ran numerous hospitals, colleges and other agencies and where churches were relatively large and close to self-support. By 1958 the two hundred churches still open in Shanghai in 1957 had gone down to twenty-three; in Beijing, sixty-five churches were reduced to four (Hunter and Chan 1993:133, 225).

Has the pressure of the Cultural Revolution and the Red Guard movement sealed the fate of these forms of institutional religion? In the most conservative of estimates Chinese Christians had increased around sixfold by the 1990s, while population slightly more than doubled; according to official figures Protestants grew from one to five million in the 1980s (Hunter and Chan 1993:71). And the cities? Some show a high church concentration, the most important being Kaifeng, Shanghai, Wenzhou and Xiaoshan. Churches officially registered with the government remain a tiny urban number.

Where do we begin to evaluate these urban realities? What do we look for when we look for religion in the city? Do we count buildings? Or are there other things to look for?

## Traditional Research Trails

An important early scholar who examined the place of religion in the city was Émile Durkheim (1858-1917). His views have been the touchstone for later studies and have been modified in both sociology and anthropology.

Durkheim retained Tonnies's polarization of rural and more complex societies such as cities but reversed its plus and minus poles. He saw rural solidarity as "mechanical," a union of beliefs and customs, ritual and symbol almost automatic in character. By comparison, he saw the evolutionary process of social development as a positive move toward the "organic" solidarity of modern society, especially cities, and toward individualism.

The problem for Durkheim was not the city but religion—a totemic expression and creation, said the French atheist, of the personality of the social community. Its purpose? To give sacral meaning and plausibility to certain practices and institutions. At the heart of that community expression was the contrast between the sacred and the profane, between those acts and things regarded with awe, veneration, fear and distance, and those regarded as ordinary and mundane. Assignment of sacral meaning declines in industrial societies, where the separating out of different spheres of life makes religion less able to maintain the overarching legitimacy it possesses in more traditional societies.

Only as traditional forms of religion decline, Durkheim argued, will urban belief in the worth of the individual and freedom develop. Religion's symbols and rituals will take on new social forms in industrial societies, specifically new ideals of moral individualism. But even in such settings they will provide only functional significance in the process of social integration and cohesion.

Durkheim's discussion of religion and the city blazed a trail that many have followed. His questions continue to dominate current discussions: What is the function of religion? What is society? Does religion decline in technologically sophisticated cultures? His methodological atheism has found its successor in contemporaries like Peter Berger who insist that "sociological theory must, by its own logic, view religion as a human projection" (Berger 1967:180).

Durkheim left us with a powerful reminder that religion, in a real sense, has a social dimension. But his reduction of religion to a merely functionalist role in society has left scholarship in a search for where that compartmentalized function lies. If it is not in the division of the sacred from the secular (as Durkheim said), where do we find it? Could it be in its clinging to the supernatural? Or in surface-level beliefs and practices? Or in its structural attachment to the institutional? As the cultural means by which we cope with our human limits? As a functional instrument to maintain social integration?

**Beyond reductionism.** Ultimately this treatment of religion as basically a functional response to an essential social need leaves us in the quandary of reductionism. Religion is narrowed to a "nothing but" surface foam, a purely methodological, fragmented perspective without wholeness, an effervescence given off by social reality. And that lack of wholeness inhibits us from seeing also a key element in the wholeness of human life that is one of the professed interests of cultural anthropology as a discipline. Polarizing the sacred versus the secular, facts versus meaning, knowledge versus values, as Durkheim and those who followed his lead did, divides life into two-realm dualisms. Where then do we turn?

We must understand religion in another way if we would think biblically. As the human response to the revelation of God, religion is more than a functionalist, isolatable act of response to, and satisfaction of, a basic human need. It is also more than the formal, institutional systems of beliefs and practices such as those we call Hinduism, Islam, Shinto. It is the holistic response of the whole human self who, in that totality, is the image of God (Gen 1:26-28).

Thus religion is not an aspect of our lives; it is our life. Our humanness depends on our religion (Lyon 1975:63). It is the voice of the heart (Prov 4:23; Mt 12:34) as it "permeates and is an integral part of the totality of life in every society" (Loewen 1975:5). It serves as the core in the structuring of culture's meaning and usage.

***Religion made visible.*** As the integrating, radical response of humanity in covenant to the revelation of God (Rom 11:36), religion cannot be totally isolated from any part of urban life or reduced radically to only a segment of that life. The biblical narrative does not yield to any such scientific compartmentalization. It underlines instead the totalitarian character of religious faith. It is "total, taking in the whole of [human] life, because God's demands are all-embracing" (Schrotenboer 1964:14). The lifestyle of the city thus becomes religion made visible, urban humanity before the face of God *(coram Deo)* in both the sacred and the secular. Urban life is religion.

There is an antithetical character also to this biblical picture. Religion shapes a creaturely worldview either for or against the Creator. It either builds a city in defiance of God (Gen 11:4) or seeks, out of covenant obedience, the welfare of the city, praying to the Lord on its behalf (Jer 29:4-7). To greater or lesser degree, the incurably religious heart displays in its constructed image of the city both the wisdom of God and the flaws of sin and humanity's self-justifying constructions of reality.

Sadly, within the Christian community itself there are still remnants of compartmentalizations and two-realm schisms that inhibit a holistic understanding of religion. The history of urban mission is dotted with these leftover dualisms—church life versus urban sociopolitical life, evangelism versus social responsibility, charity service versus community development, proclamation versus presence, individual participation versus structural transformation.

## Religion's Urban Agenda

Is this picture of humanity as *Homo religiosus* too sermonic to make useful sense of religion in the city? In seeing religion as "the heart of urban culture," are we confusing, as some Christian anthropologists argue, religion and worldview (Kraft 1996:198-201)? If religious meanings are potentially everywhere, inquires the sociologist, how do we draw these together into something we can recognize and talk about? Doesn't the use of the label religion become very subjective? "What one researcher may see as a meaningful focus of society, another may not" (Ahern and Davie 1987:30).

There is wisdom in these cautions. Such caution may be one of the reasons that many scholars have been content to see religion as a sur-face-level subsystem of belief and behavior, along with politics, econom-ics and the rest—and that the post-World War II agenda of the sociology of religion "consists mainly of descriptions of the decline of ecclesiastic institutions" (Luckmann 1967:20). After all, goes the argument, religion can be measured most accurately when it is organized and institutional-ized into something we can call Islam or Judaism or Christianity.

At the same time, is systematized religion the only way we make sense of the routines of everyday urban life? the only way we measure the mys-tery and riddle of existence? the only way we find a norm for holding things together? When people speak of others as deeply religious, does it always have to imply full participation in religious meetings and a clearly visible allegiance to institutional beliefs and practices? As images of God, isn't everybody incurably and deeply religious?

Missiologist J. H. Bavinck may offer some help here. He has suggested that the religious consciousness circles around five foci or "magnetic points." These points are questions with which we confront ourselves and our world, our urban world. They are rooted in our existence as images of God. And they are not always expressed in institutionalization or organization.

> Even when he [humanity] never takes the time and the trouble deliberately to ponder on them and so penetrate into them, still his whole way of living already implies an answer, and *is* an answer. That is why we find these five focal points in every religion and in every human life, even in that of the so-called nonreligious man. (Bavinck 1966:34)

Two of Bavinck's five magnetic points would fit fairly easily into our traditional understanding of structured, institutional religion dealing with the supernatural—our craving for salvation and our sense of a Supreme Power behind the curtain of this phenomenal world. But they also, with three others, operate just as clearly outside institutional boundaries. We focus now on the other three, to underline the wider boundaries within which religion orbits.

**I and the cosmos.** There is a sense of cosmic relationship, of connec-tion between ourselves and our environment. We feel a kinship to the world in which we live and to which we belong, a bond now misshapen by our sin. Left in the human heart now estranged from God is a nostalgia for a lost Edenic paradise. The city becomes the sacred space where fallen humanity seeks again to place itself at the center of a cosmos of peace and divine stability. Cain searches for that lost security in the building of a city (Gen 4:17). Solomon's temple in Jerusalem links cosmos and Eden together (1 Kings 6). The carvings in the temple—palm trees and open flowers—speak of the cosmos. The holy of holies becomes "a distant memory of Paradise. Above the Ark were cherubim, just as Paradise was cut off by cherubim. . . . No man was allowed to enter the Holy of Holies except the priest, and that only once a year" (Bavinck 1966:145). The temple as a whole faced east, the guardian point of the cherubim in a fallen Eden (Gen 3:24).

In the pangs of exile an unrepentant Israel hangs on to the illusionary dream of a restored temple city (Is 7:4-7). There will come, replies the Lord, a return to the city of Zion and the golden bliss of "the garden of the LORD" (Is 51:3). But it will come when God's people are given new hearts of flesh by the Spirit (Ezek 36:26-27). Then nostalgia will become reality and the ruined cities will "become like the garden of Eden" (Ezek 36:35; Amos 9:13-15).

Across the ancient Near East and in the heart of the fallen creature that sense of cosmic relationship linking the city and the lost paradise of God lingers in twisted form. The cities, like the mountains and temples, were symbolic centers of the world, the zone of the sacred. Every house in that city connected its inhabitants to the cosmic axis (Eliade 1959:6-17). Babylon was a *Bab-ilani,* a "gate of the gods," for there the gods descended to earth and its inhabitants dwelt among them. Sennacherib built Nineveh according to "the form . . . delineated from distant ages by the writing of the heaven-of-stars." The city became the archetypal repetition of the Edenic transformation of chaos into cosmos.

Beyond the world of the ancient Near East that sense of cosmic connection through the city is repeated. The erection of Baghdad by the Abbasids in A.D. 762 meant more than the providing of a military camp for Abbasid soldiers. Baghdad's four gates suggested the four main points of the compass; it was to be a "world-axis" city, the crossroads at which the world turned.

Does this religious consciousness of our urban cosmic connection still live? It "passed into the religious architecture of Christian Europe: the basilica of the first centuries of our era, like the medieval cathedral, symbolically reproduces the Celestial Jerusalem" (Eliade 1959:17).

It echoes in the Puritan hopes for New England; they saw their urban experiment as a "city in the wilderness," part of God's eschatological design for the final harvesting of the cosmos. America was to be itself "the New World, a chance to create paradise on earth. The names of colonial towns—New Haven, Connecticut, and New Hope, Pennsylvania, to name only two—convey this idealism" (Phillips and LeGates 1981:406).

Such idealism is repeated by Victor Hugo, who described the Paris of older days as "the ceiling of the human race . . . a synonym of Cosmos" (quoted in Lees 1985:77), and, without the support of a cosmological myth, by New Yorkers who speak of their city as "the crossroads of the world."

*I and the norm.* There is, second, a vague sense of norm that reminds us of rules to be obeyed, that warns us of desires not to follow. However blunted, blurred or distorted by sin, there is some sense of being wrong and of wrongdoing, some distinction between good and bad (Rom 2:14-15). John Calvin speaks of this as "only some seeds of what is right implanted in their nature" (Calvin 1947:98).

This religious sense of norm is often tied to cities, even to modern cities. In the search for better housing and a resolution to the plight of the urban poor, cities still seek to do the right thing. In their promotion of order and civic virtue, cities still protest against total anarchy. In their appreciation of the human community, they return to a sin-twisted paradise memory of righteousness and communion.

The Hindu-Buddhist world of early southeast Asia had a sense of that norm. People felt they existed in a moral cosmos. Great cities were built as physical and social microcosms that embodied that karmic moral order. In Thailand, for example, "cities were the moral and social center of society, the peak of its hierarchy culminating in the king. As the social order and the natural order were one in a moral cosmos, the hierarchy of society could not be entirely separated from the urban form of its rule. Indeed, among the Thai wherever the ruler built his house automatically became a city" (O'Connor 1978:30). Behind this hierarchical society embodied in the urban community, they believed, was the harmony of a moral order.

The regal-ritual cities mentioned at the beginning of this chapter are uniquely symbolic of that link to the tradition of cosmic norm. Whether among the Dahomey of West Africa or in traditional southeast Asia, their identity comes from their role as ideological personifications, replicas of cosmic order and harmony. They serve primarily as places where the residence of monarchs is seen as crucial to the social order and the universe. Reflecting this connection with norm, many of these cities refer to themselves with titles like "the navel of the world."

The beginnings of urban planning in the Anglo-Saxon world of the nineteenth and twentieth centuries reflect this same religious nostalgia for a utopian norm. The word *utopia* in fact originated as the title of a 1516 book by Thomas More and had an urban twist. He used the label for his vision of how a new land of towns should be organized.

A key figure among utopian visionaries was Sir Ebenezer Howard (1850-1928). Urban historian Lewis Mumford claims that his 1898 work *Garden Cities of To-morrow* "has done more than any other single book to guide the modern town planning movement and to alter its objectives" (Howard 1965:29). Howard's vision was born out of frustration over industrial cities. These morally and socially polluted centers offered little hope for the future. Instead he called for self-contained planned communities of thirty thousand inhabitants, uniting work, home and leisure in small "garden cities." Isolated from the noise and filth of concentrated industrial centers like London, they would be enclosed by an encircling "green belt" of fields and woodlands owned by the town.

Howard's utopian vision became reality in 1902 with the building of the first garden city in Letchworth, some thirty miles north of London. Following the destruction of much of London in World War II, thirty-four more modified new towns followed. They achieved some success in the United States after 1910. But many, like Forest Hills Gardens, New York, became bedroom communities for affluent commuters. Howard's socialist dream of cooperatively owned communities for all income groups did not fare well in America.

Intriguing in Howard's description of his dream is his clearly religious language of norm. What he called the master key of the plan was "its very embodiment of Divine love for man . . . the true limits of Governmental interference, ay, and even the relations of man to the Supreme Power" (Howard 1965:42). In the future of these garden cities he saw new directions: "to banish despair and awaken hope in the breasts of those who have fallen; to silence the harsh voice of anger, and to awaken the soft notes of brotherliness and goodwill; to place in strong hands implements of peace and construction" (Howard 1965:150). Heading the first chapter of the book is this quotation from William Blake:

> I will not cease mental strife
> Nor shall my sword sleep in my hand
> Till we have built Jerusalem
> In England's green and pleasant land. (Howard 1965:50)

***I and the riddle of my existence.*** Third, religion appears as we wrestle with the riddle of our existence. We possess a sense of standing between action and passivity. We are conscious that we are active beings but also that we are victims of that indefinable something which some call fate or destiny.

The urban mythologies of the ancient Near East reflect this dilemma. In a world filled with capricious gods and ambitious rulers, the recognition of a city's patron deity provided little security. In one ancient lament Nanna, the patron deity of Ur, is incapable of protecting his city from invasions and famine. His appeal to Enlil, the god of the atmosphere, meets only with Enlil's declaration of similar impotence (Kramer 1969:611-19). A second lament underlines again the powerlessness of Ur's patron gods to defend their own territories. In neither lament is anything said about any human action that provoked these decisions by the gods (Block 1988:130-33).

Humanity seems caught in an insecurity traceable to the arbitrariness of the gods. The city is in the hands of a mind-changing deity, with no hint of either divine anger or human causation. "The Mesopotamian did not presume that the gods themselves were bound by any order which man could comprehend" (Frankfort 1978:278). Given these assumptions, the penitential psalms of the Mesopotamian abound in confessions of guilt. But missing is a sense of sin. People knew themselves to be subject to the will of the gods, called to their active service. But they knew also that those decrees were arbitrary and not just. There is regret but no repentance, despair but no deliverance.

By contrast, the biblical narrative allows no urban escape clause in some arbitrary zone of kismet fatalism created by the conflict of the gods or some unpredictable divine playfulness. The hand of the covenant God is the only hand that scatters the city and tower builders of Babel (Gen 11:8). And his is the hand that will return his exiled people to rebuild the ruined cities (Amos 9:14). It is the one true God who opens the barred gates of the cities to the pagan Cyrus (Is 45:1-8). The same God gives peace to Zion by strengthening the bars of its gates (Ps 147:13). When disaster comes to the city, has not the Lord caused it (Amos 3:6)? When peace dwells inside the city walls, is it not because "Jahweh our God lives here" (Ps 122:8-9 JB)?

How does the Bible avoid the arbitrariness of boomerang effects of blessing and retribution? What prevents us from resorting to some Hindu-like law of karma to make the riddle merely an optical illusion?

Part of the answer lies in the reality that God is continually present (Is 45:15). "Life in this world is not the laborious endurance of what an unpersonal karmatic power pours out over us, but it always remains a dialogue with God. No power breaks this dialogue, or comes in between the participants as a destructive power" (Bavinck 1966:162).

Another part of the answer has to do with who God is and who we are as his images. We are called to be active, obedient agents in the purposes of God, responsible stewards of his creation. We are to reflect in our lives the justice and righteousness (Ezek 45:9), compassion and love of our heavenly Father (Is 1:16-17). Our cities are to be the "home of justice where righteousness dwells" (Is 1:21 NEB), our only escape from the meaninglessness of life's routine. "Fear God and keep his command-ments, for this is the whole duty of man. For God will bring every deed into judgment, including every hidden thing, whether it is good or evil" (Eccles 12:13-14).

What of a humanity that does not find its wisdom in fear of God (Prov 1:7), whose response to divine norm deprives the poor of justice, robs the weakest of their rights, and despoils and plunders the widow and orphan (Is 10:1-2), who live only in the urban present, unmindful of the eschato-logical future?

The religions of the ancient Near East left urban humanity only with a sense of guilt, a bondage in broken promises. Humanity was caught between action and destiny, outside the circle of righteousness, over-come by supernatural "principalities and powers" (Eph 6:12). By contrast, the Bible points us to a guilt that can be pardoned, sin that can be for-given. Cities like Chorazin and Bethsaida, turning to the kingdom power of Jesus, can find a new beginning (Lk 10:12-16). In Jesus justice and right-eousness have taken on flesh and blood. Through his life, death and res-urrection he frees us from the chaos and futility (Rom 8:18-20) to which God subjected the world after the fall into sin (Longman 1998:284).

The further Jesus is withdrawn from the center of cosmic totality, the deeper human beings struggle with what they know to be the broken cir-cle of harmony and the deeper they seek in myth and magic for what they know to be the lost balance between activity and passivity. "Life becomes an unceasing, 'Who-goes-there?' " (J. Taylor 1965:71).

Urban life is marked by this search. In African cities the quest for secu-rity and continuity takes new turns. Traditional ethnic hostilities between tribes are translated into neighborhood rivalries as tribe lives next door to rival tribe. There is competition for jobs, promotion, housing. People turn to the bondage breaking of witchcraft accusations as they did in the rural areas.

A 1968 survey of Dar-es-Salaam estimated there were seven hundred diviners operating in the city. They shared ten thousand consultations between them daily, 56 percent of which involved witchcraft accusation. In Kampala, the capital of Uganda, research in 1971

> found highly organized and successful diviners who had adapted their beliefs and apparatus to suit the stresses and conditions of modern life. New spirits had been discovered to deal with modern situations and procedures were carried out quickly and smoothly to cater for the very large number of

clients produced by the urban situation. Many of these clients were wealthy businessmen and government officials. (Shorter 1974:53)

In the West religion has taken different shapes in the struggle to reform the city's broken potential, "to go beyond a passive, complaining attitude toward the surface of city life" (White and White 1977:139-40). The social work movement initiated in nineteenth-century America was one such effort. In Chicago in 1889 Jane Addams began her Hull House, a flagship of the charity organization movement, to build character and bring moral uplift among the urban poor. The Settlement House and John Dewey's pragmatic view of education that accompanied it were to be instruments of social discipline. They were to remove the hollowness of urban life "by building within the big city little centers of neighborly communication to take up part of the void created by urban expansion" (White and White 1977:147). They were to be religious, neohumanitarian re-creations of nostalgic vision from the preurban past that was quickly fading.

Addams's vision influenced the thinking of Robert Park, founder of the Chicago school of urban sociology. With Addams he saw a breakdown of community, of face-to-face association and cooperation, in the city. His empirical study became a search for the reasons for that breakdown. In that search he faced also the urban dilemma of living between activity and passivity, a dilemma bearing all the earmarks of a religious quandary. "If the city is the world which man created," he lamented, "it is the world in which he is henceforth condemned to live" (Park 1952:73). The city he affirmed as an expression of human effort to remake the natural environment on its own. Yet at the same time he felt deeply that the lure of the great city was a flame drawing hapless moths. The city was both attractive and destructive, a fascinating challenge to the human spirit but the death of community. Park sensed a bondage that could be broken only by morality, a religious category. But this was a religious category he could connect only with the impossibility of a return to the rural past.

## Religion's Urban Typology

Given this sweeping view of religion as humanity's response action to God, is it possible to create a heuristic typology that will help us in sorting out where these "magnetic points" most frequently touch our lives? Systems like Buddhism and Judaism point to an institutionalized form of faith in the supernatural. But where do we look in the city to find ultimate commitments to the supernatural outside a deeply organized, institutionalized form? And where can we find a tool to catalog all-absorbing religious commitments organized and unorganized to work and entertainment, ideologies without apparent supernatural reference points?

Ahern and Daniel may offer some help. They developed a typology using four places or nodes in our human images of the city around which religion's "magnetic points" may cluster. Each of the four nodes are shaped by two fundamental dimensions: organized/nonorganized and supernatural/empirical. We will first look at the two nodes that are shaped more by supernatural referents than empirical referents—conventional or institutional religion which is relatively organized and common or folk religion which is relatively unorganized. Then we will move to the two nodes more shaped by empirical referents—surrogate religion which is relatively organized and invisible or diffused religion which is relatively disorganized (Ahern and Davie 1987:32). As with all typologies, we must be careful not to look at any one religion and say, for example, it is completely organized and formed by supernatural referents. The dividing lines between types are blurry so that any particular religion can have multiple influences but will lean more one way than another.

***The supernatural and religion common and conventional.*** The category of *conventional or institutional religion* is the one most quickly identified by the traditional student of religion in the city. It is the systematically organized institution of faith and practice structured around a reference to some supernatural Ssupreme power or powers. We quickly identify the system as Islam or Shinto. It is on this category that much academic research, both Christian and non-Christian, has focused in evaluating the impact of secularization on the city. Scholars like Durkheim and Max Weber pointed to these shapes when they spoke of the urban erosion of traditional beliefs and morality under the corrosive effects of calculating rationality and a disenchantment with systematic expressions of faith. Mission evaluations often still mark the decline of traditional institutions and beliefs as an open door for the church in predominantly non-Christian centers—or as a warning flag when the decline touches the church itself.

Sharing that similar supernatural reference is *common or folk religion*. Compared to conventional religion, it is much less tied to a sophisticated or geographically universal institution. Its formulations are more thematic than systematic, not a fully coherent whole but a large array of separate elements. Closer to the unanswered questions of everyday life, it responds to more local issues. Why did my child die? What is the cause of this drought or that sickness? Whom should I marry? Where do I build my house? What will guarantee my success in planting or business? Its search for answers to these questions comes through magic, divination, astrology, rituals connected to lifecycles, offerings to spirits and ancestors.

Predominant in tribal and peasant societies (Hiebert and Meneses 1995:118-42, 212-17), folk religion does not disappear in modern cities. The rise of the decentralized New Age mega-network in urban North America points to its contemporary viability. In Korean cities like Pusan and Seoul animistic practitioners carry on a busy trade (Hard 1989:45-46). To the urban populations of West Africa it offers stability and traditional connections in a world of social change (Assimeng 1989). Across that continent the picture is the same. "The insecurity of the new urban dwellers occasioned by difficulties, uncertainties, and increased crime and violence has resulted in a tenacious adherence to the beliefs and practices of magic and witchcraft" (Rader 1991:61).

The supernatural interests that are reflected in both the conventional religion and common religion nodes can sometimes blur the organizational line. Frustrations with the organizational can turn the participant away not from the supernatural but from the organizational. And sometimes the movement is in the opposite direction—from nonorganizational to organizational.

In Rio de Janeiro and São Paulo, for example, the movement called Umbanda (Uken 1992:43-49) not only has achieved its greatest success but has shifted increasingly from a relatively nonorganized common religion into a federation of congregations under the control of a central committee. In so doing it has been transformed into a political force with national ambitions. With other folk religions that some call Afro-Brazilian cults, it retains its spiritist mixtures of Catholicism and African and native Indian rituals and beliefs. In common with these systems, it has always been an urban cult. It has accompanied growing migration movements to the cities and expanded, with urban growth, its impact across all social and ethnic classes (de Queiroz 1991:93-101).

In Canada, by comparison, "interest and involvement in organized religion seems to be hitting unprecedented lows" (Bibby 1995:27). By the year 2015 the proportion of people attending a Christian church weekly will drop from the 1995 level of 23 percent (4.5 million) to around 15 percent (3.5 million). Yet approximately one-half of those who don't attend on a regular weekly basis describe both religion generally and their own religious group specifically as "very important" or "somewhat important" to them (Bibby 1995:24).

In this setting the incurable urge for things spiritual turns to other, nonorganized expressions of the supernatural. People continue to be intrigued with mystery. As of the 1990s, about 40 percent of Canadians believe that we can have contact with the spirit world. Approximately one in three people across the country say they believe the claims of astrology. "Fifty percent of the population claim to have personally experienced precognition and telepathy. . . . Six in ten Canadians openly acknowledge they believe in ESP, with approximately the same proportion maintaining that some people have special psychic powers" (Bibby 1993:132). These findings "signal unrest and receptivity to some of the key themes religion historically has addressed" (Bibby 1993:134). Significant numbers of Canadians not involved in institutional (conventional) religion are continuing their search for the meaning of life in common or folk expressions of faith.

**The empirical and religion invisible and surrogate.** In *surrogate religion* and *invisible or diffused religion*, the totalistic commitment of religious expression is directed toward the here and now of empirical reality. The transcendent, Godward dimension, the vertical look, is not lost. It is horizontalized—and the horizontal is made transcendent. Invisible or diffused religion carries on its search without organizational form; surrogate religion is the organized equivalent of conventional religion but, like invisible religion, without any explicitly supernatural reference points.

In the lands where Christendom has had a place, the vocabulary of invisible or diffused religion may give off a Christian scent. Religious memory dies hard for a Canadian journalist who has long since thrown over the evangelical faith of her childhood. She still cries when she hears "Amazing Grace." It takes her "back to something that she lost somewhere, somehow along the way" (Bibby 1995:24). To someone from the white working class of Tower Hamlets, London, a term like *believe* becomes a word symbol from the Christian faith transformed into social practice: "I believe in Christmas."

Verbal symbols without Christian trappings also surface, pointing to the same nonorganized religious orientation, the same nostalgic quest for meaning outside the boundary lines of the supernatural. A music critic comments: "David Oistrakh's inspired performance in Johannes Brahms' 'Concerto for Violin and Orchestra' sent his audience on wings of rapture. As a Moses, he seemed to guide us through the tensions and resolutions of Brahms' music to the promised land of clarity and final serenity" (quoted in Mol 1983:88-89). A 1997 ad in a North American newsmagazine asks, "What do you call an insurance company that has an unyielding grasp on the bottom line?" The answer appears on the second page of the ad: "Make performance a religion." The qualities that make an attorney in Philadelphia a "superb prosecutor" are defined as "that religious sense of protecting the city from those who were destroying it"; the refusal of the city's mayor and staff to let the city go under becomes the act of "offering, in their daily acts of living and survival, a prayer for the city" (Bissinger 1997:xiv, 92).

Outside the borders of Christendom and in cultures like those of Africa where life is seen as a unified whole, the pressures of urban modernity can have their effect. Over an extended period of time, practices associated with common or folk religions may lose some of their supernatural reference and take on a here-and-now dimension. But their religious character is not lost in the shift. The same crossover we have noted between organized and nonorganized boundaries takes place along the line separating the supernatural and empirical orientations. The religious character of the practice is not lost in the shift, only redirected.

Imposed systems of colonial law press for a transition of the religious source of authority of the tribal chief from its supernatural connections with the tribe's ancestral past to the empirical realities of adjusted politics. Chiefs still command the religious respect of their people and the traditional honors associated with the tribe's religious past, only now their religious authority is linked as well to empirical politics (Rader 1991:61). Music and dance in Africa remain theological dramatizations. But now, as in the Western past, their connections with the supernatural dimension of religion may shift. Their old meanings of appeasing the dead, celebrating mythic events and serving in life-cycle rites of passage are not necessarily lost. But other old meanings, more congenial with the empirical, are underlined—their role of transmitting values, ideals, emotions and even history.

In some cultures excessive drinking becomes more than simply a release from perceived personal or social pressures as in the West. In the Greco-Roman world of the New Testament it was a religious act more connected with the organized, supernatural world, a means of finding religious ecstasy, divine madness. Paul saw those religious dimensions and pointed to drunkenness as a negative alternative to the filling of the Holy Spirit (Eph 5:18; cf. Acts 2:15).

Today that religious dimension of drinking alcohol is not lost. But it often becomes a technique for seeking ecstatic religious experience in the enclosed world of the here and now. Many Mexican Indian festivals are marked by a period of excessive drunkenness even among people who otherwise do not drink much. In West Africa "some religious festivals involve the consumption of enormous quantities of palm wine, with resultant drunkenness" (Nida 1967:103). Among the Tarahumaras of northern Mexico socioreligious dances lasting all night become the occasion for the consumption of large amounts of beer (called *tesquino*).

Surrogate religion manifests the same nonsupernatural commitment as invisible or diffused religion, but its commitments are expressed in more organized forms. More than half of the Australians recently surveyed, for example, claim they have not attended a service of worship for more than a year. Church attendance in the main Protestant denominations was half what it had been twenty-five years earlier (Porter 1990:78-79). Is Australia, then, without religion? without organized religion?

The Returned Services League (RSL), a war veterans club, seems to be offering an institutional religious alternative to the church. Muriel Porter suggests it "has become a form of church-going for many Australians who have long since abandoned the more conventional kind." RSL clubs, found in every town and city of any size, provide a meeting place where veterans gather to relive past glories. "In quasi-religious rituals, the war dead are regularly remembered at club meetings. When old diggers [veterans] die, an RSL ritual is a frequent addition to the funeral service" (Porter 1990:57).

Anzac Day (April 25) is celebrated in the same spirit. It is a national holiday remembering Australia and New Zealand's war dead and particularly the seventy-six hundred Australian soldiers in the nation's entirely volunteer World War I army who died in the assault on Turkish troops at Gallipoli on the Dardanelles. But it is much more as well. It is a unique national day, almost mythic in character, the "one day of the year" for many. "It is observed more solemnly, indeed more religiously, than Good Friday. Regulations about its observance are stricter than for any other day" (Porter 1990:55). In a nation given to good-humored debunking of most sacred cows, Anzac and Gallipoli call for reverence, not simply patriotic recollections. Beneath the power of this surrogate myth, some theologians argue, is an unacknowledged recollection of a Christian understanding of sacrifice and resurrection, shorn now of its supernatural origin in the work of Christ and transformed into a this-world religiosity. On this day Australians find their answer to the question of "I and the cosmos."

It is not a large leap from Anzac Day to the surrogate faith called civil religion—nor, for that matter, from the local-oriented religion that marked the cities of the ancient Near East. The difference is between an organized religion that validates the supernatural and an investiture of the here-and-now of institutional government and politics through religious expression.

In the surrogate of civil religion the nation or city invests itself with religious symbols legitimizing its historical destiny and authenticating its power. Sometimes, as in the United States, civil religion is couched in the language of manifest destiny and invoked in prayer and political speeches on appropriate occasions. Sometimes, as in Korea and Japan, these symbols cluster more narrowly around the alleged divine origins of the country. Thus Japanese religious institutions like State Shinto arose in the first half of the twentieth century to promote a growing, militant nationalist spirit. Its defenders argued that it was not a religion, only a political symbol of Japanese identity associated with the emperor.

In South Africa apartheid as a civil religion transformed the developing cities into "the white man's city" with blacks, coloreds and Asians only "temporary sojourners." To counteract the pull of the cities for the non-whites, "a 'push' was created by not only forbidding in-migration from the rural areas, but also intentionally starving the city of quality services, thus causing a shortage in housing units" (Kritzinger 1995:206).

In the midst of England's urban revolution of the late nineteenth century another surrogate religion was forming. Between 1879 and 1914 the leisure revolution was making its appearance, and sports were a key part of it. Cricket and soccer, the most widely popular, were extensively professionalized. Rugby, tennis and golf all grew rapidly.

Sport was becoming the emotional center of people's lives. It was becoming a surrogate religion; it "did for some people many of the same things that religion did for others" (McLeod 1996:199). Sport was not an alternative to religion but one of its examples. It offered a deep experience of fulfillment and sustained people through the workaday grind of the urban world. Membership and passionate involvement in a local sports club provided their strongest religious form of social identity.

These surrogate religious dimensions have not diminished through the years. Our vocabulary becomes religious. Sports heroes are venerated; newspaper columnists describe a sports hall of fame as the place that "immortalizes our sports heroes. It enshrines their feats and accomplishments" (Mol 1983:88). Religious refrains of "I and the riddle of my existence" are echoed in the ritual rules of the game. "In many ways it functions like a secular religion that dramatizes the vision that life is a competition in which both sides compete equally and fairly and infractions are punished by god-like umpires. It shows us a world in which things are just and the victor reigns because of talent and achievement" (Hiebert and Meneses 1995:310).

Where do all these paths we have traced leave us? With urban mazes searching through the city for meaning and order to existence—quests that never escape their religious origins. With organized systems that structure religion around the supernatural, building temple and mosque. With unorganized common or folk religions that focus hopes for safe air travel in the "spirit of the air" embodied in a straw idol and then discard it at the Kimpo airport in Seoul as the plane is boarded. With the surrogate religion of the great England bowler Harold Larwood, who claimed, "Cricket was my reason for living." With the unorganized invisible religion that finds its answer to the yearning of the heart in sex or ideology, work or family.

Why do these mazeways continue to appear? John Calvin put it this way many centuries ago: "God himself has implanted in all men a certain understanding of his divine majesty. Ever renewing its memory, he repeatedly sheds fresh drops. . . . From the beginning of the world there has been no region, no city, in short, no household, that could do without religion" (Calvin 1960:43-44).

Who waits in the urban shadow of these dead-end mazeways distorted by sin, these blurred human paths along which we stumble through the city, blindly searching for links to the cosmos and its norm, to the riddle of our existence? Jesus still sees the city, weeps over it and in grace laments, "If you, even you, had only known on this day" (Lk 19:41-42).

# 10

## The City as Power

CITIES ARE NOT FULLY INTEGRATED and utterly coherent. They are an aggregate of accumulated traits and habits, shaped by time and history, constantly subject to change and modification. As human creations, these traits and characteristics exhibit to greater or lesser degree the responses to God's Word that the previous chapter explored. Molded often by sin and sometimes by righteousness, cities form a totality of interweaving systems and subsystems, sometimes self-correcting, sometimes self-destructing.

They are also provisions of God's common grace. Through them God restrains the development of evil, blesses his fallen creatures and works out his sovereign purposes in both judgment and grace. The city is an instrument of God's preserving and preventative grace and an exhibition of our creaturely response to that grace.

Where do we look in the shared functions of the city to see that grace and to see religion as a response both negative and positive to God's grace? Every city provides divinely initiated, creature-shaped guidelines for self-understanding; they lay down clues to understand the urban process. This chapter focuses on one of these crucial functions. The following chapters will introduce three more.

### Power Urban and Rural

Cities gather power, "the ability to achieve ends, even over opposition"

(Spates and Macionis 1982:382). Their centripetal magnetism draws social, cultural, economic and political activities into their geographical orbit. In turn, their force field expands outward in a centrifugal direction past their geographical boundaries.

Where power dominates, there is the city as a magnet, to pull it to itself. Where that urban power is twisted by human sin and justice becomes injustice, the Jerusalems of our world feel its tyrannical side (Is 59:1-4). Oppressive power then becomes its own divine curse (Judg 9:57; Jer 21:14). Where that power is defined in terms of justice and compassion (Mic 6:8), there will be urban restoration (Mic 7:11-12).

Folk cultures in a rural area tend to be localized, isolated and autonomous. Power is regional, shared along somewhat autonomous, but interconnected, lines (see figure 1).

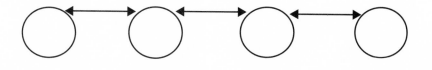

**Figure 1. Power in a folk culture**

The city, by contrast, both gathers power to itself from outlying areas and reaches out farther, interconnects more strongly. Urbanism tends to centralize power in itself, to take control and authority in every kind of direction. In its contacts with rural or village society, it does not obliterate the older links between village and village through regional networks and joint activities like markets and festivals. It becomes part of a new symbiosis whose system now links city to village. The city pulls village and rural areas to itself and, as a superhighway, connects its impact with others.

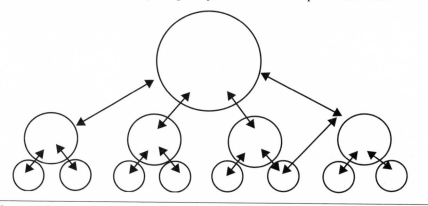

**Figure 2. The city as a power system**

John Gulick suggests that this may be the feature that enables archaeology to differentiate between cities (very small sites by modern standards) and peasant villages among the oldest remains of settlements. "The single most important presumed difference is that among the inhabitants of the earliest cities were people who wielded power over others, including others living beyond the settlements themselves, while the earliest peasant villages had no such powerful people" (Gulick 1989:68).

### Power Observed: Some Case Studies

Urbanization as a human process has continued that accumulative, power-gathering effect. The very old, historical transition we have noted from city to a networking system of cities, and from there to city-state and urban-oriented empire, is the history of urban power expansion. The reemergence of the city after the collapse of the Roman Empire and the so-called Dark Ages was, in part, a power shift. But power was still power. The feudal overlords simply found theirs surrendered to the commercial expansionism of reborn cities like Venice and Genoa. "Roman urban sites, atrophied in the Dark Ages and ruled as personal fiefs by secular or religious authorities, gained a new life as centers of trade or capitalist land ownership" (Fox 1977:97).

*Urban Latin America: Then and now.* Latin America has an urban history, then and now, that illustrates as well as any other Third World history this recognition of the city as a place of power. As early as the Iberian conquest it was manifest. Power prompted Hernán Cortés to demolish utterly the Aztec city of Tenochtitlán and erect on its rubble in 1521 his colonial alternative—the Ciudad Imperial de Mexico (today's Mexico City). "As Tenochtitlan had stood as the power center of a great empire, the new capital would symbolize Spanish ascendance throughout the region" (Lezama 1994:370). A decade later, Juan Pizarro followed the same pattern in the conquest of the Inca Empire. Inca cities were conquered and destroyed and replaced with Spanish cities.

The cities the early colonialists erected had one common feature: the exercise of exploitative administrative power. In the highland cities of Mexico and Peru, the mining of precious metals, especially silver, dominated the urban concerns of transient colonists. Coastal cities like Veracruz and Cartagena were dedicated to oceanic commerce and military defense. Into all these parasitic urban centers flowed wealth and power, funneled from the hinterland, from Indian tribute and labor, mines, and landed estates.

The ecology of these cities exhibited this same division of power and powerlessness. The *traza*, or grid plan, formed the central portion of highland cities. Normally reserved for the exclusive use of Europeans, it was the center of wealth and prestige. Indigenous Indian populations were housed in separate barrios at some distance from the center. Neighborhoods became poorer as one moved outward toward the urban periphery and beyond (Butterworth and Chance 1981:10-12).

The transition in Latin America from colonial to contemporary city has not been without change. The wars for independence and the task of stabilizing national borders on the continent in the early nineteenth century brought a half-century of political turmoil and a golden age for the elite rural landowner. "At the very time that western Europe and the northeastern United States were undergoing rapid urbanization and industrialization, Latin America experienced a period of decentralization, or even ruralization, of society" (Morse 1992:8). Large cities tended to decrease in size and impact.

By the last half of the twentieth century that urban primacy dip had vanished. Rural migrants took the place of Iberian colonialists in permanent migration to the cities. The dream of power, still defined in terms of economic opportunity, pulled them. Though the continent's cities bore the brunt of recession in the 1980s, that disastrous economic decline did not radically deter rural optimism over urban power centers. By 1990 the region continued to reflect the demographic pull of that dream. Currently Latin America boasts thirty-nine cities with more than one million people, eleven with more than three million. Is the era of the megacity as a nodal control point for the nations dawning?

In the wake of this change are two worlds—the world of the large city and the rural world, each with advantages and disadvantages. One is a world of motorized high speed, the other of oxen, pack animals and laden humans. One is a world of prestige, power, higher education and better jobs. The other is a world of the soil, its rural stability transformed into chaos by the city's magnetic attractions.

In this setting power and powerlessness still manifest themselves. "The modern state in Latin America has been an instrument of the dominant classes for their own gain and their own wealth, and they use the law to achieve their own objectives. There is a great divide between workers and the means of production. Misery becomes normal, and oppression is an instrument to keep order" (Couto 1997:90).

The crisis leaps out at you as you walk through any of the countless shantytowns *(favelas)* that form the rim of large urban centers. Here, cut off from the city's economic mainstream and many of its services, the urban poor live in makeshift shelters of cardboard, wood scraps, corrugated plastic, even mud. In these *villas de miseria* rural emigration, poverty and unemployment tear at the social fabric of the family. Single-parent households are common. São Paulo has an estimated 2.5 million abandoned children, castoffs of the disintegrating family. Some recall the advantages of their rural past: "there was less hunger, the choices were limited, life was more simple, and the family network provided daily support" (Nuñez and Taylor 1996:117).

**The rebirth of the city-state?** Is a new form to urban power emerging with the rise of the megacity in Latin America, in the United States and around the world? Economic planners like Neal Peirce suggest we may be returning to a revised version of the city-state that existed prior to the birth of the nation-state in the sixteenth and seventeenth centuries (Peirce 1993). National governments, he argues, are losing their power to innovate, to reposture a society. Throughout history it has been cities, not rural areas or nations, that have been the chief generators of wealth and creative power (Jacobs 1969). The "citistate" intensifies that reality. Are there visible hints that point to the presence of the citistate? Look in the United States for metropolitan districts that begin to run into each other, cities swallowing cities to form gigantic conurbations or cocities, hinges working within extended urban networks. An urban castle on a lake called Chicago becomes a crossroads labeled Chicagoland. Dallas stretches across the miles to become the megalopolis of Dallas-Fort Worth, and that well-placed hyphen draws together a population of 3.9 million people. Commuter links between Washington, D.C., and Boston create an urban corridor through the northeast United States.

In developing countries the primate city phenomenon points in the same citistate direction. One city absorbs its surrounding population centers and by far exceeds in size and power the second largest city in the country. Peru becomes metropolitan Lima. Lima becomes the center of all significant government and economic activity, the heart of decision-making. "In many ways, not to be in Lima is simply not to be" (Kent 1994:464). Sucre is the legal capital of Bolivia, with a 1988 population of about 105,000. But La Paz, whose department borders included 1,926,200 people and 30 percent of the national total at that time, dominates. It houses all government institutions and, by 1972, accounted for 72 percent of the nation's industrial production. Beyond its borders, it spreads to unite Cochabamba and Santa Cruz into a widening urban network, a conurbation.

What makes such megacities (sometimes called global cities) so different from their past? Demographics is only a marginal part of the picture. Scale comes closer to defining the difference. To amplify Peirce's economic definition, they have become entities that perform as critical actors, transforming their national connections and character into transnational power nodes on a sociocultural, economic, political and religious global scale.

Terms like *citistate* may still be too novel, too journalistic to aptly denote the power shift of urban domination now taking place in the world. But terms like *megacity* are less and less useful also; they focus too much on size and not enough on transglobal scale. Whatever label we use, urban interconnection and impact appear to be increasing.

## Implications for Mission

It is not always easy to predict the relationship between the city as a power center and its effect on the planting and growth of the church. In too many cases, evangelical attention to the macro-context of the urban dimension is minimal. Concerns tend to focus on local, microdimensional issues more readily observed and felt—pastoral leadership, difficulties with evangelism in a large population area, the sense of inferiority status among Christians in a Muslim setting or minorities in America's inner cities. Contexts large and local both need our attention.

**The church as a barrier to urban mission.** Ray Bakke, director of International Urban Associates, has led urban mission consultations throughout the world. In countless meetings he has asked urban pastors to define the ten basic barriers to effective evangelism of their cities. To his surprise, he has found that most of the barriers are defined as internal. "Nearly all barriers," he has concluded, "are created by church politics, policies, priorities, or personalities, and not by the big, bad city itself" (Bakke 1987:60).

Reinforcing those obstacles is the rural orientation of the church's past that blocks an awareness of urban power as a path to growth and new vitality. Again, Latin America is as good a sampler as any.

Liberation theology, with all its concern for the poor, has, in the judgment of some, largely overlooked the urban character of Latin American society. "One could read dozens of volumes by liberation theologians without realizing that Latin America has made the 'urban leap' in the last generation or so" (Berryman 1996:159). On a larger scale, the recent past of the Catholic Church has shown the same flaw. The church's structures and mindset are seen by some as the product of a rural Latin America now on the wane. Seminary students were typically from rural areas, with few candidates from either the middle class or the *favelas* on the urban fringe. Just when Brazil was becoming more urban, seminarians were coming increasingly from rural areas. Between 1960 and 1982, Brazil's agricultural population had fallen from 53.9 percent to 31.5 percent.

But during the same period the percent of seminarians whose parents were farmers increased from 44.6 percent to 56.5 percent. "Few come from the working class and few from upper-class families" (Berryman 1996:163).

The past history of Protestant work in Latin America shows a similar disconnection. Early missionaries in Venezuela, for example, were slow to move to Caracas. They "went primarily to rural areas and small towns further west, where several denominations had arrived in the early decades of the century. One writer notes that the only Protestant church established in Caracas before 1940 was the First Presbyterian Church" (Berryman 1996:126). Like the Catholic leaders, Protestant missionaries, many of whom were themselves of rural background, went primarily to rural areas. Church expansion in the city did not begin until the 1960s (23 churches). A 1992 survey found there were 231 churches but still totaling no more than 1 percent of the three million people in the area studied.

There are some indications this long hiatus in urban ministry may be changing. The 1995-1998 pastoral plan for the Catholic archdiocese of São Paulo calls for a new engagement with the urban future of the city. The document envisions "pass-through" parishes aiming at the large number of people present downtown only during the day. Another suggests the creation of spaces for evangelization in large public places such as commercial districts and railway and bus stations. Parishes and church agencies are called to renew their missionary spirit so that "inculturating themselves ever more in the urban environment, they might hear and respond to the cries of the people with solidary actions, and especially of those who are deprived of work, health care, housing, and education" (Berryman 1996:166).

Among the inhabitants of São Paulo there is another sign of growing interest in the city, this time among Protestants. By 1982, 35.3 percent of the city's Protestants were participants in a new model of church life, what has been called popularly grassroots churches. The Brazil for Christ (O Brasil para Cristo) congregation, founded in 1955, meets in a hangar-like building designed to seat fifteen thousand. By 1993 it had become a movement boasting a million members and 650 churches throughout Brazil. Started in 1962, the highly regimented God Is Love (Deus e Amor) Church, like most of the grassroots churches, is Pentecostal in flavor and has spawned a movement of 1.6 million members. Also based in São Paulo is the Renascer em Cristo (To Be Born Again in Christ) church movement. Only eight years after its founding in 1986, the mother congregation had an estimated fifty thousand followers who worshiped in thirty-one meeting places (Berg and Pretiz 1996:101-16).

Many without U.S. mission connections, others with missionary ties now broken, still others planted by missionaries from another Latin American country, these churches are products of spontaneous combustion. Not all are as large as the megachurch examples from São Paulo. Most are Pentecostal in theology (sometimes to the extreme), with a strong orientation to the poor. Some are one-man movements with a highly authoritarian style of leadership.

But spread through cities large and small—and rural areas as well—they represent a new wave in church growth. Over 40 percent of Latin America's Protestants are in these grassroots churches. In major cities those percentage figures remain high—55.2 percent in Mexico City (1986), 36.6 percent in Lima (1993), 36.2 percent in Buenos Aires (1992). In larger, more populated countries with a stronger sense of national identity and lesser cultural, religious and economic dependence they thrive. Amidst the recent history of economic, political and military disasters that have befallen Argentina, they rise in strength (Berg and Pretiz 1996:50-53).

**The city as a barrier to mission.** In other settings it is not the negligence of the church that is to blame. The city is the barrier to church growth. In cities where urban power is overtly religious in orientation and strongly institutionalized, it may be very difficult to see strong church growth or a change of faith. With major religious symbolic significance, such a city does not easily open its doors to theological outsiders.

In the five holy cities of India no churches may be built. Salt Lake City, the power center of Mormonism, has not had a strong history of dynamic evangelical church growth. The recent rise of Muslim fundamentalism and its call for a return to Islamic law in society, culture and politics is strongly tied in its origins to the city. With it has come even stronger resistance not only to Western but to Christian intrusions. The city is the unseen fuel that fires the engine of Islamic idealism (Claydon 1998:8-14).

Sometimes that inhibiting role of power may be political in character. Chinese state policy, for example, throughout its long history has sought to penetrate, regulate and control institutional religions. From the arrival of Matteo Ricci in the sixteenth century to the Ch'ing proscription of 1736, and from the Tientsin Treaties of 1858-1860 to the present, the Chinese state has so regarded institutional, independent Christianity (Hanson 1980:113). Buddhism, Catholicism and Protestantism all found their initial strong growth only during periods of social, economic and political weakness and crisis.

**The city as a path to mission.** On the other hand, when church growth takes place in such cities of power, it can be significant not only for the city but for rural and outlying areas. The city's magnetic power by its very nature carries the church in its expanding wake. Remember the efforts of Jeroboam to build alternate centers of worship at Dan and Bethel to avoid the drawing power of Jerusalem's central worship (1 Kings 12:26-33). Consider the impact of the gospel on the fledgling church at Pentecost when Jewish pilgrims "from every nation under heaven" were confronted with the power of the Holy Spirit (Acts 2:4-13). Before the day was out a handful of believers had become three thousand people scattered in diaspora return to their homelands.

Sometimes not directly perceived, that connection between the power of the city and church growth has nevertheless had its effect. There was no perceived global church-planting strategy behind the Azusa Street Revival in a depressed industrial section of downtown Los Angeles from 1906 to 1909. But that urban revival drew thousands from around the world to this American city to participate in this Pentecost experience. When they left they spread its message as emissaries of a new Pentecostal movement that "has quietly become the largest Christian movement of the twentieth century" (Cleary 1997:1). Some 400-500 million followers have spread over most of the world. And one feature of that growth, at its beginning and in its expansion, has been a continuing connection with the world's cities.

In Mexico City, where one out of four Mexicans live, 10 percent of the Protestant churches "are drawing more new people than all the rest put together. And most of these churches are Pentecostal" (Berg and Pretiz 1992:117). The world's largest congregation, the Yoido Full Gospel Church of Seoul, Korea, had a membership of 500,000 in 1988; it is a Pentecostal church. A 1992 study in Rio de Janeiro classified 61 percent of the city's Protestant churches as Pentecostal. "Even more significant was the fact that 91 percent (648 of 710) of the new churches in Rio established during the 1990-1992 period were pentecostal" (Berryman 1996:18). In 1937, of the fifty-five Hispanic Protestant churches in New York City, twenty-five were Pentecostal; by 1983 the number of Latino Pentecostal churches there was 560 (Adams 1997:167).

The same unplanned connection between city and church has reshaped the location and style of America's black churches. In the United States from 1910 to 1970 more than six million African Americans left the rural south for the urban centers of the north. The shift was the largest internal migration in American history (Lincoln and Mamiya 1990:118; Sernett 1997). They were welcomed to the city by African American churches. In storefront churches aimed at the walking poor and in established, more traditional fellowships, the migrants found the love of God, hope in Christ, community with one another and the cultural broker churches needed for a new beginning. And again, many of those welcoming churches were Pentecostal in character (Kostarelos 1995; Williams 1974).

***Intentional strategy as a path to mission.*** Intentional planning and strategy has also marked the city's power potential for the church. Ignatius of Loyola (1491-1556), founder of the Society of Jesus (1540), saw the cities as "landmarks" in the Jesuit emphasis on scholarship, education, preaching and teaching. Where else but in cities could be developed "suitably diplomatic approaches to those who could influence the currents of both thought and action" (Neill 1952:164)? "Placing his companions in the midst of the City of Man, they would thus be able to lead its citizens more easily toward the City of God. That is why he abandoned cloister, habit, and choir, and struggled to build downtown residences, schools, social centers, and churches" (Lucas 1992:215).

Out of that vision of a "preferential option" for the urban setting, Ignatius structured the Society's *Constitutions* and its later *Spiritual Exercises.* Like a garrison from which troops go out to make raids and sorties, the urban setting was to provide

> the greatest diversity of possibility "where the greater fruit will probably be reaped through the means that the Society uses." . . . The city's critical mass of population, wealth, and apostolic need provided possibilities for spiritual, social, and pastoral ministries, public preaching, and private conversations, the long-range social impact of work with those who have power to effect systemic change, and the promise of reforming a world by educating its youth. (Lucas 1992:169-70)

The global movement of the Jesuits followed that model of Ignatius as he founded his Jesuit vineyards in the busy heart of Rome and in downtown locations all over Europe. Crowded cities around the globe became the crossroads from which, it was hoped, would emerge new vineyards. In Asia Jesuit missionaries like Francis Xavier, Roberto deNobili, Matteo Ricci and Michele Ruggieri saw the radiating urban centers of Goa, Macao, Madura and Beijing as radiating centers of church growth. In Africa, where such cities of scale were then unknown, there were other power paths to explore—the Cape Verde islands as a launching pad for Christian expansion on the mainland's western shore; the Jesuit evangelizing envoys to Africa's kings like Zimbabwe's Mwene Mutapa and Ethiopia's Galawdewos.

Where cities did not exist, Jesuit efforts helped create them. Nagasaki, Japan, was founded as a Jesuit settlement in 1579, São Paulo, Brazil, in 1553 as a settlement by and for a team of six Jesuit missionaries. In 1607 the superior general of the society formed a new province, Paraguay, to reach the Guaraní Indians. To save the Indians, scattered amid forests, from Portuguese slavers and Spanish colonists, the Jesuits gathered them into "reductions" or "large towns and transformed from rustics into city-dwelling Christians by the constant preaching of the gospel" (McNaspy 1982:9). The settlements eventually numbered more than thirty cities.

Wherever it could be found, the path to power was seen as the path to the world's heart. And that path was more often urban: "for the greater glory of God and the more universal good."

More recent evangelical missions have adopted the same intentional commitment to the city. In 1980 the World Missions Department of the Pentecostal Holiness Church determined to focus its global ministry on world-class cities. Within a decade it had churches or church-planting teams in forty-one major cities. Out of its perceived understanding of the Pauline focus "on establishing strong churches in urban centers," it has restructured its focus and training strategy (Underwood 1990:26). From that commitment was born the London-based Centre for International Christian Ministries (CICM), with emphasis on equipping urban church planters, both national leaders and missionary teams. A spinoff of the CICM program soon carried the training program to Latin America, and similar programs have been initiated in Asia and Africa. The goal for 2000 was "to have strong churches in at least 100 world class cities. . . . Twenty-two of these will be targeted by the U.S. missions department, and the others by our brothers in other nations" (Underwood 1990:33).

A similar vision has directed the thinking of Mission to the World (MTW), an agency of the Presbyterian Church in America born in 1973. Its stated purpose, unchanged through the years, is "to reach the world's unreached, responsive peoples with God's Good News." This it seeks to do through concentrating its church-planting teams in major urban centers of the world. By 1989 it had teams in twelve major cities in ten nations. By 1996 sixty-one nations and their cities had been targeted for urban ministry.

Several unique features of MTW's urban mission strategy continue to shape their program. The teams operate under a closure policy that seeks to plant a presbytery (or regional church) in each target city. With the formation of the presbytery, made up of five to six established churches with pastors and trained leaders in place, the missionaries are redeployed to new target cities. In addition, there is a special emphasis on reaching middle to upper classes. This segment of the urban population, MTW argues, forms a large percentage of the world's unreached, and from them come the major decision-makers in business and government. History also shows them congenial to the cultural assumptions of Presbyterianism.

Tackling an entire city with a similar initial interest in the middle class has been an exciting experiment of the Christian and Missionary Alliance (C&MA) and its campaign Lima al Encuentro con Dios (LED). "According to Peruvian standards, 20% of Lima's population is middle class. And it is this same 20%," wrote missionary commentator Fred Smith in 1983, "that produces over 40% of the GNP. . . . They are also the reaping ground for an abundant harvest of souls. In the last decade, this social class has been the well-spring of unparalleled church growth in Peru" (F. Smith 1983:20).

That reaping history, and the emergence of the LED movement, began in 1970 in a C&MA congregation in Lima's central district, Lince. Begun in 1958 with twenty-five members, the congregation had purchased an old mansion on one of Lima's main thoroughfares. With a foothold in one of the better middle-class sections of the city, it had peaked by the late 1960s to a membership of 180. Challenged to erect a building that would seat a thousand and supported by the availability of outside start-up money, the congregation, in cooperation with the western mission and its Peruvian denomination, rose to the occasion.

Without prepackaged techniques, a basic philosophy emerged: "to reach all of Lima, concentrating for this purpose all kinds of resources—human, economic, and others—in one place (at first this was the Lince Church), to later reach out to all of Peru and even to Latin America beyond" (Palomino 1983:10). To meet those goals, LED evolved its growth principles—aggressive personal evangelism; a massive network of prayer cells; the recruiting of a skilled leadership core; an extended fifteen-month period of evangelistic campaigns; the creation of a Bible academy for instructing and consolidating new converts into the church.

By 1992 LED had proven its worth. "The program in Lima has grown from one church and 120 members to twenty-five churches and more than 10,000 members" (Smith 1997:251). Lima has become a model imitated (and modified) in cities like Buenos Aires, Bogotá, Quito, Cali, São Paulo and Santiago. In highly visible and accessible areas of such strategic cities "Encounter churches" are emerging; they function as flagship congregations, numerically large enough to support a team ministry and with the goal of hiving off a daughter congregation of eighty to one hundred members plus a full-time pastor.

In the process they are finding, as MTW has found, that middle-class people are not the only ones attracted to the gospel. In view of the response of the poor, MTW more recently has partially expanded its concerns past the middle class. And LED "has seen many of its churches spontaneously spring up in many of the lower class *barrios* of Lima. . . . It is also true that a good number of those attending the Lince and Pueblo Libre churches are from the poorer classes of Lima's society. . . . God is using many middle class converts to reach both ways on the social scale" (F. Smith 1983:28).

The LED movement has touched other fellowships as well. In 1980-1981 it gave new vitality to the largest Christian congregation in Caracas, the Las Acacias Evangelical Pentecostal Church. Begun in 1954, the congregation had about 450 regular worshipers when it moved into a 2,200-seat facility in 1980. Its implementation of the Encounter strategy, supplemented by the adoption of the Evangelism Explosion program in 1982, initiated an explosive growth cycle. By 1985 membership in the congregation had reached two thousand (Brink 1990:47-49)—at a time when there were only 25,000 evangelicals and 165 churches in a city of 3,600,000 people.

With a strong emphasis on prayer, a vision for mission that had initiated five different church-planting ministries by 1990, and a planned program of discipleship and incorporation, Las Acacias continues its pattern of urban concern. Less bound to a rigid rules-centered morality than most Pentecostals in Venezuela, the congregation has become a refuge to many estranged, hurt or wounded from other fellowships. Its relative openness has made it a haven, though not one free of criticism.

The church's urban interests have forged "a healthy balance between the dynamic, verbal proclamation of the gospel message, and the proclamation of that same message through the loving, caring deeds of a social ministry program. Name a big city need, and this congregation has designed to heal and satisfy it in the name of Jesus" (Brink 1990:49). Twenty-five percent of the budget is designated for the needs of the poor and hurting. To implement these holistic commitments is a full list of services: food, clothing and medical banks; low-cost medical and dental clinics for the poor; free courses in nutrition, sewing, cooking, crafts, literacy and secretarial services. In the planning stages in 1990 was a low-cost food co-op and a bank loan system.

The wreckage left by the hurricane path of urban power has found a Christian route to a deeper relief—cups of cold water offered in the name of Jesus.

# 11

## The City as Center

INTEGRAL TO THE CITY AS A CENTER OF POWER is its capacity for centralization and integration, for connecting. Power carries both a centripetal and a centrifugal force, drawing regions and systems into its orbit. "The big story of the city is bigger than the city itself" (W. Flanagan 1993:83).

### Biblical Examples

On a limited scale, hints of this connecting drive can be found in the cities of the biblical narrative. Frequently, as we have mentioned earlier, the Old Testament will speak of a city and (translating literally) "its daughters," *banoth* ("its surrounding settlements," NIV). Scholarship still debates the full significance of this connection. Was the relationship one of security, of agricultural, economic or political dependency? a combination of all of these? Whatever the answer may finally be, the element of connection seems clear (Num 21:25, 32; 32:42; Josh 15:45, 47; 17:16; Judg 1:27; 11:26).

Sometimes the connections are explicitly commercial. Tyre, a port city-state based on a maritime monopoly (2 Chron 8:18), boasted skilled workers in wood and stone and a hinterland noted for its cedars. In what has been called "a new development" in Israel's social interaction (Baldwin 1988:199), David made use of connections with Tyre's Hiram in the building of his palace (2 Sam 5:11-12), as did Solomon in the construction

of the temple (1 Kings 5:1-12). Ephesus, a major cosmopolitan center of
the Hellenistic and Roman cultures, was the leading seaport of Asia
Minor and its greatest commercial city in the days of Paul. The apostle
spent two years there, the gospel so radiating along those connecting
lines "that all the Jews and Greeks who lived in the province of Asia heard
the word of the Lord" (Acts 19:10).

In other places the urban drive for connections is drawn in terms of
military expansion or religiously syncretistic influence. Damascus, for
example, sitting astride several major caravan routes, followed them to
extend its power as an international trade and political center. Rezon,
whose two-hundred year dynasty began with his taking of Damascus (1
Kings 11:24-25), was Solomon's northern thorn in the side. The books of
Kings highlight the apostasy of the sixteen-year reign of Judah's Ahaz by
noting his displacement of the Lord's altar at Jerusalem with a replica
modeled on the one he found in Assyria-conquered Damascus (2 Kings
16:10-18).

By the time of the Roman Empire, political and cultural connections
were becoming prominent. In an empire of diverse languages, Greek
became the networking language of urban trade and commerce and, bor-
rowed from that fabric of metropolitan spirit, the language of the New
Testament. Antioch, because of its location on the most important trade
routes, served as the capital of the annexed Roman province of Syria.
"Apart from Jerusalem, no city of the Roman empire played as large a part
in the early life and fortunes of the Christian church" (Longenecker
1985:16). The birthplace of foreign mission (Acts 13:1-2), it became the
apostle Paul's home base (Acts 14:21-22, 26-28; 15:35; 18:22-23).

These early hints are found in cities still emerging from a predominantly agricultural world. They have become more dominating features
as that world of which they were a part has become more urban in scale
and have widened their power scale, structure activity, beliefs and knowledge into networks. Organizing networks and systems function as cues
that allow a person to move through the city as if on automatic pilot (Krupat 1985:70). They move toward larger unified systems, the incorporation
of human activities into a tighter, more all-inclusive systemic form.

## Geographical Signs of Centralization

Where do we look to find these connecting trails that lead us in and out of
the city's networking drive for centralization? The trail most visible to the
eye is geographical. Cities expand their borders past political and physical
borders, annexing land as they go. The United States' urban ecology
exemplifies this movement in recent history.

***United States patterns.*** From the beginning of the twentieth century

once independent, outlying towns, villages, and crossroad markets found themselves engulfed in an urban network. The local bank became a branch of a large city bank; local papers were replaced by metropolitan dailies; and local dairies and breweries went under, unable to compete with metropolitan-based firms. Where once such places were moderately self-sufficient, they now either declined in significance or began to perform specialized functions for the larger metropolitan area. Some previously independent communities became satellite towns, while others specialized as bedroom suburbs. The consequence was the emergence of the metropolitan unit. (Palen 1992:112)

In the early years this expansion took on political and legal form. In the first half of the twentieth century especially, the older urban centers of the Midwest and Northeast increasingly incorporated neighboring communities. When the legal drive there subsided in midcentury, cities in the Southwest picked up the slack and pushed new annexation campaigns, creating a Sunbelt boom. The area of Phoenix increased from 17 square miles in 1950 to 187 square miles in 1960. Albuquerque ballooned from 16 square miles in 1946 to 61 square miles in 1960. "Similarly, Texas' lenient annexation laws allowed Houston to expand from 76 square miles at the beginning of 1948 to almost 447 square miles nineteen years later and San Antonio to absorb 115 square miles of new territory between 1950 and 1970" (Teaford 1993:109).

Beyond the legal changes there were other shifts in American urban ecology. In 1920 city dwellers had become a majority of the population. By 1970 more Americans were living in suburbs than in cities. "Of two hundred million people, seventy-six million lived in areas around but not inside cities, sixty-four million in cities themselves" (Chudacoff 1981:264). With this movement came significant social changes. The racial and class segregation that had been part of earlier suburbanization history in the United States now extended its grip (Conn 1994a:47-48, 76-80). White blue-collar workers joined the elitist and upper middle classes from earlier decades in the search for refuge from urban diversity. Left behind in America's urban core to face the disappearance of an industrial complex that formerly supported them and a diminishing economy and tax base were the city's growing minority populations and its poor.

In the last few decades of the twentieth century, new spatial and social changes reshaped this metropolitan sprawl in other ways. The older suburbs had been home base for commuter trips flowing to work in the city. Now edge cities are arising as nodes along the growth corridors of highway and interstate (Garreau 1991). Malls become their substitutes for downtown shopping areas. Added to their combination of residential and retail developments is another new component, the office complex. They combine residential, business, social and cultural areas even more remote from older central cities. The work flow is increasingly internal, from suburb to suburb. Overlaid on earlier patterns of suburbanization and incorporating the totalizing trend of the urban, the edge city "more and more internalizes within its boundaries all the necessities of life, from work to residence to entertainment to culture" (Marcuse 1997:315).

Like the suburb before it, the edge city reinforces the class and racial partitioning of metropolitan areas. Edge cities are privatopias where black and Hispanic minorities are more likely to be found employed as service workers than as residents.

These changes have also brought a new shape to the old city. There is a new convergence of class with race, of poverty with minority status. Terms such as *hyperghetto, advanced marginality, the underclass* point to a new feeling of abandonment. The combination of poverty, decaying housing and absence of decent job prospects in a city whose economy is now oriented not toward industry but toward services offers little realistic hope for change.

Do all these trends point away from the city as a place of connection and centralization, rather than toward it? We think not. Even the edge-city phenomenon represents only another form for the contemporary city: a multinodal rather than monocentric metropolitan region (Beauregard and Haila 1997:332-33). Inner city, suburb and edge city remain linked by common metropolitan necessities. In areas of financial, business and professional services, outer cities and suburbs are neither self-sufficient nor economically autonomous from their central cities (Schwartz 1992).

**European trends.** Geographical sprawl remains more constrained, by comparison, in western Europe. Edge cities have made their appearance outside places like Helsinki and Zurich. Population growth has created emerging suburbs spilling past England's intended greenbelt boundaries or overpowering Germany's encouragement of movement into cities. In welfare states such as the Netherlands and Germany there are neighborhoods where labels like "poverty pocket" aptly describe the significant numbers of people living there without any prospects of socioeconomic progress.

There are also growing indications, at the beginning of the twenty-first century, of a fusion of race and poverty as Europe follows, not as a direct copy but through hidden influences, the American model. The days of booming economies and a consequent shortage of labor that welcomed international labor migration in the 1960s have ended. The western European welcome to the guest worker is vanishing in the face of automation and the transfer of specialized industries to other parts of the world. "As governments and employers cut benefits and protections, workers turn against darker-skinned immigrants. Class struggle tends to take on the persona of race struggle, allowing governments to ignore further the demands of workers and residents" (Goldsmith 1997:300).

But despite these similarities, "central cities in most Western European countries still function as dominant cores for their regions" (Beauregard and Haila 1997:328). Unlike the United States' neglect of national or regional land-use policy, western Europe's long-term tradition of urban planning for growth and community welfare has restrained rampant spread and slowed movement to larger centers.

---

**The Stockholm Solution**

Sweden's capital now owns about 75 percent of the land within its administrative boundaries—land originally purchased beginning in 1904 with the goal of providing green space and room for future garden suburbs. The city rarely sells its land, leasing it instead on sixty-year renewable leases to both public and private developers. Since World War II, a system of subcenters or "minicities" has been created on this city-owned land. They are "built one after another along rapid-transit lines extending in five directions from the old city center. Each subcenter contains between 10,000 and 30,000 inhabitants and is served by its own community services, schools, and shops. . . . Along each string of subcenters, 'main centers' are built at appropriate intervals. Each main center, with a larger shopping mall, theaters, and a major transit station, has a supporting population of between 50,000 and 100,000 persons within ten minutes by automobile or public transit."

J. JOHN PALEN, THE URBAN WORLD, *4th ed. (New York: McGraw-Hill, 1992), pp. 296-97.*

---

**The developing world.** In the contemporary cities of the developing world extensive boundary expansion, pressed by massive demographic shifts, often staggers the imagination and appears to overwhelm the urban infrastructure. Asia is a prime example. By annexing three areas in 1963 and two in 1973, the Seoul, Korea, administrative area jumped from 268 square kilometers in 1960 to 627 in 1980. Much of this accelerated development has taken place south of the Han River that cuts the city in two. Taipei quadrupled its city area to 272 square kilometers in 1968, with a corresponding expansion of its metropolitan area. Kuala Lumpur became a federal territory in 1974 and found its area more than doubled to 243 square kilometers. In 1958 Shanghai acquired jurisdiction over ten adjacent counties and expanded its size about ten times.

Tokyo's urban reach is encapsulated in the changing terms used to describe the capital. It has gone "from Tokyo through Dai Tokyo (Greater Tokyo, dating from the expansion of administrative boundaries in 1932)

to Tokyo-to (the Tokyo metropolis, created in 1943, and now the administrative prefectural boundary) to Tokyo-ken (the Tokyo region, which comprises the Tokyo metropolis and its three surrounding prefectures)"
(Waley 1997:401). The Tokyo conurbation functions as the financial, political and industrial center of Japan. One author has described it as the "city
of London, Silicon Valley, and the Third Italy all wrapped up into one
dynamic region" (Hill and Fujita 1993:9).

### Demographic Signs of Centralization

Integrally linked to the geographical expansion of the world's cities has
been the population explosion of the metropolis. In developed countries
dependent on industrial market economies, that growth overall has
already begun to slow down (Prud'Homme 1989:45). The twenty countries classified as "upper-middle income countries" by the World Bank, for
example, experienced an average urban growth rate of 4.4 percent during
the 1960s. This decreased to 3.9 percent from 1970 to 1982. Some scholars suggest that even the very high rates experienced in the recent past by
developing megacities like Cairo, Lagos, Mexico City and Seoul will be
rare in the future. "Urban populations did grow rapidly in most parts of
the world during the 1980s—but they actually grew faster during the
1950s" (HABITAT 1996:13). Population growth rates for most major cities
in both the Northern and the Southern hemispheres were slower during
the 1980s than in the 1970s and 1960s.

Many factors increase or decrease these proportions—1950s political
shifts toward independence of former European colonies; differences in
how nations define urban boundaries in the past and present; transitions
in the urban workforce from industry to services, from formal to informal
sectors; shifts in migration patterns; the impact of globalization on industry and trade.

In the light of these complex factors, some recent scholarship has even
begun to question the traditional resort to push or pull patterns to explain
demographic movement to the city. Are such heuristic devices now too
simplistic to be useful? Don't both choices demand a dichotomy between
regions of rural peasants and urban workers that assumes too large a gap
between migrant urban dwellers and nonmigrants (Rees et al. 1991:15-
29)? And given this dichotomy of rural push and urban pull, what explains
the yet more recent trend of movement from city to city?

With all these qualifications and more, demographics still focuses its
dynamic on an urbanizing world. Before the industrial revolution, commerce and political power formed the connecting center that drew the
population; since the Industrial Revolution, cities have become "not only

places where goods and services are produced and consumed but . . . goods in themselves. A city offers much more than what is sold in its shops. It offers beauty, excitement, novelty, encounters, and comfort" (Prud'Homme 1989:50).

**Sources of population growth.** Migration patterns explain much, but not all, of this population growth and shift. For instance, Buenos Aires grew during most of the twentieth century mainly from internal and international migration. But during the last decades of that century, natural increase accounted for two-thirds of its expansion. In fact, in the Latin American countries that have become urbanized, rural to urban migration has come to have a much smaller role in urban growth patterns (HABITAT 1996:44).

Natural growth rate and an increasing life expectancy remain important, even expanding, factors. In the earlier postindependence period of Africa, rural-urban migration was the largest reason for the expansion of its largest cities. Natural increase is now the major element there (HABITAT 1996:86). Falling death rates due to improved sanitation and nutrition give Asia the largest increase in life expectancy of any of the world's regions since 1960—from around 45 years in the late 1950s to 62.5 in the late 1980s. And in Latin America life expectancy jumped from 56 to 68 years between 1960 and 1992.

Infant mortality rates are generally lower in major cities compared to national averages (HABITAT 1996:43). Worldwide generalizations underline this: Infant mortality rates in 1992 were less than half what they were in 1960 both as a world average (60 per 1,000 live births compared to 128 in 1960) and as an average for the Southern Hemisphere (69 compared to 149 in 1960).

The result is cities with growing numbers of children and young people. By 1994 one-third of the world's population, 1.8 billion people, was under the age of fifteen. Eighty-five percent of these lived in the Two-Thirds World, most of them in the city. "Of the 600 million people living in urban slums today, 74 percent are children and young people under the age of twenty-four. . . . Some estimate the median age of Mexico City as being fourteen and one half" (Myers 1994:99).

Nevertheless, in recent years it is migration that provides, if not the most accurate picture of urban change, at least the most dramatic one. Such patterns are as old as the departure of Adam and Eve from the garden (Gen 3:23-24) and the scattering of Babel's city and tower builders (Gen 11:9). The old motivations that sent Naomi to Moab (Ruth 1:1) and reshaped the history of the people of God into exiles of deportation and assimilation under conquering Assyria and Babylonia endure. Persecution still drives the world's peoples in flight across political boundaries, much as it drove Joseph, Mary and the Christ child into Egypt (Mt 2:13-14). The world still feels the pressures of famine and natural disaster, the cause-effect patterns of military struggle and the displacement of socio-political conflict, the search for a better life.

**Migration's new shifts.** But there are new twists also. Ease of travel has increased international migration. United Nations estimates for 1992 suggest that over 100 million people lived outside the country of their birth, some permanently, others as a temporary labor force. Twenty million of these were thought to be refugees and asylum seekers (HABITAT 1996:22). Migration in the eighteenth and early nineteenth centuries flowed from richer countries to poorer ones; now the flow is from less developed regions to more developed ones. There is a growing feminization of both international and internal migration.

However, it is internal migration within Third World countries that has deeply modified past patterns. "Where do all the uprooted go, with or without their families? Millions head for the big towns, adding to the chaos of the ever-expanding suburbs, creating more and more 'favellas' " (Jacques 1986:44).

In North America the suburbs are havens for the middle and upper classes; the poor are left behind in the hole of the urban doughnut. In the developing world the outer rim of the urban doughnut becomes suburban squatter settlements for the poor and homeless. They cling to the hillsides of Rio de Janeiro and Lima. The tombs of Cairo's City of the Dead become homes for thousands of dispossessed. A World Vision report estimates "the number of urban squatters across the Philippines reached 18 million in 1982" (Power 1996:19). Figures from the 1960s give some idea of the magnitude of squatter percentages: Algiers 30, Ankara 50, Istanbul 21, Jakarta 25, Kuala Lumpur 37, Mexico City 50. That growth continues to accelerate, generally at a faster rate than total urban populations and in cities of all sizes (Gulick 1989:111-12).

The impact of this growth on the city is immense. Where they exist, national and city development programs, already stretched by limited budgets, are swamped by the new arrivals—jobs, housing, health, basic human services. Poverty has become the dominant social problem for the host city. One day's solution becomes the next day's problem.

Where does one begin in a place like Calcutta? It "has survived two successive waves of three million refugees each. The result is a city of 16 million—equal to the entire urban population of Australia—in which there are 500,000 people who live their entire lives on the street" (Linthicum 1994:2).

**Growth and the smaller cities.** The megacity, however, is not the only recipient of the migrant nor the only center of growth. Intermediate and smaller cities also are growing, in many African countries more quickly than the largest cities. Latin America tends toward the same direction. Growth rates there in the 1950s through the 1970s indicate that

> the population of many small cities increased far more quickly than those of the giants. In Peru, Chimbote's population grew 35 times between 1940 and 1972 due to the construction of a new steelworks and to a boom in the fish-meal industry. In Venezuela, the number of inhabitants in the new city of Ciudad Guayana grew almost five fold between 1950 and 1961 and more than doubled in the following decade. In Brazil, many towns in the Amazon region grew very rapidly, the urban population of Rondonia increasing 3.8 times in size during the 1970s. (Gilbert 1994:48)

By 1991, 46.5 percent of Argentina's national population was found in urban centers with under one million inhabitants; 18 percent lived in centers with fewer than 100,000 people.

The Asian pattern is similar. A very considerable proportion of its urban population lives outside large cities. By 1991 in India, to cite one example, there were as many people living in cities with fewer than 100,000 inhabitants as living in its twenty-three "million cities."

Industry is not always the reason for growth. Many of Asia's small and intermediate-size cities do not have dynamic economies. They display their urban drive for centralization in their role as minor administrative centers or as markets and centers of a local or regional road network. Tourism and weekend visitors from Mexico City caused Cuautla to grow from a small market town of 18,000 inhabitants in 1940 to over 120,000 in 1991. "There are probably hundreds of urban centres in Latin America with between 20,000 and 300,000 inhabitants that grew rapidly and became prosperous because of high value agricultural export crops" (HABITAT 1996:53).

## Sociocultural Signs of Centralization

The integrating function of a city reaches much deeper than matters of demographics, geographical territory and habit. Within its networks trade is transacted, moral principles are elaborated and either upheld or rejected, government is managed, routes to happiness are sought.

*Economic paths of integration.* The city tends to centralize economic networks in itself. Places like Casablanca, the largest city of Morocco, in common with Paris and London, subsidize the rest of the national budget. In the contemporary setting the city becomes the base for financial strength.

This centralization process is not new. As early as the thirteenth century a functional world city system of economics had begun the first phase of its development. Old World Europe was already searching for long-distance trade routes, and the search linked it primarily to the East through a number of centers and port cities. By the sixteenth century Venice and Genoa, then Seville, Bruges and Amsterdam (and later London), "successively rose in importance as they became significant centres of trade and industry. Similarly, the fortunes of Baghdad, Cairo, Constantinople, Malacca, and Hangzhou waxed and waned according to the importance they commanded in trade and economic production" (Lo and Yeung 1996:3).

With the coming of the industrial revolution, the world city system entered its second phase, dominated by Western capitalism. Colonialism reinforced the unequal exchange that provided new importance and fed growing wealth to the cities of Europe. The crumbling of political colonialism after World War II ushered in the third period of the global economy. National development, political independence and industrialization loomed large for many developing countries as they pursued their own styles of growth. The megacity phenomenon arose, fed by the still unequal process of export-oriented industrialization, the hegemony of the United States' domination of the global economy and the rise of the transnational corporation.

The fourth and present phase of economic development is popularly labeled *globalization*. But though the term is new, its history is long. What then makes its current shape different from its past? A growing specialized focus on technology that shifts industries from brawn to brain products; industrialization that slices through national boundaries and creates economic links that bypass political territories; a rapid system of telecommunications that reduces spatial distance between Tokyo and New York, Beijing and London, and couples that spatial dispersal with economic integration.

What is happening to the city in this process? It continues to act as a servicing center for its environing regions. But increasingly, as it takes on the shape of a megalopolis, it is also functioning as a hinge, linking the various functions in its local and regional orbit to places beyond (Gottmann 1990:13). Corridors of trade and cultural, technological and pop-ulation exchanges grow along urban axes such as Boston-New York-Washington, or Tokyo-Osaka, or Montreal-Toronto-Detroit-Chicago. London-Liverpool and Amsterdam-Antwerp-Brussels-Cologne follow similar hinge patterns.

Singapore becomes a borderless city. Its extended metropolitan region envelops Johore in southern Malaysia and Indonesia's Riau archipelago into a growth triangle whose global market forces reshape rural areas into urban ones. Hong Kong stretches its economic impact, direct and indirect, through the Zhujiang Delta of the People's Republic of China, by 1987 a total area of over 42,600 kilometers, seven municipalities and twenty-one counties (Chu 1996:465-96). A sudden drop in its stock exchange sends the exchanges of New York and Paris and the global financial network plummeting.

More and more the world's cities are being linked into an urban network upon which the world system depends. On a bridge over the Delaware River that marks one of the entrances to Trenton, New Jersey, hangs a large sign: "What Trenton Makes the World Takes." That sign could hang now and in the future over many other urban entrances. Cities remain centralizing nodes and, at the same time, delocalizing power cores; they are not mere outcomes of a global economic machine but the centers of the world economy itself (Sassen 1991).

***Political paths of integration.*** In keeping with the networking function of cities, politics takes on an urban character, and major political transformations echo the significance of the urban context. In the upheavals in Iran and Nicaragua since the 1980s

> urban actors, more precisely actors in key cities, particularly capital cities, played the central role. . . . The urban character of these opposition movements, the pivotal importance of the capital city, and the political significance of physical control over symbolic urban space were dramatically demonstrated in China. The dissidents were urban-based, their activities focused on Beijing, and they occupied Tienanmin Square, the capital's most prestigious location, for a month and a half in 1989. (Gugler 1996:9)

Why this urban focus? Governments have become larger, more centralizing and more tied to the city. The global village has become a global city. And that global city keeps shrinking, reduced by the ever faster speed of ideas, people and goods, by the increasing exchange of goods and services, and by pressures from foreign states and international organizations.

Urban political policies widen their economic grip. Cities are often empowered to administer and tax their surrounding areas. In regions of the world where industrialization by Western firms has been most rapid, this centralization process can take specific shape.

Following the successful model of Singapore as a compact city-state, capital cities like Bangkok, Jakarta, Kuala Lumpur and Manila were transformed between 1972 and 1975 into ministates under the executive control of ministers or governors represented at cabinet level. A greater measure of control over the informal labor sector is exercised. In tandem with this, large-scale investment in the corporate sector has taken visible shape in luxury hotels, conference centers and mass transit systems. Only thinly linked to welfare considerations, they appear to some to be "designed to impress foreign investors rather than to raise the living standards of the population as a whole" (Drakakis-Smith 1987:46).

The same effect in reverse touches downtown Los Angeles, now undergoing heightened integration as a world economy hub of the Pacific Rim trade. The California locus is still the center of longtime minority residents and a typical inner-city bipolar concentration of high- and low-scale jobs. But downtown office towers, luxury hotels, cultural facilities and high-income housing expand to symbolize its new connections with the Far East.

**Social paths of integration.** From Los Angeles comes another powerful sample of urban connection—the media, more particularly television. Sets are extremely common in low-income areas around the world and affect cultural worlds as diverse as Nairobi, São Paulo and Taipei. One estimate suggests that in 1986 there were 26 million television sets in Brazil and 9.5 million in Mexico, the vast bulk in the urban areas (Gilbert 1994:30). By 1989 *Sesame Street,* to cite one gentler example, was being produced in twelve languages and viewed in seventy countries.

Television creates its own icons and propagates its own meanings. In Africa it changes cultural expectations and stimulates new consumer tastes, deeply reflective of the interests, problems and ideals of the Euro-American society from which it is beamed (Shorter and Onyancha 1997:74). In a Maya village without electricity in the Yucatán peninsula the "Los Angelization" of a culture takes place as a family hooks up its TV set to a car battery at night. In hammocks strung up over a dirt floor they gather to watch the detective show *Kojak.* In the morning the children cut palm branches and pretend they are crashing cars on the city streets of New York. Consumer materialism, violence and casual sex are some of the sadder lessons learned or reinforced.

Lifestyle changes move from city to city and city to hinterland. The open attitude of San Francisco toward gays and lesbians leads the way for people to come out of the lifestyle closet in Taipei and Philadelphia. A revival in a charismatic church near an airport in a Canadian global city sends ripples of the Toronto blessing to London and Los Angeles. The outbreak of war in Sarajevo carries political repercussions to Washington, D.C., and Geneva. Fashion styles created in Paris find their way to the United States through modified patterns in a Sears Roebuck catalog. And from that catalog they are copied in a storefront dress shop in Seoul to change Korea's look.

Even ethnicity expands past its local, nationally bound character. Montreal joins Paris as the epitome of French culture, Miami rapidly transforms itself into a Havana beachhead in the United States.

> As the Soviet Union has crumbled, the lead cities of the reemergent republics have become their citistate centers. Ask Catalans what city is their natural capital and they will name Barcelona rather than Madrid. Scots will name Edinburgh rather than London. . . . In one sense citistates seem the natural entities to fully express the cultural and linguistic ethnicity now bubbling up at the local level across the world—even though one of citistates' greatest challenges is to accommodate diverse nationalities. (Peirce 1993:10)

Many of the social issues that are at the center of current discussion seem to revolve readily around urban discussions. Terms like *overurbanization, overpopulation* and *underemployment* come quickly to mind as we measure city scale. Poverty, always a rural reality, comes to the fore as it becomes visible and expands proportionately in the large city. North American discussions of multiculturalism and Afrocentrism, a part of urban reflection in the past, are accentuated in the transnational ethnic realities of the megacity. Old dichotomies of rural and urban, agriculture and industry move into the background as new polarizations appear: employment and underemployment, trade balances and imbalances, formal and informal work sectors.

## Rural-Urban Integration

Given these centralizing pressures, the traditional arguments for rural-urban polarization become increasingly blurred and questionable. Even in Africa, the continent least touched by urbanization, "the mushrooming rural township is evidence that African cities have an even wider periphery than their own immediate hinterland. There is a sense in which a whole country becomes an urban periphery and in which remote rural areas are peri-urbanized" (Shorter 1991:40).

Elsewhere the blurring is even more noticeable. In countries like the United States where urbanization has been a dominating nationwide trait for some time, the transition from rural to urban is minimal. But many whites' full recognition of that interlocking of city and hinterland is hindered by an antiurban bias. It is fed by the rural romanticism of the recent past (Schmitt 1990) and exaggerated by long-term racism, class prejudice, ethnocentrism, and fear of the drugs and violence of today's urban cores.

Even in other areas where rapid urbanization takes place in a basically rural setting and rural-to-urban migration rates are high, the dichotomy of town and country/village is not always apparent. In 1982 the Chinese government shifted its official definition of city and town. Given this plus a push toward industrialization and an easing of urban population controls, the average Chinese city by 1993 had evolved into an increasingly "semi-rural, semi-urban entity whose labour-force was approximately one-third agricultural, industrial, and service" (Chen 1996:70). Following global trends, the Chinese city now shows initial signs of sprawling into neighboring hinterlands.

Urbanization in Indonesia shows a similar linking of city and countryside that blurs the traditional distinctions of the past. A megalopolis like Jakarta spills over into the West Java adjoining areas of Bogor, Tanggerang and Bekasi. The acronym "Jabotabek" was coined to designate the new shape. Transport corridors radiate out to link Jakarta and Bandung, Suyrabaya and Malang, Yogyakarta and Semarang. Migration patterns underline the overlapping in another way. Most of the inhabitants of Indonesia's cities are close to their rural migrant origins; circular migration moves the population back and forth between city and hinterland. Many rural residents work for extended periods of the year in cities but keep their families and their permanent place of residence in rural areas. Java remains the most urbanized region of Indonesia with more than a third of its residents in urban areas. But quite likely one-sixth of its average daily urban workforce are temporary migrants whose roots are still rural (Hugo 1996:159-65).

What does all this mean? The ideal models of city and country created by academic scholarship in the past need modification. Those models were microvisions that assumed the city and the peasant village were static isolates. The cultural systems of today must be drawn on a larger scale, a scale that takes account of social and cultural linkages between cities and between city and country; one that sees the city integrating itself with economic, social, political and religious institutions outside its border without obliterating the still meaningful distinction between city and country.

# 12

# Urban Constancy
# & Change

THE URBAN MONUMENTS OF ARCHITECTURE sound strong echoes of two other significant characteristics of the city—the themes of stability and change. Urban life, ancient and modern, swings between these two poles: movement and settlement, diversity and constancy, innovation and tradition. The city as pace-setter is also the city as culture-preserver.

Ancient Near Eastern traditions saw urban fortifications and edifices as legitimizing visual symbols of royal power. In the face of claims to power by the factional elite, urban building projects became propaganda symbols that affirmed and stabilized a royal dynasty's right to rule in societies with restricted literacy (Whitelam 1986:166-68).

Israel's early monarchy under David and Solomon is one illustration. David's conquest of the Jebusite city of Jerusalem provided him with an urban border center neither northern nor southern. And in the expansion of this "fortress of Zion" would appear the geographical place of stability and tribal unity that, with the blessing of God, was to become "the City of David" (2 Sam 5:7).

Under David, and particularly Solomon, monuments would be built in Jerusalem that symbolized the perpetuity of the divinely ordained line. The Chronicler's account of Solomon's reign thus revolves almost exclusively around his building of the temple (2 Chron 2—7). Even his "enduement with wisdom is not wisdom in the abstract (1 Kgs. 3:16-4:34), but is specifically wisdom to build the temple" (Dillard 1987:2). In Chronicles, unlike 1 Kings 5:7, Hiram does not praise God for giving David "a son over this great people." He praises God for "a wise son . . . who will build" (2 Chron 2:12).

The city gates built by Solomon at Hazor, Megiddo and Gezer (1 Kings 9:15, 17), writes one archaeological observer, "are the finest examples of this important symbolism of royal power. . . . The enormous size of the gates (approximately 19 to 20 meters long and 16 to 18 meters wide) . . . would have presented striking visual images to a very wide audience" (Whitelam 1986:169). They promised protection from external threat, the guarantee of internal peace and the stability of royal rule.

As history has progressed, this symbolic significance to monumental architecture has continued to find expression. In China the transformation of Beijing by the Ming dynasty in the fifteenth century became an affirmation of the dynasty's harmony with the cosmos and the permanence of its imperial line. Peasants, lowly and unimportant, were allowed only houses of one story, their roofs to be painted a dull gray. At the center of Beijing was the Forbidden City, the residence of the emperor, a city within a city. Here alone were erected buildings of more than one story, their roofs painted a bright yellow to symbolize the life-giving, sunlike qualities of the emperor's rule. Here the emperor's role was "to stand in the center of the earth and stabilize people within the four seas" (Spates and Macionis 1982:137).

But monuments, like cities, can also signal change. Absalom's conspiracy against Davidic rule made use of the gate as more than a visual symbol of regal stability and power. He "would get up early and stand by the side of the road leading to the city gate" (2 Sam 15:2) to ingratiate himself with the people and to suggest a dynastic shift. The restoration of royal rule into the hands of the child-king Joash is signaled by his "standing by the pillar" (2 Kings 11:14), a reference probably to the monumental temple pillars and covenant symbols Jachin and Boaz (1 Kings 7:21).

Under Mao Zedong the Forbidden City became a museum open to all. Surrounding it now are the new monumental emblems of stability and change—the Great Hall of the People, the Historical Museum, the mausoleum that holds the remains of Chairman Mao. Names like the Pavilion of Pleasant Sounds have given way to People's Road and Anti-imperialist Street. The great walls that surrounded the city and spoke of stability are gone. In their place is a city-circling highway that speaks of movement and change.

"The homologue of historic castles and cathedrals, of the great mounds, temples, and pyramids of early civilizations, is the looming office tower at the core of the city" (Plotnicov 1987:36). The skyscraper has become the temple of stability through commerce. That symbolic power may explain why Marxist governments initially forbade its construction; its ideological identification with industrial capitalism symbolized an evocative stability in that system, which the Marxist system disallowed. Could this same symbolism also explain why cities like London, Paris and Washington have resisted commercial pressures for the heights of skyscrapers to exceed those of national monuments?

But the same skyscraper in other urban centers also speaks of change and a new direction. Philadelphia's decision in the 1980s to allow buildings to be erected higher than its city hall broke with a long-standing tradition. Its expanding skyline signaled a new emphasis on change. The Petronas Twin Towers of Kuala Lumpur, Malaysia, completed in the mid-1990s, are the world's tallest buildings. As they were being completed, the chairman of the complex spoke of them as symbols "to instill a feeling of confidence among the people of Malaysia in their capability and capacity." With a price tag said to exceed the entire budget of neighboring Cambodia, the towers are statements about achievement and change. Similar skyscraper clusterings in cities like Seoul and São Paulo, Nairobi and Kampala signal their appearance in the competing world of commerce and social change.

The symbolic monument thus continues to appear as an object of its power to stabilize and to change shifts—from God to government, from shrine to commerce.

### The City as Stabilizer

As we have argued before, the city's stabilizing function is religious in nature. Viewed as the cosmic center for which humanity has been searching since the Garden of Eden, the city reflects its stabilizing task. Its norms and laws, its traditions, fulfill our vague sense that there are certain rules we must obey. The city becomes one instrument to provide the stability of law and order for which we pine, the symbol and carrier of the social and cultural continuity we now call civilization.

Cities are religious constructions of the human heart, promoting social and cultural continuity, stabilizers and protectors of long-held tradition. Ancient and modern, they are designed by God as protectors of society and culture. They maintain and transmit a society's cultural character to the regions around them. They house institutions and spin off systems that stabilize, maintain and communicate a worldview. Their laws, politics and lifestyles are exhibition showcases of how they see themselves, God and their neighbors.

City and civilization are not synonymous, but the city has a unique power to reflect and preserve the culture of which it is a part. Cities are not bounded sets but subsystems, local displays of that supralocal context we call culture or society. They are links, mirroring dynamically a worldview, a lifestyle larger than themselves. They are symbolic centers that concentrate, intensify and orchestrate culture's re-creating forces.

**Scholarship in search of urban stabilization.** Research has not always been willing to recognize that stabilizing nature of the city. For the first four decades of the twentieth century the legacy left by the Chicago school was a picture of the city as the place where primary social relationships broke down, as a center of lawlessness, powerlessness, rootlessness and anomie. In its concern for the socially disorganizing aspects of urban life, the school underplayed the role of the city as a social integrator and a promoter of social and cultural tradition.

Studies have moved in a much more balanced direction since then—but not always without ties to that negative past. The old bipolar rural-urban contrasts have reemerged, with modifications, in various forms. One of the earliest efforts to explain the "role cities play in the formation, maintenance, spread, decline, and transformation of civilizations" came in a 1954 essay by Robert Redfield and Milton Singer (Redfield and Singer 1980:183-205). The authors proposed a typology of two cities, a distinction between orthogenetic, largely preindustrial cities of moral order out of which came the Great Tradition and heterogenetic, postindustrial cities of technical order and differing little traditions. The orthogenetic city, the authors argued, safeguarded, sophisticated and elaborated social traditions and cultural stability. The heterogenetic city sought to change them.

The model has fallen into disrepair. Assuming too static a picture of the city, it stumbled into the pit of simplism. Linking the orthogenetic city to shared convictions of right and moral order and the heterogenetic city to the technical order retains old polarities. It refuses to recognize that even technical order is really also a moral order. Further, linking the orthogenetic city to the preindustrial age and the heterogenetic to the industrial hasn't worked (Hannerz 1980:89). Time and history have brought shifts. "Many cities in Asia and Africa that were heterogenetic (in that they were established by colonial powers) have been reclaimed by the native population and re-defined as orthogenetic cities—symbolic centers of new nation-states" (Eames and Goode 1977:97).

In the meantime, a wealth of sociological and anthropological literature has appeared to underline the stabilizing dimension of the city and its retention of a strong sense of community. Sociologist Claude Fischer has underlined the role of the urban subculture not only as a base for diversity but also for sharing many of the cultural patterns and traditions of the larger society. "Intimate social circles persist in the urban environment" (Fischer 1984:36). Books like William F. Whyte's 1943 study of street life in an Italian slum in Boston (Whyte 1943) and Herbert Gans's 1962 ethnography of group and class in the life of Italian-Americans (Gans 1962) pioneered in pressing for a more positive understanding of the organizational role of the city. Subsequent scholarship has followed these leads.

**Clues in the search.** Within every city, then, will be found tendencies for both constancy and change, one stronger in some settings than in others, shifting in time and history. Are there clues or hints that point especially to the stabilizing end of the continuum? Where does one look to find examples of the city as the stabilizer of security and cultural continuity? the city as the protector of social traditions?

> The city is the place where man and nature meet. The city promises a way of regulating the environment, subduing the elements and allowing a certain control over nature. The earliest cities were established to meet the basic needs of their inhabitants—the need to worship, to feel protected and to find solace in the community.
>
> RICHARD LEHAN, THE CITY IN LITERATURE (Berkeley: University of California Press, 1998), p. 13.

Look for *uniformity of control,* for cities like Mecca and Medina, Rome and Colombo, where traditional moral and religious order is defended or, as in Kathmandu and Lhasa, where the control is imposed by a strong centralized political power and where administrative control of a unifying sort allows for little outside interaction. In short, we need to look for this where cities are capable of imposing some form of a Great Tradition on the rest of the national society. Marxist ideology has played that transformative role since World War II in Pyengyang, North Korea.

Look for *integration patterns oriented to the past,* for urban movements of change that are directed toward the past, not the future, cities where religious, philosophical and literary reflection is directed toward new arrangements of traditional positions. The rise of Islamic fundamentalism, especially in Iran, reflects something of that direction (although the earliest trend in Iran is a shift away from strict Islamic social control). Now it is being felt also in cities like Cairo and Istanbul where secular statecraft was embraced in earlier decades and is now being reexamined in the call for a return to Qur'anic law. Debates spawned by the conservative right wing of the Christian church on whether the United States was a Christian nation display some of these same features.

Look for *traditional leadership,* for cities where the predominant voice seeks to safeguard, sophisticate and elaborate social traditions and cultural values. Listen for the voices whose creative interests are centered in the old culture, the traditional ways—cities and neighborhoods of America's Bible belt, cities of lesser size where the judgments and opinions of religious teachers and pastors are still formative and influential among the general public, cities where the discontinuity between rural and urban is minimal.

## The City as Change Agent

Though cities share with rural areas a high degree of conservatism and commitment to stabilization, they are at the same time the source of cultural, social and ideological changes. And again, these changes have their roots in religion, the human heart struggling in response to God.

That struggle, as indicated in an earlier chapter, often finds expression in the human self-consciousness torn between activity and passivity. Am I agent or victim, acting or being acted upon? Out of the swing between these two choices comes change as humanity moves sometimes in one direction, sometimes in another.

So the city to which Cain turns becomes a symbol of safety and stability from divine curse for himself and his posterity (Gen 4:17). But it becomes also the place of human achievement, the center of cultural innovation. Art and technology—the invention of harp and flute, the forging of bronze and iron tools—begin their developments within the city's walls (Gen 4:20-22). The image of the city shifts from stability to mobility, new methods, new ideas, new lifestyles. Life changes, and it changes more rapidly in the city. It provides "alternative routes to a given destination" (Krupat 1985:70).

The contemporary city has not lost this impetus; like the cities that came before, it encourages and effects change and innovation. In the so-called Third World, cities are proclaimed "the 'motors of development,' the main agents of social change on a national level" (Gutkind 1974:13). Along the networking paths that have always linked them to the rural hinterland, their siren call has continued to lure and attract people to alternative choices of lifestyle and worldview. And beyond the developing and underdeveloped worlds, it is the same. Cities are catalysts for exciting change and diversity: "How yuh gonna keep 'em down on the farm after they've seen Paree?"

## Researching the Connections

Christian studies in the near past have focused on aspects of these urban characteristics with great profit for the church. The church growth school, under the leadership of Donald McGavran, has underlined particularly the demographic significance for the discipling of urban populations. Even his critics have acknowledged his emphases on other aspects of the social context—the role of existing networks of clan and kin connections as "bridges of God"; the fit of social and church environments at a time when both are favorable to church growth; the need for church mobility when new social settings have to be substituted for unproductive ones (Inskeep 1993:142-43).

More recent studies from the same church growth orientation have been more specific about the urban context in particular. They are stretching the old agenda to include questions of modernity, of systemic structures and urban infrasystems (Van Engen and Tiersma 1994). In making the implicit more explicit, they are helping reduce the factors of fear and belligerent negativism in the evangelical community particularly. The call for a holistic ministry to match the holism of the city, especially in the Southern Hemisphere, has fewer naysayers in the global urban church than it did twenty or thirty years ago.

Enriching the emphasis of the church growth school on the church's institutional character and ministry have been balancing studies of church growth and decline from the social-scientific perspective (Bibby 1987, 1993; Hoge and Roozen 1979; Roozen and Hadaway 1993; Hadaway and Roozen 1995). With minimal theological interests and oriented to the North American context, these studies suggest that growth or decline is affected by more than the institutional, more than the actions and nature of the local church. It is also affected by the contextual, the environment or setting of the local church. The church growth movement emphasizes local institutional factors—what congregations are able to do in order to grow. The social-scientific movement emphasizes local contextual factors—how the setting affects growth. Both emphases are needed for full balance. Future chapters will focus on institutional factors. Our attention turns now to the urban context.

## Some Generalizations

Evaluating that urban dimension is not easy. These social-scientific studies pay little serious attention to the city as a specific context. And when they do, the focus is narrowly on the North American context. But some generalizations do emerge that may be appropriate for larger geographical contexts.

***The dynamic of the urban setting.*** Churches can never escape the integrating influence of the city as a dynamic environment. To be sure, smaller churches and churches in rural areas are less influenced by this centralizing environment of the city. The tendency of long-established small towns and rural or suburban areas on the outer edge of a city's power field is toward the stability of the status quo. Rural churches, small-town churches and churches in suburbs without recent population growth are slow to change (Hadaway and Roozen 1995:63). Conversely, in metropolitan areas the city's power of centralization can encourage the appearance of new churches and open new challenges for ministry. The urban setting promotes an openness to change that can, combined with other factors, mean revitalization for the urban church.

Suburbanization in the United States after World War II was seen as developing a new and challenging frontier of the city, a never closed frontier always being redefined and re-created. Though distancing itself ideologically, racially and socially from the city, the movement encouraged the creation of hundreds of vital, emerging congregations.

But as those suburbs aged and slowed down, so have the congregations. Dreams for new church plants now focus on the edge cities. In retrospect, some are discovering that "the most creative new frontier was back in the central cities. . . . More than one-half of the forty largest Protestant congregations in the United States are to be found in large central cities as are more than one-half of the forty fastest growing Protestant churches in this nation" (Schaller 1993:12-13).

The recent explosive growth of evangelical and charismatic Protestantism in Latin America can be traced to many conduits. But surely one of them is the explosive growth of the cities. David Martin, a sociologist whose ideological sympathies are much less than evangelical, affirms that "by far the largest conduit for evangelical Protestantism is provided by the massive movement of people from countryside or hacienda to the megacity. . . . Evangelical Christianity is a dramatic migration of the spirit matching and accompanying a dramatic migration of bodies" (Martin 1990:284).

Across Brazil, for example, the Assemblies of God saw the stream of rural-urban migration feeding growth. The majority of urban Pentecostals were converted in chapel-centered rural settlements, and these settlements became way stations for the cities. The migratory flow was harvested on both ends of the urban-rural continuum. Comments one observer with a focus on the sociological effects of this change, "Poor people felt at home in the informal, rhythmic services. When they went to strange cities, sister churches provided fictive kin and served as a referral agency. Assisted by a strict moral code and fervent exhortations to improve oneself, many poor members and their children were able to move upward in the social structure" (Stoll 1990:108).

***Demographic growth and the urban setting.*** Population growth and change in the city still offer major potential for church growth, whether in countries developed, developing or underdeveloped. Several times in the history of the United States, for example, that thesis has been demonstrated.

The growth of industrialization in the late nineteenth century was an early example. The need for workers opened the doors for ethnic immigration, this time from eastern and central Europe. Except for the Irish, the old immigration stream, coming largely from northern Europe and the Anglo-Saxon community, was about equally divided between Roman Catholics and Protestants. The new arrivals were largely Roman Catholic, Jews and members of various Eastern churches.

Protestants responded with a half-century of intolerance and racist venom; nativism, antipopery and anti-Semitism took their place again in American life. But for the Catholic Church, it was a time of building with a priority of attention to urban immigrants. National parishes sprang up in cities, their membership defined by the language spoken (Dries 1998:24), their goal the reinforcement of the ethnic group's Catholicism.

Much Catholic clerical sentiment shared with Protestants an antiurban bias and saw the national parishes as an experiment in planned obsolescence. The mobility of the new migrant and the disunity of the city, it was feared, would lead to ethnic fragmentation and the weakening of the canonically preferred territorial parish (Cross 1962:36).

Those early fears proved to be groundless. The Roman Catholic Church today is rooted in urban areas, so much so that "urban mission" has become almost identified with "mission" itself. By 1992 60 percent of all U.S. Catholics were concentrated in 30 metropolitan dioceses, out of a total of 189 dioceses. Town and country mission has become a kind of atypical concentration (Luzbetak 1992:1).

Since the 1960s, however, things have become more difficult. Inner-city parishes are closing or merging. In Detroit alone, some thirty parishes were closed in 1989. The Catholic population in St. Louis dropped by 58 percent between 1950 and 1990. During the same period Cleveland lost 46 percent of its Catholic community. In 1960 there were sixty Catholic parishes within three miles of Chicago's City Hall; by 1995, more than 30 percent had been closed.

But signs of urban church vitality remain. Parishes mixed in race, ethnicity and income are being nurtured.

> They are entrepreneurial. They encourage in various ways the "Protestantization" of weekend church attendance. They reach out to newcomers by, for example, enhancing and enlivening the weekend liturgies. They seek to net-

work with other Catholic entities as well as other churches and agencies in their area. They regard their parish school as an asset, not a burden. They strive, not always successfully, to minister to the parish's high-rise dwellers. And, finally, they give high priority to weekday and daytime ministries. (Marciniak and Droel 1995:186)

Given these new emphases, prospects for many inner-city churches seem strong well into the twenty-first century.

The Great Migration, that demographic shift of the African American community in the years between the world wars (spoken of in an earlier chapter), provides another dramatic example of the city's centralist power acting on the church. From rural southern areas blacks moved to northern cities and, with the collapse of the cotton tenant-farmer system, to post-World War II industrializing cities in the South. As they did, the churches grew. Five northern cities (Baltimore, Chicago, Cincinnati, Detroit and Philadelphia) showed a 151 percent increase in the number of black Baptist churches. African Methodist Episcopal (AME) churches in these same cities showed an increase of 124 percent for churches and 85 percent for members (Lincoln and Mamiya 1990:119). The Church of God in Christ, with a current estimated membership of 3.5 million members, started as a rural church in Mississippi but has become a predominantly urban church; it has far fewer rural churches than the Baptists and Methodists.

On the whole, though, the growth during the Great Migration did not represent new converts but transfer of membership from rural to urban settings. "Sometimes a majority of members from a single church migrated together and it was not unusual to find migrants from the same rural county or town living in proximity to each other in new urban areas" (Lincoln and Mamiya 1990:120). This pattern of so-called chain migration from geographical areas in the South to similar ones in the North can still be observed.

***Sociopolitical shifts and the urban setting.*** Where the integrating power of the city manifests itself in economic and sociopolitical shifts, windows of opportunity for church growth can open. China's Wen Zhou county, to cite one example, has become famous for the size of its Christian community. A 1998 report points to about twelve hundred churches and six hundred other meeting points in the county, two hundred churches and numerous meeting points in the city area alone. The county boasts the highest ratio of Christians (10 percent) in the People's Republic, with young people accounting for 30-40 percent of that total (Lee 1998:15). How does one explain this growth in an area with a ratio of pastors to believers of only 1 to 17,647?

Part of the answer lies in the area's heritage of fundamental Christian theology that was tested through the persecutions of the 1950s and 1960s, when believers bravely witnessed for the gospel in word and deed in the community. Another piece of the answer is the growing wealth of that Christian community, fed by the development of the county's domestic industries. Investments made by the local population have allowed the promotion, with government assent, of share-holding enterprises in the region.

Urbanization has walked hand in hand with development. In 1978 there were only 18 satellite cities in the county; by 1993 there were 137. Linked to this urbanization has been the establishment of the area's own professional markets (e.g., costume design and mechanical engineering) and large-scale enterprises with growing employment. Also significant for the churches, the government has allowed the community a new relationship of freedom. Out of this combination of Christian heritage, community wealth and a relative degree of freedom due to that wealth, a region that once was called the region without religion has blossomed into what some now call "the Chinese Jerusalem" (Lee 1998:16-17).

The combination of social dislocation, urban change and church growth is repeated on the other side of the Pacific Ocean in the Pentecostal community of El Salvador. Largely a rural phenomenon until the 1950s, the churches began to see dramatic growth after the mid-1970s. Part of the reason involved sociopolitical realities. A deepening political and economic crisis had plunged the country into massive population displacement, violence and despair. The population of San Salvador's metropolitan area swelled from 560,000 in 1971 to over 1.2 million in 1990. Open unemployment affected 24 percent of the population in 1989. Armed conflict and military repression touched virtually every home.

In the wake of the 1980 assassination of Archbishop Oscar Romero, the Catholic Church was losing its institutional presence. Church leaders began a tactical retreat from Romero's commitments. Pastoral work, restrained by the climate of repression, became highly centralized (Williams 1997:184-85). By contrast, the Pentecostal churches, careful to maintain congenial relations with the government, used this time to launch an evangelistic offensive. Throughout the 1980s there were massive evangelistic campaigns and growing use of the media. And the message they proclaimed was within the grasp of most poor Salvadorans—the promise of a new day in Christ to those tired of hearing the empty promises of corrupt politicians, an alternative society with a new personal identity and a renewed family environment. The boom was under way.

Both these examples—from China and El Salvador—are also reminders of the importance of seeing social-economic change on a larger, macro scale. City life and its church life cannot be understood simply on a micro scale, even the scale of a city. There are larger dimensions, prime movers of society like war and government policies, that also affect the city. Large-scale and small-scale forces shape urban life (Gulick 1984). Donald McGavran has reminded us of the importance of this for church growth. When a society or culture experiences a shift of macro magnitude, its after-quakes touch the life of the city and church, often to the advantage of those alert to its Richter scale opportunity.

**Mobility, age and the urban setting.** Change on a smaller scale in the city also has a ripple effect on church growth. That growth, for example, is more likely to take place at a faster pace in rapidly developing and changing cities than in cities where the pace of change is slower. A growing city is often more receptive to the gospel than a static or declining one, an edge city in the United States more open than a forty-year-old stable suburb. Where should one start a church in one of the exploding cities of Africa or Asia? In an emerging neighborhood where roads have not yet been paved and bus lines are just beginning to appear.

For the same reasons, more church growth can be expected in changing neighborhoods of a city than in neighborhoods characterized by population stability. Do not judge potential for the church's ministry even by news of a city's general population decline. Philadelphia lost 5.5 percent of its population between 1990 and 1995, one of the largest declines for U.S. cities. But during the same time twenty-four thousand new immigrants arrived in the city, shifting neighborhood ethnic makeup and creating new urban communities (McCoy 1996). Meanwhile, African Americans are moving to the suburbs in new and significant numbers (Conn 1992b). These signs point to new possibilities for church planting and growth in mobile neighborhoods.

Paralleling this neighborhood shift is the arrival of the newcomer to the city. Unlike those who have resided in the city for some time, newcomers are often the city's contribution to potential church growth. Generally speaking, they tend to be more disoriented, not yet settled. They are looking for new roots, trying to fit into a setting that is unfamiliar.

The patterns of church growth among Koreans in their homeland as compared to the United States seem to point in this direction. In Korea the Christian community stands around 30 percent; some analysts say it is beginning to level off at that mark. However, in the United States, especially in areas like southern California, New York and Philadelphia, that figure may be as high as 70 percent. Among the Koreans of North America the church's role as a culture-broker and culture-buffer is a strong factor in explaining the difference.

Age also can be a factor in the city's contribution to church life. Young people are more open to change than older people and are quicker to adopt new lifestyles and ideas. There are also more of them in the city. The average age of a resident in a First World city is thirty-four. In the cities of the underdeveloped world it is fifteen.

**The limitations of the urban setting.** But as influential as the urban environment and even a wider, macro-scale shift are for church growth, they are not as significant as the local or denominational church's sense of calling and enthusiasm for evangelism or, for example, the stability, mobility and social makeup of the urban community that the local church has targeted for ministry and to which it seeks to fit. There are too many examples of churches that were able to meet the challenge of a status quo setting and turn it into an advantage. Sadly, there are other examples of churches that declined, no matter how potentially productive their context appeared to be.

The urban context is no simple, across-the-boards explanation for why some congregations, or even denominations, grow faster than others. "In order to grow substantially, and to continue to grow, lasting changes must be made in the identity, vision, and direction of nongrowing churches" (Hadaway and Roozen 1995:65).

Recent Canadian studies underline the danger of overdramatizing the significance of the urban setting. For one thing, Canada's urban history is more stable than its counterpart in the United States, and any comparison with its rural and suburban areas is less sharp and problematic. In contrast to the antiurban mentality of the United States, Canadians in general find urban living highly satisfying (Goldberg and Mercer 1986:140). The Canadian central city has not witnessed the suburban flight of middle-income families to the same degree as the U.S. city. Unlike those in the United States, Canada's central cities have on average been growing through the 1980s, retaining in the process the traditional family household and an employment base that brings earnings only slightly divergent from those of surrounding suburbs. With a higher proportion of foreign-born residents than the United States but a considerably lower ratio of nonwhites, Canada speaks more easily of multiculturalism than of a melting-pot culture (Goldberg and Mercer 1986:252).

Linked to that, since at least the early 1950s, membership and attendance in Canadian churches has been steadily declining in both city and country. In 1987 Reginald Bibby, the most well-known chronicler of the social history of Canada's churches, commented, "The differences in commitment many people expect to find between big city and farm simply do not exist. Canadians living in communities large and small show remarkably similar tendencies to believe, practise, experience, and know . . . Devotional life, to the extent that it exists, is just as common in the modern high-rise as in the country farmhouse" (Bibby 1987:92). Since writing those words, Bibby has made some pessimistic revisions. Canadians, he has determined, are not in the market for churches. The majority "want little of what the churches have to offer" (Bibby 1993:177).

What of the considerable number whom Bibby described as highly selective consumers searching for fragmented answers to the religious meaning and mystery of life—those looking for answers to the questions we posed in chapter nine? Questions like, What is the relation between the urban cosmos and myself? between the sense of norm and myself? between myself and the mysterious riddle of my existence? This group has stopped looking in the church. The religious memory is still strong; the search for truth and meaning continues. Canadians remain open to explanations of a supernatural variety as they try to figure out life. But the church is no longer the place to search for those answers. "It's as if McDonald's or Wendy's and Burger King are all going under at a time in history when Canadians love hamburgers" (Bibby 1993:179).

Has this change affected urban and rural patterns of church participation and membership? Active involvement is definitely lower in Canada's larger cities than in the smaller communities. In Montreal, Toronto and Vancouver, Canada's three largest cities, the proportion of active church affiliates in 1990 was about one-half the figure for communities smaller than ten thousand in population. However, the proportion of marginal affiliates and inactive affiliates is similar, regardless of community size (Bibby 1993:173-74).

Far more significant than urban size in Canada are regional differences:

> Active affiliates tend to be proportionately highest in the Atlantic region, at 40%; elsewhere, the actives make up about 20% of regional populations. Marginal affiliation decreases from east to west, dipping to just 11% in B.C. [British Columbia], with inactive affiliation increasing from east to west. Both disaffiliation and nonaffiliation are higher in B.C. than anywhere else. (Bibby 1993:173).

The lesson? Don't rely simply on an urban incubator to hatch—or dispatch—your ecclesiastical chickens.

# 13

## The Contemporary
## Church Responds

THE PICTURE DRAWN OF THE CITY THUS FAR suggests the beginnings of a tentative definition. We offer this functional one: *the city is a relatively large,
dense and socially heterogeneous center of integrative social power, capable
of preserving, changing and interpreting human culture both for and against
God's divine purpose.*

The last three chapters have focused attention on how the functions of
the urban process in power gathering, centralizing, innovating and stabilizing affect the church. In this chapter we turn over the page and look at
the church's deliberate response to the city. How has the contemporary
church reacted to this display case of sin and grace, blessing and judgment?

### The Urban Reticence of the Church

The church's positive response to the city has not always been aggressive
or appropriate. Sometimes the city can be overpowering. Perry Norton, a
city planner, describes the reactions of pastors to his conferences
designed to help participants see the urban social mirror. For these series
he constructed a mythical metropolis called Metabagdad. "We prepared a
series of maps showing such things as the major highway and street patterns, and the location of major land uses: housing, industry, commerce,
and social institutions. . . . Not only did the metropolis span parts of two

states; it was made up of several cities and towns, located within several counties" (Norton 1964:44).

Since the conference participants were mostly clergy, Norton also described the position of the church in the community and its relation to it. Local parishes were described, caught up in localized parochial concerns. A monumental problem, he writes, was imposed by the fact that the imaginary city covered several dioceses, districts and conferences.

Three reactions came from the clergy as they looked at the model. Some saw it as a staggering but liberating opportunity. From the experience they drew a new understanding of their community and a new vision for ministry. Others retreated from the picture, seeing the problems as too big, too complex for an autonomous and independent ministry. How was a local congregation to cope with the integrating unity of the metropolitan whole? The third reaction was the most severe: belligerent rejection, not simply fear and insecurity. Was the conference model demanding political action of the church? "Let the church be the church," responded this third group.

Undoubtedly these three reactions reflected theological differences. Mental models of the role of the church in ministry can define phrases like "Let the church be the church" in directions other than the caricature of a pietistic folk religion that Norton himself suggests. For churches with a one-sided commitment to sociopolitical action, the phrase can become an expression of that self-understanding. Perceptions of the church as one local, autonomous congregation can limit the reach of the church to one local, autonomous community. Also influencing theological paradigms can be the setting in which the model finds its home.

**Problems from the past.** The handicap of an ecclesiastical rural past has sometimes been an obstacle. Catholic bishop Decio Pereira comments on the church of the 1990s in São Paulo, "The church is used to working in a rural setting. . . . In the village the church is the center of everything. We transferred the rural parish to the city, [but] it is not a sufficient instrument. . . . We don't have very strong or clear models of what a ministry for the city itself would be" (Berryman 1996:15).

The same frustration is expressed by Peter Kaldor in his review of the church facing urbanization in Australia. The Christian heritage, he remarks, has for so long been based on rural life there that the emergent pattern is "a village church in an urban prison," outreach more resembling "in-drag." "Many church traditions have been based around models for the small static *village community.* They assume an essentially 'Christian' community, a good base of people for whom church-going is a natural habit, the church as a central part of the social matrix and the minister/priest/pastor a respected local figure. . . . By contrast the processes of urbanisation have produced quite a different social order" (Kaldor 1987:97).

Spot checks from Africa point in the same direction. A missionary instructor on the faculty of the ECWA Seminary in Jos, Nigeria, begins to ask why many urban church plants never make it past the first-year stage of development. Part of the difficulty, he comes to realize, "was that many of Nigeria's urban church planters come from village backgrounds. They still operate with rural worldviews" (Fritz 1993:52). Part of the answer? Join seminary, mission and denomination in an urban church-planting program that will train rural pastors to be urban pastors, to understand the urban context.

Kenya's contemporary church history duplicates the picture. "Even as cities began to grow, no available evidence indicates any sensitivity in developing leaders for effective urban ministry. . . . In research done on Nairobi city recently, the findings indicated that less than one percent of the clergy persons serving various churches had formal-orientation to urban complexity and ministry" (Mutunga 1993:162-63).

**Hopeful signs of changing attitudes.** At the same time, countering this urban hesitancy are growing signs of urban awareness in the church. In the United States the Southern Baptist Convention has taken the denominational lead in the planting and growth of urban and ethnic churches. In 1970, under the leadership of Oscar Romo, its Home Mission Board began the shift to what it came to call "a philosophy of church-centered contextualization in ministry." From approximately 1,000 congregations among 20 ethnic groups in 1970, it grew to 2,074 by 1980 and 6,558 by 1993. Within a five-year period, 75 new ethnic congregations were initiated in Houston. By 1998 there were 650 congregations among the Vietnamese, Laotians, Cambodians and Hmong. "Today," commented Peter Wagner in 1979, "Southern Baptists are probably five to ten years ahead of most other denominations in perceiving the true spiritual needs of Americans who are unmelted" (Wagner 1979:201).

On a wider geographical scale, Latin America Mission launched its program Christ for the City (CFC) in 1983. Initially aiming at ten Latin American cities, including Miami, Florida, it aimed to promote and initiate programs fostering the evangelization of Latin America's major cities and the establishing of communities of believers. In cooperation with existing churches, the project, moving more quickly in some cities than in others, includes a number of components in its strategy: careful research at its foundation; a systematic program of prayer; door-to-door evangelism; simultaneous evangelistic campaigns in every participating church;

citywide campaigns; discipleship training for new believers; a compassionate response to felt needs in the community.

### Encouragements: Urban Training Programs

There are more permanent signs, large and small, that the church is developing a macro urban vision in response to the phenomenon of urban growth. A growing number of formal, nonformal and informal urban resource and research centers have made their appearance in the last two decades. We mention only a few prominent examples from a growing number scattered across the globe (see Blackwood, Reichardt and Schreiner 1992).

*Urban resource centers.* SIM International has set up an active model in the Urban Ministries Support Group. Based in Nairobi, it aids a continent-wide constituency in exploring the effect of the urban dimension on Africa's churches. Australia has spawned the Ecumenical Coalition for Urban Ministry and the network-building Scaffolding (Bowie 1985). Mexico's Visión Evangelizadora Latinoamericana (VELA) has undertaken a massive research study of Mexico City's Protestant churches. Out of that study has already come a church directory, a collection of urban church growth case studies, and a resources manual. Its plans for the future include an updating of surveys of the whole continent of Latin America and of its major cities. Under the umbrella of the Evangelical Coalition for Urban Mission (ECUM), England has drawn together four groups wrestling with the problems connected with its urban priority areas. Its magazine, *City Cries,* serves as a networking vehicle for information on issues of race and ethnicity, urban youth, poverty and homelessness. Operating out of Montreal, Direction Chretienne, born in 1967, serves churches in the French-speaking province of Quebec and has begun to stretch its supportive ministry into the major cities of the forty-six countries now an integral part of the Francophone world.

*Formal training programs.* Urban training components, some more integral than others, are appearing in theological seminaries and colleges across the globe. Institutions like the Nairobi International School of Theology (Austin 1992a) and the Theological College of Northern Nigeria (Garland 1997) are building urban studies into their curricula. Manila's Asian Theological Seminary and Alliance Biblical Seminary recently began offering master's degrees in urban mission.

Generally, however, most existent formal and nonformal urban programs are out of geographic kilter with urban growth. While the most explosive needs are in the developing and underdeveloped worlds, the United States is easily the dominant center for such study and support institutions. And even here there is a mismatch between urban needs and seminary resources. A 1997 survey of 169 U.S. theological seminaries found only fifty-nine of the schools studied were offering urban-directed courses. And 61 percent of that total offered only one to three courses (Kemper 1997:57).

A tiny fraction of all seminary faculty are dedicated to the complex task of training a new generation to minister with the people of our cities. Despite the progress of the past two decades, it is sobering to be reminded that two-thirds of all seminaries in the U.S. still fail to offer (much less require) even one course directly concerned with urban ministry (Kemper 1997:67).

**Nonformal programs.** Nonformal programs supplement these U.S. programs in a rich way.

> Many are emerging within specific culture groups, determining their own needs, teaching their own courses and offering their own certification. . . . Seminars and workshops are growing forms of non-formal training. The Christian Community Development Association (CCDA) organizes conferences throughout the country, as well as an annual convention attracting some 3,000 urban ministers and students. The Hispanic Association of Bilingual Bicultural Ministries (HABBM) operates national conferences, develops leadership and publishes a newsletter. (Tink 1998:3)

Significant also are those institutions that seek to link together formal and nonformal programs of learning and research. Boston's Emmanuel Gospel Center is one of the better examples. It acts as a networking center to promote ethnic church planting and has already encouraged and published a fine body of literature on Boston's urban church. Building on its wide networking connections with church and seminary, it acts in adjunct as a supplemental training program with the area's theological schools. Similar linking programs are Chicago's Seminary Consortium for Urban Pastoral Education (SCUPE) and the Bresee Institute in Los Angeles. The International Union of Gospel Missions' five-day training events each spring and SCUPE's biennial Urban Congress in Chicago both offer academic credit for qualified students/participants.

## Encouragements Old and New: Networking

The integrating network of the city has also pressured for a networking counterpart in the church. In one sense this pressure is not new. Comity agreements, appearing first among Protestant missionaries in the nineteenth century, were early examples of this networking trend. Intended to prevent wasteful duplication and competition among agencies, the agreements detailed a mutual division of larger geographical areas into spheres of occupation. The end product was denominationalism by geography.

**The city and comity agreements.** Ordinarily large cities were not considered as part of these agreements. They were to be open, pioneering experiments in ecumenism. The great ports, the presidency cities in India and national capitals represented such open ground to be occupied by more than one mission. In some of Africa's countries, that openness may have been tied to the reluctance of missions to enter city work.

But as the decades wore on, the rapid expansion of these cities and the emergence of new cities out of rural areas increasingly placed great stress on these networking agreements (Beaver 1962:282-91). How were only one or two mission boards assigned to one large geographical area to adequately evangelize a growing megacity like Abidjan? How could organizers of the agreements of concord deal with the mission boards that refused to sign them? with the growing theological gulf between liberalism and evangelicalism? with the post-World War II political developments that drove millions of refugees out of northern Korea to the south and to cities like Seoul and Pusan? What of African temporary laborers who moved from what South Africa had designated their homelands to Johannesburg and Cape Town in search of permanent work, and thus in violation of the government's notorious apartheid pass laws? The push-pull pressures of urban growth from that migration played a significant part in the final demolition of apartheid (Kritzinger 1995:206-7).

Everywhere, not only in South Africa, comity fell apart as an ecclesiastical response to the strains of urban growth. A stronger strategy instrument was needed to respond to the growing centralist power of the city. Comity reminded us that if the gospel is going to significantly affect the cities of the world, cooperation and unity of some sort are necessary. But what new strategy should it be? English bishop David Sheppard's response is still as disarming as it is inclusive: "When you live in an industrial city where barely four percent of the population takes the gospel seriously and goes to church, you cannot but try to find a way to work together without dividing the forces of that small flock" (Escobar 1990:29).

Throughout the twentieth century, the search for networking alternatives to urban comity was not easy. Many obstacles barred the path and sometimes still do: indifference to the city and ignorance of urban change; theological differences; institutional rigidity; the incompatibility of urban church agendas, some rigidly structured around sociopolitical change, others around evangelism and church planting.

**The Lausanne Committee.** But in the last quarter of the twentieth century new breakthroughs spurred new movement. Playing a major part in this has been the renewing vitality of the Lausanne Committee for

World Evangelization. Out of its 1974 congress came a document, the Lausanne Covenant, that provided a firm theological basis compatible with evangelical commitments. It called for cooperation in evangelism on that foundation and pled for a mission agenda that would not isolate basic concerns for evangelism from Christian social responsibility and sociopolitical involvement (Padilla 1976:9-16).

Later Lausanne gatherings and study consultations would underline the urban need. In 1980 the Lausanne-sponsored Consultation on World Evangelization (COWE) met in Pattaya, Thailand. Out of Pattaya's Mini-consultation on Reaching Large Cities came a follow-up program with Ray Bakke appointed as a Lausanne associate. Assigned to coordinate and service an extensive program of global consultations on urban ministry, by 1990 Bakke had led such consultations in over one hundred cities on six continents and "had contributed more than anyone else to create this [urban] awareness" (Escobar 1990:24). Supported by the Lausanne Committee and by World Vision International, his enthusiasm spurred networking connections between urban churches around the globe and encouraged the implementation of plans for holistic ministry and what Lausanne has called "responsible evangelism."

Since those years the urban focus has not diminished. In 1989 Bakke organized the International Urban Associates to carry on his globe-trotting program of urban networking and empowerment. Lausanne II, meeting in Manila that same year, has been described as "an immersion into the urban labyrinth" (Escobar 1990:22).

**The A.D. 2000 and Beyond movement.** As global in scope as Lausanne but with what appears to be a more pragmatic focus closer to strategy roots in the Pentecostal/charismatic tradition has been the A.D. 2000 and Beyond movement. Its interests in urban ministry have been long-term but a bit ambiguous and fluctuating.

Early in the brief history of the movement one hundred "Gateway Cities" were identified as strategic for reaching what came to be called the 10/40 window. In this window extending from West Africa to East Asia, from 10 degrees north to 40 degrees north of the equator, are said to be located 97 percent of the people who inhabit the world's least evangelized countries. The cities selected, most of them megacities, were chosen because of the unreached people groups that might migrate to them; they were regarded as the cultural, religious, and political centers which control the spiritual condition of an entire region.

There is a certain ambiguity and imprecision in the definition of these cities, in their numbers and how they were selected. We have a sense, therefore, that they may be largely a heuristic device, actually given much less strategic importance than the 10/40 window in which they are located. More recent literature is shifting again, now speaking of three thousand "Strategic Cities" or "Million Person Target Areas" (MPTAs). MPTAs are smaller than the Gateway Cities but places that "it is estimated that most everyone in the surrounding countryside would visit . . . at least yearly" (P. Vance 1998:1).

It is still too early to tell how seriously the urban emphasis of the 10/40 window will be taken as a mission strategy. But these cities' location has already encouraged large numbers of Christians—607 prayer journeys by 1997—to travel there in teams to pray for spiritual breakthroughs. And it is still true that prayer propels workers into the cities. Future research will tell us how true that is in these urban doors of the 10/40 window. Until then, they are one more reminder that the church has not lost sight of the city as center.

**Christian leadership foundations.** In 1978 a new U.S. model for networking on an urban scale began with the creation of the Pittsburgh Leadership Foundation. Empowered with a vision to see Pittsburgh as "a city that is as famous for God as it is for steel," the foundation took on a role as empowerment, not entitlement—empowerment for the Christian community within the public sector. Under the leadership of Reid Carpenter, it positioned itself as a catalyst or resource for holistic urban change in the name of Jesus (Hartis 1992:4-5).

In the years that have followed, the foundation has been the catalyst for creating nearly fifty nonprofit organizations and ministries in metro Pittsburgh, "a leadership resource bank to start and sustain new endeavors and their leadership. Some $30 million has been raised and invested in housing initiatives, health care organizations and job creation ventures; with hundreds of millions more leveraged into their continual service" ("Birth of a Nationwide Movement" 1997:2).

Encouraged by the Pittsburgh model, other foundations have sprung up around the United States, each with its own modifications and agenda. Chicago's Mid-America Leadership Foundation, the Greater Miami Urban Coalition, the Atlanta Resource Foundation and southern California's Fresno Leadership Foundation are only a few of the expanding number of city-specific networks aiming at engaging urban Christians in self-help and partnership activities. By 1994 a national Council of Leadership Foundations had been created, with twenty-five member bodies by 1997.

The foundation movement represents a new direction in networking for the church, less specifically oriented to church growth and planting than the designs of the Lausanne and A.D. 2000 and Beyond movements.

At the same time it carries forward the holistic concerns of the Lausanne movement on a wide public and social scale. It is still too early to tell how it might fare outside the developed world. Can its networking between church and society, public and private sectors, work as comfortably or on as large a scale in settings where the church is only a closet minority? where the financial resources that can be mustered in a U.S.-based economy cannot be so easily duplicated? It remains to be seen.

### Encouragements Old and New: Mass Evangelism

Has the interest in networking led to the formation and execution of strategy plans for citywide church planting? The DAWN (Discipling a Whole Nation) movement, germinated in 1966 in the mind of James Montgomery, aims for saturation church planting. But its specific focus is on the national, not the urban, level, and its broad role of encouragement does not always allow easy evaluation of its urban effect (Montgomery 1997:62-75). Despite these difficulties, DAWN remains an exciting model of networking, one that has played a significant role in the appearance of hundreds of thousands of new congregations worldwide. It poses a challenge to see a similar program arise with the city, not the larger nation, at its heart.

In a broad sense, DAWN's promotion of networking among churches in research, planning and prayer for church growth is not unique, nor are the urban crusades and evangelistic campaigns often associated with them. Such campaigns have had a long history. In the crusades of Charles Finney, Dwight L. Moody and Billy Graham, the city has featured prominently in mass evangelism. So have many methods used in such programs.

What is unique to models of evangelism appearing toward the end of the twentieth century and the beginning of the twenty-first? Latin America provides some fertile examples.

*Mobilization.* During the 1960s Latin America Mission, under the inspiration of its director, Kenneth Strachan, coordinated yearlong evangelistic efforts in ten countries of Latin America. The programs, in which nearly every evangelical church participated, involved training members of each congregation in personal evangelism, evangelizing entire populations on a one-to-one basis, widespread use of radio and literature, and evangelistic campaigns in local churches. The climax was a citywide campaign in the capital, prefaced by an evangelical parade with thousands of believers carrying Bibles and singing as they marched through the streets (Roberts 1967).

The impetus for the Evangelism in Depth programs died out in the mid-1970s but not before they had also been tried in Africa, Japan and elsewhere. At the heart of it all was Strachan's idea of mobilization and his conviction that "the expansion of any movement is in direct proportion to its success in mobilizing its total membership in continuous propagation of its beliefs" (Strachan 1968:108). Traditional mass evangelism attempts to multiply the audience for an evangelist. Strachan's mobilization concept attempted to multiply the evangelists (Berg and Pretiz 1994:63).

Without trumpeting or touting, Strachan's convictions have touched much of Latin America's thinking on evangelism. They colored the mentality behind the Encounter with God movement initiated by the Christian and Missionary Alliance in Lima in 1973 (see chapter ten). Within grassroots churches the mobilization of all members for the missionary task is virtually a given (Berg and Pretiz 1996:229-30; Escobar 1994:132).

**Church planting.** In contrast with urban crusades and mass evangelism in the Anglo-Saxon world, that mobilization is often widely oriented around the planting of new churches. The urban campaigns of Ed Silvoso's Harvest Evangelism appear typical in this respect. They build themselves on four fundamental principles. One of the four is the multiplication of new churches (Lorenzo 1993:181). Two years after the close of one of Silvoso's first campaigns in Resistencia, a north Argentinian city of 400,000, a 1993 newspaper report pointed to 130 new congregations (Silvoso 1994:53). In La Plata, comments Silvoso, "it is not uncommon to find 'house-churches' meeting in backyards with three to four hundred members under the leadership of young pastors or somebody in his early twenties who has not been a Christian for more than three years" (Silvoso 1991:110-11).

Satellite models are also appearing. Like a centrifuge, the central sanctuary retains close connection with satellites possessing their own church buildings and congregations. The Jotabeche Methodist Pentecostal Church of Santiago, Chile, has used this model to become the second largest church in the world. With over forty satellite churches, it has 350,000 or so members, but its central sanctuary holds only 16,000 people. The bridge between the 16,000 and the 350,000 is the satellite network.

**Signs and wonders.** Linked to these crusade efforts at church planting is a strong emphasis on prayer for miracles, healing and deliverance from evil spirits. Not limited to Pentecostal and charismatic circles but certainly built there, these features have become an intentional, permanent fixture of crusade ministries like those of Argentina's Carlos Annacondia, Hector Gimenez and Omar Cabrera (Silvoso 1991:109-15).

Various labels designate this focus of the crusades: "prayer evangelism," "power evangelism," "deliverance ministries." Tied to the traditional emphases of the Pentecostal past are new terms to designate new emphases: "spiritual mapping" as the researching of a city to discover Satanic strongholds that are hindering the work of God; "spiritual warfare" as strategic-level assault to disarm those strongholds; the perception of demonic control over geographical areas through "territorial spirits."

Publicized widely by C. Peter Wagner, these emphases have also been given wide circulation through the United Prayer Track and Spiritual Warfare Network of the A.D. 2000 and Beyond movement. They have moved far past the church borders of Latin America.

### New Church Shapes: The Megachurch
Congregations are taking new forms as they mirror the centralizing role of the city and grow with it. Consciously and unconsciously, their growth is reflecting urban growth. The megachurch phenomenon is the most dramatic example, and it is not limited to the Anglo-Saxon world.

Singapore's Faith Community Baptist Church, begun in 1986, grew to 4,500 in about four years, and this in a city-state where average church membership in 1979 had risen to 301 and where land limits, government restrictions and real estate prices were mountainlike obstacles (Hinton 1985:136). Thailand's Hope of Bangkok Church, the largest and fastest growing single church in the country's history, started in 1981 with five members and by 1995 had more than ten thousand in its central congregation alone. Las Acacias Evangelical Pentecostal Church of Caracas began in 1954 with about fifteen active members. In a city with only about forty-four thousand evangelicals by 1991, it had a membership then of about three thousand, eighty to eighty-five cell groups meeting around the city, and a membership projection of close to eight thousand by 1994. It is "not only the largest but also the fastest growing Christian congregation in Venezuela" (Brink 1990:46). Brazil, affirm two authors, is best described as a megacountry of megachurches (Berg and Pretiz 1996:101).

A new label, *metachurch,* has appeared to describe these megachurches as they pass the thirty-thousand barrier. Significantly again, such bodies are strong outside of North America. By 1991 there were nine identified in Seoul, Korea, with others in Buenos Aires (70,000), Lagos, Nigeria (70,000), Santiago, Chile (50,000), Manila (35,000) and Rio De Janeiro (30,000; George 1991:50-51).

Since the 1970s the clustering of megachurches has also been a trend in U.S. urban centers. Lyle Schaller designates it as "one of the four or five most significant developments in contemporary American church history" (Schaller 1990:20). John M. Vaughan, director of the International Mega-church Research Center, defines the model as "any church with an average weekly worship or Sunday school attendance of at least 2,000 people" (Vaughan 1993:78). He suggests that about thirty Protestant churches move into the megachurch ranks every year.

The Willow Creek Community Church in a Chicago suburb is one of the more well known. Begun in 1975, by October 1991 it had added a fourth weekend service and brought its weekly attendance to over fourteen thousand (Pritchard 1994:3). Like the two-thousand-member Calvary Church in Grand Rapids, Michigan, Willow Creek has attracted attention because of its association with the seeker-sensitive style of worship, a mission strategy oriented to the unchurched (Dobson 1993; Strobel 1993). But this strategy, as popular as it seems to be growing, is not by any means that of the majority of U.S. megachurches.

Careful research into the megachurch, even the U.S. megachurch, is still needed. How accurate are the statistics? How many of the members are new converts? How true is the frequently heard criticism that many come from other fellowships, drawn by the pull of size, thus weakening smaller congregations? Is the back door of the megachurch as large as or larger than its front door?

As important as these questions are, they are not the ones we wish to ask now. We ask, What is the connection between the growth of the megachurch phenomenon and the city? Is megasize a significant strategy characteristic, a model or paradigm, or simply a descriptive urban reality? or both?

It appears that the megachurch reflects a change of shape for the church in the cities, oriented to a regional, not a local, area. Its relation to changes in American urban ecology illustrates what we mean.

As noted before, population mobility shifts are reshaping connections between city, suburb and edge city in the United States. These demographic adjustments are affecting the church and its targeted context. The megachurch's center of ministry appears to be shifting from a local neighborhood to a larger and more regional area, neither urban nor suburban but metropolitan. Many express that broad regional focus by relocating either near to or directly on a major avenue and/or interstate interchange. Older churches, particularly those appealing to an African American constituency, remain in the center of the city but show the same mega-growth traits. The community church has become a delocalized regional church. And the regional church, now defining its neighborhood not by space but by how long it takes to get there by public or private transportation, becomes a megachurch. In this way the megachurch, and even the long-established central city church, has been able to grow larger—and younger also. It draws from a larger area.

The same appears true for the megachurch outside the United States. "While most smaller churches tend to represent, at most, two or three neighborhoods, megachurches are most often regional churches" (Vaughan 1993:105). The Hope of Bangkok Church, through its care group structure, builds bridges into every subdistrict of the city. The Full Gospel Central Church on Yoido Island in Seoul, Korea, grew to more than 650,000 participants by the end of the 1980s, making it the largest congregation in the world. Its vast network of home cell groups, led by some fifty-five thousand home-group leaders, spreads its reach as a congregation throughout the entire city of Seoul. Its "care delivery system" of cell groups expands its target borders citywide and at the same time, in the eyes of its members, reduces church to no more than ten or twenty people.

This does not mean that megachurches never plan, or never should plan, for megasize. Metachurch discussions, to cite one example, are more than simply descriptive analyses and more even than a modeled response to large church problems. By reconceptualizing the church into a combination of cell groups and united times of celebratory worship, the metachurch model seeks to encourage greater growth. The intentional focus on small groups is seen as a key to strategic growth (George 1991).

In addition, in global settings where the church is perceived as a small minority, many see the megachurch as an asset to social identity and self-awareness. In Thailand, where the general Christian community represents only 1 percent of the population, the founder of the Hope of Bangkok Church saw the larger urban church as a significant planning target. "Thais by nature enjoy big, exciting, festival events. . . . In this culture, a church must be perceived as being big enough to warrant their interest. A big urban church is necessary to work in Bangkok successfully. We need to make the church visible so that it can attract people's interest and confidence" (Chareonwongsak 1997:214).

**Adjusting Church Shapes: The House Church/Cell Group**
Sometimes linked integrally to the megachurch and sometimes moving in its own direction is still another urban church phenomenon. On its own and linked to a specific neighborhood, it is called the house church. Tied more closely to a larger body or congregation, the name changes to cell group or discipleship group. Thriving now in England's urban centers among the poor, and largely displacing traditional programs in church

life, the house churches bear still different titles: "root groups," "family fellowships," "vine groups," "communities of faith," "grassroot communities" (Marchant 1985:96). Adding a deep commitment to social change within the Roman Catholic Church of Latin America, they are known as "base ecclesial communities" (Cook 1985).

Able to surmount the property barrier, the house church offers a model of the church that does not necessarily demand a professional ministry or require expensive buildings in cities where land prices can be prohibitive. They create a shared ministry, drawing out gifts as they reduce the dimensions of church to the proportions of an extended household.

Their concern for simplicity can lapse into pietism; their localized nature can yield to the temptation of isolationism. Out of the informality of worship can come a reluctance to face structural and institutional demands. But for all the problems, "the house churches are a rejection of nominalism. The social advantages of belonging are not obvious and the degree of commitment is high. Paradoxically it is an alternative for Christians who feel the church is not asking enough of them" (Millikan 1981:95). As a visual aid to the gospel, the house church is an evangelistic door to the seeker. Because it is of them and for them, its appeal particularly touches the working class and the urban poor. In cities where family cars are virtually nonexistent and public transportation spotty, the house church offers still another advantage—a church within walking distance.

These virtues can be strong assets particularly in settings like Australia. Here where most have no active connection with church life, the working class see the established church as stuffy and uncomfortable and its clergy as weak, impotent and tea party "wowsers." The house church becomes a welcome alternative. It presents an open model close to the reality of everyday life. Its loose structure and lack of ecclesiastical jargon more quickly touches the hearts of those who have slipped through the cracks of a formal fellowship (Kaldor and Kaldor 1988:94-98).

The house church does not always thrive in the city. Macro political pressures can sometimes get in the way. In the People's Republic of China of the 1990s, for example, the registered churches, more centralized and facing less overt government pressure, are said to find it easier to be urban-based. By comparison, house churches, their ecclesiology shaped around a more "diffused network, with no professional clergy and an experiential, perhaps charismatic, style of worship," move more freely in rural areas (Hunter and Chan 1993:138-39).

In lands overwhelmingly Muslim, the church faces similar obstructions on the macro level. In such hostile environments the house church has been commended as an asset. As the center of social activity, the home of the believer provides privacy and requires no additional financial expenditure (Parshall 1980:229). Problems still remain. Converts are not keen to volunteer their homes because of fear of social reprisal from Muslims or betrayal by those attending who may still be Muslims.

But unlike the Chinese city, where political and theological problems of registration are obstacles to the house church, the Muslim city offers some advantages to the model. Cities offer a greater degree of freedom than village or country, where close-knit social and kin ties tend to discourage change and experimentation. In Algiers, an Arab Muslim city of over two million people, relatively liberal policies permit greater freedom for house churches than groups outside the capital enjoy (Livingstone 1993:191-96). In the cities also are the "transitionals," a people in motion, born in villages but now living in urban centers. In places like Lebanon, Jordan and Egypt, this social group is found to be the most receptive to Christianity (Matheny 1981:5-6).

Large churches have not left the small group behind. In fact, argues John Vaughan, "the large churches that survive achieve and sustain their growth through effective subgroupings" (Vaughan 1984:264). Supplementing the ministry of the large congregation, the house church is a small, home-based group feeding, and being fed by, the time of public worship. In the even larger megachurch/metachurch, its link with corporate celebration becomes even more significant.

The traditional church paradigm, generally speaking, places its emphasis on the congregation as the front door to fellowship, ministry and evangelism and the ordained clergy as the caregivers. Discipleship is a training process heavily oriented to the time of public worship. In the mega- and metachurch model the small group provides a sense of belonging for newcomers and a side-door entrance to the church. The assimilation process moves from the small or cell group to the time of corporate celebration, not the reverse as in traditional bodies. Care-giving and discipling are in the hands of the small group, with an emphasis on the laity as the instruments of that nurturing (George 1991:70-81). In the small group one finds a stronger measure of accountability, greater flexibility and a deeper rooting in the local community and culture that is missing from the regional focus of the megachurch (Toh 1990:49-51).

With a similar concern for citywide evangelism and for the significance of the small group and its connection to corporate celebration, Ralph Neighbour Jr. puts still another spin on the word *church* and on the small group. He prefers to use the term *church* for the cell groups and to see Sunday corporate worship as a gathering of the "cell group churches." Neighbour sees megachurches as contemporary supermarkets for churchgoers, program-based designs that are ultimately inefficient. Building on what he perceives as the *oikos* or house church model of the New Testament, he sees the cell (or shepherd group) as the basic building block of society and the church (Neighbour 1990:114).

Whether Neighbour's arguments for a sharp difference between megachurch and cell church are accurate is not always easy to tell. His paradigm also calls for times of joint celebratory worship. And the examples he provides of cell churches like Seoul's Full Gospel Central Church (Neighbour 1990:23-25) are also used as examples by supporters of the megachurch (Vaughan 1993:50) and the metachurch (George 1991:22). His label "cell group church" at least has the advantage of focusing on the church's structure and not on its size.

### Reproducing Church Shapes: The Flagship Church

Making use of the integrating function of the city is still another twist in the urban church. It is not a characteristic of every megachurch, nor is it limited to the megachurch only. Here the church serves as a launching pad for new church plants. Built on the proven convictions that new churches generally grow faster than older ones (Hadaway 1987) and that new churches are the best way to win new groups of people, the paradigm calls for deliberate, built-in reproductive goals in the urban mother church (Patterson and Scoggins 1993).

The model is not new to the United States. It was a widespread practice in the 1920s and again in the years after World War II. But from the 1950s as church bureaucratization grew, particularly in the mainline denominations, new church development became the responsibility of regional or national headquarters. This, coupled with a preoccupation for church planting in the suburbs, a growing shortage of funds and increasing desire to address sociopolitical needs, minimized concern for urban church multiplication. Urban mission redefined itself within these bodies around the urgent priorities of the inner city—civil rights and social justice, housing, poverty (Green 1996). Churches became advocates, not evangelists, and the faulty choice between presence and proclamation hurt new church planting.

The last two decades of the twentieth century brought some evidence of balancing, though with reluctance on both mainline and evangelical sides. More than one-half of the fourteen high-performance center city churches featured in Lyle Schaller's 1993 study "either have or are planning to plant or sponsor new missions" (Schaller 1993:172). Particularly in the evangelical community, the urban flagship paradigm is reappearing on a global scale.

The paradigm need not be restricted by the size of the mother church nor oriented to a centralized network of churches. Out of Rhode Island, for example, has come a pattern of house churches aiming at the self-reproduction of other house churches (Scoggins 1997:222-30). Initiated in the mid-1970s with an openness to change and experimentation, the movement has spread beyond Rhode Island to Massachusetts and New Hampshire and created the Fellowship of Church Planting Teams to promote, educate and train leaders for the vision. By the mid-1990s the fellowship was coaching teams and training interns for house church planting in places like Italy, the Middle East, North Africa and Taiwan.

What appears essential to this paradigm feature is that the mother birthing the daughter churches sees itself at its beginning as a church-planting anchor. Planning for the birth of Redeemer Presbyterian Church in New York City began with that intention in the late 1980s. Initiated with the prayer and heavy financial support of its twenty-year-old parent denomination, the Presbyterian Church in America, the evangelical congregation was the first one planted as an intentional flagship church. The goal was to see flowing from it a multicultural, regional network of churches (commonly termed a presbytery in Presbyterian circles).

The growth of Redeemer Church has been remarkable (Keller 1993:31-41). By 1992, 1,100 were attending, one-third of its members joining on first-time profession of faith, another 20-30 percent Christians for less than two years. By 1998, using a modification of the metachurch paradigm, its core constitution consisted of one hundred home fellowship groups.

Not forgotten in this growth has been its role as an anchor for church planting. By 1998 Redeemer Church had been involved with planting eleven of the nineteen churches and missions that now make up its new-born Metropolitan New York Presbytery. Ten of these congregations worship in languages other than English. In the works at this writing is the initiation of a church in Harlem. The connections between city and suburb for church planting are also clearer. Senior pastor Tim Keller notes that "you can reach the suburbs from the city better than you can reach the city from the suburbs" (Keller 1993:40). With a continuous flow of young couples moving from Manhattan to the suburbs but still active in Redeemer, Keller sees this as "a trend that will continually lead to new churches around the suburban rim of New York City."

Outside the Anglo-Saxon world the flagship model has been particularly successful. Mission boards like that of the Evangelical Free Church have developed their church-planting strategy around it as they tackle world-class cities. That denomination's paradigm began in Singapore and

Malaysia as the missions there came to grips with years of limited results. By 1972 its Singapore mission, after fourteen years of work, had planted only one church. Its Malaysian counterpart, after eight years of ministry, had only one church. A new direction was needed.

Instead of sending one couple to struggle alone, the new paradigm shifted missionaries into team networks of supportive and complementary ministries in the city. Missionaries became trainers of national believers in a growing pattern of expanding team collaboration. A six-year cycle of training, modeling and church planting was developed, moving through four phases from continuing team training to the establishment of new churches. The focus of the missionary team is not to plant churches but to plant reproducing churches, which will reproduce themselves by training nationals for the task. At the end of the six-year cycle ten churches had been planted, each church planting or in the process of planting, in turn, a daughter church (Sawatsky 1985). At the end of ten years there were twenty reproducing churches.

More than idle speculation, by 1984 the strategy had achieved modest success in Malaysia and Singapore. The two church plants that existed there by 1972 had become twenty-two by 1984 (Childs 1985:38). And the paradigm was being exported by then to ten world-class cities.

But the most spectacular display of the flagship-anchor paradigm outside the United States has not arisen from foreign mission efforts. For that we turn to the ethnic churches of the world's cities. Here the typical church, as in Manila, is planting daughter churches in strawberry-plant fashion. Like the Diliman Bible Church in Quezon City, started in 1971, it may not see remarkable numerical growth. But by 1998 that congregation had planted five daughter churches that in turn have spawned three granddaughter congregations (Prescott 1998:20).

Often, but not always, a megachurch in one of these cities, with awesome resources, functions as a church-planting anchor strong enough to become a denomination and not a congregation. The Full Gospel Central Church of Seoul, in addition to its vast network of cell groups, had planted over 120 congregations by 1984 (Vaughan 1984:271).

Brazil's grassroots church scene is dotted with megachurches that have spawned enough satellite congregations to become their own denominations. The Brazil for Christ (O Brasil para Cristo) congregation, spoken of in chapter nine, is one such. Posted signs on the walls of the God Is Love (Deus e Amor) Church, also in São Paulo, warn of a seating capacity of ten thousand. The anchor church's tightly controlling structure regiments the connections of the thirty-two hundred branch churches (as of 1993) with the mother congregation. Every one of those churches "must display the name of the movement's founder . . . and the street address of the headquarter's congregation. Even a branch mission in Central America must announce that Brazilian street address on its outside sign" (Berg and Pretiz 1996:108).

Thailand's Hope of Bangkok Church turned to the flagship paradigm a decade after its beginning in 1981 and, since then, has planted over three hundred churches in Thailand and overseas. Another late starter was Calvary Church, a charismatic congregation founded by pastor Tissa Weerasingha in 1975 in Colombo, Sri Lanka. In the period from 1975 to 1983 the congregation grew from seventy-five members to over nine hundred, a figure exciting enough for Sri Lanka. In 1983 Calvary launched a church-planting program, shifting its vision, in the language of the pastor, from a "maintenance mentality" to a "reproductive mentality" (Weerasingha 1992:53). In particular it targeted the slums and shantytowns of Colombo. These areas accounted for about 53 percent of the total housing stock of the city, and a Christian population lower than the national average of 7.4 percent (1985 figures). Using the home cells as the basic evangelistic and care structure, Calvary Church has started over thirty churches and preaching points since 1983. Some of these, planted in major towns like Moratuwa and Ragama, have in turn become parenting churches. Shifting their role to follow Calvary Church's model, they are producing their own clusters of house churches. In the meantime, the mother church had more than doubled in size, reaching two thousand by 1992, making it the largest congregation in the city.

Undoubtedly there are many factors, good and bad, that affect the success or failure of the flagship churches we have sampled: strong, in some cases domineering, leadership; financial and spiritual resources; the strength or weakness of the reproductive vision; the expectation of a work of the Holy Spirit in the life of the church; the simple joy of full participatory celebration in worship; a sense that God is at work now in the life of the church.

But few such churches, we have argued in this chapter, would achieve the prominence they have without the city's centralizing, integrating background. The city's growing demographic spread allows the flagship new corners into which to spread. The growing connections of country and city, slum and suburb, open doors for connecting cell and larger celebration, rich and poor, minisatellite and megachurch.

# Part 4

Developing Urban
Church Growth Eyes

# 14

# The Social Sciences
# & Mission

A MISSION TEAM HAS LABORED FAITHFULLY IN São Paulo, Brazil, for more than twenty-five years. Out of that ministry have come twenty congregations. But is there more to do in a metropolitan region of fourteen million people? What of the hundreds of thousands of Japanese, for example, who live in the area? Could research and observation open up further doors for gospel ministry?

A call comes to Philadelphia at the beginning of a new day: "I am wondering if you could help us out. The community in which our church has been serving for the last thirty years has changed drastically, and many of our members, due to that change and the existing generational gap, are no longer coming to church. We have a major task ahead of us. We have a significant decline, and it doesn't look any better for the future. Should we move or stay?"

Such questions are common, and we should not answer them too quickly. We will need to look at our Bible and the social sciences as we map out the future of such churches, taking a careful look at the direction in which the community and the city are heading.

Even more significant are the timelines that mark the ministry of urban churches. The American community has been in transition for over twenty years. Through casual observation and some more scientific examination of trends in the community, the church could have noticed and asked how it *should have* planned for the future. Recognizing a changing community and a thirty-year ministry, how will the church now begin evaluation? And has the Brazilian mission taken account of all the possibilities of ministry to the Japanese residing in its area?

The social sciences as applied sciences for mission are not new to missionaries and urban church planters. They were mission tools prior to the rebuilding of Jerusalem by the forces of God under the leadership of Nehemiah (Neh 2—3). Nehemiah did some careful examining as he undertook the task of building the city of Jerusalem and its walls (Neh 2:13-16). The analysis was important if he was to get on with the task God had assigned him. It was not the kind of utilization of social data we are accustomed to, but it served its purpose.

> **Going Where the People Go**
>
> The mission was to plant a church among Southeast Asians in a community on the northeast side of the city. As the planners reviewed the migration patterns and immigration figures, they decided it would be wise to send missionaries to live south of the present location. A change was anticipated; those who had lived in this area for over ten years were moving south, and those coming into the city would naturally locate their new homes in the same area. Therefore the team moved one family into the southern neighborhood and left another family in the present location long considered their community. Without examining mobility patterns, the mission team would have sent its families to an area that would probably be vacated within the next five years.

A parallel process often happens in our communities, especially when indigenous leaders are expanding their ministries or relocating. They begin with a very informal observation that is helpful to them and the building and establishment of their work. Applied science is simply knowledge made useful to people (Landis 1992:9).

In its simplest form the definition for social sciences is

> all those disciplines that apply scientific methods to the study of human behavior. The social sciences include sociology, cultural anthropology, psychology, economics, history, and political science. (Tischler 1993:436)

### Values from the Social Sciences for Mission

Use of the social sciences can make Christian mission activities both more effective and more fluid. We are able to plan and strategize better when we gain an accurate understanding of the dynamics of culture and geography in an area. And a fluid policy enables us to evaluate the process and direction of a mission and make essential changes.

*Research for mission.* "Effective research enables a Christian worker to achieve specific goals that promote God's kingdom in the shortest possible period of time" (Monsma 1992:61). Using information from the social sciences helps us achieve kingdom goals—but more than that, the social sciences enhance the way our goals are initially set.

Larry L. Rose and C. Kirk Hadaway open their book *The Urban Challenge* with the statement "The United States has long been an urban nation." They go on to note, "The 1980 census revealed that three fourths of the United States population live in metropolitan centers, and many more live in smaller cities and towns" (Rose and Hadaway 1982:9). How important was this information? It was the gathering of such statistical data that helped the authors understand the context to which the American church will have to respond in the present and in the future. The challenges are clear. The cities are growing, and new people groups are migrating to the United States, primarily from Asia and Latin America. They will insist on citizenship and equal benefits but will have less interest in assimilation. The United States will now be their home and country. So the authors wisely provide models of ministry that can enhance the work of inner-city churches facing these changing demographics.

> **Changing to Meet Needs**
> The church had been ministering through its healthcare agency for many years, primarily to the elderly. Over the last ten years changes in demographics indicated that many young people under the age of fifteen were occupying the neighborhood. It was also obvious that many teens were pregnant without any support or healthcare. Statistics indicated that major needs now revolved around teen pregnancies. A pediatrician was called in to serve, and the clinic adjusted its schedule and approaches to minister to this new group of young families.

Patterns of migration, high fertility and low mortality show us where populations are expanding and provide us with the parameters for coming to grips with the challenge of the Great Commission in the city. God is concerned about the masses of people and where they might be engaged with the gospel of Jesus Christ.

In Brazil, Christian scholars have found that people in the upper-lower class and the lower-middle class levels "are the most solidly receptive to Christ and the most consistent in subsequent faithfulness" (Shipp 1986:139). This receptivity can be attributed in part to these people's desire for self-improvement and respectability. Does this information open a channel from sociology to church planting? Are some social classes more receptive than others at some times?

Church growth investigators have used this kind of sociological assistance for many years. For example, *Understanding Church Growth and Decline: 1950-1978*, edited by Dean Hoge and David Roozen, compiles significant information concerning church growth during the period

1950-1978 (Hoge and Roozen 1979). The studies in this volume alert us to factors that contribute to decline or increase in local and denominational settings. Changes in community, city and region can influence the status of the church. Too often we explain growth or decline in a church only in terms of the ingenuity of the pastor and leaders—or the lack of it. Studies can also expose the sobering reality that "evangelizing secularized 'outsiders' has been a minor source of growth for conservative churches when compared to the influence of higher birth rates and more successful retention of geographically mobile members" (Hadaway 1993a:169).

According to Kenneth W. Inskeep, two key elements influence the growth or decline of a church. One is external—the context in which one is serving. As he notes, "The social scientist tends to show more awareness of the social context of church growth by explicitly considering 'contextual factors'" (Inskeep 1993:135). These factors include demographic information and data on how the community is being formed. Internal or institutional factors, on the other hand, have to do with the structure of the institution. How does the church function? What traditions does it embrace?

The use of the social sciences does not in any way compromise our commitment to Scripture and the sovereign Lord who holds all of life and history together. Rather they help us recognize that God uses concrete, social realities to bring his redemptive message home. Very often we give most of our attention to the internal

> **Where Do People Go to Church?**
> After World War II, the Evangelical Free Church and its immigration resources saw high church growth percentages among Scandinavian immigrants to the United States. The Christian Reformed Church also grew rapidly after World War II due to large numbers of Dutch immigrants. This growth did not necessarily come from an energetic evangelistic movement. Rather, the socialization of Dutch immigrants led to growth in the CRC (Inskeep 1993:137). Where will Presbyterian churches grow most successfully? It is important to review both the external (the context) and the internal (the institution) in order to make a prediction. Kenneth Inskeep suggests that Presbyterian congregations are most successful among affluent, young, middle-class white families. Satisfaction with worship and programs for their families were such couples' major reasons for joining a church (Inskeep 1993:139).

aspect. The ultimate result is that many pastors are left wondering if they are cut out for the task assigned them, especially when no major signs of growth are evident in their congregation.

This may seem far removed from the mind of God and his will for the church. But this kind of understanding tells us about God's involvement in the affairs of humanity. Factors such as the interests and needs of particular groups of people, decisions made by government powers, abrupt changes due to famine and natural disaster, the lack of healthcare in some less-developed countries, civil war and improved medical care for newborns all have a bearing on the direction and ministry of the church.

**Church growth studies.** Some of the most persistent and open attempts to use the social sciences came from the School of Church Growth at Fuller Theological Seminary. Donald McGavran's important book *Understanding Church Growth* (1970) brought a major paradigm shift for many evangelicals by analyzing growth and decline in mission churches. McGavran made evaluation—the use of the social sciences for examining the state of the church in mission—mandatory. In his list of reasons why there is lack of growth in the church, McGavran includes both internal and external categories.

### Internal
Fearing the problems brought in by converts and churches made up of new Christians, they set very high standards and baptized few.

The ministry was too highly trained and paid, was not one with the people, and could not be supported by the churches themselves.

The mission faced with little growth did not seek expert opinion from the outside.

### External
Church and mission allowed themselves to remain stuck in an area of low potential.

They did not learn the language of the people, worked always in English, and so established the image that the Christian religion signifies mainly cultural advance. They thus got a few of the rebel young men on their way out of the tribe, but very few older men or families. (McGavran 1970:141-42)

In most of these cases the internal, to some degree, overlaps with issues related to the external context. McGavran's analysis was not popular until it became clear that he was on the right track. In the opening pages of his preface he lays out the key issues:

> The theory and theology of mission is what is in dispute. As God carries out His mission in the world and the Church seeks to be found "about His business," what *should* be done? What priorities are correct? Among many good enterprises, which has the preeminence? Which should come first and which—if any have to be—should be omitted? How is carrying out the will of God to be measured? What has really been accomplished as the Church has spread on new ground? Considerations of anthropology, sociology, theology, and organizational complexity pile up one on the other. Never was a clear mission theory more needed than today—a theory firmly rooted in biblical truth. (McGavran 1970:5)

In 1973 Vergil Gerber wrote a helpful text called *God's Way to Keep a Church Going and Growing: A Manual for Evangelism/Church Growth.* This work was intended to provide, in very subtle ways, an approach to looking at the church present and in Scripture through the lens of the social sciences. Sociological jargon was not often used. However, some of Gerber's material lacks biblical support. And too often his conclusions reveal a shallow and simplistic hermeneutics (Costas 1974). In the early edition Gerber measures the growth of the early church with graphs and measuring tools. Much of his application of the social sciences is simplistic, and there is no indication that he referred to resources in the social sciences. However, the book was conceived as a manual for churches both in the United States and in Third World countries, and this short volume indeed became the handbook for many denominations in evaluating and planning for growth.

Following the work of Gerber, James F. Engel and Wilbert Norton put out *What's Gone Wrong with the Harvest? A Communication Strategy for the Church and World Evangelism,* directed toward evaluating the church in contemporary society and offering suggestions on how to communicate the gospel effectively. This work emphasized use of media and culture analysis, drawing on Engel's background in marketing. "Secular experience has amply demonstrated that no amount of advertising, no matter how 'persuasive' (assuming that there is no deception—quite an assumption in today's world), will succeed if the program goes against the grain of consumer demand" (Engel and Norton 1975:41). Engel and Norton were convinced that the church was not adequately understanding the needs of contemporary society in order to communicate the gospel effectively.

The more recent *Church and Denominational Growth: What Does (and Does Not) Cause Growth or Decline,* edited by David Roozen and Kirk Hadaway, is a masterful work that provides some of the best information and the most comprehensive data to assist the church in understanding why churches grow and decline in our present context. Roozen's chapter "New Measures, New Perspective," for example, suggests a fresh explanation for churches' growth rates:

> The growth rate trends for conservative and moderate Protestants are the least volatile of any denominational family. Since these two families are arguably the least culturally extreme within American Protestantism, the relative stability of their growth rate suggests that the closer a denominational ethos is to the underlying mainstream of American culture, the lower the risk of steep decline on the one hand, but also the lower the possibility of dramatic growth on the other. (Roozen and Hadaway 1993:24)

Although the finding that "denominational growth is heavily influenced by the birthrate" (Hadaway and Roozen 1993:39) is somewhat simplistic, it is still worth noting. This information is crucial in terms of how a church plans its children's ministry. The churches that provide high-quality children's programs will have a better chance of growing. This will be especially true in developing communities in the U.S. and Canada, where young couples in transition are moving for employment and lifestyle reasons.

White denominations in the United States have long struggled with minority retention. They have speculated on why African Americans and Hispanics have not stayed with certain denominations. The guessing game continues to this day, but few have taken on the challenge of research to determine the causes. A 1995 study in the *Journal for the Scientific Study of Religion,* "The Persistence of Ethnic Descent: Dutch Clergy in the Reformed Church in America," by Roger J. Nemeth and Donald A. Luidens, provides helpful insights into the issue. For example:

> Although immigrant churches were important to this generation, religious ties generally were less important than ethnic ties. For the second generation, assimilation and accommodation into the American mainstream were of utmost importance. This generation rejected the ethnic group and the immigrant church as foreign. Those of the third generation, however, did not need to prove they were American. They could afford to revive cultural folkways and religious beliefs and practices without the threat of being labeled "un-American." (Nemeth and Luidens 1995:200)

Another interesting discovery was that the persistent social structures—which included where ministers were educated and where they lived—favored Dutch rather than non-Dutch clergy (Nemeth and Luidens 1995:205). Opportunities for advancement and recognition were promoted within the Dutch constituency. The study also noted that ethnicity within a strong ethnic denomination does not necessarily diminish over the years. On the contrary, within the Reformed Church in America (RCA) the "Dutchness" has increased.

> In the face of acculturation, the RCA and its sister denomination, the CRC [Christian Reformed Church], are the only institutions which maintain a sizeable Dutch presence. To the extent that Americans of Dutch extraction wish to identify with their ethnicity, they may find that association with these denominations is the only route left. (Nemeth and Luidens 1995:212)

The social sciences provide resources for thorough research that may end much of the enigma surrounding minority retention. Guessing games will not do, and spiritualizing the circumstances will not provide meaningful answers. Social-scientific assistance is needed when we want to plan for the future and recognize ongoing trends in immigration and urbanization.

## Tools from the Social Sciences for Mission

The scientific method of investigation, at the heart of the methodology of social sciences, has been defined as "a process by which a body of scientific knowledge is built through observation, experimentation, generalization, and verification. . . . To have any meaning, facts must be ordered in some way, analyzed, generalized, and related to other facts" (Tischler 1993:8). This method provides tools that are helpful for mission.

*Diagnostic.* The words *diagnose* and *diagnosis* stem from the Greek word *diagignōskein*—to distinguish. Diagnosis is "the act or process of deciding the nature of a diseased condition by examination of the symptoms; a careful examination and analysis of the facts in an attempt to understand or explain something" (Neufeldt and Guralnik 1988:379). Accurate diagnosis involves acquiring knowledge about something that is necessary in order to accomplish a particular task. A counselor, for example, needs to know what is causing the conflict in a family. The counselor discovers the causes and symptoms through serious diagnostic work. In the case of physical problems, a patient's illness will be addressed temporarily on the basis of a brief, superficial diagnosis while doctors await results of more extensive tests.

Diagnostic tools are crucial for calculating the plan and direction one is to take. Yet diagnostic work is not only used for problem-solving or preventive measures; it is also the means to understanding and planning for mission activities. A church-planting ministry is not necessarily a problem in the negative sense; it is a task that has to be figured out, calculated as if it were a math problem, and operationally planned for. Gerber uses the term "diagnostic research":

> Research is the means by which your family doctor can diagnose the health of your body. He knows that each organ in the body has a specific function. He also knows that its function is measured in terms of its purpose or goal. He can tell whether an organ of the body is functioning properly. And whether the body as a whole is fulfilling its ultimate purpose or goal. This is done through careful statistical research. He calls it diagnostic research. (Gerber 1973:45)

Several elements are part of the process: identification, engagement and recording.

1. *Identification.* When we speak of identification we are often thinking of naming something. We identify a car problem through technical means

and notice that the dysfunction is due to an electrical short. The place where we do this may be called a diagnostic center for automobiles. The identification process is crucial, because how we identify the problem will determine the solution.

Keep in mind the general heading of diagnostic work and the warning previously mentioned—that it is not necessarily a negative problem that we are trying to solve. The process of identification involves no value judgment. Perhaps we are trying to identify the area where a church should be planted, or the how-tos of reaching out to a particular people group. Identification may involve uncovering census information delineating characteristics of a particular people in the city. Identifying an area or a particular group of people is helpful in the beginning of diagnostic work.

In preparing for church planting in Vienna, for example, where do we look to identify Viennese? They are not always found easily. Back in 1900 the city numbered 1,674,957 people, but only 44 percent were born there. Between 1988 and 1991, the fall of the iron curtain drew new waves of immigrants to the city. Foreign population increased more than 28 percent, nearly 10 percent per year. Forty-four percent of the newcomers are from the former Yugoslavia, 22 percent from Turkey. Marginalized by the Viennese government and society, these people live in residential segregation and face segregation in the labor markets of the city. By 1981, 50 percent were living in seven of Vienna's twenty-three districts.

But diagnostic research does not end here. Too often it is considered finished at the point of identification. Diagnostic work in the local church is imperative. Pastors are always identifying issues that are affecting one's life and the life of the church. The question is, *what does it all mean to me?*

Consider marriage. A married man and woman may experience personal troubles, but when the divorce rate during the first four years of marriage is 250 out of every 1,000 marriages, we have an indication of a structural issue having to do with the institutions of marriage and the family and other institutions that bear upon them (Mills 1959:9).

The point has to do with symptoms and causality. The high divorce rate indicates we are facing more than an accumulation of individual problems. How we identify the problem will determine how the solution is formulated. If we only approach the individual couple and their marriage problem and pay no attention to the realities of the larger picture, we have missed the institutional factor and some of the major reasons any given couple is considering separation. This will not do if we are serious about healing and prevention. When we see only the individual problem, our plan for recovery will be limited. This may reduce the effectiveness of our ministry to dysfunctional families.

Now consider the following case. A pastor notices several homes for sale in his neighborhood, more than is usual for that area. This may mean that people are moving out for bigger homes or better living conditions. That is not cause for serious concern, since other families will eventually move in and transitions are natural in major U.S. urban centers. On the other hand, upon further investigation the pastor may find that the reason so many homes are being sold is new neighbors. The community is undergoing a drastic ethnic and racial change, and the long-term residents want no part of the people who are moving in. The issues are quite distinct then: On the one hand, the neighborhood seems to be changing primarily due to lifestyle changes. On the other hand, it is racism that is bringing about this swift change in the community. This will have serious implications for the church and its ministries. Identifying the cause of the transition is important in order to go on with the diagnostic procedure. Diagnostic work will also identify the new homeowners and their needs, allowing for a certain amount of preplanning and strategy.

Identification is the beginning component of diagnostic work. In counseling clients may offer superficial reasons as to why they are coming to a counselor. Hearing their initial explanations is important, but it is not enough. The task of doing a serious analysis is incomplete until we engage the counselee.

2. *Engagement.* The second aspect of diagnosis, engagement, involves a more thorough investigation. Here we are digging deeper and asking questions to gain more accurate and comprehensive information. This component helps clarify the need and the cause. Engagement is the process of investigation through uncovering historical data. Understanding that the real needs are found in causes, not symptoms, we must work hard at engaging the community or the individuals if we are to plan well.

Many ministries are developed in response to symptoms rather than causes. The reason is that discovering the causes may be a challenge. The time constraints are on the side of quick answers, which in the long run only provide for limited solutions.

The purpose of engagement is to get more details in the ongoing work of knowing your community and its needs or determining the context in which to plant a new church. In the engagement process we are getting much more information than census data can give us. We are asking questions in the community and doing significant interviews. The following chapters illustrate how it is done.

3. *Recording.* Thorough recording of all data is essential; it allows us to

recognize procedure and patterns as we note the essential elements in the diagnostic process. This is more than journaling; it is documentation of research for the purpose of study and reflection.

Recording as we plan our urban ministry is similar to the descriptive work done in ethnographic recording. "An ethnographic record consists of fieldnotes, tape recordings, pictures, artifacts, and anything else that documents the social situation under study" (Spradley 1980:63). The recording in this case pulls together descriptive information of events, causes and responses, dialogue, interview text, anything that will, in the mind of the recorder, be helpful for shedding light on the subject at hand.

"Analysis . . . is sorting out the structures of signification" (Geertz 1973:9). Details are important and will help us understand the constructs of how others are thinking. Try to limit labeling. Applying one- or two-word categories is too simplistic and does not lead others into the range of information needed. Instead, give full descriptions of what is going on—the function, the activity. In record keeping you are taking notes of all the parts of the diagnostic process.

**Exploration.** Second, using the social sciences in ministry requires *exploration*. This has to do with testing for the purpose of effectiveness in missions. It has three components: models, theories and on-site evaluation.

*Models* are existing examples of ministry that can help as you evaluate your mission. *Theories* are formulations refined over a long period that have stood the test of ministry and time and have proved their aptness. *On-site evaluation* is the process of testing the doing of ministry, keeping one eye on the context in which you are serving and the other on Scripture.

1. *Models.* Models are simply evaluation tools used to compare various elements that have corresponding features. Models that have led to healthy growth in a similar geographical context and institutional makeup will be important to the development of your ministry. Denominations attempt to rely on models, but very often they generalize a model without taking note of major distinctions.

A church with a bivocational pastor, for example, was growing rapidly, and the parent denomination concluded that other churches might grow comparably if bivocational leaders were employed in all the denominational church plants. This application of a model ignored location and disregarded the differentials of context.

It is always wise to note the similarities and dissimilarities of ministries. Many of our patterns of ministry will not be suitable models due to major variations in the contexts of urban church planting. Each city has a unique ethos, so a particular model may not serve well.

One of the most exciting models for urban church growth has been the Encounter with God program of the Christian and Missionary Alliance. Initiated in 1973 in Lima, Peru, by 1992 it had grown from one church and 120 members to twenty-five churches and over 10,000 members. It became a model for urban projects in Argentina, Brazil, Chile, Colombia, Ecuador and El Salvador.

The Lima church has remained a model. But participants like Fred Smith have realized wisely that modifications are necessary in contexts outside Lima. When the model was implemented in 1987 among seven churches in Guayaquil, Ecuador, a number of changes were made to fit the new context.

The Lima model sought to establish new churches; the Guayaquil experiment started with established churches. The Lima model had a large infusion of outside funds to initiate the program; in Guayaquil only in-country funds were used. Lima aimed for at least ten thousand members as soon as possible; Guayaquil modified this goal, aiming for as many members as the existing church building could accommodate in its Sunday-morning services. Lima's emphasis was on buildings and the filling of them with people; Guayaquil reversed the model, concentrating on people first and buildings to follow (F. Smith 1992:11).

The Encounter with God program is a valid model. But mass production of any model can neglect the unique contexts of church and community elsewhere. Models are helpful but should never be carbon copied.

Models can be useful and time-saving because they have already undergone the testing period and much has been learned regarding how all the components of the ministry can work together.

What the Denver church learned (see inset p. 267) would be extremely helpful to a ministry being launched in an ethnically diverse community. This knowledge would provide a head start and a reduction in expenditures as well as in frustrations. However, remember that a model cannot be transferred without careful evaluation of the similarities and dissimilarities between it and your intended ministry.

Model ministries that have been tested over time can in effect mentor and guide similar ministries. The testing has been accomplished to the benefit of new programs. Models respond to theological, sociological, psychological and philosophical constraints.

Models are also referred to as imitations. They allow us to anticipate what may happen if we follow a particular pattern. Relevant models should be researched whenever the possibility of a new ministry is being explored. When the need for appropriate models is disregarded, teams of missionaries move out without sufficient resources.

2. *Theories.* A theory is a "speculative idea or plan as to how something might be done; a systematic statement of principles involved . . . a formulation of apparent relationships or underlying principles of certain observed phenomena which has been verified to some degree" (Neufeldt and Guralnik 1988:1387). In urban ministry, a theory includes a set of rules and principles that guide and provide direction for a particular ministry project.

Theories dealing with global population growth and change have special significance for missions. They wrestle with issues like "What will stop rapid population growth? When will it stop?" (Peters and Larkin 1993:99). Trying to answer these questions is a major task. Theories, after all, mean different things to different people. One social-scientific definition is as follows: "A *theory* is a formal conceptual structure composed of laws and rules that bind together the otherwise disparate facts that come from empirical research" (Peters and Larkin 1993:100).

> **Multiethnicity and the Church**
>
> A multiethnic church in Denver discovered over a ten-year period that several elements were essential for an effective ministry bound by the gospel of reconciliation in a multiethnic community. There was a need to be intentional from the start. It was also necessary to have theological commitments that voiced the concern not only for multiethnicity but also for justice. These emphases had to be part of the doctrinal commitment of the church and incorporated into the training of new members.

Sociological theory by definition is a deductive one.

> It starts with definition of some general concepts (and, often, a few clearly stated assumptions); lays out rules about how to classify the things we observe in terms of these different categories; and then puts forward a number of general propositions about the concepts. (Wallace and Wolf 1991:3)

Church growth theory is structured by numerous principles or rules, one of which is the "homogeneous unit principle" (HUP). This principle was developed by the founders of the School of World Mission at Fuller Theological Seminary. It posits that people are more prone to welcome the gospel and respond to it when it is presented in their own social, cultural and linguistic setting. This principle was developed using social-scientific tools, primarily anthropology, with biblical support especially from the New Testament. HUP also suggests that it is best to keep the continuum of homogeneity in the life of the church if individuals within it are to grow and the church is to successfully develop indigenous leadership.

Theories are not practices but are rules and concepts that orient the practitioner to apply the principles to ministry in order to better control the outcome. In church growth and church-planting theory, a principle often referred to is *contextualization*. The gospel needs to be contextualized in order for the recipient to understand its significance with reference to his or her relationship with God. If the gospel is not received or understood, one reason may be a lack of contextualization. This is not to disregard the work of the Holy Spirit; it is an issue of mission effectiveness. Simply put, the gospel needs to be translated into the language of the people in order to gain a hearing. This principle can help in evaluating the ongoing process of the ministry. A theory can be used to test your work.

The scientific inductive approach moves from the particular to the general in order to discover patterns. Such an approach can help us anticipate changes.

3. *On-site evaluation*. Evaluation of the ministry in process needs to keep in view both the Scriptures and the context of mission. We must be faithful to both. On-site evaluation uses the goals of a mission to test its procedure and quality as it begins to develop. This must be done much more scientifically than we are accustomed to doing.

Very often we use empirical observation as we try to determine where the ministry has been and where it is headed. Leaders of a ministry that is three years old will probably use *sight* evaluation. Taking a long hard look, we notice whether numbers are growing or declining. In some cases we even take a count of the people attending our services or small group and record the information over a period of several months.

> **Community Transition**
> African Americans are moving into an area that had been an Anglo blue-collar community. Once approximately 10 percent of the community becomes African American, we can be virtually sure that the trend will continue until the neighborhood is African American. This is what sociologists call tipping.

This approach is not to be discouraged. But we must also engage in a more rigorous investigation. In one testing process, for example, "in order to reduce error variation selection criteria were used to ensure that the churches that were called growing were really growing, and that the churches that were called declining were really declining" (Hadaway 1993a:171).

On-site testing is important because it may relieve our anxieties or shake up our false conclusions regarding the church and its function in society. Leaders of a church will tend to dismiss the need for any evaluation if the congregation is visibly growing in numbers. They will assume that everything is going according to plan and will relax with a sense of accomplishment. Yet careful examination might show that the church's 15 percent growth over the previous year came from other area churches and that the reason was the simplicity of the preaching or the availability of a daycare center for infants. If the church is interested in conversion growth over against transfer growth, then expectations have not been met. More than that, the church may be attracting Christians in disregard of other local ministries.

Such patterns are habit forming and often irreversible. You have learned how to promote your ministry to Christians rather than to non-Christians, and by all appearances you have found success. Yet this will not achieve New Testament church growth, nor will it lead to formation of a significant entity in community.

A church usually follows the pattern laid out by its leaders, and over the years a distinctive ethos builds up, giving the church its uniqueness. Too often the result is major hindrances to evangelism. Very often a new church plant promotes a great deal of energy and excitement and it becomes pragmatic, meaning that the church sees the end as numeric growth. It does not matter how the growth is occurring as long as numbers are increasing. In some cases there is rapid growth because there is a certain uniqueness to the ministry that draws people to worship and participate in the life of the church. Since the leadership has a great desire to see the development of this ministry, people transferring from other local churches is not questioned. What can take place is growth in one church at the expense of other churches rather than a concerted effort of presenting the good news of Christ to those in the community who are lost, thus bringing growth to the universal Church.

How can we determine the quality of the growth, the ministry's significance and impact in the community, and the heartbeat of the congregation in evangelism? Ongoing on-site evaluation is an important aspect of the church's life. It is important to keep track of new convert growth versus transfer growth. If seeming growth is mostly from transfers, it will be important to do community analysis including house-to-house surveys to determine the needs and discern how to make appropriate changes in the ministry to increase conversion growth.

**_The prescriptive process._** The social sciences can assist the church in making significant prescriptive discoveries about its current state and the direction it should take. Keep in mind that we seek an applied science for mission. When we use the social sciences for ministry and mission, we are attempting to predict what will occur when we apply information in a certain manner to a particular setting. The prescriptive element does not necessarily mean that we understand all that is going on, but that we consider our findings are adequate to give us enough information to make certain predictions about ministry.

A small group of young adults is highly committed to meeting together every week. The group of new Christians comes together for meals and fellowship. Its members display a high regard for each other and accountability without any formal regulations. They meet under any circumstances, despite individuals' setbacks and time constraints. The group continues to work as is and becomes a successful small group ministry. The leaders of the group do not understand exactly why there is such a high level of commitment among the members but assume that their needs are being met by the security and encouragement they experience in the ministry. They now take the next step and start evaluating the process they have gone through. They survey the members of the group and find that the high level of commitment hinges on the social aspects of enjoying being together, eating together and finding support and encouragement. The leaders also monitor the process for changes. By keeping an account of what has gone on and why, as well as any changes taking place, the leadership will be in a better position to plan for the future and maintain a healthy group. Their evaluation record can also be used as a guide to reinvent the process in another setting that ministers to similar kinds of young adults.

> **A Church That Misses Change**
> A church has been in its current location for over seventy-five years. Holding a high view of evangelism, its members have trusted that the Lord of the harvest would bring growth in the church. They would say, "People get saved when the gospel is preached."
>
> But the neighborhood started to change fifteen years ago, and the language most residents now speak is not English. There is a different culture altogether, and the people in the community do not find the church friendly and caring. Church leaders decided to use a youth ministry approach to bring in the people. No success was evident. The church needs a major structural alteration if it is to stay in that community and have numerical growth.

The prescriptive dynamic leads to the development of strategy that has enough fluidity for change as evaluations monitor the process of the ministry. Too often we put into place a strategy that is too rigid and do not allow an evaluation tool to assist us in adapting it.

Prescription involves not only on-site evaluation but also planning and strategy. When conditions change—such as when the makeup of the community shifts—we must make ministry changes that are appropriate for the new context. This does not mean that we change our understanding of biblical absolutes regarding the church. But our programs and methods may need to be evaluated in light of the new context. The church needs to ask, "How do we speak to the culture and condition of the people in our community without compromising the gospel?"

The prescriptive process is always carried on in the tension of change. Since we are serving people who live in a reality that is both dynamic and concrete, we must be willing to take on the posture of servant (1 Cor 4:1), seeking to know the people and serve them with integrity.

Too often our desire for control leads us to suppress change. We want life to move in a straight line; the future should be like the past, everything predictable and sure. This is not the reality of life. Prescription gives us certain general patterns to observe. But given the inevitability and rapidity of change in our society, we must be fluid enough to discern and accommodate.

In the past change was usually quite localized; today social shifts occur on a global scale. The Third World, the Old World and the New World are increasingly linked by media and trade, and social change is faster than ever. We may not feel we have sufficient time to contemplate and reflect. It seems that long-term planning is less and less meaningful.

We must commit ourselves to studying the world as it rapidly moves into the future. For such study we need to use the skills and sciences available to us with a certain amount of precision. And again and again we turn to the Word of God, the eternal absolutes, to learn how we should live and serve in this needy and demanding world.

# 15
## Ethnographic Studies & Mission

THE YOUNG WOMAN IN THE VILLAGE was accused of prostitution. This seemed strange to the missionaries; they knew this young lady and her clear testimony for Christ. She had been converted one year earlier and had been an example to the name of Christ. Further investigation revealed that the people of the village considered this woman cursed because she had not married. It was part of the culture of that village that a woman should be married by the age of twenty-one. Given this young woman's conversion to Christ and the teaching of the Bible, the missionaries assumed that she could only marry a Christian. In this village there were few Christian men, if any. An ethnographic study would have better prepared the missionaries to handle this type of conflict within the process of discipleship (Hiebert 1987).

Gangs in East Los Angeles use recruiting approaches that harm many of the young people growing up in that community. Great importance is placed on protecting the community (barrio). The geographical boundaries marked out by a gang (turf) are considered sacred. It is honorable to defend your community even to the death. It is a responsibility and an honor to protect your turf from other gangs or intruders.

Being a gang member is a means of economic advancement. A gang is able to provide for its members' needs as they arise. This Robin Hood notion is clearly destructive.

A youth worker from a parachurch organization had questions as to how to undo the gangs' hold. Can you be a Christian and still participate in the care of your neighborhood? The youth worker needed to become familiar with the intricate rules of gang life, gang rites of passage, and how a person might disengage honorably from the activities of the gang.

In another city, people from Cambodia were moving into a community that had been occupied by Irish Americans. The church was determined to stay and minister to this migrating group of people and felt it was important to understand its culture and how these people perceived the gospel and the Christian faith. As the committee on evangelism gathered to discuss strategy, members realized that not knowing the people living in the community limited their ability to formulate a plan for effective ministry. None of them knew how to characterize the culture accurately.

The above scenarios point to the need for ethnographic studies. "Ethnography is the work of describing a culture" (Spradley 1979:3). That definition seems very simplistic and truncated, yet it is sufficient. Fieldwork is the method used in ethnography, the process of describing the culture from the point of view of the indigenous person. Spradley notes, "It offers the educator a way of seeing schools through the eyes of students; health professionals the opportunity of seeing health and disease through the eyes of patients from a myriad of different backgrounds" (Spradley 1980:vii). The people we want to learn about must be the teachers, and the ethnographer is the student. The knowledge we gain through ethnographic study makes the difference in how need is defined and how we attempt to meet that need. It is not the outside "expert" but the person walking in that community who defines need. We must learn from the true expert.

Anthropologist Charles H. Kraft remarks ruefully, "It came as a bit of a shock that most of what I had learned in Christian college and seminary, in the forms in which I learned it, was inappropriate or irrelevant to the Nigerians I worked with" (Kraft 1996:xiii–xiv). Kraft issues a call to consider the work of anthropology as a significant tool for mission and warns against irrelevancy in crosscultural outreach. His call, however, is carefully balanced: "So, I believe in anthropology for everyone—but only as a means, never an end. Respect for people of other cultural worlds is a Christian principle. But the absolutization of tolerance that often underlies rhetoric about 'multiculturalism' is in no way Christian. The Gospel, not simply tolerance, is to be communicated into everyone's world (Mk 16:15)" (Kraft 1996:xiv).

Urban anthropological research has its roots in early studies of the Chicago school in the 1920s—studies providing a "slice of life" (Lamphere

1992:15). This early research provided information that was very descriptive of the marginal world.

The ethnographic task is dependent on field research. The process is time intensive and requires immersion in the context of the people; it also takes into consideration interaction between individuals and their present historical reality. This interaction with others and the social-economic condition is necessary for determining the "native point of view" (Spradley 1979:3). Since culture is learned behavior, context often provides a unique angle in fieldwork .

This chapter aims to provide the student with theory, process and practice in matters of ethnography. The theory will help us think about the science of cultural anthropology. Can we draw conclusions from what we see? Is observing the most obvious behavior of people sufficient for us to draw conclusions? Can observation of people's behavior lead to accurate characterizations of their culture? Yes and no. The behavior of a particular group might inform us that a wife always walks behind her husband, but what does this mean? Why is she reprimanded if she does not walk behind her husband? Development of theory involves looking deeper than outward manifestations to probe meanings. Fieldwork involves learning methods of gathering this information.

Say you are researching the elderly in your community. If the community in which you are growing a church includes a high percentage of elderly residents, how should you reach out? What are the needs of the elderly and how can you meet those needs? An ethnographic study could provide some of that information. Some of the findings would inform your church of the daily activities of the elderly. Take diet. You may find that many elderly folks do not like to cook for one person, so they do not maintain a balanced diet and may be in danger of malnutrition. The church could provide a daily meal to address the potential deficiency.

The church needs to learn the appropriate language to use to converse with senior citizens without offending them. Keep in mind that the ethnographer is not trying to study people but to learn from them. When a fieldworker is just observing and studying, it is easy to be distant or detached. But when the subject becomes the teacher, the expert, the relationship changes. Establishing such a teacher-learner relationship is essential if you are to gather information that is truly accurate and helpful for ministry.

It's easy to make the great error of assuming that this kind of research is necessary only in the distant lands and cultures of the Two-Thirds World. It is just as important in the United States and other Western nations, where too many facile assumptions are made about culture and ethnicity. "Field work is the hallmark of cultural anthropology . . . whether in a New Guinea village or on the streets of New York" (Spradley 1979:3).

Case studies can increase our learning curve and our skills in ethnographic work. Keep in mind that our goal is to utilize the social sciences for effective mission strategy. Ethnography is not an end in itself.

## Theory

When you are doing fieldwork, you need to constantly keep in mind that you are the student and the subject from whom you are learning is the teacher. You are allowing members of a particular group to inform you about their lives and worldview. You do not impose your view or interpretation.

**The fieldworker as student.** As a fieldworker you must enter a particular cultural/social setting and explain your presence in such a way as to build confidence and cooperation (Georges and Jones 1980:2). You are forming relationships. And that immediately requires building trust, which is not attained easily or quickly but is essential if you are to gather accurate information.

There is a definite correlation between the subject's response to the fieldworker and how much accurate information the fieldworker can gather. How long it will take to build the right level of trust with a subject is unpredictable. The major need is that trust be established. When you have trust, you will gain information that is accurate and thorough. When we rush the process and lose sight of the principle that we are the students and the subject is the teacher, we look at the subject through our own eyes and our own worldview. This puts up obstacles to understanding and makes it unlikely that we will put together an effective strategy for ministry.

> **Singapore Battered Women**
> A missionary who had been involved in planting urban churches in Singapore was asked to consider a new work in a densely populated area where the number of battered women was high. The missionary was unfamiliar with the issues and dynamics involved in the battered woman syndrome. Therefore he decided to do some fieldwork and look at the situation through the eyes of the women and men before developing a strategy. He knew it would take at least several months to establish the trust necessary to gather accurate information. As he began doing the work, he found that personal relationships were difficult to establish; he soon realized that the task would take even more time than he had expected.

**The fieldworker in conflict.** It is very likely that the person who does field research will experience personal conflict. We cannot allow conflict to stop our work. Rather we must continue the process, recognizing conflict as part of the learning experience. It is not for us to give up, nor should we push ahead with an arrogant attitude. Conflict often proves to be our friend, expanding our understanding in unexpected ways.

It is a good idea not only to record conflicts but to include these accounts in the main body of your field report. Often this information is hidden in the footnote section. We have found that all the experiences encountered in doing fieldwork are helpful in the final strategy—including the ongoing reactions of the fieldworker. "Those who have written about fieldwork in recent years have begun to include remarks concerning the human and personal nature of the enterprise" (Georges and Jones 1980:2). Recorded accounts of personal conflict will help others developing coping skills in similar situations.

---

**Young Prostitutes of Tijuana**

The missionary was to be working among the poor of Tijuana, Mexico. He had never before lived in such a poor area of the country. Becoming aware that young girls were being sold for prostitution, he became eager to help bring an end to this practice, rooted (he assumed) in immoral attitudes and values. He reviewed his conclusions with his wife, and she encouraged him to learn from both the families of the young girls and the teenagers themselves.

So the missionary set out to learn about the community, recording information as he gathered it. He spent many hours getting to know people and listening to their concerns for their community. He had breakfast in the same small diner every morning, and its staff and other patrons befriended him. Where conversation had once been filled with cold and calculated words, it was now friendly, and self-disclosure was more evident. He was now ready for some intial questions that might lead to a greater awareness of the meaning of teen prostitution in the community.

After several months of listening and recording information from the families and the girls themselves, he was amazed to learn that his initial assumptions were wrong. The issue was not immorality. Many of the girls were going to school regularly, and actually the major cause of the prostitution was poverty.

The information that the missionary took over nine months to gather helped him find a way of doing community development that would eliminate teen prostitution and assist the community to become economically stable. The ethnographic work he had done led to a strategy that he had not originally considered.

---

One type of conflict fieldworkers face is the personal stress arising from loneliness and frustration (Georges and Jones 1980:2-3). Other conflicts arise in the effort to build personal relationships with members of the community. Tension also arises in a Christian's fieldwork when moral and ethical issues are involved. The Christian fieldworker cannot compromise the gospel.

*The interpretation of information.* A graduate student, trained in primary education, entered an urban alternative school for the poor. Noticing the old desks and secondhand, damaged books, he concluded that the quality of the school must be poor. He had no information other than the visual appearance of the school. Asking no questions to check the accuracy of his impressions, he became paternalistic and arrogant.

Another student entered the school and witnessed the same conditions. She had been living in the community and recognized that the school had high standards for teachers and higher standards for the children than other schools in the community. This led her to appreciate the work being done and volunteer her time and resources.

> **Humboldt Park Gangs**
>
> When a pastor began ministry in the Humboldt Park area of Chicago, he discovered that gangs were part of the everyday life of the community. To be effective, then, he needed to know as much as possible about gang-police relationships. The problem was that neither group had any confidence in pastors or social workers. They both believed that a pastor would be naive and gullible and would betray their strategies. The trust level was low, so that trust could be gained only slowly.

Here we have two interpretations of the same situation. What are the reasons for the two perspectives? The students' differing worldviews led them to develop different perspectives. The student who assumed the quality of education was not good came from an upper-middle-class community that provided high-quality materials for elementary students. His upbringing had also communicated the notion that members of certain ethnic groups are not as capable as others in matters of learning. The other student came from a similar background but after moving into this community had learned that some of her presuppositions were incorrect.

The operating principle here is what James Spradley calls "elaborate cultural rules for interpreting your experience" (1979:6). Marvin Mayers speaks of how culture determines our norms:

> The term "norm" . . . generally denotes what is normative, that which is the foundation for expectation within society. If someone acts in a way expected of him, given a certain stimulus within a given situation, he is carrying out that which is normative for the society. Any deviation from this expected or normative behavior is seen as abnormal in some way. (Mayers 1974:82)

This insight can help explain why one student acted so differently from the other.

Another case shows how different perspectives can lead to gross error.

Nov. 23, 1973. Hartford, Connecticut. Three policemen giving a heart massage and oxygen to a heart attack victim Friday were attacked by a crowd of

75 to 100 persons who apparently did not realize what the policemen were doing.

Other policemen fended off the crowd of mostly Spanish speaking residents until an ambulance arrived. Police said they tried to explain to the crowd what they were doing, but the crowd apparently thought they were beating the woman.

Despite the policemen's efforts the victim, Evangelica Echevarria, 59, died. (Spradley 1979:5-6)

Two groups of people saw the same event and responded differently because their interpretations were very different. The crowd saw the policemen as out of order and the woman in danger, so they attacked the police to protect the woman.

The Christian doing ethnographic work in an unfamiliar culture must beware; the possibility of understanding a situation incorrectly is all too real. Therefore it is imperative that informers or interpreters be found to assist the process.

***The need for informants.*** Informers or, as Georges and Jones call them, interpreters (1980:8) have a significant role in the fieldworker's process of learning.

Ruth Benedict, who trusted interpreters (but who never identifies them, explains how they were chosen, or indicates their roles in her investigations) implies in her writings that she had probed the minds and actions of individuals in order to determine the function of customs and the dynamic nature of the art of taletelling, but evaluation of her work is difficult without knowledge of her methods. (Georges and Jones 1980:8)

Many Christian fieldworkers try to gather and interpret information without a resource person, what anthropologists call an informant. This is a serious weakness, likely due to lack of adequate training in ethnographic work. Also, many Christians feel a certain amount of distrust of and separation from those outside of the Christian community.

The informant is essential to the process of describing culture. "Ethnographers work together with informants to produce a cultural description. This relationship is complex. . . . The success of doing ethnography depends, to a great extent, on understanding the nature of this relationship" (Spradley 1979:25). The ethnographer develops an ongoing relationship with the informant. This relationship will not only help fieldworkers get information but also assist them in understanding the facts and their meaning, and in developing hypotheses.

The informant provides the fieldworker with the language of the group being investigated. This group might be cab drivers in Manila or gang members in East Los Angeles. Terms and language and how the group appropriates them are important. A group can create a language that is not necessarily found in any literature. Spradley and McCurdy report that in a study of checker players, a fieldworker had to learn from the checker players as informants, rather than from his previous experience, what terms like "double jump" or "kings" meant (1972:11). Words familiar to the fieldworker may be used in an entirely different way in the community under investigation.

We all play the role of informant at one time or another. We are asked where we live, where we came from, where we work and whether we enjoy our work. In a community being studied, the expert is not necessarily the native who is always giving out information, what we might call a tourist-leader kind, but is often an ordinary person from the community. (The word *native* is usually used by social scientists to refer to an indigenous person.)

If you are studying the significance of grocery stores in an urban Hispanic community, you may need to get informants who are local consumers. Listen to their stories about the role the grocery store plays in their lives. Beyond storytelling, listen for indications of how the store functions in the community. Why do they go to the grocery store? Who usually serves them? What do they buy at the store? How do they feel when they buy at the store? How much time do they spend in the store and why? Similar listening should be done with the owners of the grocery stores using a different set of questions. The researcher may find it invaluable to work at the store and record the conversations that arise. In some communities the grocery store is the most important institution. The information gained there can be invaluable for a pastor or church planter. It becomes apparent that many of the needs of the people of the community are being met in the interaction between the grocery store workers and the consumers. Often the owner of a store is somewhat like a pastor, providing help and wisdom.

Working with informants is not simple; as mentioned before, sometimes it involves conflict. Nevertheless, as Spradley and McCurdy note, it is an essential part of ethnographic fieldwork (1972:41).

***Confirming and disconfirming hypotheses.*** The goal of doing ethnographic research is to confirm or disconfirm particular hypotheses. You, as a researcher, come into the field with preconceived ideas and formulas. It is a challenge for you to be objective. If you are learning the lifestyle of teenage mothers, you must not come to the teen-mother informant with preconceived ideas and language. She must define herself. You may notice, for example, that these young mothers usually do not call themselves either mothers or teenagers. A teen mother may say that she is a young woman caring for her child and never once use the word *mother.* In the early stages of motherhood, soon after the birth of her child, she is willing to say that she has a child but not willing to refer to herself as a mother. This is more than semantics; she is still defining her role and responsibility. Her social role has changed drastically, but she has not completed the transition.

You may discover in this study that the daughters of teen mothers often become teen mothers themselves. This crisis in many of our poor and urban communities needs to be studied if the church and Christian organizations are to carry out ministry that is preventive rather than crisis oriented. Through the work of ethnography you will discover how to work with these young women and the language to use with them.

## Process

How to enter the field.

1. *Selecting the field.* In the U.S. context most communities are complex, with many subgroups and often a maze of cultures. This can cause frustration for the fieldworker. We suggest that you select a clearly defined community whenever possible. This may mean you need to look for evidence of group homogeneity. If you are establishing a ministry to homosexuals in your parish, you may need to select a community for research where there is a high density of homosexuals and clear identity is maintained. An isolated individual likely will not provide sufficient information or understanding in matters of how relationships are built and preserved.

Judith Lingenfelter enumerates several steps for targeting specific groups of people.

1. Contacting the population—where are the public places where people gather?
2. Defining population divisions and characteristics through mapping, observation, and interviewing.
3. Assessing population routines and opportunities for witness by observing such things as time, space, activity, events, actors, goals, and feelings.
4. Learning the experiential and linguistic context for witness through grand tour questions, structural questions, and contrast interviewing.
5. Analyzing social organization and leadership patterns through networks, associations, and groups to target people of influence and develop witness strategies for them.
6. Analyzing values and features of worldviews that provide obstacles and opportunities for response to the gospel. (Often urban ministry *begins* here and ignores the other five stages!) (Lingenfelter 1992:193)

Lingenfelter is concerned not so much with the professional carrying out of ethnographic work as with its application for mission. "We want to see the practical applications of the research we conduct, or else the project is not worth our time and effort" (1992:193).

2. *Be objective.* It is important to recognize your biases. Too often people take on a research project under the illusion that they have no preconceived notions. This sets them up for frustration and crises with informants. We all have biases and commitments that are culturally imposed. For example, when you think about a teenage mother, you may immediately attach a moral tag on her without realizing that you have done so. This will certainly truncate the field-research process and cause conflict. She will sense that you are harsh and critical regarding her moral values and that in some way you blame her. Your judgment will not necessarily be communicated overtly but through body language and the voicing of questions and opinions. Nevertheless, it will be noticed, and the subject will respond to your attitude.

Some means of introspection or small group discussion could provide reflection and clarity on your preconceived ideas regarding the values and morality of your subjects. To do good fieldwork, you want to be as objective as possible.

"*Is it possible to be completely objective?* No, but we need to examine why this is so since it is crucial to our use of ethnographic semantics as a research method" (Spradley and McCurdy 1972:13). Objectivity or the lack of it not only affects the final interpretation but also the ongoing process of doing research. The imposition of values and biases can be harmful to the data-gathering process and may well mean that information and conclusions are inaccurate.

How can you increase your objectivity? First, be honest about your biases. This is a good start but not easy. Say you are working to gather information on West Indian people who have recently come to the southern part of your Miami community. You have had experiences with West Indian people, most of which have been negative. You start your research with a bias that informs the data recorded, and this will probably produce flawed results.

After you have become aware of some of the biases, begin to wrestle with your objectivity. This alteration is imperative. And it is achievable if you are ready to admit that you have prejudices.

3. *Be a student.* This may sound repetitive and simplistic. But in the North American context we study for the primary purpose of teaching others. You will have a difficult time reversing this process on the field. To be a student involves a certain humility. Most of your previous learning has probably not relied on a dialogical approach.

Taking the student posture usually causes tension for the researcher working with the native. We think of ourselves as teachers; we think we have information and the subject does not. We are trying to change the subject and impose our culture on him or her, a process that Paulo Freire calls cultural invasion (1989:150-66). "The teacher teaches and the students are taught; the teacher knows everything and the student knows nothing; the teacher talks and the students listen" (Freire 1989:59). This mentality has to be reversed if your work is to be effective and productive.

4. *Be open and receptive.* The informant you find may not be the one you expect. As a fieldworker you must be open to surprises. The most common, ordinary person may be the best teacher—but that is not always true. Or you may need a young person rather than someone more mature. You must be alert and open to the unusual, the unexpected. The right informant may not come along immediately, so be patient, recognizing the importance of this step. Do not go ahead of yourself.

**How to build relationships.** "Informants are human beings with problems, concerns, and interests. The values held by any particular ethnographer do not always coincide with those held by informants" (Spradley 1980:20). As a Christian you may find this to be a problem at times. You may recognize that a particular act is wrong or even illegal. The fact that Christians have a superior accountability, the Word of God, could cause some difficulties with other ethnographers. How do you respond to actions and practices that are clearly inappropriate?

Even if relationships are cut short, you should maintain your standards. The end never justifies the means. Yet ethical principles from secular anthropology still have merit. You not only need to respect the privacy of informants, you also need to safeguard their rights (Spradley 1980:21). Say you are working in a Muslim context, learning how to best establish a ministry in the community. Most Muslim countries do not allow the entrance of Christian missionaries per se, but missionaries do come in as teachers and other professionals. In such a situation, even associating with you may jeopardize the safety of the native informant. It is imperative that you safeguard the individual's name. "Informants have the right to remain anonymous" (Spradley 1980:23).

Relationships are built through process. "The key for successful personal relationships and ministry is to understand and accept others as having a viewpoint that is as worthy of consideration as our own" (Lingenfelter and Mayers 1986:118). Probably you must begin with superficial contact. Rather than discounting the value of these initial encounters, recognize them as the beginning of a process of building a significant relationship. Then you can grow into a relationship of mutual need and mutual giving. A sense of being fairly comfortable together will tell you that the trust level is growing.

Following this period there is usually an opportunity to do some personal sharing. This indicates that there is growing confidence. Sharing is still limited and superficial. As the relationship builds, however, more intimate sharing takes place—perhaps openness regarding one's family or one's trials. This is a healthy sign that things are going well and trust is growing. Spradley points out the need for disclosure of your goals as part of this process: "The more intimately one works with informants, the more important becomes the task of communicating the aims of research" (1980:23).

**How to discover worldview.** When you enter a new context, the first thing that catches your eye is likely people's behavior—the outer layer, the action, the performance. The question that follows is, why are they acting this way? You try to find out the meaning of their behavior. How do you explain their actions?

The question of meaning is extremely important: too often we come to conclusions based on behavior alone and therefore miss the true significance of what we have observed. You can make serious judgments on the basis of behavior. You must notice behavior. But more important, you must seek to discern the reason the people are making certain choices. Choices are usually the manifestation of the values of a culture.

To discover a group's worldview, you begin with the obvious, the behavior of the people, what is being done. You next consider what is behind the behavior, what are the values or what is considered good or best. This is still not enough, so you proceed to investigate the belief system that ignites the values. This gets you to the core of the matter or what we call worldview—what is perceived as true.

> Behind the observable patterns of human cultures seem to lie certain assumptions about the way the world is put together. Some of these assumptions, called "existential postulates," deal with the nature of reality, the organization of the universe, and the ends and purposes of human life. Others, values and norms, differentiate between good and evil, right and wrong. (Hiebert 1983:356)

The worldview is at the center of every culture. A knowledge of this underlying system is important for understanding people's behavior. Values are selected on the basis of what is true according to the belief system. "Worldview assumptions or premises are not reasoned out, but assumed to be true without prior proof" (Kraft 1996:55). This means that changes in worldview are very difficult to accomplish. However, that is exactly what Christ wants to do—change a person's worldview.

Anthropologists speak of worldviews as having a central core that is often religious. When we speak of a Christian worldview, though, we see a problem with the term *core* and prefer to use *center.* "Ultimately, 'core' language demands that we think in terms of gospel irreducibles. 'Center' language demands that we think in terms of gospel expansions" (Conn 1984:197). This is not a matter of nitpicking with labels. When we think of a core, we think of something that cannot be changed. What core pieces are necessary in a Christian worldview? When we make decisions about necessary elements regardless of the specific culture we are addressing, the danger is there to cloak those core beliefs with our own cultural interpretations. We should not be trying to introduce a Eurocentric or Afrocentric or any other ethnocentric core of basic beliefs and understanding into a different culture and call it Christian. Rather we want to speak of Jesus as the gospel center of a Christian worldview.

> The gospel center must always be context-specific. . . . The gospel center of God's redemptive activity in Christ has to be addressed to the specific form the human predicament takes in each given case. . . . But the center remains center, whether it be Jesus the Messiah (addressed to a Jewish audience) or Jesus as Lord (addressed to a Gentile audience). The gospel "sameness" is not eroded by the gospel's particularization when presented to Nicodemus in terms of being born again or to a rich young ruler in terms of giving away his wealth. It is simply being made specifically appropriate. If the gospel, in fact, is not big enough, wide enough, enduring enough, to speak to each dimension of the human condition in human cultures, it is not universal enough to take away the sins of the world. (Conn 1984:197)

How is this worked out practically? Edmund Clowney tells us a story of a missionary to Papua New Guinea.

> "You mean to say that God doesn't want us going on cannibal raids?"
> This response in a Bible study of Genesis 9 startled R. Daniel Shaw, a missionary to Papua New Guinea. "Not being a cannibal," he tells us, "I had never considered this passage from that perspective." The Papuan saw the implications of the text: God is not pleased when we kill those made in his image. His Samo culture divided people into *Monsoon,* those who slept in the same longhouse; *Oosoo Buoman,* their allies; and *Ton,* those who spoke the same dialect; all others were *Hatooman,* enemies. (Clowney 1995:167)

These cannibals had to change their underlying assumptions about how others might be categorized and realize that all people, regardless of their relationship, are fellow image-bearers of God.

Another story comes from Don Richardson's quest for "powerful cultural analogies" to use in presenting the work of Christ to tribal cultures. In one case, the tribes valued treachery above all else. For them the hero in the crucifixion story was Judas, and Jesus was a wimpy coward. One day two tribes were negotiating a truce, and the chief of one tribe gave his son to the chief of the other tribe to raise. This custom, which sealed the truce, was called giving a peace child. Richardson was able to build from this to present Christ as the ultimate Peace Child given by God to bring peace between him and sinful humankind. Richardson's success in discovering analogies like this "led him to believe that every culture has a providentially prepared key that will unlock it for the truth" (Clowney 1995:168).

As long as Richardson dealt with the traditional images of Father, Lord and the like, he could not bring Christ to Papuan tribes in a meaningful way. Their worldview of valuing treachery prevented it. But once he found the key, he was able to bring Christ in a way that began to truly redeem and transform the worldview.

**How to interpret the data gathered.** Always remember that you are prone to interpret out of an ethnocentric reality, a deep-lying assumption that your own culture is significantly superior to others. A great deal has been written about the dangers of ethnocentrism in interpretation because of the assumption that the scientific method is totally objective. However, "ethnocentric assumptions may unconsciously influence" the research process itself (Spradley 1980:4).

Documentation of the analysis and interpretation is like "think[ing] on paper" (Spradley 1979:76). It is the final written record of the ethnography. You will be applying the data to mission goals; you desire to use the data for purposes that go beyond thinking on paper. You look to interpretation to lead you into building relationships with people who have not encountered the transforming Christ. For you, the information is necessary to contextualize the gospel while avoiding the traps of syncretism.

Interpretation also assists you in recognizing your own attitude of superiority. As you move from examining behavior to considering how people decide what they think is true, you discover that you misjudged the situation and imposed your cultural values on the people group.

Interpretation will, in some settings, begin to assist you as a missionary or Christian worker in matters of language. Communication is crucial for effective ministry. Whether you are working in an E3 context in your own country or in another country, ethnographic work can be helpful. An E3 context is one in which you must cross major linguistic and cultural hurdles in order to evangelize effectively.

Interpretation has to do with discovering the meaning of the behavior of the people. It is knowing why they do what they do. It has to do with why they choose to pray on their knees rather than sit in a chair. It has to do with the importance of senior men or women as authority figures over youth. It has to do with why sacrificing a life for another is irreligious or religious.

### Practice

*Testing findings.* For the church in a crosscultural setting, testing what we have researched involves utilization. The missionary or Christian worker makes use of the material in the context of the people researched to see how accurate the data are. The data may need clarification, but that is to be expected.

> **East Asian Senior Citizens in Denver**
>
> A pastor working with older citizens in Denver, Colorado, is field researching the senior citizens of an East Asian culture in his community. He has learned the language necessary to communicate with the families and has done an ethnographic study with informants who have taught him the needs and language of senior citizens. The East Asian group is quite different from the Anglo population to whom he is accustomed. The data are tested in serving the community.

Spradley notes, "The best way to learn to do ethnography is by doing it" (Spradley 1979:42). The best way to test the information you have gathered is by using or applying it to the mission group you have outlined.

*Evaluating by using case studies.* Case studies that have been thoroughly completed are helpful in the evaluation process. They may not be mission bound or have a primarily scientific conclusion, but you need to study them to see if your work has missed invaluable information. In *The Cultural Experience* Spradley and McCurdy provide numerous case studies that whet your appetite for fieldwork . But they also give you a process you can use to critique your work. Certainly your conclusions and reason for fieldwork are different from those of the social scientist, but you must not shortchange the process because you are intent on mission application.

An interesting case study is "Golden Age Apartments: Ethnography of Older People" by Nancy Wright (Spradley and McCurdy 1972:119-36). Wright notes, "As Americans have ceased to care for their aging relatives within the confines of their own households, new structures for the maintenance of old people have emerged" (Spradley and McCurdy 1972:121). Reading through this material, a Christian can see readily that a strategy for the church could have been initiated based on the research described. For example, Wright takes up hardships common among the aging—such as deterioration of their bodies, death of their peers and decreased usefulness—and how the subculture forms solutions through small groups.

Preventive measures are generally preferred to crisis intervention.

Fieldwork done scientifically can help with prevention of many social ills. Take the case of teen pregnancy mentioned earlier in this chapter. Too often people function on the basis of symptoms and not causes. The real needs are in the causes. In order to meet the needs of individuals, the researcher must discover the cause of the problem. Teen pregnancy is not an isolated, individual problem; it is a systemic factor that requires much more than one-to-one counseling. What are the causes? The percentage of teen mothers is on the increase, and the church is confused as to how to end the epidemic and prevent more girls from becoming pregnant. Solid ethnographic research might assist the church in determining how to strategize and plan for effective ministry.

## Conclusion

Ethnography is an important tool for the Christian who is serving in a mission context. It allows for church growth that is guided by a kingdom perspective when the data gathered reveal comprehensive, realistic issues. Contextualization is not carried out on the rebound but is part of the initial process of planting a church crossculturally or across socioeconomic boundaries.

Mercy ministry in the local church is not just providing for basic needs but involves uncovering the causes of those needs in order to better steward time and resources. Holistic Christian community centers seek to do more preventive work than high-stress, crisis-oriented ministry.

The work of the Holy Spirit is crucial to whatever the believer in Christ does. Fieldwork, analysis, strategy setting and the whole of the missionary task are dependent on the Godhead, particularly the energizing work of the Holy Spirit.

# 16

# Demographic
# Studies & Mission

THE CHURCH FACES A MISSIOLOGICAL CHALLENGE regarding population growth
and people movements throughout the world. In the next ten years
approximately one billion people will be added to the world's population—which has already surpassed six billion (Bakke 1997:13). Most of
this addition will take place in Asia and in the developing countries.

The urbanization of the planet and the globalization of cities are
reminders that push-pull is more than a sociological reality; it is also a
theological announcement. The sovereign Lord is bringing people from
various countries and ethnic backgrounds together in a way never before
witnessed. In our missiological context we meet diverse peoples not necessarily by crossing the oceans but by crossing the streets of our urban
centers. All of our ministries will have to contend with this demographic
situation, a pluralism impossible to escape. Our ministries, seminaries
and churches will encounter a multiethnic, multisocioeconomic, multi-
religious challenge that calls us to stand by the truth of the Word of God
without wavering.

The Reformation recalls us to commitment to and action "within the
everyday world. Just as the Reformers rejected a retreat to the monasteries, so their modern heirs must reject a retreat into the narrow withdrawn
confines of Christian subculture. The world at its worst needs Christians
at their best" (McGrath 1994:56).

This chapter will help the mission student use the science of demography as an applied science for mission. However, keep in mind the following warning: "Do not take population figures as gospel truth, especially if they come from areas with less than adequate data-gathering facilities" (Peters and Larkin 1993:4).

## What Is Demography?

The term *demography,* of Greek etymology, means description of people. It is the study of population, trends and movements. Demography is an interdisciplinary study "drawing heavily on biology and sociology for the study of fertility; on economics and geography for studies of migration; and on the health sciences for analyses of mortality" (Stycos 1989:vii). It is best defined as the study of size, territorial distribution and composition of the population, the study of the change in those factors, and particularly the study of the components of such change. Population change occurs through three dynamics: (1) fertility—a birth may take place, (2) mortality—a death may occur and (3) migration—a person can either move into or out of a community. These three are the only ways populations grow or decline.

However, other factors are involved. For example, "the conception of the population problem that is rooted in macroeconomics is that rapid population growth produces slower economic growth, as measured by output per capita or per worker" (Preston 1989:3). Others are saying that "there are serious costs to high fertility that are not borne by the childbearing couple" (Preston 1989:4). Problems occur when families' childbearing affects other families' childbearing or well-being.

For Christians, demography is not an end in itself but a means to an end. Charles Kraft states, "We apply its perspectives to a task that far transcends the anthropologist's goals of accumulating insights concerning other peoples and, in the process, learning to respect them. Our mandate is still the Great Commission" (Kraft 1996:xiv). There are several ways demographics can assist us in carrying on the mission God has given us. This chapter will look at how demographics helps us discover (1) the *shalom* of God in community or the lack of it, (2) systemic as well as individual needs, and (3) the reasons a church is facing growth or decline. The final part of this chapter explains how to do community analysis.

## Discovering the Shalom of God in Community

The shalom of God has to do with having right relationships with God, our neighbor and our environment. It involves enjoying life with others and ourselves (Is 11:6-8), a harmonious relationship with God (Is 2:2-3), harmonious relationships with our neighbors and other human beings (Is 32:16-17) and a harmonious relationship with nature (Is 25:6).

Shalom is not present, for example, when life expectancy is cut short due to economic conditions.

> More than 300 million people live in nations where the average life expectancy is less than 50 years. In many of these countries one of every ten newborns dies before age one. . . . Life expectancy tends to be generally related to the level of economic development. (Peters and Larkin 1993:129-31)

Dick Taylor indicates that various types of research, including demographics, are helpful in determining the will of God for a particular community. The purpose of research, in his words, is "to discover where people in your neighborhood are being denied their rightful shalom" (Taylor 1979:23).

Demographics help the missionary discover the needs of a particular group of people. For example, demographic investigation can highlight the problem in the Sudan where Muslims from the north are raiding Christian villages in the south, kidnapping their children and forcing the children into slavery. Rumors are seeping out and making us aware there is a problem. But demographics can bring out the horrifying extent of the problem. Then missionaries can work with local Christians to formulate an effective response.

---

**Tribal Infant Mortality**

In a particular society there may be economic imbalances that are negatively affecting the lifestyle of the people. The imbalances may stem from agricultural methods that do not produce a healthy enough crop to both feed the people and allow for marketing and income. Because income is limited, there is no potential to correct the economic problem. Discovering the need and especially the causes of the need are part of the demographic task.

A missionary saw a community dwindling down to a small group of people in despair. The mortality rate for children was too high. The missionary began to research health problems and discovered that the tribe had two major needs: better use of irrigation and the use of their basic crop for nutrition and healthcare. The crops they already farmed, if used well, would be sufficient to restore good health and, hopefully, bring about a decline in infant mortality. By going from observation of population decline to seeking the cause for the high infant mortality rate, the mission team was able to help establish stability and opportunity for continued mission work within the tribe.

---

Understanding and defining needs is an essential component of demographics. What, then, do we mean by *need*?

> The definition of need is central in the conduct of needs assessment in the community. Sociologically, need can be defined as the measurable discrepancy existing between a present state of affairs and a desired state of affairs

as asserted either by an "owner" of need or an "authority" on need. In the former instance, need is described as motivational; in the latter instance, prescriptive. (Beatty 1981)

The difference between real and felt needs is important to understand. The felt needs of poor people often deal with the physical—food, housing, transportation, medicine. However, the deeper, real need has to do with valuing themselves as creations of God, reclaiming the dignity God desires them to have and finding the hope of a transformed life in Christ. Too often ministries care only for felt needs, an approach that does not lead to changed lives.

Cities around the world are attracting poor people. Their communities isolate them to varying degrees and promote vulnerability. The very nature of poverty prevents most of the poor from owning their own homes, which increases their vulnerability. In the United States the poor often live in communities located near the center city area where many from outside the city commute and work. This section of the city has become prime property and in demand by those who are seeking to relocate. It becomes a speculative area where outsiders promote community renewal. Speculators aggressively advertise for others to move in, taking advantage of the poor and displacing them. J. John Palen speaks of this phenomenon as a move from one urban turf to another of "middle-income and upper-middle-income whites (and some blacks) [who] are buying and restoring old homes and new houses—a process commonly known as 'neighborhood regeneration' or 'gentrification'" (Palen 1987:256). The advantage of gentrification is the revitalization of communities that had been deteriorating and the augmentation of the tax base, much needed in cities that have been close to bankruptcy. On the other hand, gentrification removes poor people from their residences, usually unwillingly, to benefit others who care more for their own well-being and economic advantage than for those who are being displaced. The question is, can community transformation be realized without having to displace the people Christ admonished us to care for?

In Third World countries we find two kinds of settlements inhabited by the poor—slums and squatter settlements.

*Slums* are areas of authorized, usually older housing which are deteriorating or decaying in the sense that they are underserviced, overcrowded, and dilapidated. Slums are usually located on valuable land adjacent to the central business district. . . . *Squatter settlements,* on the other hand, contain makeshift dwellings erected without official permission (i.e., unauthorized on land which the squatters do not own). . . . They are usually located on the periphery instead of near the center of cities. (Brunn and Williams 1983:32)

Gentrification in the United States is relatively new, having begun in the 1970s, and we do not see the same type of revitalization occurring in Third World cities. However, gentrification could eventually take place in Third World slums due to the value of the land on which slums rest. What seems a bit more improbable, yet it does occur, is that a squatter settlement would be bulldozed so that a developer can build townhouses for middle-class residents. This occurred in Damayan Lagi, a squatter settlement outside of Manila.

Demographics can aid an urban worker or pastor in preventing such displacement. Following are some helps for doing such preventive work.

1. Identify your community to see if it is in danger of gentrification. Is it located in a section of a North American city that is considered prime? Who might be interested in living there because it is close to their place of work (center city) or to the arts or places of recreation? Many more important questions need to be asked regarding how speculative such community change might be. If the neighborhood lies in the path of center city and the creative activities of the city, it will probably become a community in need of renewal.

2. Identify any transitions that are going on or can be predicted for the near future. Generational, ethnic, racial and socioeconomic transitions are all indicators that a community is vulnerable. A community that is stable likely has been able to organize around issues of concern—lack of city services, crime, even types of building use. But when a community is in transition, neighbors do not know each other, and there is little if any organizing. The general tenor is distrust. Speculators can enter the community with relative ease, as they will not have to expect a confrontation with current residents.

3. Identify the owning power of the community. If only 12 percent of community residents are home owners, the community may be in trouble. If there are many rentals with absentee landlords, the community may intentionally, with the help of banks, be allowed to run down without home improvements or investments to build the community with the existing residents. In the United States this is called redlining, the practice of planning on the part of banks and investors not to invest in particular communities.

In the Third World, squatter settlements are subject to the whims of politicians. If politicians view the squatters as an asset to themselves, they may do as Ankara's politicians have done. "Many [of the squatters] have been granted partial *de facto* or *de jure* rights over the years as politicians have sought favour and votes with such a large section of the community" (Drakakis-Smith 1987:90). On the other hand, authorities "can use the illegal nature of the housing or the activities of the residents to demolish and evict whenever they wish" (Drakakis-Smith 1987:93). This indicates the total lack of power of those living in squatter settlements.

4. Identify the intentions of city hall and the city planning division. A historical site in the process of redevelopment could mean removal of the poor. Often there is a push for a better community. The question must be asked, for whom is this better community being planned? Words such as *redevelopment, revitalization* and *reconstruction* should serve as red flags suggesting gentrification. In a book by Bowden and Kreinberg, *Street Signs Chicago*, we find a perfect example.

> A mile or so away, a contraption of condominiums and townhouses called Dearborn Park is rising on the vacant railroad land south of the Loop. *Chicago Magazine* hosts a bright, full page color advertisement: "THE GRAND OPENING OF CHICAGO'S NEXT GREAT NEIGHBORHOOD." Want to move into the neighborhood? Plunk down $40,000 to $140,000. The artwork shows green lawns and plump Grant Wood trees. Dearborn Park, the ad reassures, will have its very own public school. So relax. (Bowden and Kreinberg 1981:32)

5. Identify the interest of the local banks in your community. It is important to find out whether or not they are investing in the community with the existing residents in mind. If the churches and individual members of the congregation are customers of a given bank, be strategic in confronting bank management. If the church and a large number of its members have holdings in a bank, they can exert leverage on the bank to be just. For example, if a bank that refuses to loan money in a poor community is faced with the threat of losing a significant number of depositors, it may alter its position and begin a loan program in the community.

6. On a positive note, it is important to do long-range planning to increase home ownership.

7. Other agencies, such as Habitat for Humanity, could be helpful in building and beautifying your community. Starting in 1968, Clarence Jordan voiced his concerns about housing. He died the next year, and Millard Fuller nurtured the idea until "in September of 1976, twenty-seven friends and supporters of the concept of partnership housing came together at Koinonia Farm near Americus [Georgia]. . . . After three days of deep discussion and prayer, Habitat for Humanity was brainstormed into existence" (Fuller and Scott 1986:23). Established on the foundation of partnering with God and partnering with each other, Habitat builds or renovates quality homes for the poor with volunteer labor, financial contributions and required sweat labor of its new home owners, "seeing no

profit and charging no interest" (Fuller and Scott 1986:25). It started its work in Americus, Georgia, but has expanded throughout the United States and the world as it seeks to fulfill its goal "to eliminate poverty housing from the face of the earth" (Fuller and Scott 1986:20). Former president Jimmy Carter and his wife Rosalynn began their well-publicized association with the organization when President Carter gave a short greeting at the October 1982 Habitat board of directors meeting. By early 1984 they were deeply committed to Habitat.

> ### Hispanic Health Center
>
> Esperanza Health Center in Philadelphia had been planning for years to move into a particular community that was heavily populated by Hispanics. It was the center's goal to serve a very poor Hispanic population in the inner city. If Esperanza directors had relied merely on their hunch as to where they should locate the ministry, the life of the center would have been shortened due to city planning and a process of gentrification. The city planning commission, along with other agencies, was working hard to displace this Hispanic community because it stood in the way of speculation for developers and upper-middle-class people who were eager to move near their employment and the fine restaurants and entertainment available in center city.
>
> Careful study of trends kept the health clinic from moving to its initial choice of location. Instead it was placed in an area where the study indicated the center could anticipate long-term ministry because the community was stable and showed no signs of redevelopment.

Demography helps us begin to determine the will of God for a community as we discover where the shalom of God is missing. To restore shalom, something must be done. This will naturally lead to community development activities, which will be covered more thoroughly in another chapter. Development is Christian ministry that flows out of Christ's command to love our neighbor (Mt 22:39) and directs us to the atonement of Christ and the resurrection.

## Discovering Systemic As Well As Individual Needs

Demography can assist us in discerning individual and systemic needs. These days many clients of Christian counselors in Seoul, Korea, are asking for help in their marriages. In the past the possibility of divorce and separation was rarely mentioned, for various reasons. Cultural values and norms frowned on divorce, and it was not a major, recognizable problem in society. Now the problem of separation and divorce has become more complicated. Families both in the church and in the non-Christian community are facing this hardship. The problem is approached on a personal level; therefore the solution offered will be personal as well.

There is no way that a Christian counselor could or should avoid dealing with these pathologies on a personal and family level. However, demographic data would inform Christians that the percentage of divorces has increased over the last ten years and seems to be continuing its rise. It is clear that the problem is not only personal but also systemic and that solutions must include systemic remedies. The problem will probably increase rather than decrease if our diagnosis works only on the individual level. As in the United States, all the efforts to work on family issues have not provided a preventive measure that significantly affects the divorce rate in the larger society and in the church. One reason is that we have not made use of demographics, nor have we understood systemic questions and solutions.

Inside a marriage a man and a woman may experience personal troubles. But when the divorce rate during the first four years of marriage is 250 out of every 1,000 marriages, we have an indication of a structural issue having to do with the institutions of marriage and the family and other institutions that bear upon them (Mills 1959:9).

Understanding systemic influences will help us do some preventive work rather than only crisis intervention. As the church analyzes demographic information pertaining to divorce, it may alter the content of its curriculum for children and adults. Christian counseling centers may provide assistance to churches in ways that alter the trend of family instability when its staff members realize that divorce is more than an individual problem.

A simpler issue is one that urban workers often face—the lack of effective education for children. If a high school of twenty-five hundred students has a consistent dropout rate of 70 percent, or if high percentages of young people are graduating from high school functionally illiterate, we have a systemic issue that must be dealt with systemically. It is quite different for a school that consistently has good standing in retention and academic scores, yet a small percentage still falters. The strategy in that case might be much more individual than systemic.

"How do you change, not simply selfish people, but a systemic structure built around selfishness?" (Conn 1987:128). The long-standing problem for evangelicals is that we have privatized the gospel; we see sin as a purely individual problem. And "as we approach sinful systems by changing individuals alone, we miss the "holistic character" of the social structures (Conn 1987:129). The saying "we have more racism and fewer racists" becomes credible because racism has been institutionalized. Orlando Costas comments:

> To say that sin is personal, however, is not to say that its consequences are limited to the individual. In biblical faith, that which is personal is never individualistic, isolated from others. On the contrary, that which is personal is

intrinsically related to that which is collective. Men and women find their personality in society. For this reason, too, every personal action affects the community. Personal sin brings with it collective guilt. (Costas 1982:25)

---

**Systemic Unemployment**

Consider unemployment. When, in a city of 100,000, only one man is unemployed, that is his personal trouble, and for its relief we properly look to the character of the man, his skills and his immediate opportunities. But when in a nation of 50 million employees, 15 million men are unemployed, that is an issue, and we may not hope to find its solution within the range of opportunities open to any one individual. The very structure of opportunities has collapsed. Both the correct statement of the problem and the range of possible solutions require us to consider the economic and political institutions of the society, and not merely the personal situation and character of a scatter of individuals. (Mills 1959:9)

---

***Understanding why a church is facing growth or decline.*** David A. Roozen and C. Kirk Hadaway (1993) give an example of why the whole picture is necessary to account for the growth or decline of a church. Too often we make snap judgments solely attributing the growth or decline of the church to leaders' ability or lack of ability. Certainly this may be part of the story. But Roozen and Hadaway's research indicates that demographic data must also be taken into account.

In the early 1940s and 1950s European immigration to Chicago was still active, especially from Norway and Sweden. Many of the ethnic language churches were growing rapidly. The German Lutheran Church was showing signs of growth and excitement. As migration patterns shifted and the homogeneous communities that represented the European people declined, the church began to experience a leveling off. The second generation was moving into mainline America, and the old community, which kept its culture intact, was making major transitions. By the middle 1960s and early 1970s the church and community had undergone both ethnic and generational transitions. The church faced major declines.

Church growth patterns seem to take on a life of their own when a church moves past the 200-250 mark. Churches then seem to grow more through administration than through outside evangelism. In the same way, a church that is beginning to decline can perpetuate its own demise.

How would we analyze, from the symptoms alone, what took place in these churches and the reasons for the increase and the decrease? Often the story a church tells about itself is only partly accurate. It usually starts with a description of the church in its heyday, a wonderful, exciting church that was faithful to the gospel and through whose preaching of the Word many came to know the Lord. And this is probably true to a certain point. Then the rest of the story has to do with community change, with people moving away to the suburbs. (In some cases the move is reversed as people go to the city. This may be happening in certain churches in Korea and Brazil and other countries where people are moving to urban areas, leaving behind their rural roots.)

If we take a sociological peek at the above scenario, we will notice the importance of ethnicity, migration patterns and certainly the hand of the sovereign Lord. It is fundamentally a theological story of how God brings people to places where they will hear the gospel. God uses migration patterns! But he also uses affairs of government and politics.

In order to see the whole picture it is important for us to work with what God employs. What are we to do in the midst of a process of change and movement? In the above example, the migration trends might have been indicators that the church's resources for growth—that is, migration from Europe to the United States—were being depleted. Not only that, the community that once was filled with people from Scandinavia was changing; newer residents were from the Caribbean and Mexico. Research would have given the church an opportunity to anticipate the changes and plan ahead. The trends would have signaled that alterations would have to be made if the church were to continue to be effective in that community. Demographic information can warn church leaders that a decline or even possibly a closure will take place unless the church draws on missiological resources and principles.

Reginald Bibby carried out a 1978 study to offset an argument by Dean Kelley (Kelley 1972, cited in Inskeep 1993:136) about mainline churches and conservative evangelical churches. Kelley argued that the decline of mainline churches had to do with culture and the inability to promote a belief system to its members. He also asserted that conservative religion demands commitment and discipline. The rebuttal by Bibby is

> that contextual factors (birthrates) were more important to church growth than institutional factors (conservative theology) in explaining church growth . . . [and] that neither the Conservatives nor the Mainliners were very successful in recruiting active followers from outside of the Christian community. (Bibby 1978, cited in Inskeep 1993:137)

A 1979 study by Gary Bouma deals with membership in the Christian Reformed Church (Bouma 1979, cited in Inskeep 1993:136). Bouma's research showed that the growth of the CRC in the United States came immediately after World War II, when immigration of Dutch Reformed people was high. He concluded that immigration and not evangelistic efforts was the reason for growth.

Bouma noted that the CRC lost very few of its children, thanks to "successful socialization of its young people" (Inskeep 1993:138). This was, of course, a benefit to the denomination. But it also provides a strategy for ethnic-minority churches to use to continue having healthy growth regardless of immigration rates. Future growth will rely on developing the church through socialization and mobilization of its second- and third-generation emerging leaders.

Kirk Hadaway notes that overall U.S. church membership growth was high in the 1940s. This was true in most denominations, if not all. Also, marriage and birth rates climbed. The suburbs were the place for growth (Hadaway 1993b:346-57), and the church went right along with the baby boomers.

> By the middle of [the 1920s], more than 15 million persons were residing in the fringe neighborhoods of the city. Slowed down by a depression and a world war, the great push continued after 1945. By 1955, approximately 1,200,000 Americans were moving to the suburbs annually. And scholars were predicting that 85 percent of city growth during the 1960s and 1970s would be suburban.
>
> The churches followed, giving primary attention to their suburban expansion. (Conn 1994:97)

Church growth was affected by general demographic changes. "Declining rates of membership growth affected all denominational families in the 1950s and early 1960s" (Hadaway 1993b:348). Individual churches grew depending on where they were located. United Methodist churches grew if they were located in the South. The same was true of Southern Baptist congregations (Hadaway 1993b:352). Certainly this is not the whole story, but it is a significant part of growth patterns. Another element is that conservative churches are much more growth oriented than liberal churches persuaded by culture to relax their evangelistic interest.

Today churches that have taken the challenge of parish evangelism and justice seriously are growing rapidly in multiethnic communities. Others are declining in similar communities because they have found the task of reaching outside their cultural boundaries impossible. In the early 1970s Peter Wagner and others from the School of Church Growth at Fuller Seminary were pessimistic about church growth in a context of cultural diversity.

It is clear to all of us who believe in the power of the gospel and the redeeming work of Christ that salvation is of the Lord. He alone gives the increase. But God uses the conditions of the world to bring people to him through the preaching of the gospel. Demographics tell us what to expect as we think about the future of the church. The world continues to change rapidly, and we need to know how to use cultural changes and flows of people for the furtherance of the gospel. It is the Christian's responsibility to be faithful to the world in which we live and to the Word of God that gives life. In a world where many people are heading toward the cities, who will welcome them? And in the United States, how shall we prepare for the continued migration pull into this country?

***How to do community analysis.*** What happens in a poor community where there is high fertility and low mortality? Certainly there should be sizable growth. The term "demographic transition" is used to denote the period when the death rate of a population starts to decline (due to technological and medical advances) but the birth rate continues to increase or remain high. This causes tremendous biological growth, a dynamic often referred to as population explosion. Finally there is a leveling off of birth rates.

This pattern does not occur in all countries at the same time or to the same degree. "Developed and underdeveloped nations have different population histories. From the 18th century until after World War I the growth rate in the developed countries . . . exceeded that in the underdeveloped ones. . . . Since the 1920's growth in underdeveloped regions has predominated, and since 1950 the gap has become large" (Coale 1975:47). The demographic transition has essentially run its course for the developed nations, which, "during the past two centuries, doubled the average life expectancy and halved the total fertility rate" (Coale 1975:48). But population increase did not even begin in less developed countries until about two hundred years ago. A major upswing began in the 1920s; "since World War II the population increase has accelerated dramatically" (Coale 1975:51) and has still not reached equilibrium in many nations. "According to projections prepared by the UN, more than 90 percent of the increase in population to be anticipated by 2000 will be contributed by the less developed nations" (Coale 1975:51).

What are the implications of such growth for housing, education, employment and family relationships in the context of church ministry? Very often the church does not know population growth is occurring and has very little to say about it. We are not familiar with demographic tools. This is to our detriment. We should not consider individuals apart from their social reality. "Neither the life of an individual nor the history of a society can be understood without understanding both" (Mills 1959:3).

The scientific method usually consists of two major mental activities. First is *observation*. Researchers try to take note of all the things and events that are happening, what they mean and how they relate to other things concretely. Say we are noticing many young adults out on the streets in the early afternoon when people are usually in their workplace.

The observation may be significant for ministry if we can understand some of the reasons these young adults are at loose ends. Observation will assist us in making use of everyday events that we are accustomed to noticing but about which we have failed to ask questions.

The other kind of activity in scientific analysis is forming theories or opinions based on what we observe. This is called *inference.* Inference can be either inductive or deductive. Inductive reasoning moves from the specific to the general, a process of asserting some observed uniformity. Researchers, for example, examine a few U.S. communities that have gone through racial transition, particularly from Anglo to African American. They discover that the communities changed once a certain percentage of African Americans moved in. These communities had been nearly homogeneous, primarily made up of white blue-collar workers. When the community was approximately 10 percent African American, it began to tip: white residents began to sell their homes and move out. From this observation, researchers generalized their findings and developed a theory that all (or at least most) communities would respond in the same way.

Deductive reasoning starts with a theory—for example, that communities "tip" after a certain percentage of African Americans move in. That theory is then tested through study of other communities to see if the same dynamic occurs. Researchers now discover that the tipping point for other ethnic groups moving into a white community is different. For example, a community would have to become approximately 23 percent Hispanic before it turns over from another ethnic group to Hispanic. The adjusted theory is then carried over to other communities to see if it works in a similar fashion.

The deductive approach involves going from the general to the particular. We use a general principle to explain a particular situation. If the pattern does not hold up as it did in other communities, we have to make adjustments to the theory.

How would a pastor use the tipping theory? Say your church has been ministering in a German American context for many years. Currently people are moving from the southern part of the city into your community— mostly African Americans who are seeking better housing. Observation tells you that new people are coming into the area; you surmise that if the tipping theory holds true, many of your members will probably move out. This means that either you will have a totally new parish and church family or you will have to challenge the congregation to realize that racism underlies the shift and that Christians are to promote justice and not segregation.

Or the pastor may realize that the church has been declining over the years due to generational transitions. The population shift may open up a time of exciting growth for the church if it purposes to provide comfort and encouragement to the new families moving in. Hospitality and mercy ministries are excellent ways to display the beauty of the Lord.

In order to have the necessary information to establish new ministries in the city, work with justice issues, and develop church ministries with awareness as the context changes, community studies are necessary. Such a study should examine demographics but needs to be broader and more comprehensive. There are a number of steps that should be taken (Ortiz 1992:85-98).

1. *Commitment to bonding.* Commitment to bonding may seem a strange concept in this context. But it is extremely important in living the life of Christ as well as learning about our new context in a way that allows us to minister with integrity. The best analogy for this process is an infant entering a new environment, a world of new experiences, smells and sights. We are entering a unique community, even if it is in the same city in which we have been serving. We are becoming part of that new situation as an infant becomes part of its family at the time of birth.

It is important not to allow our time and involvement to be taken away from our community. Team efforts may be counterproductive to the bonding process, because our natural tendency is to stay within our own comfort zone rather than to be vulnerable in the midst of a new community. In a context of newness, team members may spend far too much time together and avoid relationship building with neighbors. Community ministries begin with our neighbors, those who may see the gospel in action through us and our families.

Bonding in a community, as for an infant, begins to happen instantly. Thus we should commit ourselves to staying in the community to enhance the bonding process. We will know that bonding has taken place when we begin to own, and feel at home with, our neighborhood.

The story of a young Christian woman who came out of a nonurban community illustrates the bonding process.

> I've lived in this, a largely Hispanic community, for the past eight months. Considering my completely different background, I feel very much at home here. I haven't been conscious of how I've been becoming a part of the community, but as I look back there are several things that have been helping me to feel a part.
>
> I live with a Puerto Rican family in the community whose extended family is very close by. Very quickly I met brothers, sisters, nieces, nephews, etc. I

never really thought of it as firsthand exposure to the culture and neighborhood until now.

Most of my time is spent in the community. I go to church here and work
here, and therefore most of my friends are here. It's as if the community is
now the base of all my activity. Not that everything is done here, but everything has a connection back to the neighborhood. Usually those connections
are people.

I think it has also helped that I knew I was a stranger. I was not only new
to the area but to the culture as well. My background isn't anything like the
people I am meeting, but we have been able to enjoy and deal with those
differences through humor. My major barrier at this point is the Spanish language, but they are willing to teach, and I am willing to learn, so one of
these days I'll catch on.

The overriding motivation for being involved with this community is that
God has called me to the city and given me a peace about being here. That's
an exciting base from which to work.

Too often we forget how important bonding is because we are citizens
of the same country, or we come from the same ethnic or tribal culture, or
we are not aware of the significant differences between communities.
Then the bonding process never takes place, our rural or suburban values
are never challenged, and our field of ministry takes a turn for the worse.
If we miss the early stages of bonding, we may never fit. We find ourselves in the community but not of it.

2. *Discovering our biases and stereotypical influences.* This step is often
the most difficult due to the introspection and individual work it requires.
But it is one of the most important. The basic idea is to discover biases
and prejudices we may have in relationship to the city, multicultural communities and the poor. Does ethnocentrism exist within us? Do we have
an oppressive sense of superiority as we observe other cultures? What
are our deep feelings about the poor?

We need to be honest where it hurts the most. How can we be Christian and at the same time racist? What do we think when we see a new
car in a poor community, or a welfare recipient that is physically healthy
and intelligent, or the welfare mother that solicits the help of men to
make ends meet?

Many other questions can be asked in order to discover who we are in
relationship to the city. What are the biases that prevent Christian Indians
of different castes from living out their need for each other in the community of faith? Can Indonesian Christians and Chinese Christians residing in
Indonesia get past their prejudices and model reconciliation? How do
Christian Yugoslavians handle the disaster carried out by their nation
under the guise of ethnic cleansing? Can Palestinian Christians in Israel

unite with Jewish Christians? We could go on. Biases and prejudices are universal, and we must understand what ours are if we are to be effective.

3. *Absorb the life of the community.* Here the primary concern is participation in the life of the community. It is best not to question people at this time if at all possible. Become involved in community festivities and regular times of play. Learn from each age group. Play or participate with young people. Become part of the community's fun life. Enjoy a festive event, eat in community restaurants, shop in the stores. And notice how the people treat each other as well as how they respond to your presence.

4. *Gather community information.* Information should be gathered from people living in the community. It is important that residents of the community be the ones to define the community. Ask questions that pertain to the major themes of the community. What are the best aspects of living in the community? What are the most difficult aspects of living there? What are their feelings in general about the community? Would they rather live somewhere else and why? Feelings are important because they provide an underlying basis that may influence perceptions.

Always keep in mind that many people will try to please you or provide the answer you are looking for, especially if they think you are a stranger in the community or are of a different culture. Other considerations should be taken into account, such as the issues of respect and disclosure among different groups.

Gathering community information is extremely important for the eventual selection of indigenous leadership. Within this framework, begin to divide the community into age segments. How do adults, senior citizens, young adults and youth perceive the community? Gender distinctions are also important. Women may have different views of the community because of their profound concern for family. At times there may be a wide gap between males' and females' perceptions of the community. Both stories are important; they should not be used to confirm or disconfirm each other.

Merchants should also be divided into various groups. The first are merchants who are from the dominant culture of the community and live in the community. The second are merchants who are of the dominant culture but have moved out of the community. Third, there are merchants from the culture that was once the dominant group in the community. These persons, in spite of the shift, decided to stay in the community. Finally, there are merchants who are of a different culture and live outside the community.

The data collected is important as we integrate into the life of the community. Community becomes more valuable as one sits at the feet of the culture, learning and interacting.

Another source for the gathering of community information is community agencies. Agencies may be indigenous or outside controlled. Indigenous agencies are usually controlled by community leaders, even though their funds may come from outside sources. The leaders attempt to direct programs to fit community needs and use people from the community to run the programs. Where indigenous leaders are employed, most of the money earned stays in the community. Paraprofessionals draw lower salaries, while the professional model excludes many community workers. The professional model employs from outside and brings in high-paying staff who live outside of the area of service. Information gathered from both institutional models is valuable regardless of the control issue.

Besides community agencies, the religious community can in many cases be a source of information. However, this information is not always helpful, especially if the pastor and many of the members live outside and have limited exposure to the community. But in Latin America we find the presence of base ecclesial communities (CEBs). Although often organized under the Roman Catholic Church, as in Brazil (Hewitt 1991), these communities use lay leaders within primarily local memberships to provide both traditional religious services and innovative activities of social involvement. Leaders of these groups are potentially quite useful in providing information about their communities.

Another effective tool for discovering some of the unique aspects of a community is focus groups. Focus groups can be used to get a general feel for various community issues. People from the community are brought together for discussion of a particular topic. A Christian community center pulled together a couple of focus groups in order to determine what programs might be helpful to community members. This was an enriching exercise for the staff of the center.

Focus groups allow us to learn much about the community as we observe the interaction of participants. We are able to catch some of the significant words used in the neighborhood, often called buzz words. The meanings for various terms are explained, and this helps the fieldworker or missionary get a better handle on the worldview the people espouse. Often the group will speak about common experiences, and this leads to a recognition of trends that will eventually determine matters of contextualized ministry. The mission person gets a quick orientation to community that may be very valuable in determining strategy. Also, a focus group may provide the missionary with new relationships that will promote the bonding aspect that is essential in crosscultural ministry.

5. *Gathering demographic material.* In urban and metropolitan areas in the United States, one of the first things to examine is the census tracts and their geographical boundaries. Much demographic information can be gathered from city hall, institutions of higher learning, radio stations, cable companies, major fast-food companies and real estate agencies. Usually real estate agencies can provide good information on community transitions and the future and condition of the community. Most other countries have some form of a census which can be used. Also, existing mission agencies will often compile demographic material on selected nations for use in strategizing.

Sometimes the key to finding demographic information is forming relationships with key government people who can then act as gatekeepers, providing access to records that are not publicly displayed. Becoming acquainted with the community is an ongoing process that helps us prepare for a ministry that honors the Word of God as the source of strength and transformation in which God's concern for the people of the community is understood.

6. *Gathering God's perspective on the community.* In all this the gatherer, walking in the Holy Spirit, discerns God's perspective on the community. How are we discerning the Holy Spirit's leading? Paul was touched deeply as he viewed the idolatrous city of Athens (Acts 17:16). At another point the Holy Spirit kept Paul and his missionary friends from preaching the gospel by the Holy Spirit in the province of Asia (Acts 16:6). Philip was instructed by the messenger of the Lord to go south, where he eventually met an Ethiopian official in need of new life in Christ (Acts 8:26-40).

In living out Christ in our communities, the yielding of our lives to the indwelling, guiding work of the Holy Spirit is imperative. The Holy Spirit will burden us with Christ's love. The conviction of serving the Lord will draw us to prayer. Sureness that we are in God's appointed place will bring joy. And at the same time, the demonic powers will force us to prepare us for battle.

7. *Formulating and interpreting information gathered.* The gatherer must now formulate and interpret the information gathered and list questions that will allow people to evaluate the interpretation. The people must participate in critiquing our information.

## Conclusion

Demographic studies seem to be technical and quite distant from the people you are researching. Yet demography is an essential discipline that complements ethnographic fieldwork. It is indispensable for any ministry that intends to work and serve in a community on a long-term basis.

One thing demographic work does that is not accomplished through other disciplines is determining needs in advance. This means ministries can plan for the future more accurately on the basis of community trends.

> Because felt needs are products of a past-to-present orientation, continuing to function on a felt needs basis will make community development increasingly irrelevant to and incapable of addressing today's major social and economic issues. The felt needs concept should be replaced by that of "anticipatory needs," products of a present-to-future orientation, which identifies what needs to be done in order to move towards a specified future. The distinction between felt needs and anticipatory needs is crucial to the practitioner because these two types of needs are very different and lead to different programming activities and patterns of relationships with community groups. (Wade 1989)

Demographic work will provide a good grasp of what is happening in the community and in the larger geographical area. It not only provides insight into the present needs of a community but also highlights trends, such as in education, family structure, employment opportunities and unemployment. We use the trends as indicators or predictors that allow us to foresee developments in the next five or ten years.

A church has learned it must plan for a massive population movement from the south side of its city, due to city planning. This relocation of a large group of people means the church should anticipate changes in the community, recognize the tipping dynamic described earlier, and plan for the stress on its congregation that is common during community transitions. The resulting serious community involvement may lead to church growth. Population growth very often will mean church growth if churches are prepared to minister with the gospel of Jesus Christ to the new people entering the community.

This type of people movement will also occur when there is natural or civil strife in a country that suffers from constant political instability. In the early 1980s there were mass exoduses from Nicaragua, El Salvador and Guatemala as people fled the death squads. Residents of Florida remember the waves of Cuban refugees fleeing the Castro regime. Rwanda has been in the throes of civil strife for many years. In 2000 Eritreans in Ethiopia were forced to leave due to the strife between those two countries. Thousands fled the strife-torn former Yugoslavia. The population movements in such cases present different needs. Their needs are more drastic; those who seek to minister may need to do a great deal of networking with other agencies to address medical and healthcare needs.

A church in the north Philadelphia area did a demographic study that informed them that better than 45 percent of the population was unchurched. They also discovered that the educational achievement of elementary students was very low and that the population makeup was predominantly African American and Hispanic. This study alerted the church that they were in a good place to consider a ministry to meet educational needs of children and families as well as developing a multiethnic church.

Cities are constantly changing, so the churches in them must remain alert in order to maintain a viable, relevant and visible presence. Churches must avail themselves of all the tools God has made available, including demographics. We have seen how demographics assists us in discovering where communities are lacking God's shalom. We have been challenged to go beyond personal issues to identify systemic barriers to participating in shalom. We have noted how demographics help us understand overall church growth and decline trends. And we have learned various procedures to follow to do an effective community analysis. Churches must anticipate and act accordingly rather than react, usually incorrectly, after transitions have taken place. This is the purpose of using demographics for ministry.

# Part 5

## Promoting Kingdom Signs in the City

# 17

## Reachable People Groups & the City

THE SMALL STOREFRONT CONGREGATION FINISHED its Sunday morning service with an altar call. A number of the members had been spending time with María, presenting God's plan of salvation to her. When María came forward to accept Christ as her Savior, these members praised God. They reminded each other that the angels rejoice each time someone comes to know the Lord. This was evangelism at its best.

In the Western world, especially in the United States, we are taught to be individualistic. The above vignette highlights this individualism in regard to evangelism. People were rejoicing that some*one* came to know the Lord. Of course we would all want to join in celebrating what God accomplished in María's life. But we ought to go further in our evangelistic thinking. María is an immigrant from El Salvador. She works as a maid at the Hotel Hilton along with many other Salvadoran women and women from the Dominican Republic and Haiti. She represents a nationality, an ethnicity, an occupational niche and a socioeconomic grouping. Our individualistic view of her salvation is short-sighted. We need to expand our vision of evangelism to recognize that María represents intertwining people *groups,* groups that must be confronted with the gospel. But it is not easy for an individualistic culture to become group oriented.

Part of the problem lies in our vocabulary. When we use the word *people* in English, we usually mean "persons" (Winter 1987:18). We talk about the three people standing in front of the store. Sometimes we think a little more broadly and talk about the people as "the public, the masses, or the common people" (McGavran 1970:296). This is what politicians mean when they herald themselves as the people's choice.

Responding to scriptural mandates to reach the nations, we once again find difficulty in word usage. Our English notion of *nations* is not helpful. We talk about the United Nations and we basically equate nations with countries or political entities. But people groups are much more than just nationalities. So what do we mean by people groups, and how do we reach them?

This chapter begins with a discussion of the nature of people groups. Where did that term come from? What exactly do we mean by it? Once the meaning is explored and established, we will look at two very important dynamics that lead to the intermingling of a plurality of people groups in urban areas around the world: immigration/migration and poverty.

Traditionally missionaries have responded to Jesus' call to be his witnesses "to the ends of the earth" (Acts 1:8) by traveling to the remotest parts of jungles, deserts, mountains and plains to reach the millions of people who have not heard about God's saving grace. However, we have witnessed a turn of events. The world is entering our cities at high rates. Missionaries are no longer primarily dealing with homogeneous tribes but rather are faced with the challenge of plurality and rapid change in increasingly dense and complex urban settings. Wherever we find people mixtures that can be divided by tribe, nationality, color or caste, we also tend to find economic stratification based on those divisions. This does not happen naturally but is a product of discrimination and injustice. So we do not speak just about the different ethnic groups. We start using terms such as *minorities* for some groups. As a part of this chapter's treatment of immigration/migration and the plurality arising from it, we will discuss what minorities are and how they are determined.

When justice, or maybe we should say injustice, comes into play, it is important to discern issues of power and perceived powerlessness. Ultimately these issues are tied up with economics: some peoples (people groups, not just individual persons) become rich and others poor. Power and poverty tend to be closely related dynamics. We want to understand exactly what poverty is, the extent of poverty in the cities of this world, how poverty is perpetuated and what can be done to alleviate it.

The chapter ends with a strategy for evangelism of people groups and church growth as we seek to bring the fullness of the gospel to the peoples of our cities. How do we approach groups that speak many different languages? What happens when the second and third generations start using the standard language of the country yet do not want to completely lose their own cultural identity? How should the church respond to the injustices that cause so much pain for so many? How do we effectively reach the poor with the hope found in Jesus Christ, who cares about them and is not satisfied with their current condition? We will pull together principles to both provide a challenge to consider these questions carefully and help in developing churches that can effectively respond.

## The Nature of People Groups

Remember María? What people group does she belong to? Does she have to belong to only one people group, or can she be a part of a number of people groups that overlap and intersect? The answer to these questions returns us to what we are trying to do—what our ministry focus is. To understand, we need to trace the usage of people group terminology back to two schools of thought—church growth and unreached people groups research.

As already noted, there are two common English usages of the word *people*. McGavran gives a more technical definition that should help us begin to catch its meaning in connection with people groups: the word *people* can be used to "mean a tribe, a caste, or any homogeneous unit where marriage and intimate life take place only within the society" (McGavran 1970:296). This is a very tight definition. If we think it through, it makes sense as long as there is a clear division between groups. But do we have clear divisions today? McGavran formulated his definition a few decades ago, and since then the world has drastically changed. Urbanization has brought many peoples together, and many have mixed on numerous levels including "marriage and intimate life." But at least this definition is a starting point.

Researchers of unreached people groups rely on Matthew 28:19-20: "Therefore go and make disciples of all nations, baptizing them in the name of the Father and of the Son and of the Holy Spirit, and teaching them to obey everything I have commanded you," and Luke 24:47, "Repentance and forgiveness of sins will be preached in his name to all nations, beginning at Jerusalem." These two verses are the only ones that use the word *nations* explicitly to indicate all the world's peoples.

But we still get confused between nations and peoples. Let's use Yugoslavia as an example. Since the demise of the communist bloc, Yugoslavia has rarely been out of the news. Fighting has been a fact of life between Serbs, Bosnians, Croatians and Kosovars. The term "ethnic cleansing" has become a part of our vocabulary. In the past Yugoslavia was thought of as a single nation inhabited by Yugoslavs; we now know that Yugoslavia was a single nation in terms of its geopolitical borders, but it was inhabited by multiple people groups, each with its own culture and biases toward each other. Now even its geopolitical borders have been split.

Out of this confusion Harley Schreck and David Barrett have proposed a definition of *people* as "a human population with a common language, shared ethnicity, and significant patterns of social interaction" (1987:6). This is a little more helpful. Even though there are many persons who claim two languages or multiple ethnicities, almost everyone has a primary language and a primary ethnicity.

Most unreached peoples researchers are interested in discovering discrete groups in order to know where to place missionaries so that all nations will be discipled. Barrett puts out long lists of unreached people groups each year. Groups that have been reached are eliminated, and new groups that have been found are added. The basic idea is to track progress in reaching the unreached. James Reapsome notes Conn's explanation of this: "The terms 'people groups' and 'unreached people groups' are . . . functional attempts at blocking out the job that still needs doing" (Reapsome 1987:64). You can almost see a giant tote board listing all the people groups with check marks next to those that have been reached. It is a strategy tool for Christians who want to be faithful in reaching the nations.

Given this ministry goal, every person in the world should belong to one and only one people group at a time (Schreck and Barrett 1987:12). This is what Schreck and Barrett call a "global" definition of people group. People can be divided into such groups a number of different ways, but the researchers are looking for a way that would make sense according to their definition of a people. For example, dividing the world between men and women would create discrete groups but would hardly be helpful for progressing toward the ministry goal of reaching all the people groups in the world. A better focus is divisions "based on ethnicity, language, and political boundaries. . . . This approach then gives us the type of global partitioning we need" (Schreck and Barrett 1987:13).

Schreck and Barrett introduce a second way of determining people groups, the "particularistic" way: a people group is "a significantly large sociological grouping of individuals who perceive themselves to have a common affinity for one another. From the viewpoint of evangelization this is the largest possible group within which the gospel can spread without encountering barriers of understanding or acceptance" (1987:7).

To understand this better, we need to draw on an anthropological under-standing of cultures and subcultures. Charles Kraft (1996) recognizes that culture can be understood at several levels. He speaks of community, regional, national and even multinational culture (e.g., Western culture). But he also notes other ways to divide cultures according to one or more shared characteristics—economic, social, religious or political. He goes even further by introducing subcultures such as "youth, blue-collar work-ers, white-collar workers, farmers, even computer specialists, taxi driv-ers, clergy, and any number of others" (Kraft 1996:41). Now we can begin to see María as a member of all the different groups mentioned earlier.

The particularistic definition has met with some criticism. The primary problem is pointed out by John Robinson of Missionary Internship: "To define people groups only in sociological terms gives little help in the task of enumeration beyond the framework of the particular sociological group in question. When one begins to try to enumerate more broadly, the tremendous problem of overlapping classifications makes it very diffi-cult to talk meaningfully about progress" (Reapsome 1987:63). Clearly Robinson is still trying to check people groups off his list of the unreached. Let's be clear. This goal is fine as long as we recognize that it is only one goal and is part of a broad missionary focus of reaching all peoples, all nations for the Lord. However, that is not the focus of those using the particularistic definition.

The particularistic understanding of making disciples of all the nations includes recognizing "that human beings live in the context of society, and in interaction with one another. In order to see disciples appear, we must evangelize persons in their social and cultural matrices" (Schreck and Barrett 1987:5). In other words, the particularistic definition points us toward exploring how to effectively contextualize the gospel so as to actually bring people to Christ. Considering 1 Corinthians 9:1-23, Schreck and Barrett continue:

> Winning "the more" (vs. 19) involves discovering and eliminating whatever offends or confuses (so far as lifestyle, message presentation, methodology) and enhancing what will maximize the number of those who become obedi-ent to the gospel. This necessarily implies a careful knowledge of the group to whom the evangelist directs his or her ministry. What are their values, beliefs, and ways of making decisions? What adjustments must be made in methods, media, or roles if there is to be a culturally authentic opportunity to respond to the gospel? (1987:7-8)

This is the approach we need to build strategies that can address the overlapping pluralism of urban life.

A second set of criticisms of the particularistic approach deals with the goal of unreached peoples missionaries, which is to establish churches among the unreached. They are not looking only to see individuals saved but are wanting to establish a lasting Christian witness among people groups. In fact, the definition of unreached people group is "a people group among which there is no indigenous community of believing Christians with adequate number resources to evangelize this people group without outside (cross-cultural) assistance" (Reapsome 1987:61). This definition reveals that it is not even enough to have churches established; the goal is to see churches run by the indigenous people, leadership development from within the group.

The particularistic approach could lend itself to this goal, but not necessarily. For example, if you are strategizing to reach taxi drivers, do you actually aim to plant and grow a church just for taxi drivers? Of course not. The taxi drivers would most likely be discipled to join churches that already exist. Making disciples of all the nations cannot be narrowed down to just planting churches. Planting churches is vitally important, as is developing indigenous leadership, but other ministry goals are also important. The global approach to understanding people groups and the particularistic approach have different purposes. They should not be seen as at odds with each other but as complementary.

A final problem with the particularistic approach has to do with the mindset of mission and church leaders. "The concept of culture or ethnicity has already found a permanent home in the worldview of many missiologists and church executives. Other legitimate ways in which people groups are formed have not been understood to the same degree. There seems to be an implicit belief that only ethnicity defines meaningful or scripturally relevant groups among humans" (Schreck and Barrett 1987:32). Such a close-minded mentality does not allow for the reality we find in cities whose "heterogeneity and social complexity" provide numerous ways for groups to be established. "Ethnicity is only one of the many forces which shape human social life" (Schreck and Barrett 1987:33). Others include "residence, class, caste, career, nationality, leisure, travel, clubs, societies, industrialization, and so on" (Schreck and Barrett 1987:16-17).

Regardless of whether the global or particularistic approach is used, the idea of dividing up the world into people groups is subject to criticism on some fronts. The primary difficulty is that using this concept is often associated with the homogeneous unit principle (HUP) of the church growth movement. McGavran asserts, "A homogeneous unit of society may be said to have 'people consciousness' when its members think of themselves as a separate tribe, caste, or class" (1970:190). Noting that "the great obstacles to conversion are social, not theological" (1970:191), McGavran comes to the conclusion that "men like to become Christians without crossing racial, linguistic, or class barriers" (1970:198). He further says, "Church planters who enable men to become Christians without crossing such barriers are much more effective than those who place them in men's way" (1970:200). McGavran acknowledges that in areas that can be called "true melting pots" the church can be a unifying force that supersedes the divisions among peoples. He cites the development and tremendous growth of Pentecostal churches in the cities of Brazil as an example. But he concludes, "If congregations increase, they do so by transfer growth. Non-Christians are not becoming Christians in numbers." Despite his statement, there are many models of multiethnic churches in the United States (see Ortiz 1996) that are growing through evangelism. Some of the models cross not only ethnic lines but also class lines, such as Rock of Our Salvation Church in Chicago.

The main criticisms of HUP, and people group strategies in general, have to do with their advocacy of separatism in the church—an ecclesial separate but equal idea. Critics see HUP as promoting racism and division in the true universal body of Christ. Of course this is not the intention of church growth theorists, but it does tend to be the result of that type of strategy. A related criticism is that HUP "allows a missiology based upon the social sciences, not upon Scripture. The Church should be the 'new humanity' created by Christ—not the broken humanity cowed and fractured by racism or division into classes or castes" (Schreck and Barrett 1987:26).

Schreck and Barrett attempt to answer such criticisms by pointing out that people groups may be homogeneous units but are not necessarily so, especially if we use the particularistic definition.

Now that we have a little better understanding of what people groups are and some of the possible dangers in targeting people groups, let's look at the process of immigration/migration which has brought great ethnic plurality into major urban centers.

## Immigration and Migration

María immigrated from El Salvador to a major U.S. city. Why did she come? Did she come alone? Why did she settle where she did? How does her arrival affect the growth or decline of her city? The answers to these questions lead us into the subject of urbanization: how do cities grow or decline?

There are really only two ways populations of cities (or any other area) can grow: people are born in the city or people move into the city. On the other hand, city population can decline when people die or move out. Natural and migrational forces are both important, but either takes on more significance depending on what stage of the urbanization process the city is in.

> The two components of urban population growth vary in relative impor-
> tance through space and time, but in general migration is more important in
> the early stages of urban population growth. . . . As the urban population
> rises, so does the contributory role of natural growth, although only up to a
> certain point. Beyond this point, . . . urban fertility begins to decline and
> migrational growth once again becomes more important, albeit at a drasti-
> cally reduced level. (Drakakis-Smith 1987:29)

Many old industrial cities in the United States are undergoing patterns of urban decline rather than growth. However, the decline affects some cities and some groups more than others. Take Philadelphia. According to U.S. census figures, the total population of the city of Philadelphia declined between 1980 and 1990. Both the white and the black populations of the city showed significant decline during that period, but the Hispanic and Asian populations grew dramatically. This example gives us a taste of the dynamic population changes that take place in our cities.

**The nations come to the cities.** What do we mean by this—that the nations are coming to the cities? In many countries the primary flow is internal, from rural areas to cities. In those cases farmers have been pushed off their land through drought or competition with large agribusinesses. They may have tried to work as laborers on one of the large holdings for a while, but that work is usually seasonal and doesn't pay enough to hold them over through the workless periods. Men may leave wives and children behind to seek work in the city with the hope of returning, but more often than not, if the family reunites it will be in the city.

This phenomenon can be seen the world over. In the United States a great black migration occurred during World War I when the cotton crop was destroyed in the South just as northern cities needed workers for the war effort. Streams of southern blacks moved into northeastern and midwestern industrial cities. In the Third World, modernization efforts have had the same effect. Poor rural peasants have no choice but to try the cities for survival.

At the same time, the lure of work or the desire to flee repressive governments has caused many people to move to other countries. Some seek freedom, some seek economic betterment, and many just seek the chance to find a job—any job. "Uprooted and transplanted immigrants, starting life anew in strange surroundings and needing community and friendship, flood into cities" (McGavran 1970:282). These words were actually written before North Americans were feeling the effects of the new immigration, which took place after 1968, when the new Immigration Act became law.

How has the new immigration affected U.S. cities? For one thing, it has brought astounding heterogeneity. For example, the 1990 census shows seven distinct Asian nationalities and ten distinct Hispanic nationalities in the Los Angeles metropolitan area with populations over twenty thousand. On the other side of the country, in the New York City metropolitan area, there were five Asian nationalities and eleven Hispanic nationalities with populations over twenty thousand. We can now understand better why the Hispanic and Asian populations of Philadelphia grew even though the overall population declined. We can also imagine the variety of sounds, smells and sights we would take in if we went through any of the urban areas that have attracted immigrants.

These changes affect the urban church as well as other urban institutions. "People from all nations are coming to America. . . . The shift to urban and ethnic missions is probably the most important development in denominational and interdenominational home-mission activity in the closing years of the twentieth century" (Greenway and Monsma 1989:61).

The phenomenon of attracting the peoples of the world is not unique to U.S. cities. Greenway tells of visiting an Anglican parish in Liverpool, England, in which twenty-two different languages were spoken. He also recalls speaking in an Amsterdam church to a congregation "composed of people from a dozen different Spanish-speaking countries" (Greenway and Monsma 1989:63).

With our new understanding of nations or people groups we can see the same kind of dynamics occurring in Third World cities. For example, Nigeria is a country of over 250 tribes, each with its own language and culture. In its major cities, such as Lagos, there are large populations of many tribes and at least some learned people from almost all the tribes. Yes, the nations are definitely coming to the cities.

***The harvest.*** When people make a major move, such as rural to urban or immigration to another country, they tend to be unsettled. They face new values, new ways of doing things, possibly a new language. At the same time they have left behind a large portion of their former support system. Families and friends are separated, possibly for the first time in their lives. As McGavran says, "Immigrants and migrants have been so pounded by circumstances that they are receptive to all sorts of innovations, among which is the Gospel. They are in a phase of insecurity, capable of reaching out for what will stabilize them and raise their spirits" (1970:219). To illustrate, "it is no accident that the tremendous growth of

Pentecostals in Brazil has taken place largely among the migrants flooding down from the northeast to the great cities of the south" (McGavran 1970:219).

Cities around the world provide a wonderful opportunity for reaching the nations, yet too often it is other religions that are taking advantage of this.

> In the 1980s the non-Christian religions are on the march in such unusual places as London, Brussels, and San Diego. Major cities have become the backdrop for a syncretistic mix of mosques, gurus, and corner altars dedicated to objects of worship hitherto unknown in those locales. In London the elegant Regent's Park Mosque is one of the most beautiful worship centers built in England in the past quarter century. In nearby Brent, England, Muslims pray in what was once a Reformed Church building. In the east of London Muslims have bought an old synagogue and are now using it as a mosque. In Brussels one can see devout Muslims all over the city dropping to their knees and foreheads to observe their noon prayer ritual. In Stuttgart, Mercedes Benz has built a company mosque for its Turkish and European convert workers. The cities of France in 1984 contain more than two million Muslims. A new mosque was completed in 1980 in Rome where its call to prayer is within hearing of the Vatican itself.
>
> San Diego reflects the North American cities flooded within the past decade with Oriental religions. Americanized gurus mix with Nichiren Buddhists and Arab Muslims on the busy streets and market places, each vying for new converts from the Catholic and Protestant Christians there. (Starkes 1984:95)

Just as all these religions are making inroads into the world's cities, evangelicals are fleeing the new and different and moving out of the cities in order to maintain their comfort levels. Ordinary Christians have been seriously negligent in answering the mandate of the Great Commission; instead they have left "mission work to professionals specifically "called" by God. We are not taking advantage of the open door, and it will not remain open for too long. "A Methodist minister in Lima, Peru, . . . said that country folk who moved to the shack-towns of that great city remained winnable for a decade or so; but when they began to earn well, built a brick house, and educated their sons and daughters, they grew hard of heart and dull of hearing" (McGavran 1970:219).

Have we abandoned the nations living so close to us and given them over to non-Christian religions? How will we explain this to our Lord? Far too many comfortable Christians will have to face the same rebuke aimed at the servant with the single talent, "You wicked, lazy servant!" (Mt 25:26).

Part of the problem is that it is easier to deal with sending missionaries to foreign lands, to be interested in the different peoples "over there," than to deal with different people in our own cities.

> Too often, it would seem, the differences of these neighbors seem threatening and not at all intriguing. We are not as concerned about meeting these people and learning the reasons for their cultural practices as we are about making sure those practices don't bother us. . . . Our crosstown neighbors are close enough to have an impact on our daily lives. . . . It may be easier to get to know and appreciate people ten thousand miles away than those who live ten blocks away. (Ronsvalle and Ronsvalle 1992:119)

We must be willing to get out of our comfort zones and reach out to the nations the Lord has brought to us.

**Ethnic consciousness.** Interestingly, as long as we are surrounded by people just like us, we do not think of ourselves as being ethnic. So when does a people group recognize itself as a people group? Did the Irish Catholics fleeing the potato famine really think of themselves as an ethnic group prior to coming to the United States? Or did that occur as they realized they had to fit into a majority culture different from theirs? Did feeling different or, maybe more to the point, being treated differently have anything to do with raising their consciousness about ethnicity? What else enters into this awareness?

It may be helpful to explore the process people groups go through when they enter a new city. First, they tend to be segregated by choice. It is only natural that newly arrived immigrants would want to settle with others from the same homeland, others who tell the same types of stories in the same language, who eat the same foods and celebrate the same festivals, and who may be helpful in the quest for a job. However, events that follow may go in either of two directions.

The first direction is what sociologists call assimilation. First-generation immigrants tend to stay with those like them for most of their lives, but their children and grandchildren—the second and third generations—will have grown up schooled in their new homeland, possibly speaking a language different from their parents'. They have been exposed to the customs and opportunities afforded the majority and have learned better how to fit in. The result is that they become different. They are not like their parents. They have become more a part of their new home. They have advanced educationally and economically and have mixed with the majority to the point that there are very few visible differences between the immigrant and the majority. This is assimilation.

There was a time when it was thought that all groups would assimilate. However, many groups maintain large pieces of their cultural heritage regardless of generation. This clinging to one's own ethnicity has caused pluralism—the second major form of immigrant adaptation. Pluralism can be voluntary or involuntary.

Consider the city of Ibadan in Nigeria as an example of both assimilation and pluralism. The tribal majority of Ibadan is Yoruba. Also residing
in Ibadan are two minority tribes, the Hausa and the Ibos. The Hausa control "long-distance trade in kola and cattle between northern and southern Nigeria" (Cohen 1988:328) and want to protect their monopoly of this
trade. In order to do this, they have established links in a chain of trade,
one of which is Sabo, a section of Ibadan that is almost completely inhabited by Hausa. In order not to share the wealth associated with this trade,
the Hausa have rules against social interaction which have been reinforced by the adoption in the early 1950s of a strict Islamic sect. When the
Hausa entered Ibadan, the Yoruba treated them as strangers and did not
reach out to them apart from trying to become part of the lucrative trade,
an attempt that met with almost no success. The Hausa maintained their
ethnic identity for economic reasons. They knew if they mixed with the
Yoruba, they would lose their control over the trade routes.

The Ibos were also initially treated as strangers by the Yoruba. But they
did not have a reason for maintaining ethnic solidarity within their tribe,
and they eventually mixed with the Yoruba. They have only a weak tribal
association, and the tribe has promoted successful adaptation to modern
urban conditions among its people. "Second-generation Western Ibos in
Ibadan speak Yoruba 'without accent' and have Yoruba as their play-
mates" (Cohen 1988:331).

This is more than just an interesting story. It has real implications for
reaching these tribes. "The degree of people consciousness is an aspect
of social structure which greatly influences when, how, and to what
extent the Gospel will flow through that segment of the social order.
Castes or tribes with high people consciousness will resist the Gospel primarily because to them becoming a Christian means 'joining another
people' " (McGavran 1970:190). It would be exceedingly difficult to reach
the Hausa who not only have a high degree of people consciousness but
also have wedded their economic aspirations to a highly restrictive
Islamic sect. However, the Ibos, who have already shown great willingness to adapt to newness, would be much more open.

In the United States, government and big business have united to
develop an economically stratified society that to a large degree is laid out
along ethnic lines. The groups on the bottom are the groups Christians
have abandoned in the inner cities, where other religions are taking hold.
The Black Muslim movement is aggressive and dynamic in many major
cities. Christians do not want to go into Philadelphia's round house,
which is the first place prisoners are sent while awaiting their arraign-

ment, but Muslim leaders daily enter and minister to these men and women. We are throwing away tremendous opportunities to "make disciples of all nations."

Groups that have been involuntarily pushed into pluralism are victims of discrimination. This can take many different forms. An extreme is the past apartheid of South Africa, which made it illegal for blacks, coloreds, Indians and whites to intermix socially and forced blacks to live in designated townships. In the United States, segregation levels for African Americans have led some researchers to write of "American apartheid" (Massey and Denton 1993). Then there are subtle ways of keeping discriminated groups "in their place"—for example, school systems that do not educate inner-city blacks and Hispanics so that they can compete with other groups to succeed in higher education.

In the process of immigration or migration, then, groups do not have equal opportunities in employment, education or overall economic well-being. But what does it take to keep a group down? Are we talking solely in terms of numbers? The answer to this takes us into a consideration of minorities.

**Minorities.** What do we mean by a minority? Quantitatively, the major ethnic group in a country (or area or city)—the one with the largest population—is the majority and all others are minorities. In the United States this means that European whites are the majority and all others—blacks, Hispanics, Asians, native indigenous people and so on—are minorities. In France the French are the majority and Algerians and Moroccans are minorities.

Although this is an important way of determining minority status, it leads to some confusion. The concept of numeric strength tends to make us think in terms of power, and usually the majority does hold the power, but this does not always hold true. In Indonesia a very small minority of Chinese have a great deal of economic power, as they control most of the assets and large business groups. However, the Indonesian majority does control political power. During apartheid years, the white minority in South Africa held both economic and political power. During the colonization era, the invading colonizers were all small minorities, but they assumed control backed up by military strength. At times, such as in the United States, the colonizers were so effective in controlling the indigenous peoples and attracting other colonizers that they actually moved from being the minority to becoming the overwhelming majority.

Maybe we need to think about minority status differently. Maybe we need to take into consideration the role of discrimination in ethnic stratification. Maybe we need to define minority qualitatively rather than quantitatively. This would mean that the groups that do not hold economic and political power, regardless of their size, can be labeled minorities. The issue is power or the lack of power.

We can even say that the issue is the degree of power held by a group or the degree to which a group lacks power. In a society as pluralistic as the United States, we could picture the various groups arrayed along a continuum based on their access to power. This would leave four groups at the powerless end: African Americans, Puerto Ricans, Chicanos and Native Americans. Other groups, such as Cubans, Chinese, Japanese, Indians and so on would be arranged along the continuum with European whites at the powerful end.

All discrimination is sin. When we speak of discrimination, we refer to overt acts. But underlying these acts are the majority's attitudes of superiority-inferiority. If we understand minority in this manner, population numbers become only one part of the explanation. The rest is really a matter of oppression. In order to meet the needs of urban minorities who experience alienation, marginalization and injustice, the church must be concerned with justice issues.

Discrimination is not just a U.S. evil. It is found the world over. It can be found in Europe, especially in Germany, where tensions have arisen with "guest workers" from southern and eastern Europe. In Southeast Asia many countries are resentful of the influx of Chinese and Indians. "In recent years ghettos have developed in selected areas [of Western European cities], which are attributed in part to the large scale influx of black West Indians to British cities; Algerians to France, especially Paris, and Italians to cities in Switzerland and Germany" (Brunn and Williams 1983:97). Discrimination tends to revolve around differences—any number of differences.

> A number of social problems are created by tensions between religious groups (Catholics and Protestants in Northern Ireland), linguistic and nationalistic differences (Belgium), and long established residents and recently arrived foreign immigrant groups. Indonesians (Moluccans) in Dutch cities; Pakistanis, Saudis, and West Indians in London; Italians and Turks in Munich . . . and Algerians in Paris, Marseilles, and other French cities have been the victims of social alienation and the focus of conflicts. (Brunn and Williams 1983:115)

Underlying discrimination there are usually economic forces—a drive to keep wealth in the hands of those who already have it. This results in wealth for a few and poverty for many. David Claerbaut contrasts the ideological concept of "each person is equal in worth before God and in the eyes of the law" with the "private norm of prejudice and discrimina-

tion [which] very clearly accords differential degrees of respect and defer-
ence to individuals based on group affiliation" (1983:129). He then relates
this to its base in economics:

> Lust for power and advantage gives rise to competition. When victory can-
> not be gained within the system economically, educationally, or occupation-
> ally, it will often be seized through forms of prejudice and oppression. To
> have advantage, even on illicit and immoral grounds, is preferred to risking
> a possible setback in status. (Claerbaut 1983:132)

The only possible result of this type of reasoning is the impoverishment of
some so that others can live a life of luxury.

## Poverty

Just what is the extent of world poverty? And what are the causes? Robert
Linthicum warned that by the close of the twentieth century, "more than
20% of all the people on the face of the earth" would be "the urban poor."
That means one out of every five people is among the urban poor. Viv
Grigg puts it another way: "If one includes the less reachable, decaying
inner-city slums as well as the street people in [Third World] cities, a reasonable estimate of the urban poor by the year 2000 is one billion people"
(1992a:25). This projection does not include the urban poor in the Western world, and neither projection includes the rural poor. These numbers
are staggering. This is not what God intended for his creation. But how do
we respond to these statistics? Too often we don't.

A big part of the problem is simply that the numbers are staggering.
They're so large that we have a problem grasping what they mean. "Over-
exposure and lack of direct involvement [create] indifference" (Ortiz
1988:4). "Too often 'poverty' is merely an abstract idea; we lose sight of
the fact that it is not 'statistics' who are hungry, but individuals with
names and faces" (Ronsvalle and Ronsvalle 1992:18). Linthicum adds,
"What is terribly important for us as Christians to realize is that behind
every statistic are millions of individual stories, stories of poverty, of sickness and despair, stories of people who are unable to influence the course
of their own lives and are powerless to change the course of their neighborhoods or cities" (1991b:7). But we do not see these people; we do not
see their faces or hear their stories. They are invisible to us, or they are
pictured as living so far away that they have nothing to do with us.

"The perpetuation of poverty by society results partly . . . from its invisibility. . . . This invisibility is exacerbated by the immobility of the poor"
(Claerbaut 1983:69). Roger Greenway and Timothy Monsma add, "The
poor are relatively immobile and tend to stay within their own neighborhoods. Middle-class people do their best to avoid these poor areas. The

result is that neither understands the other" (1989:175).

This almost makes it sound as though it is not our fault, as though we have no responsibility. After all, we can't help what we can't see. But that is not true. We can learn what poverty is, what causes poverty, where we can find poverty and how we ought to respond to poverty.

**What is poverty?** What exactly do we mean by "poverty"? "Calcutta has more poverty and more grades of poverty than any other city in the world" (Grigg 1992a:40). However, when Mother Teresa visited the South Bronx in New York City, she said the people there suffered from much worse poverty than the people in Calcutta. How could she say that? What did she mean by the word *poverty?* Grigg helps by delineating a difference between absolute and relative poverty.

> *Absolute poverty* is a term used to describe poverty when people have an absolute insufficiency to meet their basic needs—food, clothing, housing. Indeed, many who are in absolute poverty starve to death. . . . *Relative poverty* is found in the developed world and is measured by looking at a person's standard of living relative to others in the community or nation. It is sometimes called secondary poverty. It is a measure of the extent to which people are on the margins of society. . . . It is often an exclusion from opportunity and participation, a marginalization from society. (Grigg 1992a:42)

This explanation sheds some light on Mother Teresa's words. The poor in the South Bronx may not be as absolutely poor as those in Calcutta, but living in the same city as some of the most prosperous people in the United States, and maybe the world, makes their relative poverty all the harder to handle. This leads to a real poverty of identity, hopelessness and a sense of total failure and inferiority. "Being poor and hopeless in a society where most are not produces a deep sense of alienation" (McGavran 1970:236).

The word most connected to poverty is *powerlessness.* "The poor are powerless, weak, and rendered helpless. Poor people have no social or political clout with which to free themselves from need. The poor are destitute, bereft of life's necessities, and dispossessed. In short, they are the wretched of the earth" (Greenway and Monsma 1989:173). And "poverty means much more than absence of money. It is powerlessness and alienation from the key institutions of society. . . . The urban poor are almost completely cut off from the wider society and yet are oppressively controlled by it" (Claerbaut 1989:70). Linthicum explains, "To truly understand the condition of poverty today, one must understand how power is exercised in the city. Poverty is not so much the absence of goods as it is the absence of power—the capability of being able to change one's situation" (Linthicum 1991b:10). And DuBose adds that whether urban poor are concentrated in inner cities as in the United States or around the rim of cities as in much of the Third World, "we see essentially the same kinds of deprivation: social, cultural, economic, political, psychological" (DuBose 1984:51).

Our response to this situation ought to be the same as God's. The cities that house the poor have forced the poor "to live lives that break God's heart and should break ours, as well" (Linthicum 1991b:8).

**What causes poverty?** We can all spout a list of reasons why people are poor—they're lazy; they're addicts; they're mentally deficient; they have a bad culture (from the culture of poverty literature); they have poor work habits.

> Those who are financially secure or politically powerful like to suggest that it is the fault of the poor that they are poor. Those who have been amply rewarded by the reigning system of the city and country like to suggest that the poor are lazy, lack education, lack personal initiative, have too many babies, etc. In other words, they suggest that it is their own fault that the poor are so poor; they are simply inferior people. (Linthicum 1991b:9)

It is much easier to blame the poor for being poor than to understand that we benefit from the very social, political and economic powers that are oppressing others and making them poor. But as Christians we cannot allow ourselves to fall into that trap. You may object: "I know of so and so who keeps losing jobs because of being late almost every day." How does that fit in?

> Generally, society blames the poor for being poor, but such blame focuses on the effects, not the causes. Poverty is a lack of options, complicated by the depletion of indispensable goods and services. The church must stop blaming the poor and begin assuming concern for their circumstances and the causes of poverty. This will be difficult as long as we in the church hold a "we-they" attitude and do not welcome those who are poor into our worship and communities. (Hollinger and Modica 1992:230)

"The cause of urban poverty is largely injustice. . . . Injustices, oppression and oppressive structures" cause poverty (Grigg 1992a:4). Whether in the United States and the rest of the Western world or in the Third World, injustices are at the root of poverty. We must at times participate in interventions that are not popular with the political and economic forces in power.

> The cause of the poverty of the slums has to do not only with the spiritual condition of the slum dweller and the lack of resources among the poor. It has to do also with oppression and the political and economic structures of society that operate in favor of the rich. Holistic ministry cannot avoid confronting the principalities and powers that pervert and corrupt the structures

of society in ways that bring abundance to the few and grinding poverty to the many. . . . If the poverty of your squatter [or slum] area is caused by oppression, the pastoral response will involve actions that may conflict with the interests of those who oppress. (Grigg 1992b:176-78)

"Why are there poor people in the city? It is not because they are lazy, uneducated, or lack initiative. It is because they lack power. People are poor because other people are rich—and use their wealth and power to control the poor. The poor are victims of such power, and as victims, often turn to victimizing each other" (Linthicum 1991b:20). The Old Testament has much to say about the poor. "A careful examination of the Hebrew words translated 'poor' reveals a much wider meaning than we might have expected. The poor are those who are forced into submission, reduced to subservience—the oppressed and violated" (Greenway and Monsma 1989:173).

Purposeful segregation has perpetuated and exacerbated poverty among African Americans in the United States. Much has been written about the changing economy in New York City, which has caused tremendous poverty among minorities and new immigrants as big business looked first to the South and then overseas for ever cheaper labor, exploiting people groups both at home and abroad. Linthicum (1991b:7) writes about the cruelty of the Nairobi government, which forced men to burn down their own homes in a slum where many had lived for twenty-five years. Michael Duncan (1996) recalls how a Taiwanese firm bought land around Manila on which squatters had lived for close to forty years and evicted all of them in order to bulldoze the area and build plush townhouses for the rich.

When the United States won Puerto Rico as spoils of war after the Spanish-American War, big U.S. businesses bought up or took land used by rural farmers to consolidate holdings into large sugar plantations. This resulted in huge levels of unemployment in rural areas, the migration of tens of thousand to island cities that did not have enough jobs, and finally the Puerto Rican diaspora to the mainland—over a third of the Puerto Rican people left the island in search of jobs. South African apartheid kept the vast majority of people, separated by race, in deplorable townships while the ruling white minority lived in luxury.

The examples are endless. We cannot close our eyes to the fact that injustice and oppression are at the root of most poverty in this world.

Yet it is not popular to talk about injustice, not in academia and not in churches.

Over recent decades [an ongoing debate] has relegated the issue of social justice to the hinterlands of academic inquiry. And this while cities have wit-

nessed a disturbing rise in homelessness, job losses, poverty, housing deprivation, and violence (much of it against women). Indeed, the speed and
depth of the urbanization of injustice urges critical analyses not only to
rethink the relationship between spatiality, power and justice, but also to
push for a political and intellectual agenda that rallies around the development of socially just urban practices. (Merrifield and Swyngedouw 1997:2-3)

We, as part of God's universal church, must address these issues. We
must take responsibility for what is going on in our cities, our countries,
our world.

**Where do we find the poor?** Before exploring strategies for reaching
the poor, let's discuss where we can find the poor. Remember, they tend
to be invisible, immobile, often segregated. We don't see them because
we don't want to see them. So we must intentionally discover where the
poor are. In the United States and most Western countries, we generally
find the poor huddled in inner-city slums. A clarification is helpful: "The
inner city does not necessarily refer to the geographic center of the city.
. . . An inner city can be defined as a poverty area in which there is much
government activity and control but little activity by the private sector"
(Claerbaut 1983:35).

Inner-city areas are not formed through natural means as suggested by
some sociologists, but are rather manipulated by the political and economic powers of urban centers. Redlining, steering and other purported
illegal actions are still very much a reality. In one poor Philadelphia community a call reporting a theft in progress did not bring police for a number
of hours, even though the thieves were stripping a building of everything
including plumbing fixtures, but just a few blocks away in an area inhabited
by professional people a call reporting a stolen barbecue grill brought five
squad cars immediately. This is discrimination in action. It is abetted by the
ability to identify the bad areas through segregation patterns.

Slums are not just a part of Western cities.

Although much poverty can be found in the larger transitional areas of the
cities, especially in the developed nations, the greatest concentration of poverty the world over is found in the slums. . . . The slum is the major social
context for physical, emotional, and moral deterioration in the city. It is
where urban poverty is seen in its most obvious reality and its most dramatic dimensions. . . .

[A slum] is a place where men, women, and children have to live in conditions fundamentally unsuited for the most basic expressions of any reasonably meaningful way of life. It is therefore inherently dehumanizing and
demoralizing. It is both the cause and result of poverty, and it is the place
where the vicious cycle of poverty is lived out to its most inhuman expression! (DuBose 1984:58-59)

DuBose's description of a slum tends to encompass all areas of extreme and concentrated poverty. However, as noted earlier, in developing nations there is often a differentiation between slums and squatter settlements. Slums consist of dilapidated housing, usually near a city center. Squatter settlements are clusters of unauthorized makeshift dwellings, usually on city peripheries.

The difference between slums and squatter settlements is more than physical. The significance goes beyond sociological interest and has direct bearing on the reachability of the people groups involved. *"Inner-city slums* . . . may be described as *slums of despair. . . .* In terms of response it is more strategic to focus on *squatter areas,* which tend to be *slums of hope"* (Grigg 1992b:44). Why would Grigg call squatter areas slums of hope? After all, squatter areas, with their makeshift housing and few or no public services, are much worse off physically than inner-city slums. But we must understand the reason people come to the squatter areas. They are usually poor people moving from rural areas with the hope of finding work in the city and thus improving their lives. The fact that work is not readily available does not change the fact that a move to the city is a move of hope. Also, many people who move into squatter settlements do improve their lives. However, most people who live in inner-city slums have been there for some time and have resigned themselves to a life of hopelessness.

Regardless of the type of slum, we find that slums "are the final result of all the major *powers* that have come to dominate the world in the last decades—urbanization, technology, industrialization, modernization, capitalism, multinationals, nationalism, colonialism, the United Nations, World Bank—all are what the Scriptures call powers that have contributed to the process" (Grigg 1992a:83). Again, the systemic causes of poverty are at work.

Linthicum tells us, "If the church does not deal with the systems and structures of evil in the city, then it will not effectively transform the lives of that city's individuals. . . . It is widely suggested that the systems that order the life of a city are economic, political and religious" (1991b:11). He goes on to suggest, "When the systems, corrupted by evil, corrupt the city enough, even the people are seduced by those systems. They finally begin to accept for themselves the standards the systems have built their empires upon. . . . Exploited and oppressed by the systems, the people will become exploiters and oppressors of each other" (Linthicum 1991b). If we are going to address poverty, we cannot avoid confronting these powers.

## Strategies for Reaching the Nations in Our Cities

So far in this chapter we have been exploring dynamics of urbanization that operate to separate people groups along ethnic and class lines. Whether in regard to immigration and migration or poverty, injustice plays a part in maintaining separations. In this section let's consider a number of strategies that have been found to be helpful in reaching people groups in our cities.

**Congruence.** An earlier section of this chapter discussed the homogeneous unit principle. David Britt suggests a different approach. He begins by asking, "How can we hope to understand the social processes that engender or enable church growth in a context as fluid and apparently random as the pluralism of a modern city?" (Britt 1991:27). The HUP is not helpful in such a setting; it will produce a church that is incapable of changing as the community changes, since the church will be reaching only out to people who are just like its current members. Many churches in urban centers were founded to meet the needs of a particular ethnic group. Later they stay homogeneous even though many, and eventually most, of their members have moved out of the immediate geographic area. Once thriving with membership in the thousands, such a church struggles to stay alive as more and more of its congregation—now mostly senior citizens—move or pass away. These churches literally die off because they are incapable of reaching out to the new citizens of the community, people who are from a different ethnic group and maybe even a different socioeconomic class.

Britt's model involves *congruency*. It is based on the idea that a church will grow as the values of the church and the values of the community interact and combine into something new. As the community changes, the new values fit into the interaction, thus allowing the church to adapt to the new community and continue growing as its message and worship remain relevant.

**First-generation immigrant churches.** "Growing churches will be those that accept ethnic congregations, allow them space to develop their own styles of worship, leadership, and activity, and make the fullest possible use of the laity in the ongoing life of the denomination" (Greenway and Monsma 1989:66). The idea is not to Anglo-Americanize new people groups or have them behave just like yourself, but rather to "disciple them within their cultures, transformationally, until all areas of their lives have been leavened by the gospel" (Greenway and Monsma 1989:81).

But can this really happen? Can we find models of churches that have been able to do it? The answer is yes. Ortiz lays out a progression of multicongregational models, beginning with the renting model. Here a dying church attempts to remain open and subsidize its budget by renting its facilities to other congregations, usually first-generation immigrant churches that hold services in their native language. There is little desire to interact apart from maintaining a rental agreement.

The second possibility is the celebrative model. Here there is much more contact between a number of congregations sharing a single facility. The idea is that the original congregation enjoys the presence of people from other cultures and celebrates what it sees as an example of what heaven will look like. However, the congregations remain separate and have relatively little contact apart from planned combined celebrative services.

The final option is the integrative model. This type of church "is not solely concerned with seeing people of various ethnic groups come together. It also wants to see them influence the life and structure of the church" (Ortiz 1996:72). Models of this type bring different language congregations together under one church structure. They work hard to develop coequal leadership from the different congregations with built-in accountability to deal with reconciliation issues. There is no superior and no inferior. Ownership of facilities rests with all the congregations, and the overall vision and ministry approach is governed by all. In the United States the English-speaking congregation actually looks more like a multiethnic church, as it services the second and third generations from all the groups.

Many people wonder, why do we need different language churches? Why can't everyone learn the standard language of the country and worship together in it? The major acculturation issue faced by immigrants is language. Often first-generation immigrants in the United States will never learn English, or will remain most comfortable using their native tongue. This is not unique to the United States. "In Mexico, eighty-eight Indian languages have survived four hundred years of Spanish dominance and are heart-languages for hundreds of thousands today" (McGavran 1970:193). Let's explore this further.

> Hundreds of millions of men live in two worlds. The first, of great importance to them, is that of "our intimates who speak our own language"; the second, of relatively slight importance, is that world of a strange tongue in which we trade and work with outsiders. In the first the "medium of communication" is the language of the heart; in the second, the "medium of confusion" is a trade language or standard language, good enough for buying and selling, taking orders and finding one's way, but pitifully inadequate for the things that really matter. (McGavran 1970:193)

Since the gospel message is aimed at the heart, it only makes sense that it would be more effectively communicated in a people's heart language. Multicongregational churches that uphold the value of each language group and have a true plurality of leadership and decision making can reach the wide array of immigrants who mix in our large cities.

Unfortunately, most missions use what has been termed the standard language, primarily because it is easier than learning several native languages and dialects. Also, since governments usually require the use of the standard language in schools, missionaries "find it difficult to use the vernacular for propagating the Gospel" (McGavran 1970:195). Sometimes missionaries are more concerned with their own ease than with the understanding of their hearers.

### Second-generation immigrant churches/multiethnic churches.

The first immigrant generation really needs to use native languages, then, to worship freely. But what about the second and third generations? Even though second-generation immigrants are schooled in the standard language, they find intimacy in the native tongue spoken at home. However, their skills in that native language are somewhat limited. This makes it difficult for them to understand formal preaching in their native tongue, but they do not want to let go of it altogether.

The tension arising from this confrontation of languages is poignantly pictured by Richard Rodriguez in *Hunger of Memory* (1982), recounting the process he went through in order to make English rather than Spanish his "public" language. In that process he lost both his ability to speak Spanish well and the intimacy attached to that language. How can a church reach those who are second or third generation and are torn between two languages?

Certain principles for reaching second-generation Hispanics can be generalized to other second-generation groups as well. First is the need to maintain their identity. "They must be given the dignity of their culture if they are to grow as balanced and progressive individuals in their present situation" (Ortiz 1993:81). Second, second-generation immigrants need to know their own history—not from an American or Western point of view but from the point of view of their own culture. Third, church leaders must take time to understand the groups "anthropologically and sociologically so that the church can provide 'room' for them to express their cultural dynamics" (Ortiz 1993:82). Fourth, efforts must be made to develop leadership from within the group and to include the group in ministry strategy and decisions. Finally, there is the issue of language. Services will usually use the standard language for preaching but include worship pieces—songs, Scripture reading, testimonies and so on—in the native language.

When a church is situated in a community that is either multiethnic or in a transitioning stage, some further problems emerge. To thrive, a multiethnic church must intentionally include all groups at all levels of leadership and decision making, so that each of the groups feels ownership of the church. The goal is to develop a new humanity that is inclusive of all, that displays both the diversity of its people and the unity found in Christ.

## Strategies for Reaching the Poor in Our Cities

The church has often been negligent in reaching the poor. It's not comfortable to be around poor people. Even those with a kind heart struggle as the needs seem overwhelming. Where can we begin?

One place is to recognize the importance of ministry to and among the poor for God. God did not intend that there would be poor peoples in our cities. He desired Jerusalem to be "a city centered in the worship of God and practicing a politics of justice and an equitable stewardship of resources for all" (Linthicum 1991b:14). God wants justice for his people.

Grigg suggests that "the question for us as Christians is how to bring justice into the process of peasants migrating to the city" (1992a:90). But what does justice look like?

> Justice means offering the opportunity for all people to hear how much God loves them through Jesus Christ.
>
> Justice means sharing our resources so that parents need not helplessly watch their children die.
>
> Justice means loving our neighbors—near and far—at the same level of quality and care with which we love ourselves. (Ronsvalle and Ronsvalle 1992:61)

And "justice . . . involves thousands of little acts accumulating into processes and systems and relationships that are felt by the participants to be right and fair" (Grigg 1992a:90)

In the Old Testament and the New Testament alike, God expresses profound concern for the poor and delivers scathing indictments of all who would oppress them. Today we cannot pretend the poor do not exist. They are in our cities by the hundreds of thousands. The church must take responsibility and reorder its priorities in order to fulfill its responsibilities to the poor.

"Why does the Bible make such a point of the poor?" DuBose asks.

> The reason is that if we do not make a special effort to include them, they get left out. They have no power. They are the outcasts, the disenfranchised, the nobodies of the earth. They do not count. Poverty is like a disease. It carries a stigma. It is bad enough to go hungry and to have nothing—to see those you love go hungry and be humiliated by the absence of the basic amenities of life. But the greatest stigma is the psychological one—the total

estrangement, the dehumanization, the loss of dignity, and a sense of worthlessness that no creature made in God's image should be forced to feel. (DuBose 1984:67)

A few key principles should assist us to effectively minister among the poor.

**Centrality of Christ.** There can be no justice without Christ. Therefore we must establish churches among the poor that proclaim the name of the Lord.

> Establishing the church is the primary objective in developmental activity for those committed to the Scriptures. Kingdom perspectives see the development of the spiritual kingdom as the central element of societal transformation. Economic, social and political development are an outgrowth of this spiritual development. They are important, but not central nor primary. (Grigg 1992a:4)

Greenway and Monsma explain, "The weak and the poor, just as much as the rich and the powerful, need to hear the gospel, repent, believe in Christ, and be saved. The poor are not exempt from this requirement, as if their poverty somehow atoned for their sins. Central to every strategy must be the proclamation of Jesus Christ and his redemptive work for sinners" (1989:174). Grigg continues along this same line:

> More nightmarish than the poverty and the staggering growth of that poverty is to find no more than a handful of God's men, God's women ministering among these poor in each city.
> I do not mean that there are no relief and development agencies. They are many, and most of them are doing good work in their roles as diaconal agencies of the church. But the church has given bread to the poor and has kept the bread of life for the middle class. (Grigg 1992a:11-12)

Whatever ministry we carry out among the poor, then, must be based in the proclamation of the gospel. The work of John Perkins (1982) provides further principles for reaching the poor. Perkins builds his strategy around what he calls the three Rs—relocation, reconciliation and redistribution.

**Relocation: Incarnational ministry.** Although it has often been overstated, we must again repeat that ministry *to* the poor must begin with ministry *among* the poor. It is important that this hard step be taken. The most difficult step for many missionaries and urban church planters in the United States to take is to rearrange our lives. Jesus rearranged his life for us, and it is imperative that we rearrange our lives for the people he died for. This will not only mean geographical relocation but also lifestyle rearranging. In order to reach out to the poor, we must first reach in among the poor. This incarnational approach may be the stop sign to well-meaning missionaries, but it is essential.

Grigg asks, "Where are the men and women who, like Jesus, choose to live as poor among the poor, establishing and tending newly formed churches day and night, exhibiting . . . the incarnational lifestyle?" (1992a:2). Claerbaut agrees: "The effectiveness of these [ministry] approaches is greatly enhanced when the pastor and as many members of the congregation as possible live in the community" (1983:47). In short, incarnational ministry is instrumental in community transformation.

"To be incarnational Christians in the city is, most of all, to be Christ's ambassadors (2 Cor. 5:20), willing to live the gospel as Christ did, willing to speak as Christ did, willing to serve as he did" (Ortiz 1992:96). Incarnational ministry among the poor

> is mission that builds from a base among the poor, with the poor in mind, as the apostle Paul did (1 Cor. 1:26-29). It is not enough to build our ministries among the poor and for the poor. The poor must be incorporated into the family of God and take their place in Christ's kingdom for the mission of King Jesus to advance. The rich need the poor and the poor need the rich, and in the kingdom we recognize our incompleteness without each other (1 Cor. 12:21-26). (Ortiz 1992:97)

Grigg adds a practical piece of counsel: "The church will not be established among the poor unless it is tended day and night. . . . An evangelist may work from the outside; but if he does, he must find a pastor on the inside to develop the new embryo. A development worker may work as a catalyst from the outside, but the church will be established only if there is a pastor tending this work day and night from within" (1992b:161).

"How tragic it is that where the needs are greatest, the church is weakest. Where the voice of Christ ought to be heard the loudest, there is awesome silence" (Greenway and Monsma 1989:176). It is sad that "to walk the streets of poor neighborhoods, live in low-income housing, and identify with the underclass in everything one does represent more than most Christians are willing to consider" (Greenway and Monsma 1989:177).

**Reconciliation: Creation.** Creating among the poor is what Perkins considers most important, because using community people and resources provides dignity and healthy growth and development. Too often we begin with what we do not have, reaching out for outside resources rather than what is already available. If we are quick to go outside, we hinder the possibilities of creating from within. Basing ministry on the gifts of local people is essential; it begins a process of restoring the people's dignity as we work together toward reconciliation with God and with our environment.

At the core of their being, people have a bent toward creativity. And very often creative abilities are enhanced in the city; the environment draws out creativity. The poor have had to make do with very little. Imagination and stewardship are the most important elements of creating new ministry and making use of natural resources. For example, a decaying inner city community of Philadelphia was marked by drug dealers, graffiti, and overgrown, trash-strewn vacant lots where homes had been torn down. The residents were hopeless and accepted the situation as unchangeable. Outsiders came in with a variety of programs, but the neighborhood continued to decline. Then a few of the neighborhood people, together with a resident Catholic nun, had an idea. Enlisting the participation of residents on each block, neighborhood watches worked with police to drive out the dealers. Community artists—some just children—tackled graffiti-covered walls by painting murals over them depicting community pride and cultural histories. Vacant lots became gardens initially growing vegetables for consumption but later organized around cultural themes such as the Taino Indians, the indigenous people of Puerto Rico. The creativity of these low-income residents supported by the Catholic church resulted in renewed pride in their community and a sense of dignity and hope. In turn this new hope resulted in more openness to the transforming power of Christ.

Not only should we look to the community for creativity, we must be willing to let the community control the process. The Ronsvalles accepted this when they allowed their Brazilian brothers and sisters to distribute large sums of money without requiring them to report on how the money was used (Ronsvalle and Ronsvalle 1992). "The question is not, 'How do we help the poor?' but 'How do the poor themselves escape poverty?' If we learn the answer to this question, we can work with them in the processes that lead to transformation" (Grigg 1992b:167). Linthicum cautions, "Only the poor of the city can assume responsibility for solving their own predicaments" (1991b:37). This was a difficult lesson for the Duncans to learn in their diaconate work among the squatters in Manila (Duncan 1996).

From a secular point of view, Mariz asserts, "Too often underestimated, the poor have the potential to be agents of social transformation. . . . This belief that the poor are completely powerless and can do nothing to improve their lives is nearly as harmful as blaming them for their poverty" (1994:5). We should take this to heart as a warning against our paternalistic instincts. We are not to enter a community to save it from all its pain and degradation but rather to bring hope, the hope found in Christ's transforming power as individuals come to know him and then join together in bringing change to their community life.

Grigg warns that foreigners can only be catalysts in developing ministries:

> We must model in such a way that indigenous ministries, indigenous leader-
> ship and indigenous missions emerge. The aim is not mission. This is too
> small. Nor is it church growth. This is too limited. The aim is the discipling of
> the peoples—indigenous, discipling movements among the squatters in a
> city. Missions that would catalyze these must be sending workers who
> choose lifestyles of voluntary poverty among the poor. (Grigg 1992a:113)

***Redistribution: Reciprocity.*** One of the easiest concepts to recognize, yet one of the hardest to actually do, is that if we have money and
others do not, we need to share. "Giving money away is one of the surest
ways to break its power over us. . . . Since the motivating force of money
is to accumulate it, the spiritual counterforce is to give it away" (Ronsvalle and Ronsvalle 1992:50). However, if all we do is give, we will be
addressing only physical needs. We will be doing nothing towards allowing the poor to recognize they are very valuable to someone else—us.

Mutual resourcing is important. This gives people an opportunity to
learn from others and discover our great need for each other. It also
keeps the poor from being stuck in a deficit mindset that will only promote dehumanization. Mission work that begins to develop from the outside usually makes the grave mistake of having the outsiders give and the
insiders receive. This will hinder the long-range development of community life and well being. Mutual exchange of resources is much more profitable, but it is also much more demanding for leaders.

## Conclusion

In this chapter we have reviewed the existence of separations among
people, separations that are useful for mission to the unreached but also
those caused and used by the rulers, authorities and powers "of this dark
world" (Eph 6:12) to benefit themselves with no concern for the many
who are damaged and destroyed. We have strategized ways of development that lead us toward the final city established by Christ.

> Then I saw a new heaven and a new earth, for the first heaven and the first
> earth had passed away, and there was no longer any sea. I saw the Holy City,
> the new Jerusalem, coming down out of heaven from God, prepared as a
> bride beautifully dressed for her husband. And I heard a loud voice from the
> throne saying, "Now the dwelling of God is with men, and he will live with
> them. They will be his people, and God himself will be with them and be
> their God. He will wipe every tear from their eyes. There will be no more
> death or mourning or crying or pain, for the old order of things has passed
> away." (Rev 21:1-4)

This world's inner cities and squatter areas are where the poor can be found. They are the location of the disenfranchised rather than just geographical territories. The gospel must be proclaimed there as the power of God over all of life. "The migrant poor are the greatest responsive group across the face of the earth today. . . . All are in a state of rapid socio-economic and world view change and are hungry for the reality of a new relationship to a god" (Grigg 1992a:10).

Can we divest ourselves of our cultural trappings and obey the Scriptures: "Do nothing out of selfish ambition or vain conceit, but in humility consider others better than yourselves" (Phil 2:3)? Can we go against society and take the side of the poor, be one with them and bring Christ to them in word and deed? Such a renewal of people and community exemplifies the new city that God will provide for his people in the last days. The model city is the city of God.

# 18
## Shalom & Social Transformation

THE CHURCH GATHERED FOR ITS REGULAR distribution of food and other necessary items. The deacons often found this ministry to be very rewarding. It
gave them a sense of doing something that the Lord was concerned
about, the feeding of the poor.

The deacons and some volunteers had finished a very busy and productive evening when one of the volunteers asked the deacons why they
were not witnessing or placing tracts in the food bags. The question led
to a discussion that got everyone thinking. Some felt that passing out
food *was* the gospel. If anyone asked them why they were doing mercy
ministries, they would say that Jesus is concerned for the poor and they
believed it was a necessary ministry of the church. Others were of the
opinion that they would not need to say anything, that passing out food
was done in the name of the Lord and that was evangelism. This was not
satisfactory for the inquisitive volunteer. The most important part of the
individual is the soul, he said, so to pass out food without sharing the
gospel or placing a tract in a person's hand was more social gospel than
fully caring for people the way Christ would.

This is not a new conversation; it has been ongoing in mission for
decades. "The curse of Protestant world mission in the past quarter century has been polarization" (Escobar and Driver 1978:5). In social and
community development ministries in countries where the poverty level

is high, the strain of this polarization—mission and social justice, evangelism and development—is a constant. "Western cultures, particularly, see development and evangelism as separate enterprises—development is not necessarily evangelistic. The thinking is that evangelism addresses spiritual needs while development addresses physical needs" (Bradshaw 1993:5). Yet evangelism is a call to justice (Conn 1982:35).

Many think that an inevitable byproduct of evangelism is community transformation. Donald McGavran uses the concepts of redemption and lift to argue that the saving power of the gospel touches the human heart and changes the individual internally *and* socially. "He gains victory over pride, greed, laziness, drink, hate and envy. He ceases quarreling with his neighbors and chasing women" (McGavran 1970:261). Also, a lift occurs when Christians participate in community change. "The founding mission or church establishes schools, hospitals, agricultural centers, literacy classes, and many other institutions to serve and help the general public and specially the new brothers in Christ" (McGavran 1970:261).

The redeemed and lifted follow a changed lifestyle—aspects of which may be both helpful and harmful to the church. In the United States and other countries the tendency is for the newly converted to move away from past surroundings and relationships, so as to make a complete break and start a new life. The new converts become vigilant against sin. Those who receive the gospel are transformed by God's grace and now see the plight of their community through different lenses. They look at social deterioration as a danger but not necessarily as a challenge for mission. They may conclude that leaving the community is the only way they can maintain their new lifestyle. Such a departure leaves a redemptive vacuum. Further social and spiritual decline in the community may begin as the church moves its witness and incarnational ministry to a more pleasant and safe environment.

While doing community analysis in several major cities, researchers visited community churches to find out their perspective on their community. But they had difficulty locating a pastor or other leaders who lived in the community; nearly all of them had relocated. One pastor indicated that he had moved due to the poor school system. Others felt that the community was too dangerous. So rather than transformation of community when numerous people come to a saving knowledge of Christ, sometimes the result is community abandonment.

One author advocates mercy ministry as a means to evangelism. Serving the needy by providing food and other necessities provides an opportunity for evangelism or for gathering names for a visitation team who will later evangelize. "We conduct a social relief program simply to get names for our evangelism visitation team" (Keller 1989:110). Mercy ministry is connected to our understanding of grace—mercy ministry, just like grace, is unmerited favor (Lk 6:35; Keller 1989:110).

This chapter does not aim to resolve this polarization problem. Rather it takes a look at ministries that, in response to the Word of God, are reaching out to the poor and needy in their communities as a means of God's grace. The missionary arm of the church of Jesus Christ has not made the mistake of ignoring its social responsibilities. It was commanded to obey Jesus in all things (Mt 28:20). The assumption was that redemptive power and obedience would change life on both personal and community levels. Both the spiritual and physical life would be transformed by the gospel.

> Missionaries often moved by the providence of God into areas experiencing great change. They helped produce that change, often channeling it positively, and at times they helped reform some of its most harsh aspects. Thus, what we would call community development has frequently, if not always, accompanied Christian missions as either an explicit part of the missionary task or an intended by-product of mission. (Pierson 1989:7-8)

The first section of this chapter looks at biblical-theological reasons for Christians to be involved in the ministry of community transformation. This section provides a basic theological framework to help community developers in service among the poor. The second section takes up essential elements needed for this kind of ministry—some of the factors of which community developers should be aware as they begin their task. This is an overview only—numerous elements such as acquiring a financial base or particulars in training leaders are not addressed. The third area offers warnings, clarifying what community development is *not* and providing cautions for those who embark on transformational community ministry.

## Development Definitions

Definitions help us focus and understand a particular subject by reducing it to succinct statements. Following are two definitions that may help as you try to understand community transformation.

> Generally, development is the struggle of a given social segment to transform itself toward improved life quality and participation for an enlarging percentage of its members. Almost inevitably, any such segment will encounter the need to integrate, at some point, into an environing and usually threatening larger system. This larger system will usually be composed at least in part of competing elements which attempt to limit participation in its available rewards. (S. Wilson 1989:153)

Development is the process by which persons and societies come to realize the full potential of human life in a context of social justice. It is essentially a people's struggle in which the poor and oppressed are the active participants and beneficiaries. Development is the conscientization process by which people are awakened to opportunities within their reach. Development is people with an increased control over their destiny. Development is freedom, wholeness and justice. (Stoesz 1977:3-4)

Another theorist defines Christian social transformation or development in terms of the Christian's three key relationships. According to him, development is "every biblically based activity of the body of Christ, his church, that assists in bringing human beings toward the place of complete reconciliation with God and complete reconciliation with their fellows and their environment" (Moffitt 1987:236).

Community transformation is a Christian ministry that takes seriously the effects of sin over all life and all the earth—the sin of Genesis 3 that alienated men and women from God, from self, from others and from the environment. Community transformation is the reversal of this sin and the restoration of God's order in creation and God's intent for humans to be full image bearers of the Godhead. Such transformation will make people more fully human, worshipers of God by the power of the gospel in word and deed. The completion of this task will occur at the culmination of this age, when Christ returns.

## Biblical/Theological Considerations

The Fall in Genesis 3 provides a holistic picture of our sinful dilemma. The disobedience of our first parents, Adam and Eve, brings about profound alienation and spiritual, psychological and social decline. The results of the Fall touch the center of life, separating us from God. From this point on all humanity is hiding from God. No one seeks after God (Rom 3:11).

Having enjoyed a close and intimate relationship to God, Adam and Eve must now hide from God (Gen 3:8). We walk alone in this world of multiple decisions and vulnerability. The Lord says to Moses, "You cannot see my face, for no one may see me and live" (Ex 33:20). The distance has continued to grow. We cannot, nor do we desire to, walk with God. Instead we have become enemies of God (Rom 5:10). Orlando Costas speaks of sin as an issue of relationships (Costas 1982:21). That is, sin's consequences reveal themselves in relationships between God and humanity and between men and women. This great divide must be bridged by the ministry of the gospel. The divide is alienation from God. One writer suggests "the Hiding Ones" as a good title for the human race

(Keller 1989:47). "Disobedience is the open rejection of the Word of God" (Costas 1982:22).

Development must take seriously this personal alienation and know that the gospel is the radical solution for this sinful bent. Addressing corporate-systemic issues that infect society begins with the recognition that sin is both personal and public. Personal sin affects the social environment, just as the social affects the individual.

The Bible tells us that the consequence of sin is the wrath of God (Rom 1:18). God is angry and displeased with us. How shall we be saved from this dreadful reality? The sad condition of sinful humanity is approached with the efficacious gospel.

The Philippian jailer, a responsible employee, observes a violent attack on Paul and Silas, watching without sign of compassion or sympathy. He is shocked when an earthquake opens up their prison cell—a reaction that arises out of concern for his own welfare should the prisoners escape. He is a survivalist. He is certainly not worried about the condition of the two missionaries who have been singing despite the pain of the beating they endured. The story, as we know, concludes with a response to the gospel, a conversion that is radical not only in the jailer's life but also in the lives of his family. Now more fully human, he cleans the wounds of Paul and Silas and invites them to eat with him. The alienation, the great divide, is bridged by the gospel of Jesus Christ (Acts 16:22-35).

Genesis 3:10 also tells us about the great fall from fearing God to fearing human beings—an emotional, psychological fall, a dysfunctional placing of our lives in the hands of others. Now others hold the power of our identity in their control. Lack of self-esteem arises from the fear of others, from addictive people pleasing.

> Many of the people I've talked to also had an awakening when they saw the controlling power of other people. They awoke to an epidemic of the soul called, in biblical language, "the fear of man." Although they were avowed worshippers of the true God, below the surface they feared other people. (Welch 1997:14)

Such individual distortions are only a step away from injustice, attacking others intentionally.

> Sin represents a deliberately aggressive action against others. If disobedience implies rejection of the lordship of God, injustice signifies hatred and repudiation of the neighbor. Sin, then, is every unjust act—every lack of consideration for the well-being of one's neighbor, every insult to human dignity, every act of violence done by one to someone else. (Costas 1982:23)

Injustice to our neighbor flows from a false center in our hearts. We seek fulfillment and happiness in other persons and objects; we worship idols. Instead of God, we want idols to comfort us, and we will do almost anything to maintain or gain these idols (Rom 1:25). We abandon confidence in God and seek autonomy.

Social alienation begins to appear in the Fall story when the man says, "The woman you put here with me—she gave me some fruit from the tree, and I ate it" (Gen 3:12). Social alienation is visible in what Paul calls fornication, murder, invention of evil, sexual immorality, social immorality and obscenity (Rom 1:29; Eph 5:3). All of this is sin against our neighbor. "Shalom is absent when a society is a collection of individuals all out to make their own way in the world" (Wolterstorff 1983:70).

Sin affects our primary relationships with family. The divorce rate in the United States, for example, is better than 50 percent. Social alienation also takes the form of racism and sexism. "Injustice alienates people; it makes them strangers to themselves; it leaves them morally deformed" (Costas 1982:23).

According to the 1978 World Development Report of the World Bank:

> the past quarter century has been a period of unprecedented change and progress in the developing world. And yet despite this impressive record, some 800 million individuals continue to be trapped in . . . absolute poverty: a condition of life so characterized by malnutrition, illiteracy, disease, squalid surroundings, high infant mortality and low life expectancy as to be beneath reasonable definition of human decency. (World Bank 1981:11)

Sin has made its mark on all of society and life. Every human being is born with the touch of the first parents: "all have sinned and fall short of the glory of God" (Rom 3:23).

> [Since] sin is a universal problem, its eradication must be radical—salvation, to truly be effective, must be salvation of the soul and of the body, of the individual and society . . . "of humanity and of the whole creation . . . groaning in travail together" (Romans 8:22). (Costas 1982:26)

Sin also touches nature, the earth, the environment. "Cursed is the ground because of you" (Gen 3:17). The natural world is on a downslide, decaying without resolution until Jesus returns. Hunger and disease stalk the many poor nations in the world. Death comes to babies and young people because healthcare and nutrition are not available. It is impossible to separate the environment from people and their life condition (Bradshaw 1993:100). North Philadelphia makes the connection vivid. The buildings are collapsing from lack of care, absentee landlords and systemic evil that has redlined the community so home-improvement loans are not available. The streets are filled with garbage that should have been picked up by the sanitation department. No one cares. This is the environment in which many inner-city children survive.

How can the distorting, disastrous shift, from the fear of God to the fear of others, from God-confidence to self-confidence and the establishing of idols, from love to violence, be reversed? Only through the gospel. Nothing else can address the enormity of the problem of sin. We turn to Scripture and to a loving God who has called us to be his sons and daughters (Eph 5:1), created to be like him (Eph 4:24).

The man in Luke 8:26-36 was trapped in a demonic captivity that produced fear in others and personal harm to himself. Jesus asked, "What is your name?" He had none—only "Legion, because many demons had gone into him." Jesus delivered him from his oppression, so that the man ends up sitting at Jesus' feet dressed and in his right mind. The gospel reverses the bent of sin, turning us toward righteousness and mission.

A medical doctor in Philadelphia is moved by the many needs in the Hispanic community and the prompting of the Holy Spirit. She gathers members from her church to approach the ongoing medical, emotional, spiritual and social needs in the community. An outreach is established to meet the needs of the whole person. AIDS patients are being treated both physically and spiritually. Abused children and families are counseled with compassion in the name of Jesus. The gospel is brought into the moral decay of society and heals alienation by introducing men and women to the power of reconciliation found in Jesus Christ (2 Cor 5:16-20).

John Perkins has taken the call to racial reconciliation seriously. Over the years he has been salt in the Christian community. He has prophetically challenged both church and society concerning continued obstructions to God's creation. "To this day," he mourns, "our nation has not lived up to its goal of justice for all" (Perkins 1982:11).

A church in Chicago, Rock of Our Salvation, speaks about breaking down walls (Washington and Kehrein 1993). The pastor and elders of the church keep the challenge before them, persuaded by Scripture that the gospel is multifaceted and speaks to all the forms of alienation in their community. Their evangelism reconciles men and women to God and to each other.

A church recognizes a lack of God's shalom and moves to gather people from the congregation to beautify the community. They meet on Saturday and begin to make a difference. The community is appreciative that someone took the initiative and cares.

A team of Christians, American and Ugandan, tackle healthcare needs by purifying water that is then piped into Ugandan villages. A missionary, along with people from the village, labors long and hard to lay out the twenty miles of pipe that will allow the people to drink clean water. The kingdom of God is displayed as this act of compassion translates into the shalom of God.

"Shalom is the human being dwelling at peace in all his or her relationships: with God, with self, with fellows, with nature" (Wolterstorff 1983:69). Christian researchers do community analysis to discover where the shalom of God needs to be brought to the community. One church found that the children of the community were not being educated properly. The church began providing resources for the children, their families and the school. They started a tutoring program and developed new relationships. Parents and other community members were appreciative, and some of them began attending Sunday morning worship service; several gave their lives to the Lord. The church began to grow through conversion growth. Usually a church's significant impact in its community will lead to growth in the church.

Does the Lord of the harvest care about weather, crops, the ground we live on? Yes, "Christian development cannot be holistic without a concern for the environment" (Bradshaw 1993:101).

The church and especially those involved in community development must incorporate a vision of shalom. Recognizing that our Lord calls us to be involved in the restoration of society, we can minister in confidence. "To dwell in shalom is to *enjoy* living before God, to *enjoy* living in one's physical surroundings, to *enjoy* living with one's fellows, to *enjoy* life with oneself" (Wolterstorff 1983:70). No longer do we run from God. Now we enjoy our relationship to the Lord and desire to serve him (Is 2:2-3). Creation will be delivered from its curse, liberated from decay. There will be freedom in its fullness at the coming of our Lord (Rom 8:21).

Racial reconciliation is taking place in some Christian colleges because the shalom of God, through the preaching of the gospel, is taking hold and Christians have been brought to repentance. Reconciliation takes place when the gospel is preached and the kingdom of Christ is lived out in the presence of the world. We are in the system but not of it. The hands of Christians reach out in the name of Christ to touch wounded lives. The reversal of the curse of sin is evident. This healing is not total, but its completeness will be experienced at the second coming of Christ.

The task of the church is to preach the kingdom of Christ in a way that effectively reverses the Fall and brings wholeness and peace to individuals and community. A world-centered spirituality—bodies without souls— will not do. A soul-centered approach—the soul without the body—will not make much of an impact. A God-centered spirituality touches all of life. Life is not compartmentalized but seen as a whole, a covenant agreement broken but now healing. God is concerned about the total person, including relationships and environment (Conn 1982). "The church is to be an agent of the kingdom. It is not only to model the healing of God's rule but it is to spread it" (Keller 1989:54).

The basis of all Christian activity is the Word of God. Community development that pictures the kingdom of God and his righteousness and aims for biblical transformation must know its source of power and authority (Mt 28:19), the inspired Word of God (2 Tim 3). Here is our great weapon for renewal and reversal of the curse.

To seek development without centering on Christ and his kingdom as our confession is to be reductionist. On the other hand, to do evangelism while ignoring the concerns of poor and the powerless is also reductionist.

"Praise to the Lord, the God of Israel, because he has come and has redeemed his people . . . to guide our feet into the path of peace" (Lk 1:68, 79). Our covenant God is a God of shalom. This fallen order will be redeemed when the Judge of the nations returns (Ps 96:11-13). Injustice will be put away; poverty will no longer exist; there will be no poor; healthcare *will* one day be universal. Jesus is our peace, and he will not deprive anyone of justice.

## Essential Elements of Community Transformation Ministry

> There are three distinctly different responses that any church or mission organization can make to its city. The response the church chooses to make decides whether that church will play a significant role in the poor's empowerment, will provide social services out of its largess or will simply ignore the needy around it. (Linthicum 1991b:21)

Linthicum settles on the idea of ownership as we work with a community in need. We must be *with* the community. This is the posture of the incarnation: a participation with the people. Transformational development is not work done for another; it is owning a problem and working jointly to respond. As a safeguard against paternalism or a spirit of arrogance, we need to recognize that development is not necessarily something we bring in as a gift. "Outside agencies do not bring development; it is an indigenous process going on before they arrive. At best they accelerate its pace; at worst they frustrate it" (Stoesz 1977:12).

An important but often neglected qualification for this ministry has to do with our character development: *vulnerability.* This is not something we *do,* as in taking inventory of a community, but something we are *becoming.* Jesus is our example. Philippians 2 portrays how our Lord descended in order to become a servant. Psalm 69 is a messianic psalm in which David speaks about sinking into the miry depths. Our Lord leaves his place in glory to be with us. It is a total lifestyle change: having been rich, he becomes poor (2 Cor 2:8-9), coming down from glory to the cross (Phil 2:6-8).

Vulnerability is not an academic exercise taught at a seminary. It is that quality of spiritual life that allows us to come into community not as the savior but as the servant of the Savior.

This is certainly not new thinking. Spiritual exercises were part of the daily life of Pietists in the 1600s. The spiritual priesthood moved beyond knowledge of the Word to a practice of their faith that influenced their unbelieving neighbors. It was a spiritual demonstration (Pierson 1989:12). Today we embark on this process by learning dependence on others. We are weaned from the strong individualism that is promoted in many of our institutions—the idea that we can do just about everything. We develop a spirit of community and reliance on others.

As noted earlier, at this point a ministry team effort may be counter-productive. The members may depend on each other so much that bonding and reliance on the community are not developed. We may be starting off on the wrong foot.

A woman enters a poor community to live and serve the Lord. But she has undergone tremendous hardship prior to arriving. Her emotional state is fragile, and physically she is very weak. As she moves in, she finds herself dependent on her new neighbors. They come to help her move. They cook food and make sure she is getting rest. This does not sound like our typical approach to mission, but the woman's vulnerability and dependence on others mark the beginning of a productive ministry. Community members begin to trust her almost immediately and are highly willing to help and to listen to the message of Christ.

Such an approach is not the result of a superficial act but a deep realization of our need for others and dependence on community. It is a mature spiritual walk that understands the compassion and love of the servant of all, Jesus Christ.

How do we do this in a genuine manner? It begins with our spiritual development. Pride, perfectionism and good management will not wear well on God's mission field if they are not seasoned with love and dependence. Biblical humility provides the environment needed for engaging and working with people. Humility is dependence on God, knowing that we can do nothing apart from him (Jn 15:4-5). This is a process that begins early in our calling and continues for a lifetime.

Christians working in community transformation and mission need to take a good look inside before thinking about looking outside. Humility is certainly more of a character trait than a tool or skill, but it is important to reflect on this subject in preparation for service. Not only will we find favor with the Lord, but we will also find favor with the people God has called us to serve.

As you move into the community, recognize that the people are image bearers of God. They are alienated from God and need the Lord greatly. But they have much to offer you. This is God's grace in mission. Begin to take note of their skills and resources. What do they offer the project you are about to undertake? How can you cultivate each other's skills and gifts? How can their experiences and background enhance your life and task?

Too often we are blind to community members' gifts because we are task oriented and not people related. We want to get the assignment under way and see it completed as soon as possible with minimal frustration and financial cost.

Community development is more than projects and new programs. The peace of God provides for improvement of quality of life and relationships. Vulnerability will bring increased opportunities to share the gospel. As we submit to the lordship of Christ, our lives are changing (2 Cor 3:18) and our service is taking new forms. Service to God and others should not be compartmentalized into spiritual versus social or task versus relational. It should be a total way of life sharing.

Another element in community transformation is *community organizing*. How do we organize a community to be part of the process of transformation?

> A local church partnership is the best way for a Christian community development to carry out its work. Without the local church people will not grow into spiritual maturity. Christ is coming back for the church. Christian community development must be a feeder to a local church or churches. . . . A Christian community development ministry and the church must hold common values and ministry philosophy. (Kehrein 1995:179)

The church in community is the best vehicle for holistic community transformation. It is also the most effective (Mt 16:13-19). The church is able to tear down the strongholds of Satan and repair the brokenness in people's lives.

How do we provide strategy and planning to begin this process? World Vision does it this way: "Each of the field offices interested in participating in World Vision's Urban Advance draws up its own strategy, identifying the slum communities in which it will organize, and contextualizing the generic urban strategy of this development agency" (Linthicum

1991b:25). The process is the key, and we must begin with networking.

Friendship building is at the core of community organizing. Doubtless World Vision has the same idea in mind. But friendship cannot be a means to an end. In the friendship-building process we must discover needs and identify key leaders. When we begin to work with the poor, there will be a certain amount of mistrust, especially if we are outsiders. Outsiders have too often been exploiters and not friends. Focusing on friendship builds the trust that is needed in community organizing. "People are more important than things; the person is more important than the activity. Growth comes from within each person; all persons have talents waiting to be discovered and used" (Hiebert 1989:91). Engagement and friendship cultivation will be extremely profitable in the long run. Be patient and avoid the conflicts that arise when trust is not built.

Christian agencies should work through local churches whenever possible. Sometimes community development organizations have ignored the church. Soliciting partnership with the local church is one of the requirements for building high-quality, long-lasting ministries. This will not be a quick process. But a lack of tolerance and patience—moving ahead without local church involvement—will cause problems. The Christian testimony is at stake.

If a local church is the agent doing community development, it still needs to network with other local churches. Our resources are limited, and it will benefit the project if we are drawing on corporate gifts and resources.

Why do we not utilize the gifts and resources of others more? One reason is that we have failed to build relationships with other pastors and leaders. Churches too often exist as islands unto themselves. Another reason for neglecting other ministries is our mistrust and insecurity. Third, there is inherent in all of us the desire for personal and denominational recognition. This will isolate local ministries from each other and will break down the potential of networking. Denominational flags have a tendency to promote alienation from others and downplay partnership ministries in community.

Coalition building in the city should be a natural given. We are living in close proximity and are concerned for the same neighborhood. Yet too often we avoid one another. We are like street gangs trying to control our turf by keeping others out. Relationships are developed over long periods of time and by direct personal contact.

Another aspect to community organizing is *discovering community needs.* Who defines and determines the need? Is it the community people or the expert on community issues?

We often think that the needs of a community are easily discovered. We surmise that need is something that is lacking in a person's life, in a people group or in a community, and that this determines where we must work. The task of discovering needs is much more subtle. Actually the problems we can easily see are usually symptoms of much deeper issues. The real needs are found in the causes of a problem—and often they are difficult to uncover.

Discovering the real needs is a very important aspect of development. Too often the needs in a community are identified by symptomatic indicators. A great deal of time and money can be spent on programs that never address the real need.

Consider a church in a community where people had obvious needs for food and clothing. The deacons of the church decided to open its doors one evening per week for food distribution. This ministry continued for one year, and the number of people registered for the food bank increased.

It was suggested that research should be done to see why there seemed to be an increasing need for food. Statistics indicated that unemployment and unemployable rates were very high. Further investigation indicated that the skills the people currently had were not suitable for the present job market. So the church, together with several community agencies, developed a job-training program to equip the people.

This church took on the challenge of discovering the causes. The outcome was a decrease in both unemployment and the need for ongoing food distribution. Now the church provides food every other week rather than every week.

In another case, a church's community had a high rate of addictions and sexual immorality. The employment rate indicated that many community families had at least one member working at reasonable hourly wages. The underlying problem involved alcoholism and drug abuse. The church's food panty was actually supporting these habits by providing food while the money parents earned was used in unhealthy ways. Weekly food pickups were at times used for additional income for addictions rather than feeding families. The community had too many bars and liquor stores. In this case the causes had to do with social and sexual immorality.

The church became aware of the deeper issues and did two things. First, it asked for city restrictions on how many liquor stores could be in a community and for better police surveillance to cut down on drug deals. Second, it set up a counseling and rehabilitation center for families and individuals. In this ministry the gospel was shared and many came to know the Lord. Lives were changed and lifestyles were altered. Many of the men who came to know the Lord became helpers at the center.

World Vision employs a method that involves both building relationships and discovering needs, described as

> acting/reflecting/acting: A dynamic process begins. Coalitions reflect, act, evaluate, act again and reflect more deeply. Reflection includes a freedom to look at their own sinfulness and gospel solutions. The results? Root problems are addressed, systemic action taken. Self-confidence and community trust are built. And Christians who have joined with the poor in addressing these issues can naturally share their faith. (Linthicum 1991b:25)

The final aspect of community organizing we will review is reliance on *community leadership* in tandem with church leadership or a mission team.

"We are finally beginning to realize that programs do not fix communities. Only neighbors can do that. Urban neighborhoods need vested neighbor-leaders who will organize the taking of playgrounds back from the drug dealers" (Lupton, Lupton and Yancy 1995:81). This is often difficult for the church because we are fearful of working with non-Christians. We wonder whether an involvement with non-Christians will put us in conflict with Christians. Or perhaps the message of the gospel will be compromised. Some Christians find it difficult to be honest in confessing Christ when working with non-Christians. We may be concerned about offending others or coming off as superior rather than different. How can we be in the system but not part of it?

God desires us to be involved in the world and associate with non-Christians without taking on the deeds of darkness (Eph 5:11). The church can shine the light of Christ brightly as it is under inspection by the non-Christian community. It is here that many will be convinced that Jesus is the true light (Eph 5). We are always ambassadors for Christ (2 Cor 5:20) and should not compromise our identity to win approval or receive assistance. The best posture is to be Christians without arrogance. Honest relationships have the greatest potential for growth and partnership.

Community leadership is necessary for lasting effects. Why *community* leadership? Any development project, especially one brought from the outside, will need to find its contextualization niche. Also, it is impossible to do everything that is needed without people from the community. The task is enormous. "Because Christian community development ministry is so intensive, the emergence of a full-time staff is highly likely" (Gornik and Castellanos 1995:226). We will need people from the community to assist in the process of community transformation. Wycliffe Bible Translators adheres to this principle. When its linguists are in a new territory, where the Bible has not yet been translated into the language of the people, they find an informant from the community to help them carry out their task. Such work with local informants and helpers is to be done in a manner that is not exploitive but reassures others and affirms that we have need of them.

Soliciting community leaders and developing their skills is not to be a means to evangelism, even though evangelism will certainly happen in the process of the task. Developing leaders is an end in itself.

> Leadership development is not a way to accomplish ministry, it *is* the ministry. We must believe that viable community leadership already exists and needs only to be identified and encouraged to flourish. Leadership development is not someone taking on a ministry job. (Gornik and Castellanos 1995:226)

It is imperative that moving in—relocation or incarnation—be part of the process. Also, indigenization of the ministry is crucial.

> An important distinctive feature of Christian community development ministries is the guiding philosophy that relocation is essential to effective community rebuilding. This means that ministry leadership and staff are strongly encouraged to move into the neighborhood where they feel called to minister and become "indigenized" neighbors. (Lupton, Lupton and Yancy 1995:82)

### Warnings and Clarifications

*Community transformation must consider objectives and process as equally important.* Providing water for a community might be done by an outside Christian agency that brings in heavy equipment and several capable teams that begin the drilling and get the job done in a matter of weeks. They complete their goals, and the people of the community now have clean and accessible water.

Another group could take a different tack. The people of the community are brought in to consider the need and the process. After the process is determined by both the community people and the Christian agency, they begin to work together. When they have finished, there is much praise and ownership of the completed task.

It is crucial that Christian developers be sensitive to both the objectives and the process of any development project.

*Community transformation is comprehensive.* As we work with the poor, there are many issues to understand. There may be a need for a clinic to improve the healthcare of the people. But some health problems may be related to their farming techniques. To address only one area of need and not the other may short-circuit the ministry's goals. If malnutrition is causing much of the present illness, clearly the community could use some help in growing good crops. A team is needed to address such multi-faceted needs. A long-term teaching journey can accomplish long-lasting effects.

*Community transformation should not promote dependency.* A certain medical doctor was reprimanded by his sending agency for teaching the people in a rural community how to care for themselves by using a diet that would prevent certain illness and malnutrition. The doctor was taken off the field and replaced with other staff.

As we help others with the compassion of Christ, it is important that we not keep them dependent on outside resources. In the United States, for example, many community development projects are costly and require intensive fundraising which only certain people who have good contacts can accomplish. An Anglo who has moved into an African American community and who has a certain following and financial ca-pability is often the person who obtains the initial funds for a ministry. As time passes, a full-blown ministry in the community takes shape. But the Anglo leader is still the only who can gather major financial backing. The budget balloons as more ministries are added, and the need for fundrais-ing intensifies. Indigenous ownership of the community project is limited because the contacts and abilities to seek out funding agencies are still in the hands of the Anglo leaders.

We must train indigenous leaders to take on financial oversight and fundraising while keeping the ministries at a level that will not place excessive demands on these emerging leaders. Development projects often grow too quickly. Then the financial requirements require that lead-ers from the outside retain their positions and indigenous leaders stay in support roles. Leadership has not indigenized.

Leaders who move in will eventually indigenize (Lupton, Lupton and Yancy 1995:82). Over a long period of time these leaders and their fami-lies become part of the community. A big problem, however, is a high turnover among outside Christian workers. As young couples begin to grow families and miss their roots, they often leave and take up other vocations.

To indigenize is much more than living in community and becoming part of the life of the community. It is a major overhauling that changes deep-seated values and begins to burn the bridges to workers' past lives. There is a profound bonding with people and community that allows the worker to call that place home.

*Development requires indigenization.* We have been talking about own-ership and leadership; now we consider method—how things are done, when they are done and who is involved in the process. Leadership development is a high priority. If we are to have a lasting effect, promote community transformation and see greater fruit, leadership development is a must. The vision for community transformation must be grasped by many. This will remove the possibility of paternalistic work as well as a dependency role for the community. Very often this is hard because it has to do with power questions. How will decisions be made and by whom?

*Development requires justification.* Justification is too often excluded from the ongoing ministry of development. This is not to say that mission teams do not intend to share the gospel, that they are not concerned with seeing people come to a saving knowledge of Jesus Christ. However, the gospel is often forgotten in the mix of doing community work. It may even be excluded when opportunities present themselves. We have lost sight of our original goals and understanding of the holistic gospel.

It is difficult to keep this balance in development ministry due to the urgent need for physical and social change in the community. It is hard to be holistic in our everyday work. Evangelism that penetrates people's hearts and brings them to Christ must be retained as a central goal. Intentionality is important if we are to communicate what God desires for his creation. Shalom begins with the right relationship with God.

We need to share the gospel with the desire to see people come to Christ if we are to say we have done evangelism. In much of the literature of development and community transformation, after statements that the gospel touches all of life and that God is concerned for the poor, their environment and their liberation from oppression, little or nothing is said about leading people to Christ and seeing the church grow.

Tim Keller closes his book on mercy ministry with a chapter about church growth: "We must integrate evangelism with mercy ministries and provide follow-up strategies that will incorporate new believers from our mercy ministries into the church" (Keller 1989:207). Often development programs that aim to start churches along with community projects do not see much numerical growth. This could be because they have placed their focus on community development to the point that they are no longer being intentional about evangelism.

*Development requires justice.* Justice has a primary place in the ministry of development. It has to do with a corporate relationship with God and his righteousness. In Deuteronomy 6:6-9 Moses speaks about keeping the commands of the Lord, which focus on issues related to justice. The Old Testament makes clear that justice is a fundamental concern in God's relationship to humanity (e.g., Mic 6:8). God deals with all creatures on the basis of justice and expects just dealings among them. God has established human society on this principle. When there is not justice, when there is not consideration for others, what rules is egoism and therefore injustice (Costas 1982).

Christians in ministry find that often the reason underlying the need of development is that people have been sinned against. This sin will have to be dealt with as the cause of oppression or injustice. Injustice has to do with keeping a people in a dreadful condition (Ps 82:1-8). In order to get to the causes of community problems, we must speak against the injustice in society.

*Development must not lead to self-progress alone.* Development that does not promote the welfare of the whole community has missed the mark. In the training of leaders who have benefited from the resources provided in community development, the intention is that a corporateness be created to address the concerns of others. Too often when those who have been oppressed are delivered from the injustices and sin, they become oppressors themselves. Community transformation sees beyond the individual and is able to use community leaders in a manner that enhances the long-term development of the community.

*Development requires biblical obedience.* This warning has to do with the Christian's reason for doing development. Responding to social needs is certainly important, but we always need to develop a *Christian* response to social ills. The Bible has given us three reasons for poverty—injustice, natural disaster and personal sin. To ignore any of these is to ignore the resolve of the gospel. Often all three are found together.

The Christian's agency or church must know that the universal problem of sin demands a radical presentation of the gospel. To be sociologically aware alone will leave the community with a reductionist response to the needs of the people. Liberation theology has often criticized evangelicals for using theology as an academic exercise, separating truth from practice, but obedience to Scripture cannot be overemphasized.

## Conclusion

Community transformation is the arm of the church that speaks clearly of the compassion of Jesus Christ. This ministry is greatly needed in a world that does not understand the separation of spiritual needs from hunger or economic oppression. The Christian community must understand the universality of sin and the solution—the gospel of Christ. Men and women are joined to God and to each other, shalom reigns, and all can worship the Creator God.

# 19

## Spiritual Warfare in the City

THERE IS NO DOUBT THAT GOD IS CALLING the church into the city. Demographic data indicate not only high growth rates but also an increasing disparity between the rich and the poor.

> It is too soon to move away from missions to unreached tribal cultures in rural areas. We need to train and go to them. But the currents of history are going to be sweeping these people *either* a) literally into the cities geographically, as rural economies fail to sustain older ways of life, or b) into cities *culturally* as technology connects younger generations to global hyper-culture. Traditional missions to "unreached peoples" may be preparing you for a world that is passing away in 20 years. (Keller 1999:2)

The question is whether the church will pay heed to the harvest awaiting it in the city. The globalization process is bringing the world with all its cultural and religious attachments to our center cities. This cultural/ religious invasion will test the church and revive old challenges that could ignite the church toward renewal and global expansion. Evangelism will have long-distance effects when a Hindu from India comes to Christ in New York. It will have implications for those in her hometown.

### The City
The city is where religious pluralism will be most displayed and realized. The polarization of ethnic groups will be mapped, and culture as they

have known it will continue to one degree or another. "Cities [are] the most important site for church planting and missions. [They call] into being a diverse church planting movement. [We] will have to be especially attentive to multi-ethnic and multi-faith realities, especially at the neighborhood level" (Gornik 1999:3). It is also true that culture will change when the urban milieu enculturates our new friends. With this concentration will come religious conflict and also spiritual warfare.

Many view spiritual warfare as synonymous with urban ministry. "It is in the city that Satan has a stronghold," they say, "not as much in our suburban areas or rural communities." "Evil is found at its very worst in our cities. The cities are evil!" This popular antiurban view has captured the hearts of many Christians and sent them running to places where evil supposedly is not rampant and overbearing. A woman greeted an urban professor after a Sunday morning service by saying, "You're closer to God in the country (Conn 1987:9).

> Yet the 1984 annual Gallup poll on religion in America sees no large gap between center city, suburb, or rural area on a question like "How important is religion in your own life?" Fifty-three percent of those who live in the center city answer "very important." In the suburbs 51 percent feel that way, in the rural areas 61 percent. A difference to be sure, but not large enough to carry the weight of the stereotype. (Conn 1987:9)

The assumption that only the city is subject to the outrageous infiltration of evil bespeaks our distorted perceptions. It is what shapes our life. "Worldview governs everyday behavior" (Hiebert 1994:11). Note that the antiurban sentiment does not reflect the biblical perception of reality.

Yet we cannot simply dismiss the spiritual battles that occur in our urban centers. After all, they are centers of power and culture and are strategic for world impact. "The world-class cities are the location of the 'brain' of the global-economic system. Decisions about what to put on MTV, what to market, are made in the cities" (Keller 1999:2). We can expect that spiritual warfare will continue to be fierce in cities throughout the world.

## War and Conflict

"We are engaged in constant spiritual warfare with the principalities and powers of evil, who are seeking to overthrow the church and frustrate its task of world evangelisation. We know our need to equip ourselves with God's armour and to fight this battle with the spiritual weapons of truth and prayer" (Padilla 1976a:205).

Spiritual warfare involves war components such as enemy, soldiers, weapons and outcomes—who wins, who is wounded, how long is the battle and why it was fought. But often the language of warfare immediately suggests evil versus good, as though the enemy were just a force or a system and not a person. It excludes the evil leader of this battle, Satan. To see the warfare in this way is to start on the wrong foot and possibly be greatly deceived. Yet we must not see the conflict as unrelated to our own rebellion against God and quickness to sin. "We acknowledge that we ourselves are not immune to worldliness of thought and action, that is, to a surrender to secularism" (Padilla 1976:205).

To think of evil as being only systemic is erroneous, just as it is wrong for us to consider evil as only personal. Evil is headed by the devil, and he has legions. He is able to affect and infect individuals because he has the raw material with which to work—sinners.

> This Puritan preacher has in his mind's eye the general structure of his social world, and it is this that he subjects to his withering, somewhat hysterical attack. Clearly his assumption is that social structures are not something natural. They are not the reflection of true human nature. They are the result of human decision, and being made by us, they can be altered by us. Indeed, they *must* be altered, for they are fallen, corrupt. (Wolterstorff 1983:9)

Individuals who are infected also infect society as they submit to the schemes of the devil (Eph 6:11). Christians are in a battle, a fight against Christians, especially those on the front line.

## Evil Exists

When we speak of spiritual warfare, we must address matters of evil. "Warfare in itself is evil. If evil did not exist there would be no warfare of any kind" (Murphy 1992:17).

One Saturday night a pastor and deacons called for help with a young woman they believed was demon possessed. It was a frightening moment, since all I knew came from a flashback of the movie *The Exorcist.* I had a suspicion that it was a hoax. *People do not get possessed by demons in this day and age.* Even though I had read numerous books on spiritual warfare and had been reminded by professors of theology that demons do exist because the Bible says so, it seemed impossible that this was happening in contemporary society.

As I entered the church the men, all over age forty and very big and strong, were talking to a teenage mother about her attempts to commit suicide. Then they paused to pray. A voice that was unfamiliar to all of us suddenly began speaking in a mocking manner. I remained suspicious until I noticed that any reading of Scripture or references to biblical content caused an immediate flareup of anger and violence. During the flare-ups it was nearly impossible for two men to hold down this young woman and keep her from attacking.

This type of experience is familiar especially to those who have worked in Third World countries. Yet spiritual warfare is not a major topic of concern for most urban ministers and missionaries. It is a category appealed to in times of trouble or in sermons to challenge the church. But making a plan or strategy to combat satanic infiltration and possible attacks is not often done.

The city is characterized as being painfully violent and sinful. Some pastors attribute this visible anguish to Satan and his army, yet there are few accounts of churches dealing with actual spiritual battle as in the story above.

## Warning and Testing

We must be cautious and realize that all spiritual warfare must be tested. "A great deal of fiction, superstition, fantasy, nonsense, nuttiness, and downright heresy flourishes in the church under the guise of 'spiritual warfare' in our time. For many people . . . the working worldview of spiritual warfare has the ring of a horror movie or fantasy novel instead of the sound of Scripture" (Powlison 1995:13).

> Interest in spiritual matters must be both welcomed and tested. It must be welcomed because the church too often has bought into the worldview of a secular science that denies the reality of sin and spiritual realities. It must be tested because we are in danger of returning to the views of our pagan past. (Hiebert 1994:203).

Generally we have placed such conflict and spiritual warfare in the context of underdeveloped countries and poor communities where animism, spiritism and tribal customs are more apparent. This is a grave error that could have us looking in the wrong direction (Hiebert 1994:213).

Robert Linthicum speaks about young men who were worshipers of Kali, the Hindu goddess to whom the city of Calcutta is dedicated and for whom it is named. Kali is "the goddess of darkness, evil and destruction in the Hindu Pantheon" (Linthicum 1991a:65).

> Jim and Pilak hit it off together right away. As they parted Pilak pulled out a doll and pressed Jim to accept the gift as a token of his friendship. But when Jim showed it to the missionary couple in whose home he was staying, they gasped with dismay. They informed him that things were different on the mission field, that here people were involved with demonism, sorcery, and witchcraft. (Priest, Campbell and Mullen 1995:9)

## Definition

Defining spiritual warfare requires more than a simple sentence. It is important to examine both theological and anthropological elements in the definition. Our definition is developed in an integrative and general way, presenting various illustrations and thoughts on the subject rather in a limited, narrow statement. Definition in this case involves laying out the essence of spiritual warfare.

The origin of this conflict did not start with the fall of humanity. It comes between the events of Genesis 1:31 and Genesis 3:1 (Grudem 1994:412). It is not found in Genesis 3 but in a cosmic rebellion. "One point is certain: at least by the intertestamental period, when Genesis 3 was read and explained to Jewish listeners by Jewish teachers, the serpent was identified with Satan. The New Testament interpretation of the fall of man and that of the Jews is identical at this point" (Murphy 1992:18).

Satan is an angelic being who is the originator of sin and who tempted Eve (Gen 3:1-6; 2 Cor 11:3). "The devil's characteristic has been to originate sin and tempt others to sin" (Grudem 1994:415). He opposes good works yet is limited as to how far he may go without God's permission (Job 1:12; 2:6). This is simplistic but important as we move ahead in understanding spiritual warfare. Satan is fighting for the souls of people and luring them in through deception (Rev 12:9), creating an environment to tempt and seduce humans (1 Thess 3:5). One striking way he accomplishes this is through accusation, promoting guilt (Rev 12:10).

Another angle for understanding the essence of this battle is offered by Hiebert.

> The Scriptures speak of spiritual warfare (see Eph. 6:10-20; Rev. 19:19-20), but that warfare does not fit the Indo-European myth. First, *the central issue in biblical warfare is not power but faithfulness.* In the Old Testament both Israel's victories and defeats are attributed to God. Their victories are due to their faithfulness to God and his laws; their defeats to God's punishment when they forsake him (Judg. 4:1-2; 2; 6:1; 10:7; 1 Sam. 28:17-19; 1 Kings 16:2-3; 20:28; 2 Kings 17:7-23). (Hiebert 1994:208)

***Definition and world system.*** Padilla indicates that spiritual warfare is a world system (1976a:211). It lies behind much of the materialism and individualism of Western society. This system is at odds with God. And the connection of this system is with Satan and his armies (2 Cor 4:4). Here is where we find the principalities and powers, the authorities of this world. They are cosmic and exist systemically in society. Linthicum agrees that this has to do with evil throughout the universe (1991a:67) but is concerned that we not place it under the rubric of otherworldliness. He notes an interesting perspective on principalities—a prince or head person may occupy the throne, such as a mayor of a city. The person may change, but the office does not (Linthicum 1991a:67). Dominion is a territory influenced or ruled by the throne. And "the power of a throne comprises the rules, legalities, traditions, and sanctions that legitimize the throne's rule over that dominion and provides the authority by which the principality occupies that throne" (Linthicum 1991a:67). The point is that Satan works through existing systems and structures (Linthicum 1991a:68).

"Demons flow where abuse flows. Demons flow where Satanism, Satanic occult practices, and the New Age movement flourish. Demons enter the bodies and lives of abused children, especially those who have experienced SRA, and of practicing New Agers" (Murphy 1992:xiii). Murphy's concern may seem extreme and in need of biblical backing, but he is concerned that the church in the West will not be able to handle this kind of conflict because of its present worldview and dysfunctional theology (1992:xiii).

***Definition as the Christian fight.*** It may be important to understand spiritual warfare as a fight, as Paul describes it in Ephesians 6. The fight and soldier images are found throughout this section of Scripture. Paul uses a soldier metaphor to communicate the importance and urgency of conflict and war. It is a battle for our souls, Paul tells us; it is not war with flesh and blood (Eph 6:12) but with principalities and powers. Warfare is confronting things that have to do with eternal values. Warfare involves individuals as well as systems. An illustration of this is a story recounted by Scott Moreau.

> When our daughter Lauren was about one year old, she started waking up at night screaming. Being our first child, we were not sure what to make of it. She had always been a peaceful sleeper, a fact for which we had been grateful! The problem was that these were not cries of hunger. They were screams, and we had no idea what caused them.
>
> After a week, my wife, Emily, told me that she had read somewhere that children might start to experience bad dreams at Lauren's age. Realizing that one possible source of bad dreams is the intimidating work of Satan, we decided to take our stance. That night, as we put Lauren to bed, we prayed over her. We thanked God for her and for our relationship with Him. We announced to the enemy that he had no ground to stand on and that we were claiming our authority in Christ over our daughter. We declared that if the dreams were from Satan, they had to stop. They did! From that night on, Lauren slept peacefully. (Moreau 1997:163)

***Definition and causes.*** The origin or cause of spiritual warfare is often given a simplistic explanation. We immediately say the devil caused a given problem. But the issue is really more complex. Often the struggle may be divided into three areas: (1) evil inside, or our sin condition, (2) evil outside, or systemic corruption, world systems and worldviews opposed to God and his reigning power, and (3) cosmic evil that leads into confrontation with Satan and his powers and systems. We must stop being simplistic and approach these matters on various fronts.

The first area of struggle is the evil inside us, our sin condition. All evil and sin are not from Satan and his legions, but certainly some is. Satan is a defeated foe (Col 2:15). He is in eternal chains, but he has influence and power over us in our most vulnerable states. We give in to one who has no right over us. An example may be when we do not deal with our guilt biblically. In this case we give Satan an opportunity to harm us. Satan is conquered and cannot touch us unless we give him opportunity.

We are inclined to live for self. We take the position of being God and want to be in control of our lives—an attitude made vivid in the account of Genesis 3. This will surely bring major hardships in our walk with God and in our ministry. It may be that we have damaged souls due to a sexually immoral lifestyle before conversion. This could haunt us as we find difficulty in overcoming temptation, opening the way for relapse so that we begin to live again for our own pleasure.

If we are children of the King, we have been transferred from the kingdom of darkness to the kingdom of light (Col 1:13). No longer does Satan have power over us unless we submit to his whims and strategies.

Many women and men who have gone through many difficulties as they grew up in poor urban communities discover that being Christian is a constant battle because they are faced with their vulnerabilities. This is especially true for those who were abused or seriously sinned against as children. The ongoing problems will need to be addressed, keeping in mind that the individuals will have to deal with damaged souls and their sin condition. Therefore it is essential that discipleship prepare people biblically for battle in the areas of their vulnerability.

The Lord has given all believers authority over demons (Lk 9:1; 10:19; Acts 8:17). The war outside deals with our humanistic anti-God systems, society's convincing power to relativize our biblical commitments and standards and infiltrate the church.

> This moral space between law and freedom shrinks daily, for what cannot be enforced, it is now assumed, should not be a matter of obedience. We are free to do, or say, or think, or be anything that we want, short of crossing the line of illegality. Everything that is not illegal is therefore morally permissible. This attitude in itself is a recipe for profound social disorder, because there are many forms of dishonesty, of antisocial behavior, that are not illegal at all. But its most pernicious outcome, the one with the deepest effects, is hardly noticed at all: we have lost our ability to talk about Good and Evil. (Wells 1998:70-71)

Patrick Johnstone warns:

> The world, as we see it, is a battlefield at every level—political, moral, mental and spiritual—with many strongholds to be stormed. His infernal majesty is not a "push-over" and in recent years the nature and intensity of the spiritual warfare in which we are engaged has become more apparent. Yet, for these seemingly impregnable strongholds to fall, we must wield those weapons given to us by God. (1995:137-38)

Spiritual warfare is comprehensive, and it is often difficult to identify the particular cause. Very often all of the three elements are actively involved, but not always.

**Definition and its evidence.** How is evil noticed? Linthicum says he felt evil over Calcutta the moment he stepped into the city. It was an impression on his mind, soul and emotions. As we entered the great city of Hong Kong and walked the streets, we noticed aromas of drugs and saw that pornographic material was being sold in the poorest communities. The poverty was overwhelming. But as we moved toward the commercial and hotel part of the city, we saw gleaming lights and the affluent huddled together as they negotiated with one another. In both parts of the city the spirit of evil was evident—thick and easily read and experienced. There is a spirit over the city.

If you visit the high-density inner city of north Philadelphia, you will probably be stopped by drug dealers seeking new customers. Yes, this is illegal and evil. Sin is acted out publicly. But a spiritual aspect of it captures us and informs us that the legions of Satan are near. This is what Paul experienced in Corinth when he wrote about the residents' devotion to the temple idols (1 Cor 10:20). How do you test this phenomenon? Biblically, of course.

First, keep in mind that sin has probably given way to oppression. There is no doubt that the New Testament identifies the presence of demonic activity in the world and among believers, but our focus must be on overcoming sinful desires in our lives and seeking holiness. Notice Paul's admonition in 2 Timothy 2:25-26: those who disobey sound teaching are caught by the devil. You may have allowed anger to take control and have not obeyed the Lord's words in Ephesians 4:26, "Do not let the sun go down on your anger." You have not forgiven; therefore you have given the devil an opportunity. If you are bitter, you have moved away from the center to a place of vulnerability, and you must run not from the devil but from your bitterness. We deal with sin and its manifestations through repentance, reliance on God and faithfulness to his kingship.

Where cosmic power has come to attack, Paul reminds us to place God at the forefront of the battle by putting on the full armor of God and standing firm (Eph 6:13). We are not some insignificant entity that simply falls apart under the attacks of Satan or the harassments of the world. We are able to stand firm in the midst of the battle. In Colossians 2:9 Paul tells us, "For in Christ all the fullness of the Deity lives in bodily form." We have it all—the full Godhead living within us. Second Peter 1:3 reinforces our biblical stature: "His divine power has given us everything we need for life and godliness through our knowledge of him who called us by his own glory and goodness."

It is also true that Satan and his army are too much for us as humans. They are angelic, but God has worked out the ultimate authority on the cross. "Having disarmed the powers and authorities, he made a public spectacle of them, triumphing over them by the cross" (Col 2:15). First Corinthians 10:13 gives assurance that God has the ultimate say, even in our own conflict and temptation. If we live for our own pleasures, we become like those to whom Jesus referred as living like their father the devil (Jn 8:44). We need to give up our rights and submit to him who is able to do more than we imagined (Eph 3:20-21).

### The Christian Response

How do we deal with evil that is coming through the spirit of this age? This may seem quite confusing. David Wells, quoting Augustine, noted that Rome did not collapse because of Christian morality but because of pagan immorality (Wells 1998:7). Is it therefore accurate to think that Rome was not defeated by outsiders but by the Romans' own hands? What does this mean to us? Why is it that the fastest-growing religion in the United States is Islam and that it is found almost totally in the African American community (Wells 1998:19)? We have lost our stewardship responsibility to uphold the Word of God in this age and the age to follow (1 Cor 4:1-3). Yet Satan's cosmic war is successful only as long as we continue to imitate the ways and standards of the world.

We have not painted a sensational picture of spiritual warfare, even though we have used a couple of very honest and legitimate illustrations. We believe that it is not as much the casting out of demons in our cities that will enhance God's kingdom and destroy the schemes of the devil as it is the exaltation of our confession that Jesus is Lord over all of life (Phil 2:11).

David Wells states, "My concern is with the Church. The erosion of its theological character, its unwitting worldliness, its inability to think clearly and incisively about the culture, and the growing barbarism of that culture" (Wells 1998:6). Ministers and missionaries serving in the city have come to see that high growth numbers in churches does not always mean high impact. The church needs to combat the deterioration of our communities by coming back to our basic commitment to the sufficiency of the gospel for life and ministry. "Satan and demons are sterile and, therefore, cannot create anything from nothing. They can only piggyback on what is there already. . . . *We cannot assume that every problem has been caused by demons. That is too simplistic*" (Kraft 1992:41).

So our strategy is not at all what you might expect in a chapter on spiritual warfare. The church greatly needs renewal. The Lausanne Covenant states, "We believe that we are engaged in constant spiritual warfare with the principalities and powers of evil, who are seeking to overthrow the church and frustrate its task of world evangelisation" (quoted in Padilla 1976a:213). The church is the agent and community of the kingdom. The church must reclaim spiritual warfare by taking a renewed look at Scripture. It is not enough to look for method. We must search the Scriptures for understanding of how the enemy attacks and how the Christian should respond. To one degree or another every Christian is responsible for this battle, since warfare affects every Christian. "The Bible portrays human history as a drama of war and peace" (Powlison 1995:20).

We must also build new biblical structures for warfare in our local churches. The present structures are too evil centered and conflict oriented. We need structures that are kingdom centered and conflict preventive. The present state of affairs seems to display intimidation and crisis rather than authority over all evil and confidence in the sufficiency of the gospel.

Linthicum states two reasons Satan would drive his power against the city.

> First, those who provide the primary leadership to the systems are ripe for seduction. They tend to overestimate their own power because they are convinced they are in control. Second, the church is woefully ignorant of this strategy. The city church places its primary effort into individuals and its secondary effort into church and family groupings. The church thus leaves the field open to Satan for exerting spiritual influence on both the city's systems and its interior spirituality. (Linthicum 1991a:77)

The power of the gospel is the kingdom of God incarnate in Christ. It is his kingdom rule over all of life. Jesus came to Galilee, and when he spoke, the Bible tells us, demons came out of many (Lk 4:41). When Paul spoke to the young girl who had an evil spirit, when he preached the gospel, the spirit left and she was no longer under domination spiritually and socially (Acts 16:16-18). The deacon Philip preached in Samaria and "evil spirits came out of many" (Acts 8:7). The church must appropriate this power and authority of the gospel of Jesus Christ (Rom 1:16). There is no room for the church to be intimidated by Satan and his evil schemes.

We have been saying that there are three enemies and that any one or all of them may be attacking or taking hold of the church as a body or as individual Christians. All three must be considered when a particular situation in the church is being diagnosed. Here is an example. A Christian found himself apathetic toward the local church and its ministry. This was not the case in the past—the man used to be very active. In a conversation about his present spiritual state, he indicated that he had begun to look at pornography on the Internet and found that he no longer had any interest in reading Scripture and attending Christian activities. He also had been suffering tremendous mood swings that were difficult to explain since he had never been that type of person. He felt more in tune with his fellow employees than with Christian friends and had accommodated their ways to the point that he engaged in a small illegal business, setting up a pornographic website.

Questions made it clear that the man's dilemma started when wealth, status and power became primary goals for him. He then attended church only as a means to an end, to be independently secure and wealthy. He came for self-righteous reasons, hoping that God would see his "good" work of going to church. He wanted to be in charge of his life and make his own decisions.

As he began to realize that his wishes were really to be his own god and that he wanted God to be no more than a substitute runner for him, he started to repent of his self-centeredness and confessed Jesus as his Lord. He revealed his wrongdoing to his fellow employees and abandoned his relationship with the website business. He noticed that some of the other difficulties in his daily life were also being resolved. He not only dealt with his sin, but he left no room for Satan to attack him.

In this case it was clear that sin led to a control factor with the enemy and to abuse of others. Today in many of our churches that are sensitive to spiritual warfare the main approach is passivity—the devil made me do it syndrome—which relieves the individual from any responsibility. This will only cause greater conflict and more oppression. On the other hand, sometimes only the individual's sin is diagnosed and the temptations and spiritual attacks are ignored.

Another example: an elder was found to be a racist. The church's plan was to discipline him by helping him learn more about other ethnic groups and possibly even make friends with a person of a different ethnic group. The problem here is that racism is not treated as a sin. It is looked at as a social, individual behavior that does not affect the structure of the church, family or work. Thus the disciplining of this problem is not comprehensive enough.

> To say that sin is personal . . . is not to say that its consequences are limited to the individual. In biblical faith, that which is personal is never individual-istic, isolated from others. On the contrary, that which is personal is intrinsi-cally related to that which is collective. . . . Every personal action affects the community. Personal sin brings with it collective guilt. (Costas 1982:25)

The church must get it straight in order to be effectively destroying the stronghold of Satan in the church, community and society (Ps 1:1-6).

Another important element of appropriate response has to do with kingdom discipleship—where is the power? The way to destroy the schemes of the devil is to center our attention on the King of the kingdom through discipleship. A church that is centered on evil and seems to be on the defensive—always attributing worth to Satan for his activities—is a church that has lost its power and authority. In the city the church very often attributes too much to the devil.

The kind of discipleship that teaches Christians how to rebuke the devil and how to cast out demons may not be as helpful as one might think. It is not our wish to limit the use of authority over demonic works but to enhance our effectiveness by knowing what and who the enemy is and to use appropriate means to disarm and resolve the conflict. In an attempt to keep a balance Wayne Grudem speaks about standing firm when conflict with hostile spirits occurs. "Paul's readers should not run away in retreat or cower in fear, but should stand their ground boldly, knowing that their weapons and their armor 'have divine power to destroy strongholds' (2 Cor. 10:4; cf. 1 John 5:18)" (Grudem 1994:429). He goes on to say that Christians should speak directly to demons.

We must also respond to spiritual conflict in preventive ways. The way to prevent the enemy from taking control of community, church and family is to disciple the church toward a kingdom perspective on life and ser-vice. We must keep in mind that "sin is the great disorder that tries to frustrate the work of God; salvation is the re-creation that overcomes sin and regains control of God's great plan" (Costas 1982:27). Kingdom disci-pleship helps Christians to preach the gospel to themselves, to others and to the enemy. Christians begin to recognize that we have a bent toward taking charge of our lives and replacing God with self. When Christians are weak enough to admit their failures and shortcomings, repentance allows for healing. We need to acknowledge that independence and autonomy are not freedom but imprisonment. The work of Christ on Cal-vary, his death and resurrection, is the basis for our authority over demons. Here is where Satan was decisively beaten and defeated (Heb 2:14).

Discipleship is always preventive in that it equips Christians to stand firm and be wise in their dealing with life situations. But it is imperative that disciples realize they are dealing with the "murderer" (Jn 8:44) and that they are no match for Lucifer apart from God. This calls for both a spirituality that is seeking holiness and a truthtelling that confesses one's vulnerability. Often small groups are established for people who are having problems with certain addictions or habits. It is best to recognize such issues as early as possible. Opportunities for confession and prayer can lead us toward the study of God's truth in relationship to prevention and healing.

Kingdom discipleship involves living in the gospel—this means living in spirit and in truth (Jn 4:23-24). The disciplines of faith are crucial for growth and prevention of evil. Paul declares in 2 Corinthians 3:18 that as we with unveiled faces reflect on the Lord, we grow from glory to glory. There is a process, but we must be in the Word and allow the Holy Spirit to transform us into his image. Living in the gospel also means prayer and worship. Paul and Silas were in jail with what would seem to be enormous pain and discomfort. They began living in the gospel by praising the Lord (Acts 16:25). Living out the gospel as disciples is crucial as well. In John 4:32-34, Jesus rebukes the disciples and tells them that his food is to do the will of God. He is saying, in the context of harvesting, that his heart embraces mission. His desire is to reap the harvest. This food is necessary if we are to be maturing Christians. A Christianity without conversion cannot be understood.

There is one more area to grasp, and that is what Jesus warns the disciples about in Luke 21:34-36: that there will be a time of great opposition and evil. "Be always on the watch, and pray that you may be able to escape all that is about to happen, and that you may be able to stand before the Son of Man." There are two important facets to kingdom discipleship. One is to know that as we follow the Lord we will inevitably be attacked and must face evil and suffering. But the other is that we must be constantly in prayer. In 1 Timothy 2:1-4 Paul asks us to pray for peace in the midst of harvesting because "one of the great obstacles to victory is when people are swept up into social and political and militaristic conflicts that draw away their attention and time and energy and creativity from the real battle of the universe. Satan's aim is that nobody is saved and comes to the knowledge of the truth" (Piper 1999:15).

Many authors from various theological traditions have written about spiritual warfare. We can gain much from the writings of the early church fathers. Merrill Unger (1952) from Dallas Seminary opened the minds of evangelicals when he approached the subject of whether Christians might be possessed by demons. Peter Wagner went from serious church-growth planning to profound strategies for dealing with demonic conflict. Frank E. Peretti presents a dramatic and interesting fictional rendering in *This Present Darkness* (1986).

Volumes have been written to equip the church. Some of these works are extreme and probably caused more harm than good. Although in some cases the readers have been alerted to this war that is taking place in the world, others have assumed it is nonexistent and we need only to deal with sin. Still others have ignored the spiritual conflict and have resolved the warfare with scientific answers apart from truth.

Peter Wagner's *Confronting the Powers: How the New Testament Church Experienced the Power of Strategic-Level Spiritual Warfare* (1996) clearly lays out not only the strategy of Satan but also the way Christians can have victory over evil attacks. The resources are abundant. It is for the reader to search out any difficulties in matters of exegesis and interpretation.

The church needs to take on the task at hand with a growing conviction that the greatest instrument for every spiritual battle is the knowledge and application of the Word of God to holy living and service. This is an area of weakness in many of our congregations. We have not done our homework. There must be a return to serious study of the Scriptures. We must also recognize our continued idolatry and become men and women of God who delight in having the Lord tell us what to do—people of God who are single-minded.

Our leaders are falling along the wayside due to unholy living. We are not equipped spiritually for the onslaught of Satan. The disciplines of the faith for spiritual health have been ignored. It is a serious mistake to think that we might consider the possibility of knowing the Word apart from obeying the Word.

Following are some specific helps for the urban church.

1. The urban church must identify its authority over demons and Satan.
2. The urban church must review the strategy of Satan in general.
3. The urban church must identify the strategy of Satan as territorial (Poythress 1995).
4. The urban church must act in accordance with Scripture.

## Biblical Understanding of Demons, Satan and Spiritual Warfare

"To be fit and equipped for personal spiritual warfare I must know, believe, and apply biblical truths about spiritual warfare" (Moreau 1997:25). The basic theological information and initial material we have provided so far can serve as the basis for understanding Scripture in matters of spiritual warfare. Linthicum encourages us to begin with Scripture in order to understand the city and the "battle between the God of Israel and/or the church and the god of the world" (Linthicum 1991a:23). We have too often gone the route of experience and storytelling to define spiritual warfare. This will be a constant battle and will probably put the church in deeper trouble rather than allowing it to celebrate the victory established in Christ.

One area that has often been attributed to demonic activity is emotional imbalance or emotional problems. Charles Kraft notes, "The origin of such difficulties lies elsewhere" (1992:41). The church in the city has tended to go to one extreme or another—to place too much responsibility on Satan or to ignore the possibility of demonic activity in the life of the believer and the church. Therefore, as Powlison exhorts us in the subtitle of his 1995 book, we must reclaim spiritual warfare. This is the first step in biblically understanding spiritual warfare.

Powlison's purpose fits well with the process the church needs to undergo in this initial step. The reader may find some awkward points in his position, but it will surely drive you to Scripture.

> The first question engages how we understand the Christian life. *What are we fighting?* How does the evil one actually work? How does he exert—or attempt to exert—his dominion? The second question engages our practice of the Christian life. How should we fight? What is the way God delivers us—and tells us to deliver ourselves and each other—from bondage to the devil? *What is the mode of warfare?* (Powlison 1995:18-19)

Christians are instructed to arrange their lives according to Scripture (Ps 1) as well as the life of the church in society.

The second step is that *we must identify the authority the church has over demons and Satan.* "Jesus Christ died for our sins, to free us from the present evil world. His incarnation and his cross are the norms for the life and mission of the church. His victory is the basis of our hope in the midst of the conflict. His call is to equip ourselves with God's armour and to fight this battle with the spiritual weapons of truth and prayer" (Padilla 1976a:221).

We are lost when it comes to applying the authority given to us in Christ. We fret and yell as though the loudness of our voices would scare the evil one or the authority and bravado of our statements would frighten the power of Satan. Deliverance is dependent on the authority of Christ and nothing more. It is claiming what we have in Christ and what he has already accomplished. Yes, there is a steadfastness only because we believe in the finished work of Christ, but Satan flees because of Christ—his work and his person. "We must avoid two extremes: *a denial of the reality of Satan and the spiritual battle within and around us in which we are engaged and undue fascination with, and fear of, Satan and his hosts.* Our central focus is on Christ, not on Satan" (Hiebert 1994:214). We must never forget where the authority and power come from. For this the church must sharpen its biblical thinking rather than recount its personal experiences.

Third, *the urban church must review the strategy of Satan in general.* Satan would rather have us fight in the wrong areas or completely ignore him. We must again turn to Scripture to gain a better grasp of Satan's tactics. Kraft, Hiebert and Powlison all provide a healthy tension that allows sufficient understanding of Satan's schemes. Hiebert directs the church toward the preparation of leaders—such as pastors, counselors and those with gifts of exorcism—to work together (1994:214). In order for this ministry to go on there must be some understanding of demonic tactics. "The real danger is found in people who coolly and rationally reject Christ and his rule in their lives, lead others astray (Eph. 4:14; 5:6; 2 Thess. 2:3), and build human societies and cultures that oppress people and keep them from coming to Christ. Idolatry and self-absorption, not spirit possession, is still at the heart of human rebellion" (Hiebert 1994:214).

It is important to take this to a larger scale, taking up a strategy that involves territorial spirits. Both Linthicum (1991a) and Poythress (1995) acknowledge the biblical understanding of territorial spirits. When Linthicum conducts workshops on inner-city ministry, he usually asks who is the angel of the city where the workshop is to be held. Very often it is clearly described. He then begins to ask how this spirit manifests itself (1991a:75). Just as it is important to accurately diagnose a person who is physically or emotionally ill in order to apply the prescription that will lead to healing, so the church must be able to identify the strategy of the evil one. Biblical tools again are encouraged along with case studies of successful treatments.

Finally, *the urban church must act in accordance with Scripture.* The challenge for the church is not to sit back while spiritual warfare is going on but to become active in its community through preparation and prayer. This is not a time of desperation but of seeing the majesty of Christ lifted high. Paul was continuously in the fight. As a matter of fact, all of life was war (2 Tim 4:7; 6:12). "He was a man who loved peace. But the pervasiveness of war is in the fact that one of the weapons of war is the Gospel of peace! (Eph. 6:15)" (Piper 1999:14). Until we realize that we are in a battle that is serious and pervasive, we will not pray with earnest hearts. The church is armed with the most powerful weapon to destroy the deceptive tactics of Satan. We must use the gospel of peace to make Christ's name known in our communities.

**Conclusion**

This chapter is intended to point to the need for additional study and to encourage rethinking of a subject that is often ignored in most theological discussions. Spiritual warfare is a reality of the Christian life. It is ongoing but not always noticed or clearly defined. We are in combat and must use Scripture as the weight that puts the scale in balance. "Life is war because the maintenance of our faith and the laying hold on eternal life is a constant fight. Paul makes clear in 1 Thessalonians 3:5 that Satan targets our faith for destruction" (Piper 1999:14). We must be on the offensive, confident that this battle is the Lord's, and therefore we must submit to his prescribed will for his soldiers.

We may be either too overwhelmed by or too dismissive of the signs that Satan is still on the front cover of our neighborhood newspaper. The war is not over, and we must feel the strain of that reality. Prayer is our most important weapon (Eph 6). We must arm ourselves with God's weapons and Spirit as our neighborhoods come into freedom through the preaching and the living out of the gospel.

# Part 6

## Leadership & Discipleship for the Urban Church

# 20

# Contextual Traits
of Urban Leadership

MUCH HAS ALREADY BEEN WRITTEN AND taught about church leadership. However, a good portion of these resources develop a concept of leadership that makes no reference to the context to which it is meant to apply, whether suburban or urban, this culture or that culture. While the Bible's direction for leaders is truly transcultural, the way we apply it practically must vary from one cultural context to another. And any additional guidelines not directly from Scripture must always be seen relative to a particular context.

When books and talks on leadership fail to articulate the context for which they are intended, readers and hearers mistakenly assume that the direction offered will apply in any cultural context. Obviously this can lead to frustration, disillusionment and ineffectiveness when a leader attempts to apply the principles in a context different from the one the principles assume.

Most guidance available concerning church leadership tacitly assumes a suburban context. Very little is written or taught concerning leadership that consciously addresses the urban context. Again, this leaves people concerned about serving the urban church with few resources and little context-appropriate training. The matter becomes increasingly critical as the world's demographics continue to shift: more of the world is increasingly urban; less and less of it is suburban.

In this chapter we hope to address this oversight. This is a book intended to help those in urban ministry. We want to show how careful attention to contextualization helps us understand better how to apply what the Bible says about leaders to urban ministry.

## Leadership in Context

Most Christians know of books and materials written to help local church leaders who serve in a suburban or rural setting. These books are written to help such churches be more efficient and biblical. But they are very narrow in matters of culture, context and task. The books are usually for pastors, elders and deacons. They often focus only on the local church and fail to address sociological and missiological implications.

A quick browse through *The Making of a Leader* by Robert Clinton (1988) and *Leadership in Christian Ministry* by James Means (1989) readily supports our point concerning context. They are both fine and helpful books that have been used as texts in numerous classes, but they limit their instruction to a particular context without ever referring to it. This leaves the reader assuming that the book's instructions, not just the biblical principles, apply to all cultures and contexts. Matters of style and methods that reflect contextualization are universalized without the provision of any caution.

Most often when we think of leadership we think primarily of a local church setting without considering the context. If the context is mentioned, it is only for the reader to know its geographical location. The meaning of the context is rarely referred to as being important in developing a philosophy of ministry. Therefore, even though a book is geared toward Christian leadership in the context of a nonurban environment, there is no mention of this uniqueness. In reality the content of the book is geared for leadership in a suburban/rural community. The assumption is that all Christian leaders come from a nonurban context and are serving outside of the urban reality. There is also an assumption that since scriptural principles are universal they fit anywhere without contextualization. These assumptions are invalid and need redirection.

In contrast, the number of books that address or assume *urban* leadership is minimal at best. In addition to demonstrating ignorance of the importance of context, this inequity certainly indicates a lack of interest in matters of urban mission as well as a lack of understanding of the world's changing demographics.

The distinctions between rural, suburban and urban are slowly vanishing. Part of this change in the United States has to do with what Joel Garreau calls "Edge City." "Today, we have moved our means of creating wealth, the essence of urbanism—our jobs—out to where most of us have lived and shopped for two generations. That has led to the rise of Edge City" (Garreau 1991:4). This spreading out of the landmarks should not cause us to become less concerned about the city but rather more interested in understanding the urbanization process.

Demographics indicate that the highest number of evangelical churches exist in nonurban areas. We mention this as a point of concern. Where are the evangelical churches in this urbanizing world? Why does the city suffer from "evangelical absenteeism" (Conn 1994a:142)? The context, even in suburban and rural communities, is drastically changing. Rural communities are becoming small-sized cities (50,000) and are growing toward becoming larger, middle-sized cities (100,000). "The real city is the total metropolitan area—city and suburb" (Rusk 1993:5). Keep in mind that more and more the lines between urban and suburban are fading (Elliston and Kauffman 1993:128). "No longer suburbs, not quite cities, they are called 'urban villages' by some" (Conn 1994a:134-35). Suburban communities are becoming more and more culturally diverse. In 1972 one denomination "estimated that 150 of its churches were in communities 'undergoing ethnic change,' and that 600-800 of its 6,800 congregations throughout the United States would find themselves in changing communities by 1980" (Ziegenhols 1978:16).

The issue of knowing the context in which we serve must be taken seriously, especially as we see the continued urbanization and globalization of the world. In matters of training, seminaries and Bible colleges continue to prepare leadership for a context that has long passed and are not taking into regard the changing world that is becoming more urban and ethnically diverse than ever before.

### Three Kinds of Urban Leaders

The critical impact that context has on leadership requires that we distinguish three kinds of urban church leaders. Apart from understanding the important role of context in urban ministry, it is not possible to distinguish these different kinds of leaders. It is important for would-be leaders and their churches to be aware of these differences so that they can take them into consideration in their preparation and in their ministry. Each category reflects a different kind of relationship to the urban context. As a result, each has its own unique set of assets and liabilities. Urban church leaders exist who exemplify each of these categories.

The first has to do with those who enter the urban community from a distinctly different environment and culture, such as a rural or suburban context. This type we will call *relocated leaders*. The urban scene is unfamiliar and foreign to these leaders' way of living and doing ministry. They come from homogeneous communities that usually represent a different socioeconomic stratum. To them the city is awkward and at times oppressive. They have become aware of the needs in the city and have been drawn into the city due to what they sense is a call from the Lord. They need time and training to orient themselves to the new context.

The second kind are *indigenous leaders,* those who have grown up in the city and belong to a particular culture. These may be, for example, Anglo leaders who have lived on the south side of Philadelphia, are of Italian descent and are recognized as leaders. They live in a type of community which very often takes on the name of the roots of its forefathers and becomes Little Italy, China Town or Korea Town. It may be that the urban leaders come from an African American or Hispanic community. Indigenous leaders, whether trained for urban ministry or not, belong to their urban context socially and ethnically. They are urbanites and feel at home in the city, whether it is center city, where most of the commerce and business is found, or the inner city, where the social and economic conditions are quite different. They do not find high density or multicultural settings to be oppressive. But the fact that an indigenous leader is comfortable in his or her urban community does not mean that he or she will be comfortable or tolerant in a different urban ethnic community. An individual from an Asian community might find it difficult to live and work in a Hispanic community. Ethnic and socioeconomic polarization is common in most cities in the United States.

The last type of leader is found in a multiethnic milieu, working alongside other leaders in a local church. We will call this a *multiethnic leader.* This type of leader can be found in a church in a U.S. center city area or close to the center city where cultural diversity is evident. Often there is a college or university campus within the vicinity of the church that lends to this reality. Or it may be found near the center city commercial community where young professionals live within easy commuting distance and enjoy access to entertainment and the arts. This church probably will not only be multiethnic but will also display major socioeconomic differences within the makeup of the church.

**Relocated leaders.** In contrast to the indigenous and multiethnic leaders, these leaders engage in true crosscultural ministry. In this respect they are like foreign missionaries, but they serve much closer to their home context. It is the fact that they serve so close to their home context that makes the ministry accessible. It is the same fact that can lead to difficulties.

**Indigenous leaders.** The next type of leadership in urban ministry is called indigenous leadership. The story on page 383 exemplifies the development of an indigenous leader. Wayne Gordon believes that indigenous leaders already exist in any urban community:

> First we must commit to believe that the *leaders are already in our communities*. As we look at the young people in our neighborhoods, we must not look down upon their usefulness, as Paul tells Timothy, but we must see them with kingdom eyes. We must see the people around us as leaders, people who have insights and intuitions that are far more sensitive to the needs of the community than ours. Our perceptions of leadership must be different from the world's perception of leadership. (Gordon 1995:182-83)

It is problematic to use the word *indigenous* because many issues have been raised about that label in missiological discussions both in Protestant and Catholic circles.

> The difficulty with this term, at least in some places, is the history of the word "indigenous." In those parts of the world that once made up the British empire, "indigenous" connotes the old policy of replacing British personnel in colonial government with local leadership. (Schreiter 1985:5)

There was a debate during colonialism about whether or not the national church could fend for itself and create its own leadership and church structure. Out of this came a formula created by Rufus Anderson and Henry Venn that suggested the indigenous church approach should be self-supporting, self-propagating and self-governing (Conn 1984:79). As you can tell, the term is loaded with a variety of definitions and conclusions.

In this book when we speak of indigenous leaders, we mean those who have been raised in an urban context in a particular cultural and sociological milieu, who consider this context their own, psychologically and sociologically. Indigenous leaders find the city home. They have no ties to another context that might draw them to return to it, or that they have to overcome to remain in this urban setting. The most indigenous people in an inner-city community are those we call kids. They are in the community *in toto*. They find all their resources of life in the streets and blocks of the area. The music, culture and language of the city have become their own. There is no other community or culture for them. They know the community better than most because their time is spent in the neighborhood. Here they find meaning and interpret the world through the eyes of their community experience.

By contrast, a family which moves from Mexico into Chicago's La Villita, a homogeneous Mexican urban community, may not be fully indigenous. They share common cultural roots with others in the community, but the socialization process may not have taken place in matters of the urban reality. Their worldview is still rural, and the urban worldview has not taken hold. They are still looking to return to their home in rural Mexico; they consider the urban setting temporary. Their lifestyle has not changed since they lived in the rural community they call home outside of Mexico City. These people are in the city but not of it, and they don't intend to be of it ever.

The second generation Mexicans born in this Chicago community are indigenous. They not only have the cultural roots of their parents but also have been enculturated to the urban reality. They have actually become a three-cultured people—they are Mexican, urban and enculturating into the Mexican American experience. It is possible (though not inevitable) for the family of the second generation Mexican living in that community eventually to become indigenous with respect to the urban Chicago milieu. This will require that they adopt a new lifestyle and commitment to the present environment.

Similarly, an urban church leader may share nationality with those in an urban context and yet not be indigenous to it because he or she has moved from a different socioeconomic group in the same culture.

Leaders who do emerge from an indigenous upbringing are extremely valuable assets to a long-term ministry in that part of the city. They will eventually become the contextualist walking in the community filled with the Spirit of God. They are able to contextualize the gospel and bring to the neighborhood a Messiah who speaks the language of the people and who understands their needs. We believe that this kind of urban leadership is living and surviving in those pockets of the city. Finding and developing indigenous leaders is the most important thing we can do to grow the church in our urban centers. Yet for various reasons indigenous leaders are often ignored by church planters and denominational missionary groups.

Denominations are having difficulty finding this kind of leadership. They wonder where they will find urban leaders. Denominations also are finding the city resistant to their outreach. This is because they are not contextualized into the urban multicultural reality and are working out of a culture that is repellent to many of our city leaders. They do not realize that institutions are not neutral. Institutions have been formed by culture and continue to reinforce that culture within their ranks. The relocated leader may have been formed in that setting and, therefore, finds it difficult to make headway in the urban area designated to start a church. We believe that denominations would do well to take seriously and seek to develop indigenous leaders.

Indigenous urban leaders have several characteristics that other leaders do not share. Urban indigenous leaders see the city as their home and mission. Their commitment to the city and to the healing of the city is long-term and natural and becoming more God centered. There is no need to convince them about the city. In their mind's eye there are only urban pictures. Anything else is fantasy or from a make-believe world. They embody an urban lifestyle: they know the boundaries for survival, they are accustomed to the noise, busyness and crowdedness of the city, and they do not compare this way of life to another. They know the hardships related to the city and have been nurtured to live with them. The limitations of education, public services that do not care about sanitation or beautification, and violence that erupts in their presence are all a part of the urban life to which they are accustomed.

> ### The Church on the Corner
>
> The church on the corner had been there for over thirty years. As kids, my friends and I had found that the steps were ideal for hanging out. We never entered the building, but I do remember the elderly lady who wanted us to attend a class on Sunday that she claimed would be fun and exciting. I had been cautious since we were of a different religion. The community had been changing for years, and now there were few white people living in the neighborhood. The church had a few senior citizens meeting on Sunday, but as soon as a service was over, they all headed out of the community.
>
> Most of the people in my community were Hispanics and African Americans. A Spanish-speaking pastor lived in my building, and he was always sharing about the love of Christ. My father and mother began attending this Bible study that was in Spanish. They invited me, but I did not understand the language very well. Eventually there was a large group of people meeting in this pastor's apartment, and this formed the nucleus of a new church in our community. They went to the pastor of the corner church to see if they could rent the building for worship services on Sunday. This church agreed and the new church grew.
>
> Shortly after my twelfth birthday I met a person who said he worked in the church as a youth pastor. He shared with me my need for the Lord, and I accepted his invitation to know Christ as my Lord and Savior. I am now a youth pastor in that same church and find my life meaningful as I serve the Lord. This is my community, and I want its many needy people to come to know the Lord as their Savior. I am hoping to go to the evening Bible institute and learn more about the Word of God. I am going to be a pastor in my community one day. My parents still live in the same building. Many of our neighbors have come to know the Lord.

Most indigenous families understand the temporality of property and possessions. They know that the chances of having someone steal their belongings is high and can happen frequently. At the same time indigenous families share a sense of protection because everyone on their block knows them. People often believe that such protection is part of life in suburbia and rural communities, but it is seemingly more readily available in urban neighborhoods. High density or living in close proximity may seem uncomfortable and less private, but urban indigenous leaders find it a helpful resource. For the suburban dweller, a police car siren means help is on the way. For urban people it often means trouble is on the way.

*Multiethnic leadership teams.* The multiethnic leadership team is a group of leaders, usually pastors, who are serving together in a multiethnic church and in a very ethnically diverse community. Such teams have developed mostly in cities in the United States.

In the cities of a developing world country the population can also have multiethnic leadership. But in such cases usually the population and the church are homogeneous but there is an ethnic plurality of leaders because a foreign missionary team is involved in the local church and community. On these teams the missionaries should provide a supportive role rather than assume a mutually equal position.

A multiethnic milieu can develop when there is a major shift in population taking place due to civil war, tribal strife or natural disaster. In this case people from different economic, cultural and ethnic backgrounds are entering the city. It is usually the very poor who have relocated due to political and social conflict. They are refugees who have many pressing needs, and the only helping hand is the church. A multiethnic situation can also develop as a result of mass immigration from other countries to a city. A number of cities in Canada, for example, may experience a large influx of people from Hong Kong or mainland China. Here the issues are different, but they present the church with opportunities for evangelism and church growth. In either case the necessity of multiethnic leaders is essential. These leaders are concerned about the various people groups in the community and the racial struggle that this kind of pluralism presents in the city. They are interested in showing the community that God is concerned about reconciliation and harmony among all people.

Despite the need for such an effort, it can be difficult to make a multiethnic leadership team work. The leaders on this team are very often more ethnically equipped to deal with their own culture than they are to work in the city. They are concerned for the city only as a means to the end of helping their own people group. Also, their commitment to the multiethnic church's vision may only be instrumental: they unite with other leaders primarily to have access to the church's ministries for their own ethnic group. If the team members are primarily in it for what they can get in matters of church growth and facilities, the team effort will eventually break down. Circle Church in Chicago in the late 1970s discovered the difficulties of serving in the city as a team of coequal leaders. They found that communication and commitments had different definitions and expectations. Their basic philosophy of ministry was challenged. Eventually their leaders decided never to work together again (Ortiz 1991).

A multiethnic church intentionally decides to include multiple leaders, each from different cultures. Together they work to address the needs of each cultural group—the need for facilities, the need for support and the need to pursue interracial reconciliation as the name of God's kingdom. The multiethnic leadership team needs to see the larger picture of this mission. It is more corporate than the leaders might have imagined. The multiethnic team must first be committed to biblical goals in matters of reconciliation and the unity of the body. A multiethnic team usually works best when its leaders belong to the same denomination or theological tradition. Second, it must be committed to the missiological task of reaching out to the particular people groups but also to the crosscultural dimension of the community. Third, the team also has to be committed to the teaching of the Scriptures in matters of the church and its growth. Too often multiethnic leaders are content to see their own group grow without much concern for the more senior group that is presently declining. Church growth is not just for local churches but for the whole of the church.

If these things are held as of primary importance, then it will be clear that individual ethnic leaders' exclusive ministry to their own people will not do. The most difficult aspect of this leadership team is developing a means of trust and a commitment to the same goals of reconciliation. This team must work together for the long haul. It must realize that the journey is filled with challenges that pertain to our sinful self centeredness. Ethnocentrism must be challenged so that there is no longer a superior or inferior culture. Christ is all in all (Col 1:16-17). He is the superior one. The leadership must understand the many aspects of human behavior that cannot be left to thoughtless assumptions. Since we have segregated churches, communities, colleges and denominations, this task is somewhat difficult. Multiethnic leadership seeks to break down barriers that have kept us apart and distorted the authority of God's Word.

Trust takes a great deal of time and face-to-face encounters. Too often there is time together but rarely face-to-face development. As difficult as this is, the time together must be more qualitative. Face-to-face encounters must include honest discussions that review the concerns of all the groups and also the theological commitments that bind them together.

Careful attention to the issue of context in general and urban context in particular has led us to distinguish three kinds of urban leaders seeking ethnic leadership team. Each has its own unique characteristics, assets and liabilities, and thus it is important and useful to distinguish one from another. Obviously a leader who is indigenous to a context can perhaps more easily influence it for Christ. But a leader who has relocated to a context can be effective especially as he or she first acknowledges the critical influence of context and takes appropriate steps to adjust. And a leadership team seeking to serve a multiethnic city culture can be effective as they unite to serve a multiethnic context rather than individual subcultures. Taking context into consideration should not stop us from reaching out to the city but rather impassion us to prepare well to meet this critical challenge.

We have shown that the urban context must be taken seriously both as we study leadership and as we apply Scripture to city ministry. Urban leaders must become better equipped to read and exegete community and the trends that are sociologically revealing how the future will unfold. The social sciences are important as leaders look at Scripture and invite the Holy Spirit to help them apply the Word in that social reality. The urban leader must be a student of the Word. In the context of the city we begin to look at Scripture in a different way. Now the context of mission helps us to do theology. Most of our training has ignored a theology of the city or urban church history. Now we read the Bible differently in matters of context and application.

## Issues Faced by Leaders in Context

Crosscultural ministry has been with us since biblical times. The most drastic example was the coming of the Messiah (Jn 1; Phil 2). Jesus crossed the greatest cultural boundary to give us the gospel of his salvation. Mission, as we see it both in Scripture and contemporary society, is often crosscultural in nature. Paul was Jewish, yet he lived like a Gentile in order to reach more than just Jewish people (1 Cor 9:19-22).

Urban crosscultural opportunities very close to home continually increase in number. Presently the increasing global push-pull migration patterns are bringing people from different countries and communities to both new and old developing cities throughout the world. The key words are *change* and *adapt.* Cities are popping up everywhere, especially in places we did not expect.

This does not mean that we are becoming less urbanized; rather that urban culture is spreading out and colonizing the suburb, small towns and rural areas. The city is less of a place and more of a process. (Bakke 1987:31)

Cities such as London, Jerusalem and Sao Paulo, Brazil, continue to engage new people groups with enormous immigration from Asia, Africa and Latin America. Liverpool has 10,000 Chinese (Bakke 1987:32). Cities grow when they are elastic (Rusk 1993:10). By that we mean they have room to grow. Cities can have room two ways: (1) they can have a lot of vacant land within their current boundaries that is available for new uses or (2) they can have the ability to annex areas adjoining them, growing by actually expanding their boundaries.

Crosscultural realities are found everywhere a city is defined. Two-Thirds World countries are not only becoming more urban but are also experiencing the enormous globalization process. Their populations are on the move to other places. "London was the head of the world—now the world is in London" (Bakke 1987:34). This means that we will be able to reach a high proportion of Hindus from India in London or in Philadelphia simply by relocating from a reasonable car ride away.

The easy part is that we have the immediate resources to make this geographical move. The most difficult part of it is that we do not see the need to understand the urban culture and the ethnic particulars to prepare for this encounter. This is our downfall. Geographically near, a culturally and socially distant context may add up to wrong assumptions by well-intended leaders and denominations. This lack of preparation for urban ministries manifests our ignorance of the demands to serve in the urban context. "Any one who ventures into crosscultural missions without some kind of preparation is nuts" (Hale 1995:30).

The case study on page 391 points out the drastic change and commitment that are necessary for the relocated leader. The relocated leader is in a cross-social, -economic and -cultural tension and yet has probably not traveled any farther than three or four hours from his or her home church and community. How will leaders who enter the city from a context other than urban make the necessary adjustments? The following are a few possible liabilities that a relocated leader would do well to acknowledge and address.

## Potential Liabilities

*Bonding.* People who relocate into a unique culture nearby often fail to sever and re-form the ties that enable them to bond effectively with their new context. I find it difficult to accept Lupton's view that relocated leaders can become indigenized (Lupton 1993:51-55) because relocated leaders continue to have options and alternatives for departure from the new context no matter their commitments. They never become African American or Hispanic or whatever, nor are they expected to. But relocated leaders who do not bond with the new culture, rather than being shaped by the new culture, shape the new culture by turning it into the one they came from. After many years in a new context, relocated leaders would do well to check whether their value system has not changed and they have instead placed their values on others. They have suburbanized the urban community. Bonding involves struggling with how much of the culture and social context a relocated leader should adopt. "Culture is the anthropologist's label for the sum of the distinctive characteristics of a people's way of life" (Lingenfelter and Mayers 1986:17). That is certainly a simplistic and short definition, but it says enough to remind us that bonding will call for a complete change to another's way of life. Such a change is more total than just being comfortable in another context. The only one to have that ability completely was the Lord Jesus when he became a 200 percent person—he was fully God and fully Jew (Lingenfelter and Mayers 1986:17).

**Expectations.** When relocated leaders come to the urban context, they arrive with certain expectations. An expectation is a mental structure of what the individual wants to see happen in ministry and in self-development. Usually it is intended to be useful, bringing change as quickly as possible. But expectations can harm rather than help the ministry of the relocated leader. Expectations may be shaped by perceptions these leaders have of the city, the church and the leadership they seek to serve. Because our outlook on the urban context has been cultivated through the media, family and the church in negative images, we might begin our ministry with a deficient view of the city, its leadership and its church. Wrong perceptions lead to a spirit of paternalism and an attitude of being the savior of the people and the community, what is often classified as a messiah complex. "Nothing good was taking place until we arrived." These are sinful elements that we carry with us, and they need to be discarded. Certainly all of the above are encountered in the process of sanctification. As a people in a sinful world we all know that culture is fallen and that we are prone to be racist and paternalistic. We consider ourselves superior to other people groups. Similarly our history might be imperialistic, oppressive and in need of repentance.

Relocated leaders will have to undergo recontextualization and renewal of mind and heart. Otherwise, the future and effectiveness of the ministry in that particular community will be limited. There are certain things that relocated leaders should not bring with them when entering a different culture, what is often called excess baggage. They need to keep and appreciate that which is given to us by God—things such as gender, ethnicity, generation and history. When these things are accepted as God's good pleasure, relocated leaders can advance their ministry in a crosscultural milieu.

Crosscultural ministry always requires that a person deal with fear. Fear of the unknown and the known is part of the process of entry. This usually comes up as fear of danger of physical harm for self and family. *A Clarified Vision for Urban Mission* (Conn 1987) is an important book for those entering the city as missionaries and lay leaders, for it helps to provide balance and to erase common misperceptions. "The reality of crime in the urban areas of the United States is difficult to deny. But it does seem that the largely white suburbanites have a fear of city crime out of all proportion to the facts" (Conn 1987:72). This fear soon diminishes when you are living in the city and learning a new lifestyle. Coping skills are raised to a new high and the relocated leader learns to confront his or her own fears in light of God's calling.

There will certainly be fear of those who are ethnically different from

> **Moving to the Context of Ministry**
>
> The young couple from rural Wisconsin had attended a conference where the subject was urban mission. They went unaware of the needs of the city. They knew that their interest for service and mission would be in a suburban church or in a foreign mission in Africa. This conference turned their whole lives around and their hearts now pounded for the cities. They found additional assistance in determining how that call might be materialized. The suggestion was for them to apply to a seminary that would prepare them for ministry in the city. They could not find one that explicitly provided urban courses, but they were offered an opportunity to learn urban work through an inner-city church. They applied and began their move to a large city in the Midwest.
>
> As they moved in they discovered that this was a drastic move. It was one thing to speak about serving in the city; it was another to move into a poor urban community where the culture was totally different from theirs. They also realized that now they lived in the context of ministry. Ministry in the city was not something they went to but something that was always at their front door. It was clear that they lived in the context of mission, and the tension between their private and public lives was now being rearranged. Vulnerability was something they had never experienced. They were used to having control of their environment and knowing what to expect most of the time. At first, experiencing a different way of doing things, such as worship and preaching, was exciting and stimulating. But after the first year they encountered a cultural loss, because their new way of serving, worshiping and relating to others bore no resemblance to what they had known all their lives. They pondered what to do next. Was the Lord calling them to a more familiar community where they could maximize their skills and knowledge?

the incoming leaders. "White ethnocentrism continues to influence us. Non-English speaking and/or 'nonwhite' peoples have always been viewed with suspicion by whites in the New World" (Conn 1987:75). Racism is ingrained in our society and is a part of our nature that we call self-centeredness. Sin is the root that blossoms both personally and systemically.

**Energy and excitement.** Relocating crossculturally can bring an initial rush of energy and excitement that leads to a false or sinful sense of power and masks the severity of the crosscultural change. Newness, difference and quantity can at the outset promote a certain level of high energy and willingness to do things and take on challenges. Ideas are shooting out that have never been tested or evaluated. There is a rush that stimulates courage to "live for God." Ministry is now at the leaders' doorstep; there is no need for them to get in a car and go to ministry. The neighborhood has a good feel to it—people knowing people, calling each other by first names, running into someone they know every day. Hospitality is not planned but happens when they invite neighbors or people invite themselves to their apartment. Fellowship or small groups are happening several times a week because they enjoy opening their home to others and coming in from a walking distance. Discipleship is both planned and spontaneous. A problem occurs and an individual or couple comes over to talk to the relocated leaders because they live right around the corner. These leaders have now become needed and very important. Their uniqueness is appreciated. They have now come to realize how important they really are and how gifted God has made them. They have more power than they ever imagined, and the rush feels good.

As they enter into the morning service on the Lord's Day, they discover a relaxed environment. New songs are played, spontaneity is evident, and they can let it all hang out and be demonstrative about their faith and worship. The service is loud as the drums play and keep up with the tempo of the city. People are hugging and the leaders find that rewarding and an expression of friendship and commitment.

Now it is important to take inventory of what is happening. The relocated leaders are being fulfilled and encouraged and have a sense of power on their side. They think that what they are doing is special and to some degree superior. The "I need you" now has become "you need me." Others want to be like them because of the sense of enormous energy and boldness for the gospel. This is dangerous for the relocated leaders. Now they have the power in their hands, people sense their importance and usability, and instead of humility there is headship. How will they learn servanthood and submission? God has called us to servanthood.

> A minister is a servant; Christ is the one Lord, who must rule until all his enemies are put under his feet (I Cor 15:25; Col 3:1). No one is called to lord it over the flock of Christ (1 Pet 5:3); no throne is set in the church but the one at God's right hand. (Clowney 1964:41)

These leaders are now serving because of the rush and the personal reward. This is a time of evaluation and of needing assistance from indigenous leaders on how to get out of this dilemma.

**Critical spirit.** After the initial rush of energy and excitement, the next struggle is one of a critical and censorious spirit. The relocated leaders begin to feel the radicality of the crosscultural change they have made. As they look at the order of the church, the level of emotions expressed in the worship and the loudness of the music, instead of experiencing enjoyment, they compare these expressions with what they traditionally enjoyed. They find that they miss the order and quietness of worship. The spontaneity that they found liberating they now classify as unorganized. The ministry and activities that made them feel useful are now overwhelming, and they wish they had more space for themselves and less crowding in on their privacy. They enjoyed newness but now they miss their home roots. Some of what was appealing has now become a reason to question their continued service in the city. "Where do we go from here?" At this point many have made a decision to leave the city wondering whether they had made the right decision at the outset.

## Stress Points in Urban Ministry

In urban ministry there are personal stress points that are certainly not unique to the city but are often intensified in the urban context. These stress points are very personal and can cause burnout if they are not noticed and dealt with.

**Aloneness.** It is not the lack of partners in ministry—there is always enough of that. But there may not always be enough same-gender friendships and pastoral oversight. Urban leaders need edifying relationships, friends who are honest with them and with others. Leaders need to be strong and courageous in the city as they minister the gospel. But this can lead them mistakenly to think that we must not be vulnerable and disclose our needs and hardships if we are to keep our urban profile intact. If a leader unduly hides his or her needs, this will create too many secrets; it will eventually cause a leader's downfall. Urban leaders need friends and overseers who will care for them. They need small group accountability where brothers or sisters are praying and caring for each other.

**Lack of spiritual development.** Leaders are always expected to give. By nature of being giving servants, leaders are in the city in order to develop others. We can mistakenly think that therefore they are not to receive or to be developed. But the assumption that leaders grow and grow into maturity because they are always calling others to grow is incorrect. Due to the strenuous demands on urban leaders, there is more of a chance that they will neglect their own walk with God and not grow toward Christian maturity. We have found too many urban leaders damaged spiritually and eventually socially because of the lack of spiritual development and maturity in the faith. The spiritual warfare that is undertaken by leadership cannot be handled by ill-equipped leaders. A certain quality of spirituality is necessary for urban mission. There is no room for any team or church staff leadership ever to take for granted that their partners in ministry are prepared for battle and are ready to engage the enemy (Eph 6:10-18). The spirituality that is demanded is one that requires constant contemplation and devotion to God. Paul exhorts the elders at Ephesus to "keep watch over yourselves and all the flock of which the Holy Spirit has made you overseers" (Acts 20:28). The word προσεξω means to hold the mind toward something, to take heed. The verb is in the present imperative in order to charge us with the importance of constantly caring for ourselves and others (Lenski 1934:846-47). It also has the notion of caring for yourself first if you are going to care for others. If we are to call others to devotion to God, we must first be devoted to God. Be taught yourself if you are going to teach others. Be close to God in prayer if you are going to encourage others to be close to God in prayer. We should expect as leaders that we always need to grow. We should always seek to grow. In a leadership team we should expect that each member will help the other to do this. The urgency of urban ministry requires that we exercise personal spiritual care so as to meet the city's challenges over the long term.

**Imbalanced lifestyle.** The call here is for leaders to consider how holistic their lives are. Is there balance? In Luke 2:52 we notice that Jesus grew in all areas: wisdom, stature, favor with God and with man. In urban ministry there is an unspoken law that recreation is an unnecessary extravagance in light of needs that are many and profound. Leaders are placed in a guilt mode if they go outside the city for recreation. We believe that there is a great need for urban leaders to be held accountable for the purpose of steady growth and a healthy life. Change very often is as important in matters of healthy living as rest. Again, accountability is important in carrying out this imperative. At least one day per week should be used for recreation. Vacations are to be taken as well, in order for life and ministry to have long-lasting and healthy effects. If ministry occupies 95 percent of a person's life, it will not take long for that individual to find that he or she is in a deep hole of depression. The exhortation in Acts 20 is that we must care for our well-being if we are to encourage others to follow suit. It is part of what mentoring is all about. Emerging leaders will follow our example. Often this imbalance is primarily due to self-centeredness. It is the leaders' need for others that keeps them pushing ahead, not the people and community they serve. Too often our need for others hinders our love for them. "We need to need other people less and love other people more" (Welch 1997:167). "Self-serving needs are not meant to be satisfied; they are meant to be put to death" (Welch 1997:162).

Usually in the city everyone is busy and active. How are the leaders going to be held accountable? This again becomes a serious neglect in the church. We are to consider that we are accountable to Christ (1 Cor 4:2). Christ will evaluate our performance on the basis of our heart. Therefore, we are to please God and not people (2 Cor 5:9; Col 1:10).

***Need for reflection.*** The need for reflection is not an option as some might think. Reflection is necessary not only for the leaders' well-being but also for the well-being of the church. The stress point here has to do with renewal and freshness in ministry. Repetition is important and good until the activity becomes dry and stale. A ministry that is stale depletes energy rather than restores it. A time of reflection has two important features: looking backward and looking forward. It is a time to evaluate our relationship with the Lord and to consider areas of our lives that need refinement or rejection. What are the areas in which we need to grow? What are the things we need to abandon? Leaders need to seek the Lord not only in reference to personal matters but also concerning their ministry. Reflection is a time of introspection, but it should also be a time of vision casting. Stepping away and looking at the ministry, both past and future, will restore creative energy to leaders.

We must also discover the discipline of prayer. Paul solicited the prayers of the saints at Ephesus: "Pray also for me, that whenever I open my mouth, words may be given me so that I will fearlessly make known the mystery of the gospel, for which I am an ambassador in chains. Pray that I may declare it fearlessly, as I should" (Eph 6:19-20).

A spiritual retreat can afford us the time for much-needed reflection. We have abandoned a contemplative lifestyle because we have associated it with a Roman Catholic mysticism. This has been to our detriment, for contemplation need not be Roman Catholic and need not be mystical. We must restore contemplation, for it is necessary for healthy ministry.

Another reason for neglecting spiritual reflection is that we do not view it as a high priority or even as an aspect of ministry. We dismiss what many are calling spiritual formation because it is not productive enough, but in fact our spiritual need is profound. It underlies all our other needs and desires. Dr. Ed Welch notes several concerns:

> 1. We were created with biological needs. We need food and protection from harsh weather. We need God and, secondarily, other people to meet these needs.
> 2. We are sinners who have spiritual needs. Apart from the redeeming and sustaining work of Christ, we are spiritually dead. We need Jesus. We need to be taught of him and rebuked in love when we stray from him. Furthermore, . . . we need to know his immense love.
> 3. We were created as people with limited gifts and abilities. All the gifts of God are not contained in any one person. Therefore, we need other people in order to accomplish God's purposes and most accurately reflect his unlimited glory. (Welch 1997:163-64)

Urban leaders can underestimate the importance of spiritual reflection because they underestimate what it will take to do what they're called to do. Urban leaders understand what it means to serve in a mission context. But often they do not understand what it will take to live out the gospel and be faithful and fruitful in that context. Urban leaders can forget that they must fear God rather than man. Then they begin to experience various forms of fear—fear of physical harm, fear of psychological strain and fear of spiritual warfare. Indeed there is much to fear in this mission. But there is much more to embrace in matters of growing in relationship to Christ. Urban leaders must learn to trust and rely on God.

**People pleasing.** Urban leaders can be tempted to seek to please others in their ministry. "How can you believe if you accept praise from one another, yet make no effort to obtain the praise that comes from the only God?" (Jn 5:44). We are too persuaded by our context to make decisions and respond to life issues that are not in accord with the Word of God. Jesus was not willing to be conformed to the mindset of others (Mt 22:16). He encourages us not to pay serious attention to others or to our circumstances but rather to seek the Lord. Paul learned this as he ministered in the context of fear (Acts 18; Eph 6:19-20).

**Forgetting personal sinfulness.** Urban leaders can forget their sinfulness. They are often caught by surprise when they see the rage or lust in their hearts. They have a bent towards self righteousness that will mislead them and those they serve. It is profitable for them to know that they are able and willing to commit the most heinous sin. When they are aware of this, they are more willing to protect themselves from such actions by honest relationships. They must see that they are never above anyone else. This is humbling and allows them to be compassionate. Sin will never surprise them if they are aware of their own human sin capabilities. It has been our experience that leaders that have undergone suffering and serious downfalls have been able to stand firm again in Christ and be healers of the broken in their communities.

**Needs and wishes.** Urban leaders need to have God alter their wish lists. Too often their needs and wish lists are nothing more than their lust in action. God will not feed into their lust. They need to prioritize the important. Church growth at times becomes an idol. They ask God for growth because they are feeling like failures, not because the lost are eternally condemned and they are not glorifying God. The Lord needs to change their wish lists. Urban leaders need to seek holiness. It would seem that they need more skills and less contemplation, but our experience indicates that the opposite is true. The things that have eternal value are the things that help leaders to be imitators of Christ and, therefore, they can guide others to carry out his image in the city. How will we be holy and loving toward God? We will lay down our agenda and let the Word of God rule as we bow down to him (Ps 119:120). All the urban leaders are called to do urgently requires that they address these potential stress points. They must take time for spiritual reflection, for their ongoing spiritual development, for balance in lifestyle and in spiritually refreshing relationships.

## Preventative Steps

Crossing into a unique culture and into a different socioeconomic reality can be life challenging. To compensate for the potential liabilities we have discussed several preventive steps must be taken.

**Call on others.** First, relocated leaders need to call on others, especially the elders in the urban ministry, to pray and to help them sort out what is happening. This is often excluded, and the relocated leaders make decisions without church counsel. The only time there is an honest discussion is when they have made up their minds and are ready to leave. This is too late. Honest discussion with seasoned and mature leaders should begin immediately when there are questions of calling and location. This discussion could help put things into perspective.

Leaders primarily listen to God and his Word. The city at times promotes an indifference toward one another. There are many disappointments and casualties in urban work. The tendency is to become hard of heart and hearing and to die to the filling of the Spirit. But Christian leaders find that they must listen to those around them when no one else will pay attention (Jas 1:19; Prov 1:5; 19:20). Leaders have to listen to others both for the sake of serving and for their personal growth. Urban leaders are motivators who are to help inspire people to seek higher ground. They bring others to a recognition that God has called them to do his bidding, that they have it in them to serve the King of kings.

**Spend time with the Lord.** Also, it is imperative for relocated leaders to spend time alone with the Lord to review their initial calling. This is the anchor that reminds them why they came in the first place. They need to allow the Word of God to speak to them. Paul in Corinth experienced some doubts and fears: "I came to you in weakness and fear, and with much trembling" (1 Cor 2:3). The Lord responded, "Do not be afraid; keep on speaking, do not be silent. For I am with you and no one is going to attack and harm you, because I have many people in this city" (Acts 18:9, 10). The most important aspect of this passage is the covenant language the Lord used to affirm Paul. God does not offer a psychological counseling session to remove Paul's tension—"I understand what you are going through, Paul." Rather, he reminds him of his promise to be with him and to redeem many people. This must be our assurance over the ages. God has made a covenant to take care of us. It is what sustained Joshua (Josh 1:6) and will sustain all of us. A relocated leader's significant point of evaluation and possible change comes when the newness wears thin and "new and different" is more of an obstacle to ministry than it is a source of positive energy. Decisions are too often made on the basis of circumstances rather than on the basis of the promise of the Bible.

**Count the cost.** Relocating urban leaders need to have counted the cost of their ministry before they begin, the way foreign missionaries do. When missionaries plan to go overseas to reach people of a diverse culture, they prepare and train in matters of culture, language and contextualization with a sense of urgency. The seriousness of their calling and commitment is challenged before undertaking a ministry which will require them to relocate, live and serve among a different people group. Due to the need for intense preparation and the cost for travel and living expenses, they need to be convinced about their calling to serve in a distant geographical and cultural milieu. Once they are on the field, the bridges to their roots and to more familiar things will be distant, and the cost for reconsidering is prohibitive. As a result, psychologically these missionaries handle the stress and emotional challenges much better than those who relocate to a nearby city. "What is the Lord's will, and has he called us?" they ask. They have seriously counted the cost for mission. Calling is the marker that reassures the missionaries of their commitment and steadfastness. It is also imperative that calling be at the forefront of relocating into urban mission. Most of what we do for foreign mission needs to be done for domestic urban mission if we are to be effective for the long term.

**Specific training.** Comparing urban relocation with foreign mission highlights another important way to address the potential liabilities of such a venture. We must develop fuller training and orientation for leaders relocating to the city. When a person is relocating to a foreign country, his or her training and orientation is very thorough, supportive and accurate. This preparation assists the missionaries in making a healthy entrance that will insure long-term ministry. Such thorough training is currently not available for people relocating a few miles to an urban context. Urban relocation is every bit as crosscultural as the foreign mission experience, and thus thorough training is every bit as critical.

Part of the problem for denominations is that they do not have personnel experienced in urban work to train others. Models of ministry are few. The cultural distance may be as far as that of going to another country, but this truth is difficult to internalize. On the contrary, there is usually no preparation and support. Crosscultural dynamics are not understood, nor is the need for long-term commitments internalized. This will limit the effectiveness of leaders who are relocating into an urban context that is culturally different. It may also truncate the process of bonding by leading to discouragement and maybe even causing the relocated leader to leave the city before becoming part of the city.

Here again we see that the need for equipping is crucial. Even if an individual has received a theology degree, he or she is probably ill-prepared for urban ministry. The truth of the matter is that new curricula have to be developed for leaders to work with the aggressive ideological pluralism in the city and the ethnic, cultural and socioeconomic diversity. It is the task of Christians who claim the authority of Scripture for all of life to now grasp the opportunity to do theology in an urban reality.

# 21

# Selecting Candidates
# for Urban Leadership
# Development

IN THE LAST CHAPTER WE DISTINGUISHED three types of urban leaders: the relocated leader, the indigenous leader and the multiethnic leadership team. Where the critical role that context plays in ministry to a community has gone unnoticed, Christians wanting to reach an urban community have mistakenly thought that the best thing to do is to relocate a trained Christian leader to that community to minister there. We have shown that this approach is likely to be less effective than equipping and employing an indigenous leader.

Relocated leadership is not impossible, however. The key is to train a relocated leader the way a foreign missionary would be trained, to take seriously and sensitively the cultural challenge both for personal commitment and for ministry.

By contrast, starting with an indigenous leader can be strategically effective, for that person embodies his or her context and thus avoids most crosscultural difficulties faced by a relocated leader. But more often than not an indigenous leader needs spiritual formation, theological training and special insight concerning how to apply the Scripture to his or her own context. In our haste to meet the crying needs of the city, we may be tempted to utilize an indigenous leader who has not yet matured or been trained. This can cause setbacks in urban ministry as much as utilizing a contextually naive relocated leader.

Multiethnic leadership teams are made up of individuals indigenous to each ethnicity represented and often include a relocated leader as well. Multiethnic team ministry requires additional spiritual formation and preparation for ministry in light of the multiethnic reality of the city. Team members may characterize the urban setting, but the very nature of multiethnicity means that crosscultural issues must be faced by all members of the team.

It has been common for the church of Jesus Christ to overlook the important role that context plays in urban ministry. But having recognized the importance of context, the church can be tempted to err in the other direction. We can be tempted to think we have all that we need for the task if we have found and installed an indigenous leader. We can be pressured to do this by the urgency of the city's need. In doing so we omit or hurry through the absolutely critical process of preparing a leader by bringing him or her to spiritual maturity. Leadership that is not biblical leads to an equally desperate state of affairs for the city. Tremendous care and thought must be invested in training those contextually qualified for leadership. Careful training also enables relocated leaders to function capably in the city context.

It is imperative that we ask what kind of urban leadership will enhance the kingdom of God and advance the church of Jesus Christ? How should such leaders be selected? How should they be prepared in and for the mission of the city? Given the state of affairs we have described, it is obvious that a key strategy for effective urban ministry is to train indigenous leaders adequately to minister the gospel of Jesus Christ to their own urban context. In this chapter and the next two we will sketch the basic parameters of such preparation.

As Christians who uphold the Word of God, we are to be clear that all leadership functioning for the Lord must be of the Lord, prepared by the Lord and selected on the basis of his Word.

> Leadership, in Scripture, is based primarily upon spiritual maturity (1 Tim 3:1-13; Tit 1:6-9), as well as upon teaching ability and doctrinal soundness. A leader is not to teach only with words, but also with his life, to be a particular reflection of Jesus Christ. He is to be capable of "imitation" (1 Cor 4:16; 11:1; Phil 3:17; 1 Thess 1:6; 2:6; 2 Thess 3:7-9; Heb 13:7). Not only the apostles, but all leaders are to be godly examples to the flock (1 Thess 1:7; 1 Tim 4:12; Tit 2:7; 1 Pet 5:3). (Frame 1990:31)

Too often we omit the most important dimension for leadership, the spiritual quality of the leader. In the urban context we can value the indigenous leader as one of the most important elements in developing urban ministry but fail to remember the necessity of spiritual qualifications. The ministry of a biblically unqualified indigenous leader may have a healthy and prosperous beginning, but it will stop growing because the leader is not spiritually mature. We have often seen this pragmatic approach taken: a church will install a novice in a leadership role, hoping that subsequently he or she will grow spiritually. It does not occur, and the ministry is left limping along. A rookie in the Lord will be ill-equipped to lead. He or she will have a proud attitude that will give a foothold to the devil (1 Tim 3:6).

This is happening in many Latin American communities where the power of the Holy Spirit is bringing many to Christ through evangelism. The fact that many are coming to Christ is exciting. But if indigenous leaders who are new to the faith are installed, in a few years the church will most likely experience adverse consequences. There will be in-house fighting as leaders or members lord it over others, dividing the church. When we overlook biblical qualifications as we install indigenous leadership, we have become too concerned about the expedient in God's mission and no longer biblical in

---

**High Hopes in a High-Rise**

The church planter in Hong Kong had been trying to build relationships with the people in the community in which he was living, and signs of hope of starting a new ministry were dim. People were not responding as he thought and wished. After a visit to a family whom he had met in a restaurant and who lived in one of the high-rise apartments, he finally found an opportunity to share the gospel and possibly start a Bible study. When he arrived at the apartment, the people were very hospitable and open to hearing the gospel. The husband and wife both received the Lord that evening. This was a start for what might become a church in those apartments.

The men and women who had come to Christ were excited about their faith and began to invite others to a Bible study in their home. A number of people responded and attended, though some were suspicious. This suspicion was soon dispelled. People came regularly and a number of them also came to faith in Christ. The church planter began to see other possibilities for ministry at another site and decided to turn over the present ministry to the first converts who had come to the Lord one and a half years ago.

After three months under the new house cell leaders, the group began to experience problems. It seemed to be losing its members. The church planter discovered that the leader was insisting that the people make a commitment to come to the group without exception. He said that Jesus is our King and we must be faithful and obey him by coming to the group every week. When someone missed, he scolded him or her. In one case he became furious and publicly said something to the individual that shamed him. That person left, never to return. The group finally lost all its members, and the hope for a church in the high rise was put on hold.

---

our church development. The greatest error in ministry is impatience—unwillingness to wait for leaders who are ready to take on leadership responsibilities. "Leadership models for the church 'must be supported by Scripture and evaluated in terms of accountability to Christ' " (Elliston and Kauffman 1993:7). The story in the box illustrates what can happen to a church whose indigenous leader is spiritually immature.

Trouble arises when churches do not require spiritual maturity of their urban leaders. However, urban ministry benefits as we apply what the Bible says about spiritual leadership uniquely to the urban situation. Our claim, therefore, is twofold: (1) utilizing indigenous leaders is the most effective way to reach urban communities for Christ, but (2) it is imperative that anyone chosen to lead first be brought to spiritual maturity through adequate training. In the coming chapters we sketch the basic contours of this kind of training: how to select qualified candidates, how to shape a curriculum and how to train through mentoring. Biblically qualified leadership is all-important to the spread of Christ's church in the city; it's worth the careful investment it takes to bring it about.

## The Importance of Careful Selection

We've established the importance of taking context seriously as we prepare to minister to the city. We've argued for the strategic effectiveness of working with indigenous leaders to equip them for urban ministry. We're going to talk about how to equip them, considering both what they need to be taught and how they can most effectively be developed. The question before us now is *who?* How do we go about choosing candidates—indigenous leaders who can be groomed for effective urban ministry?

We do not mean to deny that the Lord is the one who chooses his servants. It is certainly understood that the Holy Spirit selects leaders for the church. But we can say that the church and mature leaders affirm the selection the Lord has done. "Existing leaders carry out their selective role in new leader discovery and recruitment" (Elliston and Kauffman 1993:82). God uses existing mature leaders as his instruments in selecting new leaders, even as he uses them to equip new leaders. Expecting the Holy Spirit to select leaders should lead the church not to irresponsibility but to greater responsibility in recruiting and training leaders. Thus we need to consider carefully what criteria should guide us in our choosing potential Christian leaders.

There is another obvious reason why we must exercise care in our selection. The task of developing leaders calls for a tremendous amount of time and effort by both the existing leaders and the potential leaders. Mentoring, the style of training that we recommend as especially suited to the task of equipping indigenous leaders for urban ministry, is much more intensive and demanding than other approaches to training. The amount of time and effort necessary to carry out this ministry reminds us that a mentor's investment in leadership development needs to count. For this to happen, we need to be diligent and careful in whom we choose to mentor.

A third reason for care is that leadership development through mentoring depends not only on the mentor but also on the mentoree for its success. The attitude and initiative that the student brings to the learning situation is absolutely critical to the ultimate success of the training effort. Thus, we must choose students who exhibit potential and readiness for the thing that needs to be accomplished.

The temptation we face in the city is the expedient model of getting things done and finding sufficient resources in the community. There is a spirit of desperation in selecting leaders, and often the sociological dimensions may persuade us to select individuals for kingdom service who are not spiritually appropriate. To move quickly without evidence of the appropriation of God's effective salvific grace is to bring a distortion of the gospel and will move the ministry into being a social agency. One area that Satan will work in is to bring heresy into the church (1 Jn 2:26-27). We would not think this needs to be mentioned, except for the ongoing nominalism and reductionary ministries existing throughout the world. We are afraid that overlooking it is one of the great mistakes in ministry.

In urban ministry we tend to be too pragmatic with emerging leaders. Or we may give authority to leadership prematurely. In Luke 22 the Lord has communion with his disciples. The fellowship is intimate and worshipful, and yet after the sharing a rivalry occurs. A power-play is revealed, accusations are made, and the Lord rebukes the disciples by saying, "You are not to be like that" (Lk 22:26). Leaders can make critical mistakes when they are trained without biblical criteria.

Elliston and Kauffman note the need to be clear on matters pertaining to the Christian witness. They ask, "What is a *Christian* leader? What distinguishes a Christian leader from other leaders? What is distinctive about an *urban* Christian leader?" (1993:2). The trap in making a wrong selection is that Christian and non-Christian leaders can have many attributes in common. We must discern the differences and wait until we are at peace with what the Lord has done in the individual's life. Potential leaders must first of all be servants of Christ before they are servants of the church (1 Cor 4:1).

It is important that the witness of the indigenous leader be of one Spirit with the body (1 Cor 12:12-13). Maturity and effectiveness for the Lord's kingdom originate only in the call of God. This search for a candidate who exhibits a readiness to serve Christ takes time and is usually done best when there is a process of discipleship and the church is in the community to see the witness of the individual.

Having said that, we have to realize that we should not expect to find the qualities we look for fully developed in our candidates. If we could find such candidates, there would be no need for us to equip them! Therefore, we make our selection with both an understanding of a prospective leader's present characteristics and in anticipation of what the leader will be like under the influence of the Word and the Holy Spirit in the future. This is also true of the relocating leader. We need to think anticipatorily, looking for certain characteristics that have the potential for maturing.

We must also expect to gauge the distance a candidate must move to achieve spiritually mature leadership and adjust our plan for his or her development accordingly. If the person is a recent convert, for example, the task will demand a longer period of preparation. It is clear in 1 Timothy 3:6 that a novice must not take on major leadership responsibility because it will conclude in major problems along with allowing the devil an opportunity to control individuals in their pride. This is one of the mistakes often made by urban churches that are seeking leaders for their ministries. Existing church leaders must assess the situation carefully.

In this chapter we offer four major criteria for selection. We believe that these criteria apply universally to any context. No matter where the church of Jesus Christ seeks to extend its reach, these criteria must be utilized in selecting its potential leaders. We do not deny that we must select leaders relative to each unique context. But that itself is one of the criteria. A viable candidate for leadership development in a particular urban setting must be a servant, a steward and a student, with a special call to his or her context.

## A Servant

Selection for the indigenous leader clearly involves acknowledging that the individual is not just contextually qualified but spiritually prepared to serve the Lord. To be an effective servant of God, a leader must exhibit biblical leadership. We must always look for leaders who focus on God and his will as revealed in Scripture. The teaching of 1 Timothy 3 should be at the top of our list of qualifications.

Paul lists characteristics that are important in matters of serving the Lord in the city. First of all, Paul tells us that leaders are first servants of Christ (1 Cor 4:1). The servant "is one who voluntarily submits to the sovereign authority (lordship) of Jesus Christ, to obey Him as directed for His benefit" (Elliston and Kauffman 1993:8). Leaders are first to be ministers of Christ before they are ministers of the church. Rather than use δουλοζ, Paul uses the word ὑπηρετας for *servant* or *minister*. It has the sense of one who runs errands. This lowly word puts us in our place; a leader candidate having this outlook will avoid major problems in the future. Leaders are Christ's servants doing what he beckons us to do. They must be those servants who sit at the feet of Jesus waiting for his instruction in humility. Too often a leader takes on the city as one who feels a great deal of ambition for the Lord and a great deal of self-power and strength. This will not do. No, they walk in submission to the Lord knowing that they are also responsible to him (v. 3).

Being a servant of Christ calls for humility. John 15:5 tells us what humility is: Jesus says, "Apart from me you can do nothing." Titus 3:2 indicates that humility is the first step toward faithful kingdom ministry. This is not an easy message for leaders serving in the city to learn. They are prone to depend on other resources, to take charge and control, rather than submit to the Lord of the harvest, allowing him in his mighty power to conquer that which is his (Eph 6:10-13). The city is a place of testing. We must learn that this complicated system called the city can be loved and transformed only in the name of Jesus. This is the place where Lydia, the slave girl and the jailer can come and worship God in the same church (Acts 16). It is important to grow and be mature in order to serve with integrity in the city. It is the servant heart and not the heart that seeks to be boss that will honor the Lord (Mt 20:28).

A readiness to serve Christ requires a readiness to serve others. Jesus said that servanthood was the most important requirement to follow him: "If anyone wants to be first, he must be the very last, and the servant of all" (Mk 9:35). "For even the Son of Man did not come to be served, but to serve, and to give his life as a ransom for many" (Mk 10:45). Much of the New Testament notion of service deals with provision of food and drink for the hungry and thirsty, shelter for the homeless, clothes for the naked and destitute, visitation of the sick and imprisoned, care for widows and orphans. In Matthew 25:45 Jesus said that not serving the least of these in these ways is a failure to do it to him.

In the city there is much more of a need to utilize this aspect of leadership than most of the other gifts or spiritual qualities. It is in this serving that people of the community, especially the poor, get a glimpse of and start to understand the compassion of the Lord. Leaders in a servant role are concerned about the development of others (Mt 20:28). The biblical notion of this word to serve or to minister is διακανεω. It has to do with provision of food, water, shelter, clothes and the visitation of the sick, the orphans, the widows and the imprisoned (Mt 25:34-46). Urban leaders need to serve their community of faith and their parish. There is no room for urban leaders who want to have followers and position. Their major characteristic must be that of serving others. For both the indigenous and relocating leader there is a need to see the heart of the individual caring for others. This kind of leader is imperative. There is no substitute for the servant, no matter the gifts of the individual—whether they include preaching, teaching or evangelism. The servant aspect should never be substituted or relinquished. We also never outgrow our servant concerns for others. The most obvious characteristic of a Christian in the city is the serving of others.

Many are trained to oppose such service rather than to embrace it in fulfillment of the Lord's will. Often much teaching on servanthood has to be done in order to keep it within the biblical framework. We have noticed that recent converts are more willing to serve others than the more "mature" Christians, who seem to feel that as Christians grow they depart from servanthood. How does one teach the willingness to serve? Primarily by modeling servanthood and by discussing the potential leader's commitment to service.

In 1 Corinthians 4:1-17 Paul indicates that the biblical characteristics for the leader include seeing ourselves as "the scum of the earth" (v. 13). This is not a very appealing description, but it helps us understand how we should think of ourselves as we relate to people who need Christ. *We must not put ourselves in a high position.* In verses 9-13 Paul contrasts his suffering with the haughtiness of the saints at Corinth. Paul is laughed at for the sake of Christ. We are fools for Jesus Christ (verse 10). This is very difficult for many of us to understand. It is hard for us to be in touch with the reality Paul is laying before us. How will this happen in urban ministry? It will happen as we confront the injustices of our society, as we confront the drug dealers who are exploiting our children. It will happen when we confront the world with the high standards of Jesus Christ. Too often leaders come into the city with a humble heart and then discover that they are able to make a name for themselves. This kind of attitude will not serve the King of the kingdom well. In verse 15 Paul indicates that Christlike leadership is marked by a spirit of *gentleness.* Such a spirit is seemingly so opposite of what often takes place in our inner cities. Leaders often think about being rough and tough and not showing emotions and vulnerability. But Paul sees himself as a father to the saints, offering a gentle heart that suffers long with his brothers and sisters.

A servant leads not by demand or coercion but by building relationships in which others know that the leader is concerned for their needs without seeking recognition. A leader does not lead by controlling and manipulating others but by supporting others and lifting them up. Leaders lead by strengthening others and developing their gifts and skills to do the work of the ministry rather than doing it all themselves. They guide and do not dominate (1 Pet 5:2-3). They seek servanthood rather than status and position.

The servant is always a servant until Christ returns. It is that preparation that is necessary as we live in a fallen and broken world (Lk 22:24-27). To have a leader in the city who is not first a servant is to have no leader at all. We desire leaders who will be servants of all. Jesus said that to be his disciple, one must "be a servant of all" (Mk 9:35; 10:44).

> **Modeling Ministry in Manila**
> The pastor lived close to the church building in the eastern part of Manila. Once, in the late hours of the night, he heard a knock on his door. He went to answer it and found it was the father of a family that lived near the church in a shanty section of the community. This part of the city was very poor, and many went to bed hungry. The young man asked if the pastor could help his wife who was expecting. She needed milk and nutritious food for both her health and that of her baby. The pastor saw the despair in the father's eyes and immediately went to get the food. He also knew that it was late and that walking home carrying the bag of food might be dangerous. So he insisted on taking the father home. When he arrived, he found the family had many other needs. The following morning the pastor called the church leaders together to see how they might help this family.
>
> What the leaders observed was a servant pastor who would impact their lives as they grew in their leadership role. This was an opportunity for the church to share the love of Christ. The other leaders remarked as they left the pastor's office, "Was not our pastor modeling what, in a true sense, a deacon should be—for that matter, what every Christian should be?" They thought to themselves that this pastor was closer to the true image of Christ in Scripture than anything they had ever witnessed.

## A Steward

Paul also tells us that leaders are stewards of the secret things of God (1 Cor 4:1). They are stewards of the truth that God has revealed, the wonders of salvation both for Jew and Gentile. Paul was bound to preach (1 Cor 9:17). A steward is one who manages the house for the owner. Stewarding is more than keeping and securing those things that are sacred. It primarily has to do with being a servant manager. Christ's stewards are his servants. I am obligated and bound to the task of sharing the good news with my community (1 Cor 9:17). Paul makes this an important element for leaders when he exhorts the Corinthian Christians in their deliberation over what is a biblical leader (1 Cor 4:1-4). The steward is another aspect of the leader that is essential. The leader must be able to teach the Scriptures and apply the gospel to the community.

In 1 Timothy 3 Paul writes to Timothy about the requirements for being a leader in the church. Most of the requirements are moral qualities. But one requirement is a professional quality—the leader must be a διδακτκον. He must be able to teach. Ministers are above all things stewards of God's Word. This will also involve a certain kind of lifestyle that is disciplined in matters of studying the Bible. This does not mean that we are not to study anything else; on the contrary, we must also study the world and in particular the community in which we are serving.

Ministry in the city demands a commitment to the Word of God. It is the major tool of the urban worker for community and life transformation. Leaders often ignore the Scriptures in practical matters, thinking that the Bible applies to theological issues and not to street issues. However, the Bible is the handbook for all of life. Leaders must be well prepared to utilize the Word of God, and they must have confidence in the gospel. They must resist the temptation to place more confidence in their methods and personalities than in the power of the Word of God.

Urban leaders who are good stewards of the gospel apply the Word holistically in their community. The kind of leader that impacts life and community is one who understands that sin is comprehensive (Gen 3) and that the only way to respond to this complexity of sin and oppression is with the gospel. As they faithfully steward the gospel, they see the transformation of all of life. The urban minister who reduces the gospel to either just the social or just the spiritual is not a steward of the gospel. Stewardship is a commitment to preach and teach the whole counsel of God (Acts 20:27). But first it requires that leadership respond to the Scriptures in obedience. This is Paul's exhortation to the elders at Ephesus: "Keep watch over yourselves" (Acts 20:28).

## A Student

When we are looking for viable candidates for leadership training in urban ministry, we must look for people who are teachable, who are willing to see themselves as students. This would seem an insignificant requirement, except for three things. First, in urban ministry, in our experience, potential leaders quite often mistakenly believe that they don't require training. Thus, they are not teachable, and they cannot be taught until they are. Second, you cannot train or develop a person who does not agree with you that he or she needs just the training that you offer. Third, unteachableness is a sign of personal spiritual needs—to trust others, to develop a submissive heart through following, to be open to team with others in ministry and to expect to study and apply the Word forever.

Why might leader candidates not believe they require further training? If they are from the community, potential ministry leaders may resist the offer of training because they think have enough background to serve already. They are urban and have lived in that context all their lives. This is a wrong assumption that has too often been made in developing leadership. In addition, we have discovered, many indigenous leaders have had poor experiences with learning institutions and have divorced themselves from ongoing learning and studying. They learn to depend on common sense or streetwise information alone, and they resist the idea that they can and must profit from training. Therefore, the growth and development of indigenous leaders might be limited and not fully appropriate for ministry or for the development of other emerging leaders in the future. This should not discourage us as we take on the challenge of leadership development. However, it may slow down the process until the leaders are motivated to discipline their lives and begin the process of being students of Christ and of the world in which the Lord has placed them.

Similarly, a relocating leader can mistakenly believe no additional training is necessary because he or she has had training in the past, even a degree in urban mission. But the task of doing theology in the city is not something they can learn in institutions that are distant from the realities of the city. They must do this in the field of ministry. It is in the context of ministry that we are discipled to do theology.

We must develop a student mindset in all leaders. Without it—if the church utilizes leaders who have resisted the kind of teaching we have in mind—the results can be drastic. The arguments of both indigenous and relocated leader candidates should be dismantled. We should never make the mistake of looking for leaders who are already trained and prepared by others and utilizing them without further development. We are mistaken if we think they are thus prepared, and we are mistaken if we allow them to think that also. The integrative urban curriculum will involve theory and practice, utilizing already existing leaders working closely with candidates. This kind of leadership development is contextually specific and biblically contextualized, teaching candidates how ministry and the church will function and live out the gospel. It will require candidates' openness to such leadership and training.

Pastors need to watch for and cultivate young hearts that are enthusiastic and willing to follow the Lord in the future. We need young people with the same willingness as Levi: "'Follow me,' Jesus said to him, and Levi got up, left everything and followed him" (Lk 5:27-28). Christians should be selected who want to be mature in Christ and want to be equipped for ministry. A potential leader must have an appetite to learn, a willingness to follow, an openness to new possibilities and a desire to grow. They are both hungry for the Word and for the preparation to serve. We have found that indigenous people who are trained for ministry by their missionaries or pastors are more effective and more apt to make a permanent commitment to their community.

Not only is such teachableness required for a candidate's formation as a leader; it is also requisite for his or her personal spiritual maturity. How teachable are the potential leaders? Can they trust God and others with their lives? If so, they are probably open to change and to new or old ideas. They are likely able to submit to authority and be convicted of sin. We believe Paul was a moldable person. "Together Barnabas and Paul taught. Here again Barnabas played a mentoring role wherein he took the lead but also provided opportunities for Paul to learn and grow over the period of a year" (Raab and Clinton 1985:23).

In the selection process we have to recognize the submissive heart. Too often we move potential leaders into leading, rather than following. It is in the following that leaders are developed. The weaker the following, the weaker the leading. Paul exhorts us not to affirm elders who are novices (1 Tim. 3:6). In other words, to bypass the process of following and learning submission is to promote pride in leadership which will eventually come to the forefront of the individual's ministry. What is necessary in determining who will progress into leadership is an evaluation of the willingness of the leaders to submit to one another (Eph 5:21). This is necessary for both indigenous and relocating leaders. The disruption of any ministry is usually due to the self-centeredness of individuals. Having a submissive heart is God's call to all of us (Eph 5:21) and is contrary to our makeup and desires. Therefore, Paul exhorts us to be filled with the Holy Spirit so that there can be biblical harmony in all of our relationships (Eph 5:18).

A closely related important attitude for city ministry is willingness to minister as part of a team. A person should seek others with whom to work. In the city it is crucial to value the organism of the church and move toward a nonclergy-dominated team. In a team approach, working coequally with others provides a healthy environment of physical and spiritual support. Gifts are used properly and Christians find themselves mutually dependent on one another. Barnabas was a team person, one who "brought Paul into the mainstream of Christianity" (Raab and Clinton 1985:84). Unfortunately

> almost all church theology is clerical; almost always ordained ministers in seminaries or in congregations are called upon to depict the meaning of the Christian life in any profound way. [Therefore, the laity is usually omitted from] the circles out of which theological interpretation of life occurs. (Marty 1975:84)

We need to see that biblical ministry, especially in the urban context, requires a team approach that transcends what can be an arbitrary boundary between clergy and laity.

Given the fact that the urban leader will never stop needing to study the Word and the context in order to apply the one to the other, leader candidates must recognize that they must cultivate teachability not just for a temporary period of training but for a lifetime of ministry. All Christians, especially leaders, have to become students of the ancient texts as well as the contemporary world. They must avoid the distortion of being solely practitioners without being students. Urban leaders must grow in their commitment to be students and learners forever. They must learn to utilize Scripture in their ministry.

### A Special Call to Leadership in the Urban Community

Another indicator for selection of urban leaders has to do with their call and commitment to the city. The call and commitment must be as specific as the target context. Thus, while this criterion for selecting a candidate for leadership training holds universally, following it will guide us to people specifically suited for and called to each context in its individual concreteness.

For indigenous leaders there is a sense of satisfaction in helping and giving to others in their neighborhood. They realize that they are committed to a cause—to bring justice, to assist their community and city. For the relocating leader there is newness and possibly a satisfaction in experiencing purpose and meaning as a Christian in this context.

The missionary or pastor should be able to observe that God has gifted potential leaders in a visible way for the task of leading and serving. They bear some visible quality of leadership. "Leadership never translates as anything less than leadership," says Calvin Miller (1987:14). Visible leadership qualities include charisma, followers, attitude, appearance, administrative ability, a multifaceted personality, willingness to serve others and visionary aptitude.

As helpful as those things are, it is wise to return to the Scriptures in matters of calling and mission. Those things that are very satisfying may be caused by emotions that can change and, therefore, the ministry can change as well. Most of the things that bring that kind of motivation, self-satisfaction and purpose may be self-centered and may cause eventual ministerial disruption (Gen 3:1-7). The reason for ministry must ultimately be a divine intrusion—God has called (Acts 13:3; 20:28). This is an important aspect of the selection process because it lays out the reason for serving in the city, but it also holds the power to remain faithful to the Lord when the spiritual war becomes overwhelming. Urban leaders here in the United States must have a calling from God as much as a missionary who is called to serve in a distant country.

A viable candidate for urban leadership development must also demonstrate an awareness of the larger, crosscultural picture. Because the urban context reflects the process of globalization, potential leaders must possess sufficient urban crosscultural attitudes and abilities so as to enhance ministry that crosses cultural barriers.

Serving in changing communities, contextualizing into multiethnic dynamics and working with people from different socioeconomic strata require flexibility. It is one of the most difficult aspects of leadership. Young leaders need to understand that in today's world, everything is changing—except the eternal Word of God. Flexibility must be learned, appreciated and applied responsibly. Because the urban setting forces people to develop survival skills, most indigenous leaders will already be flexible to some degree. They will need to direct it toward responsible and useful ends. Awareness of and openness to the changing realities of the urban community indicates a candidate's specific call to and suitability for ministry in it.

# 22

## Curriculum for
## Developing Urban Leaders

THE OBJECTIVE OF THIS CHAPTER IS to examine what goes into shaping a curriculum for developing urban leaders, relocating or indigenous, to serve in the city as effectively and biblically as possible. This is not a theoretical chapter founded simply on documentation of secondary material but rather a functional chapter on how best to develop urban leadership from a practitioner's point of view. Certainly there will be secondary material utilized, but what we offer mainly reflects our own experience training leaders for urban ministry.

### Overlooking Indigenous Leadership
It has been the our experience, as well as that of others with experience in urban ministry and leadership training, that the kind of leaders necessary for the task of urban mission already live in the targeted urban community. To exclude the community as a resource for selecting and developing leadership is to exhibit superior and paternalistic attitudes. It demonstrates lack of respect for the people we hope to serve. We are long overdue in developing mission strategies that reflect the fact that leadership for the present and future of the ministry are already in the community and that such indigenous leadership is necessary for healthy and long-term witness. It is inappropriate, inept and unnecessary to recruit from outside and impose on a community the leaders we deem

requisite to carry the mission forward, as if there were no potential leaders in that particular urban community. The downfall of urban ministries has been to shape their mission without planning to utilize indigenous leaders. Many denominations and mission societies have failed in this regard, taking more of a pragmatic approach to mission by bringing in the dream team leadership—people who have been trained in Christian leadership without reference to context—and not considering and including leaders indigenous to the community in which the work is started. Historically we have sought leaders from outside the context of the urban mission.

## Overlooking the Importance of Leadership Training and the Church's Role

Actually, in our urban mission planning, we have not always even given leadership development the high priority it ought to have in mission planning. Leadership development has taken the posture of expediency: how can we get things going as rapidly, efficiently and cost effectively as possible? Leadership is taken into account after the ministry is underway. For example, the concerns of a church planter in a major city are first to evangelize the people in the community with the hopes of gathering a nucleus of people to establish a church and then to begin to look for appropriate leadership to assist the process. Due to the shortsightedness of the mission, it then utilizes the expedient mode of furnishing leaders, requesting outside assistance. Or for example, a church in a transitioning community, since it has not engaged in intentional development of indigenous leaders from the community, may revert back to what it has always done: gleaning leaders from its denominational seminary. Thus it solicits leaders who are relocating crossculturally and really ought to be trained to address this particular context. Relocated leaders who already fit the profile of the community are usually hard to come by. As a result, the church continues to minister only to people who have long since moved out of the community, with little or no impact on its immediate context. The only way to preserve an ongoing ministry in any transitional community is to train and develop indigenous leaders to carry on the ministry of our Lord in that changing area.

Churches have generally left leadership development to seminaries. We have never thought in terms of training our own leaders. We feel inadequate for the task. We think instead that only institutions such as seminaries are qualified to recruit and train leaders for us. For example, in the book *Church Planting for a Greater Harvest* by Peter Wagner (1990) little is said to instruct churches about how to develop leaders—in fact, only a short paragraph is devoted to it. And yet the author notes, "Leadership is crucial. It is too bad that this turns out to be one of the weakest areas in pastoral ministry" (1990:54). He goes on to say that seminaries will not do the job. This leaves the reader with the impression that leadership development is a secondary item in the functional aspect of the church. It also allows that outside recruitment is an option. The major omission in this book is that indigenous leaders are not highly regarded nor are they a significant priority in church planting ministries. And yet he "agrees with John Maxwell that everything rises or falls on leadership" (1990:54). An important point in the discussion of leadership is to recognize that leadership can never be an end in itself. It is always a means to an end.

The problem is not just that we do not plan for leadership development and feel inadequate for the task. We have also underestimated the role that context plays, as well as the role of personal modeling of on-the-job experience, in mission and community leadership development.

It will benefit the church and the kingdom of God to recognize that developing leadership is a priority, that it is a necessary element for church planting, church growth and holistic ministry strategies, and that the church can and must play a key role in developing leaders in and for its own community.

## A Faulty View of Training

How would a church most effectively train indigenous leaders? Usually when we think of such training, we have in mind a classroom setting in which a teacher dispenses information concerning a field in which he is an expert to a group of novices. The students are like empty bank accounts into which a fund of information is deposited. Generally we assume that the students, having received this information, are now qualified in the field in question.

In many of our training centers and higher education institutions we have placed too much credence on the Greek (Hellenistic) model of education. This is often seen in schools of theology and Bible. Ted Ward warns against this approach:

> First of all, hierarchy is basic. There are those who *know* and there are those who *need to know*. . . . Social distance and its artifacts are a second characteristic of the Greek assumptions about human relationships. Yes, social distance is more than social circumstances and relational characteristics; it creates and thrives on its artifacts. A lectern is such an artifact; a platform is such an artifact. The third . . . is one-way communication: from the authority to those who are assumed to be in need of hearing. The fourth characteristic . . . has to do with social privilege and how one gains social privilege. Education is essentially a social privilege. (1996b:39-40)

Jesus spoke angrily against the status-seeking group called Pharisees who wanted to be heralded as the most important in the community, having the first seat and visible to all. They assumed that they were doing it all correctly and to the satisfaction of God until Jesus said, "Woe to you, Pharisees" (Lk 11:37-44; Mt 23:2). A Greek model of education can inadvertently embody pharisaical status seeking.

We sometimes think of a teacher as one who has all the information and of the student being merely a container to be filled. "His task is to 'fill' the student with the contents of his narration—contents which are detached from reality, disconnected from the totality that engendered them and could give them significance" (Freire 1989:57). We may view the teacher as one who is superior and has all the information while the student has nothing to offer and is inferior to the process. This model of teaching will not work in the urban context, where there is a multitude of divergent experiences and backgrounds. The banking approach (Freire 1989:58) will not be able to carry out the mandate of developing urban leaders for the church.

This model, a distortion of learning in any field, is especially inappropriate, ineffective and impossible when it comes to training indigenous leaders to minister in their context. Indigenous leaders are not likely to have access to seminary or Bible college classes, nor would they be equipped to benefit from them. Often such classes ignore individual urban contexts or are not in a position to shape information to fit. A classroom model tends to downplay or ignore the critical role of context in ministry, both as it shapes the setting and as it shapes the indigenous leader. And finally, since the thing that we seek to inculcate—leadership—is a skill, and since that skill is already evidenced in recognizable measure in the indigenous leaders, the conventional classroom model fails to pertain. For it assumes that the student has nothing to contribute and that all that is needed are pieces of information.

## Developing Leaders in Urban Ministry

For the reasons given above we prefer to think of what needs to occur as leadership *development.* This term communicates that we take what is already there and make it better. What is already there is an individual indigenous to an urban community, with potential for leadership. What is already there is a unique urban community with specific assets and needs. While the message of Christ and Scripture's guidance for daily living are universal, always they must be applied to specific persons in specific contexts. We believe that this means that leadership development must always reflect a specific context and leader. In this chapter we see the implications of this for a curriculum: it must be dynamic and flexible enough to be adjusted to a particular situation and learner. In the next chapter we consider the implications of context specificity for teaching: we propose mentoring individuals rather than teaching classes. Both the curriculum and the style of leadership training reflect the fact that we learn by example and by doing. Leadership development necessarily involves modeling and concrete on-the-job training.

In urban leadership development we should expect to integrate an array of educational traditions, such as nonformal education, informal education which utilizes unstructured learning of daily life (Snook 1992:17) and distance education which

> implies the absence of the physical presence of a teacher (or that the teacher is present only on occasion). It involves reproduced courses, a wide range of media, and mass production of educational materials (Kaye 1985:3, 1433). It also involves two-way communication with planned and explicit catering for individual study. Distance education is a "guided form of didactic conversation" (3:1432). (Snook 1992:20)

Because this is an integrative approach that draws from various traditions, it will depend on those traditions only to a certain degree. It will depend more on the influence of the instructor who is both a teacher and a model of ministry. It will also be more andragogical than pedagogical, relying more on the contributions of the learner instead of solely on the pronouncements of a lecturer.

Since leadership development must take seriously both the individual indigenous leader and his urban context, the leader is not removed from the context of ministry. The context becomes an important feature in the leader's learning and development (Snook 1992:6). An urban curriculum must train leaders to be Christian servants in the city. The development of urban leadership is really the development of servant leaders in the context of the church in the city. The church is not only the place of ministry but it is also the immediate reason for the development of urban leadership.

Even though it is more than training, leadership development includes training. We use the term *training* in this chapter to refer to certain ingredients or components that we utilize in developing urban leaders. For example, a trainee may be shown how to operate a thrift store. The particular activities in which the student must be trained will be determined primarily by the context, within the parameters of Scripture. Training is a process toward an end and should involve whatever the goal and context demand based on the fundamentals of Scripture.

We do use the word *teaching*. Obviously we do not mean by it the sterile stereotype of one-way inculcation of facts. Teaching in the context of developing urban leaders takes the classroom and learning experience out of the four-wall setting of an institution. It expands the process to integrate other learning traditions, and to take seriously and utilize the urban context. Teaching indigenous leaders involves imparting information. In fact, it is fair to say that an urban curriculum depends on much more than the content that comes from the usual disciplines. It incorporates the social sciences, theology and biblical studies, as well as the cultural context of the urban reality. But teaching in the urban context must also view the teachers as models, life-examples of leaders/teachers and experienced practitioners. The teacher must utilize all of these elements. And as we'll see in the next chapter, the teacher not only models urban ministry but mentors potential leaders.

When we think of developing urban leadership, we believe it is important to avoid terms such as *empowerment*. These terms are often used by whites in an African American urban context, but speaking of empowering leaders is filled with paternalistic baggage. It may promote a superior-inferior attitude, since one has to be empowered to empower others. Such an attitude undermines the very thing that it attempts.

## What Motivates an Urban Leader to Mature?

Before we discuss the urban curriculum, we should address a subject often dismissed: what will motivate a potential urban leader to utilize any curriculum to mature in ministry?. Usually the urban curriculum is not offered for academic credit, as opposed to that offered in a college or seminary. It is not a degree-oriented program. In the degree-oriented program a student is motivated to comply with the school regulations to pass with a grade in order to receive an academic degree. In the urban curriculum there is no such motivation at the heart of the curriculum.

Instead, the urban leader trainee must be motivated first by the longing to *honor God*. He or she must not prepare for urban ministry for selfish reasons or even for the good of the community. All things were created for Jesus (Col 1:16). Students who are preparing in and for urban ministry must relinquish their self-centeredness and be motivated to study and apply the content of their preparation because it honors the Lord. One of the mistakes in curriculum building has to do with excluding God from the goal of learning. A theocentric foundation insists on a process that brings adoration to God.

Another motivational element has to do with *divine calling* to service and maturity (Eph 4:13-20). The student is motivated by the fact that his or her calling is to grow and mature holistically towards God, church and community. Also, the student must realize that God is the source and power of all of life and of all wisdom (Job 28:28; Prov 3:5-7; 9:10) and, therefore, he or she must learn how to rely on the Lord.

Students are also motivated by seeing that they stand in need of maturing and equipping in order to minister effectively even in the urban context they already know well. *Awareness of personal need* motivates the learners as they examine themselves in light of the particular mission. The students need to come to grips with their shortcomings, areas where they need help and assistance as ministers of the gospel. The curriculum will help leadership grow in specific areas. This awareness motivates the leader to push ahead and gain the skills necessary for urban work.

Another motivating factor is the *needs of the field*. What are the needs of the community and how can we minister in this unique context? And how do we apply the Scriptures to the pressing issues of the community? The proposed learning process will provide students with necessary contextual skills. These areas for motivation are important and will test the leaders on their commitment and willingness to be servant leaders in the city, theocentric matters in worship and calling, and their personal and field needs orientation.

## Basic Prerequisites of an Urban Curriculum

A program to develop urban leadership, we have already seen, must utilize a model of learning other than the traditional one of one-way impartation of information. Instead, we must integrate an array of learning traditions. It must take seriously that we learn best by imitating a model. Thus, we can expect learning to be most effective when it includes mentoring by a qualified model, with on-the-job training for the learner.

A curriculum for urban leadership development must always meet certain prerequisites. First, it must maintain a *theocentric perspective*. A curriculum, whether it is for adults (androgogy) or for children (pedagogy), must start with a theocentric perspective. "For from him and through him and to him are all things, to him be the glory forever Amen" (Rom 11:36). The Christian servant leader in the city must first be able to serve God and worship him. "Missions is not the ultimate goal of the church. Worship is" (Piper 1993:11). Education involves preparing God's leaders to serve to his glory. Christian education provides leaders with the ability to do good works (2 Tim 3:17). In reality every Christian curriculum must first be used to administer the Word of God. Therefore, the urban curriculum must first be theocentric in goal and concept. This theocentric goal guides and holds in place the remainder of the urban curriculum for leadership. If this is not first established, it will short-circuit our very purpose in training leadership (Rom 11:36), no matter what the context. This error will also misdirect the leaders in their course of development and confuse the process of ministry. "The model of leadership . . . must be drawn from the Scripture and evaluated in terms of accountability to the Lordship of Christ" (Ward 1996b:35).

Second, it must be *sensitive both to the specific learner's assets and needs, and to the specific urban context* for which that learner is being prepared. As has been mentioned previously, every curriculum should be contextualized. In order to provide a training program that is able to function in the community and city that is being served, the needs of both the students and the city must be known. Urban students should have, for example, an accurate picture of the political system that controls much of what happens in their city. Also, the students themselves might vary in matters of skills and knowledge.

> What do I teach? *People! That's what I teach!* The questioner usually has in mind the content field or the subject that is being taught. Fair enough. But as Ivan Illich and many others similarly concerned about depersonalization of modern education are quick to point out, the human task of teaching and learning focuses first and foremost on the learner. Content is but the instrumentation or the tools toward human fulfillment. (Ward 1996a:8)

Therefore, the curriculum should be able to adjust to those variables. Certainly there are areas that are universal to any other kind of urban curriculum, such as the need to know Scripture and some of the other disciplines, but the uniqueness of the context and the student make a distinction between curricula. This means that a curriculum created for developing leaders for a certain urban context should never be applied without revision to a separate urban context, even if the second context is only a few miles away from the first.

Another prerequisite for an urban curriculum is that it be *flexible and dynamic*. The reason the curriculum must be dynamic is that the community, society and students are changing. Many make the error of having the students and possibly the church fit into a learning process that will not serve them or the community well. Curricula should be living. They need to move and breathe as the leaders are being trained. Urban curriculum has a life of its own and it lives in the context of mission and people. Therefore, adjustments are necessary as it goes through the process of training urban leaders.

It is a mistake to take what may work in a particular urban community and transfer it to another context. We must first evaluate a method before attempting to impose it on another context. "The specifics of equipping or training must always be contextually adapted for optimal effectiveness. No single educational program design is universally applicable" (Elliston and Kauffman 1993:3). If the direction of the curriculum is too general and not student- and context-sensitive, it may be that the curriculum will be dysfunctional and will cause major upheavals because of its irrelevance.

The need for a curriculum to be sensitive to the target context also means that a curriculum for a transitioning urban community, for example, one that once was Irish American and is gradually becoming African American, must be revised continually in light of the current state of affairs. A contextually sensitive curriculum must of necessity also be a dynamic and flexible one.

## Urban Curriculum

A curriculum provides building blocks for learning. The urban curriculum lays out numerous elements that will provide the student with the equipping necessary for urban mission. A curriculum for adults is basically "the process of planning educational experiences for adults" (Galvin and Veerman 1993:178). The approach we recommend, as mentioned previously, is the *integrative form of urban leadership development*. This approach fits into the reality of city life. The city and city life are integrative. They are revolving in that the elements are all interacting with each other and are at the same time part of each other.

Etymologically, the Latin word *ducare* from which we take *educate,* means to "lead." The prefix, *e*, means "out." Thus, to educate is to lead out (Groome 1980:5). Therefore, education has to do with taking someone from one position to another in their learning experience. Groome notes:

> Three dimensions or points of emphasis can be discerned in "leading out": 1) a point from which, 2) a present process, and 3) a future toward which the leading out is done. In this sense education has an "already," a "being realized," and a "not yet" dimension to it. While these three dimensions should never be separated in practice, they can be distinguished for the sake of analysis. (Groome 1980:5)

The components that will help us design this curriculum are the context, the mission and the students. These three are separable but intertwine and interact with each other.

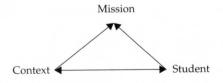

In other words, the student is shaped by and will shape his or her own context in light of the particular mission in view. The context shapes and will be shaped by the particular student and the particular mission. The mission is shaped by and shapes the particular student and the particular context in the context of mission. All three components interact with each other as we continually evaluate each one in light of the other two. The student learns how to carry out a mission while continually assessing whether or not the mission or task is appropriate for the context. The student will also ask whether his or her gifts are appropriate for the mission. All the components and their mutual shaping must continually be evaluated in light of Scripture. Artificially separating the components in the curriculum allows the student to inquire about the substance of each one. But we always keep in mind that the components must be reintegrated in practice.

There is more than content to curriculum (Baptiste and Anderson 1980:48). We must also look at values that are shared by society, instructors and peers.

The three components—the student, the context and the mission—shape the three major sections of a viable urban curriculum. In each section there will be subsections that will assist each of the tracks. The subsections are to be developed in context by the instructors in tandem with the students and in reflection on the changing community.

The first section of one curriculum has to do with what we will call *spiritual formation*. This involves the preparation of the leaders' personal lives before God, in the context of the church and community.

Another section will be *mission formation*. This is shaping a concrete mission outreach that comports with how God is working in that particular city. It is theology concretely applied in that crosscultural, cross-social structure. Verkuyl's definition of missiology reminds us of both the sovereign aspect of God's salvific work in the world and the need for the church to be the ongoing incarnation of Christ that communicates the gospel. He notes:

> Missiology is the study of the salvation activities of the Father, Son, and Holy Spirit throughout the world geared toward bringing the kingdom of God into existence.
>
> Seen in this perspective missiology is the study of the worldwide church's divine mandate to be ready to serve this God who is aiming his saving acts towards this world. In dependence on the Holy Spirit and by word and deed the church is to communicate the total gospel and the total divine law to all mankind. (Verkuyl 1978:5)

Mission formation involves laying out and then applying fundamental biblical structures. It is interested in how leaders become involved in society as Christian leaders.

The final segment is *social formation.* This primarily utilizes insights from the social sciences for urban ministry. In the process we exegete or assess the community to discovering its specifics and uniquenesses in order to contextualize.

The following is not an actual curriculum but rather a brief summary of what each section will include.

**Spiritual formation.** The urban curriculum must begin with knowledge of God and of self. "Knowledge of God and knowledge of self are preconditions of spiritual life" (Lovelace 1979:82).

> The most difficult task in urban ministry is to remain optimistic, creative, hopeful, and full of humor. Ministry demands that you give out constantly—and city ministry makes that demand relentlessly. But you cannot give out what you do not have. If you are not replenishing yourself in order to continue the spiritual warfare of the city, then you are exposing yourself to defeat, burnout, and spiritual exhaustion. After all, you can lead God's people only as far as you yourself have gone. If you have not paid attention to your soul's interior journey, you do not have the resources nor the experience either to sustain yourself or to lead your church in sustaining the battle with the Enemy. (Linthicum 1991a:235)

Spiritual formation is the holistic preparation of the leader. It involves examining and equipping the urban leader for a ministry that is initiated by the Holy Spirit and carried out by our triune God. It is a supernatural ministry; thus, it must rely on God who has called us and who will establish and carry out his ministry.

Some existing training programs assume falsely that Christian leaders have resolved personal issues and are maturing in grace, that all is well in their relationship to the Lord. In addition, they sometimes falsely assume that urban leaders understand the basics of theology and spiritual development, and have a clear understanding of the gospel. A curriculum that ignores or assumes too much concerning what urban leaders may have attained in their walk with God and their personality transformation will eventually result in heavy, negative, consequences in ministry.

It may seem that the subject of renewal does not fit into the training of an urban leader. On the contrary, it is most appropriate. Many of our indigenous leaders have built false belief systems by which they live. These may refer to such things as their self-image or the way they approach marriage. At times indigenous leaders operate out of these false belief systems in a way that will hinder the ministry. Also, they have experienced personal hardships either because others have sinned against them or because of the reality of a context that may breed violence, oppression and escape from reality through substance abuse. Therefore, their self-image may be greatly distorted and in need of renewal by the Holy Spirit. Renewal primarily has to do with returning to Scripture as an authority for life and obedient service.

A very common false belief system is legalism. Untrained urban leaders can portray the gospel as only a set of regulations; their teaching and even their lifestyle reflect a moralistic imbalance. This lacks the biblical understanding of grace and is thus a distortion of the truth. It is harmful to the Christian's growth and often leads to a guilt-ridden life.

It is most difficult to speak of the gospel to others with a perspective of the gospel that is mere legalism. Lovelace speaks of this subject and notes:

> Much that we have interpreted as a defect of sanctification in churchpeople [sic] is really an outgrowth of their loss of bearing with respect to justification. Christians who are no longer sure that God loves and accepts them in Jesus, apart from their present spiritual achievements, are subconsciously radically insecure persons—much less secure than non-Christians, because they have too much light to rest easily under the constant bulletins they receive from their Christian environment about the holiness of God and the righteousness they are supposed to have. Their insecurity shows itself in pride, a fierce defensive assertion of their own righteousness and defensive criticism of others. They come naturally to hate other cultural styles and other races in order to bolster their security and discharge their suppressed anger. They cling desperately to legal, pharisaical righteousness, but envy, jealousy and other branches on the tree of sin grow out of their fundamental insecurity. (Lovelace 1979:211-12).

We have seen leaders in the city who have protected their position as if those positions were theirs to own. Their defensiveness and legalism damaged other leaders and truncated the process of growth of the ministry.

Both law and grace must be declared with solid biblical exposition. "Faith in Christ cures unbelief, anxiety and insecurity, and in so doing it cuts the roots of envy, jealousy and a host of related egocentric fleshly patterns" (Lovelace 1979:115). "The person who knows that he received mercy while an undeserving enemy of God will have a heart of love for even (and especially!) the most ungrateful and difficult persons" (Keller 1989:60).

When indigenous leaders begin to realize the enormous love and care given to them by Christ and the truth of the all-consuming sin in their lives, they are on their way to renewal in the Holy Spirit. Those who begin to experience the grace of God begin to see that their need for control is unnecessary and sinful.

Spiritual formation also addresses the social dimension. As leaders appropriate the gospel to their personal lives, sanctification brings them to repentance. They now have a new and proper view of God and themselves (Rom 6:1-3, 6-7). They now view their relationships through the lenses of Scripture. They now see marriage more in accord with the Word of God. And their social manifestations are changing because the core of their understanding is changing. Their marriages are formed by God. Their relationships with neighbors, family and coworkers are altered. When their relationship to God is growing and maturing, the effects of the gospel in their private lives affect their public lives. In other words, spiritual development alters our social realities. Many leaders are serving with a poor understanding of how God desires their relationships to be lived out. They have come from broken homes and have at times experienced abusive relationships. They have difficulty trusting others. And they will find themselves dysfunctional in building proper relationships with new neighbors and other leadership team members. This fundamental aspect of curriculum seems biblically appropriate because it is here that leaders will grow and be victorious in the "day of evil" (Eph 6:10-14).

> If a person's understanding is clear in its hold on truth and his will is sincerely grounded in holy purposes, then he is a maturing Christian. But if the understanding is uncertain and the will is wavering and unsteady, the man is dull and his life is one of spiritual impotence. (Gurnall 1988:22)

The relocated leader must also have time to assess his or her spiritual condition. In some ways the issues may be distinctly different from those of the indigenous leader. In particular, a relocated leader may have to struggle against the mindset of wanting to save those poor people in the community. What sometimes has happened is that relocated leaders have been ushered into the city on the heels of an evangelistic rally. The evangelist has challenged them to serve in the city, saying that the city needs them, that they will change the city's current affairs and condition with a courageous and bold move to live in the city and take charge. This sets up relocating leaders to think that the city does not already have a vibrant church and leadership. It leads them to think of themselves as a messiah who will change the direction and problems of the city. On the surface this may seem heroic and not problematic, but this can infect the imagination with a messiah complex. A relocated leader can act out of this mindset, developing feelings of superiority, thinking of others, either consciously or subconsciously, as inferior. This expression of the gospel and the call of God leads to a ministry that is paternalistic and often promotes racial strife and racism. Such thinking must be renewed through the gospel; leaders must take off falsehood and put on the true righteousness and holiness of God (Eph 4:20-28).

**Mission formation.** Mission formation consists of doing theology in the context of the city. It is more than developing an urban strategy. It is learning how to use Scripture as a guide both for life and for community transformation. Mission formation as it is described here fits very closely with spiritual formation but provides further tools on how to know and do Scripture in our youth ministry, homeless ministry, elderly service or ministry to single teen mothers.

Many urban programs only minimally utilize Scripture in their planning for urban ministry. A mission can instead lean heavily on experience, intuition, the social sciences and common sense. When these tools are not subordinated to Scripture, we can hurt the ministry.

Christians should be people who think and recognize that sin is comprehensive and touches all of life—the basic relationships, environment, personal development and social development (Gen 3). They realize that it is the radical nature of the gospel that will alter the events of life and history. Thus the best way to address a community's deepest needs is to bring the gospel to bear concretely on every aspect of its life. This is why urban leaders must be equipped with the knowledge of Scripture and its use in the context of ministry.

> Theologians, as well as development workers, could well take this to heart. As in development, which seeks not simply to feed people, but to give them skills to take charge of their lives, so what we are after is a theological discipline that empowers people to be the people of God. We must seek to enable them to read and obey Scripture for themselves. If there is one generalization that could be made about the Gospel across cultures, it is that it is God's means of delivering people from all kinds of bondage and leading them to enjoy the freedom appropriate to his children. (Dyrness 1992:34).

For example, how do we figure out what it means concretely to love our enemies? Will we lean upon sentimentality or common sense? In Luke 6:32-36 Jesus provides us with the necessary equipping for that task. Love will be active and sacrificial. It will take doing good deeds to someone else who has clearly become an enemy. Common sense or experience, by contrast, would lead us to depend on self and not on the Word of God. In knowing Scripture leaders discover both the mechanics and the motivation for community ministry. Caring for the poor, for example, is not an option or a gift. The church needs to recognize that this is the essence of the Christian life (Mt 25:31-46).

Therefore, urban leaders must learn how to utilize Scripture in the context of the city. As the spiritual battle of the kingdom of darkness versus the kingdom of light takes hold (Eph 6:10-14), the reality of that war is too much for any mere human beings, even Christians, unless they apply the living and powerful Word (Rom 1:16) to their everyday life and ministry. Urban leaders who do not utilize the Bible in ministry will truncate the work of God in their cities. It is important that they uphold the Scriptures as the infallible Word of God for all of life. They must be trained to serve their communities from the Word of God. It is imperative that there be no separation between knowing and doing in matters of the Scriptures—to know is to do. This important lesson will develop and form urban leaders into being servants who understand the peril of sin and the solution.

This is not a popular approach, because on the surface it sounds too academic and not practical enough. However, the discipline of knowing Scripture equips leaders with the ability of doing Scripture. If leaders recognize that they are to be growing Christians in order to serve the Lord, it will immediately also tell them that they must be praying and studying the Scripture.

The mission formation section of the curriculum should begin by showing why Scripture is essential for urban ministry. This will give the leaders confidence that God can and will speak to contemporary issues. It should be followed by hermeneutics—how to interpret, understand and exegete Scripture. "Exegesis is the careful, systematic study of the Scripture to discover the original, intended meaning" (Fee and Stuart 1982:21). Here then is the reinforcement for the previous subject—we are developing a theology for the city using hermeneutical tools. Finally, leaders need to learn how to do theology in the community by using case studies. This will help students see the actual application of the Scriptures in everyday situations.

***Social formation.*** The final section of the urban curriculum has to do with understanding the unique context in which urban leaders are living and serving in order to theologically approach actual social issues in a particular city. Since ministry involves a specific person applying Scripture concretely to a specific context, preparation for ministry will not be completed, and theological application will not be possible apart from insight into the context at hand. The social sciences enable us to understand particular contexts, giving students the ability to recognize specific and unique elements found in their community.

The indigenous leader already has a basic understanding of the community and the city. But his understanding is general and without categorization. What is taught through the use of demographic tools helps the student see that there are underlying issues, causes and reasons for why things are happening in the community. The tools of the social sciences help leaders go further into some of the anticipated issues the church will have to face in the future. These tools help us "exegete" community.

The social formation section of the urban curriculum prepares the indigenous leader for ministry by enabling him or her to understand the community so as to utilize Scripture to address a particular societal concern. Social formation is more than using the social sciences to know community. It has to do with how to use Scripture in the social reality of the people. This aspect of training allows the leaders to utilize the integrative approach in developing an urban strategy for ministry.

How should a worship service in a community that has a high percentage of Afro-Caribbeans be conducted, especially if the group has recently come to that part of the city and is trying to survive and adjust to the new environment? The religious beliefs are numerous in the Afro-Caribbean neighborhood. The leaders will be facing beliefs from Roman Catholicism to spiritism to a combination of both. How will the gospel penetrate the newcomers' present worldview? It is as the leaders think through the unique elements of their context that they will be fully equipped to bring Scripture to bear effectively on that context.

What may be true of Mexico City may not be evident in Liberia or in Detroit, Michigan. The intention of this section is to stress both how to exegete community and how to do theology in that context. Thus, the social formation aspect of the curriculum enables urban leadership development to adapt to contexts that differ from place to place and time to time. The urban curriculum for urban leadership development is flexible enough to meet the needs of the present community and the particular leaders who are being trained for a particular city. It is important to keep in mind that the student and the environment help mold the curriculum. Therefore, adjustments are made in leadership training as the dynamics dictate change.

In concluding this chapter let us reiterate this: we cannot overemphasize the importance of searching for indigenous community leadership. Neither can we overemphasize the importance of equipping these leaders through a theocentric and context-specific curriculum. As we seek to reach urban communities for Christ, we must plan ahead and make such leadership development a priority.

# 23

# Mentoring
# the Urban Leader

IT IS ALREADY APPARENT FROM WHAT HAS been said about developing indigenous and relocated leaders for urban ministry that it will take something
other than merely a classroom or book approach to equip qualified candidates for the task. The teaching model we have had in mind in the last
chapters and which we recommend is mentoring.

*Mentoring* refers to the process where a person with a serving, giving,
encouraging attitude, the mentor, sees leadership potential in a still-to-be
developed person, the protégé, and is able to promote or otherwise significantly influence the protégé along in a realization of potential (Clinton
1988:130).*

The mentoring model fits well with demands placed on training for
urban ministry to adapt both to the context and to the needs and unique
strengths of the individual candidate. Mentoring is the style of teaching
implied in our discussion of curriculum. And it reinforces and perpetuates
the lifelong maxim of continually studying the Word and applying it in
ever fresh, concrete ways to the changing context.

---

*Portions of this chapter were previously published in Manuel Ortiz, *The Hispanic Challenge:
Opportunities Confronting the Church* (Downers Grove, Ill.: InterVarsity Press, 1993).

Mentoring is one of the most effective ways to disciple new Christians to maturity in Christ. Mentoring is also the best way to develop urban leaders. It is here that the Bible is incarnated into actual life situations. It is a life-learning curriculum. There may not be hard scientific data to document the success of this approach. But our informal, experiential observations indicate that it is effective in preparing leaders for urban ministry. We believe it should be seen as an essential part of developing urban leaders.

Mentoring is already often practiced by ethnic churches. In the African American

> **Mentoring**
>
> Sushil lived in the small community of Prembazar in India. Out of curiosity and because of the repeated invitations he received, Sushil finally decided to attend a small group, which gathered in the home of a minister to talk about the people's concerns and interests. Sushil knew that associating with the Christians near his home was not appropriate in his culture, where Hinduism was practiced by all the families. He knew that the consequences of his decision might even include his being unaccepted by his family and cast from his home.
>
> As he heard the Indian minister talk, he felt a greater desire to hear more about this great prophet called Jesus, the Son of God. After several visits he knew that he had to bow to the teaching of the Word of God and accept Jesus Christ as his Lord and Savior.
>
> Sushil thought that things would be easier and more pleasant in his life because he had trusted Christ. Instead he discovered that life became more difficult and at times unbearable. He now had the desire to share with his family about his wonderful discovery and eternal life, but he feared their rejection. He did not know how to do this.
>
> Sushil asked the pastor how to share this news with his family. The pastor told the young convert to accompany him during the early mornings so that he could learn by observation. This Sushil did. He discovered that he had many questions at the end of each day as he observed his pastor. Sushil learned the Bible from his pastor both through his teaching and through his lifestyle in the community and with his family. He also learned how to share his faith by watching the pastor in the market place as he went about sharing with many people. Sushil was being mentored by a more experienced Christian on the Christian life and ministry in this Hindu context.

church emerging leaders sit with the senior pastor and do a great deal of observation. They carry out the requests of the senior pastor with sincerity, aspiring one day to be pastors themselves. There is a high level of respect for the senior pastor, and there is no room for usurping authority. Opportunities come to the mentoree as he or she is found diligent and willing to serve. Moving into leadership depends not so much on outstanding skills or abilities but on the individual's willingness to be a servant as displayed by a high regard for authority in the church. In a similar way the Hispanic church brings along leaders as they follow the senior pastor in ministry and display a heart for God and the ministry. These leaders learn more from observation than from lectures or literature. Neil Braun relates a similar illustration: "When a man felt a call to preach, he would tell the church. He would then be asked to preach; and if his sermon indicated promise, he would be licensed to preach in that church or perhaps in a small area around it" (Braun 1971:54).

The mentoring process is a complex and developmentally important relationship. It is complex because it involves people in relationship to one another. It is developmentally important because the mentor supports and facilitates the clarification and realization of the mentoree's dream. He is a teacher, sponsor, guide, model and counselor.

Elliston and Kauffman speak of mentoring in several terms. One has to do with *mirroring*. "Existing leaders again mirror the work of the Holy Spirit empowering new leaders by delegating authority to them to lead, and influence toward God's purposes" (Elliston and Kauffman 1993:92). The other word they use is *empowering*. "Empowerment is the process of enabling, equipping, and allowing people to influence significantly in a situation and the recognizing [of] that contribution" (Elliston and Kauffman 1993:92).

Mentoring is a relational activity that can best be done in a one-to-one relationship. However, it may also be productive with a small group of two to five. Our experience is that it is actually best accomplished with two mentorees and a mentor.

In what follows we will examine the Bible for guidelines concerning mentoring. Then we will define the task and the responsibilities of the mentor as we lay out the actual process.

### The Biblical Parameters for Mentoring
Any approach to ministry that involves the church should be based on a biblical theological foundation. Mentoring is certainly not a new approach to training. It has clear roots in the Old and New Testaments.

In the New Testament Paul uses the word *imitate* (2 Thess 3:7, 9; Phil 3:17). This word has to do with doing what another is doing. A related word that is familiar to many of us is the word *mimic*. We mimic or imitate someone else who has given us reason to want to imitate him or her. The biblical concept also has to do with "molding" or "marking." Here the idea is to mold something like a potter would do when given clay to make a piece of art or a useful utensil.

Paul is an example to follow, but he himself is following the ideal, the Lord Jesus. Since following the Lord Jesus is the calling given to the church, it is important that we understand that what Paul says about mentoring, and what we do in the way of training leaders by mentoring, is always set in the context of what the Lord has in mind for the church. Setting mentoring in the context of God's work in and through the church for his glory, we believe, helps us to avoid unbiblical approaches in mentoring.

Thinking through what the Bible says about the church of Jesus Christ yields three basic parameters that must characterize our outlook as we engage in mentoring future church leaders. The first is that *the church, the body of Christ, is an organism.* Mentoring begins with the understanding that the church is a growing, dynamic organism with a divine and a contextual structure (Eph 4:15-16). Paul speaks of the church as "growing up" (Eph 4:15), "built up" (Eph 4:12), "joined and held together by every supporting ligament . . . as each part does its work" (Eph 4:16). He is describing the church as a living entity. "An organism that does not grow is in reality dead" (Costas 1983:97). The church is the body of Christ (Eph 5:23), and it has been called into being by God. The mentoring process, therefore, has the high calling of preparing and equipping to continue Christ's body, his ongoing incarnation in the world.

Too often pastors select new leaders based on their popularity and desire alone. This approach violates the Word of God. Jesus calls leaders to be his stewards (Jn 15:16). True mentoring prepares those chosen by God to enhance the growth of the church as a whole. There is no room for leaders who do not see the church as the body of Christ, a covenant people divinely called to grow.

Donald MacNair states, "The pastor is the building block of a living church. What he does and the way in which he does it has a significant bearing on the church's vitality" (MacNair 1978:43). The Antiochan church was blessed with faithful and capable leadership (Acts 13:1). The leaders were called prophets and teachers. Their primary ministry was to equip the church in which the disciples were first called Christians (Acts 11:26). The listing of these servant-leaders reminds us of both the divine initiation of selecting and installing these men and the contextual relevancy in discharging the gospel to a diverse congregation (Acts 13:1-3). Mentoring is influenced both by divine and contextual structure, not only by an analysis of community and world but also by an analysis of God's providence and power.

A second parameter for mentoring is that according to Scripture, *Christ is the one who prepares people for ministry.* He sovereignly chooses the people to whom he graciously gives gifts, and the fact that he has graciously given the gifts is the most important factor in the success of those people's ministry.

> But to each one of us grace has been given as Christ apportioned it. This is why it says: "When he ascended on high, he led captives in his train and gave gifts to men." (What does "he ascended" mean except that he also descended to the lower, earthly regions? He who descended is the very one who ascended higher than all the heavens, in order to fill the whole universe.) It was he who gave some to be apostles, some to be prophets, some to be evangelists, and some to be pastors and teachers. (Eph 4:7-11)

In the first four chapters of Ephesians, Paul communicates the astounding joy of God's grace. The sovereign election of God is announced (Eph 1:3-5), and it is this very grace that is given to the church for service (Eph 4:7-13). Christ has apportioned his grace to each member (Eph 4:7). This grace works in us and finds its fruit in the church's call to world evangelization.

The task of mentoring depends on Christ as the giver of grace. Christ is the one who selects a person for a unique ministry (Eph 4:11). When Paul was humbled on the way to Damascus, he was ordered by the Lord to "get up and go into the city, and you will be told what you must do" (Acts 9:6). In Ephesians 4:11 the emphasis is on the giver. He himself and no other is the giver. God is the one who calls and prepares.

> The church is thus a God-created and indwelled community. It is the body of Christ, integrated by many members with diverse functions. It is the fellowship of the Spirit, set apart for service by its grace and purifying fire. (Costas 1986:463)

A mentor does not vote for someone to be a servant-leader or manipulate another for the Lord's field of service. The task of mentoring is to discover whom God has touched and anointed.

Not only is Christ the one who selects people for ministry, but Christ is the one who prepares his people for service. A willing heart is important to the process of mentoring, but it can never supersede the preparation of Christ. Our potential as God's children depends on Christ and a yielded life. Often we are too quick to judge the potential of servant-leaders based on personality traits, psychological manifestations and academic qualities rather than on their yieldedness to Christ. For a potential leader to begin without dependence on Christ as the giver of grace, or for a mentor to approve such a beginning, is to tolerate a ministry that is person-centered rather than Christ-centered. By doing this we limit the movement of God's church in the world.

The reality that Christ is the one who chooses and graces leaders for his church gives us tremendous hope as we participate in church ministry. The Lord not only equips the church but selects and empowers those for significant ministry in the world. It is divinely apportioned and therefore perfect and just.

Finally, we need to remember a third biblical parameter of mentoring, that *Christ calls us to prepare others for service* (Eph 4:12-13). Mentoring must concern itself not merely with leaders but with *servant*-leaders. In the New Testament, leadership is viewed as service or *diakonia* (1 Cor 12:28; 16:15-16; 2 Cor 3:7-9; 4:1; 5:18; 6:3; Eph 4:11-13; Col 4:17; 2 Tim 4:5). For the leader truly called by the Lord, service is what the calling is all about. It is what Peter exhorts the presbyter to do, to tend the flocks of God (1 Pet 5:1-4). The ruling aspect is present, but the christological mandate is to serve (1 Cor 3:5; 2 Cor 1:24). In this milieu of preparing, repairing and equipping, God has specifically recognized and called certain people to be the emerging pastor-teachers, evangelists, church planters and preachers of the Word (Eph 4:11). Christ calls the people he places in these roles to prepare the church for service, unity and growth (Eph 4:12-13). The process takes time (2 Cor 3:18) and will culminate in glory (Rom 8:29-30).

Mentoring can never be a step to higher ground—only to holy ground. Therefore, in mentoring the goal is not to equip for position but rather for function, that is, for service, so that the body of Christ may be built up (Eph 4:12). Mentoring others is a major responsibility of following the giver of gifts, Christ, within the church historically and culturally.

We can observe these biblical parameters and other important features of mentoring in some examples of leadership training in the Bible. We begin with Jesus. Jesus seemingly selected the unqalified and gave them his Spirit. His choices do not seem to have been particularly appropriate from a human point of view, but Jesus knew them. He called them first to himself and then to service in the world (Lk 5:10).

For the disciples, we see that the training process begins with observation as Jesus ministers (Lk 5). He then empowers them to follow his ministry (Mt 10:1) and sends them out (Mt 10:5). The disciples observed and served. This is the order and the components which characterize leadership training by mentoring.

We also see from Jesus' example that mentoring is not a selfish task; it is the task of calling others to do the work of the ministry. It is even calling others to do greater things that will bear more fruit (Jn 14:12).

The account of Barnabas and Paul offers some insights about mentoring as well. Barnabas became the link between Christianity and the Gentile world. As a Jewish Levite coming out of Cyprus, he would have had the important quality of being flexible within a multicultural situation.

In Acts 4:36-37 we notice his willingness to be committed to the body of Christ. When Barnabas met Paul and discovered what God had already done in him, he affirmed Paul in the presence of the apostles (Acts 9:27). The mentor is usually the one who knows the individual best and can affirm conversion, gifts and use of gifts. Colaboring is also part of the curriculum. Barnabas brought Paul to Antioch because he needed help discipling the new and growing congregation there. Barnabas was Paul's link to ministry. It was arranged by God, making it possible for Paul to observe and serve with Barnabas.

Keep in mind that Paul was mentored by a person who was good, full of the Holy Spirit and faith (Acts 11:24). Barnabas was a man of integrity, sensitive to the guidance of the Holy Spirit. He had made the effort to find Paul because he had discovered God's potential in him. Paul was mentored by a man prepared by God for this missiological task of mentoring. Barnabas discovered God's selection and prepared Paul through colaboring (Acts 11:22-30; 13:1-3; 14:23; 15:1-4).

The period of mentoring ended with Paul's disagreement concerning Barnabas's decision to take Mark with him on his missionary journey. But as a result, new mentoring relationships were established: Barnabas and Mark, Paul and Silas. Paul was then sent out to serve but also began to mentor another disciple (Acts 16). It is obvious that the mentoring process continued as an essential part of the spread of the church.

Paul's approach to training further leadership resembles Jesus'. Paul does not merely talk to his disciples about growing and serving; he builds a relationship with them and involves them in his own ministry (Phil 1:1; 1 Thess 1:1). He displays the grace apportioned him. Paul was always concerned with making an impact on others. "You know how we lived among you for your sake. You became imitators of us and of the Lord" (1 Thess 1:5-6). As a mentor, Paul entrusts the gospel to reliable men (2 Tim 2:1-2) so that the ministry may go on. Paul mentors Timothy by colaboring, observing what God is doing and then sending him to do the significant service of God.

## Qualifications of a Mentor

In the examples of Barnabas and Paul, we see several qualities which must characterize a mentor.

*The mentor must first of all be devoted to Christ and thus to personal holiness.* Barnabas and Paul displayed a life of holiness and commitment to Christ. The mentor must first follow God before he can call others to follow him. Charles Hodge describes this expression of devotion and love:

> Love to God, however, is not mere complacency in moral excellence. It is the love of a personal Being, who stands in the most intimate relations to ourselves, as the Author of our existence, as our Preserver and Ruler, as our

Father, who with conscious love watches over us, protects us, supplies all our wants, holds communion with us, manifesting himself unto us as he does not unto the world. The feelings of dependence, obligation, and relationship, enter largely into that comprehensive affection called the love of God. This affection is still further modified by the apprehension of the infinite wisdom and power of its object. These attributes are the proper objects of admiration; and, when infinite in degree and united with infinite goodness, they excite that wonder, admiration, reverence, and complacency, which constitute adoration, and which find in prostration and worship their only adequate expression. (Hodge 1959:211-12)

These moving words cause us to stop and recognize our greatest goal in life: to be conformed to the image of Christ (Rom 8:29). The apostle Paul lists qualities of a godly leader that are thereby those of a godly mentor. "The mentor must be (1) temperate; (2) worthy of respect; (3) self-controlled; and (4) sound in faith, in love and in endurance" (Scott 1995:129).

Many mentors, after years of mentoring others, stated that the most important and the most difficult aspect of mentoring was the priority of holiness—to provide emerging leaders with a model of what it means to be sanctified to God for his glory. Too many mentors have been described as providing resources for the mentoree's ministry rather than for his living. Both are essential, but the one without the other nullifies the whole.

Devotion to Christ and to holiness is that feature of our ministry that will make it most effective. As Hodge notes, "It is impossible that those who have correct views and feelings in regard to God should not feel and act correctly in regard to their fellow men" (Hodge 1959:214). The modeling aspect of mentoring is extremely powerful. "Everyone who is fully trained will be like his teacher" (Lk 6:40). It is imperative that those who are mentored also become holy (1 Pet 1:16). Therefore, a mentor must devote time and practice to living righteously before the Lord.

The mentor is to be committed to continual growth in his or her life. This involves more than intellectual growth. The mentor must continue to grow in ministry and especially in biblical character and spiritual traits as noted. The mentor's involvement in family and leadership in the church and community should evidence a maturing individual. The mentor displays the fruit of Christ in life and ministry.

*The mentor must be mentored.* Given Barnabas and Paul's example, we should expect that mentoring remains a vital key to every believer's spiritual formation, whether he or she is being mentored or is also mentoring. The one aspect so vital to fruitful mentoring is that the mentor continues to grow within a milieu of experienced and mature Christians. A good mentor is one who is being mentored.

*The mentor must be passionate about the advance of the gospel.* The accounts of Paul, Barnabas, Timothy and Peter depict men who are passionate for the gospel of Christ. Paul exhorted Timothy to fan into flame the gift of God (2 Tim 1:6). In the same context Paul encouraged his son in the faith not to be ashamed to testify about our Lord (2 Tim 1:8). The call to serve is ongoing for the mentor who is completely in love with Christ.

*The mentor must be active in service.* Ruling is secondary to service. This is true for the mentor as well as for the mentoree. Both Paul and Barnabas were active servants. While Paul was preaching in Tarsus, Barnabas found him for another task that would use his gifts (Acts 12:25-30). The mentor also realizes that he or she must continue in ministry.

The point here is that we cannot mentor others from a theoretical position. Nor can we teach without practice. The mentor is a practitioner. This is important, because we tend to intellectualize and avoid the actual doing of ministry. We become intellectual missionaries and evangelists and teachers without ever getting real practice. For the Christian, mentoring must be "one beggar telling another beggar where to find bread." To mentor without touching the level of hands-on ministry is inappropriate and filled with suggestions of years passed and speculations.

*The mentor must be deeply committed to those he or she is mentoring.* Paul clearly expresses his emotional attachment to Timothy (2 Tim 1:3-4). The mentor is never so concerned about the mission that he loses perspective on the individuals Christ has given him or her. Barnabas and Jesus also displayed this deep concern for those God had entrusted to them.

*The mentor is committed for the duration of the race.* Both Paul and Barnabas were engaged in the task of mentoring until the very end. Jesus also displayed this kind of loyalty. The privilege of mentoring others for God's service is great, but the responsibilities are lifelong—in sickness and in health. A temporary commitment is impossible.

*The mentor must be well prepared theologically.* The Word of God is the strength and power of biblical ministry. The mentor must possess well-developed exegetical and hermeneutical skills in order to prepare emerging leaders to be exegetes of the Word of God. To have a prosperous and successful ministry, future leaders will have to know what the Word of God tells us (Josh 1:8). The need of many of our pastors is to learn how to do biblical exposition. This calls for biblical exegesis that takes into account systematic theology as well as biblical theology.

> The truth is that one cannot really practice, say, biblical exegesis without taking into account the concerns of systematic theology; similarly, it would be artificial to suggest that we must not or cannot address the problems

posed by practical ministry until we have fully explored the area of biblical theology. (Silva 1987:21)

In many of our urban churches, the issue is not so much the infallibility of the Word of God but the appropriation of the Word of God in context. Preaching too often is contextualized inappropriately when, in the absence of solid exegetical and hermeneutical training, the text is misapplied because context is given the upper hand. Giving in to the pressure to be relevant without using good hermeneutical skills is dangerous. Without such training, we can convince ourselves that our present-day concerns are the exact concerns of the biblical text.

On the other hand, we must not deny our pressing issues and needs. Moisés Silva reviews the subject of contextualization:

> It would be a mistake, however, to jettison the basic concept of contextualization simply because it has been abused. The fact is that every attempt we make at understanding the Bible (or any other ancient document) necessarily involves transferring a particular text from one historical context to another. When contemporary Christians read a portion of Scripture (already partially contextualized by the English version!), they can make sense of it only from the context of their own knowledge and experience.
>
> The question, therefore, is not *whether* we should contextualize, for we all do it, but rather, *how* to do it without compromising the integrity of the Bible. (Silva 1987:100).

Silva notes:

> Of course, we must be very careful not to read into the text present-day concerns that are not really there, but it is proper and even necessary to approach the Bible with a strong awareness of our needs. The problems faced in the gospel ministry often alert us to truths in Scripture that might otherwise remain veiled to us. Proper exegesis consists largely of asking the right questions from the text, and the life of the church can provide us with those very questions. (Silva 1987:22)

*The mentor must be sociologically and anthropologically prepared.* God speaks his eternal Word to people in concrete, historical situations. If we are to proclaim the good news with the intention of seeing all of life confess Jesus Christ as Lord, then we must consider the dialogue between the Word of God and the social sciences to be important. Too often we have omitted this dialogue and overemphasized the interaction between theology and philosophy. Our major need is to understand the historical and social context in which we are ministering. The awareness of transitions and social evils provides the context in which the Word will be presented, along with the dynamics of cultural distinctions. The urban context is a complicated reality that needs serious study. In many cities the church is vulnerable because it does not understand the social dynamics or the power of God to bring reconciliation. As a result, we have white flight, black flight and brown flight—church people fleeing to another context much more sociologically and theologically comfortable. Mentors must be skilled in guiding emerging leaders not only through demographic work but also ethnographic documentation.

*The mentor must be flexible.* Paul was able to shift gears when he was called by Barnabas. Paul served with an interesting and diversified group of men (Acts 13:1). In order for the Holy Spirit to use him in their lives, Paul had to be flexible. We also see that Paul was able to adapt to a new partner in mission, Silas (Acts 15:40). Paul was not hindered by inflexibility from going to Syria and Cilicia to strengthen the churches. The mission goes on when we are willing to adjust to changing circumstances. Mentoring without flexibility makes it difficult to hear God's voice in a complex world.

A close look at the words and actions of mentors in the Bible has thus provided us with a well-developed picture of mentoring as it fits into the overall mission of the church. We have a better sense of what it involves and what it requires. And in the process, our working claim is confirmed: mentoring is not only the most effective method of training future leaders; it is also the most biblical, central to the ongoing task of Christ's body in the world.

### The Mentoring Process, Level One: Building a Relationship

We distinguish three levels of the mentoring process. The first is building a solid but informal relationship between mentor and mentoree. The second is preparing the mentoree for leadership ministry through observing and modeling the mentor. It involves an array of informal and formal activities which promote the student's learning and development. The third level is examining the mentoree's beginning ministry. Here the emerging leader is given much more autonomy to do ministry while still being supervised in a limited way by the mentor.

These levels have an order of priority, in that the first must come before the second, and the second before the third. However, the priority does not prohibit a chronological overlapping of the three levels. In fact, it will quickly become clear that a clean separation of the levels would be both impossible and unwanted. Nevertheless, we can reasonably expect that a mentor and mentoree would begin level one before beginning level two because level one is the proper foundation for level two, even as two is of three.

Mentors must realize that the timeframe for mentoring is to some degree flexible and depends on the individual candidate's ability to embrace and grasp the teaching that is shared through verbal communication and observation of the mentor's life. All three levels may take different periods of time for different candidates. Each student must be mentored for the length of time called for by his or her specific strengths, needs, commission and context. This process is much more organic than organizational, and it depends a great deal on dynamics formed in the relationship. It is important for both mentor and mentoree to exercise patience. It is possible to short-circuit the process by losing sight of the needs of those being mentored as we feel the pressure to get on with the task of ministry.

The three levels of mentoring are of such a nature that it is impossible to designate the length of time each will take. The first level is the most important and usually takes one or two years at the outset before the mentoree can move into levels two and three. And as we said before, the three levels often can overlap chronologically. Thus, they should not be placed in a structure that will not consider the uniqueness of each individual. An example of a structure that is too rigid is one that creates a mentoring curriculum that insists that the first phase be accomplished in a six-month period or placed on an academic calendar. The mentoring approach should be very fluid and allow the relationship to create its own timeframe. This is another reason why it is always best for one leader to mentor one or two students at a time and no more.

The first level of mentoring is developing a solid informal relationship between mentor and mentoree. This relationship must be characterized by mutuality, holism and friendship.

**Mutuality.** A relationship must be mutually desired. It is not imposed but rather enjoyed and desired over time. Sometimes a friendship occurs immediately, but more often it requires numerous personal contacts before one wishes to be more involved. Because the relationship is reciprocal, it enriches both parties; mentor and mentoree are sharing their lives together.

The Scriptures confirm such mutuality in ministry. We are all attaining to unity of faith (Eph 4:13), we are all disciples. Christ is the one who teaches us (Mt 23:10); we are all being transformed into his image (2 Cor 3:18), we are all called to go and make disciples (Mt 28:19-20), we are all to be witnesses for Christ (Acts 1:8), we are in need of each other (1 Cor 12:21-26). We are to exercise our spiritual gifts (Eph 4:10-11) out of mutual concern and submit to one another as we yield to God's lordship (Eph 5:21). In other words, Christian living and growth take place in reciprocity, as we build relationships.

Many in our urban centers care less about institutional commitments and more about commitments to relationships and to a community. Thus this mutual aspect of the mentoring relationship dovetails with felt needs and foci in the city.

Too often when we think of leadership development, we downplay any mutuality in the teaching relationship. The mentor does not take into regard the mentoree's experiences and history. The mentor should utilize the mentoree's life and ministry as being significant for mutual growth.

In order for this to happen the mentor must be able to build relationships. This is not as easy as it seems. Many existing leaders have learned to work alone and be distant from others without a team effort. Therefore, this characteristic must be one that is visible and developing in the mentor's life.

**Holism**. The second aspect of the relationship between mentor and mentoree is that it encompasses all aspects of life. Whole-life relationships must go both ways. Just as we enter into the everyday life of others, we should also allow others to see our daily life and family interaction. As ministers, our credibility will dramatically increase when others can examine our family life and our daily walk, not just our preaching and teaching. Praying and sharing Scripture is good, but it is not enough. We must bring people into our lives, not just the segment that we erroneously call ministry.

Jesus "became flesh and made his dwelling among us" (Jn 1:14). That is, he lived out his life as a servant, in appearance as a man, humbling himself (Phil 2:8). His ministry was not separated from his life. His life in action *was* his ministry.

> In Scripture we find that the Gospel is essentially the person and work of Jesus Christ. It is not a message or formulation, but the person Jesus Christ. There are several features of his incarnation which are important considerations for the communication of the Gospel:
>
> *Incarnation is specific to a context.* Jesus did not come as a universal man: he came as a Jew to Jews. Incarnation is limited to a context, it is not general and universal.
>
> *Incarnation is involved in a context.* Jesus did not just speak to Jews, he became a Jew. He identified himself with all aspects of being a Jew.
>
> *Incarnation takes the cultural context seriously.* Jesus did not become a Jew as a convenient illustration of general truths. He faced real problems, debates, issues, struggles and conflicts which concerned the Jewish people. He entered into sharp debate with the Pharisees and Sadducees about how to be obedient to God. He took the side of social outcasts, the women, the Samaritans, and the lepers. Within that real Jewish culture, its economic, social and political relationships, he was incarnate.

*Incarnation takes humanity seriously.* Jesus did not address the Jews imper-sonally, as one abstracted from their cultural context. He came to his own, and spelt out his claims in terms that spoke uniquely to Jews—their social, economic and political relationships, not just their personal rights and reli-gious beliefs. The Jew's holistic view of life as ordered under God admitted no such division. Jesus addressed himself to economic questions, to the political groupings in Israel, and relationships of injustice that prevailed.

On these issues his concern was not so much *effectiveness*, in terms of winning a large following, as *authenticity*, that people should clearly under-stand the nature of his mission and of God's kingdom. (Samuel and Sugden 1987:62)

When Jesus calms the storm in Luke 8:22-25, we learn a lot about him. Not only is he Jesus, the tired person who needed a nap, but he is also the sovereign Lord who "rebuked the wind and the raging waters" (8:24). "Where is your faith?" he asked his disciples. In fear and amazement they asked one another, "Who is this? He commands even the winds and the water, and they obey him" (8:25). Jesus used daily circumstances to teach. Sometimes these circumstances were intense, as in the storm, and other times they were quite ordinary. We can take a similar approach in our own contemporary situation. Intense and faithful relationships can and should be built holistically if we are living among the people we are serv-ing. Incarnation is important to developing relationships.

We should not separate the social from the spiritual but rather see God as involved in the totality of life. We have found that times of casual, relaxed discussions and recreational activities can be the most important part of building a relationship. We are not as self-protective, and we feel free to disclose more of who we are. We share many sides of our person-alities that we do not often reveal in "spiritual" moments. This allows for an interweaving of two lives. Working together or visiting the sick can be great times for sharing and learning.

**Friendship.** The capstone of this solid relationship is that it is a rela-tionship of friends. This component to mentoring is more difficult than we imagine. The mentor must enter into the life of the mentoree. The mentor cannot be distant. A friend in biblical terms is one who becomes a soul partner, one who shares intimately with another. This is very difficult for many who have never learned to develop friendship. Friends need each other; friends are willing to confess to each other; friends have conflict but are willing to reconcile; friends are vulnerable to each other; friends learn from each other; friends never allow for superior-inferior dimen-sions. This is a very supportive role for both as they engage in the men-toring process.

In order to bring such a mutual, whole-life friendship about, a mentor must possess and cultivate a few capacities that deserve mention. First, a significant aspect of relationship building is *listening*. Myron Rush says:

> When I first got into the consulting business, I assumed that the key to good communication was one's ability to verbalize his thoughts and feelings. Over the years, I've changed my thinking. I now believe that the key is the ability to be a good listener. (Rush 1983:163)

Interestingly, the very opposite tends to occur when missionaries or pastors work with emerging leaders. Pastors do the talking, and the trainee is expected to listen. As Christian leaders, we are trained to speak and not to listen. We've been programmed to believe that listening is not leading, not taking responsibility, not being productive. So we keep on talking. Paulo Freire speaks of this dimension in educational terms which ultimately dehumanize the students:

> (a) the teacher teaches and the students are taught;
> (b) the teacher knows everything and the students know nothing;
> (c) the teacher thinks and the students are thought about;
> (d) the teacher talks and the students listen—meekly. (Freire 1989:59)

This attitude may damage potentially fruitful relationships. No one has everything to give and nothing to receive. Again we are reminded of the need for reciprocity. We urgently need to learn how to listen. It may be more important for the missionary or pastor to listen first so that he or she can learn to receive and feel mutual worth.

Listening provides an environment in which others can be who they are and express their uniqueness without fear of rejection. "Listening is the key to developing understanding" (Rush 1983:163). It requires concentration and undivided attention. To do otherwise is to manipulate the situation, causing the other to wonder if he or she is really important to you. Listening involves respecting the other person as an individual made in God's image and significant to God's mission.

Rush indicates that there are two kinds of listening—perceptive and passive. Perceptive listening focuses on what is behind the verbal and nonverbal message. It listens "for the thoughts and feelings" (Rush 1983:164). Passive listening merely takes in the words themselves and often leads to misunderstanding. Perceptive listeners must "have an honest desire to hear what the speaker is saying." They should provide feedback "to assure the sender you have heard correctly, and the sender will be responsible to say so if you have not." An important part of the feedback is to make sure you are not judging the message (Rush 1983:166-69).

Rush gives us several rules for effective listening:

a. Don't interrupt the speaker.
b. Don't start forming your response while the speaker is still talking.
c. Do ask questions for clarity.
d. Don't assume you already know what the speaker is going to say. (Rush 1983:171)

Second, the mentor must cultivate *honesty.* The importance of being honest in a relationship hardly needs support. But although it is easy to admit that honesty belongs in every relationship, it is not very easy to accomplish.

The apostle Paul sets an example of expressing himself openly: "I came to you in weakness and fear, and with much trembling" (1 Cor 2:3). Rather than cover up who we are, honestly sharing ourselves will more likely enhance our relationships. It also helps us to learn how to be honest without being arrogant or damaging to the spirit of those we are serving. Paul tells us, "Therefore each of you must put off falsehood and speak truthfully to his neighbor, for we are all members of one body" (Eph 4:25).

Failing or making a mistake in public may have more positive fruit than expected. Emerging leaders, who often feel inferior to their mentors, may recognize that we all have much to learn. Normally we hope that developing leaders will not discover our frailties and shortcomings. But hiding them tends to make our position look impossible to reach.

When it comes to building relationships, we cannot rush matters. The mentor must exercise *patience.* Emerging leaders may not yet be ready to learn how to lead. Patience allows for a healthy, growing environment. Prior to more task-oriented experiences, building the fundamental relationship between mentor and mentoree requires patience. All relationships take time to grow. The ability to listen is cultivated and learned in process. Honesty takes trust, and trust grows with time. In some ways relationship building is never-ending. We simply move from one phase to another.

While there are many other aspects to building relationships, we have tried to zero in on the ones most important to the process of leadership development. And we must always keep in mind that we are disciples together and that Christ is our teacher (Mt 23:10).

Our methods may have to be adjusted to each person. In some cases it may take longer than expected to build a solid and lasting relationship. Certain cultures respond to relationships differently, and it is wise to review the cultural dimensions on how to enter this process. People will not want to be viewed as a target audience, but rather as human beings with many needs who desire respect and compassion. They do not care about theological paradigms or concepts as much as they want to know that we care for them. Compassion requires solidarity, a "suffering with." Vulnerability must be mutual. It is imperative that we live in the community and participate in its life, using the same stores, schools and means of recreation. We are as enriched and as limited as they are. We begin to internalize their suffering and powerlessness.

### The Mentoring Process, Level Two: The Learning Experience

The second level of the mentoring process might be considered mentoring proper. It is the guided, interactive, learning experience in which mentor and mentoree engage together in an array of formal and informal activities.

In developing emerging urban leaders within the church, our direct participation is essential. The mentor guides and facilitates the mentoree into a learning experience by providing the environment for learning through teaching, praying and fellowship.

Mentoring encompasses five main activities: modeling, supervising, teaching, observing others and sending. Modeling involves allowing and teaching emerging leaders to observe and discuss *our* life and ministry, how we live out the gospel in context. Supervision consists of directing and overseeing young leaders as they live out the gospel and carry on ministry, followed by dialogue. Teaching refers to lecturing, or providing formal and informal means of instruction, with sufficient dialogue. The mentor also enables mentorees to observe other ministries outside of their community, state and country, in order to see the global dimensions of God's work in the world. Again, this includes plenty of dialogue. Finally, mentoring culminates in sending: assigning new leaders to various mission endeavors, allowing them to do ministry in their unique way while keeping biblical principles intact. These activities also show the various roles we will need to play in building mature and fruitful new leaders. In some cases these five activities occur simultaneously rather than in chronological order.

*Modeling*. The mentor must first of all model the ministry for which he or she is preparing the mentoree. Webster defines model as "a person or thing considered as a standard of excellence to be imitated" (Neufeldt and Guralnik 1988:871). The mentor as a model of urban ministry is worthy of imitation. This does not necessarily require a success story, although this is certainly what we are looking for in training. It may also include stories that have many hardships and failures that have become intrusions of the Lord to promote a more growing ministry in the city. Some urban ministries are effective without having enormous numbers attached to them.

Rather, they may have had gradual and enduring effective ministries. But mentoring involves allowing emerging leaders to observe *our* life and ministry, how we live out the gospel in context, followed by dialogue.

Observing is something we all do, yet it is also a skill that needs to be taught. Spradley tells us that "we are all *observers*, even when acting as ordinary participants. But what we watch and listen for remains limited to our immediate purpose of accomplishing some activity" (Spradley 1980:56). Because we do not observe as closely as we should, it is easy to miss much of what is happening. Mentorees must be taught to observe the mentor's modeling.

One way to teach observation is to set up situations where we model good leadership and then question or dialogue with the prospective leaders afterwards. For example, after we witness to a person on the street, we can ask questions such as, What did you notice about the person I was speaking to? What was their culture? What socioeconomic range were they in? Were they single, married, a parent? Were they receptive to the gospel? Why or why not? What were the felt needs of that individual? Why did I use a particular passage of Scripture and specific words to communicate? How would you do it and why?

The young leaders must learn to observe with all their senses. It is not enough to see; they must develop perceptive listening skills so they can pick up on various needs and truths about the individual. Sometimes these needs are immediate and should not be ignored. For example, a woman we are speaking with mentions she is going to the clinic with her child. The clinic is two miles away and she is expected at a certain time, but she has no means of transportation. A ride to the clinic may be the most constructive initial approach to sharing the gospel. Or, if parents strike up a conversation about the needs of their children's education, we should take time to listen and respond to their concerns. If we are not observant, we will insensitively push ahead with our agenda without considering the immediate need of the individual. Emerging leaders learn not only to observe the model but to observe and respond to their surroundings.

One resource that gives mentorees some help in understanding human needs (though it should not dictate our understanding of biblical teaching on human nature) is Maslow's hierarchy of human motives, which in order to be used most effectively will also require that we understand our culture. Notice that the needs get more basic as we go down the list:

7. Aesthetic needs

6. Desire to know and understand
5. Need for self-actualization
4. Esteem needs
   a. self-esteem
   b. esteem from others
3. Love and belongingness needs
2. Safety needs
1. Physiological needs

Maslow's basic point in his theory and model is that *all* seven of these needs are intrinsic to human personality—but not all of them are center stage, in the forefront of consciousness, and *currently* motivating a person's life. The need that is in the forefront of consciousness and that is currently motivating the individual will be the lowest need that is basically unfulfilled.

For instance, the basic, rock-bottom human needs are physiological—nutrition, elimination, sex, sleep. If these needs are not met, a person spends most of his time in an attempt to fulfill them; and until these physiological needs are met, he ignores his other needs that are present in the background of his personality. In wartime, when people are starving and homeless, they do not expend much energy asking philosophical questions or painting landscapes. (Hunter 1979:41-42)

After modeling some aspect of ministry, we can initiate dialogue with questions that teach the emerging leader observing skills. We can first ask how the emerging leader might have handled the situation. Why witness? Does God have a concern for the whole person? Much of the dialogue falls under the heading of theological and missiological understanding for the purpose of praxis. The discussion will often lead into contextualization and help an emerging leader become a capable contextualist.

In cases where it may be impossible to have the young leader with us, we can still share what we are doing. For example, much of the training we give in counseling would need to be conveyed by cognitive teaching, using case studies. But we can also train our young people in observation by sharing about our own preparation and expressing the feelings we experience during counseling. Counseling is not merely an academic discipline but rather a shepherding aspect of ministry that involves the pastor deeply, requires compassion and often brings about stress.

We can also share on a personal level about private aspects of ministry, such as preparing messages. We can talk about how we selected the theme, developed the ideas and exegeted the Scriptures and what response we desired. We can also share the strain and inadequacy we may have felt during the preparation, the constraints of time, perhaps even the spiritual battle that led us to profound prayer.

Our observation training should not be limited to areas of ministry that run smoothly but should include areas that involve conflict and stress.

Emerging leaders must also observe how we handle matters of discipline, forgiveness and reconciliation. Because modeling is so important in helping others learn observation skills, the privatistic lifestyle fostered in North American culture often hinders leadership development.

The mentor is a model and thus should expect to be evaluated constantly. The mentor as model must remain vulnerable and humble, because constant evaluation is a key part of how the mentoree learns. In a discussion we heard leaders from Sri Lanka share that public failure by leaders was a good thing because it displayed the frailty of leaders and gave hope for others who thought it would be impossible to serve.

**Supervision.** The basic idea here is gradually to reverse the direction of observation. The emerging leader begins to do ministry, and the missionary or pastor does the observing in order to provide supervision and guidance. Young leaders need to practice what they have been learning from observing the pastor at work. A key aspect of supervision is knowing how much responsibility to give the new leader and when. It can be destructive to allow the individual to do too much too soon.

Most emerging leaders should begin by learning to share their faith, lead a person to Christ and conduct the early stages of discipleship. The missionary or pastor must also observe his young people closely to identify personality traits that need healing or restructuring under the lordship of Christ. For example, the way leaders handle finances and manage their homes will directly affect their ability to serve. Many pastors have fallen short in their ministry because of domestic mismanagement. Supervision will enable us to pinpoint areas that need special resources and attention. In this way we will assist the growth of the emerging leaders and broaden their ministerial responsibilities.

Here are a few guidelines for supervision. Begin with acts of ministry that will not produce ego trips and puff up the individual to the point of grieving the Holy Spirit. Emerging leaders should be deeply aware of the sovereign God's involvement in salvation and service, and humility should result. Also, as responsibilities increase, we should monitor their levels of anxiety and fear of failure, which can cause them to avoid or postpone getting involved.

Second, observe the mentorees' attitudes. What are their attitudes concerning submission and authority? How do they view service that calls for seemingly unimportant or behind-the-scenes tasks? Do the mentorees, for example, view setting up the chairs or cleaning the restrooms as someone else's job, or do they willingly pitch in as the Lord's servants? Attitudes toward family should be noted and evaluated. Many emerging leaders will come from hurting families with a history of poor relationships. They must be encouraged to love and honor their families, even when they disagree with their approach to life.

Third, watch their teamwork. Are they lone-ranger types, or do they work well with others? Leaders must be able to work well on a team. The ability is best learned by watching others and then by practicing it themselves at various levels of ministry. Those with no role models or previous team experience will have greater difficulty accepting and delegating responsibilities and maintaining an overall spirit of cooperation.

Finally, observe the mentorees' stewardship as they accomplish their tasks. Note the quality of the work and how long it took. Are they responsible and accountable for their use of time and resources? How well do they evaluate their own accomplishments? Young leaders who are truly concerned about their calling will strive to take responsibility for their assignments. And as they mature, they can take on more responsibility.

**Teaching.** In teaching the mentor acts as a guide as well as a resource person, while maintaining a healthy learning environment.

The mentor as teacher must keep in mind that the responsibility of learning is left in the hands of the mentoree. Therefore, in the process of learning, the mentor becomes more aware of the mentoree's needs in various facets of life such as ministry, family, community and self.

How the mentor as teacher views the teacher-student roles can either assist or hinder the student in the learning process. McKeachie has delineated a number of ways a teacher can look at his or her role. Notice that many of these indicate the role as relative rather than absolute.

☐ *Expert-neophyte.* As an expert, the teacher is to transmit information—the concept and perspectives of the field or subject—while recognizing areas of inadequate expertise.

☐ *Formal authority-subject.* As a formal authority, the teacher is to set goals and procedures for reaching goals, and as a subject, the teacher is to be open to students' suggestions where appropriate.

☐ *Socializing agent-socialized agent.* As a socializing agent, the teacher is to clarify goals and options beyond the class or course and to prepare students for these. As a socialized agent, the teacher is to be open to the suggestions and influence of students and others within and beyond the teaching setting.

☐ *Facilitator-self-teacher.* As a facilitator, the teacher is to promote creativity and growth in the students' own terms and help them overcome obstacles to learning. The teacher is to be sensitive to his or her own creativity and growth.

☐ *Ego ideal-ego in process.* As ego ideal, the teacher is to convey the excitement and value of educational inquiry in given areas and recognize areas where ideals and practices are lacking.

☐ *Person-person.* As a person the teacher is to convey the full range of human needs and skills relevant to and sustained by one's education activity, to be validated as a human being and to validate the students as persons (McKeachie 1978:81-82).

Intellectual training can utilize two approaches, informal-local and formal. The first consists primarily of teaching students informally in their community. The second, the formal, is an institutional approach involving seminaries or Bible schools. The informal-local approach can take place in a home or church in a weekly two- or three-hour block of time. For example, a two-hour Sunday-school class can be used for leadership training. Informal does not mean structureless. The two-hour class should be well structured, and the participants should be serious about the training and sharing. The teaching could revolve around case studies written by the leaders or by the pastor or missionary. These case studies should reflect common situations in the local community. Mentor and mentorees discuss the biblical and pastoral implications of each case study. Or the mentor can assign each young leader to present a ministry issue they are facing or a theological theme with which they are wrestling, and the group can discuss it together.

The formal approach to training is more difficult for urban indigenous leaders. A nearby seminary may be able to provide courses that will help students do theology in an urban context. In order for this to be viable and valuable, classes should be taught in the community and the courses contextually adapted.

Unfortunately many religious institutions lack the ability to contextualize the content and be sensitive to the culture. And some seminaries have a banking concept of education which just provides information in lectures. Instruction is deposited in students as money is deposited in a bank. It is one-way, and the content is often detached from the real world of the student (Freire 1989:57). Narration (with the teacher as narrator) leads the students to memorize mechanically the narrated content. Worse yet, it turns them into containers, into receptacles to be filled by the teacher. With this model, the more completely they fill the receptacles, the better the teachers are. The more meekly the receptacles permit themselves to be filled, the better the students are (Freire 1989:58). As we have said before, this model not only is pedagogically unsound; it also is especially ill-suited to training urban leaders.

**Observing others.** Many of our community leaders have an island mentality—that is, they confine their focus and experience to a given geographic area. Many will never leave their immediate community boundaries during their lifetime. In ministry this mentality limits the exposure of young leaders to new experiences and resources for growth. It also omits the global picture of missions.

Leaders need multiethnic, multicultural, domestic and foreign experiences in order to evaluate different approaches to ministry from outside the community. They should take field trips both within the city and out of state to observe how others are doing ministry. They should interact with those they visit, with one another and with their pastors, comparing and evaluating how ministry is accomplished in different contexts. And occasional trips outside the United States will give them a fuller understanding of global mission. Every experience, every discussion, becomes a learning event.

**Sending.** This aspect of developing emerging leaders allows them to begin a ministry apart from the mentor without being completely independent of him or her. New leaders learn to seek and share with the mentor for their own growth and development. They are neither dependent nor fully independent but rather interdependent. At this juncture emerging leaders must face the responsibility of finding and using their own ministry resources. Roland Allen describes how this process must have occurred in the Bible:

> With the appointment of elders the churches were complete. They were fully equipped. They very soon became familiar with all the orders of ministry both permanent and charismatic. They no longer depended necessarily upon St Paul. If he went away, or if he died, the churches remained. They grew in numbers and in grace: they were centers of spiritual light by which the darkness of surrounding heathenism was gradually dispelled. In Galatia "the churches were strengthened in the faith and increased in number daily." From Thessalonica "the word of the Lord sounded out" in Macedonia and Achaia. From Ephesus the Gospel spread throughout all the neighboring country so that many churches sprang up, the members of which had never seen St Paul's face, and he himself could write to the Romans that he had "no more place in those regions."
>
> They were no longer dependent upon the Apostle, but they were not independent of him. (Allen 1960:111)

Meetings with the emerging leaders should be scheduled and organized. A commitment to meeting is important and should be expected. This will help them work into ministry gradually. There is a wide gap between dependent and independent ministry. Things that were done before under supervision and were accomplished with confidence and joy now have become extremely difficult. The emerging leaders' confidence may be shaken and their joy inconsistent. During this time the mentor reviews preaching and teaching messages and interacts on all levels of ministry. Most important, the mentor provides support. As the new leaders' confidence builds, the mentor's role shifts to become primarily a resource who is called upon when needed. Meetings are less frequent and voluntary. And on occasion, the mentor may even call the new leader for resources.

## The Mentoring Process, Level Three: Examination

The final level of mentoring is the examination of the mentoree. This is one of the most difficult aspects of the mentoring process because it has to do with shifting the authority on to the mentoree. The mentoree initiates and requests evaluation and assistance. This shift tests the mentoree on how much he or she has learned teamwork, trusting other leaders and submission. The mentoree gives approval for the mentor to examine the mentoree's life and ministry. In the case of a youth worker who has been mentored, the mentoree is now asking for evaluation on how he or she has presented the message to a junior high group. Was the message biblical? Was it contextually appropriate?

Mentoring may continue even as the relationship, due to relocation, finds itself geographically distant. Here the phone or letters are used for advice, encouragement and other points of interaction. The process has changed but there is still value to continuing. This was true of a pastor who trained men and women and after a number of years left to take on other responsibilities. The process was to use the telephone on a particular evening in the week to review the content of the message for Sunday morning and to talk about other matters pertaining to ministry. This process continued for an additional two years and was a great encouragement to the new pastor in ministry. Mentoring is time consuming, as was previously mentioned, and the commitment is for longer periods. The advantage of this approach is that the mentoree will also have learned a valuable tool in mentoring others.

Evaluations are intended to develop and encourage each other. This has to do with the shifting of authority and also the commitment to pursue maturity in life and ministry. In some ways it is a mutual aspect of evaluation. Evaluation often lends to a superior-subordinate relationship. One evaluates the performance of the other and provides a helpful critique. Evaluation in the mentoring process is done by both mentor and mentoree. It is a time of self evaluation which is always part of the process of mentoring. Our lives and ministry are valuable and therefore worthy of evaluation. The goal of evaluation must be established from the beginning because it is an ongoing process.

Evaluation happens at every stage of the process. This is done through debriefing, reflection and informal conversations. The outcome of evaluation is change. It may be a change of attitude, an awareness of different perspectives or an adjustment in method, theology or strategy. The evaluation is a key tension dynamic that allows for life and ministry transformation.

In conclusion, it is important to note that mentoring is an art. It is something that the mentor enjoys and finds great reward in doing. Therefore, the mentor perfects the process. This does not mean that the mentor overwhelms the process with organizational aspects but rather develops in areas that have been flaws in previous or ongoing relationships.

Not everyone is able to be a mentor. Mentoring demands a driving heart to see others emerge into the leadership role. The mentor receives great joy at seeing others develop and even move beyond the mentor's abilities. Yes, it does involve patience, flexibility and tolerance, but the major force behind mentoring is the joy of seeing others grow in God's grace.

# 24

## Equipping the Laity
## for Urban Ministry

IN THE LAST FEW CHAPTERS WE HAVE STRESSED the importance of training leaders for urban ministry, and we have examined that process in detail. In this final chapter we turn our attention from leadership to laity. Another strategic approach to effective urban ministry consists of mobilizing and equipping an urban church's entire membership for outreach to its own city context. Involving laypeople in community outreach has proven a powerful influence on cities ever since the church of Jesus Christ began.

Roland Allen speaks of mobilization of the laity for urban ministry as the

> expansion which follows the unexhorted and unorganized activity of individual members of the Church explaining to others the Gospel which they have found for themselves; I mean the expansion which follows the irresistible attraction of the Christian Church for men who see its ordered life, and are drawn to it by desire to discover the secret of a life which they instinctively desire to share; I mean also the expansion of the Church by the addition of new churches. (Allen 1962:7)

Laity mobilization must be a high priority of the church if it is to be stable and dynamic in this age of despair and instability.

"At no time in history has it been more true than now that he who wins the city, wins the world," Roger Greenway once noted (Greenway

1978:11). We believe that only a strong lay movement will enable us to reach the cities throughout the world with the gospel of Jesus Christ. For the world to be reached, the cities must establish a high priority in their vision for evangelism and church planting. This will involve intensive training and mobilization.

As we consider mobilizing laity for urban ministry, we do not mean to imply that leadership and laity are two distinct categories. In fact, as we have said before, viewing lay members of a church as members of the ministry team alongside clergy is both appropriate and healthy. Inasmuch as the leadership training described in the last three chapters can be applied to lay leaders as well as to clergy or future clergy, we should expect a great deal of overlap between those chapters and the current discussion. The distinction only represents a difference in focus.

## Obstacles to Urban Church Outreach

Ignorance of the need for training a city church for city ministry, fear or selfishness, common misperceptions about the nature of church ministry and the extent of Christ's kingdom, and the realities of the urban context—these factors have often thwarted church community outreach. It may sound outrageous to suggest, first of all, that a church in the city might not have the skills to reach its neighborhood. But the fact is that very often they are unprepared. For example, the church may consist of second-generation Christians who did not participate in the early stages of the ministry in their church. The church in its initial stage had to walk the streets and depend on community resources for its establishment and growth. Many of its present leaders came from the community. But now that the church is established and the community has undergone several transitions, very little is being done in the community. Its members have lost their commitment to and skills for working with people in the neighborhood. They also lack confidence in their resources and ability to serve in the urban setting, even though they may understand that ministry in the community is vital for the continued life and growth of the church. This shortcoming of the church may promote an avoidance of the community and an ultimate decision to relocate. Feeling ill-equipped for ministry to the neighborhood may be the reason why many churches leave the city.

Many churches do not identify with a community. They perceive no concrete points of contact that they might use as bridges to ministry. This has resulted from the stark inevitability of a continually changing culture in the city. In order to understand its need for equipping, a church must see how seriously we must take any contextual factors when we plan outreach.

The congregation may be convicted that the community in which the building is located needs to be the context for service, but for various reasons they find it very difficult to be motivated to serve there. One reason is that most of the members no longer live near the community and have lost touch with the people. Another reason has to do with the class struggle. Even though the church members may have the same ethnic makeup as the community, there could be a gap between the socioeconomic status of those in the church and those in the community. Also, fear reigns in the hearts of the congregants. The community has deteriorated socially and spiritually, and now it seems unmanageable and something to be feared and avoided.

In a poor *favelado* on the outskirts of Rio de Janeiro, for example, the masses of impoverished peasants are increasing daily. The established Roman Catholic Church is more interested in siding with the status quo than in addressing the issues of the poor. There are very few Protestant churches, but they too are becoming institutionalized and are not interested in confronting the issues. As a traditionally religious people with a history of grassroots involvement, these masses are looking for an alternative that will impact reality as they know it.

Misperceptions concerning the nature of the church and its mission also thwart community outreach. The contemporary church, different from the early church to some degree, prepares God's people for a personal and private relationship to Christ. The educational program of the twentieth century church often prepares the congregation for personal piety and, in one sense, ingrownness. The church seeks the truth not to use it but to affirm its position in truth. But the church becomes ingrown if its approach to Scripture is to know truth apart from doing. The church has separated the possibility of knowing the Word of God from obedience. Neil Braun notes:

> The *laos* of God is called to ministry. The word "ministry" in English has come to refer to clergymen or to their work, but in the New Testament *diakonia* (ministry) is not the function of one class. It is the role to which all believers are called. . . . All members of the church, says Kraemer, the laity not less than the clergy, are to proclaim the "new reality in Christ, to manifest the hope of the world now set forth in Christ." (Braun 1971:105)

But instead what is happening is that there is an attitude that prevails within the laity that they are only in the church to be cared for. They chose a particular church based on whether it could provide for all their needs. C. John Miller speaks to this concern.

> The local church was intended by Jesus to be a gathering of people full of faith—strong in their confidence in him—not a gathering of religious folk

who desperately need reassurance. Perhaps seeking personal comfort is not wrong in itself. But it is desperately wrong when it becomes the primary reason for the existence of the local church. When that happens, the local church is no living fellowship at all, but a retreat center where anxious people draw resources that enable them merely to *cope* with the pains of life. The church then becomes a religious cushion. (Miller 1986:20)

While these obstacles of ignorance, selfishness, fear and contextual change need to be taken seriously, only if a church also denies the Lord's call to surmount such obstacles for the sake of spreading his kingdom will the obstacles successfully prevent community outreach. It can, instead, happen this way. A church in the inner city of Pittsburgh had gone through an ethnic and generational transition. The people remaining in the congregation were middle-aged to elderly. The congregation reviewed its options. One possibility was to move out of the area and begin a new church in a suburban community. Another was to call in a pastor who was urban wise and had a vision for the inner city. This pastor would develop a new congregation while the existing church would make plans for an easy transition to another community. The new pastor would do most of the direct ministry, and the existing members would be passive recognizing that they would not be part of that church. Another suggestion was made to bring in an experienced urban pastor to assist them in reaching the community and building a new church together. After periods of prayer and sharing, the church took on this challenge. They were willing to stay in the community (many still lived in the area) and get the necessary training for developing their church in the community where there were still many who had never heard the gospel. It is important that we see that the Lord intends to use all believers to reach their own communities.

**Laity Mobilization in New Testament Times**
The New Testament indicates that God used the laity, the people of God, in the initial stages of the church's ministry. In Acts we notice the movement of the Holy Spirit in establishing local congregations. "It was the scattered Christians of Cyprus and Cyrene, he asserted, who founded the church destined to spearhead missionary work to the Gentiles (Acts 11:20). Such churches as those in Laodicea, Colossae, and Hierpolis were the result of the efforts of laymen, not of the apostles" (Braun 1971:135). One such congregation was the one in Jerusalem that witnessed the severe persecution of Stephen (Acts 8:1). This led to a displacement of God's people into other regions (Acts 11:19). Some landed in Antioch.

Antioch was a large city that became the "third largest city in the Roman Empire and a major center of cultural and economic exchange"

(Kee 1997:147). In the process of relocation they shared the gospel first to the Jews, and then some broke rank and shared the good news with Greeks also (Acts 11:20). The need for leadership was evident when Barnabas was sent to them and, in turn, Saul was solicited to come and join the mission of preparing the church to continue the work of Christ in Antioch (Acts 11:25-26).

Not only was there a need for gifted and mature leaders, there was also an awareness of the accomplishments of God's people who carried on the task started by the Holy Spirit. When God's people were driven by the realization of the death and resurrection of Christ as well as the joy of being stewards of the message that transforms lives, there was kingdom expansion. Here, in Luke's account, the disciples were first called Christians (Acts 11:26), Christ's adherents or servants. "Evidently their sources were sufficiently good for them to recognize that this Jewish sect was characterized by its belief in Jesus the Christ and by living out lives in the name of this Christ. It was natural that they should be referred to, then, as the Christ-ones, 'Christians' " (Dunn 1996:156).

The gifts are distributed for the purpose of displaying kingdom power and kingdom abilities (Eph 4:11-13 ). It is the utilization of the gifts in the power of the Holy Spirit that corrects the sin curve of Genesis 3:8-19. It is a comprehensive, holistic straightening out and restoring of life and community. The gifts are used for character change, and the more we are like Christ, the more renewal and restoration occurs.

## Laity Mobilization Today

Actually, today there are more and more churches following this biblical pattern by training their people to reproduce the church in the city and equipping their members to become the major force in this move. This is what happens when a church directly takes on the challenge of urban mission and finds that the responsibility for the growth of the church and the reproduction of the church depends on the total body of Christ.

Deliverance Evangelistic Church in Philadelphia is such a ministry. This church is alert and has over one hundred ministries in which its members can get involved. Church planting ministries occur as members and leaders are groomed in the Deliverance Bible Institute to be equipped for service in their communities.

A Nazarene church in the mid-Wilshire area of Los Angeles stayed through the waves of ethnic changes to their community and began to build a growing multiethnic church. The church was led by a pastor who understood the need to claim a context for ministry and have a laity that was trained for ministry. For many years the leadership conducted a training institution for the preparation of urban church workers.

Comunidades Eclesial de Bases (CEBs) have been started as part of the Roman Catholic Church throughout Latin America by pastoral agents who can be "seminarians, nuns, or lay people. . . . CEBs [are] Catholic groups of poor [lay] people that attempt, through meditation and prayer, to foster a view of religion that is socially and politically engaged" (Mariz 1994:17).

If we look at other settings, such as a nonurban context outside of the United States, we can find remarkable testimonies about laity movements that bring encouragement to the church universal.

> During the years 1945 to 1962, a remarkable case of expansion took place in central Nigeria (Grimley and Robinson 1966:138-57). In 1945 a Church of the Brethren congregation established some years before in a village called Lassa, besides the Yedseram River, had eighty-eight members scattered across several villages. Under the blessing of God the Lassa congregation began to grow. In 1951 it was able to foster the birth of a new church in nearby Gulak, giving up thirty-five of its members in order to do so . . . besides engaging in many other evangelistic and church planting endeavors. The 88 members of 1945 had grown to 4,619 by 1963, twice that many persons related to the churches (Grimley Robinson 1966:138-57). In such ways is the will of Christ still being carried out in some areas of the world. (Braun 1971:20)

This example is not in an urban setting, but it shows what the church can accomplish when the laity are mobilized.

In the United States the Bear Valley Baptist Church in Denver grew due to its pastor's emphasis on the unleashing of the congregation to do the work of the ministry. Vernon Grounds says about the pastor of the church, "His message . . . is clear and simple: unleash the church! Forget about bringing people in. Focus on getting God's people out where there are sin and pain and need" (Grounds 1982:5).

The question with which we are challenged in this chapter has to do with the preparation of laity for urban ministry in the local church. First, we highlight the importance of leadership being committed to mobilization and fostering a vision which includes the laity in urban ministry. Next we look into how the needs of the church and community must be matched with the gifts of God's people in order to have effective ministry. Once gifts and needs have been identified we suggest ways in which a church can equip its laity. Finally we bring a warning as to what can hinder this process.

### Leadership Committed to Mobilization

Equipping the laity for urban ministry begins with the vision of the pastor and the leadership. The leadership of the church must have a commitment to mobilize the church for worship, the Word and mission to world. "There can be no question that if the churches are to move into an era of church multiplication based primarily upon lay evangelism, the training of the laity must be assigned high priority" (Braun 1971:140). It is the church's leadership which must cultivate the sense that laity mobilization is a high priority.

The pastor's leadership and vision is key. John Mott reminds us:

> The secret of enabling the home church to press her advantage in the non-Christian world is one of leadership. The people do not go beyond their leaders in knowledge and zeal, nor surpass them in consecration and sacrifice. The Christian pastor, minister, rector—whatever may be denominationed—holds the divinely appointed office for inspiring and guiding the thought and activities of the church. By virtue of his position, he can be a mighty force in the world's evangelization. (1998:21)

Leadership that follows the instructions of the Bible brings the church to maturity and to service.

In the city, as in other places, the vision for renewal always has to be in the mind and heart of the leadership. Leaders must have a vision that promotes the eschatological view of the city that there will be a new city (Rev 21:1—22:5) and that we are moving toward that end. They must see the city as a city formed by God for God. It is as the city should be. Robert Linthicum notes, "One of the most unique aspects of the book of Revelation is the detail with which it describes the quality of life in the new Jerusalem. I believe it is described in such detail to give us hope as we in urban ministry seek to be faithful, though we are often overwhelmed" (Linthicum 1991a:286). The vision for the city lies at the hands of the pastor and leaders.

The most obvious obstacle to equipping the laity for urban ministry has to do with the leadership of the pastor. The problem lies not so much in the congregation as in the leadership. Frank Tillapaugh notes, "The biggest obstacle to unleashing the church is not rural psyches, entrenched lay-power structures, lazy, unmotivated people or small facilities. It is the senior pastor" (Tillapaugh 1982:102). If leaders are the ones who must initiate this process, it must be clear and convincing to them that the church must be motivated and equipped for the ministry. The biblical pattern calls leaders to equip the saints for work of the ministry (Eph 4:12-13). The ministry is done by the church and not by a select group alone.

The pastor's personality and his view of utilizing the laity can actually hinder or thwart urban ministry. "The pastor's personality also can inhibit the use of lay people as caregivers, even though the overworked pastor gains from their involvement. Often the qualities that attract people to the ministry and make them effective are the very ones that get in their way of sharing this ministry" (Detwiler-Zapp and Dixon 1982:9). The pastor may be one who seeks the reward of the congregation and therefore does not want to share the ministry. Being needed and rewarded for service is one of the joys of ministry. This attitude will greatly hinder the development and use of the congregation.

A pastor may also hinder laity mobilization simply because of their own inexperience. Many pastors are never trained in training others or mobilizing other Christians for service. Their skills are inadequate and thus limit the church's growth in body life.

Leaders must understand that for the church to be in renewal and growing, it must be equipped for change, for meeting the new challenges and the ever changing context of the church and surrounding communities. An urban church does not have to be motivated by the urgency of its own membership's growth versus decline; the church should be equipped for high impact on community, neighborhood and city. With leadership in place and giving direction to the church, the following elements assist the equipping of the laity for urban ministry.

### Fitting the Needs with God's People

Equipping the laity for urban ministry begins when members ask the question, "For what am I being prepared?" The question is best answered both biblically in terms of gifts and the purpose of the church and also in light of the needs of a church's particular community. A survey of both the church and the community that reveals members' gifts and community needs thus precipitates the move towards equipping Christians for specific ministry.

***Uncover the community's needs.*** Through an analysis of the church and community we discover the reason why we are being prepared. It is important to take notice of what is going on in the community. The demographic material in chapter sixteen will be useful in enabling a church to assess concretely the needs of its community. It does not always need a formal investigation, but members of the church should keep their eyes alert to what is happening in their community. They can discover a great deal this way and can provide webs into the community for ministry.

The mistake churches often make is one of ignorance of the needs. We encourage people to get involved and be committed to service, but there is no clear direction for ministry. Basically they do not know what they are to do. "We are not sure why we are being equipped," they say. Tilla-

paugh says that too often the people are frustrated because there is training but no outlet for their potential (1982:17).

Knowing the needs of the church and the community in concrete ways
helps to empower people. They have to know that a need exists, what it is
and how they will be used to meet that need. Ministry opportunities must
be presented.

**Uncover the church members' gifts.** Discovering the needs of the
community is not enough to have a ministry. The church must then fit
those needs with the people God has given them. This requires knowing
the gifts and personalities God has provided for that particular church as
embodied in its members.

In the 1970s the U.S. church began to take seriously the idea that each
member of a church is given unique spiritual gifts that he or she should
be contributing to body life. The body life concept, practiced in Peninsula
Bible Church in Palo Alto, California, by Pastor Ray Stedman, gradually
took hold. This movement did much to mobilize and train the laity. The
essence of this movement was to have the church, to its fullest membership capacity, involved in ministering to each other and to the community. While it is possible to apply this claim about spiritual gifts too rigidly,
the principle is definitely biblical.

We believe that the Lord has provided the essential gifts for the church
in community to do the necessary work of the ministry. The gifts are
divinely distributed (1 Cor 12:7; Eph 4; 1 Pet 4:10) to all Christians at the
time of regeneration. All Christians have a duty to exercise their gifts (1
Pet 4:10).

In Ephesians 4:16 (cf. 1:22) it is clear that the ministerial power of
Christ is delegated to the church in the form of spiritual gifts. This is the
continuing work of Christ in the world. This enablement of the church is
for service. Therefore, there is a plan for the church to be equipped to
minister in its particular context. When the church utilizes the power of
God in community, more and more people come under the lordship of
Christ. The result of this is that the church grows qualitatively and quantitatively.

The difficulty in many urban churches is that they believe they must
hire professional staff in order for the church to grow and function efficiently. Unfortunately, hiring professionals actually truncates the opti-
mum use of all members in the church. It promotes a specialized,
consumer approach to ministry. The urban church, therefore, should not
have as a priority the recruitment of specialized staff from outside the
community. They should first patiently examine and develop what is
already available and incorporate people from the community as they

respond to the gospel and become growing and mature Christians.

Gifts are discovered in the context of need both in the church and in the community. Knowing the needs begins the process for ministry and gift discovery. Many of the people in the church find that as they serve there is an increasing desire to do more and even improve their gifts through training. They do not find or sort out their gifts first and then decide to serve but rather they find high energy results in the milieu of ministry when they are being obedient to the Lord in the exercise of their gifts.

An example of this is a church that realized that some of the children in the surrounding community could not read and did not have social outlets. The church saw that they could use their Sunday School to meet the needs of the children in the community holistically. They could be motivated to learn to read and meet new friends. The task was enormous, but it was worth undertaking because it provided access to the community.

This church, having seen the need and envisioned the solution, sought laypeople to carry it through. Was there a person who could give this ministry leadership? The need was mentioned at a prayer meeting and in the small groups during the week. A public school teacher from the community, who had been a member in the church for some time, was convicted and offered her assistance.

But she realized she needed to learn how to communicate the gospel to children. She also recognized that there is a difference between secular and Christian education. With her own need in mind, she developed a teacher training class for Sunday School teachers to train them in evangelism and Christian education. Since the teachers had long been bewildered as to how to keep their children involved, the new training classes promoted stability and growth in their Sunday School.

Another challenge arose when a number of people from the church who lived in the community observed that there were many senior citizens on their block. A young man at a church fellowship began to share how there seemed to be no resources for the elderly in the community. A few people at his table began to talk and pray about what might be helpful. They talked with the deacons, and a team was assigned to follow up on some of the needs of the elderly.

The team conducted a survey in the community. It indicated that there were high numbers of senior citizens with multiple needs. One pressing need was to be able to get out of the house during the week and find some means of social activity. The team decided to use the church facility for a gathering place, providing snacks and refreshments for elderly people who would come. This led to many other avenues for ministry and relationship building. The ministry to the elderly grew, and some began to attend the Sunday service.

In a Brazilian *favelado*, the poor were being exploited. They had no voice and had accepted a fatalistic view of life that said they must just make the best of things. They did not see that God was opposed to injustice and oppression. Giving these people hope for a changed existence became part of the driving force behind the establishment of CEBs, as believers assessed both their own gifts and the concrete needs of their community.

The fascinating aspect of this delegation of gifts and the uniqueness of the people is that the Lord has provided the church in the city with all it needs for kingdom ministry. It is for the church to gather God's people and equip them for service. We have discovered that in the inner city church the Lord has made a way to contextualize the gospel by providing the necessary people resources. The people are suited for the context. They may not fit well into another context, such as that of a rural community, but they are effective in their particular urban environment. The urban context may have to emphasize ministries of compassion, cross-cultural sensitivity, deep expressions of mercy and patience. This should prompt us to consider that the church needs to be incarnational, gathering and utilizing the people of God in that community and city. This will assist the church to grow and effectively contextualize the gospel in that setting.

Utilizing those whom God has already provided in the church as well as developing those who are coming to a saving knowledge of Christ means a church must have a strategy for comprehensive training and the development of their gifts and skills. This would be true in such matters as evangelism, hospitality and helping people through crises. Some of this thinking has been assisted by Tim Keller (1989).

We saw when we talked about the important role a pastor's leadership plays in laity mobilization that a pastor can also hinder that mobilization. The same is true of the congregation: it plays an important role in mobilization for urban ministry, but it can also hinder it. Many churches are formed in such a manner that they hire the professional to do the work of the ministry. The pastor does it all. There is a definite consumer mentality in the church. The members have come to see what they can get out of the church—what the benefits of the church are and its ministry—rather than asking what they could do to serve and be productive. This approach leads to overworked leadership and eventual burnout as well as an underdeveloped and immature laity.

The congregation's time constraints can also be a hindrance. Few members have time for an additional night or activity. Ministry demands time, and time has become a commodity that will not easily be relinquished. At the present at least a part of two days are used for participation in the life of the church—Sunday for worship and Wednesday night (or some other evening) for small groups. Any additional time becomes problematic to the point that people feel more like part of the staff or leadership than the laity. This means that they view any serious engagement in ministry as unusual and the responsibility of a high caliber of leader. In the North American church, many people think of any member who is involved in actual hands-on ministry as an exceptional Christian. This outlook can hinder community outreach.

With each of these misconceptions, as with any sin, we must look to the Spirit and to the proclamation of the Word of God to reshape hearts. Here the pastor can be God's instrument, as can church members who model ministry.

### Releasing the People and Power

Another important feature of equipping laity for urban ministry is their training and spiritual oversight. The elders of the church must see to it that individual members receive training in the use of their gifts. They must also oversee all the ministries of the church because God holds them accountable as elders for the church's life and ministry. The church should not use an irresponsible, spontaneous approach to utilizing the gifts of its people where the church goes ahead and activates the gifts without oversight and mentoring.

*Elder oversight.* Oversight of the elders allows for individuals to be confirmed in the direction they are going. The objective affirmation by the elders is of utmost importance. This affirms the ministry Christians are doing in the name of Christ. It also corrects and forms ongoing activities and the aspirations an individual may have for a particular ministry. Coordination of ministries places people in the most appropriate place for service on the basis of maturity, gifts and skills.

There should be a warning here. Churches are prone to be too pragmatic at this juncture and ignore spiritual qualifications and prayer for God's direction. This has often led to a misuse of gifts and skills.

If church members sense that they receive little supervision in their tasks, they can become frustrated and withdraw their involvement. Supervisors can help promote a positive learning experience.

Supervision does not mean superiority but alludes to the pastor's perspective as one who has an "overseeing" vantage point. As a supervisor, the pastor is responsible for keeping an eye on the whole and for seeing separate events and interactions as a part of the ongoing learning process. By keeping track of individual threads, the supervisor may begin to see emerging patterns and offer learners a broader view. (Detwiler-Zapp and Dixon 1982:64).

Too often members are left to fare for themselves with very little evaluation or coaching. This shortcoming promotes frustrated laity who will soon resign from serving due to their bad experience and will probably never volunteer again. On the positive side, however, carefully exercised spiritual oversight should greatly encourage lay ministry.

*Training for ministry.* Also, it is wise to mentor people in the use of their particular gifts as part of the training component. Mentoring assists the growth of the individual but also provides accountability. Churches should keep in mind that there are areas of ministry in which all Christians should be involved, such as giving, teaching and evangelism, and that training should also be provided for those areas of service. Here is a key point of intersection between our focus in this chapter and the concept of mentoring presented in earlier chapters.

For example, a person who has matured in matters of hospitality will be of great benefit to those desiring to serve in that capacity. A teacher in the church may provide great insight to other teachers. This is also true of the gifted evangelist, the administrator and so on.

There are numerous avenues which a church can utilize to bring about the training necessary for responsible use of the gifts. We will discuss several of these—the Bible institute, small groups, church ministries, adult Sunday school and the work place.

*A lay Bible institute.* The institute provides for both the application of the biblical content and a greater insight into Scriptures. The use of Scripture and how to interpret the Bible becomes part of the learning. Pastors and elders as well as other mature Christians do the teaching. Many churches establish an institute for biblical studies and ministry in order to develop the laity and emerging leaders. The training equips them for ministry in their local church.

In Latin America training for laity is essential and has always received high priority. The whole church is involved in ministry, and churches are planted by laity as well as pastors and emerging leaders. This is true with the Catholic CEBs as well as with grassroots Protestant churches. This is also true in many of the Hispanic communities in the city in the United States. Part of the success in Latin America was intensive training for all believers (Braun 1971:141). In this intensive training Christians were equipped in matters of church life and polity as well as Christian living and evangelism (Braun 1971:141). The Bible institute is the way many urban churches equip laity since they often do not see seminary or Bible college as an option. This form of equipping produces a great deal of mobilization.

However, in order for a Bible institute to offer a valuable means of training for urban ministry, its content must undergo serious evaluation. Most of the education that is provided in local churches today is primarily transmissional. It provides biblical information for the purpose of conforming the church to be unified in doctrine. The church needs to be more transformational and mission oriented. If you notice how curricula are chosen for the church and how the teachers are selected, you will realize that not much thought has been given to mobilizing the Christian for ministry. Rather, the educational process is primarily for clarification and information. A revised approach is necessary to equip the church to be fully active in God's service.

*Small groups.* Small groups in the community of the church present a good place to begin and to continue the process of training. In the home meetings of the church the opportunity for service becomes tangible. It is in the small group that members become involved with the needs of the community as people share their concerns.

For example, when a mother comes to a group and begins to share about her needs concerning her husband who is facing a court hearing, the members of the small group begin to pray and some offer assistance on where she could possibly find legal help. Others go to be with her as they share compassion and hospitality during this time of difficulty. In this type of process the small group learns to network, pray fervently and become supporters. The Bible is active as Christians counsel and share their possessions.

Another example is when a wife informs the group she is losing her husband to AIDS. The church visits the husband and provides food and support for the family. There are numerous financial needs and generosity is displayed by the members of the group who, when the time comes, absorb the expenses of the funeral.

Then there is the husband in need of assistance as his wife undergoes cancer treatment. The group members provide food for the family on a daily basis. The church is totally involved. The church is both active and learning how to serve.

In Latin America the CEBs are small groups that mobilize their members with a specific focus in mind—to confront and change the oppressive conditions in which they find themselves. Although it is true that the CEBs grew out of Catholicism, Guillermo Cook (1985) points out that Protestants would do well to learn from their example. Cook reports that CEBs throughout Latin America share four fundamental orientations: "(1) a new way of seeing reality, (2) a new way of being a church, (3) a new way of approaching Scripture, and (4) a new way of doing mission" (1985:89). All of these encompass the necessity of mobilizing the lay membership to participate at all levels of the ministry.

Cook reports that there were an estimated 150,000 CEBs in Latin America in 1979, over half of which were located in Brazil. CEBs have grown out of a sociological milieu characterized by "poverty and marginalization, as well as socio-economic and political dependence" (p. 14). They began in rural areas, but "*comunidades*, although fewer in number in large cities than in rural areas, are an attempt to provide the necessary ideological 'space' for a revitalized and more relevant Catholic religiosity" (Cook 1985:53). These alternatives to traditional Catholic forms "forced Catholic activists back to Scripture and to their own tradition in search of theological foundations and a liberating spirituality. Their Christian commitment, and not a political program per se, impelled them to identify with the struggles of the poor" (Cook 1985:76). Both the liturgy of the Word and the Eucharist are opened up "to the full participation of the entire community with active lay involvement" (Cook 1985:82) thus reinforcing the community aspect of the CEBs. These churches are growing, and they're growing through lay ministry. We agree with Cook that the Protestant churches can learn a great deal from the CEBs.

Gifts become more obvious as the people of God function. Small groups allow for a certain amount of freedom to serve. There is less concern about being successful and more concern about serving in the name of Christ. Many members take their first step toward service. Both the equipping and mobilization are taking place simultaneously.

*Adult Sunday school.* Sunday school can be a very effective time for the equipping of laity intending to serve. It is also a time when a high percentage of committed members are available. Sunday school should do more specifically to equip the congregation in areas of ministry. What are the needs of the congregation in the city, and how can we equip the church to do that ministry?

Sunday schools have had traditional goals and aims that need evaluation. Classes normally are provided with a study of a biblical theme or book in the Bible. There is application of the text, but very often the application is individual and personal, and not necessarily geared to the church and doing ministry. As a result, the kind of teaching necessary to train laypeople for ministry is often left to another night of the week, placing a time stress on members of the church.

Adult classes should be specifically equipping the church for the work of the ministry. Sunday school curriculum should be determined by the needs of the church and the community and the equipping needs of the laity. This does not ignore biblical data but rather provides the biblical data in the context of the church's mission. Sunday school is a time to enhance the congregation's understanding of how God intends to use his people in this world and how Scripture is applied specifically to particular situations.

An example of this is to have a class on mercy ministry that lays out the biblical instruction with an end of applying the Word to a particular ministry in the church. Recently a church did a class on prayer. Commonly a Sunday school class on prayer is given for the sake of knowing how Jesus prayed and how we must pray as Christians. However, this church provided the biblical content for prayer and showed how prayer is a ministry of the church and how it can be utilized. The class met to study, and this led to a prayer ministry of the church where fifteen people were used by the church to pray for others and to use prayer for reaching out to the community. When there is a need in the community, members of this prayer team go out to pray for the family. This does not exclude the work of the elders pertaining to prayer, but it allows for the mobilization of the church toward a prayer ministry.

Hospitality is rarely a subject discussed but is often something the members of the church want to get involved with. A Sunday school prepared curriculum material that would help students be more effective in their ministry of hospitality. The elders who were emerging from the congregation needed preparation, so a class was formed to help them see the biblical requirements of elders and how elders should function.

Using the Word of God for all of life and service encourages the church. Sunday school offers a key venue for training laity for ministry.

*Church ministries.* The church also needs to utilize all the members already involved in its programs. A new Christian feels awkward in doing anything that may need expanded biblical knowledge, but cooking and serving food is something that is safe and will introduce the individual to the compassion of the Lord and to the process of serving and being involved as a joy and responsibility.

The church has a GED program and teachers are needed for special subjects in the evening. Here people are sharing and teachers are becoming aware of the needs of the people in the community. A homeless ministry provides food for those living on the streets during the cold months of the year.

*The work place.* One of the most difficult tasks for the church is how to balance work and ministry. The opportunities for service in the marketplace are numerous. The major problem is that Christians tend to separate life into compartments. This is the compartment for the religious or spiritual, and this is the one for the social. In one way or another the church teaches that one has nothing to do with the other. In learning the importance of calling, the people of God begin to grasp an understanding of the sovereignty of God. The Christian professional, such as a medical doctor, senses the calling of God to serve in his or her professional capacity. All work is ministry. All work is part of the kingdom vocation, whether it is church, family, work or society.

In this chapter we have recognized three important ingredients necessary to mobilizing the laypeople of an urban church to reach out to their own community. These three are the pastor's vision for that outreach, the church's effort to ascertain and match the needs of the community and the specific Spirit-given gifts of its members, and the elders' faithfulness to train people for the task and to exercise spiritual oversight of the people as they engage in ministry. Even as we have noted common obstacles to laity mobilization, we have also seen it modeled in the early church, and we have taken to heart several accounts of churches carrying it out today. Mobilizing church members to reach their own community enables a church to bridge the contextual gap naturally, the very thing that must be done if we are to carry forward the urgent business of reaching urban communities for Christ.

# Works Cited

Abu-Lughod, Janet
    1971    *Cairo:1001 Years of the City Victorious.* Princeton: Princeton University Press.
    1987    "The Islamic City: Historic Myth, Islamic Essence, and Contemporary Relevance." *International Journal of Middle East Studies* 19:155-76.
    1991    *Changing Cities.* New York: Harper/Collins.

Adams, Anna
    1997    "Brincando el Charco/Jumping the Puddle: A Case Study of Pentecostalism's Journey from Puerto Rico to New York to Allentown, Pennsylvania." In *Power, Politics and Pentecostals in Latin America,* edited by Edward Cleary and Hannah Stewart-Gambino, pp. 163-78. Boulder, Colo.: Westview.

Adams, Robert
    1966    *The Evolution of Urban Society.* New York: Aldine.

Adler, Moshe
    1995    "Ideology and the Structure of American and European Cities." *Journal of Urban History* 21:691-715.

Ahern, Geoffrey, and Grace Davie
    1987    *Inner City God: The Nature of Belief in the Inner City.* London: Hodder & Stoughton.

Ahlstrom, G. W.
    1982    "Where Did the Israelites Live?" *Journal of Near Eastern Studies* 41:133-38.

Allen, Roland
    1960    *Missionary Methods: St Paul's or Ours?* London: World Dominion.
    1962    *The Spontaneous Expansion of the Church and the Causes Which Hinder It.* Grand Rapids, Mich.: Eerdmans.

Anderson, Gerald
    1995    "American Protestants in Pursuit of Mission: 1886-1986." In *Missiology: An Ecumenical Introduction,* edited by F. J. Verstraelen, pp. 374-420. Grand Rapids, Mich.: Eerdmans.

Arndt, William, and F. Wilbur Gingrich
    1957    *A Greek-English Lexicon of the New Testament and Other Early Christian Literature.* Chicago: University of Chicago Press.

Ashley, Timothy
    1993    *The Book of Numbers.* The New International Commentary on the Old Testament. Grand Rapids, Mich.: Eerdmans.

Assimeng, Max
 1989    *Religion and Social Change in West Africa*. Accra, Ghana: Ghana Universities Press.
Austin, Thomas
 1992a   "Integrating City and Seminary." *Urban Mission* 10 (2):28-38.
 1992b   "Integrating Urban Mission into the Curriculum of Nairobi International School of Theology, Nairobi, Kenya." D.Min. project, Westminster Theological Seminary.
Avi-Yonah, M.
 1950-1951 "Development of the Roman Road System in Palestine." *Israel Exploration Journal* 1:54-60.
Bairoch, Paul
 1988    *Cities and Economic Development: From the Dawn of History to the Present*. Chicago: University of Chicago Press.
Bakke, Ray
 1987    *The Urban Christian: Effective Ministry in Today's Urban World*. Downers Grove, Ill.: InterVarsity Press.
 1997    *A Theology as Big as the City*. Downers Grove, Ill.: InterVarsity Press.
Baldwin, Joyce
 1988    *I and II Samuel: An Introduction and Commentary*. Downers Grove, Ill.: InterVarsity Press.
Baptiste, H. Prentice, Jr., and James E. Anderson
 1980    "Developing Curriculum in an Urban Context." In *Urban Education: The City as a Living Curriculum*, edited by Claude Mayberry Jr., pp. 44-67. Alexandria, Va.: The Association for Supervision and Curriculum Development.
Barrett, David
 1986    *World-Class Cities and World Evangelization*. Birmingham, Ala.: New Hope.
 1987    *Cosmos, Chaos and Gospel*. Birmingham, Ala.: New Hope.
 1996    "Annual Statistical Table on Global Mission." *International Bulletin of Missionary Research* 20:24-25.
Barrett, Stephen
 1997    "Growth Through Change." *Urban Mission* 14 (3):29-39.
Batey, Richard
 1991    *Jesus and the Forgotten City*. Grand Rapids, Mich.: Baker.
Bavinck, J. H.
 1960    *An Introduction to the Science of Missions*. Philadelphia: Presbyterian & Reformed.
 1966    *The Church Between Temple and Mosque*. Grand Rapids, Mich.: Eerdmans.
Beatty, Paulette T.
 1981    "The Concept of Need: Proposal for a Working Definition." *Journal of the Community Development Society* 12 (2):39-46.
Beauregard, Robert, and Anne Haila
 1997    "The Unavoidable Incompleteness of the City." *American Behavioral Scientist* 41 (3):327-41.

Beaver, R. Pierce
1962    *Ecumenical Beginnings in Protestant World Mission: A History of Comity.*
        New York: Thomas Nelson.
Bebbington, David
1989    *Evangelicalism in Modern Britain.* London: Unwin Hyman.
1993    "Evangelicalism in Modern Britain and America: A Comparison." In
        *Amazing Grace: Evangelicalism in Australia, Britain, Canada, and the
        United States,* edited by George Rawlyk and Mark Noll, pp. 183-212.
        Grand Rapids, Mich.: Baker.
Beker, J. Christiaan
1980    *Paul the Apostle: The Triumph of God in Life and Thought.* Philadelphia:
        Fortress.
Benjamin, Don
1983    *Deuteronomy and City Life.* Lanham, Md.: University Press of America.
Bentley, Peter, Tricia Blombery, and Philip Hughes
1992    *Faith Without the Church?: Nominalism in Australian Christianity.* Kew,
        Australia: Christian Research Association.
Berg, Mike, and Paul Pretiz
1992    *The Gospel People.* Monrovia, Calif.: MARC.
1994    "Five Waves of Protestant Evangelization." In *New Face of the Church in
        Latin America,* edited by Guillermo Cook, pp. 56-67. Maryknoll, N.Y.: Orbis.
1996    *Spontaneous Combustion: Grass-Roots Christianity, Latin American Style.*
        Pasadena, Calif.: William Carey Library.
Berger, Peter
1967    *The Sacred Canopy.* Garden City, N.Y.: Doubleday.
Berlin, Adele
1996    Introduction to *Religion and Politics in the Ancient Near East,* edited by
        Adele Berlin, pp. 1-6. Bethesda: University Press of Maryland.
Berryman, Phillip
1994    "The Coming of Age of Evangelical Protestantism." *NACLA Report on the
        Americas* 27 (6):6-10.
1996    *Religion in the Megacity: Catholic and Protestant Portraits from Latin
        America.* Maryknoll, N.Y.: Orbis.
Bibby, Reginald W.
1978    "Why Conservative Churches Really Are Growing: Kelley Revisited."
        *Journal for the Scientific Study of Religion* 17:129-37. Cited in Kenneth W.
        Inskeep. 1993. "A Short History of Church Growth Research." In *Church
        & Denominational Growth: What Does (and Does Not) Cause Growth or
        Decline,* edited by David A. Roozen and C. Kirk Hadaway, pp. 135-48.
        Nashville: Abingdon.
1987    *Fragmented Gods: The Poverty and Potential of Religion in Canada.* Tor-
        onto: Irwin.
1993    *Unknown Gods: The Ongoing Story of Religion in Canada.* Toronto: Stod-
        dart.
1995    *There's Got to be More!: Connecting Churches and Canadians.* Winfield,
        Canada: Wood Lake Books.
Bibby, Reginald W., and Merlin B. Brinkerhoff
1973    "The Circulation of the Saints: A Study of People Who Join Conservative

Churches." *Journal for the Scientific Study of Religion* 12:273-83. Cited in C. Kirk Hadaway. 1993. "Is Evangelistic Activity Related to Church Growth?" In *Church & Denominational Growth: What Does (and Does Not) Cause Growth or Decline*, edited by David A. Roozen and C. Kirk Hadaway, pp. 169-87. Nashville: Abingdon.

1983    "Circulation of the Saints Revisited: A Longitudinal Look at Conservative Church Growth." *Journal for the Scientific Study of Religion* 22:253-62. Cited in C. Kirk Hadaway. 1993. "Is Evangelistic Activity Related to Church Growth?" In *Church & Denominational Growth: What Does (and Does Not) Cause Growth or Decline*, edited by David A. Roozen and C. Kirk Hadaway, pp. 169-87. Nashville: Abingdon.

Birth of a Nationwide Movement

1997    "Birth of a Nationwide Movement." *IUA Newsletter* 1997:2.

Bissinger, Buzz

1997    *A Prayer for the City*. New York: Random House.

Blackwood, Vernon, Barbara Reichardt, and Sally Schreiner

1992    *SCUPE Urban Researchers and Resource Centers Directory*. Chicago: Seminary Consortium for Urban Pastoral Education.

Blauw, Johannes

1962    *The Missionary Nature of the Church*. London: Lutterworth.

Block, Daniel

1988    *The Gods of the Nations*. Jackson, Miss.: Evangelical Theological Society.

Boer, Harry

1961    *Pentecost and Missions*. Grand Rapids, Mich.: Eerdmans.

Boer, Jan

1984    *Missions: Heralds of Capitalism or Christ?* Ibadan, Nigeria: Day Star.

Bonar, Horatius

1880    *Does God Care for the Great Cities? The Question and the Answer from the Book of Jonah. A Word for the Paris Mission*. London: Nisbet.

Booth, William

1890    *In Darkest England and the Way Out*. New York: Funk & Wagnalls.

Bosch, David

1981    "Evangelism." *Mission Focus* 9 (4):65-74.

1991    *Transforming Mission: Paradigm Shifts in Theology of Mission*. Maryknoll, N.Y.: Orbis.

Bouma, Gary D.

1979    "The Real Reason One Conservative Church Grew." *Review of Religious Research* 20:127-37. Cited in Kenneth W. Inskeep. 1993. "A Short History of Church Growth Research." In *Church & Denominational Growth: What Does (and Does Not) Cause Growth or Decline*, edited by David A. Roozen and C. Kirk Hadaway, pp. 135-48. Nashville: Abingdon.

Bowden, Charles, and Lew Kreinberg

1981    *Street Signs Chicago: Neighborhood and Other Illusions of Big-City Life*. Chicago: Chicago Review Press.

Bowers, W. Paul

1976    *Studies in Paul's Understanding of His Mission*. Ph.D. diss., Cambridge University.

Bowie, Vaughan
1985   "Scaffolding: Urban Mission in Australia." *Urban Mission* 2 (5):46-51.

Braaten, Carl
1977   *The Flaming Center: A Theology of Christian Mission*. Philadelphia: Fortress.

Bradbury, Nicholas
1989   *City of God?: Pastoral Care in the Inner City*. London: SPCK.

Bradshaw, Bruce
1993   *Bridging the Gap: Evangelism, Development and Shalom*. Monrovia, Calif.: MARC.

Brandfon, Frederic
1981   "Norman Gottwald on the Tribes of Jahweh." *Journal for the Study of the Old Testament* 21:101-10.

Braun, Neil
1971   *Laity Mobilized: Reflections in Church Growth in Japan and Other Lands*. Grand Rapids, Mich.: Eerdmans.

Brierley, Peter
1989   *Christianity in Europe. MARC Monograph No. 22*. Bromley, U.K.: MARC Europe.

Briggs, Asa
1993   *Victorian Cities*. Berkeley: University of California Press.

Brink, Paul
1990   "Las Acacias Evangelical Pentecostal Church, Caracas, Venezuela." *Urban Mission* 7 (3):46-50.

Britt, David T.
1991.   "From Homogeneity to Congruence: A Church-Community Model." *Urban Mission* 8 (3):27-41.

Bromiley, Geoffrey W., ed.
1965   *Theological Dictionary of the New Testament*, vol. 3. Grand Rapids, Mich.: Eerdmans.
1967   *Theological Dictionary of the New Testament*, vol. 4. Grand Rapids, Mich.: Eerdmans.

Brooke, C. N. L.
1970   "The Missionary at Home: The Church in the Towns, 1000-1250." In *The Mission of the Church and the Propagation of the Faith*, edited by G. C. Cuming, pp. 59-83. New York: Cambridge University Press.

Brookes, Dean
1990   "Growth in Australian Churches." D.Min. diss., Fuller Theological Seminary.

Brown, Callum
1995   "The Mechanism of Religious Growth in Urban Societies: British Cities Since the Eighteenth Century." In *European Religion in the Age of Great Cities, 1830-1930*, edited by Hugh McLeod, pp. 239-62. New York: Routledge.

Bruce, F. F.
1954   *Commentary on the Book of Acts*. Grand Rapids, Mich.: Eerdmans.
1968   *This is That: The New Testament Development of Some Old Testament Themes*. Exeter, U.K.: Paternoster.

Brueggemann, Walter
1977    *The Land*. Philadelphia: Fortress.
1984    "A New Creation—After the Sigh." *Currents in Theology and Mission* 11:83-100.
Brunn, Stanley D., and Jack F. Williams
1983    *Cities of the World: World Regional Urban Development*. New York: Harper & Row.
Buccellati, Giorgio
1967    *Cities and Nations of Ancient Syria*. Rome: Instituto di Studi del Vicino Oriente, Universita di Roma.
Bulmer, Martin
1984    *The Chicago School of Sociology: Institutionalization, Diversity, and the Rise of Sociological Research*. Chicago: University of Chicago Press.
Butterworth, Douglas, and John Chance
1981    *Latin American Urbanization*. New York: Cambridge University Press.
Cadbury, Henry
1961    *The Making of Luke-Acts*. London: SPCK.
Calvin, John
1947    *Commentaries on the Epistle of Paul the Apostle to the Romans*. Grand Rapids, Mich.: Eerdmans.
1960    *Institutes of the Christian Religion*. Philadelphia: Westminster Press.
Candeleria, Michael
1990    *Popular Religion and Liberation: The Dilemma of Liberation Theology*. Albany, N.Y.: State University of New York Press.
Chandler, Tertius, and Gerald Fox
1974    *3000 Years of Urban Growth*. New York: Academic Press.
Chareonwongsak, Kriengsak
1997    "Megachurches for Christian Minorities: Hope of Bangkok." In *Planting and Growing Urban Churches*, edited by Harvie M. Conn, pp. 211-21. Grand Rapids, Mich.: Baker.
Chen, Xiangming, and William L. Parish
1996    "Urbanization in China: Reassessing an Evolving Model." In *The Urban Transformation of the Developing World*, edited by Josef Gugler, pp. 61-90. New York: Oxford University Press.
Childe, V. Gordon
1950    "The Urban Revolution." *Town Planning Review* 21:3-17.
Childs, Lloyd
1985    "Teams Multiply Churches in Malaysia/Singapore." *Urban Misson* 2 (5):33-39.
Christiano, Kevin
1987    *Religious Diversity and Social Change: American Cities, 1890-1906*. New York: Cambridge University Press.
Chu, David K. Y.
1996    "The Hong Kong-Zhujiang Delta and the World City System." In *Emerging World Cities in Pacific Asia*, edited by Fu-chen Lo and Yue-man Yeung, pp. 465-97. New York: United Nations University Press.
Chudacoff, Howard
1981    *The Evolution of American Urban Society*, 2nd ed. Englewood Cliffs, N.J.:

        Prentice-Hall.
Claerbaut, David
    1983    *Urban Ministry.* Grand Rapids, Mich.: Zondervan, Ministry Resources
            Library.
Clarke, Andrew
    1990    "The Good and the Just in Romans 5:7." *Tyndale Bulletin* 41:128-42.
Claydon, David
    1998    "Urban Islam: The Unseen Engine in Fundamentalism." *Urban Mission*
            15 (3):8-14.
Cleary, Edward
    1997    "Introduction: Pentecostals, Prominence and Politics." In *Power, Politics,
            and Pentecostals in Latin America,* edited by Edward Cleary and Hannah
            Stewart Gambino, pp. 1-24. Boulder, Colo.: Westview.
Clinton, Robert J.
    1988    *The Making of a Leader: Recognizing the Lessons and Stages of Leader-
            ship Development.* Colorado Springs, Colo.: NavPress.
Clowney, Edmund P.
    1964    *Called to the Ministry.* Phillipsburg, N.J.: Presbyterian & Reformed.
    1971    "The Final Temple." In *Prophecy in the Making,* edited by Carl F. H.
            Henry, pp. 69-88. Carol Stream, Ill.: Creation House.
    1988    *The Unfolding Mystery: Discovering Christ in the Old Testament.* Colorado
            Springs, Colo.: NavPress.
    1995    *The Church.* Contours of Christian Theology. Downers Grove, Ill.: Inter-
            Varsity Press.
Coale, Ansley J.
    1975    "The History of the Human Population." *Scientific American* (Septem-
            ber): 41-51.
Coggins, Richard
    1987    "The Old Testament and the Poor." *Expository Times* 99 (1):11-14.
Cohen, Abner
    1988    "The Politics of Ethnicity in African Towns." In *The Urbanization of the
            Third World,* edited by Josef Gugler, pp. 328-37. New York: Oxford Uni-
            versity Press.
Companjen, Johan
    1993    "In Need of a New Identity." *World Evangelization* (January): 8-9.
Conn, Harvie M.
    1982    *Evangelism: Doing Justice and Preaching Grace.* Grand Rapids, Mich.:
            Zondervan.
    1984    *Eternal Word and Changing Worlds: Theology, Anthropology, and Mission
            in Trialogue.* Grand Rapids, Mich.: Zondervan, Academie Books.
    1987    *A Clarified Vision for Urban Mission.* Grand Rapids, Mich.: Zondervan.
    1989    "Urbanization and Its Implications." In *Muslims and Christians on the
            Emmaus Road,* edited by J. Dudley Woodberry, pp. 61-83. Monrovia,
            Calif.: MARC.
    1992a   "The Kingdom of God and the City of Man: A History of the City/Church
            Dialogue." In *Discipling the City,* 2nd ed., edited by Roger S. Greenway,
            pp. 247-77. Grand Rapids, Mich.: Baker.
    1992b   "The Suburban Black Movement." *Urban Missions Newsletter* 35 (Sep-

tember): 1-3.

1994a    *The American City and the Evangelical Church: A Historical Overview.*
         Grand Rapids, Mich.: Baker.

1994b    Foreword to *God So Loves the City: Seeking a Theology for Urban Mis-*
         *sion,* edited by Charles Van Engen and Jude Tiersma, pp. i-viii. Mon-
         rovia, Calif.: MARC.

1997     Introduction to part one of *Planting and Growing Urban Churches,*
         edited by Harvie M. Conn, pp. 25-33. Grand Rapids, Mich.: Baker.

Cook, Guillermo

1985     *The Expectation of the Poor: Latin American Basic Ecclesial Communities*
         *in Protestant Perspective.* Maryknoll, N.Y.: Orbis.

Cooper, Paul

1994     "Urban Mission Down Under." *Urban Mission* 11 (4):3-4.

Costa, Frank J., Ashok K. Dutt, Laurence J. C. Ma, and Allen G. Noble

1989     "Trends and Prospects." In *Urbanization in Asia,* edited by Frank J. Costa
         et al., pp. 3-17. Honolulu: University of Hawaii Press.

Costas, Orlando E.

1974     *The Church and Its Mission: A Shattering Critique from the Third World.*
         Wheaton, Ill.: Tyndale House.

1979     *The Integrity of Mission: The Inner Life and Outreach of the Church.* New
         York: Harper & Row.

1982     *Christ Outside the Gate: Mission Beyond Christendom.* Maryknoll, N.Y.:
         Orbis.

1983     "A Wholistic Concept of Church Growth." In *Exploring Church Growth,*
         edited by Wilbert R. Shenk, pp. 95-107. Grand Rapids, Mich.: Eerdmans.

1986     "The Mission of Ministry." *Missiology* 14:463-72.

Cotterell, Peter

1989     "The Church in Europe." *Evangelical Review of Theology* 13 (1):37-48.

Couto, Alva

1997     "Latin American Social Contexts." In *Serving with the Poor in Latin*
         *America,* edited by Tetsunao Uamamori, Bryant Myers, C. René Padilla,
         and Greg Rake, pp. 87-99. Monrovia, Calif.: MARC.

Cox, Harvey

1966     *The Secular City: Secularization and Urbanization in Theological Perspec-*
         *tive.* London: SCM Press.

1973     *The Seduction of the Spirit: The Use and Misuse of People's Religion.* New
         York: Simon & Schuster, Touchstone.

Cross, Robert D.

1962     "The Changing Image of the City Among American Catholics." *Catholic*
         *Historical Review,* 48:33-52.

Cundall, A. E.

1969-1970    "Judges—An Apology for the Monarchy?" *Expository Times* 81:178-
             81.

Curtis, A. H. W.

1978     "The 'Subjugation of the Waters' Motif in the Psalm: Imagery or
         Polemic?" *Journal of Semitic Studies* 23:244-56.

Danker, Frederick

1976     *Luke.* Proclamation Commentaries. Philadelphia: Fortress.

Davis, Kingsley
    1960    "The Origin and Growth of Urbanization in the World." *The American Journal of Sociology* 55:429-37.
de Queiroz, Maria Isaura Pereira
    1977    "Afro Brazilian Cults and Religious Change in Brazil." In *The Changing Face of Religion,* edited by James Beckford and Thomas Luckmann, pp. 88-108. Newbury Park, Calif.: Sage.
de Vries, Jan
    1984    *European Urbanization, 1500-1800.* Cambridge, Mass.: Harvard University Press.
DeRidder, Richard
    1975    *Discipling the Nations.* Grand Rapids, Mich.: Baker.
Detwiler-Zapp, Diane, and William Cavenes Dixon
    1982    *Lay Caregiving.* Philadelphia: Fortress.
DeWitt, Dale
    1979    "The Historical Background of Genesis 11:1-9: Babel or Ur?" *Journal of the Evangelical Theological Society* 22:15-26.
DeYoung, James
    1960    *Jerusalem in the New Testament.* Kampen, The Netherlands: J. H. Kok.
Dillard, Raymond
    1987    *2 Chronicles.* Word Biblical Commentary. Waco, Tex.: Word.
Dillard, Raymond, and Tremper Longman III
    1994    *An Introduction to the Old Testament.* Grand Rapids, Mich.: Zondervan.
Dobson, Ed
    1993    *Starting a Seeker Sensitive Service.* Grand Rapids, Mich.: Zondervan.
Dougherty, James
    1980    *The Fivesquare City: The City in the Religious Imagination.* Notre Dame, Ind.: University of Notre Dame Press.
Douglass, Truman B.
    1962    "The Job Protestants Shirk." In *Cities and Churches: Readings on the Urban Church,* edited by Robert Lee, pp. 87-94. Philadelphia: Westminster Press.
Drakakis-Smith, David
    1987    *The Third World City.* New York: Methuen.
    1990    *The Third World City.* London: Routledge.
Dries, Angelyn
    1998    *The Missionary Movement in American Catholic History.* Maryknoll, N.Y.: Orbis.
DuBose, Francis M.
    1978    *How Churches Grow in an Urban World.* Nashville: Broadman.
    1983    "The Practice of Urban Ministry: Urban Evangelism." *Review and Expositor,* LXXX (4):515-21.
    1984    "Urban Poverty as a World Challenge." In *An Urban World: Churches Face the Future,* edited by Larry L. Rose and C. Kirk Hadaway, pp. 51-74. Nashville: Broadman.
Dumbrell, William J.
    1975    "Midian—A Land or a League?" *Vetus Testamentum* 25:323-37.
    1983    "'In Those Days There Was No King in Israel, Every Man Did What Was

Right in His Own Eyes': The Purpose of the Book of Judges Reconsidered." *Journal for the Study of the Old Testament* 25:23-33.

Duncan, Michael
  1996    *Costly Mission: Following Christ into the Slums*. Monrovia, Calif.: MARC.
Dunn, James D. G.
  1970    *Baptism in the Holy Spirit*. London: SCM Press.
  1996    *The Acts of the Apostles*. Valley Forge, Penn.: Trinity Press International.
Dyrness, William A.
  1992    *Invitation to Cross-Cultural Theology: Case Studies in Vernacular Theologies*. Grand Rapids, Mich.: Zondervan.
Eames, Edwin, and Judith Goode
  1977    *Anthropology of the City*. Englewood Cliffs, N.J.: Prentice-Hall.
Edwards, Douglas
  1988    "First Century Urban/Rural Relations in Lower Galilee: Exploring the Archaeological and Literary Evidence." In *SBL Seminar Papers*, edited by David J. Lull, pp. 169-82. Atlanta: Scholars Press.
Eliade, Mircea
  1959    *Cosmos and History: The Myth of the Eternal Return*. New York: Harper/ Torchbooks.
  1963    *Patterns in Comparative Religion*. Cleveland: World Publishing [1958].
Elliston, Edgar J., and J. Timothy Kauffman
  1993    *Developing Leaders for Urban Ministries*. New York: Peter Lang.
Ellul, Jacques
  1970    *The Meaning of the City*. Grand Rapids, Mich.: Eerdmans.
Engel, James F., and Wilbert Norton
  1975    *What's Gone Wrong With the Harvest? A Communication Strategy for the Church and World Evangelism*. Grand Rapids, Mich.: Zondervan.
Engels, Friedrich
  1950    *The Condition of the Working Class in England in 1844*. London: Allen & Unwin.
Engnell, Ivan
  1967    *Studies in Divine Kingship in the Ancient Near East*. Oxford: Basil, Blackwell & Mott.
Escobar, Samuel
  1990    "From Lausanne 1974 to Manila 1989: The Pilgrimage of Urban Mission." *Urban Mission* 7 (4):21-29.
  1994    "Conflict of Interpretations of Popular Protestantism." In *New Face of the Church in Latin America*, edited by Guillermo Cook, pp. 112-34. Maryknoll, N.Y.: Orbis.
Escobar, Samuel, and John Driver
  1978    *Christian Mission and Social Justice*. Scottsdale, Pa.: Herald.
Eslinger, Lyle
  1985    *Kingship of God in Crisis: A Close Reading of 1 Samuel 1-12*. Sheffield, U.K.: Almond.
Estragó, Margarita Durán
  1992    "The Reductions." In *The Church in Latin America: 1492-1992*, edited by Enrique Dussel, pp. 351-62. Maryknoll, N.Y.: Orbis.

Faith in the City
    1985    *Faith in the City: A Call for Action by Church and Nation: The Report of the
            Archbishop of Canterbury's Commission on Urban Priority Areas*. London:
            Church House Publishing.
Falk, Peter
    1979    *The Growth of the Church in Africa*. Grand Rapids, Mich.: Zondervan.
Fee, Gordon D., and Douglas Stuart
    1982    *How to Read the Bible for All It's Worth: A Guide to Understanding the
            Bible*. Grand Rapids, Mich.: Zondervan, Academie Books.
Ferguson, Sinclair
    1996    *The Holy Spirit*. Contours of Christian Theology. Downers Grove, Ill.:
            InterVarsity Press.
Feyne, Sean
    1980    *Galilee From Alexander the Great to Hadrian—323 B.C.E. to 135 C.E.*
            Wilmington, Del.: Michael Glazier.
Filbeck, David
    1985    *Social Context and Proclamation: A Socio-Cognitive Study in Proclaiming
            the Gospel Cross-Culturally*. Pasadena, Calif.: William Carey Library.
Filson, Floyd
    1970    "The Journey Motif in Luke-Acts." In *Apostolic History and the Gospel*,
            edited by W. Ward Gasque and Ralph Martin, pp. 68-77. Grand Rapids,
            Mich.: Eerdmans.
Finke, Roger, and Rodney Stark
    1992    *The Churching of America, 1776-1990*. New Brunswick, N.J.: Rutgers
            University Press.
Finkelstein, Israel
    1988    *The Archaeology of the Israelite Settlement*. Jerusalem: Israel Exploration
            Society.
Fischer, Claude
    1984    *The Urban Experience*, 2nd ed. Orlando: Harcourt Brace Jovanovich.
Fishman, Robert
    1987    *Bourgeois Utopias*. New York: Basic Books.
Fitzgerald, Aloysius
    1972    "The Mythological Background for the Presentation of Jerusalem as a
            Queen and False Worship as Adultery in the Old Testament." *Catholic
            Biblical Quarterly* 34:403-15.
Flanagan, James
    1988    *David's Social Drama*. Sheffield, U.K.: Almond.
Flanagan, William
    1993    *Contemporary Urban Sociology*. New York: Cambridge University Press.
Fleming, Daniel
    1986    "'House/City': An Unrecognized Parallel Word Pair." *Journal of Biblical
            Literature* 105:689-97.
Flender, Helmut
    1967    *St. Luke: Theologian of Redemptive History*. London: SPCK.
Flight, John
    1923    "The Nomadic Idea and Ideal in the Old Testament." *Journal of Biblical
            Literature* 42:158-226.

Floristan, Casiano
    1992    "Evangelization of the 'New World': An Old World Perspective." *Missiology* 20:133-49.

Foreman, Charles
    1982    "Evangelization and Civilization: Protestant Missionary Motivation in the Imperialist Era. II. The Americas." *International Bulletin of Missionary Research* 6 (2):54-56.

Fox, Richard
    1977    *Urban Anthropology: Cities in Their Cultural Settings*. Englewood Cliffs, N.J.: Prentice-Hall.

Frame, John M.
    1990    *Perspectives on the Word of God: An Introduction to Christian Ethics*. Phillipsburg, N.J.: Presbyterian & Reformed.

Frankfort, Henri
    1978    *Kingship and the Gods*. Chicago: University of Chicago Press.

Franklin, Eric
    1975    *Christ the Lord—A Study in the Purpose and Theology of Luke-Acts*. Philadelphia: Westminster Press.

Fredericksen, Andy
    1993    "Evangelizing Taiwan's Factory Workers." *Taiwan Mission* (January): 16-18.

Freire, Paulo
    1989    *Pedagogy of the Oppressed*, translated by Myra Bergman Ramos. New York: Continuum.

Frick, Frank
    1977    *The City in Ancient Israel*. Missoula, Mont.: Scholars Press.
    1997    "Cities: An Overview." In *The Oxford Encyclopedia of Archaeology in the Near East,* vol. 2, edited by Eric M. Meyers, pp. 14-19. New York: Oxford University Press.

Friedrich, Gerhard, ed.
    1967    *Theological Dictionary of the New Testament*, Vol. V. Grand Rapids, Mich.: Eerdmans.

Fritz, Paul
    1993    "Infant Mortality in Nigeria's Urban Churches." *Urban Mission* 10 (3):52-58.
    1995    "Going Downtown: Ministering to Rural Immigrants in Urban Africa." *Urban Mission* 13 (1):33-41.

Fritz, Volkmar
    1995    *The City in Ancient Israel*. Sheffield, U.K.: Sheffield Academic Press.

Fuller, Millard, with Diane Scott
    1986    *No More Shacks! The Daring Vision for Habitat for Humanity*. Waco, Tex.: Word.

Gaffin, Richard Jr.
    1978    *The Centrality of the Resurrection*. Grand Rapids, Mich.: Baker.

Galambush, Julie
    1992    *Jerusalem in the Book of Ezekiel: The City as Jahweh's Wife*. Atlanta: Scholars Press.

Galvin, James C., and David R. Veerman
    1993    "Curriculum for Adult Education." In *The Christian Educator's Handbook on Adult Education*, edited by Kenneth O. Gangel and James C. Wilhoit, pp. 178-89. Grand Rapids, Mich.: Baker.

Gans, Herbert
    1962    *The Urban Villagers: Group and Class in the Life of Italian-Americans.* New York: Free Press/Macmillan.

Garland, Sidney
    1997    "Teaching Missiology at the Theological College of Northern Nigeria." D.Min. project, Westminster Theological Seminary.

Garreau, Joel
    1991    *Edge City: Life on the New Frontier.* New York: Doubleday, Anchor Books.

Geertz, Clifford
    1973    *The Interpretation of Cultures.* New York: Basic Books.

Geller, Daniel
    1980    "Responses to Urban Stimuli: A Balanced Approach." *Journal of Social Issues* 36:86-100.

George, Carl
    1991    *Prepare Your Church for the Future.* Grand Rapids, Mich.: Revell/Baker.

Georges, Robert A., and Michael O. Jones
    1980    *People Studying People: The Human Element in Fieldwork.* Berkeley: University of California Press.

Gerber, Vergil
    1973    *God's Way to Keep a Church Going & Growing: A Manual for Evangelism/Church Growth.* Glendale, Calif.: Regal.

Gilbert, Alan
    1994    *The Latin American City.* London: Latin America Bureau.

Gili, Juan
    1989    "The Challenge of Southern Europe." *World Evangelization* 16 (60):17.

Gilliland, Dean
    1983    *Pauline Theology and Mission Practice.* Grand Rapids, Mich.: Baker.

Glaab, Charles
    1963    *The American City: A Documentary History.* Homewood, Ill.: Dorsey.

Goldberg, Michael, and John Mercer
    1986    *The Myth of the North American City: Continentalism Challenged.* Vancouver: University of British Columbia Press.

Goldsmith, William
    1997    "The Metropolis and Globalization." *American Behavioral Scientist* 41 (3):299-310.

Gordon, Wayne L.
    1995    "Indigenous Leadership Development." In *Restoring At-Risk Communities: Doing It Together & Doing It Right*, edited by John M. Perkins, pp. 181-93. Grand Rapids, Mich.: Baker.

Gornik, Mark R.
    1999    "Globalization and Urban Mission: Some Brief Reflections." Unpublished paper.

Gornik, Mark R., and Noel Castellanos
1995    "How to Start a Christian Community Development." In *Restoring At-Risk Communities: Doing It Together & Doing It Right*, edited by John M. Perkins, pp. 211-36. Grand Rapids, Mich.: Baker.

Gottmann, Jean
1990    "Introduction: The Opening of the Oyster Shell." In *Since Megalopolis: The Urban Writings of Jean Gottmann*, edited by Jean Gottmann and Robert A. Harper, pp. 3-20. Baltimore: Johns Hopkins University Press.

Gottwald, Norman
1977    *The Tribes of Jahweh*. Maryknoll, N.Y.: Orbis.

Gowan, Donald
1987    "Wealth and Poverty in the Old Testament: The Case of the Widow, the Orphan, and the Sojourner." *Interpretation* 41:341-53.

Grant, Robert
1986    *Gods and the One God*. Philadelphia: Westminster Press.

Green, Clifford, ed.
1996    *Churches, Cities, and Human Communities: Urban Ministry in the United States, 1945-1985*. Grand Rapids, Mich.: Eerdmans.

Greenway, Roger S.
1973    *Calling Our Cities to Christ*. Nutley, N.J.: Presbyterian & Reformed.
1978    *Apostles to the City: Biblical Strategies for Urban Missions*. Grand Rapids, Mich.: Baker.
1994    "Protestant Mission Activity in Latin America." In *Coming of Age: Protestantism in Contemporary Latin America*, edited by Daniel Miller, pp. 175-204. Lanham, Md.: University Press of America.

Greenway, Roger S., and Timothy M. Monsma
1989    *Cities: Missions' New Frontier*. Grand Rapids, Mich.: Baker.

Grigg, Viv
1992a   "Church of the Poor." In *Discipling the City*, 2nd ed., edited by Roger S. Greenway, pp. 159-70. Grand Rapids, Mich.: Baker.
1992b   *Cry of the Urban Poor*. Monrovia, Calif.: MARC.

Grigg, Viv, ed.
1995    *Transforming Cities: An Urban Leadership Guide*. Auckland, New Zealand: Urban Leadership Foundation.

Grimley, John B., and Gordon E. Robinson
1966    *Church Growth in Central and Southern Nigeria*. Grand Rapids, Mich.: Eerdmans. Cited in Neil Braun. 1971. *Laity Mobilized: Reflections in Church Growth in Japan and Other Lands*. Grand Rapids, Mich.: Eerdmans.

Groome, Thomas H.
1980    *Christian Religious Education: Sharing Our Story and Vision*. San Francisco: Harper & Row.

Grounds, Vernon
1982    Foreword to *Unleashing the Church: Getting People Out of the Fortress and Into Ministry* by Frank R. Tillapaugh. Ventura, Calif.: Regal.

Groves, C. P.
1955    *The Planting of Christianity in Africa*, Vol. III. London: Lutterworth.

Grudem, Wayne
  1994    *Systematic Theology: An Introduction to Biblical Doctrine*. Grand Rapids,
          Mich.: Zondervan.
Gugler, Josef
  1996    "Regional Trajectories in the Urban Transformation: Convergences and
          Divergences." In *The Urban Transformation of the Developing World*,
          edited by Josef Gugler, pp. 1-14. New York: Oxford University Press.
Gulick, John
  1984    "The Essence of Urban Anthropology: Integration of Micro and Macro
          Research Perspectives." *Urban Anthropology* 13 (2-3):295-306.
  1989    *The Humanity of Cities: An Introduction to Urban Societies*. Granby,
          Mass.: Bergin & Garvey.
Gurnall, William
  1988    *The Christian in Complete Armour*, vol. 2. Carlisle, Penn.: Banner of
          Truth.
Gutkind, Peter
  1974    *Urban Anthropology: Perspectives on 'Third World' Urbanization and
          Urbanism*. Assen, The Netherlands: Van Gorcum.
HABITAT [United Nations Center for Human Settlements]
  1996    *An Urbanizing Word: Global Report on Human Settlements 1996*. New
          York: Oxford University Press.
Hadaway, C. Kirk
  1987    *New Churches and Church Growth in the Southern Baptist Convention*.
          Nashville: Sunday School Board of the Southern Baptist Convention,
          Research Services Dept.
  1993a   "Church Growth in North America: The Character of a Religious Mar-
          ketplace." In *Church & Denominational Growth: What Does (and Does
          Not) Cause Growth or Decline*, edited by David A. Roozen and C. Kirk
          Hadaway, pp. 346-57. Nashville: Abingdon.
  1993b   "Is Evangelistic Activity Related to Church Growth?" In *Church &
          Denominational Growth: What Does (and Does Not) Cause Growth or
          Decline*, edited by David A. Roozen and C. Kirk Hadaway, pp. 169-87.
          Nashville: Abingdon.
Hadaway, C. Kirk, and David A. Roozen
  1993    "Denomination Growth and Decline." In *Church & Denominational
          Growth: What Does (and Does Not) Cause Growth or Decline*, edited by
          David A. Roozen and C. Kirk Hadaway, pp. 37-45. Nashville: Abingdon.
  1995    *Rerouting the Protestant Mainstream: Sources of Growth and Opportuni-
          ties for Change*. Nashville: Abingdon.
Haenchen, Ernst
  1971    *The Acts of the Apostles—A Commentary*. Philadelphia: Westminster Press.
Hahn, Herbert
  1966    *The Old Testament in Modern Research*. Philadelphia: Fortress.
Hale, Thomas
  1995    *On Being a Missionary*. Pasadena, Calif.: William Carey Library.
Halligan, John
  1975    "A Critique of the City in the Jahwist Corpus." Ph.D. diss., University of
          Notre Dame.

Hallo, William
1971 "Antedeluvian Cities." *Journal of Cuneiform Studies* 23:57-67.
Hammond, John, and Barbara Hammond
1975 *The Rise of Modern Industry.* New York: Harper & Row.
Hammond, Mason
1972 *The City in the Ancient World.* Cambridge, Mass.: Harvard University Press.
Handy, Robert T.
1969 "The City and the Church: Historical Interlockings." In *Will the Church Lose the City?* Edited by Kendig Brubaker Cully and F. Nile Harper, pp. 89-103. New York: Word.
Haneda, Masashi
1994 "Introduction: An Interpretation of the 'Islamic' City." In *Islamic Urban Studies: Historical Review and Perspectives,* edited by Masashi Haneda and Toru Miura, pp. 1-10. London: Kegan Paul.
Hannerz, Ulf
1980 *Exploring the City: Inquiries Toward an Urban Anthropology.* New York: Columbia University Press.
Hanson, Eric
1980 *Catholic Politics in China and Korea.* Maryknoll, N.Y.: Orbis.
Hard, Theodore
1989 "Does Animism Die in the City?" *Urban Mission* 6 (3):45-46.
Hartis, Gerry
1992 "Empowering Without Entitling." *IUA Newsletter* (autumn): 4-5.
Hartley, Loyde
1996 "Urban Church Literature: A Retrospection." In *Churches, Cities, and Human Community,* edited by Clifford J. Green, pp. 308-63. Grand Rapids, Mich.: Eerdmans.
Hewitt, W. E.
1991 *Base Christian Communities and Social Change in Brazil.* Lincoln, Neb.: University of Nebraska Press.
Hiebert, Paul G.
1983 *Cultural Anthropology.* Grand Rapids, Mich.: Baker.
1987 "Conversion or Social Convention?" In *Case Studies in Missions,* edited by Paul G. Hiebert and Frances F. Hiebert, pp. 161-63. Grand Rapids, Mich.: Baker.
1989 "Anthropological Insights for Whole Ministries." In *Christian Relief and Development: Developing Workers for Effective Ministry,* edited by Edgar J. Elliston, pp. 75-92. Dallas: Word.
1994 *Anthropological Reflections on Missiological Issues.* Grand Rapids, Mich.: Baker.
Hiebert, Paul, and Eloise Hiebert Meneses
1995 *Incarnational Ministry: Planting Churches in Band, Tribal, Peasant, and Urban Societies.* Grand Rapids, Mich.: Baker.
Hildebrandt, Jonathan
1993 "Church Expansion and Africa's Cities." *Urban Mission* 11 (1):37-44.
Hill, Richard Child, and Kuniko Fujita
1993 "Japanese Cities in the World Economy." In *Japanese Cities in the World*

*Economy*, edited by Kuniko Fujita and R. C. Hill, pp. 3-25. Philadelphia: Temple University Press.

Hinton, Keith
1985 *Growing Churches Singapore Style: Ministry in an Urban Context*. Singapore: OMF Books.

Hobsbawm, E. J.
1968 *Industry and Empire: The Making of Modern English Society*. New York: Pantheon.

Hodge, Charles
1959 *The Way of Life*. Ft. Washington, Penn.: Banner of Truth.

Hoekendijk, J. C.
1967 *The Church Inside Out*. London: SCM Press.

Hoge, Dean R., and David A. Roozen, eds.
1979 *Understanding Church Growth and Decline: 1950-1978*. New York: Pilgrim.

Hogg, W. Richie
1977 "The Role of American Protestantism in World Mission." In *American Missions in Bicentennial Perspective*, edited by R. Pierce Beaver, pp. 354-402. South Pasadena, Calif.: William Carey Library.

Hohenberg, Paul, and Lynn Lees
1995 *The Making of Urban Europe, 1000-1994*. Cambridge, Mass.: Harvard University Press.

Hollinger, Dennis, and Joseph Modica
1992 "The Feminization of Poverty: Challenge for the Church." In *Envisioning the New City: A Reader On Urban Ministry*, edited by Eleanor Scott Meyers, pp. 221-34. Louisville, Ky.: Westminster/John Knox.

Howard, Ebenezer
1965 *Garden Cities of To-Morrow*. Cambridge: MIT Press [1898].

Hugo, Graeme
1996 "Urbanization in Indonesia: City and Countryside Linked." In *The Urban Transformation of the Developing World*, edited by Josef Gugler, pp. 133-83. New York: Oxford University Press.

Hunter, Alan, and Kim-Kwong Chan
1993 *Protestantism in Contemporary China*. New York: Cambridge University Press.

Hunter, George G., III
1979 *The Contagious Congregation: Frontiers in Evangelism and Church Growth*. Nashville: Abingdon.

Hutchison, William
1987 *Errand to the World: American Protestant Thought and Foreign Missions*. Chicago: University of Chicago Press.

Inskeep, Kenneth W.
1993 "A Short History of Church Growth Research." In *Church & Denominational Growth: What Does (and Does Not) Cause Growth or Decline*, edited by David A. Roozen and C. Kirk Hadaway, pp. 135-48. Nashville: Abingdon.

Isichei, Elizabeth
1995 *A History of Christianity in Africa*. Grand Rapids, Mich.: Eerdmans.

Jacobs, Jane
1969    *The Economy of Cities*. New York: Random House.
Jacobsen, Thorkild
1946    "Mesopotamia." In *The Intellectual Adventure of Ancient Man*, edited by
        H. and H. A. Frankfort, John Wilson, Thorkild Jacobsen and William
        Irvin, pp. 124-219. Chicago: University of Chicago Press.
Jacques, Andre
1986    *The Stranger Within Your Gates: Uprooted People in the World Today*.
        Geneva, Switzerland: World Council of Churches.
Johnstone, Patrick
1995    "Biblical Intercession: Spiritual Power to Change Our World." In *Spiritual Power and Missions: Raising the Issues*, edited by Edward Rommen,
        pp. 137-63. Pasadena, Calif.: William Carey Library.
Jongeneel, J. A. B.
1995    "The Protestant Missionary Movement up to 1789." In *Missiology: An
        Ecumenical Introduction*, edited by F. J. Verstraelen, pp. 222-28. Grand
        Rapids, Mich.: Eerdmans.
Kaldor, Peter
1987    *Who Goes Where? Who Doesn't Care?: Going to Church in Australia*. Sydney, Australia: Lancer.
1992    *First Look in the Mirror: Initial Findings of the 1991 National Church Life
        Survey*. Homebush West, Australia: Lancer/Anzea.
Kaldor, Peter, and Sue Kaldor
1988    *Where the River Flows: Sharing the Gospel in Contemporary Australia*.
        Homebush West, Australia: Lancer/Anzea.
Karp, David, Gregory Stone, and William Yoels
1991    *Being Urban: A Sociology of City Life*. New York: Praeger.
Kaye, Anthony R.
1985    "Distance Education." In *International Encyclopedia of Education*, vol. 3,
        edited by Torsten Husen and T. Neville Postlethwaite. Cited in Steward
        G. Snook. 1992. *Developing Leaders Through Theological Education by
        Extension*. Wheaton, Ill.: Billy Graham Center.
Kee, Howard Clark
1997    *To Every Nation Under Heaven: The Acts of the Apostles*. Harrisburg,
        Penn.: Trinity Press International.
Kehrein, Glen
1995    "The Local Church and Christian Community Development." In *Restoring At-Risk Communities: Doing It Together & Doing It Right*, edited by
        John M. Perkins, pp. 163-80. Grand Rapids, Mich.: Baker.
Keller, Timothy J.
1989    *Ministries of Mercy: The Call to the Jericho Road*. Grand Rapids, Mich.:
        Zondervan, Ministries Resources Library.
1993    "An Evangelical Mission in a Secular City." In *Center City Churches: The
        New Urban Frontier*, edited by Lyle Schaller, pp. 31-41. Nashville: Abingdon.
1999    "Globalization, International Missions and Redeemer: Reflections."
        Unpublished class outline.

Kelley, Dean M.
    1972    *Why Conservative Churches Are Growing*. San Francisco: Harper & Row.
            Cited in Kenneth W. Inskeep. 1993. "A Short History of Church Growth
            Research." In *Church & Denominational Growth: What Does (and Does
            Not) Cause Growth or Decline*, edited by David A. Roozen and C. Kirk
            Hadaway, pp. 135-48. Nashville: Abingdon.
Kelley, John
    1977    *The Church in the Town: Re-thinking the African Urban Apostolate*.
            Eldoret, Kenya: Gaba Publications.
Kemper, Robert
    1991    "Trends in Urban Anthropological Research." *Urban Anthropology*
            20:373-84.
    1997    "Theological Education for Urban Ministry: A Survey of U.S. Seminar-
            ies." *Theological Education* 34 (1):51-72.
Kempinski, Aharon
    1983    "Early Bronze Age Urbanization of Palestine: Some Topics in a Debate."
            *Israel Exploration Quarterly* 33:235-41.
Kent, Robert B.
    1994    "Peru." In *Latin American Urbanization: Historical Profiles of Major Cities*,
            edited by Gerald M. Greenfield, pp. 446-67. Westport, Conn.: Greenwood.
Kitchen, K. A.
    1966    *Ancient Orient and Old Testament*. London: Tyndale Press.
Klaiber, Jeffrey
    1992    *The Catholic Church in Peru, 1821-1985: A Social History*. Washington,
            D.C.: The Catholic University of America Press.
Kline, Meredith
    1963a   "Divine Kingship and Genesis 6:1-4." *Westminster Theological Journal*
            24: 187-204.
    1963b   *The Treaty of the Great King*. Grand Rapids, Mich.: Eerdmans.
    1972    *The Structure of Biblical Authority*. Grand Rapids, Mich.: Eerdmans.
    1983    *Kingdom Prologue*, vol. II. Published privately by the author.
Kostarelos, Frances
    1995    *Feeling the Spirit: Faith and Hope in an Evangelical Black Storefront
            Church*. Columbia: University of South Carolina Press.
Kraemer, Hendrik
    1958    *A Theology of the Laity*. Philadelphia: Westminster Press. Cited in Neil
            Braun. 1971. *Laity Mobilized: Reflections in Church Growth in Japan and
            Other Lands*. Grand Rapids, Mich.: Eerdmans.
Kraft, Charles H.
    1992    *Defeating Dark Angels: Breaking Demonic Oppression in the Believer's
            Life*. Ann Arbor, Mich.: Servant Publications, Vine Books.
    1996    *Anthropology for Christian Witness*. Maryknoll, N.Y.: Orbis.
Kramer, S. N., trans.
    1969    "Sumerian Lamentation." In *Ancient Near Estern Texts Relating to the Old
            Testament*, edited by James Pritchard, pp. 611-19. Princeton, N.J.: Prince-
            ton University Press.
Kritzinger, J. J.
    1995    "Missiology and the Challenge of Urbanisation in South Africa." *Mis-*

*sionalia* 23 (2): 201-15.

Krupat, Edward
   1985    *People in Cities: The Urban Environment and Its Effects*. Cambridge: Cambridge University Press.

Kselman, Thomas
   1995    "The Varieties of Religious Experience in Urban France." In *European Religion in the Age of Great Cities, 1830-1930*, edited by Hugh McLeod, 165-90. London: Routledge.

Lamphere, Louise
   1992    Introduction to *Structuring Diversity: Ethnographic Perspectives on the New Immigration*, edited by Louise Lamphere, pp. 1-34. Chicago: University of Chicago Press.

Landis, Judson R.
   1992    *Sociology: Concepts and Characteristics*, 8th ed. Belmont, Calif.: Wadsworth Publishing.

Lapidus, Ira
   1969    Preface to *Middle Eastern Cities,* edited by Ira M. Lapidus, pp. v-vii. Berkeley: University of California Press.
   1986    "Cities and Societies: A Comparative Study of the Emergence of Urban Civilization in Mesopotamia and Greece." *Journal of Urban History* 12:257-92.

Latourette, Kenneth
   1943    *A History of the Expansion of Christianity*, vol. 5. New York: Harper & Row.

Lawton, William
   1988    *Being Christian, Being Australian*. Homebush West, Australia: Lancer/Anzea.

Lee, Jonathan H. Y., trans.
   1998    "The Chinese Jerusalem—A Report on Wen Zhou County." *Chinese Around the World* (May): 15-17.

Leeds, Anthony
   1994    *Cities, Classes, and the Social Order*, edited by Roger Sanjek. Ithaca, N.Y.: Cornell University Press.

Lees, Andrew
   1985    *Cities Perceived: Urban Society in European and American Thought, 1820-1940*. New York: Columbia University Press.

LeGrand, Lucien
   1990    *Unity and Plurality: Mission in the Bible*. Maryknoll, N.Y.: Orbis.

Lenski, R. C. H.
   1934    *The Interpretation of the Acts of the Apostles*. Minneapolis: Augsburg.

León, Abelardo Sánchez
   1992    "Lima and the Children of Chaos." In *Rethinking the Latin American City,* edited by Richard Morse and Jorge Hardoy, pp. 201-7. Washington, D.C.: Woodrow Wilson Center Press.

Lewis, Oscar
   1963    *Life in a Mexican Village: Tepoztlan Restudied*. Urbana: University of Illinois Press.

Lezama, José Luis
    1994    "Mexico." In *Latin American Urbanization: Historical Profiles of Major Cit-
            ies,* edited by Gerald M. Greenfield, pp. 350-95. Westport, Conn.: Green-
            wood.
Lincoln, C. Eric, and Lawrence Mamiya
    1990    *The Black Church in the African American Experience.* Durham, N.C.:
            Duke University Press.
Lingenfelter, Judith
    1992    "Getting to Know Your City." In *Discipling the City,* 2nd ed., edited by
            Roger S. Greenway, pp. 183-94. Grand Rapids, Mich.: Baker.
Lingenfelter, Sherwood G., and Marvin K. Mayers
    1986    *Ministering Cross-Culturally: An Incarnational Model for Personal Rela-
            tionships.* Grand Rapids, Mich.: Baker.
Linthicum, Robert C.
    1991a   *City of God, City of Satan: A Biblical Theology of the Urban Church.* Grand
            Rapids, Mich.: Zondervan.
    1991b   *Empowering the Poor: Community Organizing Among the City's 'Rag, Tag,
            and Bobtail'.* Monrovia, Calif.: MARC.
    1994    "Working with the Urban Poor." *Together* 44 (October-December): 1-4.
Livingstone, Greg
    1993    *Planting Churches in Muslim Cities.* Grand Rapids, Mich.: Baker.
Lloyd, Peter
    1979    *Slums of Hope?: Shanty Towns of the Third World.* New York: Penguin.
Lo, Fu-chen
    1996    Introduction to *Emerging World Cities in Pacific Asia,* edited by Fu-chen
            Lo and Yue-man Yeung, pp. 1-13. New York: United Nations University
            Press.
Loewen, Jacob
    1975    *Culture and Human Values.* Pasadena, Calif.: William Carey Library.
Longenecker, R. N.
    1985    "Antioch of Syria." In *Major Cities of the Biblical World,* edited by R. K.
            Harrison, pp. 8-21. Nashville: Thomas Nelson.
Longman, Tremper, III
    1998    *The Book of Ecclesiastes.* The New International Commentary on the Old
            Testament. Grand Rapids, Mich.: Eerdmans.
Longman, Tremper, III, and Daniel Reid
    1995    *God Is a Warrior.* Grand Rapids, Mich.: Zondervan.
Lorenzo, Victor
    1993    "Evangelizing a City Dedicated to Darkness." In *Breaking Strongholds in
            Your City,* edited by C. Peter Wagner, pp. 171-93. Ventura, Calif.: Regal.
Lovelace, Richard F.
    1979    *Dynamics of Spiritual Life: An Evangelical Theology of Renewal.* Downers
            Grove, Ill.: InterVarsity Press.
Lowenstein, Susan
    1965    "Urban Images of Roman Authors." *Comparative Studies in Society and
            History* 8:110-23.
Lucas, Thomas
    1992    "The Vineyard at the Crossroads: The Urban Vision of Ignatius of Loy-

ola." Ph.D. diss., Graduate Theological Union.

Luckmann, Thomas
1967    *The Invisible Religion: The Problem of Religion in Modern Society*. New York: Macmillan.

Lupton, Robert D.
1993    *Return Flight: Community Development Through Reneighboring Our Cit-ies*. Atlanta: FCS Urban Ministries.

Lupton, Bob, Peggy Lupton, and Gloria Yancy
1995    "Relocation: Living in the Community." In *Restoring At-Risk Communi-ties: Doing It Together & Doing It Right*, edited by John M. Perkins, pp. 75-106. Grand Rapids, Mich.: Baker.

Luzbetak, Louis
1992    Personal correspondence. May 13: pp. 1-3.

Lyall, Francis
1984    *Slaves, Citizens, Sons: Legal Metaphors in the Epistles*. Grand Rapids, Mich.: Zondervan.

Lyon, David
1975    *Christians and Sociology*. London: InterVarsity Press.

MacKenzie, R. A. F.
1963    "The City and Israelite Religion." *Catholic Biblical Quarterly* 25:60-70.

MacNair, Donald J.
1978    *The Living Church: A Guide for Revitalization*. Philadelphia: Great Com-mission.

Maddox, Robert
1982    *The Purpose of Luke-Acts*. Gottingen, Netherlands: Vandenhoeck & Ruprecht.

Malamat, Abraham
1982    "How Inferior Israelite Forces Conquered Fortified Canaanite Cities." *Biblical Archaeology Review* 8 (2):24-35.

Marchant, Colin
1985    *Signs in the City*. London: Hodder & Stoughton.

Marciniak, Edward, and William Droel
1995    "The Future of Catholic Churches in the Inner City." *Chicago Studies* 34 (2):172-86.

Marcuse, Peter
1997    "The Ghetto of Exclusion and the Fortified Enclave." *American Behav-ioral Scientist* 41 (3):311-26.

Mariz, Cecília Loreto
1994    *Coping with Poverty: Pentecostals and Christian Base Communities in Bra-zil*. Philadelphia: Temple University Press.

Martin, David
1990    *Tongues of Fire: The Explosion of Protestantism in Latin America*. Oxford: Basil Blackwell.

Marty, Martin
1970    *Righteous Empire: The Protestant Experience in America*. New York: Dial.
1975    *The Pro and Con Book of Religious America: A Bicentennial Argument*. Waco, Tex.: Word.
1984    *Pilgrims in Their Own Land*. Boston: Little, Brown.

Massey, Douglas S., and Nancy A. Denton
    1993    *American Apartheid: Segregation and the Making of the Underclass*. Cambridge, Mass.: Harvard University Press.
Matheny, Tim
    1981    *Reaching the Arabs: A Felt Need Approach*. Pasadena, Calif.: William Carey Library.
Mathews, Basil
    1951    *Forward Through the Ages*. New York: Friendship.
Maust, John
    1984    *Cities of Change: Urban Growth and God's People in Ten Latin American Cities*. Coral Gables, Fla.: Latin America Mission.
Mayers, Marvin K.
    1974    *Christianity Confronts Culture: A Strategy for Cross-Cultural Evangelism*. Grand Rapids, Mich.: Zondervan.
Mays, James
    1983    "Justice: Perspectives from the Prophetic Tradition." *Interpretation* 37:5-17.
Mayur, Rashmi
    1985    "Supercities, the Growing Crisis." *The Futurist* 19 (4):27-30.
McCoy, Craig
    1996    "How Best to Halt an Out-and-Out Exodus?" *Philadelphia Inquirer,* March 24, E1, E3.
McGavran, Donald
    1955    *The Bridges of God: A Study in the Strategy of Missions*. New York: Friendship.
    1970    *Understanding Church Growth*. Grand Rapids, Mich.: Eerdmans.
McGrath, Allister E.
    1994    *Spirituality in an Age of Change: Rediscovering the Spirit of the Reformers*. Grand Rapids, Mich.: Zondervan.
McKeachie, Wilbert J.
    1978    *Teaching Tips: A Guidebook for the Beginning College Teacher*, 7th ed. Lexington, Mass.: D. C. Heath.
McLeod, Hugh
    1995    Introduction to *European Religion in the Age of Great Cities,* edited by Hugh McLeod, pp. 1-39. London: Routledge.
    1996    *Religion and Society in England, 1850-1914*. New York: St. Martin's.
McLoughlin, William
    1978    *Revivals, Awakening, and Reform*. Chicago: University of Chicago Press.
McNaspy, C. J.
    1982    *Lost Cities of Paraguay*. Chicago: Loyola University Press.
McSwain, Larry L.
    1982    "The Cultural Captivity of Urban Churches." In *The Urban Challenge: Reaching America's Cities with the Gospel*, edited by Larry R. Rose and C. Kirk Hadaway, pp. 50-62. Nashville: Broadman.
Means, James
    1989    *Leadership in Christian Ministry*. Grand Rapids, Mich.: Baker.
Meeks, Wayne
    1983    *The First Urban Christians: The Social World of the Apostle Paul*. New

Haven, Conn.: Yale University Press.
Meeting on African Collaboration
1983    "The Pastoral Care of Young People in Urban Areas." In *Young People in African Towns: Their Pastoral Care,* edited by Roger Tessier, pp. 1-17. Eldoret, Kenya: Gaba.
Mendenhall, George
1975    "The Monarchy." *Interpretation* 29:155-70.
Merrifield, Andy, and Erik Swyngedouw
1997    "Social Justice and the Urban Experience: An Introduction." In *The Urbanization of Injustice,* edited by Andy Merrifield and Erik Swyngedouw, pp. 1-17. Washington Square, N.Y.: New York University Press.
Miesner, Donald
1978    "The Missionary Journeys Narrative: Patterns and Implications." In *Perspectives on Luke-Acts,* edited by Charles Talbert, pp. 199-214. Danville, Va.: Association of Baptist Professors of Religion.
Miller, C. John
1987    *Outgrowing the Ingrown Church.* Grand Rapids, Mich.: Zondervan, Ministry Resources Library.
Miller, Calvin
1986    *Leadership.* Colorado Springs, Colo.: NavPress.
Milligan, W. J.
1984    *The New Nomads: Challenges Facing Christians in Western Europe.* Geneva, Switzerland: World Council of Churches, Risk Books.
Millikan, David
1981    *The Sunburnt Soul: Christianity in Search of an Australian Identity.* Homebush West, Australia: Lancer/Anzea.
Mills, C. Wright
1959    *The Sociological Imagination.* New York: Oxford University Press.
Moeller, Berndt
1979    "The Town in Church History: General Presuppositions of the Reformation in Germany." In *The Church in Town and Countryside,* edited by Derek Brown, pp. 257-68. Oxford: Basil Blackwell.
Moffitt, Robert
1987    "The Local Church and Development." In *The Church in Response to Human Need,* edited by Vinay Samuel and Christopher Sugden, pp. 254-63. Grand Rapids, Mich.: Eerdmans.
Moholy-Nagy, Sibyl
1968    *Matrix of Man.* New York: Praeger.
Mol, Hans
1983    *Meaning and Place: An Introduction to the Social Scientific Study of Religion.* New York: Pilgrim.
1985    *The Faith of Australians.* Sydney, Australia: Allen & Unwin.
Monsma, Timothy M.
1989    "African Urbanization—the Future." *World Evangelization* 16 (61):20-22.
1992    "Research: Matching Goals and Methods to Advance the Gospel." In *Discipling the City: A Comprehensive Approach to Urban Mission,* 2nd ed., edited by Roger S. Greenway, pp. 61-68. Grand Rapids, Mich.: Baker.

Montgomery, James
    1997    *Then the End Will Come*. Pasadena, Calif.: William Carey Library.
Moreau, A. Scott
    1997    *Essentials of Spiritual Warfare: Equipped to Win the Battle*. Wheaton, Ill.: Harold Shaw.
Morse, Richard
    1992    "Cities as People." In *Rethinking the Latin American City*, edited by Richard Morse and Jorge Hardoy, pp. 3-19. Washington, D.C.: The Woodrow Wilson Center Press.
Mott, John R.
    1998    "The Pastor and Modern Missions: A Plea for Leadership in World Evangelization." *Mission Frontiers Bulletin* (July-August): 21-24.
Motyer, J. A.
    1966    *The Richness of Christ: Studies in the Letter to the Philippians*. London: Inter-Varsity Press.
Mumford, Lewis
    1961    *The City in History*. New York: Harcourt Brace Jovanovich.
Murphy, Ed
    1992    *The Handbook for Spiritual Warfare*. Nashville: Thomas Nelson.
Mutunga, Stanley
    1993    "Contextual Leadership Development for the Church: An Investigation into Rural-Urban Migration to Nairobi." Ph.D. diss., Fuller Theological Seminary.
Myers, Bryant
    1994    "State of the World's Children: Critical Challenge to Christian Mission." *International Bulletin of Missionary Research* 18 (3):98-102.
Na'aman, Nadav
    1981    "Hezekiah's Fortified Cities and the LMLK Stamps." *Eretz Israel* 15:15-21.
Neighbour, Ralph
    1990    *Where Do We Go From Here?: A Guidebook for the Cell Group Church*. Houston: Torch.
Neill, Stephen
    1952    *The Christian Society*. London: Fontana Library.
    1964    *A History of Christian Missions*. Grand Rapids, Mich.: Eerdmans.
    1966    *Colonialism and Christian Missions*. New York: McGraw-Hill.
Nemeth, Roger J., and Donald A. Luidens
    1995    "The Persistence of Ethnic Descent: Dutch Clergy in the Reformed Church in America." *Journal for the Scientific Study of Religion* 34 (2):200-13.
Neufeldt, Victoria, and David B. Guralnik, eds.
    1988    *Webster's New World Dictionary of American English*, 3rd college ed. New York: Webster's New World.
Newbigin, Lesslie
    1953    *The Household of God*. London: SCM Press.
    1978    *The Open Secret: An Introduction to the Theology of Mission*. Grand Rapids, Mich.: Eerdmans.
    1989    *The Gospel in a Pluralist Society*. Grand Rapids, Mich.: Eerdmans.

Nicholls, Bruce, ed.
1986    *In Word and Deed: Evangelism and Social Responsibility.* Grand Rapids, Mich.: Eerdmans.

Nida, Eugene
1967    "Drunkenness in Indigenous Religious Rites." In *Readings in Missionary Anthropology,* edited by William Smalley, pp. 103-6. Tarrytown, N.Y.: Practical Anthropology, Inc.

Niemeyer, Larry
1989    *Summary of the Nairobi Church Survey.* Nairobi, Kenya: Daystar University College.

Norton, Perry
1964    *Church and Metropolis.* New York: Seabury.

Nuñez, Emilio Antonio, and William Taylor
1996    *Crisis and Hope in Latin America,* rev. ed. Pasadena, Calif.: William Carey Library.

O'Brien, Peter
1995    *Gospel and Mission in the Writings of Paul.* Grand Rapids, Mich.: Baker.

O'Connor, Richard A.
1978    "Urbanism and Religion: Community, Hierarchy, and Sanctity in Urban Thai Buddhist Temples." Ph.D. diss., Cornell University.

Olyan, Saul
1996    "Honor, Shame, and Covenant Relations in Ancient Israel and its Environment." *Journal of Biblical Literature* 115 (2):201-18.

Ortiz, Manuel
1988    "The Dilemma of Demographics." *Bulletin of Westminster Theological Seminary* 27 (2):4.
1991    "Circle Church: A Case Study in Contextualization." *Urban Mission* 8 (3) (January): 6-18.
1992    "Being Disciples: Incarnational Christians in the City. In *Discipling the City: A Comprehensive Approach to Urban Mission,* 2nd ed., edited by Roger S. Greenway, pp. 85-98. Grand Rapids, Mich.: Baker.
1993    *The Hispanic Challenge: Opportunities Confronting the Church.* Downers Grove, Ill.: InterVarsity Press.
1996    *One New People: Models for Developing a Multiethnic Church.* Downers Grove, Ill.: InterVarsity Press.

Overman, J. Andrew
1988    "Who Were the First Urban Christians?: Urbanization in Galilee in the First Century." In *SBL Seminar Papers,* edited by David Lull, pp. 160-68. Atlanta: Scholars Press.

Ozment, Steven
1975    *The Reformation in the Cities: The Appeal of Protestantism in Sixteenth-Century Germany and Switzerland.* New Haven, Conn.: Yale University Press.

Padilla, C. René
1976a   Introduction to *The New Face of Evangelicalism: An International Symposium on the Lausanne Conference,* edited by C. René Padilla, pp. 9-16. Downers Grove, Ill.: InterVarsity Press.
1976b   "Spiritual Conflict." In *The New Face of Evangelicalism: An International*

*Symposium on the Lausanne Conference*, edited by C. René Padilla, pp. 205-21. Downers Grove, Ill.: InterVarsity Press.

Palomino, Miguel Angel
  1983    *Lima al Encuentro con Dios: A New Kind of Urban Missiology*. n.p.

Palen, J. John
  1987    *The Urban World*, 3rd ed. New York: McGraw-Hill.
  1992    *The Urban World*, 4th ed. New York: McGraw-Hill.

Park, Robert
  1952    *Human Communities: The City and Human Ecology*. Glencoe, Ill.: Free Press.

Parshall, Phil
  1980    *New Paths in Muslim Evangelism*. Grand Rapids, Mich.: Baker.

Patterson, George, and Richard Scoggins
  1993    *Church Multiplication Guide*. Pasadena, Calif.: William Carey Library.

Peil, Margaret
  1982    *African Cities and Christian Communities*. Eldoret, Kenya: Gaba Publications.

Peirce, Neal, with Curtis Johnson, and John S. Hall
  1993    *Citistates*. Washington, D.C.: Seven Locks Press.

Peretti, Frank E.
  1986    *This Present Darkness*. Westchester, Ill.: Crossway.

Perkins, John
  1982    *With Justice for All*. Ventura, Calif.: Regal.

Peters, Gary L., and Robert P. Larkin
  1993    *Population Geography: Problems, Concepts, and Prospects*, 4th ed. Dubuque, Iowa: Kendall/Hunt.

Phillips, E. Barbara, and Richard LeGates
  1981    *City Lights: An Introduction to Urban Studies*. New York: Oxford University Press.

Pienaar, D. N.
  1981    "The Role of Fortified Cities in the Northern Kingdom During the Reign of the Omride Dynasty." *Journal of Northwest Semitic Languages* 9:151-57.

Pierson, Paul E.
  1989    "Missions and Community Development: A Historical Perspective." In *Christian Relief and Development: Developing Workers for Effective Ministry*, edited by Edgar J. Elliston, pp. 7-22. Dallas: Word.

Piper, John
  1993    *Let the Nations Be Glad! The Supremacy of God in Missions*. Grand Rapids, Mich.: Baker.
  1999    "A Battle Call to Advance God's Kingdom." *Mission Frontiers* (March-April): 13-15.

Pirenne, Henri
  1952    *Medieval Cities*. Princeton: Princeton University Press.

Plotnicov, Leonard
  1985    "Back to Basics, Forward to Fundamentals: The Search for Urban Anthropology's Mission." In *City and Society*, edited by Aiden Southall, Peter J. M. Nas and Ghaus Ansari, pp. 29-55. Leiden, The Netherlands:

Institute of Cultural and Social Studies, University of Leiden.

1987    "The Political Economy of Skyscrapers: An Anthropological Introduction to Advanced Industrial Cities." *City and Society* 1 (1):35-51.

Porter, Muriel

1990    *Land of the Spirit? The Australian Religious Experience*. Geneva, Switzerland: WCC Publications.

Power, Grant

1996    "Battling the Odds for Urban Land and Housing." *Together* 51 (July-September): 18-21.

Powlison, David

1995    *Power Encounters: Reclaiming Spiritual Warfare*. Grand Rapids, Mich.: Baker Books.

Poythress, Vern S.

1995    "Territorial Spirits: Some Biblical Perspectives." *Urban Mission* 13 (2):37-49.

Prescott, Ian

1998    "Metro Manila: Great Growth and Great Challenges." *Urban Mission* 15 (4):18-25.

Press, Irwin, and M. Estellie Smith

1980    Introduction to *Urban Place and Process: Readings in the Anthropology of Cities*, edited by Irwin Press and M. Estellie Smith, pp. 1-15. New York: Macmillan.

Preston, Samuel H.

1989    "The Social Sciences and the Population Problem." In *Demography as an Interdiscipline*, edited by J. Mayone Stycos, pp. 1-26. New Brunswick, N.J.: Transaction.

Pretiz, Paul

1995    "Evangelical Presence in Latin America's Cities." *Latin America Evangelist* (June): 7-11.

Priest, Robert J., Thomas Campbell, and Bradford A. Mullen

1995    "Missiological Syncretism: The New Animistic Paradigm." In *Spiritual Power and Missions: Raising the Issues*, edited by Edward Rommen, pp, 9-87. Pasadena, Calif.: William Carey Library.

Pritchard, Gregory

1994    "The Strategy of Willow Creek Community Church: A Study in the Sociology of Religion." Ph.D. diss., Northwestern University.

Prud'Homme, Rémy

1989    "New Trends in the Cities of the World." In *Cities in a Global Society*, edited by Richard Knight and Gary Gappert, pp. 44-57. Beverly Hills, Calif.: Sage.

Raab, Laura, and Bobby Clinton

1985    *Barnabas—Encouraging Exhorter: A Study in Mentoring*. Altadena, Calif.: Barnabas Resources.

Rachel's Tears

1996    *Rachel's Tears* 1 (4-5):1-4.

Rader, Dick

1991    *Christian Ethics in an African Context*. New York: Peter Lang.

Reapsome, James W.
    1987    "Definitions and Identities: Samples from the Ongoing Discussion." In
             *Reaching the Unreached: The Old-New Challenge*, edited by Harvie M.
             Conn, pp. 61-73. Phillipsburg, N.J.: Presbyterian & Reformed.
Redfield, Robert
    1941    *The Folk Culture of Yucatan*. Chicago: University of Chicago Press.
Redfield, Robert, and Milton Singer
    1980    "The Cutural Role of Cities." In *Urban Place and Process: Readings in the
             Anthropology of Cities,* edited by Irwin Press and M. Estellie Smith, pp.
             183-210. New York: Macmillan.
Redman, Charles
    1982    "Archaeological Survey and the Study of Mesopotamian Urban Sys-
             tems." *Journal of Field Archaeology* 9:375-82.
Rees, Martha, Arthur Murphy, Earl Morris, and Mary Winter
    1991    "Migrants to and in Oaxaca City." *Urban Anthropology* 20 (1):15-29.
Ridderbos, Herman
    1962    *The Coming of the Kingdom*. Nutley, N.J.: Presbyterian & Reformed
    1975    *Paul: An Outline of His Theology*. Grand Rapids, Mich.: Eerdmans.
Riis, Jacob
    1971    *How the Other Half Lives*. New York: Dover. [1890].
Ro, Bong-rin
    1989    "Theological Education for Urban Ministry in Asia: Declaration of the
             Eighth Asia Theological Association Consultation." In *Urban Ministry in
             Asia: Cities, the Exploding Mission Field,* edited by Bong-rin Ro, pp. 1-3.
             Taichung, Taiwan: Asia Theological Association.
Roberts, W. Dayton
    1967    *Revolution in Evangelism*. Chicago: Moody Press.
Rodriguez, Richard
    1982    *Hunger of Memory: The Education of Richard Rodriguez*. New York: Ban-
             tam.
Roels, Edwin
    1962    *God's Mission*. Franeker, The Netherlands: T. Wever.
Rohrbaugh, Richard
    1991a    "The City in the Second Testament." *Biblical Theology Bulletin* 21:67-
             75.
    1991b    "The Pre-Industrial City in Luke-Acts: Urban Social Relations." In *The
             Social World of Luke-Acts,* edited by Jerome Neyrey, pp. 125-49. Pea-
             body, Mass.: Hendrickson.
Rondinelli, Dennis A.
    1988    "Giant and Secondary City Growth in Africa." In *The Metropolis Era*
             vol.1, *A World of Giant Cities,* edited by Mattei Dogan and John D.
             Kasarda, pp. 291-321. Beverly Hills, Calif.: Sage.
Ronsvalle, John, and Sylvia Ronsvalle
    1992    *The Poor Have Faces: Loving Your Neighbor in the 21st Century*. Grand
             Rapids, Mich.: Baker.
Roozen, David A.
    1993    "Denominations Grow as Individuals Join Congregations." In *Church &*
             *Denominational Growth: What Does (and Does Not) Cause Growth or*

*Decline,* edited by David A. Roozen and C. Kirk Hadaway, pp. 15-36. Nashville: Abingdon.

Roozen, David A. and C. Kirk Hadaway, eds.
1993    *Churches and Denominational Growth: What Does (and Does Not) Cause Growth or Decline.* Nashville: Abingdon.

Rose, Larry L., and C. Kirk Hadaway, eds.
1982    *The Urban Challenge: Reaching America's Cities with the Gospel.* Nashville: Broadman.

Rush, Myron D.
1983    *Richer Relationships: How To Be A Conflict-Solver and A Friend-Winner.* Wheaton, Ill.: Victor.

Rusk, David
1993    *Cities Without Suburbs.* Washington, D.C.: The Woodrow Wilson Center Press.

Samuel, Vinay, and Chris Sugden
1987    "Agenda for Missions in the Eighties and Nineties: A Discussion Starter." In *New Frontiers in Mission,* edited by Patrick Sookhdeo, pp. 61-70. Grand Rapids, Mich.: Baker.

Sanjek, Roger
1990    "Urban Anthropology in the 1980s: A World View." *Annual Review of Anthropology* 19:151-86.

Sassen, Saskia
1991    *The Global City: New York, London, Tokyo.* Princeton: Princeton University Press.

Sawatsky, Ben
1985    "A Church Planting Strategy for World Class Cities." *Urban Mission* 3 (2): 7-19.

Schaller, Lyle
1990    "Megachurch!" *Christianity Today* 34 (4):20-24.
1993a   Introduction to *Center City Churches: The New Urban Frontier,* edited by Lyle Schaller, pp. 11-20. Nashville: Abingdon.
1993b   "Thirty Recurring Themes." In *Center City Churches: The New Urban Frontier,* edited by Lyle Schaller, pp. 169-87. Nashville: Abingdon.

Schmitt, John
1985    "The Motherhood of God and Zion as Mother." *Revue Biblique* 92:557-69.

Schmitt, Peter
1990    *Back to Nature: The Arcadian Myth in Urban America.* Baltimore: Johns Hopkins University Press.

Schreck, Harley, and David Barrett
1987    "Two Ways of Understanding Peoples and Their Evangelization." In *Unreached Peoples: Clarifying the Task,* edited by Harley Schreck and David Barrett, pp. 3-42. Monrovia, Calif.: MARC.

Schreiter, Robert J.
1985    *Constructing Local Theologies.* Maryknoll, N.Y.: Orbis.

Schrotenboer, Paul
1964    *The Nature of Religion.* Christian Perspectives. Hamilton, Canada: Association for Reformed Scientific Studies.

Schwartz, Alex
1992    "Corporate Service Linkages in Large Metropolitan Areas." *Urban Affairs Quarterly* 28 (2):276-96.

Scoggins, Dick
1997    "Reproducing House Churches: An Autobiographical Pilgrimage." In *Planting and Growing Urban Churches,* edited by Harvie M. Conn, pp. 222-30. Grand Rapids, Mich.: Baker.

Scott, Daniel D.
1995    *The Church as a Mentoring Community for University Students.* D.Min. project, Westminster Theological Seminary.

Seeking the Peace
1989    "Seeking the Peace of the City: The Valle de Bravo Affirmation." *Urban Mission* 1 (September): 18-24.

Selman, M. J.
1985    "Ur." In *Major Cities of the Biblical World,* edited by R. K. Harrison, pp. 275-84. Nashville: Thomas Nelson.

Sernett, Milton
1997    *Bound for the Promised Land: African American Religion and the Great Migration.* Durham, N.C.: Duke University Press.

Sherwin-White, A. N.
1963    *Roman Society and Roman Law in the New Testament.* London: Oxford University Press.

Shiloh, Yigal
1980    "The Population of Iron Age Palestine in the Light of a Sample Analysis of Urban Plans, Areas, and Population Density." *Bulletin of the American Schools of Oriental Research* 239:25-35.

Shipp, Glover
1986    "Research as a Tool for Urban Evangelism in Developing Countries." D.Miss. diss., Fuller Theological Seminary.

Shorter, Aylward
1974    *East African Societies.* London: Routledge & Kegan Paul.
1991    *The Church in the African City.* Maryknoll, N.Y.: Orbis.

Shorter, Aylward, and Edwin Onyancha
1997    *Secularism in Africa. A Case Study: Nairobi City.* Nairobi, Kenya: Paulinist Publications Africa.

Sider, Ronald J., and James Parker III
1986    "How Broad Is Salvation in Scripture?" In *In Word and Deed: Evangelism and Social Responsibility,* edited by Bruce Nicholls, pp. 85-108. Grand Rapids, Mich.: Eerdmans.

Silva, Moisés
1987    *Has the Church Misread the Bible? The History of Interpretation in the Light of Current Issues.* Grand Rapids, Mich.: Zondervan.

Silvoso, Edgardo
1991    "Prayer Power in Argentina." In *Engaging Your Enemy,* edited by C. Peter Wagner, pp. 109-15. Ventura, Calif.: Regal.
1994    *That None Should Perish: How to Reach Entire Cities for Christ Through Prayer Evangelism.* Ventura, Calif.: Regal.

Sjoberg, Gideon
  1960    *The Preindustrial City: Past and Present.* New York: Free Press/Macmillan.
Sklba, Richard
  1976    *The Faithful City.* Chicago: Franciscan Herald Press.
Smedes, Lewis
  1970    *All Things Made New: A Theology of Man's Union with Christ.* Grand Rapids, Mich.: Eerdmans.
Smith, Fred
  1983    "Growth Through Evangelism." *Urban Mission* 1 (1):19-29.
  1992    "Encounter with God—the Quayaquil Model." *Urban Mission* 9 (3):6-12.
  1997    "Encounter with God: The Guayaquil Model." In *Planting and Growing Urban Churches,* edited by Harvie M. Conn, pp. 251-57. Grand Rapids, Mich.: Baker.
Smith, John
  1988    *Advance Australia Where?* Homebush West, Australia: Anzea.
Snook, Stewart G.
  1992    *Developing Leaders Through Theological Education by Extension.* Wheaton, Ill.: Billy Graham Center.
Soulos, Mersina
  1994    "Sydney, Cross-Cultural Ministry, and the Anglicans." *Urban Mission* 12 (4):32-36.
Southall, Adrian
  1961    "Social Change, Demography and Extrinsic Factors." In *Social Change in Modern Africa,* edited by Aidan Southall, pp. 1-13. London: Oxford University Press.
Spradley, James P.
  1979    *The Ethnographic Interview.* Fort Worth: Harcourt Brace Jovanovich.
  1980    *Participant Observation.* Fort Worth: Holt, Rinehart & Winston.
Spradley, James P., and David W. McCurdy
  1972    *The Cultural Experience: Ethnography in Complex Society.* Prospect Heights, Ill.: Waveland.
Spates, James, and John Macionis
  1982    *The Sociology of Cities.* New York: St. Martin's.
Spindler, Marc
  1987    "Europe's Neo-Paganism: A Reverse Inculturation." *International Bulletin of Missionary Research* 11:8-11.
Spykman, Gordon
  1992    *Reformational Theology: A New Paradigm for Doing Dogmatics.* Grand Rapids, Mich.: Eerdmans.
Stambaugh, John, and David Balch
  1986    *The New Testament in Its Social Environment.* Philadelphia: Westminster Press.
Stapleton, Kristin
  1996    "Discovering History in Chinese Cities." *The Urban History Newsletter* 13:1-3.
Starkes, M. Thomas
  1984    "Non-Christian Religion and Culture in the Cities of the World." In *An*

*Urban World: Churches Face the Future*, edited by Larry L. Rose and C. Kirk Hadaway, pp. 95-115. Nashville: Broadman.

Stek, John
1978    "Salvation, Liberation, and Justice in the Old Testament." *Calvin Theological Journal* 13:133-65.

Stockwell, Clinton
1993    "The Church and the City: A Five-Stage History." *Urban Mission* 11 (1):29-36.

Stoesz, Edgar
1977    *Development Monograph Series 1: Thoughts on Development*, rev. ed. Akron, Pa.: Mennonite Central Committee.

Stoll, David
1990    *Is Latin America Becoming Protestant?* Berkeley: University of California Press.

Stonehouse, Ned
1953    *The Witness of Luke to Christ*. Grand Rapids, Mich.: Eerdmans.

Strachan, Kenneth
1968    *The Inescapable Calling*. Grand Rapids, Mich.: Eerdmans.

Strobel, Lee
1993    *Inside the Mind of Unchurched Harry and Mary*. Grand Rapids, Mich.: Zondervan.

Stycos, J. Mayone
1989    Introduction to *Demography as an Interdiscipline,* edited by J. Mayone Stycos, pp. vii-ix. New Brunswick, N.J.: Transaction.

Suttles, Gerald
1968    *The Social Order of the Slum: Ethnicity and Territory in the Inner City*. Chicago: University of Chicago Press.

Talbert, Charles
1974    *Literary Patterns, Theological Themes and the Genre of Luke-Acts*. Missoula, Mont.: Scholars Press.
1982    *Reading Luke: A Literary and Theological Commentary on the Third Gospel*. New York: Crossroad.

Taylor, Dick
1979    "A Practical Guide for Beginning Local Ministry." *Sojourners* (June): 23-24.

Taylor, John V.
1965    *The Primal Vision*. London: SCM Press.

Teaford, Jon
1993    *The Twentieth-Century American City*, 2nd ed. Baltimore: Johns Hopkins University Press.

Theissen, Gerd
1978    *Sociology of Early Palestinian Christianity*. Philadelphia: Fortress.
1982    *The Social Setting of Pauline Christianity*. Philadelphia: Fortress.

Thompson, J. A.
1983    "The 'Town' in Old Testament Times." *Buried History* (September): 35-42.

Tillapaugh, Frank R.
1982    *Unleashing the Church: Getting People Out of the Fortress and into Minis-*

*try*. Ventura, Calif.: Regal.

Tink, Fletcher
1994     "From Order to Harmony: Toward a New Hermeneutic for Urban Mission." Ph.D. diss., Fuller Theological Seminary.
1998     "Urban Training Update." *City Voices* (Spring): 3-6, 7.

Tischler, Henry
1993     *Introduction to Sociology*, 4th ed. Fort Worth: Harcourt.

Toh, Serene
1990     "Home Cell Groups in St. John's-St. Margaret's Church, Singapore." *Urban Mission* 7 (4):45-52.

Tonnies, Ferdinand
1957     *Community and Society*. East Lansing, Mich.: Michigan State University Press.

Tsai, Kuo-shan
1985     "The Evangelization of the Urban Industrial Workers in Taiwan in Missiological Perspective." D.Miss. diss., Fuller Theological Seminary.

Tunnicliffe, Geoff
1990     "Mission Toronto '90." *World Christian* (February): 18.

Uken, Charles
1992     "Planting Blue-Collar and Service-Sector Churches: Lessons from Brazil." D.Min. project, Westminster Theological Seminary.

Underwood, B. E.
1990     "God's Urban Strategy." *Urban Mission* 8 (2):26-33.

Unger, Merrill F.
1952     *Biblical Demonology*. Wheaton, Ill.: Scripture Press.

Van Engen, Charles, and Jude Tiersma, eds.
1994     *God So Loves the City: Seeking a Theology for Urban Mission*. Monrovia, Calif.: MARC.

Van Leeuwen, Arend
1964     *Christianity and World History*. London: Edinburgh House.

Vance, James
1990     *The Continuing City: Urban Morphology in Western Civilization*. Baltimore: Johns Hopkins University Press.

Vance, Patricia
1998     Personal correspondence. September 1:1-2.

Vaughn, John
1984     *The World's Twenty Largest Churches: Church Growth Principles in Action*. Grand Rapids, Mich.: Baker.
1993     *Megachurches and America's Cities*. Grand Rapids, Mich.: Baker.

Verkuyl, J.
1978     *Contemporary Missiology: An Introduction*. Grand Rapids, Mich.: Eerdmans.

von Harnack, Adolf
1909     *The Acts of the Apostles*. London: Williams & Norgate.

Vos, Geerhardus
1948     *Biblical Theology*. Grand Rapids, Mich.: Eerdmans.

Wade, Jerry L.
1989     "Felt Needs and Anticipatory Needs: Reformulation of a Community

Development Principle." *Journal of the Community Development Society* 20 (1):116-23.

Wagner, C. Peter
1979    *Your Spiritual Gifts Can Help Your Church Grow.* Glendale, Calif.: Regal.
1990    *Church Planting for a Greater Harvest.* Ventura, Calif.: Regal.
1996    *Confronting the Powers: How the New Testament Church Experienced the Power of Strategic-Level Spiritual Warfare.* Ventura, Calif.: Regal.

Waldrop, Judith
1990    "You'll Know It's the 21st Century When . . ." *American Demographics* 12 (12):22-27.

Waley, Paul
1997    "Tokyo: Patterns of Familiarity and Partition of Difference." *American Behavioral Scientist* 41 (3):396-429.

Walker, Peter
1996    *Jesus and the Holy City: New Testament Perspectives on Jerusalem.* Grand Rapids, Mich.: Eerdmans.

Wallace, Ruth A., and Alison Wolf
1991    *Contemporary Sociological Theory: Continuing the Classical Tradition,* 3rd ed. Englewood Cliffs, N.J.: Prentice Hall.

Walls, Andrew W.
1990    "The American Dimension in the History of the Missionary Movement." In *Earthen Vessels: American Evangelicals and Foreign Missions, 1880-1980,* edited by Joel Carpenter and Wiblert Shenk, pp. 1-25. Grand Rapids, Mich.: Eerdmans.

Walsh, J. P. M.
1987    *The Mighty From Their Thrones: Power in the Biblical Tradition.* Philadelphia: Fortress.

Ward, Barbara
1976    *The Home of Man.* New York: W. W. Norton.

Ward, David
1989    *Poverty, Ethnicity, and the American City, 1840-1925.* New York: Cambridge University Press.

Ward, Ted W.
1996a   "Servants, Leaders, and Tyrants." In *With an Eye on the Future: Development and Mission in the 21st Century,* edited by Duane Elmer and Lois McKinney, pp. 27-42. Monrovia, Calif.: MARC.
1996b   "With an Eye on the Future." In *With an Eye on the Future: Development and Mission in the 21st Century,* edited by Duane Elmer and Lois McKinney, pp. 7-26. Monrovia, Calif.: MARC.

Warfield, Benjamin
n.d.    *The Lord of Glory.* Grand Rapids, Mich.: Zondervan.

Washington, Raleigh, and Glen Kehrein
1993    *Breaking Down Walls.* Chicago: Moody Press.

Wauzzinski, Robert
1993    *Between God and Gold: Protestant Evangelicalism and the Industrial Revolution, 1820-1914.* Rutherford: Fairleigh Dickinson University Press.

Weerasingha, Tissa
1992    "How to Develop an Urban Church Planting Movement." D.Min. project,

Westminster Theological Seminary.

Welch, Edward T.

1997    *When People are Big and God is Small*. Phillipsburg, N.J.: Presbyterian &
        Reformed.

Wells, David F.

1998    *Losing Our Virtue: Why the Church Must Recover Its Moral Vision*. Grand
        Rapids, Mich.: Eerdmans.

Wessels, Anton

1994    *Europe: Was It Ever Really Christian?* London: SCM Press.

White, Morton, and Lucia White

1977    *The Intellectual Versus the City*. New York: Oxford University Press.

White, Randy

1996    *Journey to the Center of the City*. Downers Grove, Ill.: InterVarsity Press.

White, Ronald, and C. Howard Hopkins

1976    *The Social Gospel: Religion and Reform in Changing America*. Philadel-
        phia: Temple University Press.

Whitelam, Keith

1986    "The Symbols of Power: Aspects of Royal Propaganda in the United
        Monarchy." *Biblical Archaeologist* 49 (3):166-73.

Whyte, William

1943    *Street Corner Society: The Social Order of an Italian Slum*. Chicago: Uni-
        versity of Chicago Press.

Williams, Melvin

1974    *Community in a Black Pentecostal Church*. Prospect Heights, Ill.: Wave-
        land Press.

Williams, Philip J.

1997    "The Sound of Tambourines: The Politics of Pentecostal Growth in El
        Salvador." In *Power, Politics and Pentecostals in Latin America,* edited by
        Edward Cleary and Hannah Stewart-Gambino, pp. 179-200. Boulder,
        Colo.: Westview.

Wilson, Bruce

1983    *Can God Survive in Australia?* Sutherland, Australia: Albatross Books.

Wilson, Robert

1986    "The City in the Old Testament." In *Civitas: Religious Interpretations of
        the City,* edited by Peter Hawkins, pp. 3-13. Atlanta: Scholars Press.

Wilson, Samuel

1989    "Defining Development in Social Terms." In *Christian Relief and Develop-
        ment: Developing Workers for Effective Ministry,* edited by Edgar J. Ellis-
        ton, pp. 145-58. Dallas: Word.

Wink, Walter

1992    *Engaging the Powers*. Minneapolis: Fortress Press.

Winter, Bruce

1989    "'If a Man does Not Wish to Work . . . ': A Cultural and Historical Setting
        for 2 Thessalonians 3:6-16." *Tyndale Bulletin* 40:303-15.

1994    *Seek the Welfare of the City*. Grand Rapids, Mich.: Eerdmans.

Winter, Ralph D.

1987    "Unreached Peoples: The Development of the Concept." In *Reaching the
        Unreached: The Old-New Challenge,* edited by Harvie M. Conn, pp. 17-

43. Phillipsburg, N.J.: Presbyterian & Reformed

Wirt, Sherwood
1968    *The Social Conscience of the Evangelical.* New York: Harper & Row.
Wirth, Louis
1980    "Urbanism as a Way of Life." In *Urban Place and Process: Readings in the Anthropology of Cities,* edited by Irwin Press and M. Estellie Smith, pp. 30-48. New York: Macmillan.
Wolterstorff, Nicholas
1983    *Until Justice and Peace Embrace.* Grand Rapids, Mich.: Eerdmans.
World Bank
1981    *Development Report* (August).
Wright, George Ernest
1969    *The Old Testament and Theology.* New York: Harper & Row.
Zanotelli, Alex
1988    "Facing Problems of Rapid Urbanization." *African Ecclesial Review* 30:277-84.
Ziegenhols, Walter
1978    *Urban Churches in Transition.* New York: Pilgrim Press.
Zimmermann, Frank
1967    "Ir, Kir and Related Forms." In *The Seventy-Fifth Anniversary Volume of the Jewish Quarterly Review,* pp. 582-92. Philadelphia: JQR.